Intellectuals and Tradition

THE VAN LEER JERUSALEM FOUNDATION SERIES

INTELLECTUALS AND TRADITION
S. N. Eisenstadt and S. R. Graubard, *Editors*

SCIENCE AND VALUES: Patterns of Tradition and Change
A. Thackray and E. Mendelsohn, *Editors*

INTERACTION BETWEEN SCIENCE AND PHILOSOPHY
Y. Elkana, *Editor*

SOCIETY AND POLITICAL STRUCTURE IN THE ARAB WORLD
M. Milson, *Editor*

INTELLECTUALS

AND

TRADITION

Edited by

S. N. EISENSTADT
Hebrew University,
Jerusalem

and

S. R. GRAUBARD
Brown University
Providence, R.I.

Advisory Committee

HUMANITIES PRESS
New York

Reprinted from *Dædalus,* Journal of the American Academy of Arts and Sciences, Spring and Summer 1972. Published in book form in the United States of America by Humanities Press, Inc., 450 Park Avenue South, New York, N.Y. 10016 with permission of the editors of DÆDALUS and the Editorial Board of the Van Leer Jerusalem Foundation.

Library of Congress Catalog No. 72 86067

ISBN 391 00257 0

Printed in the United States of America

Intellectuals and Tradition

PART I

Intellectuals and Change

PART II

Preface
Intellectuals and Tradition

WORDS ARE generally highly selective in the associations they tolerate; it is not common, for example, to find the word "intellectuals" linked with "tradition." As S. N. Eisenstadt, in his introductory essay indicates, intellectuals are conventionally taken to be rebels or critics, potential or actual opponents of the established order. To view them as something other than iconoclasts or heretics, to dwell on their importance as "the creators and carriers of tradition," is to present them in an unaccustomed role. Yet, this is precisely the one selected by many who have written for this volume.

There is in this volume an implicit and explicit denial of the all-too-facile distinction between intellectuals in a premodern or "traditional" society and those who exist in a so-called "modern" society. It is not an accident that the volume deals so extensively with intellectuals outside the West European and American orbits. Whether the subject be Japan, China, or Russia, the effort is always to link the conditions of intellectual life in an earlier period with those that prevail today.

S. N. Eisenstadt sets the tone for the volume when he argues that every tradition—every interpretation of social reality—posits certain questions and provides certain answers, thereby effectively excluding the possibility of other questions and other answers. Tension is inherent in intellectual life, precisely because every intellectual construction of reality will be challenged. If a construct of "rational society" is developed by one group of intellectuals, this will only provide an incentive for others to view the matter in another way.

Eisenstadt suggests that every tradition has both symbolic and structural-organizational dimensions. Traditions are the creation of intellectuals, but also of men of power (politicians and bureaucrats), and they are often in conflict. The conflict ought not to be seen as simply a struggle between intellectuals who deal mostly with symbols and political men who deal mostly with organization. Eisenstadt shows that each creates both, and that there is, in fact, a "mutual interdependence" between intellectuals and political authorities. It is his view that the political authorities of a society seek to be legitimized by intellectuals, religious or secular; their legitimacy derives largely from recognition by the elites of a society. Intellectuals and intellectual organizations, in turn, generally require the protection of political institutions; this is a condition of their survival. It is Eisenstadt's argument that the intellectual and political authorities seek to maintain the maximum autonomy for themselves, while at the same time achieving the maximum control over the other.

v

The tension which derives from this necessity of interdependence and the persistent concern with independence influences substantially the intellectuals' moral dilemmas; it governs their responses to the problems of participation in society. The range of possibilities of participation for the intellectual may be: total withdrawal from society, with a readiness to concentrate on private contemplation, all the way to a willingness to submit to authority totally, even to assume power itself. The ideal that is most commonly sought for is somewhere in the middle—to be both a critic of society and a participant in it.

Eisenstadt insists that it is a mistake to believe that intellectuals oppose tradition as such, or that they seek a society in which traditions will have no major role. Intellectual attitudes toward tradition will differ markedly; some will accept it, others will reject it. It is well to realize, Eisenstadt says, that the majority of intellectuals have been "active or passive cultural and political conformists." The variations between societies in this respect may be large, and it is important that we know more about these differences.

When the intellectual is rebellious, Eisenstadt says, the rebellion may be as much against intellectual authority as against political authority. In modern society, the relationship between various forms of protest and general social and cultural innovation is crucial. Eisenstadt reminds us that the breakthrough to modernity involved strong revolutionary orientations on both the symbolic and the organizational levels.

Edward Shils, in his general consideration of the problem of intellectuals and tradition, distinguishes between three types of intellectuals: those who are productive, those who are reproductive, and those who are essentially consumers. His concern is principally with the first two—with those intellectuals who produce intellectual works and those who engage in the interpretation and transmission of such works. It is impossible to think of intellectuals without considering their works; these need to be placed in a frame which includes previously produced works of the same order which served either as models or points of departure. Shils writes: "An intellectual tradition is a set or pattern of beliefs, conceptions of form, sets of verbal (and other symbolic) usages, rules of procedure, recurrent and unilaterally linked with each other through time." The intellectual needs to conceive of himself as having an obligation to produce works. Unless this obligation is felt, and unless intellectual institutions and communities exist to support the intellectual in his efforts, there can be no intellectual production.

We are reminded that the term "intellectuals" is of recent creation—it is less than a hundred years old—and that before this time men were satisfied to call themselves writers, poets, dramatists, philosophers, and the like. Even now, not all who create intellectual works are prepared to call themselves "intellectuals." Fundamental to all intellectual effort is the belief that the intellectuals' concern is with important, even ultimate things. The confidence in the charismatic quality of intellectual works brings intellectuals into association with other powerful individuals. Shils maintains that the intellectual comes to see himself as participating in a social category of powerful individuals—economically and politically powerful. The contacts are sometimes positive, often hostile. There is the mutual interdependence that Eisenstadt wrote about. The powerful require the intellectual; the intellectual requires and constantly finds himself beguiled by the powerful.

Shils treats two of the more significant traditions that have developed in modern times—those that make intellectuals support anti-institutionalism and antitraditionalism. As Shils explains, the word "tradition" has itself become polemical, and is no longer properly analyzed. One of the strongest intellectual traditions since the French Revolution, he says, has been "the acceptance of the legitimacy of revolution and of the iniquity of tradition." Not all intellectuals, however, have accepted this view. Many have chosen other ways, and have served the state in important roles. To an extent that was never true before, Shils says, "intellectuals have become an estate of the realm,"·and this has meant the wide diffusion of their traditions. All these developments require a kind of analysis that has not yet taken place.

The greater number of articles in this issue of *Dædalus* deal with specific intellectual groups in particular societies. Frederic Wakeman's interest is principally with intellectuals in late Imperial China. While the possibilities for an intellectual in China were many—from being a civil statesman and policy-maker on one extreme, to being an anchorite or eremite on the other —there were two familiar intellectual types missing from the Chinese scene. Confucianism militated against the emergence of the technocrat, and there was no room for the prophet as Max Weber had defined him. Again, what is so obvious in the case of Imperial China is the mutual interdependence of state and intellectuals. Wakeman writes: "As authority required Confucian legitimization, so did literati need imperial protection against iconoclastic peasant rebels." This, however, did not make the literati entirely happy with their dependence on the state. They wished to preserve some area of true independence, though they were never capable of developing the principle of group rights for themselves. In Wakeman's view, they lacked corporate identity and had no institutional autonomy, but "sought a measure of social independence as members of the local gentry." Even in this respect they were threatened by the development of the examination system, which made their position as gentry considerably more precarious. The examination system, with vast numbers of candidates eligible for a small number of higher posts, kept most intellectuals from questioning established authority. The obligations were wholly one-sided. As Wakeman points out, "hierarchical subordinates could not expect imperial gratitude in exchange for their loyalty." The power of the emperor grew, and the possibility of resistance to him diminished.

Since there was no likelihood of the individual acting alone, or of being very effective if he took such action, the only hope of success lay in some sort of collaborative action. While Confucian tradition accepted the idea of the merit of intellectual association, anything that smacked of "parties" or "factions" was thought dangerous. With the obvious conflict between these two tendencies in traditional Chinese thought, it was usually the opposition to factions that won out. Any combination of intellectuals that could be tarred with the brush of being factious, of belonging to factions (tang), became immediately suspect.

Wakeman develops in considerable detail the implications of what he calls "the second major intellectual phenomenon of the sixteenth century: the feeling that orthodox school-work was irrelevant to true learning." The actions of the imperial system determined the possibilities of intellectual life. While it is impossible to convey in brief compass the events of these tempestuous decades, many intellectuals, in Wakeman's words, particularly those "of a more yielding temperament," substituted "quietism for activism." This, however, was not true for all, and Wakeman gives considerable attention to the activism that developed in the Tung-lin Academy, founded in 1604. His concern is to show how a group of activists formed a clique, and how they aspired toward a general policy influence. Inevitably, they depended on a set of Neo-Confucian symbols, like loyalty, for their program, and were, according to Wakeman, undone in the end by their inability to create their own symbolic and concrete forms. As Wakeman explains: "Even in their own institutions they could offer nothing in the way of alternatives to the harmonious familistic images that sustained the state by making dissent a sign of selfish factionalism." The academies never became centers of important intellectual dissent; while many of them still flourished as late as the nineteenth century, the great majority "taught the texts necessary for examination success or subsidized degree candidates."

Only after China's defeat by Japan in 1895 were new kinds of institutions founded. These so-called study societies were sometimes short-lived. They expressed in one way or another the concern with saving China from imminent dissolution at the hands of the imperial powers. This activity was particularly conspicuous during the years 1897-1898 and 1906-1908. The study societies sought to infuse their scholars with a new kind of intellectual resolve. Their interest was no longer in mutual philosophical cultivation; rather, they saw themselves as intellectuals who understood the value of utilitarian skills. Theirs was a new concept of the idea of nation; they saw their own relation to the nation in a new way. For them, man's unique distinction, separating him from all other animals, was his capacity to form social organizations. Implicit in all this was a repudiation of the traditional theory of imperial sovereignty. That men were themselves capable of creating a nation, and that the ruler of such a nation needed to rule in the name of the people were ideas that gained currency. All this, however, had to be expressed within the framework of traditional values. It is not the least of

Wakeman's achievements to suggest how this was accomplished. As he puts it, "Popular sovereignty undermined the very foundations of the throne, but it was presented as a means of uniting the throne with the people, of creating the kind of ultimate 'we-ness' even Ku Hsien-ch'eng would have appreciated." Wakeman explains that this was "not just masking novel political innovations with a classical cosmetic." Important conceptual changes had taken place; there was a new theory of popular sovereignty and a new concept of royal descent. For a moment the intellectuals seemed to have gained extraordinary influence.

This was not to last. By mid-century the possibility of intellectual dissent was seriously compromised. To attempt to differ from the established political position was to open oneself to the charge of being an elitist, of betraying the democratic dictatorship that embodied the will of the people. As Wakeman puts it, "The ultimate cost of the Chinese quest for intellectual autonomy was political estrangement."

In a second study of intellectuals in China, Benjamin Schwartz explains why the attempt to structure the experience of intellectuals in terms of a conventional triad—"tradition/development/modernity"—as is too often done, is doomed to failure. As Schwartz indicates, the ways in which one traditional culture differs from another may be more significant than anything they share in common. The differences between the caste structure of an Indian village and the structures of Chinese peasant life are absolutely critical. Yet, it is common for such differences to be underestimated. Schwartz is suspicious of those who think that the symbolic world of the great religions of the past touched only a small number of people, and that they have not significantly affected the outlook of intellectuals in developing or modern societies. Schwartz writes: "In fact, quotations from the Confucian classics were probably more immediately available to the discourse of the masses in China than passages from George Lukacs, Lévi-Strauss, or Herbert Marcuse are to our own masses."

It is wrong to see the "great traditions as essentially static, integrated, unproblematic wholes which can be described in a few well-chosen propositions." Confucianism in China, for example, Schwartz says, had a complex history with much contradiction and conflict embedded within it. The idea that there was a single Confucianism, or that one can add Taoism, Buddhism, Legalism to Confucianism and make of these a single traditional intellectual mind-set, is what Schwartz finds untenable. He will not accept the conventional notion of the Chinese literati of the early nineteenth century as the "somnabulant mandarins complacently embedded in the unchanging essence of Chinese tradition." Schwartz refuses to see tradition as a simple integrated system; he is equally suspicious of the efforts to make modernization seem a coherent whole with simple uniformities. The emphasis in his essay is always on the tensions and conflict that existed within traditional society.

Looking at the Chinese scene, he sees the first decade of the twentieth century as absolutely crucial. The decade saw the end of the imperial examination system and the admission of great numbers of people into Westernized schools. All this, he reminds us, took place in an urban environment that was changing at an unprecedented rate. The young coexisted with another generation trained in a totally different way, who were in fact remarkably open to every variety of modern Western thought. Because the latter were familiar with Chinese traditional thought and with many varieties of modern Western thought, a "complex dialectic of conscious and unconscious relations between the culture of the past and modernity" developed. Schwartz explains that this attitude was confined not only to the pre-1911 generation, but continues also into the present. Some who reached intellectual maturity after the 1911 revolution came to see the traditional culture "as a vast, inert, and uniform incubus strangling the vital spirits of the nation," but this did not mean that those who despised the past had only a high regard for the urban culture of modern Europe. Chinese intellectuals, confronted with resolving the tensions of modernity present in the West, found it relatively easy to resist certain types of political and economic liberalism. Reading the works of Western intellectuals, they had a full armory of arguments from Western books with which to attack Western ideas.

Schwartz deals only briefly with the intellectual influence of Mao Tse-tung. He shows how Mao's hostility toward intellectuals had early roots. Mao saw the intellectuals as urban men, isolated from the realities with which he had dealt from his first days as a revolutionary. He detested the intellectuals' vanity and their efforts "to complicate simple truths and to seek ironies and ambiguities." While despising them for their weakness and their unwillingness to join in the revolutionary battle, it did not occur to Mao before 1949 that the intellectuals might be dispensed with entirely.

It is clearly impossible to guess what the future will bring. While the Maoists have succeeded in silencing the older generation, there is no way of telling what a new generation of Chinese intellectuals will choose to say. Under relaxed conditions, Schwartz writes, one may expect Chinese intellectuals to renew their interest in the West. He reminds us that the West of 1972, however, is not the West of 1919. Schwartz writes: "[The West] is more deeply involved than ever in its own intellectual and moral crises. One would thus expect a new Chinese intellectual generation to be far less passive and far more critical in its relations to various tendencies in the West."

Robert Bellah, writing about intellectuals in Japan, begins by considering the ways in which Chinese culture and social institutions came to be imported into Japan in the seventh and eighth centuries. The Chinese educational and examination system, however, did not long survive in the Japanese environment. Japan's aristocrats simply refused to accept the social changes that such a system would have required. The metaphysical and political side of Chinese thought had little interest for the Japanese; insofar as the Japanese were influenced by Chinese thought at all, the interest was largely confined to literature. Until the seventeenth century, the Buddhist monks and Shinto priests were the principal intellectual forces in the country. Two periods of great vitality and originality are conspicuous before the seventeenth century—the earlier one was dominated by poetry and fiction (794-1192); the later one was dominated by religion (1192-1333). As Bellah points out, "no major work of political or social philosophy was produced in the entire period."

This situation changed dramatically after the seventeenth century. While the Europe of Spinoza, Descartes, Hobbes, and Locke was closed to Japan, Confucianism brought a new message to the country. Confucian scholars, acting as teachers, advisers, and administrators, became increasingly important. Because of its explicit endorsement of established authority, there was little likelihood that a group of critical Japanese intellectuals would develop. Japanese society was not much exposed to skeptical criticism. Bellah dwells at length on the one intellectual who did attempt such criticism—Ogyū Sorai—whose work, though superficially conservative, was in fact highly critical. Sorai was to have great influence on Japanese intellectuals in the eighteenth and nineteenth centuries, but it is important not to exaggerate the influence of his ideas. When, for example, with Yamagata Daini, an attempt was made to carry Sorai's principles into practice, the result was abortive and Daini was executed.

Bellah suggests that it is difficult to know how important was the role of the intellectuals in the process leading up to Meiji Restoration. As he says, "Behind the Meiji Restoration stood no Locke or Rousseau, no Marx or Lenin, no Gandhi or Mao Tse-tung, but only a group of open-minded young men, ready to learn, committed to Japan, but with no determinate vision of the future." Bellah sees that those few Japanese who could use a European language in 1868 were enormously advantaged. Many were taken into the government; others established their own schools, teaching English and European studies rather than traditional Confucianism. In the early Meiji period, the intellectuals came mainly from the Samurai class; their background and that of officials in the government were essentially the same.

In more recent times, movement between the intellectual class and the political class has become increasingly difficult. The intellectuals have great influence through the mass media, but are not in a position to share authority with the political elites. The Meiji Restoration created the possibility of traditional institutions being questioned. This, however, has not meant that the intellectuals have come to dominate society. Two models of Japanese society have developed—one which emphasizes hierarchy and is openly elitist; the other which emphasizes *Gemeinschaft* and is obviously communitarian. While most modern Japanese intellectuals have been critical of the first and very accepting of the second, there have been important variations in their approach to both. There can be no question that the appeal of the idea of *Gemeinschaft* to the Japanese intellectual has had something to do with the enormous popularity of Marxism in intellectual circles. While intellectual protest in modern Japan has been common, the bureaucracy has continued to rule. As Bellah writes, "Postwar democracy was not the popular enactment of the democratic visions of the Japanese intellectuals. It came from the occupation through the hands of the bureaucrats. Though enjoying an unprecedented degree of freedom the Japanese intellectuals have most of the same problems they have always had. They have yet to find the organizational forms through which they can have a decisive impact on their own society."

Michael Confino, writing about intellectuals and intellectual traditions in eighteenth- and nineteenth-century Russia, challenges most traditional interpretations of that period. While he accepts the idea of an "intelligentsia," and reminds us that the term was invented in the late 1860's and was used to characterize a group of men and women with certain moral and political ideas, he sees the necessity also of speaking of "intellectuals." The intellectuals were the professionals of the society—the bureaucrats and scientists, the professors and teachers—but also the free-lancers and artists. Not all intellectuals were part of the intelligentsia, though there was some overlap on occasion.

Confino suggests that the first major change in intellectual life took place under Peter the Great. These changes were secular and nonreligious, and they received their institutional support from new structures. To be an intellectual in Russia under Peter was to go along with the tsar's reforms. Only those who were prepared to oppose those reforms could be said to be genuine dissenters; very few chose this route. Intellectuals served Peter loyally, favoring his revolutionary changes; after his death, when the tsar stood for conservation and consolidation, they stood behind these policies also. Toward the end of the eighteenth century, with the emergence of a larger group of educated nobles, the development of historical writing, an increase in the number of scientists, and, particularly after the French Revolution, with the exaggerated fear of Western ideas on the part of those in authority, a few, like Radishchev, came forward to criticize existing institutions. This company of "critics" was miniscule. Confino writes: "Well into the 1840's, most Russian intellectuals, following patterns established in the eighteenth century, remained state servants and maintained a basic identification with the autocracy and its attitude on the major problems of social and cultural order. Alternatively, they kept their thoughts to themselves or preserved them for future generations, sometimes in beautifully written personal diaries."

The Decembrist uprising, which was largely a revolt of the military, gave the so-called "first generation" of the Russian intelligentsia a legacy they prized. Confino shows how small was this so-called first generation, and how much they represented only themselves. They did not, Confino tells us, "form 'centers' for the implementation of their ideas and did not try to organize and carry out a political action." They did not try to find disciples; their purpose was not to proselytize. A few individuals had made an existential choice. Confino argues that it is a mistake to call this group the first generation of the intelligentsia; this was "a myth" created by intellectuals of a later time.

The so-called second generation of the Russian intelligentsia, sometimes called the "generation of the sons," emerged in the late 1850's. This generation is often defined by its support of nihilism. According to conventional opinion, there was a large social difference between the two generations, the second being substantially less noble, with commoners predominating, who showed themselves considerably more radical in their political opinions. Confino raises questions about the accuracy of this portrayal. He writes: "The nihilists . . . were chiefly young men and women of gentry origin." While the commoners had a role in shaping the intellectual outlook of this generation, Confino insists that theirs was not a leading role. Just as important, perhaps, there were no substantial ideological differences with the men of the first generation. The principal criticism made of the "fathers" was that they had been insufficiently activist. They possessed the knowledge requisite to action, but had chosen not to move.

Nihilism, Confino emphasizes, despite its protestations, was not really a political movement at all; its concern was largely with a moral despotism that the nihilists found objectionable. The nihilists were rebels, not revolutionaries, Confino insists; their importance lay in their creation of a life style and a moral code that emphasized the "here and now," and that represented a sort of counterculture. Nihilism had a short life; it was already waning by the end of the 1860's. It succeeded in creating a counterculture that pretended to be a popular movement—which it was not. Nihilism was the rebellion of sons and daughters of the gentry, in which commoners also took part.

Confino is concerned to say something also about the use of the term "intelligentsia" in more recent times. He reminds us that Lenin used the term disparagingly; for him, it was equated with all that was weak and compromising in intellectual life. Confino questions the conventional opinion that intellectuals played a leading role in the revolutionary parties of the first decades of this century. He suggests that they were always a minority within these parties, and that a new assessment of their role needs to be made. Intellectuals, he explains, were among the victims of the Revolution.

Thomas O'Dea treats the role of the intellectual in the Catholic tradition. His particular concern is to show how the Catholic church, after the Council of Trent, finding itself on the defensive, came to emphasize discipline, loyalty, and resistance to every novel political or social doctrine. Increasingly, the church saw the bourgeois universe, with its characteristic values and objectives, as essentially hostile to its own. Science was particularly fearsome to the church, and it is against this background of fear that the church's attitude toward Galileo needs to be seen. There was, in O'Dea's words, "an attitude of caution and reserve toward scientific breakthroughs."

In 1789 the church experienced yet another shock: the Revolution in France. This made the church hostile to revolutionary movements, and for the greater part of the nineteenth century there was an open hostility to everything that smacked of modernity. Within the church, there were important attempts to alter this attitude but none of them succeeded. The church, basing itself on two firm positions—that of the Counter Reformation and counterrevolution—became increasingly isolated from some of the most significant modern intellectual movements. O'Dea's purpose is to indicate how that situation was altered in this century, with the convening of the Second Vatican Council.

O'Dea's brief historical summary serves to introduce a larger topic: how the intellectual's role developed within the church. O'Dea contrasts Jewish religious rationality with Christian religious rationality, which adopted the Greek mode of thought. He writes: "Jewish religious rationality was basically ethical and legal, while Christian religious rationality became basically ontological, thus further revealing and intensifying the abiding Socratic tension." Christian education, O'Dea tells us, came to rest on the older classical literature and the new, specifically Christian literature. The church, "the schoolmistress of Europe," formed the Western mind. The church was the central institution in European culture; its role was to recruit an intellectual elite from many strata of society, keeping the elite within the church. There were tensions throughout the late medieval period, but the first open break came only with the Reformation. As O'Dea explains: "That movement represented an attempt to renew religious life by emancipating it from the now rigid and overinstitutionalized ecclesiastical context in which it had become embedded. Yet it was also an attempt to return to the conditions of the earlier now hardly appropriate sacral society."

The Catholic church, in O'Dea's words, was put on the defensive; it was increasingly concerned with matters that did not seem central to the interests of modern man. The Catholic intellectual, O'Dea says, was progressively pushed out of the mainstream of intellectual life. Not only did the church become alienated from science and modern scholarship, but it showed itself hostile to the new political movements that developed.

Only in very recent times has the church made a consistent effort to withdraw from these "counterpositions." The Second Vatican Council, like *Pacem et Terris*, represents efforts by the church to undo much of what it had become since the time of the Reformation. Mr. O'Dea recognizes that this effort has produced the greatest crisis in the church since the sixteenth century. As he explains, the position of the intellectual in the church is now entirely altered, but it is impossible to know what the results of the new freedom will be.

Intellectuals and Change

Leszek Kołakowski, in considering how the belief in the universality of Reason has fared over historical time, is concerned to distinguish between anti-intellectualism, which is a disparagement of Reason itself, and the more limited attacks on *scientism*, which Kołakowski defines as the belief that all meaningful problems may be resolved with scientific methods. While distinctions between the two are sometimes blurred, their separateness ought to be recognized. Kołakowski is particularly concerned to question those beliefs that "raise questions about the cultural continuity of man and the unity of the human species." Marxism, he says, "in its fundamental presuppositions, conceives of socialism as a continuation of the spiritual work of mankind, as the inheritor and not the destroyer of the existing bourgeois culture, in its intellectual, artistic, and technological dimensions." Marxian socialism, Kołakowski writes, was until the Russian Revolution "access to universal culture." This universalism came to be challenged by the growing nationalism of the Soviet state under Stalin, but so accustomed had socialists come to viewing Marxism in its more universal frame that many could not believe what the evidence so plainly told them. The intellectuals of the interwar years, Kołakowski writes, needed to believe that there was still extant "a power representing or embodying traditional longing for cultural universalism whose agent would be the working class." Those intellectuals who were converts to Hitlerism or Stalinism Kołakowski sees as persons fascinated by barbarism, the cult of force, and the cult of authority. None of these were new things. There had been similar conversions for similar reasons at other times in history. Today, Kołakowski writes, "socialism of the Soviet brand is no longer a center of attraction for conversions of this type. It has been replaced by Maoism and the cult of backward countries, the latter, for some intellectuals, being saviors who are showing new ways to humanity." Kołakowski sees these new enthusiasms as having nothing in common with the enthusiasm that once permeated traditional Marxism. He deplores what he sees as their contempt for knowledge, their cult of violence, their spirit of vengeance, their racism. Kołakowski's concluding sentence is an admirable testimony to his own beliefs; he writes: "The idea that mankind should 'liberate' itself from its intellectual heritage and create a new 'qualitatively different' science or logic is a support for obscurantist despotism."

There is no easy transition from Kołakowski's essay to any of the others in this issue of *Dædalus*. An effort has been made to group the articles by subject, bringing together the two that treat intellectuals in the Arab world and the Middle East, the two that deal with intellectuals in early modern Spain and in Latin America in the twentieth century, and concluding with the long article on intellectuals in the United States and the Soviet Union, together with two commentaries that have been solicited on this fairly controversial subject.

Menahem Milson, after briefly considering the *'ulama'*, the Islamic religious scholars of the premodern period, reflects on what has happened to the Arab intellectual since Europe's presence, starting with Napoleon's invasion of Egypt, became more consequential. The idea of Muslim superiority, once unquestioned, was significantly threatened in the second half of the nineteenth century. European power, exerting itself through a superior military technology and state organization, made Islamic practices seem anachronistic and insufficient. Although certain members of the *'ulama'* and of the governing classes urged modernization on the Muslim states as a way of recovering their position, by the end of the century the *'ulama'* had lost their place as an uncontested intellectual elite in the Arab world and had been replaced by a Westernized intelligentsia, less inclined to dwell on its Islamic identity and more disposed to emphasize its Arab character. This movement, Milson explains, was intimately related to the rise of Arab nationalism.

The Arab intellectual felt great ambivalence toward Western culture; even when committed to modernization as a way of restoring lost power and national pride, he recognized that such a commitment involved a certain loss of self-esteem. In continually emphasizing what the West had borrowed from Islam, particularly in certain scientific fields, there was an implicit concern to minimize Islam's indebtedness to the West and to reiterate a loyalty to traditional Islamic culture. The failures of European civilization were much commented on by Arab intellectuals. They tended to see Western civilization as essentially materialistic, and contrasted it with the spiritual qualities that were said to inhere in Arab civilization. Milson considers also "the crisis of the educated," the deep-seated feelings of alienation that commonly appeared among Arab intellectuals. Whether the estrangement was caused by a sense of isolation from other family members who had not become equally Westernized, or by a separation from the masses, it was exacerbated, the author says, by yet another factor: the intellectuals were politically peripheral. They were divorced from all major power, whether in the area of planning or of implementing change. Once heavily involved in the independence movements, they were no longer useful to the military men who came to lead so many of the Arab states. They are not even used by the new authorities as the legitimators of their power. As Milson explains: "The military officers can address the masses directly, using the same ideological formulations which were originally produced by the intellectuals." The intellectuals, having once provided the ideology, are now marginal men.

Nikki Keddie, in analyzing the role of intellectuals in the modern Middle East, starts by considering the conditions that had been common until the later Middle Ages. While a first tentative effort at Westernization was made early in the eighteenth century, this movement never became important. Napoleon is credited with persuading many nineteenth-century Muslims that their survival depended on changes in their military technology, and that this demanded educational reform. The movement for change took many forms; Keddie's interest is to show how the situation developed in Egypt, and also in Istanbul, the center of the Ottoman world. An earlier belief in constitutionalism and parliamentary institutions as the Western models most worthy of emulation gave way in time to a greater emphasis on the importance of nationalism. The successes of Mustafa Kemal Atatürk were crucial in conveying this message. Arab nationalism— an invention of the twentieth century—was soon blended with socialism in various parts of the Middle East. Agreeing that the Arab intellectuals have become a marginal class politically, Keddie argues that their alienation and frustrations ought not to be overemphasized. As she explains: "They hold major positions on newspapers, and have influence as writers and professors. The secular authorities rarely heed them, but this is hardly a situation unique to the Arab world." Keddie believes that "intellectuals in the Arab countries have a more difficult task than their peers elsewhere," and one of her principal concerns is to indicate why this is the case.

Juan Linz, in reflecting on intellectual roles in sixteenth- and seventeenth-century Spain, is in fact considering the plight of intellectuals in a post-Reformation Catholic world still dominated by religion. Most Spanish intellectuals, Linz explains, were prepared to accept the established political order; this did not in any significant way affect their creativity. While there was consensus on a "fairly well-delineated range of beliefs, values, and ideologies," this proved to be no impediment to innovation in other spheres. There was, in short, no fundamental conflict between authority and the intellectuals. While the Spanish achievements during the period were not uniformly distinguished—the showing in philosophy, science, and music, for example, was considerably less remarkable than that demonstrated in literature and the arts—the reasons for such variations in accomplishment are by no means obvious.

Linz, insisting that Spanish society in the sixteenth and seventeenth centuries was neither feudal nor bourgeois, sets out to establish the social composition of the intellectual class. While one out of four intellectuals was a university teacher in the sixteenth century, the number similarly engaged in the seventeenth century proved to be miniscule. The rise of Madrid—a city without a university—as the cultural center of the nation was only one of several factors that help to explain this change. Just as important, perhaps, was the extent to which both state and church, in their complex bureaucracies, provided men with the income, experience, and leisure that made possible an intellectual life. Many of the leading intellectuals were of course clerics. Linz estimates that in the sixteenth century some 40 per cent of the intellectual elite were members of the clergy; the number declined somewhat in the seventeenth century.

Linz writes also of the political roles of intellectuals, reminding us that such a characterization would have been meaningless to Spaniards of the sixteenth and seventeenth centuries. Linz pays particular attention to the debates that took place over many years concerning the rights of the Spanish crown to conquer America and reflecting on the status of the Indians that were found there. The Spanish kings encouraged this debate, seeking to legitimate their own policies through the support of intellectuals. According to Linz, the situation became very different in the seventeenth century. The debate was no longer so much about goals as about means; questions relating to administration and economics became the chief concern of intellectuals. Linz writes: "A changing society in crisis, which does not encourage criticism of its ultimate values, which feels no guilt for its actions, seems to be particularly favorable to the emergence of empirical social science analysis and reformism." He asks whether there may not be an analogy between the Spanish experience and that of post-Napoleonic France, post-Bismarckian Germany, and post-depression United States.

François Bourricaud, recognizing the difficulties of writing about Latin America as a whole, precisely because the social and economic differences between states are so substantial, still sees the necessity of making certain kinds of generalizations. He suggests that nineteenth-century Latin American provincialism, tempered by a certain reliance on a few major external centers, in Europe or the United States, came to an end sometime in the 1920's. That decade—and not the nineteenth-century decade of independence—is for Bourricaud the critical watershed, after which time questions of dependence and identity become dominant. The intellectuals' concern, he explains, was not so much to raise questions about the critical function of intelligence as to provoke debate about what the social mission of those who styled themselves intellectuals ought to be. Bourricaud, questioning the conventional portrayal of the Latin American intellectual as "a guerrilla-obsessed, revolution-loving romantic," or "a lover of the past, forever hostile to technical progress and the modern organization of industrial societies," prefers to see them as petit bourgeois, who are at one and the same time political radicals, cultural conservatives, anti-imperialists, authoritarian and elitist. Conservatism, Bourricaud tells us, is weak as a political ideology but has a strong position in Latin American culture.

"Activism" of one kind or other is clearly the *summum bonum* of intellectual life.

Bourricaud draws attention to what he calls "pulpit idealism" or Arielism, which, while condemning industrial society, especially of the Anglo-Saxon variety, constantly emphasizes the virtues of youth and finds its principal support in the student movements of the first decades of the twentieth century. He distinguishes between this Arielism and intellectual movements that took root in the years after World War II. It was then that an earlier populist trend that had emphasized the necessity of industrialization, agrarian reform, and a diminished dependence on imperialism became more generalized. There was a growth of interest in the social sciences in the universities and a proliferation of governmental programs and agencies charged with economic development. The intellectual's role, in short, was to change the world. Bourricaud writes: "It is no longer a matter of writing, or speaking from the heights of a pulpit, or even of participating in the organization—by education or indoctrination—of the popular masses. There is only one duty left: to make the revolution!" Bourricaud adds: "I am well aware that in Spanish the word *revolución* is extremely ambiguous, since it equally designates the most commonplace military coup d'état and the most decisive social transformation." Bourricaud considers the events that have in more recent years dampened the enthusiasm of those who once had such high hopes for development; he reflects on the growing anomie among Latin American intellectuals and their fascination with violence, guerrilla warfare, and urban terrorism. The developers, through their experiences, have indeed become more radical, but they seem no less separated from the masses and the popular culture that they continue to extol.

In considering the role of intellectuals in the United States and the Soviet Union, S. M. Lipset and Richard Dobson ask whether these societies are not becoming increasingly dependent on their intellectuals precisely at a time when these intellectuals are becoming more openly critical of the political and social order they are expected to extol. Reflecting on the situation in the United States, Lipset and Dobson show how long-standing is the adversary role of intellectuals in America. They agree with others that for almost the whole of the twentieth century the "political weight of American intellectuals has been on the progressive, liberal, and leftist side." While they would not deny the substantial differences between the intellectual climate of the 1960's and that of the 1930's, the authors choose to emphasize the consistency of the general leftist orientations of intellectuals both inside and outside universities. As for the Soviet Union, the authors' chief concern is to explore what they call "the widespread diffusion of opposition tendencies among Soviet intellectuals." Again, while not wishing to exaggerate the character of this "adversary role," Lipset and Dobson speak of the "rebirth" of a critical intelligentsia since the death

of Stalin. They suggest that "the guiding role of the Communist party
of the Soviet Union is being challenged by a new intelligentsia—not the
stratum of white-collar workers hailed by Stalin in the thirties as the
creation and servant of the party—but by a conscious, amorphously organized group of intellectuals who dare to speak their minds and engage
in independent activity in support of their ideals."

Lipset and Dobson seek to explain how the social structures of two
such very different societies have contributed to the formation of a critical
intelligentsia. The institutionalized reward structure for scientific and
scholarly work is held to contribute to the formation of such a class. More
important, however, is that scholarship imposes a demand for a certain
freedom from outside interference, and, in itself, helps to breed independence. While this is true of the scientist and scholar, who ought to be seen
as "knowledge-producers," it is not equally true for writers and artists.
Lipset and Dobson consider the role of patronage and markets in leading
such people to become participants in the so-called "adversary" class. They
are careful to distinguish between the substantially different conditions
that prevail in the United States and the Soviet Union for men and women
engaged in these pursuits. Their conclusion, however, is that "the Soviet
'adversary culture' gains strength from and unites intellectuals in the
academic world and those in the arts."

Lipset and Dobson argue that the growing influence of "intellectuals
and the university community on the body politic of many nations is not
a function simply of increased numbers, of the vital services provided, or
even of increased general social prestige." Rather, they say, the influence
is tied to intellectuals' capacity to exert greater authority over other elites—
in government, the churches, business establishments, the mass media. The
authors reflect on how the intellectuals have influenced the churches in
the West and how the Communist party's ideology in the Soviet Union—
at least in its cruder dogmatic forms—has been challenged by the development of science. While accepting the fact that the links between the intellectual community and the political elite are significantly weaker in the
Soviet Union than in most Western countries, the authors seek to emphasize the gravity of the problem in all the societies that they have examined. Since post-industrial society depends on trained intelligence and
on research and innovation, Lipset and Dobson see the greatest significance
in the fact that the political leaders appear to be "at odds with their intellectuals."

Jill Conway, in considering these views on the character of the American
intellectual, asks whether the principal theses can be supported by historical
evidence. She raises the fundamental question whether an activist society
whose intellectual tradition is essentially pragmatic is capable of producing an adversary culture. She is not certain that it can even conceive
of one. Radical criticism, she argues, has not been paramount in the uni-

versities; indeed, the research that has been conducted there has proved exceedingly useful both to government and business, and has in fact been dependent on both for its financial support. The fundamental criticism of the society that Lipset and Dobson think to be so manifest seems quite obscure to one who looks at these phenomena from across the Canadian border.

Martin Malia, examining the arguments from another perspective, asks whether it is not important "to point out certain historical and social factors which could limit or diminish the recent impact of critical intellectuals in both East and West." Believing that the differences between national traditions and social and political patterns are critical in determining the character and role of any intellectual class, Malia dwells on what he sees as the substantial differences between the Soviet Union and the United States. In this respect, the capacity of the American system to withstand criticism and "co-opt" the critic is contrasted with the Soviet situation where there is, in Malia's words, "a national heritage that combines the most exalted kind of critical ideals with a virtually complete lack of institutional means for implementing them." The number of active dissenters in the Soviet Union is obviously very small, Malia writes, and while there can be no accurate knowledge of their precise number, their activities are scarcely known to the overwhelming majority of the Soviet people. Also, their protest is almost always in literary terms; the principal critics are poets and novelists, and not, as in the West, social scientists. Malia finds no great threat to the Soviet system in such an intellectual opposition.

S.R.G.

S. N. EISENSTADT

Intellectuals and Tradition

THIS ISSUE brings together two themes in sociological and historical analysis that have often been conceived as being antithetical: "intellectuals" and "tradition." The concern with intellectuals is of long standing in the history of social thought and analysis. Until now its main focus has been on intellectuals as critics of existing regimes, as their potential or actual opponents, as innovators and revolutionaries, as creators of social or cultural orientations and activities opposed to tradition.

This has been true even more in the historical approach to intellectual history, epitomized best in the tradition of the history of ideas which concentrated on the study of the internal dynamics and interrelations of systems of ideas and rarely examined the relations of the social and political context in which these ideas were formulated to the development of the ideas themselves. In these studies, also, the emphasis tended to be on intellectuals as originators of new ideas, as iconoclasts or heretics. Intellectuals were most often conceived as the guardians or would-be guardians of a society's "conscience"—but only when that conscience was thought to be opposed to the established order.[1]

Those who viewed culture from a conservative perspective, such as religious leaders and theologians, leaders of churches or sects—to whom Max Weber, for example, devoted so much attention in his study of the sociology of religion—were rarely seen as intellectuals. If they were viewed as intellectuals, they were often designated as "conservatives," as supporters of the given tradition or status quo, as being part of the establishment. By implication, they had betrayed their special calling as intellectuals. Even the conservative intellectuals studied by Karl Mannheim in his seminal essay on the *Conservative Mode of Thought* were seen as especially interesting because they were opposed to the liberal and "rational" bureaucratic premises of modern society.[2]

In all of this literature there was relatively little concern with the intellectuals as creators and carriers of traditions, as participating in the symbolic and institutional frameworks of such traditions, or as performing their function as the conscience of society within the framework of existing traditions.

1

Thus, the body of beliefs and knowledge created by them—their intellectual works, the products of their intellectual activities—were given much less attention, being often treated as epiphenomena rather than as independent factors of social life.

Similarly, while there was a great concern with the degree of the intellectuals' autonomy and independence, their often difficult relations with the holders of power, and their potential revolutionary roles, this concern rarely became—as in the work of Karl Mannheim and later Edward Shils—connected with the analysis of the modes of intellectual attitudes with regard to their own products. As for associating this with the realm of intellectual activity and creativity more generally, or with different intellectual traditions, this was rarely done.[3]

This approach was, of course, very closely related to a certain conception of tradition—a conception with strong roots in the history of modern sociological analysis and in its central concern about the distinctiveness of the modern social order. This conception of tradition was especially prevalent in the work of many of the founding fathers of sociology—deToqueville, Marx, Durkheim, Weber, and others.

From the beginning of this century, the concern with the nature of modern society became transformed in sociological thought into a confrontation between modern and nonmodern, or modern and premodern societies. Ultimately the confrontation became one between modern and traditional societies—as more or less completely closed types. These types were described in various ways, among the most famous of which were Ferdinand Tönnies' distinction between *Gemeinschaft* and *Gesellschaft* and Robert Redfield's later more anthropologically-oriented distinction between primitive, folk, and urban societies.

Whatever the methodological and substantive criticisms raised against these and similar typologies, they dominated the thinking on the subject for decades and inspired much investigation. From these studies emerged the picture of traditional and modern societies which has prevailed in sociological thought for many years.

In such work, traditional society was generally depicted as a static one with little differentiation of specialization, with a low level of urbanization and of literacy. Modern society was seen as having very high levels of differentiation, or urbanization, with literacy and exposure to the mass media being commonplace. In the political realm, traditional society was represented as being based on a traditional elite ruling by virtue of some Mandate of Heaven, while modern society was seen as being based on wide participation of broader strata of the population who did not accept the traditional legitimation of the rulers and who held those rulers accountable in terms of secular values and efficiency. Above all, traditional society was conceived as society bound by the cultural horizons set by its tradition, while modern society was seen as culturally dynamic, oriented to change and innovation.

Some time ago dissatisfaction developed with this dichotomy, with this too narrow conception of tradition, which assumed an equivalence between tradition and traditionality. The dissatisfaction stemmed also from the unstated assumption that modern societies, being oriented to change, were antitraditional or nontraditional, while traditional societies, by definition, were necessarily opposed to change.[4] It was not only that the great variety and changeability in traditional societies were rediscovered, but there developed also a growing recognition of the importance of tradition in modern societies—even in its most modern sectors, be it "rational" economic activity, science, or technology. Tradition was seen not simply as an obstacle to change but as an essential framework for creativity.

Hence, the view developed that tradition need not be restrictive. However permanent tradition may be, it is not simply the dead hand of the past, but, as Shils demonstrated many years ago in his article on "Tradition and Liberty,"[5] a framework without which cultural creativity is impossible.

These considerations called for a shift in the sociological and historical analysis of intellectuals. If they were the major creators, the carriers and bearers of the greatest products of tradition—the great religious and intellectual symbols and monuments of their day—it is not easy to reconcile this role with the emphasis on their critical stance, except when, as in modernity, their activities in the opposition served to create some new tradition.

Clearly, the relations between intellectuals and tradition are more complex than has been generally assumed. To study these relations, in a very preliminary way, is one of the principal objectives of this volume.

I

While no single definition of tradition has been agreed upon let alone developed as a result of our study, we have started our discussion with certain tentative approaches to tradition, trying to identify the enduring elements of a tradition behind their continuously changing symbolic forms and structural expressions. We attempt to see tradition as the reservoir of the most central social and cultural experiences prevalent in a society, as the most enduring element in the collective social and cultural construction of reality.

This reservoir, however, is not an undifferentiated one; it has a structure of its own; it focuses mostly around:[6]

(1) the major ways of looking at the basic problems of human existence and of social and cultural order, of posing major questions about them, especially concerning such problems as: the definition of the relative importance of different dimensions of human existence and their bearing on cultural and political identity; the perception of the interrelation and mutual relevance of the cosmic, the cultural, the social, and the political orders; the patterns of participation in the formation of social and cultural orders; the bases of legitimation of such orders;

(2) the possible answers to these problems that develop within a given society or civilization; and

(3) the organization of various institutional and symbolic structures for the implementation of different types of solutions to these problems.

Such construction of social and cultural reality, of any tradition, is closely related to the charismatic dimension of human endeavor and social activity.[7] It is here that some of the problems of the position of intellectuals, including the tensions between intellectuals and political authorities, become most fully articulated. Charismatic qualities and activities, as displayed by great leaders such as the promoters of great religions or great empires, may be of crucial importance in the construction of tradition and the expansion of the human social and cultural environment that takes place through such constructions.

The charismatic construction of reality—the construction of a meaningful environment—is not limited to what is generally defined as the intellectual dimension, such as the pursuit of learning or rational knowledge. It pertains also to other symbolic elements of human existence—the aesthetic, mythical, ritual elements—as well as to the realm of social solidarity and justice. Each of these dimensions is also susceptible to symbolic rational elaboration and can serve as focuses for the definition of collective and personal identities and bases for participation in a meaningful environment.

Such responses to the quest for some ordering experience, although always containing a strong symbolic element within them, are not created only by intellectual specialists, religious, expressive or aesthetic, and ideological. Indeed, as we have seen, many of the great traditions of mankind have been created by persons who, however adept in using symbols in their activities, played social roles not defined in terms of such specialization but spanning a much wider range of activities.

Institutionalization of the symbolic orientations inherent in the construction of traditions does, however, promote some such specialization among intellectuals and other elites, particularly the political elite. Symbolic and institutional responses to the quest for the charismatic order tend to become, in any society, centered in some specific institutional loci that are important from the point of view of the construction of tradition in general and that of the place of intellectuals in it in particular. Among these loci the most important are the so-called centers of a society. In such centers the major spheres of social and cultural identity are crystallized,[8] and the sources of authority and power are established. The exercise of authority and power is closely related to various organizational needs and must be considered in terms of what has often been called, in sociological literature, its functional prerequisites.

Thus, any tradition, especially those embedded in macrosocial orders, has both symbolic and structural-organizational dimensions. Each of these dimensions develops a dynamic of its own, while, at the same time, both are intimately interdependent through specialization of roles and the interpretation of symbolic and organizational dimensions across such specialization of roles. This fact accounts for a powerful potential for tensions and conflicts within every tradition in general and between political authorities and intellectuals in particular.

It may seem, as has often been assumed in sociological literature, that the roots of such conflict can be explained by the fact that in every society tensions develop between the symbolic and the structural-organizational dimensions of tradition. These tensions express themselves, first, in competition between specialists in each of these dimensions, that is, intellectuals dealing primarily in symbols as opposed to politicians and bureaucrats dealing primarily with organization. But though this is probably true—and though each such activity tends to have its distinct organizational and institutional basis —in fact, such tensions have much deeper roots. They are inherent in the very process of the institutionalization of the charismatic dimensions of tradition and manifest themselves on several different levels, the direct organizational competition between intellectuals and other elites being only one.

Potential for the development of such tensions lies in the fact that any tradition, any construction of cultural reality, implies posing certain types of questions about the basic problems of human existence in the social and cultural context, as well as a range of permissible answers, thus excluding other possible questions and answers.

First, any such social or cultural construction of reality usually emphasizes some dimensions of human existence—be it the aesthetic, the political, or the ritual experience—as setting up the limits of the permissible and meaningful parameters of experience. In the process, it may suppress other dimensions or relegate them to secondary or subterranean levels. Thus in almost any great tradition there tend to develop, at its very core, some accepted ideals which, although antithetic to some of its primary orientations, are derived from its parameters. While these ideals point in different and seemingly opposing directions, they nevertheless tend to reinforce one another. The interrelation between the Brahmanic ideal and that of the renouncer in Indian civilization, between the active engagement of the church in the world and the monastic ideal in Western Christianity, between the Caesaropapism and the monastic withdrawal and submission in Eastern Christianity are illustrations of such antithetic yet mutually reinforcing ideals.

Second, potential for tension is based in the fact that within any tradition or social order the possible relations between different components which coexist there go beyond their actual coalescence in the given institutionalized system. In any given historical situation, there exists a greater variety of possibilities for setting up of the components of those clusters and of their organizational derivatives than that which has become actually institutionalized. Hence, any such component may become a focus for tension and heterodoxy.

This possibility is inherent in almost all characteristics of tradition, in its symbolic as well as its organizational aspects. Thus, for instance, the very specification of the basic parameters of a cultural tradition in its relation to various collectivities is open to redefinition and recrystallization in terms of any of these parameters or of new orientations developing from them. Similarly, attempts at such redefinition may develop with regard to the degree to which any given collectivity becomes the embodiment of the major orientations, along with the relative evaluation of the different dimensions of human existence.

All these tensions are increased by the close relation of the processes of institutionalization of the various dimensions of tradition with the organizational aspects of the social division of labor in general, and with the distribution of power and control over resources in particular. The holders of power usually tend to support such interpretations of tradition. Therefore, the restrictions and exclusions entailed are necessarily closely associated with, although not necessarily identical to, maintenance of the distribution of power and wealth. Hence each of these aspects of the institutionalization of the social and cultural construction of reality—the symbolic and organizational aspects and especially the combination of the two—tends to limit the scope of participation by various groups in the society in the central symbolic spheres, in the control over resources, and in access to meaningful participation.

These constrictions may also be rooted in the fact that once an innovation is accepted it may become routinized, "deflated," more and more removed from its original impetus. Those who participate in its perpetuation—its originators and their initial close collaborators—tend to become less interested in it. Such constrictions may also stem from the fact that the originators of these cultural innovations—great religions, new political systems, new economic enterprises—may fear the further spread of such a spirit of free creativity. The one-time innovators may attempt to impose limitations on the spread of this spirit and on the attempts of other people or groups to participate in such creativity or to extend its scope. There then develops among such groups hostility and alienation toward the very acts of creativity.

II

Within the symbolic dimension these may find expression in conflicts about changing conceptions of sources or bases of social order—for example, revelation versus reason, the degree of "givenness" of the cultural tradition, the nature of "ultimate" authority which legitimizes and sanctions the social order, or the relative importance of different dimensions of human existence. These tensions in the symbolic realm are closely related to those in organizational spheres—those rooted in competition over power and resources and in structural and organizational pluralisms and manifest in movements of rebellions and sociopolitical protest. The more intellectual expressions of these tensions may become strongly interwoven with such movements. Indeed the most often recurring themes of protest in any human society are closely related in the various combinations of structural organizations and symbolic restrictions inherent in the institutionalization of any tradition.

Among these themes is, first, the tension between the complexity and fragmentation of human relations inherent in any institutional division of labor and the possibility of some total, unconditional, unmediated participation in the basic social and cultural order. Parallel to this are the tensions inherent in the temporal dimension of the human and social condition, that is, the tensions between the deferment of gratification in the present as against the possibility of its attainment in the future.

Hence many movements of protest tend to emphasize the suspension or negation of the structural and organizational division of labor and to proclaim the ideal of "communitas," of direct, unmediated participation in the social and cultural orders. They also emphasize, together with such participation, the suspension of the tensions between productivity and distribution and merge these two through a basic commitment to unconditional participation in the community.

Similarly, many such movements place strong emphasis on the suspension of differences between various time dimensions—between past, present, and future—and of the relation between time dimensions and patterns of gratification and allocation of rewards.

The two institutional-symbolic positions around which the ambivalence toward traditions and orders tend to converge are: first, those of authority, especially as vested in the various political and cultural centers; and second, the system of stratification in which the symbolic dimensions of hierarchy are combined with structural aspects of division of labor. Thus symbols of authority and of hierarchy are common causes of ambivalence and demands for change.

Such protest tends to be directed against restrictions on development of all spheres of human endeavor or on participation in all of them. Protesters, therefore, often emphasize orientations contrary to those prevalent in a given tradition. That is, they emphasize aesthetic and otherworldly orientations in rational traditions, or this-worldly orientations in a Confucian tradition. As the themes of protest become related to the problem of participation in the social order and to the distribution of power and control within the social order, as well as to the search for a meaning in terms of the identity of various groups in a society, it focuses on demands for incorporation of new dimensions of human existence into the central parameters of a tradition, for incorporation of broader groups into the more central zones of a society, or for widening the scope of participation by such groups.

Although such themes of protest may be limited to relatively simple populist, antirational, and anti-intellectual movements, tendencies to heterodoxy, antinomy, and rebellion are most clearly articulated by intellectuals. Through the activities of intellectuals—especially in the more differentiated societies and more rational traditions—elaborated antinomian sects and ideologies grounded in the negation of the rational premises of their respective traditions may develop.

These antinomian tendencies often are accompanied by support for other dimensions of human existence, such as the mystic or ritual, and, as we have pointed out above, by the more extreme expressions of subjectivism and privatization. They may also emphasize symbols of primordial attachment, though expressed in intellectual terms. But it would be wrong to assume that they are directed against political authority only. They may also be directed against intellectual authority and it is in this tendency that the antinomian orientations of intellectuals become most clearly articulated.

In the intellectuals' articulation of the major themes of protest the antithesis between rational and antirational orientations are most fully worked out. It is indeed the intellectuals who, while often building on broader populist tendencies, tend to articulate most fully, from within the very centers of tradition, from the very depths of their rational elaboration, the most extreme antinomian tendencies. With their emphasis on the negation of rationality, these tendencies and themes become focused on the symbols of some of the other dimensions of human existence and social life, and very heavily stress the various primordial dimensions of human life.

III

The preceding analysis implies that the tension and ambivalence that have characterized the relations between intellectuals and power and authority throughout the history of human society are not merely due to specialization of roles. They stem first of all from the combination of such specialization with common participation in the construction of both the symbolic and the organizational aspects of institutionalization of traditions. Political authorities and intellectuals alike tend to participate in both the organizational and symbolic aspects of formation of tradition in general and of centers in particular. They participate in the institutionalization, in symbolic and organizational terms, of some of the crucial aspects of the quest for the ordering of social and cultural experience. Their participation is especially marked in the crystallization of the common societal and cultural collective identity or identities, based on sharing common attributes or on participation in common symbolic events, and in the articulation of collective goals, that is, of organizational goals conceived as the goals of the polity.

The competition between these two groups is rooted in the very nature of intellectuals and political authority, in their mutual interdependence. Political authorities need the basic legitimation provided by intellectuals, religious or secular, and that provided by elites. Intellectuals and intellectual organizations need the protection and help of political institutions for the establishment and maintenance of their own positions. Each group attempts to maintain maximum autonomy and maximum control over the other.

Political authorities may quite naturally attempt to control the activities of intellectuals and to claim for themselves the sole right to represent the major religious and cultural symbols of the society. At the same time, they may expect a certain level of involvement in central political activities on the part of the intellectuals. Against this, intellectual elites often attempt to become the major representatives of the pure social and cultural orders, to usurp central political offices, and to remove their organizations from the political control of the rulers.

To attain these broad objectives intellectuals may attempt to gain official recognition and protection from the state—either as the established religion or dogma, if possible, or as a secondary one. They may attempt to maintain their autonomy in the performance of major activities, especially internal government, organization of activities, and recruitment of members; in the propagation of activities and maintenance of institutions; and in the independent determination and transmission of major values and dogmas. They may attempt to preserve and extend the material bases of their institutions and to enhance their general position in the society. Some may obtain positions of political and administrative importance, motivated, aside from personal ambition, by the desire to serve as the rulers' spiritual guides to assure loyalty to their own values and symbols and to increase the political and economic power of their own groups. Ultimately they may overthrow the existing regimes and establish religious or secular theocracies.

Intellectuals, especially the more technical and professional ones, tend to be ambivalent with regard to the more mundane, instrumental entrepreneurs. On the one hand, they may be envious of the entrepreneurs' power or wealth and want to share in it, while on the other hand they may look down on them as being in need of some broader legitimation that the intellectuals can provide. These tendencies may, of course, be resisted by instrumental entrepreneurs, though they may feel that in some situations, especially in situations of change, they are in need of some such legitimation. Thus, the more professionally and organizationally oriented intellectuals may become allied with some of the institutional entrepreneurs—seeing in their activities a chance to extend the scope of their own influence.

The basic poles of interdependence and tension between intellectuals and other authorities and elites in general and political authorities in particular shape the intellectuals' moral dilemmas and their responses to the problems of participation in society. On the structural-organizational level, the most extreme response is withdrawal by the intellectual elite from the existing order, establishing their own segregated, separate units or withdrawing into private activity or contemplation. This may occur with or without the performance of any active roles in the public sector. At the other extreme are two possibilities: total submission to those in power or total usurpation of power.

Between these extreme organizational responses there may develop many more differentiated types of response. In less extreme cases, intellectuals may attempt to combine, in various ways, their respective cultural activities together with different degrees of criticism, on the one hand, and participation in the formation, maintenance, and change of cultural traditions and political orders, on the other.

These organizational responses may be linked with the intellectual themes of protest analyzed above, as well as with the various traditions of intellectual response to the problem of the basis of intellectual activity and its place in the over-all cultural tradition—the scientistic, romantic, populist, apocalyptic, and anti-intellectual modes designated by Shils.[9] In their pure form, virtually all these traditions can become combined with the more extreme organizational and emotional attitudes of intellectuals. But they also become ingredients of the responses in which different modes of critical and participatory activities and orientations are combined. These various types of response may be combined with different degrees of organizational autonomy in the pursuit of intellectual activities.

IV

This brings us to two major problems in the analysis of the relation between intellectuals and tradition: first, the entire complex of problems related to the critical stance of the intellectual; and second, the problem of the place of the intellectual in the construction of broader social traditions.

The range of problems involved in the critical stance of the intellectual includes the social, cultural, and political conditions affecting their innovative activities in general and their critical ones in particular, and the relationship between their critical stance and social political radicalism.

The second problem—that of the place of the intellectual in the broader process of construction of traditions—is related to the first but not identical with it. It deals with such questions as: What are the mechanisms through which intellectual creations become articulated with the enduring elements in the social construction of reality which guide the orientations of collective and individual action, invest these actions with broader meaning, and mold the commitments of other nonintellectual groups in the society? More specifically, how did the various intellectual products and activities—and the various themes of protest, antinomy, heterodoxy, and dissent, elaborated and conceptualized by intellectuals—become integrated into broader social and cultural traditions?

These two problems tend to converge around the assessment of the role of the intellectual in social, cultural, and political change in general, and in modernization in particular.

The very linking of the problems of the critical attitudes of intellectuals to their place in the construction of tradition indicates that we should be wary of the rather common assumption that intellectual attitudes are necessarily opposed to tradition as such, and that intellectuals always perceive their role in terms of creating a society in which traditions do not play an important part. The critical stance is a condition of the mind which may express itself in assent to and acceptance of traditions, ideas, beliefs, and authority as well as in rejection. Moreover, as we have mentioned above, there is no necessary relation between the pursuance of intellectual activities, even in relatively independent and autonomous ways, and the development of different types of broader critical attitudes. The majority of intellectuals productive in intellectual fields in various societies have been in many ways active or passive cultural and political conformists. Needless to say, however, there developed many variations in different societies, variations which have yet to be systematically investigated.

Several variables in social conditions influence the scope and nature of intellectual activity in the construction of traditions, the types of intellectual traditions developed, and the scope and direction of the critical role of the intellectuals. One such variable is the degree of structural and organizational differentiation, especially the degree of development of specialized intellectual roles. A second is the degree of pluralism in the symbolic systems of a society or a tradition: the degree to which there exists in a tradition a conception of the symbolic order of society as a complex of separate and autonomous though interacting domains, as opposed to an undifferentiated, totalistic concept implying either lack of distinction between, or the hegemony of, one symbolic domain (for example, religious, cultural, or political) over all others. A third includes several aspects of the contents of such traditions, as well as the basis of the legitimation of the social and cultural orders. Especially important is the degree to which the possibility of change exists in the tradition as against a conception of the tradition as given and immutable.[10]

Societies do, of course, vary greatly with respect to the degree of social structural differentiation and spheres of cultural activities. Thus, for instance, in many primitive societies these various realms are—symbolically, conceptually, and institutionally—not fully differentiated from one another in terms of the roles that specialize in the creation and transmission of symbols. As is well known, both types of differentiation—symbolic and organizational —tend to increase as we pass from primitive to archaic, historical, and modern societies, although certainly not always in the same degree.

Cutting across degrees of structural differentiation and extent of differentiation of the various symbolic spheres is the degree of flexibility and autonomy of different symbolic orders, the relative predominance of the different spheres within the over-all symbolic structure or cultural tradition, and the degree of openness to the participation of different groups. Here several possible constellations can be distinguished. First there are those cases in which each such different symbolic sphere is seen as autonomous but closely interrelated with the others, in the sense that participation in one enables access to another without, however, the first imposing its own criteria on the second. The second possibility is that of relative closeness of each such order and of purely adaptive or power interrelationships among them. Last, and some times connected with the previous possibility, one center or symbolic sphere may predominate over the others in being able both to regulate access to them and to impose its own values and symbols on them. The exact nature or contents of such institutional and symbolic flexibility or rigidity necessarily differs from one society to another.

Thus, in primitive societies such rigidity is manifest in the close inter-dependence of its various units (clans, kinship group) and in the organizational and symbolic overlapping, or even identity, in the definition of these units. There is little differentiation between the symbols of belonging to one or another institutional sphere (political, economic, or ritual) and between the situations and roles in which they are enacted.

In more complex societies, in which there exists a much higher degree of organizational differentiation of institutional and symbolic spheres, such flexibility or rigidity is especially evident in the institutional autonomy of such spheres (in terms of their specific goals) as against a relatively tight symbolic or institutional control of one central sphere over all the other spheres.

Traditions also vary greatly, regardless of the degree of structural or symbolic pluralism prevalent within them, in the extent to which they are conceived as given and immutable, or alternatively, open to change and modification. They also vary in relative stress on learning, as opposed to inspiration or revelation, as the major source of knowledge and order, as well as in the degree of commitment to the tradition's values and symbols on the part of individuals. Here the major distinction is between a high level of commitment to it, as against a more adaptive "resource" attitude toward it.

V

The various combinations of all these aspects of structural and symbolic differentiation, and of the contents of traditions analyzed above, greatly influence the whole range of intellectual activities—their symbolic and organizational patterns and the different types of critical stances.

Thus, in general, the greater:

(1) the differentiation within the basic units of the society, and especially between the periphery and the structures of the centers and within them;

(2) the internal socioeconomic differentiation within both the centers and the periphery and a concomitant development of some wider strata or classes;

(3) the differentiation in the symbolic definition of relations between prevalent, existing units and the symbolic expression of the various centers;

(4) the general displacement of symbolic spheres and their anchorage in primordial symbols, development of varied autonomous symbolic systems, and development of varied autonomous symbolic spheres in religion and philosophy;

(5) the differentiation and *specialization* between societies,

the greater also the range of activities and organization in which the intellectuals may engage. Thus, the greater the specialization of their roles and the scope of their creativity, the greater the possibility of the development of relatively autonomous intellectual activities and institutions and of the development of critical stances, especially in relation to political authorities.

The greater the degree of structural economic and technological development of a society, the greater the degree to which the political elites become dependent on the technical resources, knowledge, and skills of various specialist groups. These specialists are, both personally and on the bases of their knowledge, associated in various ways with intellectual groups and institutions. Such conditions also tend to increase the intellectuals' ambivalence toward authority and to increase the possibility of their total submission to authority and renunciation of their own autonomous identity.

Under such conditions, the tension inherent in all societies and traditions —between different types of rationality, between them and other dimensions of human existence, and between these and the possibilities of meaningful participation in social life—become intensified as do the tendencies of heterodoxy. As we have seen, while the tendencies to heterodoxy, antinomy, and rebellion are most clearly articulated by intellectuals, they are not directed solely against political authority. They may also be directed against intellectual authority, and, indeed, in such situations intellectuals tend to articulate the most extreme antinomian tendencies.

In situations of social change leading to growing differentiation, the tendencies to heterodoxy and the attempts to reformulate different parameters and institutional aspects of tradition become fully apparent.[11] In these historical situations there also arises the possibility of extending the scope of critical orientations and substantive rationality on the one hand, and the possibility of the development of restrictive antirational tendencies on the other hand.

These latter tendencies may be due first to the fact that the greater the critical potential in any society, the greater the attempts by the carriers of tradition and the holders of power to limit the range of such criticisms. Second, there may arise among intellectuals or other groups what may be called irrational—magical, demoniac, constrictive, and alienated—answers to such new problems, often in terms of antirational antinomianism.

These general possibilities for the growing scope of intellectuals' activities, as well as for development of the different types of critical attitudes analyzed above, are indeed closely related to the general trends of differentiation already mentioned. But the specific contents and organization of these activities, and the connection between different types of creative and critical behavior and attitudes, are not influenced by the general trend to differentiation. Rather, they are affected by the constellation of relations between the different aspects of differentiation and by the other aspects of tradition we have discussed.

Here it is very important to stress that the various aspects of social and symbolic pluralism or differentiation and different contents of cultural traditions analyzed above do not necessarily appear in steady association. We may find societies—of which Japan is one of the most important illustrations—in which a high degree of structural differentiation is accompanied by a relatively small degree of differentiation in the symbolic field and with a strong emphasis on the givenness of the social and cultural order. In contrast, in other societies—such as the early Christian and many of the initial Islamic societies—some openness of social traditions and a strong emphasis on learning may be combined with a relatively small degree of structural differentiation.

Moreover, the contents of a cultural tradition—for example, its relative stress on learning as opposed to inspiration or revelation—may vary, independently of the degree of symbolic openness or of emphasis on the givenness of tradition. These contents naturally influence the direction and type of intellectuals' activities, their major form of organization, and—of special importance from the point of view of our discussion—the relations between different types of criticism and between them and other types of intellectual and broader cultural activities.

Of special interest is the distinction between heterodoxy and criticism in the intellectual field and that in the political-social field. Some traditions, for example, the Chinese, may generate far-reaching and sophisticated critical stances in the field of pure intellectual or symbolic criticism, but at the same time allow very limited criticism in the structural-political field. In other traditions, such as in Latin America, radicalism is associated with a level of intellectual criticism that is, relatively, only slightly sophisticated.

Societies may also differ greatly in the degree to which they segregate such intellectual movements from broader political and social ones. Here again China is probably the most important illustration of such segregation, when compared with other societies—Western Christianity probably being the outstanding example—which tend to facilitate close association of intellectuals with social and political movements. Moreover, as we have indicated above, societies may vary greatly in respect to the degree to which they develop within autonomous intellectual activities and organizations—also, in the degree of their combination with various intellectual stances.

All these variations are, in principle, influenced by the different constellations pointed out above. But exactly how the intellectual criticism and critical activity is addressed to the symbolic aspects of traditions related to political dissent, social and political nonconformism, and sociopolitical radicalism remains a fascinating question which is in one way or another raised in all the essays presented here. They attest to the importance of these problems and the richness of the materials available for their analysis.

VI

Such a full analysis is still very much before us, but it may be worthwhile to present here the preliminary results of an analysis of relations between intellectuals (in this case mostly religious elites) and political authorities in one type of traditional society—the historical bureaucratic empires. This analysis attempts to show the extent to which religious institutions, organizationally autonomous, participated in the central political struggle. The more closely the religious organizations were identified with state organs and institutions, the more their political participation was confined to the accepted, legitimate level; the less they were identified with political institutions, the more they developed articulated political activities beyond the existing institutional framework.

Similarly, the greater the extent to which a polity or state constituted a basic referent of religious activity, the greater the extent to which the political activities of religious groups were contained within the framework of existing political institutions and the smaller the possibility of their undermining this framework. On the other hand, the stronger the universal and transcendental elements within these religious groups, the greater the possibility of their developing various kinds of intensive political orientations and activities beyond the existing institutional framework.

Finally, the more that activist orientations within religions were mainly otherworldly, the more passive the attitude toward political activity, deflecting active forces from participation in the central political area, often directing them into segregated religious spheres. The greater the emphasis on involvement in the secular world and the stronger the specific ideological formulations, the greater the active political involvement. The combination of these elements and the vicissitudes of political struggle influenced the exact level of political participation and orientation of these religions in each specific case.

Within the framework of these relations the various modi vivendi between the religious and the political regimes were worked out. Within this basic framework there also developed opportunities for the various religions to undermine rather than support the political systems of the centralized empires, either through open opposition and active promotion of change or through political passivity and the withholding of political support.

This possibility was rooted, first, in the fact of partial differentiation of the political and religious systems. As a result, these two systems were closely interwoven or even identical at the local level, while highly interdependent and sensitive to one another in the central political sphere. Potential for undermining the political system was also encouraged by the relative autonomy of the religious sphere, by the fact that the mutual interdependence between these two spheres was to some extent asymmetrical. This asymmetrical relation was a historical fact: most of the religions analyzed had origins independent of their polities; their chances of surviving the regime were therefore quite likely. Many of these religions had flourished under other political systems: Buddhism, Islam, and especially Christianity developed and functioned under various types of relatively undifferentiated or decentralized regimes, whether patrimonial or feudal. Although a centralized empire was not a necessary condition for the existence of these religious organizations and systems, the existence of some combination of wider, relatively flexible, and traditional religious orientations was a basic prerequisite for the institutionalization of the political systems of the empires.

These factors, plus the ultimately religious character of these societies, forced their rulers to depend on religious organizations for the maintenance of their traditional legitimation and for provision of the more flexible resources. True, the rulers could destroy any given religious organization, but the basic autonomy of the religious organizations and their transcendental orientations made them relatively independent of any particular polity. Only when a given polity constituted a central referent of the orientation of a given religion—as in Confucianism and to a smaller extent in the Mazdean Church—was the dependence of the religion on this polity relatively great and its fate closely bound to that of the polity.

VII

The problem of the relationship between various forms of criticism, protest, and general cultural and social innovation on the part of intellectuals seems to be especially salient on the modern scene. Indeed, the kinds of conditions that facilitate the varied and independent activities of intellectuals become much more fully developed—and complicated—in modern societies.

Of special importance from the point of view of differences between the premodern and the modern period seem to be the much higher level of differentiation of intellectual roles; growing secularization; the breakdown of traditional types of legitimation opening the field to intellectual creativity and influence; and the increasing impingement of criticism and protest on the very centers of the society. The growing proportion of specialized intellectuals in the general population and the growing mass of their product no doubt causes increasing impact on the conceptions of social, cultural, and political order, on the symbols of identity, the perception of meaning, and the interpretation of the relation of social arrangements to transcendental contents. Reinforcing these effects is the increasing intellectualization of the trades and professions, that is, the increasing use of abstract and symbolic elements in the manipulation of nature, men, and social reality. The mass media not only stimulate the illusion of the growing impact of intellectuals, they also change the balance between them and politicians in influencing beliefs, attitudes, and orientations.

Moreover, the very breakthroughs to modernity contained a strong revolutionary orientation and the constitution of modern politics and cultural traditions is often perceived as being deliberately and consciously created. The many protest movements that ushered in the modern period, unlike those in more traditional societies, were characterized by a continuous combination of protest with institution building and center formation. These combinations were also characteristic of the great modern social movements, in which intellectuals played such important roles.

This tendency was reinforced, as S. M. Lipset has shown, by an apparent paradox that tends to develop in the dynamics of education systems. Modern systems of education, on the one hand, draw men into the orbit of the societal center and generate intensified participatory activity; on the other hand, they engender a tendency to a more fully articulated protest and dissent.

For all these reasons, modernity is often perceived as brought about only or mainly by intellectuals, and the process of modernization is often implicitly identified with their alleged role in destroying old traditions and in forming new ones. This uniqueness of the place of intellectuals in the creation of modern traditions is to some degree an illusion created by the perspective resulting from our own awareness and involvement in intellectual traditions and activities.

In fact, the context of modernization does not necessarily change the nature of the problem of the relation between intellectuals and tradition. True, intellectuals tended to play important roles in most modern reform or revolutionary movements. But they have not necessarily been the only or even the most important leaders of such movements. Nor have they necessarily been the most important generators of change or of successful symbolic institutional innovation. Rather they constitute important reservoirs of catalysts of change. They are important in the articulation of the themes of change and serve as legitimators of change.

Even in some of the more outstanding cases of participation by intellectuals in the creation of modern tradition—notably the cases of Africa, South America, and nineteenth-century Russia—it is quite clear that once intellectuals have contributed to the shaping of new symbols of collective identity, these are taken up by other elites. Intellectuals are then relegated to a more specialized and less central role, culturally and politically. This was true, for example, of the new African and Pan-African federations. These problems are not entirely different from those that existed in constitutions of premodern traditions—whether concerning the origins of the Christian faith and its conceptualization and codification into a system by the early church intellectuals or, in a sense obversely, the attempts to elaborate intellectual elements in the Japanese tradition, whose initial crystallization was most clearly not based on intellectual rationalized symbols.

VIII

Here we come to our second problem, that of the place of intellectuals in the construction of tradition. Obviously, by definition, intellectuals, as experts in symbols and their operation, play a vital part in the formulation of the symbolic dimensions of traditions. It is primarily through intellectual works that we see broader traditions, that we attempt to discern or extract them from the fantastically intricate network of sociocultural, political, and economic phenomena. However, societal traditions contain elements that are not specifically intellectual creations. Intellectuals themselves live and work within wider sociocultural traditions, traditions that constitute part of their environmental constraints, that mold their behavior and the forms of their activities. They contribute to these wider traditions, not only through their works, but also unconsciously—through their actions, reactions, and interactions, through their daily behavior.

Thus we return to the question of what the mechanisms are through which intellectual creations become articulated with the more enduring elements in the social construction of traditions. We are as yet far from a full or systematic answer to the question, but some indicators have emerged during the preparation of this volume. Of special importance is the place of so-called "secondary" intellectuals, what have been alternatively designated as "minor" or "spurious" intellectuals. They may be defined either in terms of the quality of their intellectual work—from the vantage point of cultural originality as against cultural borrowing—or in terms of their occupational roles as teachers, government civil servants, or those engaged in mass communications and popular entertainment. While the relative status and mobility patterns of various intellectual genres are clearly subject to cultural variability, it has become more and more apparent that secondary intellectuals may indeed play a central role in the broad process of construction and transmission of tradition. It may well be that it is they, through their activities in teaching, entertainment, and communications, who serve as channels of institutionalization, and even as possible creators of new types of symbols of cultural orientations, of traditions, and of collective and cultural identity.

It is true that with regard to the broader problem of the place of intellectuals, and of different types of secondary intellectuals, in the construction of tradition, we have but few systematic explanations. The problem constitutes one of the major new avenues for research and study, one that may help us to go beyond the double optical illusion: the illusion that, on the one hand, all traditions are created by intellectuals and are most fully manifest in high intellectual works and products; and, on the other hand, that the major creative aspects of intellectual activities are confined either to purely specialized tasks or to purely critical orientations.

REFERENCES

1. A good collection of materials representing this approach can be found in G. B. de Hussar, ed., *The Intellectuals: A Controversial Portrait* (New York: Free Press, 1960).

2. Karl Mannheim, "Conservative Thought," in *Essays on Sociology and Social Psychology*, ed. P. Keskemeti (London: Routledge & Kegan Paul, 1963), pp. 74-165.

3. See Karl Mannheim, *Ideology & Utopia* (London: Routledge and Kegan Paul, 1933); Edward Shils, "The Intellectuals and Powers: Some Perspectives for Comparative Analysis," *Comparative Studies in Society and Culture*, 1 (October 1958), 5-23; Shils, "Intellectuals," *International Encyclopedia of the Social Sciences* (New York: Macmillan, 1968); Mannheim, *Essays on the Sociology of Knowledge*, ed. P. Keskemeti (London: Routledge and Kegan Paul, 1952).

4. I will present the development of their approaches to tradition and modernity in greater detail in a forthcoming publication.

5. Edward Shils, "Tradition and Liberty: Antinomy and Interdependence," *Ethics*, 68 (April 1958), 153-165.

6. This formulation follows S. N. Eisenstadt, "Some Observations on the Dynamics of Traditions," *Comparative Studies in Society and History*, 11 (October 1969), 451-475, but goes beyond it. For a preliminary statement of an analysis of tradition and situations of change, see: Eisenstadt, "Tradition, Change and Modernity: Reflections on the Chinese Experience," in Ping-Ti Ho and Tang Tsou, eds., *China in Crisis*, 1 (Chicago: University of Chicago Press, 1968), 753-774. See also the most recent article by Edward Shils, "Tradition," *Comparative Studies in Society and History*, 13 (April 1971), 122ff.

7. See S. N. Eisenstadt, *Charisma and Institution Building: Introduction to Selections from Max Weber*, Heritage of Sociology Series (Chicago: University of Chicago Press, 1968), ix-lvi; Edward Shils, "Charisma, Order and Status," *American Sociological Review*, 30 (April 1965), 199–213; Shils, "Society and Societies," in Talcott Parsons, ed., *American Sociology* (New York: Basic Books, 1968), pp. 287-304.

8. See Eisenstadt, *Charisma and Institution Building*; Shils, "Charisma, Order and Status"; Shils, "Society and Societies."

9. Shils, "The Intellectuals and Powers."

10. These distinctions follow largely the analysis presented in the General Introduction and the various specific introductions to S. N. Eisenstadt, ed., *Political Sociology* (New York: Basic Books, 1971).

11. These points are more fully elaborated in S. N. Eisenstadt, "Innovations and Tension Between Different Types of Rationality," paper presented to the International Seminar on the Social and Political Implications of Scientific and Technological Innovation in the Field of Information, Olivetti Foundation, September 7-12, 1971, Courmayeur, Italy.

EDWARD SHILS

Intellectuals, Tradition, and the Traditions of Intellectuals: Some Preliminary Considerations

INTELLECTUAL ACTIVITIES are directed simultaneously toward their objects and toward intellectual works. The objects are as diverse as the universe and all its contents. Ostensibly, intellectual works are about objects; in fact, they are about objects perceived within frames set by works. In their relations to works, intellectual activities may be classified into productive, reproductive, and receptive activities. The normally anticipated outcome of an intellectual's productive activity is the publication of a coherent, conventionally self-contained intellectual work, printed or in manuscript. By self-definition, the process of intellectual production is incomplete without its culmination in an end product which is a work. The work itself becomes a work when it is presented in a conventionally complete form, when it takes a physical form capable of entering into the "possession" of others— that is, capable of being received, assessed, and acknowledged.

A work is an objectively existing pattern of symbols of remote reference which record the "state of mind" of the producer; the "state of mind" might be cognitive, normative, analytical, descriptive, or expressive—formative, auditory, or visual. It is not ordinarily, in itself, a link in a chain of empirical, executive action; in any case, when it is, it is not that feature which constitutes it as an intellectual work. The remoteness of reference of the symbols can be remoteness through actual or implied abstraction, or by distance in time or space. The referents of the symbols may be the physical universe, unseen powers, the earth, its contents and inhabitants, or society and particular men —at any level of abstraction and at any point in time. They might not have an experiential referent. A work which consists of patterns of symbols usually has a physical form or precipitate—manuscript or book or journal article or painting or musical score or sculpture. Certain works require enactment after reaching intellectual and then physical form, for example, musical and dramatic works.[1]

A principle formulated and written down by a legal philosopher might be incorporated into the decision of a judge in a *particular* case; a general proposition regarding a property of a certain class of substance might be

21

incorporated into a technological action in the production of a particular piece
of machinery. Analytically the principle and the proposition are distinct from
the judicial decision and the maker of machinery. The former *are* intellectual works or parts of intellectual works; the latter *use* intellectual works
or parts of them in a sequence of actions with practical intentions to maintain
or modify. The dividing line between practical actions and intellectual works
is fluid. The constitution of the intellectual work is independent of its intention; a work intended to be "used" or "applied" is a work nonetheless; it is
not a practical action.

Works fall into a variety of genres: in literature—novels, lyric poems,
epic poems, ballads, short stories, essays, and so on; in science—treatises,
reports on particular investigations (monographs and papers), reviews of
literature, and so on. There are marginal forms of work which do not quite
correspond with this definition. For example, oral narratives, "preprints,"
works circulated in mimeographed form, posthumous works, and suppressed
works which do not reach the stage of printed presentation. These are,
however, only variants around the norm of work completed and published by
the author regardless of whether it is explicitly attached to his name. The
various divisions among works are defined very roughly by differences in
forms, techniques, and subject matters. Genres are defined by common forms
and techniques: fields, disciplines, subfields, and specializations distinguished from each other by their subject matter and procedures. (The divisions of genres and the divisions of fields are not coordinate.) Often, but
not always—and increasingly in modern times—the fields and disciplines are
associated with corresponding institutional divisions and the specialization
of the persons who produce works in particular genres or fields.

I

Those who produce intellectual works are intellectuals. Those who engage
in their interpretation and transmission are intellectuals. Those who teach,
annotate, or expound the contents of works are intellectuals. Those who only
"consume," for example, read intellectual works in large quantities, and who
concern themselves receptively with works are also intellectuals. Each of
these is a different intellectual activity and they coexist in the same persons
in varying combinations. Productive intellectuals are almost invariably receptive and reproductive intellectuals as well. Practically all intellectual works
reproduce to some extent other works—this is one of the constitutive elements of any intellectual tradition. Obviously there could not be reproduction without reception. Receptive intellectuals—the audience—usually reproduce the contents of works but they do not produce works; if they did,
they could become productive intellectuals. The three intellectual functions
correspond roughly to the threefold division of types of intellectuals: productive intellectuals, reproductive intellectuals, and consumer intellectuals,

all of whom are concerned with intellectual works. For the most part, in our studies of intellectuals, we are concerned with productive and reproductive intellectuals.[2]

II

Any intellectual work is produced in the setting of an intellectual tradition or traditions, for example, a setting of families of previously produced works which serve as models or points of departure. An intellectual tradition is a set or pattern of beliefs, conceptions of form, sets of verbal (and other symbolic) usages, rules of procedure, recurrently and unilaterally linked with each other through time. The linkage is an identity between two or more temporally sequential works. An intellectual tradition exists in a stock of works which those who participate in the tradition "possess," that is, assimilate into their own intellectual culture and to which they also refer. Intellectual traditions are not necessarily continuous in time; there can be periods of recession in which a tradition is dormant or latent. This state of latency—not extinction—is made possible on the existence of differentiated sets of stocks of works which are handed down or made available to the productive, reproductive, and receptive intellectual through teachers, historians, critics, and editors, and through printed books, journals, and manuscripts made available through libraries, bookshops, and other distributive institutions.

Intellectual traditions are differentiated into the traditions of particular genres, fields, and disciplines. Each of these divisions of works has a variety of traditions of its own, containing and referring to its procedures and its subject matters; each has its own monumental works which embody some of the qualities the works and the adherents of the traditions prize most highly; each has its own monumental figures. There are manifold relationships including identities among these traditions. Traditions become differentiated internally and often split up into separate and distinctive traditions; traditions previously separate and distinct sometimes are fused. The traditions which neighbor on each other sometimes fuse with each other, at least the parts which are adjacent do so. Sometimes traditions which are remote in substance and space from each other come together—at least unilaterally. Numerous separate and distinct traditions very often share certain elements with each other. These shared elements may be substantive or procedural elements, or they may be elements of the ethos of intellectual activity in general, or of a major field or section of intellectual activity, or of a body of general culture.

Traditions refer to and are effective through individual works and a vague overtone or disposition which runs through many works and possesses a force of its own.[3] Every tradition is characterized by common patterns to be found in the works which constitute it and represent it to its adherents. The patterns of beliefs, forms, usages, and procedures which refer to the sub-stantive objects that are taken into or dealt with in works we will call primary or substantive traditions.

Every work which appears inevitably has its point of departure in an existing tradition. Every productive intellectual produces his work under the influence of beliefs, forms, usages, and the ethos of procedure and produc-tion which he has received and which he in part reproduces. These form the primary tradition to which he is attached or by which he is dominated. Wholly reproductive intellectuals and productive intellectuals with feeble imaginative and ratiocinative powers are dominated by their traditions and leave them unaffected. Many poor intellectuals by their feeble use of their traditions and exercising feeble mental powers could, without concert but by the effect of massive numbers, bring about a decay of their traditions. Intellectuals with greater imaginative, ratiocinative, observational, and ver-bally and visually formative powers—that is, intellectuals with "creative powers" or "genius" or "originality"—create works which extend and change their traditions.

The strength of a tradition—the extent to which its carriers are formed by it and thus give it persistence—is partly a function of the institutional procedures and structures by which it is inculcated and sustained, and partly a function of the pattern of the tradition itself—particularly of the ethos which it contains. It is also partly a function of the tasks accepted by pro-ductive intellectuals, itself something which is defined by tradition. The intellectual tasks which intellectuals undertake in the production of a work are often "given" by traditions but not by any means exclusively so.[4]

The attachment of an intellectual to a tradition can be a function of his "training" and participation in an institution which is the custodian of one or a number of primary intellectual traditions and of the activity of the auxiliary intellectual institutional system, which includes publishing, patronage, criti-cism, distribution, and so forth. Such intellectual institutions operate through training, through the provision of a sustaining environment of other persons who embody and exercise standards of performance, and through the allo-cation of facilities and rewards for intellectual exertion and accomplishment. Not all intellectuals, however, acquire their acquaintance or maintain the connections with their primary intellectual tradition through institutions to the same extent.

There is, nevertheless, a minimal institutional setting. It might be only an acquaintance with an individual who embodies and exemplifies some elements of an intellectual tradition or recommends particular works, or it might be membership in a family which has mastered a particular intellec-tual activity and transmits and cultivates skill and forms and arouses moti-vation in one or more of its offspring for the further performance of such intellectual activity. The relationship of an apprentice to a master is a more organized, even if structurally elementary, institutional form of the transmission of tradition. There have been productive intellectuals, particularly in the production of certain genres, such as novels and poems, who have had practically no institutionalized training. Where, as in the case of literary production, there is resistance to institutionalization, we may speak of "uninstitutionalized" intellectuals. But even these uninstitutionalized intellectuals have had a minimal contact with certain elements of the intellectual traditions through some institutions of elementary schooling, that is, by learning how to read and write and having their attention focused on certain major works, for example, certain epic poems, novels, and so on. The formation which the potential intellectual receives in school is not training for the production of works; it is rather some knowledge of a few works and cultivation of some of the sensibilities which enable him to make contact on his own with intellectual traditions, that is, constellations of intellectual works, and which enable his propensities to be aroused. Before this first contact and behind these constellations lies an enchainment of intellectual institutions which have made their coalescence possible. The tradition in question could not have been formed without an institutional structure to form and transmit it. Thus the uninstitutionalized intellectual is the beneficiary of a considerable amount of anterior institutionalization.

Furthermore, the uninstitutionalized intellectuals are, at least in modern times, surrounded by a complex of auxiliary intellectual institutions. They come into contact with them through the distributive institutions and the institutions of assessment. (I refer here to publishing, bookshops, libraries, journals, book reviews, honorific and sponsoring academies, and so forth.) The relatively uninstitutionalized intellectuals sometimes mingle convivially with institutionalized intellectuals, for example, in clubs and salons where literary and scientific intellectuals meet each other; they also encounter the works and ethos of the institutionalized sector of the productive intellectual stratum in a variety of settings. Increasingly they have to cope with the auxiliary or distributive intellectual institutions.

The traditions of these auxiliary or distributive intellectual institutions are sometimes but by no means always identical with major elements of the ethos or substance of the primary intellectual traditions of the productive intellectuals. An editor or director of a publishing house or of a literary review might be very congenial and indeed helpful in guiding young writers in a fruitful direction. In contrast with this, certain editors, critics, and publishers might be antagonistic to a certain trend of literary production. Censorship is the most dramatic instance of the antagonism of an auxiliary institution to an intellectual tradition. All these institutions exercise a "directive" influence of their own through selective policies of financial support, selective acceptance for publication, selective reproduction, and discriminative critical assessment. All of them have selective consequences through facilitation, promotion, obstruction, and suppression and through encouragement and discouragement.[5]

It is difficult to tell whether these restrictive influences are in the end successful in curbing or diverting the movement of production guided by the primary tradition where there is antagonism between it and the restrictive or repressive auxiliary institutions. Censorship in the eighteenth century was not enduringly effective. The puritanical restrictions of the nineteenth and early twentieth centuries were broken by the middle of the twentieth century. It remains to be seen whether the restrictions in Communist countries will continue in the future with the power which they have had for many years. Whatever the ultimate outcome, it is clear that the antagonistic auxiliary institutions, especially when confronting a primary tradition which has only a rudimentary institutional foundation, as it does in literature and painting, can constrict and inhibit production which is guided by the disapproved primary tradition.

III

Intellectual works are, of course, not produced only under the influence of primary intellectual traditions, the primary intellectual institutions which sustain and nurture them, and the auxiliary institutions which influence the fate of particular completed works and of conceptions of works unborn. They are also products of intellectual propensities, that is, the need to be in contact or communion with an order or pattern of symbols which have an "objective" validity to which the producing intellectual orients himself and which provide standards for his intellectual conduct. This order (or pattern) is either believed by the intellectual to be "given" and his task is therefore its discovery, or it is thought to be susceptible to "creation" by the intellectual's exertion of his powers. The intellectual propensities and powers—very obscure words to use to refer to such crucial phenomena—include such qualities as imagination, observational and ratiocinative capacity, sense for the sounds of words and form of works, and so forth. They also include the intellectual's motivation and capacity for sustained and assiduous application to the tasks which are accepted by him.

Intellectual works are produced in roles which include in their constitution the obligation to produce works. Once a person begins to conceive of himself as a poet or a scientist—a conception formed in part by the activity of producing, or aspiring to produce, a work—he regards it as an imperative flowing from his self-image to exert himself to produce works. The obligations of the role reinforce and give direction to the motivating propensity; they help to shape the powers of production. The roles are often enmeshed in intellectual institutions and communities which sustain and intensify propensities, help to focus them, and embody the particular currents of tradition in demanding forms. The intellectual institutions affect the propensities and powers by the exercise of authority which sanctions and rewards intellectual performances, by the presentation of models of individuals who incorporate standards, and by the opportunity for frequent and intimate association with other persons performing the same kind of actions and standards. All these by their presence fortify propensities and can if the standard is high enough impel exertion of the powers. Their absence or feebleness can dull propensities and cause talents to wither. These are the most elementary functions of intellectual institutions; some of these functions can be performed by amorphous communities in which there is no institutionalized authority but in which there is frequent and intimate association with like-minded persons and models incorporated into individuals. (Literary circles, salons, cafés can perform these functions.)

The productive intellectual acts within the framework of intellectual traditions—primary intellectual and secondary or auxiliary intellectual traditions. (The "stronger" his powers, the more likely he is to go beyond them and impose his own beliefs and thereby change what he receives from them.) He also incorporates into his image of the world and responds to his preintellectual and extraintellectual experience in society—in the family, the economy, the state. These preintellectual and extraintellectual experiences provide him with subject matter in some genres; they might also set problems for him to deal with. The extraintellectual experiences also result in attachments and repugnances which influence his relationship (for example, selection and emphasis) to elements of his primary intellectual traditions. It is relevant to mention at this point also the nonintellectual traditions with which he enters into contact through his membership in society and in the particular sector in which he spends his life. The nonintellectual traditions of the larger society—moral, religious, political—may be called the tertiary traditions of the intellectual.

Primary and auxiliary intellectual institutions exist in a setting composed of the institutions of the larger society—for example, ecclesiastical institutions, economic institutions, political parties, the state, and the system of stratification. These all influence the attachments and images of society which are possessed by intellectuals and therewith influence the production of works and the contents and shapes of primary intellectual traditions. These macrosocial institutions influence intellectual institutions through their impact on the flow of financial resources, the provision of careers, the flow of persons into careers, the direct exercise of authority, and the fostering of a matrix of beliefs about what is important in life and society. The authorities of these macrosocial institutions also set and select tasks for intellectual works through their exercise of authority, through their control of occupational opportunities and financial support, and through experience with problems which some intellectuals, by identification and sympathy, regard as their own. These externally set tasks are never viewed by intellectuals independently of the framework of their own primary (and secondary) intellectual traditions. Even when tasks are set or problems are given by an external instance, they are never exclusively externally given; the intellectual's treatment of an

externally given problem is always constitutively influenced by the procedures, categories, and interpretations which he draws from his own intellectual traditions.

IV

Intellectual traditions are substantively continuous but they do not necessarily develop in temporally continuous or substantively unilinear shape.
Innovations are constantly made, although at different rates in the different
parts of the same traditions and in different traditions.

The ethos of intellectual production in each primary tradition emphasizes
the need to be in possession of the tradition and, in some traditions, such as
the tradition of modern science, the simultaneous need to modify it. The traditions undergo revision, sometimes with the deliberate intention of modify-
ing the tradition to cause it to conform more closely with a transcendent
standard of truthfulness. Sometimes it is modified because the individual
who has absorbed it has the "need," that is, "originality" or "genius" to produce something true to the "facts" as he experienced them or more expressive
of his vision or imagination, which then turns out to be different, but not
because novelty as such was his aim. There are also innovations motivated
primarily by the aim to be "original." Finally there are those who are motivated by the need to "destroy" what has been received. By no means all of the
efforts to modify tradition—especially those which seek primarily to be
original or to destroy it—turn out to have the desired effect. Often they have
no effect at all.

The traditions are presented to their recipients at a moment in time but
the traditions themselves have an existence through time. They have a form
which moves and grows through time. This process of growth in traditions is a
process of modification, element by element. A tradition is such because of
the substantive continuity of its development and the relatively greater
stability—the relative unchangedness of certain elements. It is in this relative
stability that an important element of tradition resides. In the Christian community of believers, for example, belief in the divinity of Jesus Christ and in
His redemptive mission have been stable elements handed down from the
original Christian belief for nearly two millennia, although many other
elements of original Christian beliefs have undergone great changes. Many
subsidiary traditions have developed, the carriers and proponents of which
have often been extremely antagonistic toward each other, while nonetheless
sharing the beliefs in the divinity of Jesus and His redemptive mission. In
other traditions there is a gradual replacement or pronounced modification
of practically every element of the tradition even including sometimes its
ethos. Even the ethos of traditions undergoes elaboration and change of
emphasis. Yet these "totally changing" traditions too must be regarded as
single traditions if there is continuity in their development. By continuity I

mean reference to antecedence and factual even if unwitting incorporation of what is presented from the past, immediate or remote, into new worlds.

No tradition begins *ab ovo*. Every tradition grows out of another tradition and that is the way it has been since the beginning of intellectual activity. No intellectual tradition if it survives long enough to preside over the production of significant works ever dies completely. Even where its content is not explicitly referred to and identified as such, it goes on living through incorporation in the life of what comes after it.

V

With the precipitation of intellectual traditions and the production of a considerable stock of intellectual works, intellectual roles were accelerated. These roles were not necessarily identical with professional roles, although the frequent coincidence of intellectual roles and professional roles is of great importance for the development of primary and secondary intellectual traditions. Those who produced intellectual works came to see themselves as incumbents of intellectual roles; they saw the roles defined as those in which intellectual works were produced. They saw such roles as distinctive and different from other roles. The performers of these roles did not call themselves "intellectuals"—the term is less than a hundred years old—they called themselves writers, poets, dramatists, philosophers, theologians, historians, antiquarians, natural philosophers. Even now by no means all who perform intellectual roles call themselves "intellectuals."

The intellectuals' roles and the institutions and communities in which they have been integrated have formed the social matrix for a set of secondary traditions. These secondary traditions have been about all sorts of things and not just about particular objects of the work, the production of which was associated with the roles. Many of these secondary traditions have touched in one way or another on authority—authority in general, transcendent authority, and earthly authority.

One of the elements in primary intellectual traditions—the element of ethos—has defined intellectual activity as being concerned with fundamental—important and ultimate—things. The ethos of intellectual activity has defined the highest performance as being endowed with charismatic properties. The conception of "genius," the notion of "inspiration," both bespeak the charismatic overtones which are oriented to the greatest intellectual accomplishments. Accordingly, intellectual roles of the most creative intellectuals have been defined as correspondingly endowed with charisma; their incumbents have been correspondingly perceived.

Most of the secondary traditions of intellectuals, being concerned with authority, have been concerned with the locus of the charismatic and its institutional manifestations. The greatest secondary intellectual traditions of modern times, for example, populism, nationalism, scientism, equalitarianism, individualism, progressivism, "genuiness," and spontaneity, are traditions which assert the locus of the charismatic and its institutional manifestations. They assert that charisma is located in a particular part of society or in a particular kind of activity. Some of the secondary traditions also entail some conception of the significance of intellectual works in society and the rights, obligations, and powers of those who perform the intellectual roles. This belief in the charismatic qualification of intellectual works, of the roles of their producers and the producers themselves, has brought intellectuals into unavoidable contact with earthly authority. It has made for a sense of membership in the same social category as the other claimants of charismatic qualifications, namely the powerful. It brought intellectuals into symbolic contact with the economically powerful—landowners, industrialists, merchants, financers. These contacts have been both affirmative and hostile.

Intellectuals have been drawn and forced into social relationships with the mighty of the earth by a variety of factors. One factor has been their own social origins. When literacy was rare, the literate and the intellectuals who grew from their midst were either offspring of families of some earthly importance or they were taken into their presence so that they grew up in their midst and continued in their maturity to associate with them. Also, regardless of their class origin, intellectuals have been brought into contact with the powerful by the demand of the latter for the services of the literate, as court historians, astrologers, chaplains, civil servants—as legitimators, as conjurors with spirits, and as functionaries. Quite apart from these factors, intellectuals have been brought into contact with the powerful because they needed to be in contact with them to obtain their livelihood as their employees and as their clients and stipendiaries.

But even if these factors had not been operative, intellectuals would have been in contact with the mighty because they have been fascinated by them. Intellectual activities are "serious"; the charismatic is "serious" and intellectuals being concerned with the charismatic have, willy-nilly, been drawn into preoccupation with those in authority because all great, very powerful authority is believed by those who possess and those who contemplate it to have a charismatic element resident in it.

VI

In richer and highly differentiated societies with more numerous intellectuals and more specialized intellectual activities, intellectuals formed institutionalized and informal communities of their own. Thereupon, they tended to associate less with the mighty than they did when the way of life of intellectuals was less differentiated and the numbers of intellectuals smaller. Nonetheless, their preoccupation with the mighty, even where more of them led a life separate from the mighty, remained an ineluctable element because it was established in their secondary traditions and was constantly fed by their own primary propensity to be drawn by charismatic things.

These experiences have affected the contact of intellectuals with their own traditions. The rulers have had their own traditions and the institutions and situations of rulers and the otherwise powerful have their own exigencies. Demanding services from intellectuals for the accomplishment of their ends and for their legitimation, the powerful gave tasks to intellectuals which were not always those which were given by the traditions of intellectuals. Thus, a certain conflict arose between the obligations and commitments of intellectuals intrinsic to their primary and secondary traditions and the demands, often accepted by intellectuals, of their nonintellectual associates. This conflict has in turn fed the secondary traditions and it has also influenced in various ways certain contents of the primary traditions in those genres and fields in which intellectual activity has drawn on the intellectual's own experience in society.

VII

From their own experience and from certain secondary traditions, particularly those which developed in modern times (for example, scientism, populism, equalitarianism, progressivism, "genuineness"), intellectuals have developed two particular secondary traditions which are of interest to us here. One of these is the tradition of anti-institutionalism and the other is the tradition of antitraditionalism. The anti-institutional tradition has regarded institutions as restraints on spontaneous expression and as inhibitors of the development of "genuine individuality." Institutions have been regarded by this tradition as the repressive instruments of authority, which are thought to represent the "dead hand of the past." As "progressivism" developed as a secondary tradition, the past was devalued. The present was considered to be the beginning of the future and not so much a moment in the forward extension of the past. Traditions, according to this view, were the means by which institutions imposed the patterns of the past on the present. Tradition was thought to be inadequate to the present and its development into the future. It was thought to legitimate iniquitous institutions—iniquitous in their injustice and repressiveness. Modern intellectuals, particularly those working in certain genres, those whose productive activities had not been highly institutionalized, have been especially prone to the espousal of the anti-institutional and antitraditional secondary intellectual tradition. It has, therefore, been difficult for an understanding and mature appreciation of tradition to be aroused and developed among contemporary intellectuals. "Presentism" and "futurism" together, although in different ways, have caused a certain blindness of the mechanisms of tradition in society and in intellectual production. "Tradition" has become a term of polemic and not an object of analysis.

The anti-institutional and antitraditional attitudes of intellectuals themselves, of course, also belong to traditions. They are paradoxical traditions which have been nurtured in bohemian literary intellectual communities and in the intellectual sectors of revolutionary movements. Since the French Revolution the acceptance of the legitimacy of revolution and of the iniquity of tradition has become one of the strongest traditions of intellectuals. This coexistence of the tradition of the antitraditional raises particularly complex problems for analysis.[6]

Nonetheless, intellectuals have by no means unanimously or unambivalently espoused these antitraditional traditions. Many intellectuals have accepted civil traditions and many have espoused and entered into the services of earthly authority. Intellectuals have served authority not only as civil servants. Many have played important political roles, and not always in oppositional or revolutionary parties or movements. Some have become presidents of states, prime ministers, and members of cabinets. There have been many outstanding intellectuals among parliamentarians.

They have for the past quarter century played particularly important roles as economic advisers. As statistics become more and more an instrument of government and administration, eminent statisticians in their capacities or through their pupils have played a vital role in government.

The transformation of technology into a "science-based" activity in numerous fields of industry, agriculture, and communications has changed the standard of life of modern societies, even in underdeveloped countries and some, even much of this, is the result of the application of the work of intellectuals. The development of mass communications industries, themselves partly based on the work of scientists, has required large staffs of literary and journalistic intellectuals, and these in turn have helped to diffuse the idiom and the traditions of those sectors of the intellectual stratum, albeit in a simplified form, into a wider section of the population.

Modern politics have become increasingly "intellectualized," as, on the one side, economic policy and social welfare have become the main issues of civil politics and as, on the other, antitraditionalist traditions have become integral to the armament of ideological politics.

Increasingly since the Second World War, as higher education has become a major criterion in the claim to and allocation of deference, intellectuals have correspondingly come to acquire more and more prominence. The potentialities of scientific research for military technology have also brought about a great prosperity in certain fields of scientific research and a great increase in the number of scientists.

As a result, to a greater extent than ever before, intellectuals have become an estate of the realm. This has, perhaps for the first time in history, brought about a diffusion into the wider population of many of the secondary traditions of intellectuals, as well as some of their primary traditions.

This might have profound consequences for the primary traditions of intellectuals by increasing the quantity of intellectual works, intensifying competition, and possibly bringing certain fields into a condition of exhaustion of their intellectual potential.

The foregoing observations apply primarily to the wealthy large-scale industrial societies of the West. They have an almost equal application to the poor countries of Asia and Africa and in a different way in Latin America. The Latin American countries possess, of course, many of the same secondary intellectual traditions as the richer, industrially more advanced countries of Europe and North America. The Asian countries, including the Islamic Middle East, are distinctive in that they have intellectual traditions which are more or less separate and distinct from the modern Western intellectual traditions, both primary and secondary.

Aside from historical continuities such as Greek with Arabic philosophy, they share with the Western countries the possession of an elaborate written culture with great and famous accomplishments. They also share with the earlier history of the Western countries certain identities arising from approximate identities of the roles of intellectuals in a largely illiterate society ruled by bureaucratic oligarchical regimes. The black African societies, insofar as they are not Islamic or Christian, differ from Latin American and Asian countries in their lack of a written indigenous intellectual tradition and in their smallness of scale and poverty, which in the past inhibited the formation of a substantial and differentiated intellectual stratum.

Yet, despite their differences, these three continents now share certain characteristics. They have all become in varying degrees intellectual provinces of the Western intellectual metropolis. They have acquired in varying degrees systems of intellectual traditions derived from contact with or in emulation of the Western intellectual metropolis. In the course of these developments, they have now acquired many of the secondary intellectual traditions of the metropolis. To this they add something which arose out of their common distinctiveness, namely a defensive or protective attitude toward their indigenous culture, resentment against the metropolitan culture, as well as a dissatisfied sense of its superiority. The difficulties are aggravated in those countries which still use the language of the metropolis for their intellectual production and for reproduction at the university level. The burden of intellectual dependence is most painful and distracting there. Those who use their indigenous language, such as Japan and China, still have to live in the presence of intellectual dependence. Having however accepted this superiority, the ruling class and the rulers of their societies have attempted in various ways to implant systems of intellectual institutions. Deferential to the metropolitan model, all of them have in common a faltering achievement of implantation.

All of these changes set new tasks for the analysis of the mechanisms of formation and change of intellectual traditions and the circumstances which affect their operation.

REFERENCES

1. I leave open, in view of the marginality to the present discussion, whether the dramatic or musical work is constituted by its enactment or the physical precipitate in the form of a book or a musical score.

2. There are marginal cases of persons who perform intellectual activities which are based minimally on works and who do not produce works. "Primitive man as a philosopher," the wise, reflective, uneducated person are instances of this type but they are of marginal interest to us here.

3. Traditions often become disembodied from constellations or sets of particular works and are referred to in ideal-typical or propositional form. Traditions are sometimes presented normatively so that adherence to them is obligatory. They are sometimes operative through their sheer prominence which gives them a normative intimation.

4. Tasks are at times set from outside the primary intellectual traditions and intellectuals often accept such tasks. There is sometimes a tension in the intellectual community between the disposition to have tasks set by primary intellectual traditions and the disposition to accept tasks set outside the particular intellectual community and its traditions.

5. Auxiliary institutions by their selective functions exert influence on the careers of particular works and therewith on the increment and direction of flow of primary traditions. The mere existence of the stock—the existence of particular works in the stock of works of a field or genre—does not determine the place of the work in the tradition. Its treatment by the auxiliary institutions helps to determine whether a given work sinks to obscurity in the stock or comes forward into effective possession.

6. Of course, the structure of the tradition of science has a similarly paradoxical structure. The interpenetration of the tradition-receiving and the tradition-modifying actions in scientific research is of very great significance.

FREDERIC WAKEMAN, JR.

The Price of Autonomy: Intellectuals in Ming and Ch'ing Politics

CLASSICAL CHINESE has no word for "intellectual." "Literatus," "scholar," "gentry," yes, but not "intellectual." Yet most of the bureaucratic elite of Ming (1368-1644) and Ch'ing (1644-1911) China did "make a living by plowing with the pen" (*pi-keng hu-k'ou*), and—in the broadest definition intellectuals can give themselves—did have direct access to the legitimizing values of their society. In fact, it is not difficult to draw up a typology of intellectual species in late Imperial China running along a line from public involvement to private *Abstand:* (1) civil statesman and policy-maker, (2) practical reformer and administrator, (3) ethical idealist, (4) aesthete, (5) anchorite or eremite.

The first would be a Confucian civil servant who naturally validated authority by his very participation in government, but who also often viewed himself as a "realistic" reformer forestalling dynastic decline. Since such intellectuals were sometimes forced to ally themselves with eunuchs and corrupt courtiers in order to effect change, their prestige was usually impaired in the eyes of purer, though more ineffectual, outsiders. The second ideal type considered himself a pragmatic reformer of existing government. During this period there even developed a special school of "statecraft" (*ching-shih*) whose practitioners prided themselves upon their intimate knowledge of local government. As conscientious magistrates in office, or students of actual administrative conditions after retirement, they established a tradition of intellectual engagement in governance which would be a powerful source of reform during the late nineteenth century. In partial contrast to that was another sort of literatus whose unbending moral integrity and idealism came the closest to orthodox intellectual dissent. This form of moral opposition to state authority had deep roots in the Confucian canon, but it only became a habitual commitment during the Sung period (960-1279) when scholar-officials increasingly separated moral principles and political practice, preferring resignation to compromise. Finally, even more renunciatory, were the last two ideal manifestations of intellectual behavior: aestheticism and metaphysical quietism.

Ideal types are made to be broken, and in China these paradigms seldom existed purely. The statecraftsman could verge toward ministerial compromise, as in the case of the seventeenth-century scholar, Ni Yuan-lu. The statesman could lose himself in the metaphysical intricacies of the *Book of Changes*, as in the case of the sixteenth-century grand secretary, Chang Chü-cheng. Even more important to the survival of the traditional order, the range itself between public and private merged in single individuals. Whether expressed by "Confucian in office, Taoist without," or by Joseph R. Levenson's demonstration that an "amateur ideal" characterized both literati-painters and gentlemanly civil servants, this official toleration of private spheres—of the capacity for withdrawal—within public men was even institutionalized in the compulsory three-year mourning period upon the death of a parent. Obviously, therefore, the most expressive form of dissent was embodied in the third intellectual type. For, it was he who restlessly occupied the interface of private and public: not so attracted by quietism as to abnegate political responsibility, and not so involved in office as to forego moral indignation. Accordingly, the ethical idealist retained a visible capacity of choice, which in turn made him the most expressive bestower of legitimacy within that particular political culture.

This was also because two other familiar intellectual types were missing from the scene. One was the technocrat, commanding a body of abstruse or specialized knowledge, whose absence here underscored the Confucian gentleman's belief in moral generalism. The other, more telling, was the Weberian prophet. Not to be confused with the ethical teacher or priest, the prophet is classically defined by his personal access to grace completely outside of sacramental control, and can pose an enormous threat to traditional structures. Such men did seem to exist at times such as the fall of the Han (206 B.C.–A.D. 220) when the Chang family created a Taoist kingdom within the empire, or even during the Ming and Ch'ing when leaders of the White Lotus sect of Maitrayan Buddhism enrolled hundreds of thousands of rebelling peasants. But as the former promised health and survival in exchange for belief, they were more compensatory magicians than true prophets; and as the latter took advantage of harsh times to predict the disintegration of civil life as the Kalpa came to an end, they were merely chiliasts. Once emperors again sat on the throne and famine ceased, such antinomian figures were barely heeded and the normative order was easily restored.

This civil reintegration itself signified the mutual dependence of state and intellectuals. As authority required Confucian legitimization, so did literati need imperial protection against iconoclastic peasant rebels. True, there was a populist strain in Confucianism, but it defined mass revolt as merely an omen of heaven's withdrawal of the mandate from a particular reigning house. And since that higher legitimacy was interpreted by those same intellectuals, it was in their interest to divorce that source from the monarch. However, this strength was also a great weakness. They were spared the paramount despotism of the entirely sovereign state, but they were at the same time denied the possibility of detaching sovereignty for themselves alone. They mediated, rather than defined, legitimacy.

Consequently, the relationship between intellectuals and the state was profoundly ambivalent. At once guardian and critic, the literatus did claim a continuous right of independent judgment within a strictly defined perimeter of values shared with authority, but he could not dispense with the traditional state as such. He did not consider himself to have, like our solely modern intellectual, the right to express any idea he wished, and to extrapolate so limited a definition of the genre to Chinese thinkers would be both uncharitable and myopic. What he did have, though, as a single intellectual, was the self-defined right of evaluative dissent. Yet this was only an individual autonomy, purchased often at the cost of mortal sacrifice. The literatus could not, even with *confrères*, conceive of group rights for intellectuals.

Was there then no capacity for transvaluation? There were certain utopian strains within the canon to justify a redefinition of sovereignty and intellectual legitimacy. One was the populism mentioned earlier. Another was the notion of intellectuals banding together to unify the country. These two themes, influenced by foreign theories of the nation-state, ultimately did engender an intellectual revolution to sever the antique link between literatus and throne. Ironically, this break would ultimately disserve the Chinese intellectual, as he surrendered his brokerage in hopes of complete autonomy. I will try to clarify this gamble by contrasting the rhetoric of two famous groups of Chinese intellectuals: the Tung-lin academicians of the seventeenth century and the scholarly reformers of the 1890's.

The Social Basis of Intellectual Endeavor during the Ming

Lacking corporate identity, intellectuals of the Ming tried to strengthen their status identity as gentlemen. Deprived of institutional autonomy, they sought a measure of social independence as members of the local gentry.

The term "gentry" is an omnibus word, meaning both a bureaucratic status group and a *rentier* class. During the Sung this class maintained itself with the income from large estates (*chuang*) farmed by servile labor. By the fifteenth century, however, these great integrated holdings in areas like Chiang-nan (the fertile region south of the Yangtze between modern Shanghai and Nanking) had been parceled into scattered plots tilled by tenants. This tenurial evolution was economically complex and socially gradual, but state policy was one immediate cause for the change. For, after the Ming founder, Chu Yuan-chang (T'ai-tsu, the Hung-wu Emperor, reigned 1368-1398) selected Nanking as his imperial seat, at least 59,000 "wealthy households" of Chiang-nan and Che-chiang were moved to the capital and their lands converted into "official fields" which the government rented to tenants. There were three motives behind this decision. One was to punish wealthy gentry for supporting one of his rivals. A second, much more ostensible, was to succor the common peasant. As the "economic treatise" (*shih-huo chih*) of the dynastic history of the Ming explained it:

Thus, he punished the influential (*hao*) and powerful who at the end of the Yuan had made fools of the poor and the weak. He established laws which [did] much to honor the poor and fetter the wealthy. He formerly ordered the Ministry of Finance to register 14,300-odd households of wealthy people (*fu-min*) [living in the areas administered by] the nine provincial administration offices of Chekiang and the eighteen prefectures and districts of Ying-t'ien (i.e. Nanking), so as to summon them to the court in succession [and have them] move their families to reside in the capital. [These] were called "wealthy households" (*fu-hu*).[1]

Finally, the emperor simply desired to resettle war-ravaged areas and populate his new capital. These immediate motives could temporarily combine but their effect was constant: as the powerful gentry from areas like Chiang-nan were momentarily separated from local bases of prestige and power, their social dependence upon central authority increased. If they were to be an elite, their station would derive from their function as imperial servants and not their independent control of social resources. In fact, this bureaucratic dependence would be even more extreme as the throne regulated the dispensation of prestige by strengthening the civil service examination system, and curbed corporate official interests by abolishing the prime ministership in 1381-1382.

The early Ming saw the examination system replace the National University and the practice of personal "recommendation" (*yin*) of fledgling officials as the dominant channel of bureaucratic recruitment and upward mobility. This made the perpetuation of gentry status both more precarious and more frustrating. As the dynasty refused to set quotas for district candidates but did restrict the number of higher degree holders, the lower ranks became swollen (between 1400 and 1600 the number of *sheng-yuan*— district graduates—rose from 30,000 to 600,000). And even if a student did pass the provincial exams, he had to anticipate years of further study and probable disappointment in the metropolitan tests. The stake of this zero-sum game was so high that the dizzying dream of high office, almost like a national lottery, kept all of those lower degree holders from fundamental alienation. Besides, they did share gentry status, though its growing ubiquitousness led higher-ranking members to cultivate an aristocratic refinement, based upon connoisseurship, which was supposed to characterize fellow *chün-tzu* (the "superior man" or "gentleman").

The examination system also reinforced orthodox Sung Neo-Confucianism. Given the primacy of deferential values like *chung* (loyalty to one's superior) in the Sung texts he favored, the first Ming emperor

drove the foundations of his autocracy deep into the very matter which gave the gentry its basic identity and its social position—ideology. He thus presented to the scholars individually and collectively a conundrum which endured as long as the dynasty: that being orthodox and loyal entailed the loss of all their political effectiveness and of any ability to function as a class either positively in making administrative policy or negatively in resisting the growth of that centralism which was their undoing.[2]

Obligation to these values was remarkably one-way: hierarchical subordinates could not expect imperial gratitude in exchange for their loyalty. Rather, their social insecurity was matched by personal political instability as they lost institutional counterweights to the emperor's increasing personal power.

Despotism and Its Servants

The tendency toward a more centralized despotism did not characterize the Ming period alone. The Sung had already abolished the office of the prime minister or chief chancellor (*tsai-hsiang*), who, as he reviewed imperial edicts, represented the power of the bureaucracy to check monarchic authority. Of course, ensuing imperial councillors did periodically recover a decisive ministerial role, but the throne continued to fight against the formal expression of bureaucratic interests by symbolically treating its highest officials as though they were personal assistants. Within that same ideological nexus, subordinates retained their self-respect by hearkening back to Confucius' paradigmatic *chün-tzu*: the superior man whose ultimate value to a ruler was his moral independence and critical courage. But beyond this symbolic interplay an organizational evolution during the Ming tilted the balance in favor of the despot. At the provincial level single governors were replaced in 1376 by regional commissions which reported directly to the emperor. The center's bureaucratic independence was similarly weakened four years later, when one of Chu Yuan-chang's ministers plotted to usurp the throne. After he was discovered and executed, the emperor first reduced the classic ruler-minister relationship from one of relative moral equality into one of servility and degradation by reviving the Yuan (1280-1367) practice of flogging ministers in court (*t'ing-chang*). Then he altered the central administrative structure by stripping generals of permanent commands, and by dividing the chancellory's function among each of the six ministries. Any who wished in the future to restore the chancellory would—he announced—be killed by slicing.

To handle the routine daily flow of memorials the emperor thereafter employed a personal staff of "grand secretaries" housed in the *nei-ko* ("inner pavilion") of the Forbidden City. However, these men soon acquired an active policy-making function. After the Yung-lo emperor (reigned 1402-1425) fell into the habit of consulting them on extraordinary matters, they customarily received memorials directly. Gradually, one of the grand secretaries assumed responsibility for drafting imperial decrees.

But although this *shou-fu* (chief grand secretary) thereby resembled a chancellor, his actual rank as secretary was quite low. Despite his functional prominence, therefore, he could not represent the interests of the outer bureaucracy because he remained an employee of the inner court. Nor could the grand secretary even monopolize proximity to the emperor. Still more "inner" than he could be were the eunuchs.

The Ming founder had decreed that there be no more than one hundred eunuchs in the palace. By 1600 there were more than 70,000 of them in the Forbidden City. Ostensibly severed from the sorts of external social alliances which the regular civil service cultivated, they seemed a perfect instrument of despotic rule, so that their numbers and influence grew thanks to the duties they performed as spies, as purveyors, and as secretaries for the person of the emperor.

Their police function was aggrandized after 1420 when they were ordered to establish an Eastern Depot (*tung-ch'ang*) to survey the regular secret police (the Embroidered Uniform Guard). In addition, eunuchs were increasingly detached to the regular military establishment, actually commanding strategic garrisons. At the same time, by managing the emperor's privy purse, they acquired an important fiscal function, which permitted them to commandeer the great naval voyages of the early fifteenth century, the mining of precious metals, and the collection of commercial taxes in the empire's urban centers. But the eunuchs were merely palace servants—dangerous but tolerable—as long as they were forbidden the one skill necessary to classical bureaucracy: documentary literacy. By 1432, however, they had established their own clerical school within the palace, and had interposed a eunuch directorate of ceremonials (*ssu-li-chien*) between the emperor and the *nei-ko*. As its officers shielded the monarch from external contact (between 1471 and 1497 there was not a single ministerial audience with the throne), eunuchs naturally came to control the selection of personnel for the *nei-ko*, which of course made it necessary for grand secretaries to ally with them. Even so powerful a bureaucrat as Chang Chü-cheng, who dominated the *nei-ko* and the ministries from 1572 to 1582, could not hold his position without the help of the powerful eunuch Feng Pao.

Chang Chü-cheng and the Consequences of Centralization

From 1572 to 1582 the central government was dominated by the grand secretary Chang Chü-cheng. As policy-making settled on this single and quite able figure, the empire recovered a stability that it had not known for 150 years. Rising government costs and a declining rural tax base were met with new cadastral surveys and the famous Single-whip Tax Reform. The Mongols were held in military check by encouraging Chinese commanders to train their own personal armies. Funds were even found to repair the

Huai and Yellow rivers' waterworks after severe floods in 1575. Behind all of these decisions was Chang Chü-cheng's conviction that only a strong and independent *nei-ko* could force a top-heavy bureaucracy to reform existing institutions. Never before or since had the secretariat been so powerful, but Chang had so imperiously wielded his authority that after his death the entire civil service expressed a strong animus against an active executive.

This reaction to central authority was most frequently expressed by the demand that censorial criticism be boldly revived. Ku Hsien-ch'eng, one of the founders of the Tung-lin Academy, even argued that since the censors themselves were no more than "obeisant, sycophantish, cautious, and placatory" functionaries, *any* scholar-official should have the opportunity to present his political views to the emperor.[3] If the dynasty widened the "pathway of words" to include all the empire's *ling-shih* (leading scholars), then the gap between inner and outer courts, between the ruler and his intellectuals, would be bridged by the larger "we" of ideal political unity.[4] While Ku could understand the practical benefits of concentrating (*chü*) power in the hands of chief ministers, and the danger of making administration ineffectual by scattering (*san*) it, he argued for a careful balance in which the greater power (*wei ch'üan*) resided in the outer court. A way of maintaining this proper balance was to recognize the right of outsiders— those "leading scholars"—to criticize institutions like the *nei-ko*. But this solution in turn raised for Ku and others the key dilemma of intellectual politics during the Ming. Scholars alone, acting as individuals, were respectably impotent. Scholars together, constituting a faction, were dubiously partisan.

Public Duty and Private Factions

Well before this time two contradictory concepts of intellectual association had been carefully derived from the classical tradition. One deprecated "parties" or "factions" (*tang*), equating them with selfish partiality. This judgment was corroborated by the canonical "Great Announcement" (*Hung fan*) of the antique *Book of Documents*.

> Without deflection, without partiality (*wu tang*),
> Broad and long is the Royal path.
> Without partiality (*wu tang*), without deflection,
> The Royal path is level and easy.[5]

The second tradition sanctioned comradely groups by quoting Confucius' disciple, Tseng-tzu: "The superior man on grounds of culture meets with his friends, and by their friendship helps his virtue" (*chün-tzu yi wen hui yu, yi yu fu jen*).[6] To "delight in the company of one's friends" (*le ch'ün*) thus implied mutual effort toward apolitical self-cultivation and communal joy in the higher cultural life.

As the two values conflicted, the latter usually yielded to the former, hobbling most combinations of intellectuals with the factional epithet of *tang*. However, during the great reform struggles of the eleventh century, some respected scholar-officials like Ou-yang Hsiu did try to defend *tang*. His famous memorial "On Factions" argued that only "superior men" (*chün-tzu*) organized true parties. Mean men (*hsiao-jen*) might well form cliques, but these were based on utility instead of friendship and therefore had to be transitory. If the sovereign learned to distinguish between true and false factions, then he could use the genuine parties of *chün-tzu* to draw together men's resolve for the common good of the realm.

By using Confucius' own classification of men into superior and mean, Ou-yang Hsiu's essay disposed later politically involved intellectuals to rigidly judge a group entirely one or the other. This instantly tainted an entire faction with the misdeeds of any of its leading members. Furthermore, cliques had to be leader- rather than program-oriented since even amicable policy debates were avoided within any group of self-styled *chün-tzu* lest they appear to clash like Ou-yang's "mean men." Since the groups were not coalitions formed around complex but common political programs, they defined themselves mainly in terms of their opponents. As that meant a constant defense of their own group, even the best-meaning soon descended to the same level of strident and vitriolic debate as their opponents—a rhetoric which both used and further blackened the term *tang*. Consequently, those who lived through the turbulent factionalism of the late Ming were already somewhat jaded about the potential for amicably disputative party debates. One seventeenth-century writer, Hsia Yün-i, would write:

Since the period of the three dynasties each dynasty has had its cliques (*p'eng-tang*). The party men of the Han dynasty were all superior men. The party men of the T'ang were largely small men, but were still quite capable. The party men of the Sung were by majority superior men. And so, ever since the theory of parties and cliques arose, it was necessarily involved with the progression of the dynastic cycle. For, when we come to the decline and fall [of dynasties], if there are to be eminent and intelligent scholars who can be pushed to the fore by [the urgency] of their times, then there must be cliques to look over them. In this way spirit and wisdom can both be used for mutual reflection and defense, and [men] will not idly stand by and watch the affairs of state sink into error. However, when we point to men as members of cliques then we also have the following: this clique declines and that clique arises—and the ones that come later are not as good as the ones that come earlier, so that disaster overtakes the imperial ancestors decidedly because of this.[7]

For Hsia, then, cliques had no other function than mechanically to bring good or bad men to power. Morality still counted the most; and cliques, institutionally endemic, were not alone capable of ensuring that. In fact, their ultimate effect was detrimental. As they evolved along with the historical necessity of the dynastic cycle, struggles worsened; and cliques ended by bringing out the worst in men so that they became in turn a cause of the decline which those original cliques of superior men had been so intent upon forestalling. In Hsia Yün-i's mind this was the lesson taught by the history of the Tung-lin academy and party.

Academies

Academies (*shu-yuan*) filled the vacuum left by both defunct government schools and declining Buddhist monasteries during the disorder of the tenth century. As they developed during the Sung, these private intellectual centers represented an alternative to the National University's curriculum of officially sanctioned commentaries on the classics. Their rural locations, their monastic aura of contemplation, symbolized a withdrawal from official life and examination preparation. This privatism condemned academies in the eyes of many regular officials, and especially after 1030 many were replaced by the government schools or staffed by the regular educational bureaucracy. Still, they were a sign of intellectual florescence, so that the Ming founder actually encouraged them when he established his dynasty in order to evoke a cultural restoration in the wake of civil war. After 1375, however, the spread of regular local schools (*she-hsueh*) and the emphasis on civil service examinations led to a temporary neglect of academies. Not until the mid-sixteenth century was there an abrupt change, when—during the Chia-ching reign (1522-1566)—were founded one-third of all academies recorded for the entire dynasty.

This sudden rise was caused by two major phenomena. First, there was a marked heightening of both level and expectations of literacy. As copper plate printing made books accessible to most, there appeared—above all in urban areas—a *couche* of students whose numbers far exceeded the current amount of official school-room desks. Private schools appeared to meet this need.

Today everywhere throughout the country, schools have been established; and education is enlightened. Academies are like the family, village, and district schools. All are for the purpose of cultivating virtue and achieving talent. If the matter rests in the hands of officials then it is difficult for people to approach [the schools]. If teaching can reach the people, then it is easy for them to achieve [talent]. How can one do without these schools?[8]

Although these new academies were expected to retain the rural ambiance— rambling gardens, rustic studios—of their Sung paragon, many of the best known and most prestigious were actually located in those cities where mercantile endowments could be solicited for building and scholarship funds. Such an urban setting further linked them with that new *couche* of students who flocked to the cities in such great numbers—numbers which could be misused by popular lecturers or educational officials to swell their clienteles. The authorities huffily reported that:

Recently *mores* have become quarrelsome and superficial drivel. People are much more contemptuous. They use young students to assault and berate prefects. They use licentiates to attack and accuse civil officials. They revile their [educational] superintendents by displaying couplets on every street corner. Their popular ballads, full of vengeance, hatred and envy, are engraved on printing blocks.[9]

Their envy was of course fed by frustration—frustration at the incredible competition for a limited number of official posts, frustration at the rote learning required for the examination system, frustration at the discrepancy between the promise of personal enlightenment and the actual grind of philosophic study. These attitudes all formed part of the second major intellectual phenomenon of the sixteenth century: the feeling that orthodox school-work was irrelevant to true learning. As vehicles for the intuitionist philosophies of idealists like Ch'an Jo-shui, Ch'en Hsien-chang, and above all the great fifteenth-century master, Wang Yang-ming, academies seemed to promise an institutionalized opportunity for genuine self-enlightenment, rather than merely being a form of bureaucratic advancement.

The Ming authorities naturally tried to control this great surge in education. One form of supervision was conceived in the person of educational intendants; but because they were themselves literati, their reliability was questionable. Meant to be overseers, they were often prone to attract disciples among their charges. There was even a distinction then between crowd-pleasing and familiar lecturers and ethically sterner, more "conservative" scholars who maintained their hierarchic distance. The former type usually prevailed, if only because he stood to profit so much from a following—a potential clientele—among fledgling bureaucrats. That is, education and bureaucracy mutually invited the formation of vertical factions, and the intendant was correspondingly sensitive in either role (patron to client, master to disciple) to intellectual associations. It is not surprising, then, that Chang Chü-cheng had forbidden intimate relationships between educational intendants and local academies.

If intendants could not be trusted absolutely, then perhaps the simplest course was to prohibit academies altogether. The most famous case of this occurred in 1575 at the behest of Chang Chü-cheng who had so often deplored the "boastfulness" of "private" scholars. The imperial edict which he inspired declared that:

The sages condescended to educate the nation through the classics and thus transform mankind. If one were able to acknowledge the classics in his own person, then why would he need to establish other affiliations by assembling colleagues for empty chat? Henceforth each education intendant shall so supervise instructors and students that they sincerely seek after and personally exemplify the long-taught classical principles, terminating their past practices. They must not be permitted to form separate academies in which to assemble hosts of colleagues, then summon local ne'er-do-wells to chat emptily and neglect their occupations, thereby forming cliques of place seekers and establishing a pattern of patronage.[10]

By 1579 his campaign terminated with the imperial confiscation of all private academies. After Chang's death in 1582 the prohibition was partially lifted. But the restored or newly founded academies of the next three decades were already too closely linked with bureaucratic politics to avoid involvement in the great factional disputes of the time.

Activism and Quietism in the Tung-lin Academy

The Tung-lin Academy (founded in 1604) and the political movement that bore its name were profoundly influenced by the philosophical dispositions of two types of intellectuals. The first—perhaps best symbolized by the academy's prime founder, Ku Hsien-ch'eng—reacted to the moral ambiguities of late Ming idealism by propounding a philosophy of heroic action. The second—represented by Ku's student, Kao P'an-lung—accepted the ambiguity of most human acts but urged that the good could ultimately be found through meditation before action. Despite the dichotomy of activism/quietism, both wings agreed upon the necessity of social involvement and opposed escapist mediation.

Ku Hsien-ch'eng, born to a merchant family in Chiang-nan, began his classical studies under a tutor strongly opposed to the "neither good nor evil" doctrine of the innate mind which was believed by the followers of Wang Yang-ming. He soon pleased his teacher by rejecting the personally more relaxed emotionalism of the intuitionists in favor of the harsher rationalism (mind as master of the senses, holding the passions in check) of Sung Neo-Confucianists. He was thus encouraged to believe that constant effort was required to keep the mind "straight" by adhering to the path of righteousness. In his philosophy, as in his later bureaucratic involvement, this exertion was to be unhesitatingly partisan: one chose what was right and held to it unwaveringly. Consequently, an act of will would dissolve those long-winded arguments of metaphysicians who declared man to be immersed in a totality of being that was beyond good or evil; and genuine self-cultivation required an outward projection to set the world aright.

From ancient times the sages and worthies have taught men, saying that they must do good and do away with evil. By doing good, one consolidates that which we certainly have. By doing away with evil, one does away with what is not originally in us. Both our original substance and our [active] cultivation are good. They do not diverge at all. Therefore, how can [Wang] Yang-ming not teach men to do good and do away with evil? Thus, those who say there is neither good nor evil, yet also say that one must do good and do away with evil [are inconsistent]: if they hold to the former idea they must of necessity deny the latter one. How can this be? If the essence of the mind is to possess neither good nor evil, then all that which is called good and evil is not something which we ourselves certainly possess. If it is not something which we ourselves certainly possess, then both [good and evil] are ordained by emotions and knowledge, and both cannot be kept from blocking off our original essence. But how are we going to decide how to act [at all]? . . . The mind's substance is without good and evil, and we therefore possess neither good nor evil at all. Yet if we choose to do [good], then it is even more impossible to avoid *being* good. If we choose to do [evil], then it is even more impossible to avoid *being* evil. If there is both good and evil, then it is impossible to say that [our original substance] is neither good nor evil.[11]

Despite his bent toward the Sung School of Reason, Ku Hsien-ch'eng did concede that Wang Yang-ming had stimulated the pursuit of sagehood by shedding light on the problem of intuition. In fact, he admired Wang's bold conviction that each individual's mind was a self-sufficient norm of action, that all cosmic principles were present in the human essence. But Ku refused to accept such consequences of this individualism as Wang's famous declaration that Confucius' authority was unnecessary to prove something right if it was approved by one's own conscience. If one rejected the authority of Confucius would not Buddhist heresy or eccentric self-indulgence ensue? What Wang Yang-ming had said might apply to true sages, but what of ordinary men who could not depend upon their intuitive sense of right and wrong? Would they not have to continue to rely upon "the instructions of antiquity"? Forced to choose between the "inhibition" of the Sung rationalist, Chu Hsi, and the "dissolution" of Wang Yang-ming, he would choose the first as the safer of the two extremes. But this was not a comfortable choice. That is why Ku Hsien-ch'eng—lacking a transcendental certainty, a conviction of the necessity of specific imperatives—resolved his ethical doubts by seeking to confront "critical situations" (*kuan-t'ou*).[12]

The doctrine of "critical situations" was conceived by another Tung-lin philosopher named Shih Meng-lin. Like Ku Hsien-ch'eng, Shih was reacting against late sixteenth-century Wang Yang-ming Confucianists. The most notorious of these, Li Chih, had promised that anyone could become a sage by acting spontaneously. These injunctions to "live in the present" (*tang-hsia*)—said Shih—perniciously encouraged a laxness of behavior in men who did not really possess the discipline and inner strength to attain sagehood. Indeed, he argued, such "contemporary doctrinaires" were so obsessed with being entirely "natural and spontaneous" that they "expended no effort at all."

This [kind of] "living in the present" is on the contrary a pit to ensnare. [They] do not realize that original essence (*pen-t'i*) and effort cannot be separated. If there exists an original essence then naturally there exists effort. Without effort there is no original essence.[13]

Virtue did not exist apart from activity, by which Shih really meant conduct. The *Analects* had said that men must habituate good behavior by constant "study" and "practice" (*hsi*). This willed self-refinement—not self-expression—was for Shih Meng-lin the essence of true spontaneity (*tzu-jan*):

This effort is precisely [our] original essence. Such [a virtue] as humaneness was originally of a single essence with respect to respect, reverence and loyalty. How could they be separated? This, then, is the genuine "living in the present"; it is then the genuine "spontaneity."[14]

Virtue was defined as the norm of behavior. Filial piety was to be filial; and, true to the grammar of classical Chinese, the noun was identical with the verb. But how could one confirm that any particular conduct was virtuous? Presumably, sagehood brought its own sense of certainty. Yet, perhaps excepting those rare moments of enlightenment when principles were internalized, there was no illuminating substantiation of reward—what we might call a sense of grace. And so for thinkers like Shih Meng-lin conviction was sought by testing the integrity of one's commitment in extreme circumstances: *kuan-t'ou*. There was inspiration for this to be found in the canon: Confucius insisting that one must cleave to virtue even in moments of danger, and to sacrifice one's life in order to preserve one's virtue intact (*Analects*, 4.53, 15.8); and Mencius arguing that one must not be bent by force and that one must be prepared to give up one's life for the sake of righteousness (Mencius, 3.2:2, 6.10:1). As Shih interpreted these famous passages:

Furthermore, "living in the present" must entirely be in critical situations, requiring the highest strength. People today who live in ordinary conditions and conciliable times are capable of treating themselves with respect and reverence, and are also capable in dealing with others of extending their sincerity. [But] when there arrive critical situations of profit or harm, critical situations of honor or disgrace, critical situations of praise or slander, critical situations of life or death, then all fall short. Thus, ordinary respect, reverence and loyalty are none of them true effort (*kung-fu*); and if one does not employ true effort then there is no true original essence.[15]

Shih's theory of "critical situations" appealed to those, like Ku Hsien-ch'eng, for whom "integrity" (*ch'eng*) was ultimately in doubt. We might go so far as to explain the suicidal heroism of the Tung-lin scholars by arguing that late Ming intellectuals *needed* to fail politically, because only then would they finally encounter the *kuan-t'ou*, the "critical situations," certain to convince them that they had been true to themselves. Furthermore, their concern with emotional self-control—quiescence—in these "critical situations" likened them to fellow literati grouped under that other ideal type of Tung-lin scholar: the quietist, Kao P'an-lung.

Kao faced the contradiction between "inhibition" and "dissolution" by trying to minimize the distance separating Chu Hsi (Reason) and Wang Yang-ming (Mind or Intuition). Wishing for doctrinal unity instead of dialectical debate, he grieved that:

At present everyone has his own [version of the] *Great Learning*. Consequently it is [like] a prefectural court where we have gathered to litigate. How can there be so many [different] causes under heaven? For our own dynasty before the Hung[-chih] and Cheng[-te] period (i.e. 1488-1521) the learning of the empire stemmed from one [source]. But since the Chia-ching period (i.e. 1522-1566) the learning of the empire has stemmed from two [sources]: one being venerable Master Chu, the second being Lord Wang Wen-ch'eng's (i.e. Wang Yang-ming) scholarship and character.[16]

Though he accepted the basic difference between the two schools, Kao refused to believe those of Wang's disciples who argued that Chu Hsi was only concerned with rote learning and concrete things. Chu Hsi was just as devoted to the search for enlightenment as Wang, except that he rejected empty meditation in favor of realizing moral principles in one's daily social relations. For him, as for Kao, true enlightenment was "silently to remember what one has learned" (*mei erh chih chih*) so as to recover the pure good of our fundamental nature.[17]

Kao P'an-lung's doctrines of "silent remembering" and quiescent (*ching*) enlightenment were drawn both from the fifteenth-century Neo-Confucianist, Hsueh Hsuan, and from a revelation which he himself had experienced in 1594, shortly after being removed from office for protesting the dismissal of a "righteous" minister. After spending the summer traveling in the South, Kao had decided to return to the Yangtze provinces by boat. Leaving Kwangtung behind in late summer he headed north at a leisurely pace, with time set aside for touring famous temples and resting in the better river inns. By early autumn his boat had neared the Fukienese border. At a place called Chiang-t'ou his servants moored for the night. As his boat swung at anchor the full moon arose, sharply setting the mountains against the southern sky. Kao abandoned himself to the evening until he was struck by a strange disquiet. Impulsively he stood up to cry, "This landscape tonight is like other ones, but my inner-scapes, what are they likened to?" Like the great poet Su Tung-p'o at the Red Cliffs, he was suddenly choked with the ache of his separation from pure being, tempted to immerse himself in the night sky, to fall like a drunken poet into the moon. Yet he resisted, convinced that he must retain his self apart, even though his mind "was without comfort."[18]

The night passed and the voyage continued. Shaken by his experience, Kao grew determined to face his loneness by spending each morning in *ching-tso,* ("quiet sitting," or meditation) and the afternoons reading. At night he unwrapped his lute to relax himself with music and wine. Finally their vessel reached the town of Ting-chou in Fukien, where he decided to break his journey by lodging in an inn. There, he one day came across a line by the Sung philosopher, Ch'eng Hao, in a collection which he was reading: "In the midst of the many thousand affairs of the various offices, in the midst of millions of tools of war, one can still have joy, though one drinks water and uses the bended arm as a pillow. The myriad changes are all man's own creations. In reality there is not a thing." And at that Kao had his "sudden awakening."

"So that is the way it is! Indeed, there is not a thing!" Thereupon as if cut off, all the entanglements of my worries were gone and suddenly something like the burden of a hundred pounds fell with a crash to the ground . . . and thereupon I became fused with a great change. There was no longer a separation of heaven and man, interior and exterior.[19]

His revelation of Nothingness was by no means unique in the corpus of Chinese philosophy, though there was a distinguishing quality in Kao's realization that one must accept the hubbub of worldly affairs and embrace its transitoriness in order to find the quiescence of sagehood. Still, one always had to return to the contemplation of the study, the quiet of the library, in order to recover that inner strength.

As a man, it is impossible for one to possess the strength to pacify and settle the self without principles. For, each man's defects and difficulties are his own. The great worthies and sages had to have a great inner strength just to remain at peace in the midst of daily affairs. A mere student, though, is short of vigor and volatile, and must devote tens of years to building a thick and strong foundation of pacifying strength. The ones who encounter the most difficulty in this are those who were not instructed when young and hence became imbued with vulgar worldly concerns. For, in the vulgar [world] principles are difficult to grasp. One must bury one's head in books to allow oneself to be immersed in righteousness and reason.[20]

In short, Kao refused to escape from the world of "vulgarity" into pure eremitism. Instead, he tried to accommodate both by creating an intellectual asylum in the academy, where collegians helped each other recover the long-lost strength of the sages.

This was nowhere better expressed by Kao P'an-lung than in his preface to the "Treatise on the Tung-lin" (*Tung-lin chih*).

Heaven and earth are vast; past and present are far apart. How could the students of sages and worthies regard one time and one place as sufficient? Alas, the learning of the Ch'eng's is limited to the Shao-sheng period (i.e. 1094-1097); the learning of Chu is limited to the Ch'ing-yuan period (i.e. 1195-1200). Risky indeed! One's own self cannot be preserved for more than a hundred-odd years.[21]

Personal mortality was contrasted with the continuity, the *ch'uan* (transmission), of the *Tao* (Way) of particular "schools of learning." "Whatever changes is preserved in time. Whatever does not change is preserved in the Way." And through the Way even the temporal self could be revived, the true inner self recovered. This meant, on the one hand, that human regeneration demanded the revival of the parcel of human relationships honored by the sages: filial piety, loyalty, duty.

If people are vile then they will gradually be extinguished. How do we keep people from being vile? [Ku Hsien-ch'eng] told [me]: "In learning—learning and nothing else—men will recover the significance of being men, just as the eye, originally clear, recovers its clarity; the ear, originally keen, recovers its keenness; the mind, originally humane, recovers its humaneness; the physique, originally revered, recovers its reverence; lord and minister, father and son, elder and younger brother, friends and companions—all originally intimate, righteous, orderly, distinguished and trustful—recover their original intimacy, righteousness, order, distinction and trust. What was originally like this is called *hsing* (nature). To know that this was like this, and to recover this similarity, is called learning. If one does not learn then people are vile. If people are vile then their spirit is as cut off as breath might be to the body; and in this way the spirit of a thousand autumns could expire in a single day."[22]

Obviously, such reverential norms did not threaten established authority. Furthermore, the goal of the Tung-lin intellectuals was so vague (the regeneration of mankind) and its expression so diametrically specific (filial piety) that they did not—like proselytizers (concrete) seeking salvation (abstract)—conceive of means for the end. Or, to put it another way, the mission lacked steps to realize itself. In fact, given the Confucian ideal of social emulation ("If a superior love propriety, the people will not dare not to be reverent; if he love righteousness, the people will not dare not to submit to his example." *Analects,* 13.4), the mission could be as well realized through self-cultivation as through social action. And so, alongside activists in the academy's ranks, stood the immediate friends or disciples of Kao P'an-lung: metaphysically-oriented colleagues like Hsueh Fu-chiao, Ku Ta-chang, and Yeh Mou-ts'ai; or students of a later generation like Wu Kuei-sen, Chin Ch'ang, Ch'eng Chih, Wang Yu-yuan, and Kao Yü.[23] While some of these men did not take part in the wider Tung-lin political movement, their associations with the academy at least suggested how easy it was for intellectuals of a more yielding temperament to substitute quietism for activism.

The Tung-lin's Political Position

The functional focus of early Tung-lin protest was narrowly restricted to personnel evaluation because its bureaucratic stronghold was in that administrative arena. In 1583—two decades before the academy was actually founded—the Ministry of Personnel was suddenly filled with a new wave of bright young men determined to undo the centralization policies of the just-deceased Chang Chü-cheng. Among these was Ku Hsien-ch'eng himself, who (after a three-year mourning leave) served from 1586 to 1593 as a supervising secretary under the head of the scrutiny office, Chao Nan-hsing (1550-1627). There he and his superior fashioned personnel scrutiny into a powerful weapon of bureaucratic struggle by promoting "righteous" allies in other metropolitan offices. However, after the Ministry of Personnel tried to pack the *nei-ko* with officials of their camp in 1594, the emperor angrily accused them of partisan favoritism and purged the ministry.

Reduced to the status of a commoner, Ku Hsien-ch'eng returned home— accompanied by others dismissed along with him: Ch'ien I-pen, An Hsi-fan, Chang Na-pi, Yü K'ung-chien, Hsu Yao-hua, and so forth.[24] It was this circle which then began to hold "discussion meetings" (*chiang-hui*) at various locales in Chiang-nan, and responded positively to Kao P'an-lung's suggestion in 1603 that they find a more permanent center by restoring the old Tung-lin Academy at Wu-hsi. Ku, understandably cautious, first encouraged prominent members of the local gentry to send supporting letters to the magistrate, prefect, and governor. These officials confirmed local opinion by polling the district's students, and found their own contributions novelly matched by public donations. The academy's first public meeting was held between November 29 and December 1, 1604.

At one level, the academy was merely an assemblage of local intellectual coteries loosely attached to the central place. That is, each of the well-known scholar-officials constituting the Tung-lin's inner core brought with him a circle of personal followers and students, often organized into subacademies or literary clubs. Above these *cénâcles* there did exist a larger grouping, represented by large annual meetings that attracted literati from neighboring provinces. These meetings, which were opened and closed with devotional songs and prostration before the portrait of Confucius, consisted of lectures on the classical *Four Books*. Socratic debate or criticism of authority were expressly forbidden by the academy's rules. Rather, the solemn meetings were intended to elevate men from their daily routine into the realm of higher values, so that the *chiang-hsueh* (lectures) preached an ascertainable and unvarying truth.

The reforming impulse of Tung-lin members was ambiguously directed toward public influence because organization on a broader scale was restricted by the moral sustenance each member offered the others as part of the "happy few." Wishing to sustain each other's ethical independence, they were mutually encouraged to swim against the prevailing currents of vulgarity and profit, so that their preachings were personally exhortatory rather than ideological. It was even decided to prohibit private political ("vulgar") discussions within the academy itself, so as to avoid outer charges of intrigue and inner violations of integrity. Thus, as time came on, a split developed between the "pure" academy and the outer movement which bore its name.

The primary extension of the Tung-lin group into politics was the work of Ku Hsien-ch'eng himself, via both a stream of letters sent to friends throughout the empire, and a series of widely disseminated pamphlets. In fact, his interference—for he was still a commoner and had no bureaucratic rights as such—in two major appointment cases in 1607 and 1610 created a countrywide sensation. As the Tung-lin adherents were thus accused of factionalism, the classic Sung arguments over the nature of *tang* (parties) were heard once again. A familiar theme was sounded now much more stridently: political sanity depended entirely upon the spirit of superior men (*chün-tzu chih ch'i*). A Tung-lin patron, Chao Nan-hsing, maintained that:

The empire will be ordered and at peace as the spirit of the *chün-tzu* is constantly expressed. The empire will be endangered and disturbed as the spirit of the *chün-tzu* is constantly repressed. Since Wan-li *jen-ch'en* (1592) the spirit of the *chün-tzu* has gradually been repressed, until by *ping-ch'en* (1616) and *ting-ssu* (1617), it was severely so.[25]

Just as the academy concentrated their spirit in society, so did the *tang* naturally group superior men together in the political realm. Chao still had to confront the odious connotations of *tang*, but by seeking classical instances of *tang* in a nominal sense (did not the *Analects* mention *fu-tang*, "patriar-chal groupings," and *hsiang-tang*, "village groupings"?) argued that they were also "natural" groupings of *chün-tzu* joined by common predilection.[26] Thus not only was the invidious distinction between great and small men maintained; there was also a highly elitist conception of intellectual politics, consonant with the philosophical elitism of the Tung-lin school (which, re-member, was reacting to the "every man a sage" doctrines of men like Li Chih).

This elitism accounted for Ku Hsien-ch'eng's own opinion that a circle of disciples (*men-hu*) could not be expanded beyond a certain radius. For, only a necessarily restricted coterie of superior men could avoid the petty "divergences of opinions" (*i chih ch'i*) characteristic of larger groups of mean men.

Whoever can subdue his divergence and opinionation does not have to await being pacified but can pacify himself. Whoever can subdue his [state of] arousal will be of still greater benefit to his country.[27]

Such self-control, even if only practiced by a few members of the coterie, might then inspire the rest, thanks to the intimacy of restricted membership.

Such a belief severely restricted the political capacities of the Tung-lin intellectuals. If the reforming mission of "superior men" depended upon so small and so particular an association then it was bound to be publicly im-potent. Group solidarity—emotional intimacy—outweighed the expediency of larger confederations because virtue, not issues, was at stake. And since moral integrity was such a crippling concern, Ku and his friends were haunted by the necessity of compromise. Believing, as they did, that the po-litical world was neatly divided into black and white, they were stricken by the recognition of grey zones. Ku had admitted that he could not label all courageous enough to engage in political struggle as ardent "martyrs," just as he could not characterize the more timid as being "hypocrites and imposters." Yet while he also condemned those who "held fast to their own proposals" so rigidly that the realm was transformed into a battlefield, the only absolute antidote he could conceive of was public concern (*kung*), since the root of conflict was selfishness.

What is meant by *kung*? Right means right and wrong means wrong without ambiguity (*mo-leng*). Being right one will know its [opposite] wrong; being wrong one will know its [opposite] right, without prejudice.[28]

Fanatically opposed to fanatics, Ku was to die in 1612 confident that he did know both sides, confident that others—not he—were the worst partisans. His belief was never really tested; for the most dogmatic days of the Tung-lin were still to come.

The Height of the Tung-lin Struggle

After Ku Hsien-ch'eng's death the fortunes of the Tung-lin group went through five phases.

(1) 1615-1620: continuing scrutiny struggles controlled by the three op-
    position cliques.
(2) 1620-1621: thanks to a new emperor, Tung-lin recovery of power.
    One brief year of stability.
(3) 1621-1624: though clearly paramount, the Tung-lin group conflicts
    more and more with its eunuch opponent, Wei Chung-hsien.
(4) 1625-1626: Wei Chung-hsien purges Tung-lin members.
(5) 1626-1629: yet another new emperor restorès the Tung-lin affiliates
    who blemish their image by executing members of the opposition.

These conflicts centered on three contemporary issues: military policies in
Manchuria where founders of the future Ch'ing had initiated plans to conquer China, the continuing involvement of academies in politics, and the
struggle over imperial succession.

The third was the most bitter. Contemporary accounts referred again
and again to the famous "three cases": the cudgel case of 1615, the red pill
case of 1620, and the palace removal case of 1621. The first two concerned
the survival of an heir favorable to one or the other side, and the last was a
fight to control a newly acceded boy emperor. Nothing better symbolized
the political vulnerability of the Tung-lin intellectuals than their bickering
fixation on this particular issue. Drawn together in the first place to restore
orthodox values such as loyalty, the prime concern of the Tung-lin group
was ostensibly the "proper relationships" between ruler and minister, and its
political programs were always cast as appeals to the throne. Given the discrepancy then between a Neo-Confucian idealization of the enlightened
ruler and contemporary reality, such pleas were only to be pitied. The
T'ien-ch'i emperor, who ascended the throne in 1620 at the age of fourteen
and had only reached twenty-one when he died in 1627, was hopelessly in-
decisive. Dominated by his former wet nurse, who was in turn sexually manipulated by the eunuch Wei Chung-hsien, the emperor relinquished his
control over government to while away his days playing football and building dollhouses. But the postures of ministerial righteousness were so frozen
that even the most courageous victims of eunuch purges continued to defend themselves with a rhetoric of personal submission to the throne. For,
their loyalty—framed as devotion to a person—was to an institutional ideal
that encompassed their entire world-view. Alternatives were unthinkable.

The classic example of this has always been Yang Lien, arrested in
1625 by the secret police for having attacked Wei Chung-hsien's arrogation
of imperial authority.

Thus throughout the palace all know there is a Chung-hsien but none know there
is an emperor, and throughout the capital all know there is a Chung-hsien but none
know there is an emperor . . . If I should be able to get rid of just Chung-hsien
alone, so as not to deprive the emperor of his reputation as a Yao or a Shun, then
I should have fulfilled the command of the former emperor and might face the
spirits of the imperial ancestors. In the loyal and righteous service of my lifetime,

the extraordinary grace conferred by the two prior rulers might be recognized. And if some small recompense is wished, I should even die without regrets.[29]

We have no way of knowing if Yang Lien did experience regret at that last moment of agony when eunuch torturers pounded nails through his skull, but I suspect that even then his loyalty remained unshaken. The weakness of an *actual* emperor only made it all the clearer that one was dying for a disembodiment—and thus in the end, solely for one's own commitment to the idea itself.

Yang Lien was to be avenged. A new emperor on the throne, Wei and the wet nurse dead, the Tung-lin faction would recover power only to mar its own image of constant integrity by killing some of its opponents. Even former partisans of the Tung-lin grew disillusioned, so that Kao P'an-lung, reflecting long after the event, came to doubt the applicability of ethical absolutes to politics. The one thing he realized from the years of acrimony was that there was no quick method to identify good and evil, no easy way to extend one's good will and thereby transform things outside of us. It was a mistake to believe that all members of one camp were either purely virtuous or purely corrupt. Yet the only political device conceivable to him itself tended to create absolute moral types.

This [group] considers the other a *tang*. The other considers this a *tang* as well. A *tang* is a category (*lei*). If one wished the empire to be without *tang* then he would have to do without the category of superior men and of mean men. Then, would it not be impossible to speak of *tang*? No matter what kind of *tang* the superior men have, the ruler hates *tang*. Consequently, the *tang* of mean men turn their eyes toward it [treating it] like a *tang*. Once entrapped, the superior men are finished.[30]

The Nature of the Tung-lin Struggle

The Chinese political conflicts of the early 1600's concerned the degree to which a monarch's personal agents controlled the bureaucracy. Not only were Tung-lin intellectuals *not* struggling for the recognition of their legally independent rights; they were also barely fighting to attain a bureaucratically independent right to make political decisions. Rather, their major goal involved clique aspirations toward a general policy influence expressed abstractly with Neo-Confucian symbols like loyalty, and concretely with personnel control, that is, the bureaucratic function most crucial to the clique's survival. Thus, they were undone in the end by a lack of pluralism, both symbolic and concrete. Even in their own institutions they could offer nothing in the way of alternatives to the harmonious familistic images that sustained the state by making dissent a sign of selfish factionalism.

And even though the institutions themselves embryonically expressed autonomous intellectual interests, the academies' genesis as coteries of intellectuals blurred the distinction between informal association and formal (that is, associative and disassociative) membership, making it difficult to acquire both a socially and politically separate organizational individuality. Indeed, it was in the gentry's short-sighted interest to avoid creating institutions which might have brought society and polity together, since those organizations could as well be co-opted by the central authority. As patrons in the anthropological sense, the gentry—among which we must include most intellectuals—bridged the interstices between center and locale, increasingly mediating power as the Ming and Ch'ing wore on. As this was an informal, often illegal, function, the gentry was served by the gap between lower social levels and higher forms of authority. The "we-ness" Ku Hsien-ch'eng had advocated would have united society and polity. The reward for his failure was less emotionally satisfying, but more socially advantageous to a later generation of gentry brokers.

Study Societies at the End of the Ch'ing

Clubs and academies did not disappear with the Tung-lin. The *Fu-she* (Restoration Society) played a prominent role in the last days of the Ming, and there were several attempts during the early years of the Ch'ing to revive these intellectual alliances. However, the Manchu founders of the dynasty and some of their Chinese advisers were convinced that most *soi-disant* academies and literary societies were secretly interested in promoting the same kind of political turmoil to which they partly attributed the decline of the previous dynasty. Consequently, the government issued special regulations in 1652 forbidding scholars to meet over political or philosophical issues; and by the eighteenth century very few literary societies still existed. Academies were now financially administered by local officials; and their curriculum, which was devoted to preparing students for civil service careers, was carefully supervised by government-appointed directors of studies. The Tung-lin itself, rebuilt in 1629, soon ruled that such topics as the differences between the Schools of Reason and of Mind should not be discussed. Deprived at first of an official endowment, the academy gradually fell into ruin. Its subsequent physical recovery (the provincial authorities were ordered in 1685 to repair such academies) was illusory. However much lacquer was applied to the façade, its lecture hall completely lacked spiritual innards. Razed by the T'ai-p'ing rebels in 1860, rebuilt again at government request in 1864, it had become by the later Ch'ing heavily endowed but intellectually sterile.

Thus, though academies flourished numerically during the nineteenth century (there were perhaps as many as 4,500 in existence throughout the empire over the course of that period), the great majority of them still just taught the texts necessary for examination success or subsidized degree candidates. There were exceptions, to be sure. The most important was the Cantonese *Hsueh-hai t'ang* (Hall of the sea of learning) inspired by the

great classicist, Juan Yuan, who sought to revive the notion of a community
of scholars united by *jen* (humaneness). In fact, it was out of this circle of
intellectuals that came the famous reformer, K'ang Yu-wei.

Inspired by Juan Yuan's revival as well as the censorial ideal of "pure
talk" (*ch'ing-i*) associated with such historical heroes as the Tung-lin scholars, K'ang insisted after China's defeat by the Japanese in 1895 that the nation's strength depended upon unity, and the latter in turn upon assembling
the divided scholars of the realm in study societies. Up to now this had been
impossible because of the early Ch'ing prohibition. But was that caution not
now anachronistic? As he boldly memorialized the emperor on June 30,
1895:

> Turning to the periods of the Han and Ming [we see] that the conduct of *ch'ing-i*
> harmed traitors in power but was of great benefit to the country. But when the
> Ming dynasty's defectors (*erh-ch'en*) entered the service of [this] ruling house,
> they feared that people would criticize them and therefore strictly forbade [pure
> talk]. However, as this is not their time why must we continue to pursue their
> errors?[31]

Pending imperial sanction of study societies (*hsueh-hui*), K'ang and other
younger literati sought the personal sponsorship of high officials. With their
hesitant approval, the students met in August 1895 in Peking to form the
Ch'iang hsueh-hui (Study society [for self-]strengthening) to "inspire customs, enlighten knowledge, and unite the great mass."[32]

This, and a branch office founded later that year in Shanghai, were the
first in a series of nationally prominent societies organized by intellectuals
devoted to strengthening the country against imperialism. Conservative official approval was fickle, especially as the study groups came at times to
resemble a mass movement. Because of that and K'ang Yu-wei's iconoclastic reputation, it was an easy matter for a censor to force the disbandment
of the *Ch'iang hsueh-hui* late that same year. But as the international
situation once again worsened in 1898 there sprang up successor organizations which were more willing to forego bureaucratic endorsement. The
best known of these was the *Pao-kuo hui* (Preserve the nation society),
founded by K'ang Yu-wei and 186 others in Peking on April 12, 1898, to
"preserve the sovereignty and territory of the entire nation, preserve the
independence of the people and the race, and preserve the existence of the
divine teachings [of Confucius]."

The *Pao-kuo hui* was only one of a particular type of study society devoted to renovating the "spirit" (*ch'i*) of scholars bent upon rescuing China
from what seemed to be imminent dissolution as the powers scrambled for
concessions. There were other categories of associations which I have broken
down by kind in table 1 (page 58). It is easy to discern a general pattern of
society activity between 1895 and 1911. As the list following—which incorporates data on 138 different *hui*, representing 46 per cent of the total
300 societies founded—clearly shows, during this period the two eras of

highest activity were the years 1897-1898 and 1906-1908. One would assume an immediate difference between these two peaks if only because the
first reflected spontaneous nationalist sentiment in the wake of the scramble
for concessions, while the latter came thanks to the imperially sponsored
reform program after 1902. Table 1 details the differences a bit more meaningfully. The early peak was overwhelmingly characterized by an abstract,
non-issue oriented stress on arousing the will or spirit of the intellectual
elite (*shih* or *chün-tzu*). Though much more autonomous than Ming societies these were still symbolically rather than organizationally directed, so that
the absence of concrete goals suggests a transitional generation somewhere
between the Tung-lin and—as the time scale telescopes—the provincial
gentry leaders of the early 1900's. Traditional, and only semiautonomous,
ideology enabled the transition.

Geographic focus (table 2, page 61) also passed from the will-preserv-
ing societies' capital-fixation to new local foci of political involvement.
Peking, gathering place for metropolitan-degree candidates, had been
during the heyday of the early reform clubs the hub of a wheel whose
spokes were members of the national elite so that their "provincial" societies were mainly capital figments. But by the later period, intellectuals
had abandoned a vague concern with imperial self-development for the
concrete management of local affairs. A new kind of society (category 3)
expressed a new concern with nationalist issues specifically influencing
local or provincial politics: railway and mining rights.

This tabular contrast does not mean that one entirely different form of
political interest simply superseded the other. For, the early *hsueh-hui* were
themselves the vehicle of this evolution: a cultural as well as institutional
transition for Chinese intellectuals. The cultural facet, obvious enough in
their wish to wed occidental "skills" with oriental principles, might even be
expressed by the daily timetable of a typical study society. Ch'ang-te's
Ming-ta hsueh-hui, for example, ordained mornings for Western readings,
while the afternoon was to be devoted to Chinese studies.[33] Such schedules,
which were printed in great detail in the reform press, marked an important institutional transition from symbolic to organizational orientations,
from ritual lecturing to patterned study. Other rules defined membership
identity and formalized institutional roles. Since substantial annual- fees
were required, bookkeeping and auditing procedures were developed. Special attention was devoted to placing the *hsueh-hui* officers under the control
of elected gentry board members. "A *hsueh-hui* is not under the control
of a single individual"; managers must be checked and "not allowed arbitrarily to usurp [authority]."[34]

Study societies even enjoyed organizational extension via branch associations. The outstanding example of such a network was the *Nan hsueh-
hui* (Southern Study Society) which established local affiliates throughout
Hunan, tightly linked to the provincial headquarters. This differed sharply

TABLE 1. Types of Clubs Founded

Type of club	1895	1896	1897	1898	1899	1900	1901	1902	1903	1904	1905	1906	1907	1908	1909	1910	1911
1. Renovate the spirit of scholars in order to preserve the country	2		8	19													
2. Constitutional study and promotion of local self-government (ti-fang tzu-chih)										2	1		2	1			
3. Recover railway and mining rights											2	8	10	5			
4. Reevaluate the classics in terms of statecraft, practical needs, utilitarianism												1			3	1	
5. Preserve Confucianism (sheng-chiao)			2	1								1	1	1			
6. Scientific study (especially mathematics and geography), translation of Western books		1	3	3					1		1	6	3				1

7. Antifootbinding, antiopium; elevate local customs	1	8	3		1		1	2	1
8. Agricultural study (*Nung hsueh-hui*)	1	1			1	3	4	2
9. Manage schools established by the new dynastic reform (*chiao-wu hsueh-hui, chiao-wu tsung-hui*)		5	2	5	1	3	1

SOURCE: Wang Erh-min, "Ch'ing-chi hsueh-hui hui-piao" (A classified list of the study societies of the Ch'ing period), *Ta-lu tsa-chih* (The Continent Magazine), Part I, 26.2:14-20 (January 31, 1962); Part II, 26.3:16-23 (February 15, 1962).

Year	Number of hui founded
1895	3
1896	4
1897	24
1898	31
1899	0
1900	0
1901	0
1902	1
1903	1
1904	3
1905	10
1906	21
1907	28
1908	13
1909	4
1910	2
1911	3

from the Tung-lin Academy's horizontally crystallized coteries, because the *Nan hsueh-hui* extended down and out, paralleling the provincial bureaucratic establishment. Organizational charters—not just overlapping membership—cemented the structure together. The society did depend upon personal connections at the very top between a reformist governor and its own leaders; but as the *Nan hsueh-hui* supplanted the functions of the commissioner of education, it presaged the later interpenetration of provincial government by gentry associations during the early 1900's.

The New Ideology of Association

The general aim of these societies was expressed by those three founding slogans of the *Ch'iang hsueh-hui:* to inspire customs, to enlighten knowledge, and to unite the great mass. "To inspire customs" (*k'ai feng-ch'i*) was partly an appeal for physical education to create a new martial *chün-tzu* robustly modeled on the samurai instead of the effete literatus. But the fundamental meaning of the slogan was to eradicate such popular evils as opium smoking and footbinding. Influenced by Christian social work, the reformers also wished to infuse Confucianism with a spirit of proselytism in order to revive the sage's doctrine of humaneness (*jen*) which "grieves over the difficulties and hardships of all within the four seas."[35]

To transform ethical teachings (*chiao*) into a religion (also *chiao*) was hardly a fundamentalist revival, just as self-deprecating comparisons with Japanese samurai and Western preachers were not the mark of once-confident Confucianists. Besides, the original Sung notion of a "superior man's" obligations to transform his grief over the lot of mankind into the actual rectification of social evils reflected a determination then to instill

TABLE 2. Geographic Focus of Clubs

Geographic focus	1895	1896	1897	1898	1899	1900	1901	1902	1903	1904	1905	1906	1907	1908	1909	1910	1911
1. *Hui* founded in the capital	1		4									1	2	1		1	1
2. *Hui* founded in the capital with provincial identity and titles				2	5												
3. Province-wide (e.g., the Kwang-tung Society) *hsueh-hui* or *tsang-hui*				6						1	4	1	9	4	3		
4. *Hui* founded either in provincial capitals or in Shanghai	2	4	10	7					1	1	5	10	14	4	1		2
5. *Hui* founded by and in districts			11	9						1	1	6		10			

SOURCE: Wang Erh-min, "Ch'ing-chi hsueh-hui hui-piao."

Confucianism with the charitable spirit of popular Buddhism. Buddhist influences, especially the paragon of the Boddhisattva who postpones Nirvana to serve mankind, persisted in the ideology of nineteenth-century reformers like T'an Ssu-t'ung. But, judging from the frequent references in reform newspapers to the alarming spread of Christianity, it was this Western creed of charity that renewed the emphasis on good works, drawing literati out of meditative autolatry. Nor was it just a matter of competition. These intellectuals characteristically identified the strength of the West with its Way—and that particular *Tao* was clearly one which energetically sought to convert others. "To inspire customs" therefore meant both reforming vulgar traits of the populace and inspiring common men with a new *religious* sense of Confucian morality. In each case the intellectual's role was redefined. No longer was he, as Confucius really directed, to concentrate on the moral education of the ruler. Nor was he to be content with mere personal cultivation of his own self. Instead, he was to engage in social action by breaking the coterie mentality.

We will endeavor to carry this out by uniting officials, gentry, scholars *and commoners* as friends in a literary society, using the mighty doctrine of Confucius as our major [creed].[36]

This was far removed from the Tung-lin scholars' spiritual hermeticism.

The society's second motto, "to enlighten knowledge" (*k'ai chih-shih*), distinguished the reformers from official self-strengtheners who wished only to adopt modern technology. The *hsueh-hui* were instead devoted to exposing Chinese intellectuals to all the cultural and political facets of the West. Many societies opened translation bureaus, or published journals describing parliaments, explaining constitutional law, and recounting the biographies of Western statesmen like George Washington. Often a society would sponsor bookstores or schools, and some associations promised to send students to Japan. Many argued that such novel studies were in the best tradition of the seventeenth-century's "statecraftsmen," and insisted that men had lost sight of the "practical" connection in Confucianism between government service (*shih*) and education.[37] Even regular academies asked to be allowed to alter their curriculum from examination preparation to "the study of what is useful."[38] But here, too, extreme innovations were being introduced in the guise of a revival of "true" pragmatic Confucianism. After all, the academies became stultified in the first place because they had indeed been teaching "something useful": how to get into the traditional civil service. It was the context that had now changed. For all practical purposes, "useful" now meant Western learning; and the *hsueh-hui* (study society) itself was even sometimes identified with the occidental university.

The third slogan, "to unite the great mass" (*ho ta-ch'ün*), evoked, familiar images of intellectuals. As the rules for one study society explained:

The doctrine of the sages strongly emphasizes taking delight in the company [of one's peers] (*le ch'ün*), honoring one's calling, being intimate with worthies, and seeking out friends. At the gate of Confucius there assembled three thousand and seventy disciples to discuss every [aspect] of statecraft and the great vocation [of government], so that there was not a single skill nor single capability which was not studied and practiced. Thus, the period of study [was devoted to] actual practice, extending even to [the art of] governing the country and bringing peace to the empire. Today, occidental government emerges from a [kind of] learning which frequently attains the bequeathed meaning of [their] divine canon (the Bible). Indeed when men's talents flourish, the fortune of the country accompanies them. In China, since the prevalence of the examination essay, the ancient learning has become neglected and uncultivated. The reason for establishing this society is our genuine desire to sweep away the practice up until now of such limited and narrow [scholarship], and to collect the talents of our time to aid in reform. Along with our study of Chinese moral principles we will blend the occidental art of enriching [the country] and strengthening [the army]. If we concentrate the massed strength of men, matters will easily improve. If we unite the minds of the learned, knowledge will daily burst forth. [Then we] can preserve both the [Confucian] doctrine and the [Chinese] race along with our sagely learning and ancestral customs. Furthermore, they will spread and flow over the entire globe, so that every country will be willing as our comrades to look into this [doctrine of] moral conduct.[39]

But though it was still believed that the "spirit" of superior men would save the age, the aristocratic ideal of the *chün-tzu* had attenuated. Instead of assembling gentlemen in search of mutual philosophical cultivation, the societies were pledged to create a new kind of intellectual: *yu-chih chih shih* (scholars of resolve). Furthermore, the "scholars" so resolved now encompassed many beyond the earlier status coteries. The *Nan hsueh-hui* (Southern Study Society) founded at Ch'ang-sha in the winter of 1897 adopted the slogan: "Whether official, gentry, scholar, or commoner (*shu*)— once enrolled, they are all members, all equal."[40] Membership replaced status; the *hsueh-hui* created its own "scholars of resolve," instead of the contrary. And as these men now defined their own corporate legitimacy, they could properly be called "intellectuals" in the modern sense.

This declaration of intellectual autonomy was necessarily accompanied by a new derivation of intellectual status. As national defense required technical expertise and a "pragmatic" approach to government, utilitarian skill replaced moral mastery as a prime value. The consequent abolition of the traditional examination system in 1905 would differentiate the intellectual from both the state and the traditional gentry. Such political and social independence virtually demanded an ideology of voluntary intellectual incorporation, which was symbolized by the transition from coterie to club.

Three centuries earlier the Tung-lin patron, Chao Nan-hsing, had been forced to legitimize predilective *tang* (parties) by equating them with natural primary groups like family or clan. Partly a denial of the injurious competition of pluralistic interests within an ideally harmonious society, partly a defense against legalistic and despotic intrusions into society, this animus toward the *Gesellschaft* denied the principle of voluntary organization. Other scholars, like the seventeenth-century statescraftsman, Ku Yen-wu, went so far as to condemn all associations (*she*) which had not evolved naturally and involuntarily within society. Coteries like *t'ung-nien* (men who had passed their examinations in the same year) were acceptable, but for him even intellectual clubs were illegitimate.[41] Now, as the spread of study societies legitimized associations, the entire basis of the state was redefined. During the Tung-lin period political dissent was limited by the accepted definition of the *kuo* as a kingdom, ruled by an emperor who held heaven's mandate. The *kuo* was transmitted, not made or formed. Now, the example and theory of study societies suggested a new theory of the *kuo* as a country—indeed, a nation—formed by *association*.

The key to this fundamental change in Chinese political conceptualization was the notion of *ch'ün*. Like many single words in classical Chinese, it had a variety of meanings bound to the various strands of the rich tradition which these reform intellectuals had inherited. We have already denoted one of these in *le ch'ün*—delighting in the company of one's peers. But there was another, even more fundamental concept of *ch'ün* embodied in an important secondary tradition which went back to the philosopher Hsün-tzu (fl. 298-238 B.C.), who once wrote of man:

His strength is not equal to that of the bull; his running is not equal to that of the horse; yet the bull and the horse are used by him. How is that? Men are able to form social organizations (*ch'ün*), the former are not able to form social organizations.[42]

Ch'ün—the formation of social organizations—was thus the single faculty distinguishing man from the beasts.

Although Hsün-tzu's definition of *ch'ün* influenced Han (206 B.C.–A.D. 220) political thought, this meaning virtually lapsed in later eras. It was not until the late nineteenth century that it was dramatically revived by K'ang Yu-wei, who inspired his student, Liang Ch'i-ch'ao, to apply this concept to the definition of the state as such. Arguing that all social organizations were formed by men in concert, Liang went so far as to insist that the country itself was a consequence of *ch'ün*. Men could—together—create (*ch'eng*) a nation; and that startling realization in turn meant that the ruler of such a social aggregate had to rule it in the name of the collective, even in the name of the people.

Therefore, if one uses a *ch'ün* method to rule the *ch'ün*, the *ch'ün* will be realized. If one uses an individualistic method to rule the *ch'ün*, the *ch'ün* will fail. And if one's own *ch'ün* is defeated, that is to the profit of other *ch'ün*. How can we then speak of individualistic [state]craft? Everyone knows that they have their own selves. They do not realize they also share the empire. The ruler selfishly [looks] to his own regime. The official selfishly [looks] to his own field. The artisan selfishly [looks] to his own occupation. The merchant selfishly [looks] to his own commerce. The individual selfishly [looks] to his own profit. The household selfishly [looks] to its own prosperity. The lineage selfishly [looks] to its own clan. The clan selfishly [looks] to its own surname. The settlement selfishly [looks] to its own land. The village selfishly [looks] to its own hamlet. The teacher selfishly [looks] to his own learning. For this reason the people are as 400 million [entities], so that the country too will be as 400 million [entities], which means no country at all. Whoever knows how to rule well realizes that the ruler and people together make up a single person within a single *ch'ün.*[43]

As *ch'ün* and *hui* (nominally, association; verbally, to associate) were obviously related, the societies themselves were the one device that might bring the people together "into a single entity." In fact, "country" (*kuo*) and "society" (*hui*) were practically synonymous.

Although we want to make all as one, which course are we to follow toward this unity? I have searched through the Three Dynasties in the distant [past], and gazed extensively across the Occident. Those with *kuo* of needs have *hui:* [their] superior men associate (*hui*) in such as this; [their] officials associate in such as this; [their] scholars associate in such as this; [their] people associate in such as this. Every morning, lectured to; every evening, shaped [into one]. Even though the empire is vast, and the myriad creatures many, we can strengthen our country.[44]

Of course, neither Hsün-tzu's definition of *ch'ün,* nor the concept of voluntary association, can alone account for Liang Ch'i-ch'ao's challenge to the traditional theory of heaven-derived imperial sovereignty. As those earlier excerpts show, he was deeply influenced by the discovery of social Darwinism, then being propagated in China by the translator Yen Fu. Furthermore, like so many other reform-movement intellectuals, he was aware of constitutive examples of association (*hui*) in Japan and the West.[45] But it was the connotations, the particular ring, of such classical concepts as *ch'ün* or *hui* which partly sanctioned, partly filtered, the introduction of constitutionalism to the Chinese. However revolutionary the implications, the initial perception was only conceivable in the framework of traditional values.

Witness, for example, the editors of a Hunanese reform newspaper arguing for a national assembly (*kuo-hui*):

If we do not establish a *kuo-hui* then there will be no uniting the citizens' voices. If we do not establish a board of learning then there will be no accumulation of a general record of the myriad affairs. When asked, "What would it be like to establish a *kuo-hui* now?" we answer, "the *kuo-hui* [represents] the people's public duty (*kung-i*)." "But is the *kuo-hui* not then [a representation of] popular rights?" We say that the [imperial] order we have now received, the instructions we have taken, of the public duty to enlighten each other and revive learning is a public undertaking (*kung-shih*) of the people. Considering the public duty to be a public undertaking, and the public undertaking to be a public association (*kung-hui*), what [else] can we call it [but] popular rights? It precisely means popular rights! Besides, popular rights is popular duty. "People" cannot be separated from "having rights." The people devote themselves to their duty, and the people engage in their own undertakings, while the ruler's authority (*chün-ch'üan*) draws together these myriad undertakings. Popular rights is to manage one's own undertakings. If the people lack rights they cannot devote themselves to [public] duty. If they do manage their own undertakings, then the sovereign's authority will also reach its utmost. The people can devote themselves to their under- takings, and manage their duties. Such an undertaking therefore means that there is nothing which is not governed. Now, by advocating the *kuo-hui*, we are founding schools; and by advocating schools we are founding a *kuo-hui*. The people [will then] honor their ruler. The people [will then] move in agreement with their own company (*ch'ün ch'i ch'ün*). The country will not be struck some day with the actual disaster of mortal defeat, and the people will avoid the calamity of becoming followers and slaves of some other race. In this way there can be no severing [the connection] between the ruler's sovereignty and popular sovereignty.[46]

Popular sovereignty undermined the very foundations of the throne, but it was presented as a means of uniting the throne with the people, of creating the kind of ultimate "we-ness" even Ku Hsien-ch'eng would have appre- ciated. For, when the reformer Wang K'ang-nien argued in 1896 that the doctrine of popular rights had deep roots in the Chinese past—

The word *chih* (to rule) in Chinese just means that the ruler governs the people. Only in the Occident were there democratic countries as well as countries ruled jointly by monarch and people. Among Chinese Confucianists none fail to be shocked and astonished by this . . . However, why be astonished when our own ancient precepts about governing all meant consulting the people (*chi yü min*)?[47]

—he was returning to the very same source which had caused Ku to ponder the meaning of *tang* (parties); the *Hung-fan* of the *Book of Documents*.

If you have doubts about any great matter, consult with your own heart; consult with your nobles and officers; consult with your masses of the people (*mo chi shu-min*); consult the tortoise and the milfoil. If you, the tortoise, the milfoil, the nobles and officers, and the common people all consent to a course, this is what is called a great concord (*ta-t'ung*), and the result will be the welfare of your person, and good fortune to your descendants.[48]

Why then—asked Wang—should his readers or even the emperor himself be so prejudiced against popular sovereignty?

Wang K'ang-nien was not just masking novel political innovations with a classical cosmetic. The Confucian tradition which nurtured him was a cluster of symbols that apparently encompassed many different situational usages. The shared ideal of social harmony that was used in the late Ming to crush political formations could be employed in the late Ch'ing to sanc- tion them. On the one hand this made it almost impossible for the last Manchus on the throne to refute the intellectuals' argument for parlia- mentary assemblies, since they were as bound by the symbol of unity be- tween ruler and ruled as were the constitutionalists. But from another, classically liberal point of view, the very value that intellectuals had used to abet change ultimately denied them procedural means of political expres- sion. The "great harmony" would be contradicted if "selfish" interests were encouraged, so that a conflict theory of constitutional politics could not be expressed. Early republican intellectuals still formed cliques, still substituted personalities for programmatic disputes, still sought plurality in the place of pluralism.

Yet in spite of the seeming permanence of such primary values, certain vital conceptual changes did take place. The most important was the transformation of Confucian populism (ruling for the sake of the people) into a theory of genuine popular sovereignty. The change began traditionally enough when mid-nineteenth-century writers like Feng Kuei-fen stressed the importance of holding the people—definers of the Mandate of Heaven—in awe.[49] As popular dissent subtly changed from an omen of heaven's judgment of misrule to an actual denial of the particular sovereign's right to reign, reformist intellectuals came to conceive of monarchy as a national stewardship. A new theory of historical descent virtually snatched the *kuo* away from heaven and the ruling house. Because "our dynasty possesses a people of 10,000 years," and because "the ruler conserves a position of 10,000 years," the country was itself a thing to be preserved, an obligation to be served.[50] And as the country was the collective form of the human beings that had formed it, populism ceased being merely symbolic.

Once again, it was the intellectuals who had abetted this transformation. But their importance was only transitional. By creating an immanent definition of popular sovereignty, they automatically ceased to function as interpreters—brokers—of a transcendental source of legitimacy. Within the perimeter of shared assumptions about sovereignty during the Ming, intellectual dissent may have been organizationally limited but it was at least symbolically ultimate. Now, hoping for everything, the Ch'ing reformers gave up the little they had had. For, by the mid-twentieth century, intellectual dissent would smack of elitism, of betrayal of the democratic dictatorship which embodied the masses. Unable to claim, much less monopolize, the virtue of the people, Communist intellectuals were even forced to revive the heroic model of the Tung-lin scholars—only to stand accused of "right opportunism" and selfish privatism. The ultimate cost of the Chinese quest for intellectual autonomy was political estrangement.

This article was prepared while I received sabbatical support from the American Council of Learned Societies and the Center for Chinese Studies of the University of California, Berkeley. I am grateful for suggestions for revision from Professors Frederick W. Mote, Nicholas V. Riasanovsky, and Irwin Scheiner; from Frederic Wakeman, Sr., and Miss Judith Whitbeck; from the Research Scholars Group at Berkeley; and, of course, from the members of the Conference on Intellectuals held in Jerusalem. Research assistance was provided by Jonathan Grant and Chun-kao Poon. Indeed, Mr. Poon's own seminar research on late nineteenth-century study societies inspired some of the comparisons made here.

REFERENCES

1. *Ming shih* (History of the Ming), ed. the Kuo-fang yen-chiu yuan (Taipei, 1962), *chüan* 77, p. 818. See also *Ming shih-lu, T'ai-tsu shih-lu*, 24:7a.

2. Robert B. Crawford, Harry M. Lamley, Albert B. Mann, "Fang Hsiao-ju in the Light of Early Ming Society," *Monumenta Serica*, 15, fasc. 2 (1956), 321.

3. Ku Hsien-ch'eng, memorial to the throne, probably dated around 1586, included in Kao P'an-lung, *Kao-tzu i-shu* (Bequeathed writings of Master Kao), in *Ch'ien-k'un cheng-ch'i chi*, 262:3b.

4. *Ibid.*, 262:46.

5. *Shang shu*, Part V, Book IV, 14 (Legge, *Chinese Classics*, vol. 3, p. 331). This was usually related to another passage from the same classic: "That the multitudes of the people have no lawless confederacies *(yin-p'eng)* and that men [in office] have no selfish combinations *(pi-te)*, will be an effect of the sovereign's establishing his highest point of excellence." (*Ibid.*, Part V, Book IV, 10; Legge, vol. 3, p. 10.) *Yin-p'eng* was usually glossed to mean "corrupt parties" *(hsieh-tang)*; and *pi-te* was taken to signify "selfish combining" *(ssu hsiang pi-fu)*. The ideal, properly Confucian, was that old one-to-one relationship between the ruler and his minister. If a monarch's rule were moral then his ministers would have no reason to form selfish combinations based on "excessive" friendship. Thus, factions implied as such that a ruler had failed to govern well.

6. *Lun Yü*, Book XII, ch. 24 (Legge, *Chinese Classics*, vol. 1, p. 262).

7. Hsia Yun-i, *Hsing ts'un lu* (Record of a fortunate survival), reprinted in *Yang-chou shih-jih chi* (An Account of ten days in Yang-chou) (Taipei: Kuang-wen shu-chü, 1966), pp. 11-12.

8. From the Kwangtung provincial gazetteer of 1558, cited and translated in Joanna Flug Handlin, "On the Relationship Between the Rise of Private Academies and Eclecticism in Sixteenth-Century China," seminar paper, University of California, Berkeley, 1968, p. 7.

9. *Ming shih-lu*, *Lung-ch'ing shih-lu* (Veritable records of Lung-ch'ing), *chüan* 24, cited in Fu I-ling, *Ming-tai chiang-nan shih-min ching-chi shih-t'an* (An economic exploration of urban dwellers in Chiang-nan during the Ming dynasty) (Shanghai: People's Press, 1963), p. 110.

10. Cited and translated in Tilemann Grimm, "Ming Education Intendants," in Charles O. Hucker, ed., *Chinese Government in Ming Times: Seven Studies* (New York: Columbia University Press, 1969), p. 135.

11. Ku Hsien-ch'eng, *Chih-i tu-pien*, cited in Hsieh Kuo-chen, *Ming-Ch'ing chih chi tang-she yun-tung k'ao* (A study of party and club movements during the Ming and Ch'ing periods) (Taipei: Commercial Press, 1967), pp. 47-48.

12. Ku Hsien-ch'eng, cited and translated in Heinrich Busch, "The Tung-lin Academy and Its Political and Philosophical Significance," *Monumenta Serica*, 14:1-163 (1949-1955), 103, 115-117, 113.

13. Cited in Li Hsin-chuang, *Ch'ung-pien Ming-ju hsueh-an* (Recompilation of the *Ming-ju hseuh-an* [of Huang Tsung-hsi]) (Taipei: Cheng-cheng shu-chü, 1955), p. 483.

14. *Ibid.*

15. *Ibid.*

16. Kao P'an-lung, *Kao-tzu i-shu*, in *Ch'ien-k'un cheng-ch'i chi*, 258:7a.

17. *Ibid.*, 258:3b-4, 9-10a.

18. Cited in Hsieh Kuo-chen, *Ming-Ch'ing chih chi tang-she yun-tung k'ao,* p. 51.

19. Cited and translated in Heinrich Busch, "The Tung-lin Academy," p. 129.

20. Cited in Hsieh Kuo-chen, *Ming-Ch'ing chih chi tang-she yun-tung k'ao,* p. 50.

21. Kao P'an-lung, *Kao-tzu i-shu,* in *Ch'ien-k'un cheng-ch'i chi,* 258:22b.

22. *Ibid.*, 258:23a.

23. There are capsule biographies of all these men in, respectively, Huang Chih-chün, *Chiang-nan t'ung-chih* (The provincial gazetteer of Chiang-nan), photolithographic reprint of the 1737 edition (Taipei: Ching-hua Book Co., 1967), 142:32; 153:11b-12a; 142:32b; 163:22b-23a; 163:26a; 164:13b; 164:16a; 163:25a.

24. *Ibid.*, 142:31b, 33a; 146:11a; 163:22b, 31a.

25. Chao Nan-hsing, *Chao Chung-i-kung wen-chi* (The collected writings of Duke Chao Chung-i [Nan-hsing]), in *Ch'ien-k'un cheng-ch'i chi,* 264:6a.

26. *Ibid.*, 269:27b-28b.

27. Kao P'an-lung, *Kao-tzu i-shu,* 262:15a.

28. *Ibid.*

29. Yang Lien, cited and translated in Charles O. Hucker, *The Censorial System of Ming China* (Stanford: Stanford University Press, 1966), pp. 203-204.

30. Kao P'an-lung, *Kao-tzu i-shu,* 263:2a.

31. K'ang Yu-wei, Fourth Memorial to the Emperor, June 30, 1895, in Chien Po-tsan and others, comps., *Wu-hsü pien-fa* (The reform movement of 1898) (Shanghai: Shen-chou kuo-kuang she, 1955), 2:181-182.

32. Throughout this section I have used a basic list of the reform societies compiled by Wang Erh-min, "Ch'ing-chi hsueh-hui hui-piao" (A classified list of the study societies of the Ch'ing period), *Ta-lu tsa-chih* (The Continent Magazine), Part I, 26.2:14-20 (January 31, 1962); Part II, 26.3:16-23 (February 15, 1962).

33. "Ch'ang-te ming-ta hseuh-hui chang-ch'eng" (Bylaws of the Ming-ta study society of Ch'ang-te), in *Hsiang-hsueh hsin-pao* (hereafter cited as *HHHP*), a reform newspaper edited by T'an Ssu-t'ung, T'ang Ts'ai-ch'ang, and Hsiung Hsi-ling. The first issue appeared on April 22, 1897. It was suppressed in the eighth lunar month of 1898 when the reform movement was crushed. I have used the reprint of the full run published in Taipei in 1966 by the *Hua-lien ch'u-pan she,* 2878 pages.

34. "Hsiao-ching shu-yuan hsueh-hui chang-ch'eng" (Bylaws of the Hsiao-ching academy and study society), *HHHP*, p. 250.

35. "Liang-yueh kuang-jen-shan t'ang sheng hsueh-hui yuan-ch'i" (The origin of the divine study group and hall of vast and humane goodness of the Liang-yueh), *Shih-wu pao,* June 20, 1897, p. 2014. *Shih-wu pao* (The China Progress), ed. Liang Ch'i-ch'ao, ran from August 22, 1896, to April 1, 1898. I have used the reprint issued by *Ching-hua shu-chü* (Taipei, 1967), 3831 pages.

36. *Ibid.* I have added the emphasis.

37. "Ni she-li Su hsueh-hui ch'i" (A petition to establish a *hsueh-hui* in Su-chou), *HHHP*, p. 309.

38. See, for example, the request of the K'ang-shan gentry to change their *shu-yuan* into a *hseuh-hui* (*HHHP*, pp. 239-241); and that of the Jen-i academy in Kiangsi to change its course of studies (*HHHP*, pp. 227-230).

39. "Ch'ang-te ming-ta hsueh-hui chang-ch'eng," *HHHP*, p. 339.

40. Wang Erh-min, "Ch'ing-chi hsueh-hui hui-piao," 26.2:17. See also Wang Erh-min, "Nan hsueh-hui" (Southern Study Society), *Ta-lu tsa-chih*, 23.5:19-22 (September 1961).

41. Ku Yen-wu, *Jih-chih lu* (Record of daily knowing) (Taipei: Commercial Press, 1957), 4 *shang*, pp. 106-107.

42. *The Works of Hsüntze*, trans. Homer H. Dubs (Taipei: Ch'eng-wen Publishing Company, 1966), p. 136.

43. Liang Ch'i-ch'ao, "Shuo ch'ün tzu hsü" (Personal preface to "On *ch'ün*"), *Shih-wu pao*, May 11, 1897, pp. 1727-1728. Liang declared that K'ang had told him to take *ch'ün* as the essence, and *pien* (reform) as the function, of government. There is an excellent study of Liang's use of *ch'ün* by Professor Hao Chang, *Liang Ch'i-ch'ao: An Intellectual Transition in China, 1890-1907* (Cambridge, Mass.: Harvard University Press, 1971).

44. Liang Ch'i-ch'ao, "Nan hsueh-hui hsü" (Introductory comments on the Nan hsueh-hui), *Shih-wu pao*, February 14, 1898, pp. 3447-3448.

45. Liang had of course read Huang Tsun-hsien's history of Japan (*Jih-pen kuo-chih*), first printed in 1890, which declared that a *kuo-hui* (national association or assembly), copied from the West, had strengthened Japan by creating "a united sound from ten thousand mouths." (3:17b in the 1898 edition reprinted by the *Che-chiang shu-chü*.) He had also seen Mackenzie's account of Stein's *Tugenbund* referred to as *hui* in Timothy Richard's influential translation, *T'ai-hsi hsin-shih lan-yao* (Grasping the essentials of occidental history), 24:1. (This reference was kindly supplied by Miss Susanne Paul.)

46. "Tsung-lun" (editorial), *HHHP*, pp. 821-822.

47. Wang K'ang-nien, "Lun Chung-kuo ts'an-yung min-ch'üan chih li-i" (A discussion of China's utilization of the benefits of popular sovereignty), *Shih-wu pao*, October 27, 1896, p. 556.

48. *Book of Documents*, Part 5, Book 4, paragraphs 25-26. (See Legge, *Chinese Classics*, p. 327.) Liang Ch'i-ch'ao referred to the same section, as well as to portions of Mencius, to show that this process of consulting in ancient China was like the West's version of a parliament. "Thus even though it did not bear the name of *i-yuan* (parliament) it was so in reality." Liang Ch'i-ch'ao, editorial in *Shih-wu pao*, November 5, 1896, p. 66.

49. Feng Kuei-fen, *Hsien-chih t'ang chih-i* (Determinations from the Hsien-chih hall) (1876), pp. 10a, 84.

50. "Tsung-lun," *HHHP*, p. 805.

BENJAMIN I. SCHWARTZ

The Limits of "Tradition Versus Modernity" as Categories of Explanation: The Case of the Chinese Intellectuals

THE STUDY of the role of intellectuals in developing society has been going on for some time now. To the extent that it has turned the attention of scholars to the concrete study of intellectuals in non-Western societies, it has, of course, been a spur to fruitful inquiry. To the extent that it has attempted to structure the whole experience of these intellectuals in terms of the conventional triad—tradition/development/modernity—without a deeper investigation of the range of meaning of these terms, to the extent that it has been unduly preoccupied with proclaiming supposed universal laws or models of how intellectuals behave or ought to behave in developing societies,[1] it may have actually impeded deeper inquiry.

If the two terminal categories of this triad, tradition and modernity, do not refer to definite, internally consistent, and mutually exclusive entities but are useful only as a short-hand way of referring to vast inchoate and by no means internally integrated areas of human experience, the unreflective use of these terms can only lead to what Whitehead called the fallacy of misplaced concreteness. One of the most dire results of misplaced concreteness is that it obstructs our contacts with true concreteness. To be sure, there are many who have in mind more specific polarities when they speak of the polarity of tradition versus modernity. To some the crucial variable may be agrarian society versus industrial, to others authority versus freedom, to still others scientific outlook versus prescientific mentality, and so forth. However, all seem to share the assumption that every other aspect of the society or the culture—always conceived of as integrated wholes—is a function of whatever variable they happen to consider crucial.

What is proposed here is not the elimination of the use of the adjectives "traditional" and "modern." The adjective "traditional" remains a short-hand way (until we find a better one) of dealing with the whole past experience of any society such as China before the impact of the modern West; furthermore, within this past one can indubitably find ongoing, recognizable, coherent traditions. The modern West has certainly witnessed the emergence of qualitatively new developments as well as the acceleration of other de-

71

velopments to a point where quantity almost seems to pass over into quality. There is, however, no reason to assume any preestablished harmony among elements called "traditional," on the one hand, or "modern," on the other— nor any necessary a priori incompatibility between modern elements and traditional elements.

It is worthy of note that in the triad the only truly dynamic term is the middle term, "development." Tradition is treated as a kind of static setting whose essential features can be described in terms of a few well-chosen propositions. It is not, of course, denied that diachronic change did take place within traditional societies. It is simply assumed that such changes are not important or relevant. Furthermore while modernity is not contrasted to change—on the contrary some might say that the acceptance of change as a value is one of the earmarks of modernity—the change always tends to be regarded as incremental change within the framework of an established modernity. The recent futurological discussions on the year 2000, in spite of their constant stress on change, particularly in technology, were for the most part based on the extrapolation of certain variables which are regarded as established and irreversible. Indeed certain kinds of incremental change are themselves regarded as an inexorable fixity.

There has, to be sure, been some change in recent years[2] in the treatment of tradition. There has emerged the notion that in some societies, some traditions, far from impeding certain aspects of modernization, may have actually facilitated them. There is some acceptance of the view that the variables which differentiate one traditional culture from another may, from the point of view of certain vital questions, be more important than the features which they share in common. Yet in vast numbers of textbooks which still provide the intellectual food of innumerable schools of secondary and higher learning, the vulgar concept of traditional society has become almost a fixed dogma and has encouraged the philistine view that the total past experience of mankind is irrelevant and, on all important matters, homogeneous. Furthermore, while there has been some progress among those who deal in these matters toward a more complicated view of traditional society,[3] the notion that we all know precisely what we are talking about when we discuss the modernity pole of this triadic formula still remains, on the whole, unchallenged.

Tradition and Modernity—Some General Reflections

As suggested above, the difference between traditional and modern society is most often made to depend on some crucial variable. Among the most convincing and indisputable of these polarities is probably that of agrarian society versus industrial society. If one can assert that all peasant societies are alike in their *essential* features and that all change over time in such societies is inconsequential, one can of course go on to discount all the differences in the "high cultures" and in the historic development of these societies which in any event are assumed to affect only the ruling strata or intellectuals.

I shall not dwell here on the features which all peasant societies may share in common. While there are no doubt many, there is a tendency to accept uncritically any dogmatic assertion in this area. I would question the assertion that even on the level of the rural village, differentiating cultural features are inconsequential. The difference between the caste structure of the Indian village and the various structures of Chinese peasant life are of crucial importance from any point of view. While it is often asserted that the political superstructures of these societies have little effect on the daily life of the villager, the differing political histories of China and India have in fact had a great deal to do with the endemic nature of widespread peasant rebellions in China and their relative lack in India. What is more, the iron wall which many erect between the "high cultures" and the "little cultures" is not easily maintained under close inspection. In fact, in all these societies Confucianism, Hinduism, Islam, Buddhism tended in countless ways to cut across the folk culture/high culture barrier in both directions.

When we turn our attention to the so-called "high cultures" or Great Traditions themselves, the question of whether they concerned themselves with "significant" or "real" questions is, to be sure, ultimately a philosophic question, but it also bears most directly on whether traditional modalities of thought, attitudes, and sensibilities derived from the past may continue to affect the outlooks of intellectuals in modernizing and even in modern societies. One of the most facile ways of dismissing the high cultures of the past is to assert that they encompassed a kind of closed symbolic world of concern only to the limited strata who were involved with them and that they had little or no effect on or meaning for the lives of the masses. In fact, one might make precisely the same observation concerning the culture of academic and literary intellectuals in modern societies. The questions discussed and issues raised in our own intellectual media and the language in which they are discussed are more often than not quite inaccessible to the man in the street, in spite of his literacy. In fact, quotations from the Confucian classics were probably more immediately available to the discourse of the masses in China than passages from George Lukacs, Lévi-Strauss, or Herbert Marcuse are to our own masses. Yet this observation can hardly be used as a way of determining whether our intellectuals deal with problems of the "real world" or problems of concern to mankind in general. Given our own particular criteria of relevance, the issues which divided Ch'an Buddhists from Neo-Confucianists in Sung China, or Chu Hsi from Wang Yang-ming, may or may not appear significant. However, the fact that their discourses and debates may or may not have found an echo in every village can by no means be used as a criterion for judging the general human significance and relevance of their preoccupations.

I have here spoken of issues, questions, and debates. These words tend to imply the existence of both synchronic and diachronic conflicts and tensions within the Great Traditions. This, of course, is quite contrary to the view of these Great Traditions as essentially static, integrated, unproblematic wholes which can be described in a few well-chosen propositions. It is by no means my intention to deny the presense of persistent and predominant tendencies within traditional cultures or to deny that there were in them limits to the range of alternative approaches to human experience. Yet the more closely we examine these Great Traditions, the more we are impressed with the broadness of the range and the variety of alternatives within them; also, the more we are conscious of the significance of change over time.

Even if we focus our attention on one coherent dominant tendency within the culture such as Confucianism in China, we soon find that Confucianism itself has had a complicated and turbulent history replete with unresolved problems. To be sure, it is possible to treat Confucianism in a kind of static sociological-anthropological way by asserting that the heart of Confucianism is the Confucian family ethic and that this has remained fundamentally unchanged over time. The Chinese social structure is marked by the centrality of the family; Confucian values provide the operative norms of this structure. Hence, whatever debates may have gone on among Confucian literati and Confucian philosophers can hardly have affected the central social function of Confucianism. They were probably concerned with matters of secondary importance.

One of the characteristic features of this particular sociological view of the role of norms within a social system is that it tends to ignore the gap between norms and the way things actually work. Yet many of the most eminent ethical philosophers down through the ages have been concerned not only with the contents of given value systems but precisely with the question of how and to what extent any values are ever realized. Within the sociological perspective, the whole persistent tragic sense of tension between the ideal and the actual which has existed among sensitive spirits in every higher civilization simply disappears from view. In China, the lament that the ways of the world were far removed from the higher values of Confucianism was so persistent down through the ages that it became a cliché of Chinese literature, while those literati (probably the vast majority) who were complacently prepared to define the current state of affairs as Confucian were dismissed by the more creative intellectuals as *su ju* (vulgar or conventional Confucianists).

Even if one assumes that Confucian family morality was more or less successfully actualized over large areas of Chinese society and over long stretches of time, there is a serious question whether Confucianism can be simply equated with the family ethic. The centrality of family values existed before Confucius and was rooted in pre-Confucian Chinese religion.

If Confucius had, what seemed to his followers, a fresh message to proclaim, it did not lie here. He may have accepted filial piety as an ultimate value, but he placed it within a new context. His contribution lay in his attention to the problems of inner self-cultivation—what might be called the subjective springs of morality—on the one hand, and on the manner in which he related himself to the whole sociopolitical realm on the other. The family becomes simply one element within this larger frame.

If Confucianism is viewed in this light, one can immediately understand why the efforts to realize its higher values led to enormous and even tragic problems for serious thinkers and sensitive spirits. How is the Confucian ideal of individual self-realization ever to be attained? What is the relation of knowledge to ethics? What indeed is the relationship of personal ethics to action within the political realm? Is centralized bureaucratic organization compatible with Confucian values? What is the relationship of technical administrative capacity to morality? Was the bureaucratic state structure which had emerged after the Ch'in compatible with the Confucian stress on personal relations? Weber calls the Chinese system "patrimonial bureaucracy" but many Confucian idealists down through the ages found it far too bureaucratic and far too little patrimonial. To what extent are Confucian ethical sociopolitical values realizable at all in the world out there? What is the relationship of the aesthetic to the ethical realm? Some of the general problems which arise in the history of Confucianism when separated from the framework of specific Confucian assumptions within which they are constrained may be recognized as real issues even by those of us who live in the heart of modern Western society. As in all societies, of course, these issues became deeply enmeshed in complex ways with conflicts of material and political interest, but in this respect traditional China was no different from any society, traditional or modern.

I have dwelt here on the kinds of tension and conflict which can be found within the dominant strain of Confucianism. When one adds to this the counter-Confucian tendencies which have often been vaguely grouped under the headings of Taoism, Buddhism, and Legalism, and the complex relations of these tendencies to various aspects of Chinese folk culture, the picture of an immobile traditional setting simply fades from view. Incidentally, the notion that the countertendencies of Chinese culture simply faded away in the last few centuries of Confucian orthodoxy also becomes more doubtful the more we immerse ourselves in the concrete specificities of Ming and Ch'ing history.

Thus, a common conventional picture of the Chinese literati who first confronted the modern West in the early nineteenth century is that of somnabulant mandarins complacently embedded in the unchanging essence of Chinese tradition. Here again we must, of course, draw a sharp distinction between the unreflective mass of conventional literati and the serious thinkers. The latter were in fact profoundly troubled by the situation in late eighteenth- and early nineteenth-century China and profoundly involved in the intellectual debates of their times. Thus at the end of the eighteenth century a strong reaction had set in against a kind of prevailing scholarly positivism which was found to be increasingly irrelevant to the problems of the time. There was, on the one hand, a revival of interest in problems of statecraft and, on the other hand, a revival of interest in philosophies of personal ethics. There was even some revival of interest in Buddhist transcendentalism. Within this context, the problems created by the "sea-barbarians" were simply a somewhat novel problem in statecraft. Thus what we are dealing with here is not so much paralytic immobility as a sense of assurance that somewhere within the rich and cumulative range of experience provided by the Chinese past could be found ways of coping with all of her contemporary problems. The past provided not so much an integrated tradition as a reservoir of conflicting responses to human experience. (There was in fact no Chinese word for "tradition" in this large and vague sense; the term *chüan-t'ung* as a general term, while Chinese in origin, came back to China from Japan as a neologism.) It is only at the end of the century that we find a generation which finally began to question whether this range of experience was any longer adequate to the situation which now confronted China and which thus became open to new ideas from the West.

If tradition cannot be reduced to a simple integrated system, what can we say of modernity? Since our focus here is on intellectuals, we must be interested in modernity not merely as descriptive of certain processes of action but also as embodied in certain modes of thought and sensibility. For purposes of convenience, I shall here draw a distinction in somewhat ad hoc fashion between modernization as referring to processes of development in economic, political, legal, military, and other realms of action and modernity as referring to certain modes of thought and modes of sensibility. In dealing with modernization as a system of action I shall treat it in terms of Weber's conception of "rationalization," for it seems quite clear that the Weberian conception has been the dominant influence in the American social scientific use of this term. Modernization refers to all those realms of life in which man can achieve the ends of world mastery by the individual and collective employment of rationally effective means. To the extent that modernization is linked to an idea, it is precisely this idea of the mastery of the world of nature as well as of the social world of man.[4] While many of Weber's conceptions of the prerequisites of *Zwecksrationalität* in various areas have been challenged, the validity of the general framework will be assumed for purposes of this essay.

What then as been the relationship of modernization in this sense to all those ideas, ideologies, attitudes, and orientations which have emerged in the modern world since the seventeenth and eighteenth centuries? One might presumably resolve this question quite easily by asserting that all ideas which facilitate or are congenial with the process of modernization should be labeled modern while all ideas which are contrary to or uncongenial to the process of modernization might be considered nonmodern or antimodern. Leaving aside the highly controversial nature of this question in itself, the overwhelming force of general usage has tended to label as "modern" all sorts of tendencies and ideas which may stand in a very questionable relationship to modernization (such as the modernist movement in literature). The force of ordinary usage here seems to be quite sound and defensible, for in fact there is even less warrant for assuming that modernity is an integrated whole than that tradition is. The eighteenth-century enlightenment itself contained many mutually contradictory tendencies. Yet all of these tendencies were new tendencies.[5] Some may insist on using the word "modern" as a eulogistic value term descriptive only of the particular values which they happen to cherish, but the term can never shed its primary sense as a time-reference term. Rousseau was not less modern than Voltaire nor was Immanuel Kant a whit less modern than Jeremy Bentham. Many of the conflicts central to the French Revolution may have been quite tangential to the business of modernization as here defined. In fact, Saint-Simon, the father of the term "industrialism," in looking back over the revolutionary days felt precisely that all the sound and fury, all the frenzied moralism of the Jacobins, had been a diversion from the serious technological business of mankind. Yet would any one really deny that revolutionism has continued to be an important part of the experience of modern man or that Rousseau's pathos—which sees the whole question of society as a social ethical drama—has been as much a part of the experience of modern man as the pathos of those who have seen the problem wholly in terms of social technology?

What indeed is the relationship between modernization—the mastery of the world—and other values such as liberty, equality, democracy, and collectivity, which figure so prominently in the sociopolitical "isms" of the modern world? One cannot assume an a priori logical relationship because rational men have differed from each other profoundly concerning these matters. One can conceive of liberty, equality, and democracy without modernization. Montesquieu, Jefferson, and Rousseau were, of course, convinced that obsessive concern with economic growth was detrimental to democracy, while Max Weber himself, who was a political liberal (and probably never thought of raising questions concerning the modernity of liberalism), was profoundly agonized by the implications of the bureaucratization of society incident to modernization for the survival of political liberty. He saw not a functional relation but a profound tension between these two elements of modernity.

To be sure, the nineteenth and twentieth centuries have been rich in social philosophies which assert on various grounds all sorts of necessary functional relationships between the process of modernization and particular political social values. One might say that an underlying shared assumption of these ideologies is that all the factors of progress must be harmonious with each other either immediately or ultimately. Such political and social values are often presented as either a necessary concomitant or function of the modernization process or a final outcome of this process. One way of viewing mature Marxism is to see in it the assertion that the process of modernization, here described as the capitalist mode of production,[6] must itself lead to the realization of socialism, while American social scientists have often seen in liberal values as they understand them the final culmination of the process of modernization. The doctrine of the "end of ideology" does not involve a rejection of given sociopolitical values. It rather involved the assumption that the modernization process, in its mature phase, will itself achieve these values without the intervention of moral and ideological passions. This is, of course, not the place to undertake a consideration of the modes of reasoning which enter into these various ways of linking modernization to sociopolitical philosophies. Suffice it to say that these controversies remain unresolved and that a non-Western intellectual looking in at the intellectual scene in Europe and America during the whole span of the twentieth century could not help but be aware of profound conflict and confusion on all these matters.

Beyond the unresolved controversies concerning sociopolitical ideals and modernization, what are we to say of such an important and recurrent movement of the modern spirit as romanticism? Romanticism may share with modernization a certain Faustian striving for mastery, but in this case it is not so much the mastery of the machinery of material and social technology as the conquest of the world of affective experience and sensibility. Of course, what it rejects most emphatically is what it regards as the desiccation of feeling in the cool and gray pathos of the machine-like world of modernization as a socioeconomic process.

What are we to say finally about the whole modernist movement in literature and art, which often reflects a range of attitudes toward modernization running the gamut from vehement negativity to indifference? C. P. Snow loudly lamented the lack of congeniality between one of his two cultures and the other, but it never occurred to him to impugn the modernity of the literary culture. One is reluctant to use the cliché word "alienation," yet it does say something about the nature of much of our profoundest modern literature.

One could of course extend ad infinitum the discussion of the tensions, conflicts, and incommunicabilities within the world of modernity. One could point to such diverse phenomena as the complete noncommunication between the worlds of Anglo-American linguistic philosophers and French existentialists; to the ambiguous relations to modernization of the various movements spawned by Freud in spite of his own self-conception as a thoroughly modern engineer of the soul. Enough has been said, it seems to me, to make it quite clear that the word "modernity" refers to no simple entity.

It may, of course, be true that at a deeper level many of the disparate movements and clashing ideas of the modern West may rest on certain unexpressed common assumptions. Perhaps they all share a pervading anthropocentrism, a tendency to view the nonhuman universe as meaningless and valueless. The various specific social and political ideologies may share with the more technocratic orientation a tendency to think in terms of the management and transformation of macroscopic social structures and of institutional frameworks (systems) rather than in terms of personal self-transformation or personal ethics. Yet whatever may be the underlying common premises, the horizontal tensions and conflicts among the various currents and countercurrents of the modern world make it impossible to think of modernity as any kind of completed or synthetic whole.

Chinese Intellectuals, Tradition, and Modernity

If Chinese tradition refers to a vast and variegated experience which we have only begun to study in depth and if modernity refers to a complex and unresolved state of affairs, this does not suggest that we are likely to discover a simple development model which will adequately explain the behavior of the Chinese intelligentsia during the period of transition (a period which, it seems to me, has hardly ended) from one to the other.

What makes the construction of such a model even less likely is that in dealing with the concrete experience of intellectuals within any given society we must introduce between tradition and modernity another crucial variable, namely the concrete specificities of history. In China the end of the examination system in 1905, the Japanese incursion into China, Mao's all-out cultural revolutionary assault on the intelligentsia—to mention certain events at random—are specific historic movements which must figure in any effort to understand the experience and the responses of Chinese intellectuals within the time period with which we are concerned. None of these specificities are reducible to the vague abstractions "tradition" and "modernity." One's interest in Chinese intellectuals cannot simply be in their role within some preestablished sociohistoric scheme. One must be intrinsically interested in the situations in which they find themselves and in how their ideas and passions relate to their situations. Out of this may emerge either an enrichment or stretching of the triadic scheme or perhaps even an abandonment of it in favor of more adequate conceptions.

Whether we deal with large tendencies, groups, or single individuals, the tradition/modernity polarity will in itself seldom, if ever, be adequate to the subject of our investigation.

Thus, if we consider what might be called the transitional generation which reached its creative peak in the last decade of the nineteenth century and first two decades of the twentieth century and which included among its leading figures such luminaries as K'ang Yu-wei, Yen Fu, Chang Ping-lin, Lin Shu, Liang Ch'i-ch'ao, Wang Kuo wei, T'an Ssu-t'ung, and others, we find a group whose early life had been profoundly molded by "traditional" China. To a degree, this remains true of the younger generation of Ch'en Tu-hsiu, Hu Shih, Lu Hsün, and even of the student generation of May 4th (a generation now in its seventies). Depending upon a wide variety of social and geographic circumstances, many of the latter also spent their earliest childhood years in traditional China. Nevertheless, if one's conception of psychology allows one to concede that the second decade of the life cycle may be as crucial as the first, one must give enormous weight to the different life experiences of the two generations. The first decade of the twentieth century was to witness the demise of the imperial examination system and the scramble of the young to find new educational paths (largely in westernized schools) into an unknown future. All of this took place largely within an urban environment which was itself undergoing unprecedented change at an ever accelerating pace. In contrast, the older generation of intellectuals had still faced all the rigors and frustrations of the examination system and still had some expectation that the political system would continue to hold together.

It still was at home in the medium of classical Chinese,[7] with its rich burden of allusion, metaphors, and quotations derived from the culture of the past, and continued to be comfortable with traditional life styles. Some of its leading figures found the traditional family system quite tolerable on a personal level even when they were already prepared to criticize it severely on the abstract intellectual level. Few of them seemed to find traditional family practices as unendurable as they were to become for some young men and women of the next generation.

Above all, this generation lived sufficiently within the Chinese cultural stream to see it not as a harmonious integrated tradition but more as an arena of tensions, alternatives, and conflicts. It was thoroughly familiar with the intellectual tendencies of eighteenth- and nineteenth-century China and the animosities aroused by the relations among the various schools of literati even continued to shape their relationships to each other. The youthful K'ang Yu-wei had turned against the narrow "irrelevance" of the still dominant scholastic philological school (K'ao cheng-p'ai) which, in his view, had so little to say about the sufferings of men and the higher truths of Confucianism. He had for a time turned back to the thinkers of the Sung and Ming who had placed such stress on personal self-realization and had even been attracted by the radical transcendentalism of Buddhism. In the end, however, he believed that he found in a certain strain of early Han dynasty thought (the New Text School) the basis for a kind of redemptive philosophy of history which offered new hope for the collective future of mankind. At this point, to be sure, he was probably already in contact with Western theories of progress which he must have read back into his New Text philosophy. Yet the point is that this new Western element was fed back into a mental world still formed by the *Problematik* of nineteenth-century Chinese thought.

And yet, it was precisely this generation[8] which was to move well beyond the available range of Chinese thought and which was to prove eminently receptive to ideas from the West. Indeed, the more closely we examine their writings, the more impressed we are with the degree of openness and responsiveness to every variety of modern Western thought.

A common pervasive preoccupation of most of them[9] (particularly after the Sino-Japanese War of 1894-1895) was the concern with China's survival as a sociopolitical entity. As a group which still thought of itself, first and foremost, in typical traditional terms as a state service class, one might say that its public concern with the nation's survival and its private status anxiety moved in the same direction. It was thus this generation that directly confronted the dread question: Were the resources of the culture of the past adequate to preserve China as an independent political entity? One of their number, Yen Fu puts the matter quite baldly: "We have no time to ask whether this knowledge is Chinese or western, whether it is new or old. If one course leads to ignorance and thus to poverty and weakness . . . we must cast it aside, if another course is effective in overcoming ignorance and thus leads to the cure of our poverty and weakness we must imitate it even if it proceeds from barbarians."[10] Having put the matter in this way, having subordinated other values to the survival of the nation state, they have crossed the divide between what Western students of China call "culturalism" (what the Chinese call *pao-tao* or "preserving the Way") and modern nationalism. This is true even of those conservative nationalists such as Chang Ping-lin who continue to place heavy emphasis on the importance of preserving traditions of the past in the interests of identity. We are often struck by the degree to which Western ideas and "isms"—equality, liberty, socialism—came to be viewed in China in terms of their efficacy as a means to the achievement of national wealth and power as well as ends in themselves.

This concern with nationalist goals implies more than nationalism as such. It implies nothing less than a positive orientation to modernization and the Faustian-Promethean values underlying modernization. One is astonished by how Weberian are the prescriptions which one finds in the writings of K'ang Yu-wei, Yen Fu, and Liang Ch'i-ch'ao. Whatever their differences, they are all concerned with the rationalization of the economic, bureaucratic, military, and legal spheres of life.

Yet while Western ideas and ideologies are often viewed as instrumental to national goals, they are also viewed in terms of their own intrinsic meanings. One finds an influx of a wide variety of specific sociopolitical "isms" of eighteenth- and nineteenth-century Europe (albeit in a somewhat crude and simplified form) as well as all the puzzles involved in Western theories concerning the relationship of such ideologies to the process of modernization. Thus alongside of the scientific pathos of Yen Fu, who looks to nineteenth-century England as the teacher of piecemeal social engineering, we find the passionate revolutionary pathos of those who steep themselves in their own versions of Rousseau, the epic of the French Revolution, and the activities of contemporary Russian revolutionaries.

This openness to the variety of Western thought when combined with the ongoing sense of the variety of Chinese thought leads this generation to perceive not only antitheses but also affinities, similarities, and compatibilities between specific elements of Chinese traditional thought and specific varieties of modern Western thought. Some of this is, to be sure, disingenuous and even puerile and quite explicable in terms of the need to salvage national pride. Much of it is no doubt simply wrong and yet may reflect the brute fact that these people are inevitably forced to use the categories of thought and language available to them to assimilate the new ideas of the West.

I would submit at this point that there are no a priori grounds for assuming that all such attempts to find affinities and compatibilities are wrong in principle. There may indeed be elements of Chinese traditional thought which are similar to or compatible with elements of modern Western thought.[11] Only a careful, profound, and subtle study based on a thorough knowledge of the history of ideas and feel for language in both cultures can in the end determine whether any proposition of this type is valid or invalid and we find ourselves only at the very beginning of such transcultural investigations. When Yen Fu in his reading of T. H. Huxley[12] confronts the problem of whether human behavior can be wholly explained in terms of biological propensities or whether culture must be introduced as an independent variable, it occurs to him that *on the most general level* this debate had gone on in Chinese culture and that the Hsün-tze had adopted a position strikingly similar to that of Huxley. He had also believed that the anarchic biological propensities which man derived from nature can be brought under the control of the countervailing force of human culture. At the same time, Yen Fu is also acutely and even insistently aware of what is radically new in the Darwinian interpretation of biological reality. When others see identities between Rousseau and the book of Mencius, we cannot dismiss their claims out of hand but must examine the extent to which they may or may not be founded. We should not be deterred by culturalistic-historistic dogmas that there cannot possibly be any comparison between the thoughts of a Chinese literatus living several centuries before Christ and the neurotic social philosopher in eighteenth-century France.

Again, when T'an Ssu-t'ung finds in Buddhist philosophy as well as in Taoism and even some strands of Confucianism a kind of transcendental ground from which he can carry out an all-out attack on the ontological foundations of many of the forms and structures of contemporary Chinese society, he can find such grounds because they did indeed exist and had even been used in the past for similar purpose. When he uses this anti-formalistic mysticism as a kind of bridge to a cult of energy and dynamism of the Western type he has obviously added something new. Finally, while China may have never known revolution in the Western sense there were available utopian motifs and apocalyptic themes which could be fused in a potent blend with certain revolutionary tendencies out of the West as they indeed do in the writings of some anarchists and revolutionaries before 1911.

The complex dialectic of conscious and unconscious relations between the culture of the past and modernity is not confined to the pre-1911 generation, although it was most clearly illustrated in the life of experiences of that generation. It continues on into the present in complex and unresolved forms.

To be sure, in the generation which reached intellectual maturity after the 1911 revolution,[13] the concept of Chinese tradition or culture as an integrated whole to be rejected as a whole, does indeed emerge. Here we have a generation obviously less inside the Chinese past than the older generation. It was also a generation which keenly experienced the failures of the 1911 revolution and the political disintegration which followed that revolution. The experience of the years 1911-1919, certainly lent plausibility to a totalistic view of the traditional culture as a vast, inert, and uniform incubus strangling the vital spirits of the nation. One Chinese scholar, Lin Yu-sheng, has suggested that this totalistic rejection of Chinese culture in the May 4th period (which was, of course, not universal at this time or later) may itself be an unconscious reflection of a predominant traditional tendency to regard the cultural and political orders as one and indivisible. (This had not led even in the past, however, to any necessary consensus on the true nature of this cultural-political order.) With the collapse of the political order all aspects of the culture of the past lost their credibility. A totalistic view of culture led dialectically to a totalistic rejection of culture and beyond that to the yearning for a new totalistic cultural-political order of the future. Even in this generation, as Mr. Lin would gladly concede, when one focuses one's attention on its more creative individual representatives such as the writer Lu Hsün, one finds that the totalistic rejection of the past is often complicated by countermotifs. One finds here a vehement fury against the "man-eating" Confucian society of the past combined with a sensibility which is still under the spell of many aspects of Chinese folk culture and even of certain strains of the high culture of the past. Alongside of the rejection of the past we find a profound suspicion of many aspects of modern European urban culture and particularly of the contemporary Chinese "all-out Westerners" who represent this culture in China.

Nevertheless, in general the rejection of the Chinese past did lead to a search for answers in the modern West. So powerful had the categories of Western thought become that even those who now chose to defend tradition sought their arguments not in Chinese literature but in the writings of Bergson and Babbit, Eucken and Russell. The modern West, however, yielded no unitary answers. One could find totalistic formulas which would sum up the Chinese past but one could not find unitary formulas which would sum up all the conflicting ideas and "isms" of modernity. Chinese intellectuals were confronted with all the conflicts and unresolved tensions of modernity as well as with the difficulty of applying any variety of modernity to Chinese conditions. Ch'en Tu-hsiu, one of the great spokesmen of totalistic anti-traditionalism, drifted from a kind of French liberalism to Marxism-Leninism to a quasi-Trotskyite version of Marxism-Leninism to a kind of belief in social democracy, while Hu Shih had come to regard himself as a spokesman of John Dewey's variety of liberalism. Accidents of individual fate often partially conditioned such philosophic decisions. The fact that Hu Shih was a student at Columbia University under John Dewey led him to a quite different version of modernity from that of many of his peers who studied in Tokyo. This reminds us once more of the degree to which the varieties of modernity in the West itself have been defined by the confining boundaries of disparate national cultures. Again, others of a more literary-poetic bent such as Hsü Chih-mo, Yü Ta-fu, and Kuo Mo-jo fell under the spell of Western romanticism. They saw China's cultural crisis much more in terms of the mystery of their individual existence than in terms of national destiny or the tasks of modernization.

We shall not attempt to recount the troubled intellectual history of China (that is, the intellectual history of the small but crucial intelligentsia) between 1920 and the rise of the People's Republic. Suffice to say that the intellectuals who rejected the past did not arrive at common conclusions concerning the essence of modernity nor did the totalistic rejection of the past abolish the continuing influence of that past, for good or ill, on the shaping of the present. For one thing, the vast majority of the Chinese rural population still continued to live habitually within the framework of a popular culture inherited from the past and continued to look to types of local intellectuals such as secret society leaders, Buddhist monks, Taoist priests, leaders of Confucian uplift societies, and popular sects. The latter did not look to Bergson or Babbitt for justification although some Western notions did creep into their fund of ideas. Not only were the intellectuals forced to confront this fact but their own relationship to the past continued to be complex on many conscious and unconscious levels. Nor can one dismiss the ideas of such neo-traditionalists as Feng Yu-lan, Liang Sou-ming, or Hsiung Shih-li merely on the ground that they defended Chinese traditions in terms of Western categories.

One can perhaps make a certain case for the assertion that the intellectual history of China after 1920 conformed to a certain pattern common to all developing countries. Certain types of political and economic liberalism were not to flourish among the Chinese intelligentsia although they continued to be represented. All the objective factors which have proved inimical to Western liberalism elsewhere could certainly be found in China. One might add here that however much the "higher civilizations" of the past may have differed from each other in terms of their ethical orientations, they have, on the whole, shared in common a negative attitude toward the pursuit of individual material self-interest and have, on the whole, striven for the achievement of consensus in commonly shared truth rather than for pluralism and dissent. From this point of view, to the extent that Western liberalism is identified with a capitalist ethic and/or pluralism as an ideal it is probably the most exotic and subversive product of modern Western thought. The resistance to these aspects of liberalism has, as we know, gone on in the heart of the modern West itself and antiliberal tendencies in China whether of right or left have from the outset been able to draw much of their doctrinal sustenance from the West itself. In this sense, antiliberal intellectuals in China and the developing world in general have been thoroughly contemporary with powerful ongoing tendencies in the Western world.

One must add that the word "liberalism" is a semantic monster burdened with an enormous accumulation of accretions of meanings. Looking at the fate of Chinese intellectuals on both the mainland and Taiwan from the perspective of 1971, one becomes aware of the fact that they had, after all, not remained untouched by all strands of liberalism and that Mao Tse-tung is not entirely wrong when he accuses them of a kind of ineradicable liberalism. It would appear that even intellectuals who had long since committed themselves to the Chinese Communist movement had to a greater or lesser degree continued to believe in intellectual autonomy and in the much abhorred doctrine that "all men are equal before the truth."

In any event neither the dichotomy liberalism/antiliberalism nor the dichotomy tradition/modernity are, it seems to me, ultimately illuminating in attempting to explain the specificities of Chinese developments since 1949, particularly as they affect the intellectuals.

This is, of course, not the place to consider the intellectual biography of Mao Tse-tung. Yet if we are to say anything about the fate of the intellectuals in the People's Republic we must say something about their main protagonist.

Mao's mistrust of the intellectuals[14] has early roots and was highly developed by 1949. The urban intellectuals were isolated from the realities with which he had been contending since the early Hunan-Kiangsi days. Their individualistic vanity led them to insist stubbornly on the validity of their own mistaken ideas. They had a built-in tendency to complicate simple truths and to seek ironies and ambiguities. They could not give themselves unreservedly to the battle and submit to the general will of the masses as Mao understood that will.

Nevertheless, it never seemed to occur to Mao before 1949 that the intellectuals were dispensable. Their thoughts would have to be transformed but they were necessary to the tasks which lay ahead. If the tasks of revolution in China had been reducible to simple maxims, the tasks of building socialism would probably be difficult and complex (as Soviet experience had demonstrated). Indeed, as we know, during the Hundred Flowers experiment of 1956-1957, he even experimented with the possibility of an enlarged area of freedom for intellectuals on the assumption that they had been "basically transformed." The results of that experience were, of course, to reconfirm his worst suspicions of them and to lead to the grander visions of both the Great Leap Forward and the Cultural Revolution—visions which projected the truly radical possibility of a Chinese road to modernization without intellectuals. The older intellectuals continue to embody all the corruptions, ambiguities, and cultural superfluities of both traditional Chinese culture *and* the modern West. They are the inveterate enemies of that new morality which would show the world that modernization and national power were not incompatible with a life of collective simplicity.

When one asks whether this vision is traditional or modern, one emerges with no clear answer. To the extent that it involves commitment to further modernization, it is, of course, modern. To the extent that it embodies primitivist yearnings, it may draw on Mao's early and ardent admiration for that type of Chinese literature which depicts the untutored yet pure-hearted tough guys (*yu-hsia*) of Chinese history as contrasted to the corrupt mandarins. It may owe something to the primitivist critique of the over-complexity and corruption of "higher civilization" which finds expression as early as the Book of Lao-Tzu and which remains a persistent motif of Chinese culture ever after. It may even draw on the facile moralism of certain varieties of Confucianism. One can look here to the Sage-Kings of hoary antiquity who transformed the hearts of men through their mana-like virtue.

Through Marxism-Leninism and other Western influences, one can also point to Western sources, to the kind of deep resentment of the vanity, insincerity, and selfishness of fellow intellectuals which one finds in Rousseau. One can point to many highly relevant attacks of Robespierre on the treachery of *les esprits* and their exasperating inability to align themselves with the general good. One can even point to *The Greening of America*.

If one asks oneself how it is conceivable that the primitivist critique of high civilization can be found in undeveloped traditional societies and the modern West, it must be pointed out that development may be very much a matter of perspective. To the author of the Lao Tzu, Chinese society of his time was already overcomplicated and full of needless artificialities and therefore corrupt. In all of this we may be dealing with an orientation which transcends the dichotomy of both East and West, of both tradition and modernity.

But what of the intellectuals themselves? Their experience since 1949 has indeed demonstrated that the Chinese intelligentsia, like intellectuals everywhere, do dwell on complexities, are attuned to ambiguities and ironies, and do indeed tend to develop a strong stake in their own ideas. In this sense they are the enemies of simplicity although in other contexts they may also be the great yearners for simplicity. When given the opportunity they continue to find meaning in the culture of the past, they continue to be attracted by various tendencies in the West, and they continue to stress theoretical complexities.

What then of the future? If Mao's experiment does not succeed and a new generation of intellectuals does emerge (the Maoists have practically succeeded in stilling the voice of the older generation), where will it go? If it reacts against the Cultural Revolution will it finally achieve modernity? The entire drift of what has been said above would suggest that the only proper approach to these questions is one of Socratic ignorance—an openness to unforeseen possibilities. Since Mao has carried out an across-the-board attack against the Chinese cultural past, the whole gamut of modern Western culture, and the pretensions of technological expertise, one might, in China, expect, at least for a time, a common front among the representatives of all these tendencies. What they share in common, after all, is a defense of cultural complexity and the values of high culture. Under conditions of relaxation one would expect to see Chinese intellectuals renew their interest in the West, but the modern West of 1972 is not the West of 1919. It is more deeply involved than ever in its own unresolved intellectual and moral crises. One would thus expect a new Chinese intellectual generation to be far less passive and far more critical in its relations to various tendencies in the West. (This is already visible in some of our Chinese students.) Some tendencies out of the past might witness a strong revival, and the dialectic of relationship of traditional and modern factors would continue to produce novel combinations. Since China's objective situation remains vastly different from that of the West (for example, the overwhelming weight of its agrarian population), China may indeed have to develop its own patterns of modernization. Thus neither tradition nor modernity provide the image of China's future in a world where the future of modernity itself remains unclear.

REFERENCES

1. In all thinking in terms of "development models" one often finds, even in the same author, a constant oscillation between a descriptive-determinist approach and a prescriptive-projective approach. One speaks of how intellectuals will necessarily behave in terms of the laws of development or how they ought to behave if the

project of modernization is to succeed. In the one case the intellectuals are included within the whole impersonal process. In the other, modernization is conceived of as a project and the intellectuals are conceived of as standing outside. They navigate the ship of history for the rest of mankind.

2. Particularly among students of Japan. Also noticeably in the work of Professor S. N. Eisenstadt.

3. It is interesting to observe that Max Weber, whose concept of "traditional modes of domination" is one source of the prevailing more generalized concept of traditional society, was himself almost obsessively concerned with the *differences* among the higher civilizations of the past.

4. This leaves open the question of the ulterior purposes of this mastery, which, it seems to me, is left somewhat vague in Weber.

5. It is, of course, impossible to say that any of them were new in any absolute sense. They may all have deep roots in Western culture, as Carl Becker insisted. Whether absolutely new or not, there were serious and profound differences in the world visions of Voltaire, Rousseau, Montesquieu, Hume, and the Marquis de Sade.

6. Of course, Marx's concept of modernization incorporates the moral conflict element of class struggle.

7. Here again, the term "classical Chinese" covers a complex history of stylistic conflicts—conflicts in which the transitional generations continued to participate.

8. We are here speaking, of course, of the creative minority.

9. But not all. Wang Kuo-wei was very soon to turn away from the preoccupation with national power to his more fundamental concern with universal problems of human suffering. Significantly he was greatly attracted to Schopenhauer.

10. *Yü Wai-chiao pao chu-jen lun chiao-yü shu* (Letter to the editor of *Wai-chiao pao* on education) cited in my *In Search of Wealth and Power: Yen Fu and the West* (Cambridge, Mass.: Harvard University Press, 1964), p. 49.

11. This does not necessarily have optimistic implications. It may not be the best elements of both cultures that are compatible.

12. See Schwartz, *In Search of Wealth and Power.*

13. We may loosely call this the "May 4th Generation" if we include both the older vanguard figures such as Ch'en Tu-hsiu, Li Ta-chao, Hu Shih, and so forth, and the students of 1919.

14. In Chinese terms he must himself be classed as an intellectual or marginal intellectual. He is not a peasant leader in the Zapata sense.

ROBERT N. BELLAH

Intellectual and Society in Japan

AT THE beginning of the Chinese tradition as at the beginning of the European stands an intellectual who derived a conception of order in society from a conception of order in the Soul.[1] Both Confucius and Plato developed an idea of the Good (Chinese: *jen;* Greek: *agathon*) which provided a norm or measure for centuries of subsequent political thought. Though Confucian thought was long influential in Japan and much later Greek thought has not been without consequence, no such profound intellectual conception stands at the beginning of the Japanese tradition. Rather, the givenness of society, radically challenged in their very different ways by Confucius and Plato, has survived as the central focus of reflection in Japan.

I

Shōtoku Taishi (573-621), prince-regent under the Empress Suiko, is perhaps an archetype of the Japanese intellectual. A semilegendary figure associated with the beginning of the effort to establish a centralized imperial state on the Chinese model, he is credited with the first explicit statement of the normative order of Japanese society (the so-called Seventeen-Article Constitution) as well as with the first writings that give evidence of a profound grasp of Buddhism in Japan. For present purposes the authenticity of the documents is less important than their symbolic significance in subsequent Japanese thought. The Seventeen-Article Constitution ransacks the resources of Chinese culture to express the essential ideals of Japanese society.[2] Article one stresses harmony (*wa*), perhaps the quintessential Japanese social value, and subsequent articles extol in various ways the virtues of group solidarity, individual submission to group interests, and the self-sacrifice of high and low alike for group ends. Though almost all the language is in some sense Confucian, except for article two which is explicitly Buddhist, the Confucian idea of the Good (*jen*) is mentioned only once, in article six, and that in passing.

Shōtoku Taishi has the peculiar distinction of being not only the first

89

in a long line of intellectuals to express in foreign concepts the nearly inarticulate sociocentric emphasis of Japanese culture; he was also the first
to use foreign ideas to cast doubt on the self-sufficiency of that emphasis.
If he was the first "official intellectual" he was also the first "critical intellectual." The form of his criticism was his deep Buddhist piety expressed in
his oft repeated phrase, "The world is empty and vain; only the Buddha is
true."[3] Of course the dichotomy of "official" and "critical" is too simple.
The proclamation that there is a transcendent reality which renders empty
all earthly values had little sociological implication other than the establishment of a Buddhist monastic community (sangha) independent of
political control. On the other hand the Seventeen-Article Constitution
was obliquely critical in that it stated an ideal of general submission to the
emperor when in fact Soga no Umako had dominant power at court and the
Soga clan had for some decades effectively dominated the imperial family.
Indeed the constitution may have been written after 645 when the Soga
were overthrown and attributed to Shōtoku Taishi in order to help legitimize the Taika reforms dating from that year. In any case Shōtoku's difficulties with the Soga seem to have been real enough, so that he found himself in the typical predicament of the Japanese intellectual: having to deal
not only with the relation between foreign culture and the Japanese tradition, but also with the problem of arbitrary political forces which frustrate
political idealism. His decision to withdraw more and more into Buddhist
devotion in his later years was also prophetic.

There were clearly some remarkable minds at work in Japan during the
seventh and eighth centuries when virtually the whole range of Chinese
culture and social institutions were imported into Japan. Along with the
rest came the Chinese (Confucian) idea of education and the competitive
examination system for officials. But the educational and examination system was one of the earliest casualties of the process of erosion of Chinese
institutions which set in almost at once. A secular intelligentsia oriented
to bureaucratic office on the Chinese model did not develop, largely because the aristocratic clans managed to keep effective control of the land
and to appropriate the newly established ranks and offices. The court aristocracy was literate as the rising local military families later would also be,
but neither showed much interest in the theoretical aspects of the Chinese tradition, either metaphysical or political. Rather they inclined toward
poetry and fiction if they became interested in literature at all. Their writings tended to be in Japanese rather than in Chinese and to be a vehicle
more for emotion than thought. Theoretical culture was kept alive among
the monks and was of course mostly Buddhist, though Confucian texts
continued to be studied. The split between abstract foreign culture carried
by relatively isolated intellectual coteries and emotional native culture
more widely shared among the people has never been entirely overcome.

Until the seventeenth century intellectual life, with the partial exception of belles-lettres, was largely confined to the religious—Buddhist monks and later Shinto priests. Shinran (1173-1262) in the Pure Land tradition and Dōgen (1200-1253) in the Zen tradition carried Japanese Buddhism to its highest peaks. Both broke through the givenness of Japanese society in their demand for absolutely transcendental loyalty, but it proved difficult sociologically to capitalize on these breakthroughs. Shinran's intense spirituality in the preaching of absolute "other power" had an electric influence during his lifetime but no very stable organization crystallized after his death. It was not until the time of Rennyo (1415-1499), the so-called second founder of the True Pure Land sect, that a powerful organization was created and that was in part because Rennyo included a great deal of Confucian ethics in his teaching along with "other shore" piety. In the fifteenth and sixteenth centuries in some areas True Pure Land sect believers actually established independent political control, but not until they had come to mirror in large part the hereditary leader-follower social pattern of the environing feudal society. Loyalty and self-sacrifice were to be devoted to Amida and the sect leaders, not to the feudal lords, but the structure of relations was quite similar. Any chance that these religious structures might develop alternative patterns of social life was lost when the secular power of the religious sects was crushed by the great military dictators of the late sixteenth century, Oda Nobunaga and Toyotomi Hideyoshi.

The vigorous and independent life of the Zen monastery at the time of Dōgen later declined and the Zen monastery tended to become an educational center for the dissemination of Neo-Confucianism. Closely in touch with currents of thought in China the Zen monks, particularly of the Rinzai school, were broadly educated and made excellent advisers for shogun and daimyō. In fact Zen became associated with the samurai class and made significant contributions to its gradually developing status ethic, later called Bushidō.

To sum up the picture of Japanese intellectual life before the establishment of the Tokugawa shogunate in 1600 we may say that there were two periods of marked vitality and originality: poetry and fiction in the Heian period (794-1192) and religion in the Kamakura period (1192-1333). Some works of history were written from the early eighth century on which contained some political and social reflection, but no major work of political or social philosophy was produced in the entire period. Confucian morality continued to percolate throughout the society, to rationalize leader-follower relations, and to alter some features of traditional Japanese society, such as lowering the status of women in the samurai class. But the givenness of society was largely its own justification. When in the course of the centralization of Japan leading up to the establishment of the Tokugawa shogunate the decision was made first to restrict and then to extirpate Christianity it was partly parallel to the destruction of the secular power

of the Buddhist sects, partly because of the fear of the foreign powers behind the missionaries, but partly because Christianity was seen as a threat
to the givenness of the social order. Fabian, Catholic apostate turned Buddhist, criticized the first of the Ten Commandments, "Thou shalt venerate
Deus alone," as undermining the social order by advocating rebellion
against lords and fathers. Rather, he said, "It is the way of man to live in
accord with the rules of the Shogun who is the ruler of Japan, so long as one
lives in Japan."[4]

II

Whatever the continuities, in its intellectual life, Japan at the beginning
of the Tokugawa period was significantly different from the time of Shōtoku Taishi. Buddhism had stirred the hearts of the masses and had brought
even the remotest villages into touch with universal ideas and national
movements. In a somewhat inchoate way the needs of the peasants had
begun to be articulated by the popular sects and resistance against samurai pressure had occurred, even though ending in defeat. Both Buddhism
and particularly Confucianism had contributed to the development of a
rigorous status ethic among the samurai and to the construction of a model
of political relations which now had to be generalized to the whole country. Even if the emperor as descendant of the sun goddess still reigned
and the round of village ritual with its Shinto observance only lightly
colored by Buddhism continued as it had for centuries, the native tradition alone was far too inarticulate to provide a conscious conception of the
new order which was to arise from the Tokugawa peace. One source from
which ideas might have come was now excluded. The door had been firmly
shut on a Europe which was about to produce a Spinoza and a Descartes, a
Hobbes and a Locke. The only available tradition which could provide
a self-picture for the new society was Confucianism, and it was to Confucianism that the early Tokugawa shogunate turned.

It should not be imagined, however, that the Tokugawa system was the
creation of intellectuals, Confucian or otherwise. As Ogyū Sorai later
pointed out, Tokugawa Ieyasu, the founder of the house, was a Sengoku
daimyō, a feudal lord of the warring period, and the system he constructed
was what you might expect from such a man.[5] Although it did not meet the
systematizing standards of Sorai, the system put together by Ieyasu and
his vassals and retainers, with only a modicum of advice from intellectuals,
was a powerful and effective one, as has so often been the case in Japan.
Warfare between feudal lords was eliminated and strong political control,
direct in the central domain of the shogunate itself, indirect elsewhere,
extended throughout the entire country. The natural consequences were
a rapid advance in the agricultural and merchant spheres of the economy,
rapid urbanization, and a general cultural efflorescence.

What the Confucian scholars were not asked to construct they were asked to explain and defend. It is no accident that the school of Confucianism which Ieyasu chose to patronize and which later became the official school of the shogunate was that of Fujiwara Seika (1561-1619) and his pupil Hayashi Razan (1583-1657), followers of the Chu Hsi or Sung Confucian school in China. Sung Confucianism had for some time been the official orthodoxy in China largely because it gave nearly absolute endorsement to established authority in family and state. The system developed by Chu Hsi and his immediate followers was one of great complexity and profundity, but its use in later centuries, perhaps not unlike the use of Thomism in the Catholic church, was largely defensive. It tended to identify the existing social order with the order of nature itself and to preach an ethics of submissiveness within the inherited status system. But as is usual in Japan no single intellectual tradition provided the legitimation of authority. Ieyasu made a great point, as Nobunaga and Hideyoshi had before him, of his reverence for the emperor. The Kyoto court, though deprived of any real power, was lavishly subsidized and the emperor was recognized as the ultimate source of legitimacy for the shogun. Seika and Razan duly included a solemn exposition of Shinto myth (explicated in edifying Confucian concepts) as part of their teaching. In addition, Buddhism, though not contributing any appreciable element to the intellectual foundation of the regime, was patronized organizationally. As part of the system of thought control leading to the extirpation of Christianity all Japanese were required to become members of a Buddhist parish. This "establishment" of Buddhism among the masses was occurring just when Buddhism as a system of ideas was losing its hold among the elite.

Nonetheless it was only gradually that the intellectual role, almost identical with that of Buddhist monk in previous centuries, began to establish itself independently. Though sharply critical of Buddhism, Fujiwara Seika was himself a monk and it was not until 1691 that the head of the shogun's Confucian school was allowed to be a layman. The founder of the school of philological studies which resurrected the language and thought of ancient Japan, Keichū (1640-1701), was a monk and Matsuo Bashō (1644-1694), the greatest of the haiku poets, lived a semimonastic existence. But by the end of the seventeenth century a number of independent secular bases for intellectual life had been established. The Tokugawa peace brought a new interest in education and literacy and the demand for teachers was high.[6] The samurai, no longer primarily warriors but civil administrators, were admonished to combine literary arts (*bun*) with the military ones (*bu*). Though the samurai class was largely a salaried bureaucracy, not, as in China, a landed gentry, it took on something of the character of a stratum of literati for the first time in Japanese history. Confucian scholars as teachers, advisers, and administrators became increasingly important throughout the period. Official schools of the shogunate or the fiefs provided employment to significant numbers of such scholars.

But in addition to the official intellectual world, urbanization and the growing cultural interests of wealthy townsmen and peasants provided the social basis for a "free intelligentsia," independent of either monastic or governmental structures, for the first time in Japanese history. Well-known scholars were able to establish their own schools in the cities and larger towns and to make a good living from their students and from lecture tours. Medicine was a high status free profession which was followed by such diverse intellectuals as Andō Shōeki, Motoori Norinaga, and Yamagata Daini. Literacy, estimated to have reached approximately 40 per cent by the end of the Tokugawa period,[7] was sharply on the increase during the seventeenth century and provided a basis for the first time for a mass publishing industry which could support full-time writers.

It would be surprising if in this welter of cultural activity we did not begin to see the emergence of "critical intellectuals." Political criticism and protest are evident during the Tokugawa period but they occur so spasmodically and in so devious and muted a form that their absence is a larger problem for explanation than their presence. Part of the answer, of course, is the oppressive hand of the shogunate. Its encouragement of the Chu Hsi school implied a criticism of other intellectual tendencies, though only when the shogunate perceived a direct political threat was there actual suppression of nonorthodox scholars and even then with nothing like the severity shown toward Christianity. Censorship of the theater and popular books was concerned as much with enforcing Confucian morality as with political orthodoxy. Perhaps as important in minimizing dissent as pressure from above was the view shared by all schools (in China as well) that political criticism was a form of faction, and faction a form of rebellion. Only with the greatest difficulty in the Tokugawa period would it have been possible to legitimize political dissent, criticism, and controversy. No conception of a free marketplace of ideas in this sphere existed.

One form of social criticism was allowed, however. Indeed it was almost required. This was the conservative form of criticism which denounced the present for not conforming to the purer customs of an earlier day. Both Chinese and Japanese governments welcomed such criticism, especially when it denounced sons for being insufficiently filial and retainers for being insufficiently loyal. Denunication of the wealth and ostentation of prosperous townsmen and peasants was also highly approved. Only when such criticism became strident and led to insistent demands for government intervention, especially if the criticism and demands came from nonorthodox scholars, was the government inclined to crack down. Kumazawa Banzan (1619-1691), a follower of the school of Wang Yang-ming, the Ming Dynasty rival of Chu Hsi, was placed under house arrest during the last years of his life; his protector, the daimyo of Okayama, was pressured into abandoning the teachings of his school[8] after Banzan intemperately offered direct reform proposals to the shogunate. Yamago Sokō (1622-1685) opposed the teachings of Chu Hsi and argued for a return to the teachings of Confucius himself, unencumbered by later interpretations. He was thus one of the founders of what came to be called the Ancient Learning (*kogaku*) School. The vigor of his views earned him exile. Nonetheless neither the Wang Yang-ming nor the Ancient Learning School was suppressed and they continued to produce important (and occasionally critical) scholars in the eighteenth and nineteenth centuries.

Conservative criticism, unless it became too strident, was no threat to the status quo because it never questioned the givenness of the social order. It criticized latter day fallings away from that order, not its fundamental principles. With Ogyū Sorai, however, criticism, though conservative on the surface, reached a profound level and the implications of his teachings changed the Tokugawa intellectual world in the eighteenth and nineteenth centuries.[9] Sorai was the son of a physician and was educated to follow his father's career. However, at a fairly young age he abandoned medicine for Confucian studies. Sorai was the greatest representative of the Ancient Learning School and like his predecessors he rejected the teachings of the commentators in favor of a return to the primary texts of Confucianism. His greatness, however, transcends membership in any school. Sorai was almost unique in the history of Japanese Confucianism in the extent to which he identified himself with the Chinese culture in which he was steeped. His Sinophilia was so great that he willingly called himself an "Eastern Barbarian" (a term used in China to refer to the Japanese) and upon moving his residence in Edo announced that he was pleased with his new residence in a more easterly quarter of the city "because it is closer to China."

Looking coldly at Tokugawa society and its problems from his Chinese perspective, Sorai was perhaps the first Japanese intellectual to subject the foundation of his own society to skeptical criticism. He developed his own conception of the Confucian Way. For Sorai the Way governing society was not derived from the natural order of the cosmos (as the followers of Chu Hsi taught) nor from the nature of the human heart (as the followers of Wang Yang-ming taught) but from the sage teachings of the ancient Chinese kings. The Way of society is a humanly constructed order and even though the ancient kings had the highest wisdom, every age must to some extent construct its own institutions. Sorai takes the Confucian notion of the Good, *jen*, as the most basic teaching, as a norm for social and personal order:

In Confucian doctrine Jen occupies the most important place. Why is this so? It is because Jen is that which advances and embodies the Way of the Former Kings. The Way of the Former Kings is the Way of giving peace and security to the world.

Jen is the term used to refer to those qualities in a man which promote the growth and development of mankind and give peace and security to the people. This is the great virtue which was possessed by the Sages. "The great virtue of the universe is life." The sage conforms to this.

Jen is the Way of "nourishment." Hence in ruling the state one should "raise up the straight and set aside the crooked, and thereby make the crooked become straight." In personal conduct, too, the individual should nourish his good qualities, and thereby his evil qualities will disappear of themselves.[10]

While Sorai spent much of his life as an independent teacher with his own school, he served the Daimyo of Dewa, a member of the shogunal government, for a period and late in life was a frequent adviser to the shogunate. Much of his thinking, therefore, was directed to problems of government and its reform. Perhaps the most profoundly shocking of Sorai's opinions was that the shogun was the legitimate ruler of Japan and the emperor was superfluous, an almost unheard of view before modern times. Sorai traced much of the troubles of the regime to its founder Tokugawa Ieyasu, also a rather shocking procedure in terms of the pieties of the period. Whereas Ieyasu should have founded a new regime on broad and systematic foundations, he was, said Sorai, after all just a Sengoku daimyo, and merely projected on a national scale the experience he had had in extending power from his own domain as a base. Sorai felt the time had probably passed when the regime could undergo a fundamental reform and went to his death full of gloomy forebodings about the future of the country under leadership which he regarded as incompetent.

The particular measures which Sorai advocated were a mixture of radical and conservative elements. He advocated a strong central bureaucratic administration under the shogun with the feudal lords all but eliminated. Offices would be filled by merit rather than heredity, which meant primarily that lower ranking samurai would have a better chance, though Sorai had no objection in principle to townsmen or peasants holding office, providing they were men of talent. In these respects Sorai can be said to have anticipated the Meiji period. In other ways he was extremely old-fashioned. He was suspicious of the money economy and would have liked virtually to eliminate merchants and cities. The samurai would return to the land, and therefore no longer need money payments, and an idyllic rural existence would be enjoyed by a population of samurai and farmers. Such notions were reiterated by other thinkers of the period since they conformed to old Confucian ideals, but even many Confucian scholars recognized that they were utterly impractical. It was not, however, Sorai's particular proposals which were influential but rather his whole way of thinking which opened up for conscious reflection aspects of the cultural and social order previously closed to thought. The implications of Sorai's views had become sufficiently clear by 1790 to lead the shogunate to issue its famous ban on heterodoxy, aimed chiefly at the followers of Sorai, which led to the expulsion or conversion of scholars other than those of the Chu Hsi school in the shogunal university and the fief schools. In various ways, however, the views of Sorai continued to influence thought in the nineteenth century, making a significant contribution to the open-minded reflection about institutional change which characterized the leaders of the Meiji Restoration.

The curious influence of Sorai's thought was paradoxically present in a man who was almost his opposite, Motoori Norinaga (1730-1801),[11] the greatest figure in the National Learning School (Kokugaku), which was as radically committed to ancient Japanese culture as Sorai was to ancient Chinese. The logic of Sorai's return to the ancient texts and the radical commitment to the Way he found in them was followed by Norinaga, even though the texts in question were different and commitment to them had different consequences. Norinaga was one of the best educated of Tokugawa intellectuals and was influenced by many traditions other than that of Sorai. Especially important to him was the philological tradition going back to Keichū, mentioned above, and the Confucian Shinto tradition of Yamazaki Ansai (1618-1682). Whereas Sorai had been of samurai origin and became an adviser to the shogun, Norinaga was of merchant background and remained all his life a doctor and private teacher. Norinaga studied Confucianism in Kyoto with a teacher deeply influenced by Sorai. In the end, however, Norinaga concluded that the Confucian Way is the Way of governing the empire or a country and not the Way for an ordinary person or "small man" like himself.[12] Neither Norinaga nor later leaders of the school devoted themselves directly to political thought, partly because the leaders were all commoners and the movement appealed mainly to merchants and wealthy peasants,[13] though it was not without influence among samurai especially late in the period.

While remaining largely apolitical the thought of Norinaga and his followers had at least latently radical consequences. The ancient Way that Norinaga discovered in the ancient Japanese texts was not, like that of Sorai, a humanly constructed Way. On the contrary it was divinely instituted, indeed, a Way of the gods. Norinaga harshly rejected the notion that rulership should depend, as in Confucianism, on virtue. The Japanese emperor rules because of his descent from the sun goddess, regardless of virtue or the lack thereof. By implication the whole social order is validated by Norinaga's logic—not, as in Chu Hsi Confucianism, because it is alleged to conform to natural reason, but because it rests ultimately on arbitrary divine decree. Nonetheless Norinaga's critique of foreign, especially Chinese, culture had some subtle implications. For Norinaga true Japanese culture is natural, emotional, and even "feminine," whereas Chinese culture (in Japan largely samurai culture) was artificial, calculating, and "masculine."[14] However much the latter might fit the Chinese it was, in Norinaga's opinion, pernicious in Japan. It was Norinaga's dissatisfaction with ruling class culture that was for a long time the major subversive influence of the National Learning School. Norinaga's reverence for the emperor did not preclude profound loyalty to the Tokugawa regime, which after all also professed a high regard for him. Only at the very end of the Tokugawa period were National Learning School ideas used to undermine the Tokugawa regime,[15] and then mainly by outsiders since most official teachers of the school remained steadfastly apolitical.

Sorai's ideas had more explosive consequences in the hands of a man like Yamagata Daini (1725-1767),[16] who combined them curiously with the Shinto Confucian tradition of Yamazaki Ansai. Daini agreed with Sorai that the samurai should be returned to the land, but as commoners. Daini argued that the whole period of military rule had been a mistake and that only an abolition of the samurai class and the combing of the country for talent under the restored rule of the emperor could solve the nation's problems. Daini, himself of samurai origin, had been an official of the shogunate as well as a private doctor and teacher. In 1766 he apparently planned a rising against the shogunate involving samurai and armed peasants. He was arrested and executed. Daini had no immediate followers and the significance of his thought and action should not be exaggerated, but he was the first to move from critical thought to direct action and his example was not lost on the restorationist intellectuals at the end of the Tokugawa period.

The great fief of Mito, belonging to a collateral house of the Tokugawa family, had been the center of historical research even in the seventeenth century. The later Mito School under the leadership of Aizawa Seishisai (1782-1863) and Fujita Tōko (1806-1855) and perhaps under the influence of an infusion of ideas from the school of Sorai directed its attention to the Tokugawa institutional system and its need for reform. The Mito School, officially committed to Chu Hsi Confucianism and Shinto, worked out the theory of the National Polity (*kokutai*) and the duties and obligations of subjects (*taigi meibun*) which would become the major ingredients of the orthodox version of the Meiji emperor system after 1890. This did not mean that the Mito School was itself subversive. As in the case of the National Learning School, the ideas of the Mito School were not used against the regime until the shogunate began to prove unable to cope with the foreigners after 1853.

One significant late Tokugawa opposition intellectual did not apparently owe anything to Sorai. He is worth discussing as an example of the critical possibilities within the Wang Yang-ming school of thought, which would be influential at the end of the Tokugawa period and in early Meiji as well. His name is Ōshio Heihachirō (1793-1837)[17] and his influence is by no means dead even today. Ōshio was of samurai origin and a hereditary retainer of the shogunate. He served for some twenty years as a magistrate in Osaka, where he was noted for his zeal and honesty. After 1830 he passed on his post to his adopted son and occupied himself as a full-time teacher.

His teaching took the form of a rather ardent monism in which the usual distinctions between inner and outer, self and nonself, active and passive are overcome. From this point of view self-cultivation is identical with public moral action and the evil actions of men in society is experienced as pain interior to the self. In the light of his radical monism he viewed evil in society as the result of mistaken distinctions and differences. The people and the emperor should be united in unbroken harmony but instead the shogunate and the samurai class stand between and oppress both emperor and people.

The intensity of Ōshio's convictions finally led him to carry out an uprising which was perhaps the most significant in the Tokugawa period before the 1860's since, unlike numerous peasant rebellions, it had a conscious ideology. More religious than political, this ideology nonetheless broached themes that would have abiding significance. The rebellion itself was ill-planned. Though about one quarter of the city of Osaka was burned it took the troops of the shogunate only two days to restore order. Ōshio and his son fled and about a month later committed suicide by sword and fire when capture was imminent. If Ōshio expected success at all it was not through rational strategy but through the suasive effect of a pure moral act, striking enough to bring in a new dispensation at one blow. Conspiratorial planning would have been precisely the kind of "partial" and "separate" action which he was attempting to overcome. Similar problems, arising from the structure of Japanese values and group life, affected many later activists, including Mishima Yukio, who took Ōshio as his role model.

So far we have considered mainly elite thinkers and movements. There were also a number of movements in the Tokugawa period whose leaders were intellectuals of a sort even if they did not have a highly sophisticated education. Ishida Baigan (1685-1744)[18] and Ninomiya Sontoku (1787-1856) who worked, respectively, among the townsmen and peasant classes are perhaps the best known. Such movements, even though using mainly Confucian vocabulary, were concerned with inculcating self-discipline and self-respect among the common people and providing motivation for improving their material situation.[19] Similar in consequence though deriving more from Shinto and Buddhist concepts was the spate of popular religions which sprang up in late Tokugawa times: Tenrikyō, Konkokyō, Kurozumikyo, Maruyamakyō, and the like. None of these movements was explicitly concerned with political change and a number of them, for example Shingaku in its later phases, were co-opted by the shogunate as part of its apparatus of ideological control. Most of them espoused an ideology of harmony and obedience which would have made rebellious actions almost unthinkable, but they did nonetheless give expression to the autonomous drive for self-improvement and dignity among the commoner classes and implicitly opposed the callous and utilitarian attitudes toward them of at least some samurai thinkers. These movements together with such mass phenomena as the periodic great pilgrimages to the Grand Shrine of Ise, sometimes involving several million people, also served to break down the narrow confines of village and fief and to develop the beginnings of a common consciousness among the Japanese people. In contributing to the development of an incipient national consciousness they did among the commoners what the major elite intellectual movements discussed above did for the upper classes.

A survey of Tokugawa intellectual life up to about 1850 would hardly make one believe that a regime was about to fall. On the contrary it would be more apt to convince one of the effectiveness and perhaps the oppressiveness of a regime which was able to maintain the loyalty of the vast majority of its intellectuals and to blunt criticism so that it dealt more often with surface symptoms than with basic principles. Few of Sorai's successors had his critical perspicuity. From the vantage point of 1850 Yamagata Daini and Ōshio Heihachiro could be viewed as isolated and insignificant figures. The main currents of intellectual life followed the channels which the regime had marked out for them. If leading thinkers did not loudly extol the shogunate, and most of them did, they at least proclaimed the virtues of harmony and obedience. In those few cases where opposition did break out it took the form of dramatic and, at least in the immediate outcome, futile expressive gestures—rebellion and/or suicide—rather than sustained organization of a political opposition, for which the society supplied few cultural or social supports.

It is no surprise then that there is little consensus on which Tokugawa intellectual movements provided the main impetus for the Meiji Restoration. None of them provided much impetus in that direction until the shogunate itself began to display flagrant incompetence in the 1850's and 1860's. Under pressure, most of the prominent traditions, including Chu Hsi Confucianism, could rationalize a change of regime. But what was presented as an alternative was neither very clear nor very radical. The idea of a restoration of the emperor was powerful emotionally (the Tokugawa shogunate had itself claimed to be an imperial restoration) but lacked content. The notion of a greater degree of centralization and greater utilization of talent from all classes had long been at hand in the well-understood system of Chinese centralized empire. Basic issues about Japanese society—the place of the emperor, the nature of authority, and obedience in family and state—were not raised.

It is difficult to state with precision what was the role of intellectuals in the process leading up to the Meiji Restoration. Certainly intellectuals, almost exclusively samurai intellectuals, first saw the need for a radical change of regimes and organized the first efforts to bring about such change. The initial attempts, however, were not much more effective than the earlier efforts of Yamagata and Ōshio. Small groups of samurai or rōnin conspiring in the cities were unable to mobilize any effective support to sustain an opposition movement. Only when the great western fiefs turned against the regime was there a power base sufficiently strong to succeed. Of course the work of the intellectuals in creating a national climate of opinion favorable to restoration and a revival of national consciousness was essential. But the young administrators who moved into commanding positions in the new Meiji government were not among the most ideologically fervent. Behind the Meiji Restoration stood no Locke or Rousseau, no Marx or Lenin, no Gandhi or Mao Tse-tung, but only a group of open-minded young men, ready to learn, committed to Japan, but with no determinate vision of the future.

III

The curious thing about Japan compared to most non-Western nations is how well the young men succeeded. They and their successors have continued to rule Japan for a hundred years—through enormous successes and occasional severe setbacks. They have never been successfully challenged by a political opposition led by ideological intellectuals. They have never been overthrown. Unlike most major nations in the world the word "revolution" can be used in Japan with respect to the future or not at all.

It would not be correct to say that intellectuals had nothing to do with the formation of the Meiji state. Most of the Meiji leaders were themselves at least part-time intellectuals, but their ideas were put at the service of practical exigencies rather than vice versa. Their real creativity lay in organizational ingenuity rather than in the production of novel concepts. As was true in the Tokugawa period many of the autonomous intellectuals were co-opted by the government, especially in the early Meiji period, and served it well, including some who had begun as sharp critics of the regime such as Katō Hiroyuki and Mori Arinori. But the Meiji leadership was concerned with Japanese survival first of all and then with increasing wealth and power. It had no quarrel with the givenness of Japanese society except where it impeded these goals. It was not committed to a new conception of man or a new idea of society but rather to a defense of the old ones insofar as erosion of old conceptions and ideas threatened the more pragmatic goals.

Since the government was both effective and moderately repressive, intellectuals in the Meiji period and later have had some of the same problems as intellectuals in the Tokugawa period. The content of many of the modern ideologies has had a high degree of social relevance and has conceived of intellectuals as socially responsible, as did Tokugawa Confucianism. Since intellectuals have always been kept on the margins politically the tension has been severe. The traditional temptations of dramatically expressive but practically ineffective opposition or withdrawal into the private sphere of aesthetics or religion have remained strong throughout the modern period. The most powerful control on freewheeling intellectuals has been the strong sense of national identity, with its deep symbolic implication of life-giving maternal acceptance, that has been building up since the seventeenth century and has with almost mathematical regularity pulsated periodically ever since. Opposition which has not been justified in emotionally nationalist terms has been difficult to sustain, especially in periods, such as the present, when nationalistic sentiments are on the rise.

Even though there are important continuities in intellectual life between the Tokugawa and the modern periods there are of course very great differences. Above all, the range of cultural possibilities in Japan was enormously broadened by the reception of Western culture after 1868. The Japanese capacity to accept foreign culture without losing its own coherence and continuity, already severely tested by the reception of Chinese culture, was stretched to the breaking point. But in spite of enormous problems the flexibility of the Japanese pattern has once again been demonstrated.

Before discussing a few of the intellectual tendencies in modern Japan and the role they projected for intellectuals (even a sketch of Japan's convoluted modern intellectual history would be far too ambitious for this essay) we may consider briefly the occupational basis and career pattern of modern Japanese intellectuals.

Those few Japanese who could use a European language in 1868 were in an enormously advantageous position. Many were quickly taken into the government. Others established their own schools on the old Tokugawa private school model, teaching English and European studies rather than Confucianism. Fukuzawa Yukichi (1835-1901) founded such a school in 1868 and it eventually became Keiō University, one of Japan's two greatest private universities. Other schools were much more transient. For awhile during the 1880's Christian schools and universities were predominant—they were the best financed and the best staffed schools in the country and ambitious young men flocked to them. But while private schools and universities continued to exist, the government system of higher education became preeminent after about 1890. Graduation from one of the great national universities was subsequently a necessary key for entry into the intellectual elite, and eventually for entry into any kind of elite, as is true in most modern societies.

While the universities had a certain degree of academic freedom and were not used, as were the lower schools, for nationalist indoctrination, there were still severe limits on intellectual life in the universities before 1945. In 1892 Professor Kume Kunitake of Tokyo University was dismissed for teaching that Shinto was a "survival of a primitive form of worship." In 1920 Professor Morito Tatsuo was dismissed from Tokyo University for publishing an article on the social thought of Kropotkin. During the twenties further firings occurred, including the dismissal of most of the economics department at Kyoto University. Many famous professors lost their jobs in the 1930's. In spite of these pressures the universities, especially after the growth of radical student movements beginning in 1918, were a major source of dissent until all opposition was silenced in the late 1930's. Even then students who could not read Karl Marx read Max Weber as the next best thing and continued to think radical thoughts. After 1945 the university has clearly been the main source of criticism and dissent with respect to Japanese society and politics.

Intellectuals have played an important role in the Japanese popular press, newspapers and magazines, from the early Meiji period. Fukuzawa Yukichi was also one of the first to publish a newspaper and he wrote regularly for it during his lifetime. During the Meiji period many significant intellectuals lived mainly from their work on newspapers and magazines. Even as late as the 1920's and 1930's an outstanding intellectual such as Miki Kiyoshi (1897-1945) supported himself outside the university by journalism alone, and one could find a few examples in the postwar period as well. But after 1920 most influential intellectuals, however often they wrote for the popular press, tended to have a university appointment as their main occupation. Before 1945 government censorship was a constant problem. The press along with the universities was a major source of political and social criticism.

In the early Meiji period the intellectuals came mainly from the samurai class and there was much similarity of background between them and government officials. Even though the critical intellectuals tended to come from families who were formerly Tokugawa retainers or at least from fiefs other than Satsuma and Chōshū, which provided the main body of government leaders, there was some circulation between the two groups. The educational system had not yet crystallized and there was much movement between journalism, politics, and teaching. As late as 1917 Nagai Ryūtarō left Waseda University to go into politics and in 1920 Nakano Seigo left a successful career in journalism to enter the Diet. But over time such transitions have become increasingly difficult. The vertical structures of Japanese society have become stronger and more differentiated and it has become more difficult to move between them.[20] This does not mean that intellectuals have become less influential. The vast expansion of higher education and of the mass media has tended to give intellectuals, professors and writers, larger audiences than ever. But such intellectuals are largely cut off from personal contacts with other elites. Even though in the late thirties Prince Konoe, the last premier before Tōjō, collected a brain trust around him, the Shōwa Study Group, which supplied him with ideas and slogans, the wholesale movement of intellectuals into positions of administrative responsibility such as occurred in the American New Deal would have been impossible. Since the war the barriers have only increased. The government has its technical advisers, such as the "defense intellec-

tuals," but significant use of intellectuals in executive and diplomatic posts
in the manner of John F. Kennedy would be unthinkable in Japan. These
developments represent general trends in modern Japanese society rather
than any special encapsulation of the intellectuals.

These are, again, mainly elite intellectuals. Even when, as in recent
times, elite intellectuals have been drawn from many class backgrounds,
the samurai origin of the intelligentsia has continued to affect its attitudes.
A certain aloofness and disdain toward the common people can be detected
though the intellectuals are denouncing the government in the people's
name. It has been possible for a Japanese Marxist to believe that he has a
correct understanding of the role of the working class even if the workers
themselves are too stupid to realize it. Compounding the aloofness of the
intellectuals is the fact that they have been far more profoundly penetrated
by Western culture than any group in Japan and suffer disequilibrium from
this exposure. As before intellectuals were specialists in alien Chinese
culture, now they are specialists in alien Western culture. Many have
vacillated between extreme acceptance of some aspect of Western culture and wholesale rejection of it. The common man has largely escaped
the inner agonies, the identity problems, and the (sometimes multiple)
conversions from one to another intellectual position which has been the
lot of the intellectuals. Alienation of intellectuals because of class differences and differences in degree of exposure to foreign culture are common
in non-Western (and often Western) countries and not especially extreme
in Japan. Since the war the gap has closed as ever larger percentages of the
population attend college and as the media disseminate elite culture to
the masses. Nonetheless many Japanese intellectuals have felt the obligation to "go to the people" as an uncompleted project.

There have also been, as in the Tokugawa period, secondary intellectuals, occasionally of great influence. These were secondary school teachers, village postmasters, and the like—men of some education but not
graduates of the best national or private universities. Often they provided
the local base for conservative or nationalist political or ideological movements. Suspicious of the city, foreign culture, and the modern sector of
the economy, they sometimes contributed to the defeat of movements
favored by the elite intellectuals. Occasionally such men have broken out of
their anonymity to affect the national scene, as in the case of Makiguchi
Tsunesaburo (1871-1944), founder, and Toda Josei (1900-1958), postwar
president and major organizer, of the phenomenally successful new religious and political movement, Sōka Gakkai. Makiguchi was the principal
of an elementary school and Toda was one of his teachers.

The first major Western current of ideas to affect Japan in the early
Meiji period was the democratic and liberal thought of France, England,
and the United States. Perhaps the spirit of this new thought can be expressed in the famous opening words of Fukuzawa Yukichi's *An Encourage-*

ment of Learning (*Gakumon no Susume*), a book that sold over 3,400,000 copies during Fukuzawa's lifetime and set the tone of an era:

> It is said that heaven does not create one man above or below another man. This means that when men are born from heaven they are all equal. There is no innate distinction between high and low.[21]

According to Fukuzawa such distinctions as exist in the world are, or should be, now that the artificial status distinctions of the Tokugawa period have been swept away, based on real achievements, not on innate differences. And, since real achievements require knowledge, education—practical education, not merely the "study of obscure Chinese characters"[22]—is the royal road to self-advancement and dignity in the world. There are highly individualistic implications to Fukuzawa's teachings, but, as *Encouragement of Learning* quickly makes clear, there is a national context which, if anything, takes precedence over individual considerations. In a section entitled "National Independence Through Personal Independence" he writes: "As I have said above, all nations are equal. But when the people of a nation do not have the spirit of individual independence, the corresponding right of national independence cannot be realized."[23] Thus Fukuzawa's call for personal independence and achievement is as much or more for the sake of the nation as for the sake of the individual.

The political expression of such teaching as Fukuzawa's, and the many translations of Western liberal writings such as the Declaration of Independence and works of Rousseau and Mill, was the Popular Rights Movement (Jiyū Minken Undō) which demanded representative constitutional government in Japan. There is no question but that there was a genuine widespread enthusiasm for "freedom" in the early Meiji period, a natural response to the long period of narrowness and rigidity under the Tokugawas. What freedom actually meant of course varied from group to group. For some of the ex-samurai leaders of the movement it undoubtedly meant a new mode of access to political power from which they were excluded by the dominance of the Satsuma-Chōshū ruling clique. For many of the common people in the towns and villages it meant autonomous self-assertion of relatively oppressed groups in the face of arrogant and unresponsive bureaucratic control. Perhaps the major contribution of the movement was the way it swept ordinary Japanese all over the country into the arena of national politics and modern thought. Irokawa Daikichi has recently stressed the role of wealthy peasants (*gōnō*) as mediators of modern consciousness in the village context.[24] As he observed, involvement in the movement did not necessarily mean a break with traditional village collective consciousness but an intense autonomous concern to express that consciousness and defend that collectivity in the face of external powers and authorities. In a sense the Popular Rights Movement was the successor of late Tokugawa popular movements in breaking down village and local parochialism and bringing some kind of national consciousness to the common people. As such it contributed to what is currently called "political mobilization" more than any number of bureaucratic decrees from Tokyo could have done.

The widespread enthusiasm for the Popular Rights Movement in the late 1870's and early 1880's began to give not only the government, but even astute intellectuals like Fukuzawa, cause for alarm. Rules for political struggle did not exist and the dangers of "factionalism" in the Confucian sense were acutely felt. As early as 1875 Fukuzawa was pointing out that too great a concern for the part can lead to the destruction of the whole.[25] By 1881 he was turning his attention explicitly to the imperial house as the fulcrum of unity for the nation and people: "At this moment we are most anxious about the imperial house. The groups called political parties each have different doctrines; some are termed liberal or progressive and some conservative. Although we say that these are struggling over issues, in truth they are struggling for power: each is trying to seize the handle of power for itself . . . In Japan who can fully control the world of human feelings and preserve habits of virtue and righteousness? Only the imperial house."[26] In that same year the government announced that a representative assembly would convene in 1890, thereby relieving much of the pressure for immediate constitutional government.

For our purposes the most important thing about the liberal movement of the first twenty years of Meiji is that it opened up, even if hesitantly and indecisively, some questions about the givenness of Japanese society which had not been asked before. Very few of the Popular Rights thinkers went so far as to advocate a republican system. Very few criticized the root values of loyalty and filial piety. But the whole idea that the political institutions of Japanese society might be radically restructured by a movement from below was dramatically novel. It gave a role to popular initiative and creativity that was certainly not present in the largely intra-elite maneuverings that led to the Meiji Restoration itself. At the same time it led to serious questions about the viability of Japanese society, questions such as those raised by Fukuzawa. Much of the subsequent history of social thought and the involvement of intellectuals in politics in modern Japan has been organized around that point counterpoint.

We cannot expect to trace in this essay all the subtlety of those developments. We are fortunate in having in Irwin Scheiner's recent *Christian Converts and Social Protest in Meiji Japan*[27] a brilliant account of how Christian social thinkers deepened the conceptions of the Popular Rights Movement and gave them in the 1880's and 1890's a theoretical and religious basis alternative to the emperor system. Kenneth B. Pyle has also recently made a significant contribution to our understanding of the rise in the period 1885-1895 of a critical school of "Japanist" thought which was by no means a simple apologetics for the official governmental ideology.[28]

But here we must confine our remarks to the so-called Meiji emperor system which was not fully worked out until the 1890's and which Maruyama Masao and others have argued remained a kind of orthodoxy from that time until 1945.

In the first place the simultaneous acceptance of the idea of a constitution and representative assembly and the construction of the mature emperor system is a kind of prototype of the way bureaucratic dominance has been maintained in modern Japanese society. It is echoed again in 1925 when the Diet voted for universal suffrage at almost the same time that it passed a greatly strengthened Peace Preservation Law which severely hampered political dissent. Even in the postwar period the combination of democratic reforms (from on high) and continued bureaucratic dominance and unresponsiveness to popular needs shows much the same form. In each case the intellectuals have in a sense "lost while winning."

The Meiji government managed to make the constitution itself a keystone of the refurbished emperor system. Above all it made the constitution an expression of the givenness of Japanese society rather than a challenge to it. The preparation of the constitution was kept completely secret until it was unveiled on February 11, 1889. The day was significant for it was Kigensetsu, the national holiday celebrating the mythical founding of the nation in 660 B.C. The constitution was the gracious gift of the emperor and its preamble derived sovereignty exclusively from the "sacred and inviolable" imperial house. When Nakae Chōmin (1847-1901), leading Popular Rights thinker and translator of Rousseau, insisted in the first Diet session of 1890 that the constitution be submitted to the Diet and voted on article by article, he was ignored.[29] He later resigned in disgust. Even though it was obvious that the constitution was a carefully contrived document—and indeed Itō Hirobumi (1841-1909), its chief architect, had undertaken the most careful research, including trips to Europe to talk to constitutional experts—it was to be received almost as a natural object, protected from criticism by the charisma of the emperor. There was a tendency after 1890 to include under the term kokutai, "national polity" defined as the unique Japanese relation between emperor and people, all those things which could not be touched, which university professors could lose their jobs for criticizing, which were to be forever removed from any popular tampering. Not only were the imperial house, Shinto religion, and the military establishment part of the kokutai, but later when socialist agitation became acute, private property also was declared to be one of its constituent elements.

It is important to disentangle to some extent the image of the emperor from the emperor system as such. The imperial institution is far older than the Meiji emperor system and has survived the collapse of the latter in 1945. It has indeed been argued by some that the emperor system was a perversion of the true imperial institution. At any rate it does seem possible to extricate two rather different symbolic pictures of the emperor which have had different consequences in modern Japanese social thought. What the Meiji government tried to create was what might be called a samurai image of the emperor. He was a man in a resplendent military uniform, riding on a white horse, remote and unapproachable. As such he stood for governmental authority and military duty. He was a heroic leader but a cold and demanding one. Credit for Japan's success in its first modern half-century was attributed to the genius and leadership of the Meiji emperor. This image might be called the image of the emperor as a father figure.

But even in the Meiji period, when the actual emperor came closer to this image than either of his two successors, this was not the whole story. Much in the emperor's role evoked an older and deeper image than the samurai or father figure emperor. For one thing the commonest form of communication from emperor to people was the thousands of *waka* poems which he composed for many occasions. Unlike the stiff Chinese formality of imperial rescripts, the *waka* were written in poetic and emotional Japanese and spoke of cherry blossoms, autumn leaves, and other delicate things. Often they expressed deep concern for the welfare of the subjects and the future of the country. This was the emperor whom politicians were always wishing to "shield from anxiety" and nearness to whom, symbolically or actually, was the greatest reward in Japanese public life. Perhaps it is not going too far to see in all this an image of the emperor as a mother figure. Of course the Meiji leaders, probably without being consciously aware of the distinction I am drawing, also made use of this aspect of the emperor's image. But full control of this image evaded them, and repeatedly aspects of it were used by those in opposition.

Perhaps we can even argue that these two aspects of the emperor image represent two dimensions of Japanese social structure. The first image represents the external relations between groups of differing power in Japanese society. In particular it represents the samurai-bureaucratic-elitist notion that some groups should dominate other groups, that those below should submit with stoic obedience to those above no matter how heavy the demand. This was the military image of Japan which was very much part of the emperor system between 1890 and 1945.. The second image, however, represents the internal nature of Japanese group life, its warm, accepting, *Gemeinschaft* (Japanese: *kyōdōtai*) nature. While the first image denotes separation, hierarchy, duty, the second denotes unity, fusion, fulfillment. The problem with the second image is that it is drawn from the structure of primary groups in Japan, or at most of particular institutional structures, such as a village or company or government ministry. The second model has never accurately described Japan as a national community, though, especially when conscious of the outside world, most Japanese do feel a strong emotional sense of Japanese identity overriding differences of status. The second model, then, even though it is thoroughly "traditional," operates in some degree of tension with the actuality of Japanese society with its strong elitist authoritarian tendencies. We have already seen that the *Gemeinschaft* model of Japanese society, the fusion of emperor and people, could lead to direct political action in the cases of Yamagata Daini and Ōshio Heihachiro. It has continued to do so in the modern period. Perhaps the 1877 rebellion of Kyushu samurai, led by Saigō Takamori, had something of this quality and was not simply a revolt of the disgruntled seeking to retain their ancient privileges.

Most modern Japanese intellectuals, with some notable exceptions, have been critical of the first, elitist and hierarchical, model of Japanese society. They have been much more ambivalent about the second, *Gemeinschaft,* model. Some contemporary Japanese intellectuals, called, with more than a little pejorative overtone by their critics, "modernists," have been as opposed to the structure of primary group relations in Japan as to the elitist authoritarian control structures.[30] Indeed they have argued that the two augment and complete each other. These modernists would stand outside both aspects of the traditional *kokutai* ideology and argue for the importance of universalism and individualism in a truly modern, democratic Japan. They draw mainly from Western sources, Christian, liberal, and radical, but they also refer to the more transcendent aspects of Buddhism and Confucianism for some support in the Japanese past. Whereas in the 1930's such modernists were being attacked for being too pro-Western and undermining traditional Japanese society ("overcoming the modern" was a major slogan among intellectuals during the Second World War), today they are attacked for being too pro-Western and undermining Third World values and solidarities.

But many Japanese intellectuals and intellectual movements have not been able to make up their minds on this issue. For populists, socialists, and even Communists the symbol of the "people" or the "working class" has been redolent of the warm, maternal fusion of Japanese *Gemeinschaft.* Through the mediation of this symbol, men who have been sharply rebellious and antiauthoritarian have been able to modulate themselves into a form of "restorationism" and start talking about the unity of emperor and people.[31] Highly sophisticated students of Japanese philosophy or art have been able to move from conceptions of the "unity of subject and object" in Japanese religious or aesthetic life to a social philosophy of harmonious union of government and people under the emperor.[32] Even a radical Christian like Uchimura Kanzō (1861-1930), whose followers were among the few Japanese consistently to oppose the militarist imperialist policies of the late thirties and early forties, was in a state of tortured ambivalence whenever he experienced direct conflict with the national community.[33] Of the many leftists who underwent a "change of thought" (*tenkō*) in the 1930's under government pressure, most phrased their change as a return to the national community understood as *Gemeinschaft.*[34] The contemporary rise of what may be called a populist tendency in the Japanese intellectual world, though bitterly critical of the Meiji emperor system and bureaucratic arrogance, may also be a form of neo-*Gemeinschaft* thinking, a matter which becomes apparent from its attacks on "modernists" and dogmatic Marxists.

Perhaps the context of the two models of Japanese society, bureaucracy and *Gemeinschaft*, will help us understand the enormous popularity of Marxism among Japanese intellectuals since 1920. Many reasons have been adduced.[35] Marxism has been seen as a natural successor to Confucianism since both are collectivistic and concerned with social welfare. Marxism's claim to be "progressive" made it popular in Japan where there has been a perennial desire to "keep up with the times." That Marxism would create a society *more* advanced than the West was an added inducement. Another feature of Marxism which made it attractive to politically marginal intellectuals was that it offered a powerful theory to oppose a powerful government. The breadth, abstractness, and coherence of Marxism as a system of total world explanation have worked in its favor. But one other feature of Marxism which has probably made it attractive in Japan (as elsewhere in the non-Western world) is its nostalgia for the lost world of *Gemeinschaft* and its promise of a new *Gemeinschaft* after the revolution. One thing which tends to reinforce this interpretation is that Marxism has been far more effective as a world-view or a theory than as a form of organization. In particular the Japanese Communist party has always been small relative to the large number of Marxist intellectuals. The hierarchical, bureaucratic, disciplined nature of the party has been repellant to most of those for whom Marxism was an alternative to the bureaucratic authoritarian side of Japanese society.

The modernist critics of Japanese society hold that one of its greatest weaknesses, in either its bureaucratic or *Gemeinschaft* forms (the two are not mutually exclusive for Japanese bureaucracy is formed of a network of *Gemeinschaft* groups), is its lack of individualism. If by individualism one means, as they do, the kind of institutionalized individualism found in a civil society or voluntary organization, they are right. But Japanese society has developed its own forms of individualism not lacking a sense of autonomy (*shutaisei*). Japanese bureaucracy would not have been so effective if it could not stimulate and utilize a great deal of individual initiative, even though it maintains important constraints.

Even more striking is the kind of romantic individualism associated with "restorationism," the effort to make the whole society into a radical *Gemeinschaft*. Indeed some of the most remarkable individuals in modern Japanese history (as in Tokugawa history) fall into this category. Kita Ikki (1883-1937) wanted to "remove the barriers which have separated the emperor from the people."[36] After an adventurous life in the underworld of Meiji socialism, the Chinese revolution, and Taisho radical nationalism he was almost against his will adopted as the intellectual mentor of the young officers who staged the attempted coup of February 26, 1936. Probably innocent of any knowledge of the coup he was executed with its leaders. Nakano Seigo (1886-1943)[37] started out as an extreme liberal in the Taisho period. During the 1930's he experimented with a variety of organizational forms designed to bring about the union of emperor and people and the overthrow of the oppressive bureaucrats and capitalists. For him the restoration of the emperor was a symbol of the release of autonomous individualism among the people. He was a devotee of Wang Yang-ming thought and Ōshio Heihachiro was one of his heroes. He was one of the few Japanese openly to criticize the Tōjō government during the early years of the war and committed suicide under police pressure in 1943. The latest example of this Japanese form of romantic individualism is, of course, Mishima Yukio, who was influenced by both Ōshio and Nakano. He preached a "positive nihilism" which would sweep away all the corruptions and distortions of postwar Japanese life and return the Japanese people to a pure unity with the emperor.[38] Organizational ineffectiveness and the dramatic expressive gesture (standing alone against the entire nation even if it means death) are the hallmarks of this tradition.

Much more could be said about forms of intellectual protest and opposition in modern Japan. But it is the bureaucracy which has continued to rule. It has shared its power with some other groups. First it created the great corporations, known before the war as the *zaibatsu,* and allowed them to have a continuous influence on subsequent policy. Then it created a parliamentary system and eventually political parties to go with it. Not without strain it accommodated itself to sharing political power with the established parties. In the postwar period the alliance of bureaucracy, corporations, and the Liberal Democratic party has been singularly successful. The 1946 constitution was almost as much a meteorite from the sky as the Meiji Constitution had been. It, together with other reforms of the occupation period, made important gains in the fields of civil liberties and popular rights. The arbitrariness of the bureaucracy has been seriously hampered by these gains, but the givenness of Japanese society has not been broken through. Postwar democracy was not the popular enactment of the democratic visions of the Japanese intellectuals. It came from the occupation through the hands of the bureaucrats. Though enjoying an unprecedented degree of freedom the Japanese intellectuals have most of the same problems they have always had. They have yet to find the organizational forms through which they can have a decisive impact on their own society.

IV

If there is one among the many omissions in this essay that is more serious than the rest it is the degree to which I have ignored the apoliti-

112   ROBERT N. BELLAH

cal tradition among Japanese intellectuals. That tradition is in many respects more important than the political traditions and more revealing as to the interior structure of Japanese life. Perhaps I can make up in small measure for this defect by quoting the poem by Dōgen with which Kawabata Yasunari began his Nobel Prize acceptance speech in 1968:

> In the spring, cherry blossoms,
> In the summer, the cuckoo,
> In autumn, the moon.
>
> And in winter,
> Cold, clean snow.[39]

REFERENCES

1. On the relation between order in society and order in the soul in Plato see Eric Voegelin, *Order and History*, III, *Plato and Aristotle* (Baton Rouge: Louisiana State University Press, 1957), Part I.

2. I have relied on the paraphrase and commentary of Muraoka Tsunetsugo in his "Kenpō Jūshichi-ken no Kenkyū" (A Study of the Seventeen Article Constitution) in *Nihon Shisōshi no Shomondai* (Problems in the History of Japanese Thought) (Tokyo: Sobunsha, 1957), pp. 7-71. A translation of the constitution can be found in Ryusaku Tsunoda, William de Bary, and Donald Keene, *Sources of Japanese Tradition* (New York: Columbia University Press, 1958), pp. 50-53.

3. Even J. H. Kamstra in his *Encounter or Syncretism: The Initial Growth of Japanese Buddhism* (Leiden: Brill, 1967), accepts the authenticity of this saying, pp. 379-381. Kamstra offers an extreme demythologization of Shōtoku and goes further in this direction than any Japanese scholar. For a reasoned defense of the authenticity of most of the texts attributed to Shōtoku see *Futaba Kenkō, Kodai Bukkyō Shisōshi Kenkyū* (A Study of the History of Ancient Buddhist Thought) (Kyoto: Nagata Bunshōdō, 1962).

4. Nakamura Hajime, *A History of the Development of Japanese Thought from A.D. 592 to 1868* (Tokyo: Kokusai Bunka Shinkokai, 1969) I, 142.

5. J. R. McEwan, *The Political Writings of Ogyū Sorai* (Cambridge, Eng.: Cambridge University Press, 1962), p. 33.

6. R. P. Dore's *Education in Tokugawa Japan* (Berkeley: University of California Press, A Publication of the Center for Japanese and Korean Studies, 1965) is an excellent description of scholarship and education in the Tokugawa period and I have relied on it extensively in this section.

7. *Ibid.*, pp. 317-322. I have given a summary figure where Dore gives a cautious series of estimates based on school attendance.

8. John W. Hall, "Ikeda Mitsumasa and the Bizen Flood of 1654," in Albert M. Craig and Donald H. Shively, eds., *Personality in Japanese History* (Berkeley: University of California Press, A Publication of the Center for Japanese and Korean Studies, 1970), pp. 65-66.

9. On the central significance of Sorai in Tokugawa thought see above all the very influential book of Maruyama Masao, *Nihon Seiji Shisōshi Kenkyū* (Studies in the

History of Japanese Political Thought) (Tokyo: Tokyo University Press, 1952). This book has influenced not only my treatment of Sorai but my entire treatment of Tokugawa thought.

10. McEwan, *Ogyū Sorai*, p. 9. The three paragraphs are independent passages from different places in Sorai's writings and are not continuous.

11. We now have in English an excellent book on Norinaga, perhaps the best book on any premodern Japanese thinker: Shigeru Matsumoto, *Motoori Norinaga, 1730-1801* (Cambridge, Mass.: Harvard University Press, 1970). Maruyama, *Nihon Seiji Shisōski Kenkyū,* treats the relation between Sorai and Norinaga in chap. 1, sec 4.

12. Matsumoto, *Motoori Norinaga,* p. 32.

13. On Kokugaku at the end of the Tokugawa period and its influence among the upper stratum of peasants see Sonoda Minoru, "Bakumatsu Kokugaku no Shisōshi-teki Mondai" (Problems in the History of Kokugaku Thought at the End of the Tokugawa Period), *Kokugakuin Daigaku Nihon Bunka Kenkyūsho Kiyō,* no. 18 (1966), 1-31.

14. See Matsumoto, *Motoori Norinaga,* especially chap. 2 and conclusion. In the contrast between Sorai and Norinaga we already have the contrast between the bureaucratic model and the *Gemeinschaft* model of Japanese society which will be discussed below.

15. On late Tokugawa political thought see Harry Harootunian, *Toward Restoration: The Growth of Political Consciousness in Tokugawa Japan* (Berkeley: University of California Press, A Publication of the Center for Japanese and Korean Studies, 1970).

16. I am indebted to Tetsuo Najita for his paper "Restorationism in the Political Thought of Yamagata Daini (1725-1767)" presented at the colloquium of the Center for Japanese and Korean Studies, University of California, Berkeley, December 2, 1970, for my knowledge of Yamagata Daini. His series of papers on the restorationist strand in Japanese thought, others of which will be cited below, have influenced my whole conception of the relation between thought and action in Japan.

17. Tetsuo Najita, "Ōshio Heihachirō (1793-1837)," in Craig and Shively, eds., *Personality,* pp. 155-179.

18. Robert N. Bellah, *Tokugawa Religion* (New York: Free Press, 1957), chap. 6 and appendix 1.

19. On these movements see Yasumaru Yoshio, "Nihon no Kindaika to Minshū Shisō" (Japanese Modernization and Popular Thought), *Nihonshi Kenkyū* (Japanese Historical Studies), no. 78, pp. 1-10; no. 79, pp. 40-58 (1965). Yasumaru is rather critical of my argument in *Tokugawa Religion,* feeling that I attempt to explain too much with a notion of "traditional values" and ignore the particular historical circumstances of the various movements. Though there are important theoretical differences between us this article is an important supplement to my book.

20. Chie Nakane, *Japanese Society* (Berkeley: University of California Press, A Publication of the Center for Japanese and Korean Studies, 1970). This is a somewhat revised translation of *Tate-Shakai no Ningen-kankei—Tanitsu Shakai no Riron* (Human Relations in a Vertical Society—A Theory of Homogeneous Society) (Tokyo: Kōdansha, 1967).

114   ROBERT N. BELLAH

21. Fukuzawa Yukichi, *An Encouragement of Learning*, trans. David A. Dilworth and Umeyo Hirano (Tokyo: Sophia University Press, 1969), p. 1.

22. *Ibid.*, p. 2.

23. *Ibid.*, p. 23.

24. Irokawa Daikichi, *Zohō Meiji Seishinshi* (A History of Meiji Consciousness), enlarged ed. (Tokyo: Kōga Shobō, 1968). See also his *Meiji no Bunka* (Meiji Culture) (Tokyo: Iwanami, 1970) and *Minshu Kempō no sōzō* (Creation of a Popular Constitution) (Tokyo: Hyōronsha, 1970). The latter contains drafts of constitutions drawn up in the local areas in the 1870's and 1880's. I have profited from several conversations with Professor Irokawa during his stay in Berkeley in January and February of 1971.

25. Albert M. Craig, "Fukuzawa Yukichi: The Philosophical Foundations of Meiji Nationalism," in Robert E. Ward, ed., *Political Development in Modern Japan* (Princeton: Princeton University Press, 1968), p. 117.

26. *Ibid.*, pp. 133, 134-135.

27. (Berkeley: University of California Press, 1970). See especially chap. 8, "Loyalty and Criticism."

28. Kenneth B. Pyle, *The New Generation in Meiji Japan: Problems of Cultural Identity, 1885-1895* (Stanford: Stanford University Press, 1969).

29. Ryūichi Kaji, "The Introduction of French Political Ideas—Nakae Chomin: The Man and His Thought," *Philosophical Studies of Japan*, Japan Society for the Promotion of Science, 7 (1966), 67.

30. See the collection of writings edited by Hidaka Rokurō, *Kindai-shugi* (Modernism), *Gendai Nihon Shisō Taikei*, 34 (Tokyo: Chikuma Shobō, 1964). This collection features such writers as Otsuka Hisao and Maruyama Masao. For a vigorous if somewhat wide of the mark attack on this school see Irokawa Daikichi, *Meiji no Bunka*, chap. 8, "Seishin kōzō to shite Tennōsei" (The Emperor System as a Spiritual Structure). Irokawa accuses the modernists of elitism in their critique of Japanese *Gemeinschaft*.

31. William D. Wray has an interesting discussion of the left wing socialist Asō Hisashi in this context in his "Asō Hisashi and the Search for Renovation in the 1930's," *Papers on Japan*, 5 (Cambridge, Mass.: Harvard East Asian Research Center, 1970), 55-99. The right wing socialist Abe Isō took up the slogan of "a second restoration" in the period 1929-1930. See Tunoda, de Bary, and Keen, *Sources*, pp. 816-820.

32. Nishida Kitaro spoke of the imperial house as the "contradictory identity of subjective unity and the multiplicity of individuals." Quoted by Ueyama Shumpei in *Kindai Nihon Shisōshi Kōza* (Symposium on the History of Modern Japanese Thought) (Tokyo: Chikuma Shobō, 1959), vol. 4, p. 80. Nishida argued that "it was neither the whole opposing the individual nor the individual opposing the whole, but rather that with the Imperial Household as the center, the individual and the whole mutually negate themselves." Quoted by Tatsuo Arima in *The Failure of Freedom: A Portrait of Modern Japanese Intellectuals* (Cambridge, Mass.: Harvard University Press, 1969), p. 11. Okakura Tenshin took a similar view. He always insisted on the aspects of harmony, oneness, and *advaita* as basic in Japanese culture and society. He said, "The true infinity is the circle, not the extended line. Every organism implies a subordination of parts to a whole. Real equality lies in

the due fulfillment of the respective function of each part." Quoted by Maruyama Masao in "Fukuzawa, Uchimura, and Okakura—Meiji Intellectuals and Westernization," *The Developing Economies,* vol. 4, no. 4 (Tokyo, 1966), 14.

33. Lois M. Greenwood, a graduate student at Berkeley, has recently underlined this aspect of Uchimura's behavior in a very interesting paper, "Uchimura Kanzō: A Study in Japanese Identity," unpublished.

34. Patricia Golden Steinhoff has discussed this aspect of *tenkō* in her 1969 Harvard doctoral dissertation on the subject.

35. Two suggestive efforts to account for the appeal of Marxism in modern Japan are that of Albert M. Craig in John Fairbank, Edwin Reischauer, and Albert Craig, *East Asia: The Great Transformation* (Boston: Houghton Mifflin, 1965), pp. 552-554, and Yuzuru Okada in the Introduction to vol. 2, no. 1, of the *Journal of Social and Political Ideas in Japan,* devoted to the subject of Japanese Intellectuals, p. 4.

36. George M. Wilson, *Radical Nationalist in Japan: Kita Ikki, 1883-1937* (Cambridge, Mass.: Harvard University Press, 1969), p. 69.

37. An extraordinarily interesting discussion of Nakano is to be found in Tetsuo Najita's unpublished paper, "Nakano Seigo and the Spirit of the Meiji Restoration in Twentieth Century Japan."

38. See the article which appeared just two months before his death: Mishima Yukio, "Kakumei no Tetsugaku to shite no Yōmeigaku" (Wang Yang-ming Teaching as a Revolutionary Philosophy), *Shokun* (September 1970).

39. Yasunari Kawabata, *Japan, the Beautiful, and Myself,* trans. E. G. Seidensticker (Tokyo: Kodansha, 1969) (Japanese original and English translation). I have taken the liberty of altering Seidensticker's translation of the poem.

MICHAEL CONFINO

On Intellectuals and Intellectual Traditions in Eighteenth- and Nineteenth-Century Russia

As a genre this essay stands half-way between an interpretative paper and a program of research. As such it is therefore ill-defined and probably has the shortcomings of both and the virtues of neither. For a period extending over two hundred years, it is possible to mention only a few of the sources and secondary works used; to do more would result in a bulky volume and bring the essay to a third genre, the bibliographical one, which was not exactly its purpose. I raise questions for which, at the present moment, I have no clear answer, and I doubt at times whether the questions themselves are methodologically justified or worth being explored. This is indeed a discussion paper, intended to invite comments and criticism. It is based on the hope and assumption that in the development of a subject of study, there are junctures where tentative hypotheses, generalizations, and queries may be no less useful than a new monograph giving precise answers on points of detail.

This, therefore, is no more than a tentative reconsideration of certain features and of the pattern of coordinates into which intellectuals and intellectual traditions are usually set within the Russian context. One of these features is the existence in Russian history and historiography from the late 1860's on of the term "intelligentsia." Created by intellectuals, it conveyed at one and the same time a sociological concept, a psychological characterization, and a moral code. However, none of the definitions given during the past sixty years or so has been found entirely satisfactory, and recent research has clearly shown the vagueness of the term, its many ambiguities, and the strains between the outlook and self-image of those who used it and the social and intellectual reality it is supposed to represent.[1] Thus, it is understood that the intelligentsia was a group of sorts—but what sort of group? It is agreed that it cannot be defined in terms of an economic group; it was not a class. It was not an estate. Was it a stratum—and of what kind? It cannot be delineated by the professions of people supposedly within it; some had none, and most professionals were not included. It cannot be defined by level of education; the range covered by its members

117

ran from autodidacts to university professors, but not all autodidacts (of course) and university professors (so much the more) were necessarily considered members of the intelligentsia. It could not be defined by a set of ideas: many were radicals (of different shades), not all were revolutionaries, some liberals were "in," some others were "out."

In spite of these difficulties, the accumulated research provides a set of features and attitudes which seem to characterize the Russian intelligentsia, and these seem to be accepted by most authorities in this field. Briefly summarized, these features are: (1) a deep concern for problems and issues of public interest—social, economic, cultural, and political; (2) a sense of guilt and personal responsibility for the state and the solution of these problems and issues; (3) a propensity to view political and social questions as moral ones; (4) a sense of obligation to seek ultimate logical conclusions —in thought as well as in life—at whatever cost;[2] (5) the conviction that things are not as they should be, and that something should be done.[3] On the assumption (in view of point 4) that the intelligentsia not only felt that something should be done, but also did something, the aggregate result of these features is the delineation of a group (of sorts) in a state of potential or actual dissent (not necessarily political). In the absence of a better method of classification and definition, these features, then, will identify the intelligentsia and differentiate it from other segments of the society in which it lived. And in this sense the term "intelligentsia" will be used here. I will use the term "intellectuals" in a broad sense, as given in other essays in this volume,[4] and as a stratum including bureaucratic intellectuals, professionals, as well as scientists and the teaching staff in institutions of higher learning, religious specialists, teachers, freelancers, and, of course, artists. I will assume therefore that the terms "intellectuals" and "intelligentsia" are not synonymous,[5] and leave the clarification of this assumption to later parts of this essay. For somewhere, sometime in this period of Russian history, "intellectuals" and "intelligentsia" may meet, or overlap, but in the beginning this distinction is necessary in order to avoid confusion.

Intellectuals in an Age of "Revolutionary" Reforms

As in the case of several fields of development in the course of Russian history, a major turning point in terms of structure and content of intellectual life occurred during the reign of Peter the Great. The beginning of the eighteenth century represents, therefore, a meaningful starting point and offers a relatively clear dividing line between "Old" and "New" Russia.

Until that period the main channels and agents of intellectual accomplishments were ecclesiastical centers and personnel. Largely under church control, intellectual life was undifferentiated institutionally and qualitatively —religious. To be sure, during the seventeenth century there was a noticeable process of secularization of learning and wisdom, but in the main it remained very slow and limited in terms of intellectual growth and the number of individuals whose intellectual aspirations had some effect on the advancement of knowledge and on altering the traditional pattern of cultural isolation and antirationalism.

The substantial change in intellectual life that took place under Peter the Great stemmed from several innovations. The government promoted and encouraged the creation of new types of intellectuals and men of learning—laymen, trained in the West, or according to the then prevailing Western standards. It created new institutions and societal centers of intellectual life, rather than attempting to adapt the old ones to new goals and orientations. Peter I nourished a distrust of theological philosophy, which he considered a foe of secular learning and science, and of the clergy's attitude toward modernity in general and his institutional reforms in particular; accordingly, he chose to circumvent the church's institutions of learning and established new ones for the diffusion of knowledge. All were financed by the state and under tight government control.[6]

The new trends in intellectual life were secular and nonreligious, located in new institutional structures (Academy of Sciences, School of Mathematics and Navigation, Engineering School, Ciphering Schools). Another innovation was the increased concern with science—above all, applied and practical science. The cultural realm proper remained, at best, a secondary goal; changes in it occurred mostly as a by-product of Peter's reforms in general (institutional, social, and economic), not necessarily of changes in the structure of intellectual life.

The role of intellectuals (a tiny group including, for instance, A. Kantemir and V. Tatishchev) and their attitude toward the old tradition and the new one should be viewed within the context of the over-all orientation and ethos of the tsar's reforms. Under Peter change became institutionalized; rejection of traditional tradition became a policy; creation of a "new" tradition became a major goal.[7] All this was done by decree: an Academy of Sciences by decree, a *Kunstkamera* by decree, a translation of Vlacq's *Tabulae sinuum* and of Pufendorf's works by decree, new manners and shaving off beards by decree, Russian students in foreign universities by decree, and intellectuals by decree. The new intellectuals had to be created. They were created by these same reforms. Their assignment, their *raison d'être*, was to destroy the old tradition and create a new one. They themselves understood it in this sense and fulfilled precisely this role in the "revolution from above" initiated by Peter. On the other hand, Peter conceived of this revolution almost as permanent (for at least one generation), all-pervading, total,[8] with continuous change as one of its basic ingredients, and with its impetus initiated and directed by the state. The role left, therefore, for these "intellectuals by decree" (not because of their small number, but structurally and "genetically") was to implement and further these politics of change and policy of changing one tradition with another.

The corollary of this policy, brought about by a "revolution from above," was that everything seemed possible. Moreover, everything was legitimate: the tsar (a "usurper" and "Antichrist"), the powers, and the new tradition being, in a way, illegal and illegitimate, everything became legal and legitimate, including the legitimation of the "Antichrist's" authority by the theologian Feofan Prokopovich; there was no possible change or innovation too daring or too wide in scope. Everything was permitted, even recommended, and dissent against tradition was encouraged and rewarded. This was, indeed, a golden age in Russia for crooks and intellectuals, native and international alike.

Everything was permitted except conservative attitudes and traditionalism. Strictly speaking, those were in Petrine Russia the true dissenting attitudes. If so, then, according to a recent model,[9] the only true intellectuals of the period were the tsarevich Alexei and a quasi-conspiratorial group from among the most conservative Orthodox clergy. Being in conservative-traditionalistic dissent, they got—according to Voltaire, although himself a dissenter—the fate they deserved: severe trial and physical liquidation. Thus, for his refusal to serve in the army and to reject tradition, the antirevolutionary religious-minded tsarevich died as a rebelling and dissenting intellectual, this inversion being very much in the vein of A. Besançon's *Tsarévich immolé*, symbolizing the inverted oedipus complex inherent, in his view, in the course of Russian history.[10] To the extent that the father killing the son symbolized a generational conflict, this event also shows that in Russian history resistance to change and defense of tradition were not always the attitudes of the older generation.

Intellectuals in Times of Stabilization and "Enlightened Despotism"

Although Peter's "revolution," carried on in the style of a "crowned terrorist" and a *Jacobin avant la lettre*,[11] lasted longer than Robespierre's revolution of reason and rejection of dogmas (both of which came to a dialectical end with the dogmatic Cult of Goddess Reason), it nevertheless subsided and finally died sometime around the sudden death of the tsar himself in 1725. The developments from that moment on, during the rest of the eighteenth and early nineteenth century, will be sketched under two headings: first, an overview of some general trends; second, an analysis of events at the end of the period.

The over-all trends are the consolidation of the political regime in the early 1730's and of the estates system in general and the mechanism of the Table of Ranks in particular, with its important role in elite formation. These trends were parallel to a stabilization in the whole sphere of intellectual activity. Thereafter and throughout the eighteenth and early nineteenth centuries changes were small, inconspicuous, and chiefly quantitative.

All personnel in intellectual fields and centers were legally and existentially state servants.[12] The group as a whole was a tiny one. Scientific pursuits were mainly concentrated in the St. Petersburg Academy and the Moscow University (founded in 1755). Foreigners represented a large majority of the scientists; among the latter, particularly the Russians, specialization was low, and there existed an overlapping between the scientific and aesthetic fields. The classical example was Lomonosov—a mathematician and physicist and also a *littérateur* writing indigestible odes in a pseudo-classical style. The aesthetic field included essentially literary works, in prose and verse, mainly by representatives of the educated part of the nobility. The members of this last group appeared in all fields as dilettantes; their education was usually informal and oriented toward the arts. Intellectual endeavors within the church concerned only a few ecclesiastical dignitaries, the rank and file clergy being notorious for their appalling ignorance.

An important feature of the period was the consolidation of the new tradition—that is, its official establishment as the only acceptable one, a social code for the political, bureaucratic, and intellectual elite. The existence of a deep and all-pervading ignorance, rude manners, and superstition among the major part of the nobility, as well as a different, popular way of life and thought among the peasantry—that is, 96 per cent of the population—does not belie this assessment, since such behavior was considered by the elite as deviant.[13] Theirs was the norm, the "European" behaviors and states of mind. A remark concerning the church is also to the point here. Although the political elite used the church extensively as a submissive "ally" and instrument, they nevertheless considered scholasticism and religious thought an aberration; they thought the intellectual and spiritual food bestowed by the church as appropriate only to the simple folk, or, at a higher level, as a device for checking and fighting "dangerous" ideas. They gave the church the external marks and symbols of authority necessary for the performance of that task.

Intellectuals displayed a conspicious continuity in their attitude toward established tradition stemming from Peter's reform: under Peter they served loyally as instruments of change when change was the basic orientation of the powers; they now served loyally as instruments of conservation and consolidation when conservation (of the new tradition) was the chief orientation of those in authority.

This latter orientation did not imply a total rejection of Peter's political and intellectual heritage, but only of his style of action, his "revolutionary" way, and his overt terroristic manners. It was more a matter of form than of content. By discarding unnecessary roughness, Peter's heirs also opened the way for a reconciliation with the church (already submitted to tsar and government through an evolution brought to an end by Peter's reforms) and with the remnants of groups still dreaming about a return to the ways of pre-Petrine Russia. This reconciliation was arrived at successfully, thus excluding any serious ideological conflict, for a number of reasons. First, Peter succeeded in neutralizing the church and submitting it to the state, but, it should be remembered, he did not reject any of the cardinal beliefs of Russian Orthodoxy. The reconciliation meant, therefore, giving the church the role of guardian of morals, thought, and behavior (of the noneducated and the too educated); and going a step further, replacing neutralization of the church with its mobilization in the service of tsar and state. Second, the political powers and the church began to discern that borrowing from the West did not in itself determine values, content, ideologies. There were many different kinds of Europe to be borrowed from and many different ways of Westernizing. There were some things to be taken from the West, but in respect to others, Russia's borders had to remain closed and her customs officers' eyes open. The church, like the customs officers, filled this role of watchdog; so did the Academy of Sciences and the university. For the powers this stand did not amount to an abandonment of the Westerniz- ing orientation; it meant, rather, a course of selective Westernization, a policy of judicious shopping. It meant also, essentially, an instrumental and utilitarian attitude toward knowledge and science, and a close control on the import of ideas. In both cases, Western devices and innovations, intellectual and scientific pursuits, were tested not primarily as sources of cultural progress, but rather as a means of acquiring for Russia a Great Power position on the European scene (and such was also the intellectuals' way of looking at things). For this reason the growth of national conscious- ness in eighteenth-century Russia did not entail a rejection of Westernization or any serious ideological conflict. Throughout the eighteenth century the powers in Russia were a strong Westernizing force (in their own way), as they were also in the nineteenth century, the basic patterns remaining essentially the same.

Most of the nobility showed, as a rule, a conspicuous lack of interest in intellectual pursuits, higher learning, or formal education;[14] those noblemen who achieved eminence in these fields in the eighteenth century were atypi- cal of the class and/or began their studies as commoners (raznochintsy) and arrived at the status of nobility through state service in the army or in the bureaucracy. University study was also recognized as active government service and taken into account for advancement in the Table of Ranks. While the great majority of the gentry remained appallingly ignorant,[15] the elite had a vague interest in general education and were amused with the latest intellectual fashions. All in all, the system produced a number of enlightened state servants and heads of families capable of instilling an interest in books and respect for knowledge in their children.

The intellectuals' attitude toward the major problems in Russia at that time reflected their loyalty to those in authority. They were committed to uphold the new tradition and to support the political and social status quo, autocracy and serfdom, and imperial Russian foreign policy. Similar to that of the powers, their attitude toward Westernization, modernity, intellectual pursuits and knowledge, was utilitarian and instrumental. This included also—philosophically and existentially—their outlook about man and about the nature of human destiny: they were themselves (and accepted this human condition) instruments in the hands of a higher authority—the powers; they were themselves (most of them personally and directly) masters of the "souls"—the serfs, using them as instruments for social advancement and source of income; and all of them (whether serfowners or not) were living in a society in which nearly half the population were deprived of all civil and most human rights. Western enlightenment had yet no effect in this respect and did not lead to criticism of existing social institutions. If two of its basic tenets were liberty and property, then well till the end of the eighteenth century the intellectuals did not ask for either of the two to be respected and extended to the whole of society. Using exaggeration for the sake of emphasis, Mikhail Speransky wrote at the beginning of the nineteenth century: "I find in Russia only two classes—serfs of the autocrat and serfs of the landlords . . . In Russia there are in reality no free people excepting beggars and philosophers."[16] Certainly few intellectuals wanted to become beggars; most could not be philosophers.

The intellectuals' loyalty to the powers went beyond state policy and general principles; their commitment to the status quo was also reflected in their specific scholarly subjects, whether scientific or humanistic. Academicians and university professors, often serving as censors, were no exception to this rule, and foreigners were often among the most loyal to the policy of the powers.

To be sure, quite a number of intellectuals, including Catherine II, were "Voltaireans"; some understood what this meant; others did not; still others apparently adopted a selective way of reading Voltaire's works, very much along the lines of the powers' selective Westernization. Alexander Herzen did not exaggerate much when saying that whereas Voltaire's philosophy had freed Frenchmen of old prejudices and transformed them into revolutionaries, in Russia it reinforced the slave-like dependence of the people on the whims of the absolute monarch.[17]

Catherine II, main symbol of the powers and "enlightened despot," had a keen interest in Voltaire, in other prestigious Western enlighteners, and in enlightenment in general. It is probably on that account too that I. I. Betskoi, an enthusiastic promoter of educational ideas and practices in her time, is said to have remarked that "Peter I created men in Russia, but Catherine II gave them souls." In so doing, she reserved the supreme prerogative of determining what kind of souls were to be given, then entrusted this task to her intellectuals. They were, therefore, not only masters of the "souls," but also "engineers of the souls" *avant la lettre*—an omen that was to go a great way.

A series of important trends and events occurred near the end of the century that influenced, directly or indirectly, intellectuals and intellectual traditions in Russia:

(1) The emergence of a somewhat larger group of educated noblemen and the growth in scope and content of their intellectual interests (namely, in history, philosophy, and *belles lettres*).

(2) The progress of Russian historical writing, being at one and the same time a scholarly undertaking (collecting sources), a means of finding new aspects of Russian culture to give historical depth to the new tradition and to the growing feeling of national unity, and, since historiography sided as a rule with serfdom and autocracy, a weapon of official ideology and new traditionalism.[18] In the main, historians were either Russian noblemen or foreign scholars, usually from German-speaking countries.

(3) The increase in the number of scientists and the diversification of their interests. Science began to be conceived of as a functional component of Russian culture; most scientists were still foreigners and the Russians— not of noble origin.

(4) An overt and aggressive fear of Western ideas on the part of those in authority from the mid-1770's, especially after 1789, leading to tighter control of institutions of learning, more restrictions on imports of books, and a sharp increase in censorship, turned into a professional system for implementing the ideological curbs imposed by state and church. This attack on freedom of thought was enforced by an expanding system of secret police.

(5) Attempts at intellectual independence and qualitative dissent, although examples are few. Two cases were significant in their own time and in view of later developments: Nikolai Novikov (1744-1818) and Alexander Radishchev (1749-1802); both were noblemen and government officials. Novikov devoted himself to several fields of intellectual activity— journalism, publishing, education, literature—and worked for the dissemination of enlightenment and the "moral regeneration of the elite."[19] In Catherine's Russia he became one of the leaders in the Freemasonry movement. Then he was imprisoned for four years (1792-1796), and thereafter withdrew gradually from all public and social activity to live on his estate, looking after his serfs and trying "new husbandry." Mysticism and Freemasonry provided Novikov with inner freedom while he lived in the midst of political and social servitude. He rejected them in his mind and soul, and opened to himself a rich and boundless world of thought and feeling, while staying politically inoffensive. It was dissent by withdrawal and intellectual and psychological escapism.

Radishchev studied jurisprudence, literature, and medicine at Leipzig University. A critic of Russia's social and cultural order, he put his thoughts on paper, published them in 1790, stood trial, and, on Catherine's request, was sentenced to a ten-year exile in Siberia. Among Catherine's intellectuals, Radishchev stands as a solitary figure, striving for freedom of thought and of man, and against the institution of serfdom, monarchical absolutism and tyranny; also against scholasticism and superstition, war as a means of national policy and international relations.[20] In the main, *mutatis mutandis*, these same issues were faced by intellectuals in later generations. But in his own day Radishchev felt alone and frightened, and after his return from exile he apparently could find no way out but suicide. In a sense, there was in this end a common denominator with Novikov's withdrawal. For some intellectuals at that time, and also in later times, the alternative seemed often to be, in their view, between different kinds of suicide. Radishchev preferred this one.[21]

At his trial Radishchev declared that he had acted alone and had had no accomplices; over the next fifty years there were few successors. Well into the 1840's, most Russian intellectuals, following patterns established in the eighteenth century, remained state servants and maintained a basic identification with the autocracy and its attitude on the major problems of social and cultural order. Alternatively, they kept their thoughts to themselves or preserved them for future generations, sometimes in beautifully written personal diaries.

True, there was the uprising of the Decembrists in 1825 which introduced two qualitatively new features: a preestablished program for social and political reforms and the secret society as a means of structuring dissent and implementing the program. But the Decembrists were army officers, not intellectuals, with the exception of the poet Ryleev and the generous dreamer Kuchelbecker. The remaining more than one hundred men sentenced by Nicholas' courts were primarily soldiers, although some of them were well educated and familiar with philosophy, history, and literature. Nevertheless, they were professional soldiers, not intellectuals.

There might be a mild paradox here. For many a witness the intellectuals' attitude seemed understandable, while the Decembrists' one—puzzling. Said the Count Rostopchin: "I can understand why the Parisian rabble would rise in order to obtain rights; I can't understand why Russian noblemen would rebel in order to lose privileges." In Rostopchin's day many Russian intellectuals, although moved by the Decembrists' trial, could not understand either. Some did a decade later, partly because of the emotional imprint that this event left in educated society, and partly because of trends and developments within the wider social and intellectual context. The few who found a message and a legacy in the Decembrist uprising,[22] emerge in traditional historiography as "the first generation of the Russian intelligentsia" to which I shall now turn.

The Idea of a Free and Autonomous Intellectual Activity[23]

There are several features to be accounted for when discussing the phenomenon called "the first generation" of the Russian intelligentsia. First, the word "intelligentsia" did not exist in this period; it seems that writers, thinkers, bureaucrats did not need such a word. Those who supposedly belonged to the intelligentsia were designated, by themselves and by others, with the current equivalents of "intellectuals" ("educated men," "enlightened people"). It does not seem that anybody felt the need of a term to name them differently than, say, the Slavophiles, or Pushkin and Lermontov (whom, by the way, nobody ever proposed to see as belonging to the "intelligentsia").

Further, the dozen persons usually mentioned as representing the first generation of the intelligentsia represented only themselves.[24] Quantitatively they *were* the so-called "first generation." They were not part of a wider group. All evidence and personal testimony show that there were three circles of close friends: the Moscow Circles—Ogarev's, Stankevich's, and the Slavophiles'. "Thirty years ago," wrote Herzen recollecting these days, "the Russia of the *future* existed exclusively among a few boys, hardly more than children, so small and inconspicuous that there was room for them under the heels of the jackboots of the autocracy."[25] On Herzen's retrospective historical perspective regarding these circles' roles I shall not comment; the facts indicate that thirty years earlier they consisted of "a few boys." It is not much to make a "generation," at least quantitatively. It remains to be seen whether it might have been a "generation" qualitatively.

These men, the men of the 1830's and 1840's, were no *déclassés*, uprooted, rootless, or alienated. They were not going nowhere out of ennui, *Weltschmerz*, or Byronism; at any rate not more than well-integrated young bureaucrats and army officers, and certainly much less than fashionable *à la* Pushkin and Lermontov. They were not ascetics isolated from the world and humanity; they liked good company, good entertainment, good food, good books. They did not sever the ties that bound them to their families, their milieu, their class—the nobility, society in general, or society in Moscow in particular, with all its social conventions and mundanities.[26] They were frequent callers at aristocratic parties and literary salons *à jours fixes*, at Prince Odoevsky's, at Chaadaev's, and at Madame Elagina's, the headquarters of their supposed worst enemies, the Slavophiles—a clear indication that attachment to ideas and differences of opinions were not basic determinants in shaping their social and personal relations.

True, their circles were bound not only by ties of friendship, but also by ideas. These ideas covered a broad spectrum, with nuances ranging from right-Hegelian liberalism to socialism. Their common features were: attachment to liberty of conscience; belief in science and education; hope for Russia's integration into liberal, progressive, and enlightened Europe. More specifically, they aspired to freedom of man (meaning, first and foremost, emancipation of the serfs) and freedom of speech (primarily, of the press). On the first point, the main differences between this group of intellectuals and those in authority concerned the timing and manner of carrying out peasant emancipation, with timing gradually becoming the crucial issue. On the second point, the government consistently held a diametrically opposite view on the issue per se and on the underlying assumption of free and autonomous intellectual activity. On that issue the men of the forties clashed with autocracy and were therefore considered dangerous elements (and so were the Slavophiles too). Although this widened the gulf between them and the political regime, the men of the Moscow circles still hoped that progressive reforms and liberal evolution could be initiated and successfully carried on by the powers in general and by an enlightened tsar in particular.

This is not to belittle, of course, the fact that they rejected, in their mind and soul, established traditions in the political-institutional sphere (autocracy and government by bureaucracy) and in the social-cultural one (serfdom and its by-products), which seemed to them by now as a repulsive offspring of Asiatic tyranny and ignorance, and German drill and pedantry.

However, while in Russia, they did not form "centers" for the implementation of their ideas and did not try to organize and carry out a political action. They did not try to find adepts, to proselytize. Their dissent was and remained their own; it did not spread beyond the small circle bound by ties of friendship and ideas. In Herzen's words: "There were no secret societies, but the secret agreement of those who understood was immense."[27] True, there was the perennial problem of "thought and action." But some died young, before they had to consider translating their thoughts into action (Stankevich and perhaps Belinsky); others faced this dilemma, viewed action (like Pushkin[28]) as consisting of the spoken and written word, found this freedom negated in Russia, went to the West, and stayed there for the rest of their lives (Herzen, Ogarev, and Bakunin); still others chose the half-way point of a veiled emigration (Turgenev); a few (Granovsky) remained in Russia, trying to navigate safely in the narrow path left between voicing discontent and personal safety, or between keeping one's thoughts to oneself and keeping one's moral integrity—a hard cruise in the "dark night [that] fell upon Russia and lasted seven years."[29] In Granovsky's words: "It was easy for Belinsky, for he died at the right time."[30]

But in all that there was no break, no chasm, no major change; there was only an existential choice for a few individuals. It could be argued that emigration was a kind of escapism and of dissent by withdrawal; it could be considered a new feature, a new tradition of Russian intellectuals, because it was prompted by political and ideological reasons. And in a sense it was, though emigration as such (mostly veiled and for different reasons) was a current device in the way of life of the Russian nobility. In this respect, the "men of the forties" set an innovation, a new pattern, although they actually emigrated as Russian aristocrats, remaining in the West as political exiles.

Later in their lives, they maintained much of the psychological make-up of Russian *grands seigneurs*—a paternalism in relations toward children and wives, coupled with aristocratic permissiveness in their own sentimental affairs; a certain respect for the tsar and the establishment in spite of some verbal abuses; a somewhat sentimental acknowledgment of the historical role of the educated nobility, created and raised by Peter the Great, and a view of themselves as its heirs in general, and as heirs of the immediately preceding generation—the Decembrists—in particular. In this conception of their cultural, social, and political antecedents there was no room for feelings of guilt, and these men were not "guilt-stricken noblemen," a fact that must be stressed in view of later developments. As Isaiah Berlin put it, they represented a phase "neither mystical nor introspective, but on the contrary, rationalist, bold, extroverted, and optimistic."[31]

There is, therefore, not sufficient evidence to consider this group of men the first generation of the intelligentsia. They do not represent a generation, and do not present most of the features usually attributed to the intelligentsia.[32] The view that they were a generation of the intelligentsia is apparently a myth created by intellectuals of a later period. The first generation has to be looked for at some other time.

As Isaiah Berlin aptly remarked, these men were "the first Russian intellectuals, men of ideas, who conceived of intellectual activity as free and autonomous, and consequently, as standing in no need of any external justification."[33] In this respect they were certainly among the first, and they stand out from most intellectuals of their own day, as well as from the later intelligentsia, for it cannot be argued that the intelligentsia conceived of intellectual activity as being in no need of external justification. Quite often —just the opposite, although with changing external justifications.

There were, no doubt, a number of common ideas shared by the men of the forties and the men of the sixties—by the "fathers" and the "sons." It remains to be seen whether these common ideas suffice to create an ideological continuity, a sociological genealogy, and a psychological filiation.

The First Generation of the Russian Intelligentsia

The "second generation" of the Russian intelligentsia, also called the "generation of the sons," emerges in the late 1850's. Its first phase, which has nihilism as a central phenomenon, lasted during the 1860's and for that reason the intelligentsia of this phase is also called "the men of the sixties."[34]

Two sets of changes leading to a break in intellectual tradition are usually cited in explaining the emergence of nihilism: (1) a shift in the social origin and composition of the group, (2) the new ideological trends in the intelligentsia in general, and in this movement in particular. Both changes led to a wide gap between this generation and the previous one, and to a bitter opposition of sons against fathers.

The first point in this interpretation is the disparity between the two generations with regard to the social origin of their members. The first generation was noble; the second is said to have been characterized by a massive influx of commoners, *raznochintsy*, coming from the ranks of the people—priests, peasants, artisans, merchants.[35] This assumption provided a basic explanation of the process under discussion: ideological radicalization was closely connected with, and even resulted from, a democratization of the social basis of the intelligentsia. The more numerous the commoners, the more radical the ideas. Quantity was thus turning into quality; new ideas were founded on a new social basis and had a sociological explanation.

It seems, however, that during the ninety-six years of its existence, this interpretation has not received, as far as I know, the support of convincing and precise data. Rather, available evidence indicates that within the ranks of the so-called intelligentsia the gentry represented quantitatively a large majority during the 1860's and 1870's. Qualitatively, they kept a leading role in all intellectual developments. The nihilists themselves were chiefly young men and women of gentry origin. Finally, from the 1840's through the 1860's the percentage of *raznochintsy* in institutions of learning seems to remain steady or to fall slightly.[36]

Raznochinets prishel ("the commoner arrived"). The author of this famous expression, N. K. Mikhailovsky, was probably the first formulator of the myth it conveyed.[37] It contributed to the historical justification of the populist movement and fitted its theory of progress through the extension of culture. This was, indeed, a great idea, *bene trovata*. It was democratic, it was plebeian, it was equalitarian. But, for the 1860's, it was an anachronism. Most certainly, the *raznochintsy*, although a minority, had a role in shaping the intellectual and psychological features of this generation, but theirs was not a leading role, and their influence was not the result of a mechanism defined by the simplistic equation: "low social origin → radicalization." If their percentage was more or less steady in the 1860's as compared with the 1830's and 1840's, how is their increased influence in the 1860's to be explained? Why then and not twenty years before?

Now to the other point of this interpretation. Nihilism, first stage of the "second generation" of the intelligentsia, has usually been presented as a new and radical set of ideas, viewed as an "ideological movement" (say, within a continuum which would include later on populism and Marxism), and discussed in the framework of an ideological and political conflict between the nihilists and the men of the forties.[38] Thus, the emergence of nihilism might mean a rejection of political, social, and cultural traditions, including the ones (or some of them) formulated and established by the previous "generation of the intelligentsia"; the main cause for this rejection, and for the phenomenon as a whole, would be the new set of ideas taking over and influencing this generation. What was that set of ideas (the "ideology"), typical of and specific to nihilism? The central tenets of the nihilist outlook were a positivist, philosophical materialism, fading into scientism; a belief in the intrinsic value as well as in the progressive social function of the natural sciences; a somewhat rudimentary aesthetic realism. Some nihilists were populist-minded, standing somewhere between Herzen and Lavrov (and on that account Franco Venturi calls them "the *enfants terribles* of Populism");[39] some were not populists and may be viewed as "non-socialist radicals";[40] some believed in the redemptive role of the peasant commune and in the evil inherent in capitalism and industry; some, more typical, as Bazarov and Pisarev, despised the peasantry for their ignorance and superstitions and believed in an intellectual elite, enlightened capitalism, and industrial development. All had great faith in education. None can be meaningfully classified along the lines of Westerners versus non-Westerners. They all were both and neither.

What, then, was basically new in this set of central tenets? What were the elements that created a new tradition? Why and how did this set of ideas (most of which were not new indeed) bring about a conflict between sons and fathers?[41]

The nihilists did not raise many substantial ideological issues against the "first generation"; even on points where differences could be seen, they were considered marginal. The main attack leveled at the men of the forties was that they were "men of knowledge without will" (or "idle men" and "superfluous men"), that is, people who refrained from action, an issue on which the nihilists elaborated at length.[42] The nihilists' reproaches stemmed from a certain conception of what one's behavior ought to be after posing and answering the great questions of existence and the major problems in social, cultural, political, and personal life. The essence of this criticism was that the men of the forties, although knowing the correct answers (and among them that things are not as they should be), did not feel that something ought to be done; they lacked a sense of duty to arrive at ultimate conclusions, a sense of personal responsibility and genuine concern for these problems; they failed to see that these social and political problems were also moral ones. This failure led them to a sort of moral indifference, and, since they had the knowledge, this indifference amounted to a lack of personal integrity and intellectual impotence. They behaved as Oblomov in Dobroliubov's interpretation, or as Chernyshevsky's *Russkii chelovek na rendez-vous*.[43]

More important than the issue of whether this criticism was justified is the question: according to what sort of code and values was this criticism raised? It appears that the code contained precisely the set of attitudes usually attributed to the intelligentsia. If so, these attitudes may have emerged and crystallized at this juncture; in such case, how is this emergence to be explained?

One of the common denominators between the men of the forties and the nihilists is that both represent in Russia different phases of "the modernist revolt."[44] They stood in conflict with various aspects of the political, social, and cultural order, a conflict between two sets of dialectically opposed values: on the one hand, hierarchy, tradition, authority; on the other hand, equalitarianism, individualism, secularism, positive rights. This attitude toward man and society fascinated the generation of the sixties and had a great impact on the ethos of subsequent groups of Russian intellectuals. How did it happen that twenty to thirty years before, this same set of values, although advocated by a much more gifted, talented, and intellectually powerful group of men, went almost unnoticed, or at least did not bring about a break, a chasm, a major change? In the sixties, according to agreed interpretations, this same set of values led to an alienation of intelligentsia and students not only from the powers, authority, and tradition, but also from their intellectual and ideological forerunners: the men of the forties. As "types of ideas"[45] they remained the same, but the pattern of dissent was suddenly different. Or, if there were no basically new ideas, nor a major change in the social composition of the group, what were the circumstances that gave these old ideas a new function and led to the creation of a new tradition?

One answer might be that the nihilists took action while the men of the forties did not. But that, obviously, is a technical and simplistic explanation, even if one believes that "revolution is at the end of a gun." Even then, it would remain to be explained why some acted while the others did not. Certain relevant features must be considered:

(1) A representative sample indicates that a considerable number of the so-called nihilists were born around 1840, in gentry families, and formed—when they met in and around the universities from 1857-1858 on—a clearly delineated age group.

(2) All had followed the same *gimnaziia* curriculum, shaped and restructured by Nicholas' reforms after 1848-1849. Behind these reforms was a growing fear of liberal and subversive ideas; they resulted in a sharp curtailment in the teaching of history, philosophy, literature, and classical studies (considered as a source of dangerous republican thought). The vacuum created by the reduction in the humanities was filled in with a massive dose of natural sciences—zoology, botany, mineralogy, human anatomy, and human physiology, in addition to the more traditional physics, chemistry, and mathematics. Natural sciences and the Orthodox catechism were the main training provided the future nihilists in high school. No wonder they were not able to appraise Pushkin's poems and Shakespeare's plays. No wonder they were accused of rejecting facts that could not be proved scientifically and of disparaging things tainted by human subjectivity, and above all traditional morals and officially recommended spiritual values.

(3) A specific sequence of events occurring while they were in their late adolescence (1855-1860) had a psychological impact that cannot be

overemphasized:[46] First, defeat in the Crimean war. There were two sacrosanct pillars of Nicholas' autocracy and orthodoxy: the army and the bureaucracy. The former was defeated in a war waged on Russian soil; the latter proved appallingly inefficient and corrupted. God took no sides in the conflict and the Russian Orthodox Church appeared helpless to save Holy Russia from debacle. This happened after twenty-eight years of official praise of state institutions, particularly the army. Near the end of the war a symbolic event took place: Nicholas died. The defeat spread consternation and bewilderment; Nicholas' death caused an outburst of joy in educated society.

Second, the accession of the new tsar—greeted as the beginning of a new era, full of great hopes and bright promises. The tsar himself encouraged these hopes, and in March 1856 publicly declared in Moscow that serfdom was to be abolished. The future nihilists were by then fifteen to seventeen years old. Serfdom, of course, had to be abolished; but serfdom had always been officially presented as one of the perennial institutions of Russia, her essence, might, and wisdom. If this was wrong, then what was true?

Third, freedom was in sight. Expectations grew and public debate began. Soon thereafter the powers let it be understood that the planned emancipation was their exclusive concern, not the public's, and forbade any allusion to it in the press. It was the first of a series of disappointments ending in sheer consternation when details about the draft law became known in 1859-1860. Later, emancipated peasants believed that this was not "the genuine law"; educated people had no choice but to realize it was.

Fourth, the manifesto of emancipation of the peasants from the bonds of serfdom (February 19, 1861) was written by the Metropolitan Filaret and released through the church, which exhorted, around the country, that all men are created in God's image, and no man shall be the slave of another man. For 150 years the Russian Orthodox Church preached that serfdom had been ordained by God, and that it was a Christian's duty to accept his earthly fate. What, then, was to be believed? And who was to be blamed for the servitude of the peasants?

(4) Most of these events were the subject of heated debates in gentry circles. In many families, some of these suddenly obsolete truths had been, over the years, conveyed to the children by the father, himself a serf owner, who usually stood as a staunch defender of autocracy, orthodoxy, and serfdom, and who extolled these principles before or after his oftenheard, but always engaging, reminiscences of deeds and adventures in the army, in the service of the tsar.

This is certainly the most complicated part of these developments, requiring a detailed inquiry into causes and motivations. It seems, however, that in hundreds, perhaps thousands, of gentry families sons and daughters in their late adolescence were in sharp conflict with their parents and rejected the authority of their fathers. Kropotkin writes in his *Memoirs* that "in nearly every wealthy family a bitter struggle was going on between the fathers, who wanted to maintain the old traditions, and the sons and daughters, who defended their right to dispose of their life . . . Girls, bred in the most aristocratic families, rushed penniless to St. Petersburg, Moscow, and Kieff, eager to learn a profession which would free them from the domestic yoke, and someday, perhaps, also from the possible yoke of a husband."[47] Remembering these days, the noted mathematician Sophia Kovalevskaia (then herself a mild rebel against her father, General Korvin-Krukovsky) says: "Of whatever gentry family you inquired . . . you would hear one and the same answer—that the young quarreled with the parents,"[48] that they had left home.

They usually went to university towns, the boys to study, the girls to fight for the right to study. Quite often they refused financial support from their families, for, as Nekrasov, the only poet they declared respectable, put it in a verse: "It is bitter, the bread that has been made by slaves," so they "refused to eat that bread, and to enjoy the riches that had been accumulated in their fathers' houses by means of servile labour,"[49] lived in distress doing any kind of job, and declared poverty an ideal and work the duty of decent and honest men and women. They gathered in groups, set up *kruzhki* and *kommuny*, met there their fellow *raznochintsy*, shared board and room and books and studies (formal and self-organized), in a spirit of mutual aid, comradeship, and the usual joys, sorrows, and quarrels of young people. The nihilists were on the make. This was, then, a revolt of sons and daughters against their biological fathers, but not against vague ideological "fathers of the forties," whom these young people often had never heard of before they left home. This was also their first "action." What were the others? What did they want? What did they achieve? Why is this episode important for the traditions of the Russian intellectuals, and for the intellectuals' attitude toward tradition?

Nihilism was not a political movement. It was parallel to political organizing and activity, not identical with them.[50] In the words of a nihilist, later a terrorist, Stepniak-Kravchinsky: "Nihilism was negation in the name of individual liberty, negation of the obligations imposed upon the individual. Nihilism was a powerful and passionate reaction, not against the political despotism, but against the moral despotism that weighs upon the private and inner life of the individual."[51] The principal points of the nihilist creed were:

(1) Individualism, meaning personal dignity and the importance of the personality, a clearly elitist streak. This attitude resulted in a permanent contribution to the slang of Russian intellectuals: *Pisarevshchina*. Nihilists seldom spoke on behalf of social groups or classes, but mostly of the individual.

(2) A particular interest in questions of moral principles and rejection of a number of conventional morals. Their approach and motivation were existential rather than intellectual, and their starting point was, as a rule, a discrepancy found (or believed so) between established moral imperatives and the actual behavior of people professing them.

(3) Rejection of religion.

(4) Freedom of women (as daughter, wife, and person).

(5) Translation of these aspirations into forms of everyday behavior and dress that differed from the current fashion in society in general, and in aristocratic society in particular, and rejection of customary civility and polite speech.

The common denominator of all these manifestations was rejection of authority (of the fathers, the church, officials) and rejection of restrictions that made these youths feel underage (some of them were) and under too much supervision, the kind of supervision exercised in gentry families toward grown-up children. This set of attitudes and beliefs satisfied the desire for freedom and independence of a given age group from a definite social milieu. It was also a sort of game that provided simple answers to the intellectual and existential problems of these youths. The simple answers were found as they discovered action as the shortest way to fulfillment. Their ultimatum may be summarized as: smash everything that can be smashed, and do it now; the things that will stand the blows are those worth standing; those that will crumble to pieces are rubbish; at any rate, hit out right and left; there will and can be no harm from it. Strike at tyranny, strike at religion, strike at all the corrupt foundations of official morality.[52] For the time being the blows were only literary and, so to speak, personally existential, for the core of this attitude is in "everything" and "now." "Everything" meant the nearest things in these youths' existence: dependence upon the family and official advisers; submission of the woman; hypocrisy in human relations and family life; parasitism and social idleness. All that was to be destroyed, and it had to be done "now," that is, *in themselves*, in their own existence. Therefore it led them, *personally*, to undertake various attempts: to attain material and intellectual independence (Pisarev's "critically thinking personality"); to emancipate women, above all, to secure their access to a higher education; to inject frankness and honesty in human relations; to feel a desire to be useful to society; to reappraise moral rules of behavior (in order to destroy "the gap" between rules and behavior). This, in turn, led them to work out or to adopt more liberal and permissive theories and canons of behavior, much more puritan than was customary in aristocratic milieus (in reality, they rejected one sort of "gap" to adopt another). Last but not least, they wanted all this to be conspicuous and manifest, which accounts for their different external forms of social behavior: a new slang (not necessarily "dirty" words, but "other" words), a different fashion and various distinctive emblems, such as tinted spectacles, capes, round Garibaldian caps, short hair for girls (quicker to comb than curls), and long hair for boys, accompanied by some negligence of personal hygiene, justified by "lack of time, needed for studying," the time spent in the bathroom being "not only wasted, but serving deceit and vanity."[53]

The "nihilist revolution" was a personal and individual "revolution" (and for that reason the new adepts needed external distinguishing marks). Actually, the nihilists were rebels, not revolutionaries, but their "here and now" created a style of life and a moral code—a *kodeks*, in their own words[54]—which represented a sort of counterculture. For that reason this style and code could become the basis of the ethos, characteristics and features of the intelligentsia and of intellectuals in this generation and in subsequent ones. These features are similar to the ones usually attributed to the intelligentsia.

Nihilism proper began to wane around 1866-1867. The causes need detailed elaboration, but one seems fairly clear: the nihilists grew older, reached the age of twenty-five to twenty-six;[55] the universities ceased to be their rallying centers and to serve as a means of structuring their dissent which, in the meantime, began to be incorporated into the traditions of wider circles of educated people.[56] In their biographies, one finds, later on, some of them in the revolutionary movements; others—in some remote Russian village. For, on the basis of the nihilist ethos of translating one's thoughts into personal deeds, both life styles were possible: that of a terrorist, for a man who believed that the political regime has to be changed, but found political activity impossible in autocratic Russia; that of a village physician, for one who thought that peasants were in a greater need of medical care than town people. By then, all that pertained already to the features of the intelligentsia. The word itself emerged at the end of the 1860's, a time of growing populist influence.

A brief assessment of the *raznochintsy*'s possible role and influence may be added now. As mentioned, in the 1860's the *raznochintsy* still represented a minority among intellectuals in general and university students in particular; their percentage in the period under discussion remained relatively stable as compared with the 1840's and 1850's. Moreover, during these last two to three decades, as well as in past times, the attitude of the *raznochinskie* intellectuals (nearly all of them state servants) toward the major problems of culture and society was consistently traditional and loyal to those in authority; they often displayed more conformity than, say, the gentry in the same rank or in similar status groups. The change in the sixties was not, therefore, a result of quantitative growth, but perhaps partly, of a different distribution of *raznochinskie* intellectuals in various occupations, with more of them in autonomous intellectual activities. The change was not a result of some intellectual feature or political orientation determined by their lower social origin. Historically, conformism, not dissent, was their traditional pattern.

The circumstances that gave a role and an influence to a number of young *raznochintsy* seem to have been, therefore, of another kind. The impact of the series of occurrences from 1855 to 1861 described above led to a weakening of confidence in authority in general, and in the church in particular. For a number of *raznochintsy* studying in theological seminaries, a major consequence was loss of religious faith. As a result, they left these institutions and converged around the universities. The encounter of the *raznochintsy* with the rebelling young gentry gave the *raznochintsy* the courage to transfer their dissent to nonreligious spheres, and provided an opportunity for a valorization of several of their existential and psychological features.

Until that time *raznochintsy* were not proud of their poverty and modest social origin. An eloquent case in this respect is Dobroliubov, who wrote in shame of his poverty.[57] The "poor by deliberate choice" gentry-nihilists provided a new outlook. Indeed, only rich youths playing at being different could have made poverty an ideal. The *raznochintsy* took over willingly, washing out at once a wretched fact, and adding their own nuance: respecting asceticism as a result of their theological education, having experienced it at home and in the seminaries, and living this way anyway through lack of means, they canonized frugality as a virtue and affluence and riches as a sin. Furthermore, they themselves, "unlike others," did not have to feel ashamed and guilty for being born rich—an outlook to remain in the intelligentsia's *Weltanschauung* for several decades.

For the *raznochintsy* roughness had been a usual form of behavior. Lack of good manners, which had previously made them feel uncomfortable in society, never being quite sure whether they behaved *comme il faut*, was now justified and made respectable. It was not a regrettable gap, but a decoration—not a lack of education, but a new style. The gentry-nihilists knew what good manners were and rejected them as part of a game; the *raznochintsy* added a stress which made of it a serious matter. (However, this element in the intelligentsia's ethos was soon refined.[58]) The *raznochintsy* brought not only roughness, but also bitterness for the humiliations they had experienced. For that reason too, the nihilists' talk on individuality, personality, and man's dignity was a welcome innovation.

The *raznochintsy* also brought a dogmatic manner of thinking inherited from theological studies and the neophyte atheism of men who, not long before, really did believe. In a sense, the encounter between the rebelling gentry sons and the young *raznochintsy* was a mixing of the structure and dynamics of the natural sciences with the statics of dogmatic thought turned secular and filled in with a poor humanistic culture.

To sum up. The central phenomenon was not the rise of the *raznochinets* as a bearer of a new tradition, but rather the revolt of gentry sons and daughters, by means of which the *raznochintsy* obtained a role and became a part of the phenomenon. For the *raznochintsy* the rebelling young gentry played the role of catalyzer. For both the universities provided a means of structuring the "movement." The importance of the sixties as a formative period in the history of the intelligentsia (or, simply, of the intellectuals) is not in the relative rise of the *raznochintsy*, but perhaps in the breakthrough resulting from the absolute increase in numbers of young noblemen in the universities, and later on in the sciences and the professions, and in their willingness to "get their hands dirty," coupled with the emergence of several new existential and intellectual features.

It has been pointed out that "essentially the values and 'ethos,' the mentality and psychology, of the group are worked out and set by the first generation."[59] But in the case of the Russian intelligentsia, this was not done by the men of the 1830's. It was done, I believe, by the men of the sixties, who emerge as the "first generation." They had such an influence, not because of the specific nature and content of some set of theories, but because, in a sense, they created a counterculture: as a result of specific historical events occurring at a given point in their lives (late adolescence), combined with a generational conflict, developing within families of a given stratum of society, the nobility; at the level of manners, dress, vocabulary, behavior, attitudes toward everyday life habits, coupled with a reevaluation of the meaning of life, the aim of man's travail on earth, the nature of human bonds.[60]

It is the creation of this counterculture that has to be seen as the decisive reason for the main characteristics of this phenomenon, namely, that this age group did emerge and crystallize as a new generation, and that its attitudes, psychological make-up, and intellectual orientations could be conveyed to the next generation in spite of the subsequent emergence of new ideas and other philosophies. Their message, frame of reference, and intellectual orientations were a way of life, a vision of the world, and a moral code; these were, indeed, a specific "way of looking at the basic problems of social and cultural order, and of posing the major questions about them."[61] This was also a basic orientation implying that, in the search for answers, one has to attempt to correlate and conform one's way of life to one's way of looking at the problems. This did not necessarily imply a given type of solution; the answer could have been populist, anarchist, or liberal, elitist or anti-elitist.[62] It did imply, however, a number of basic trends, attitudes, frames of mind, and behaviors, which were, precisely, the core of this counterculture, and of a new tradition capable of being bequeathed to coming generations.

Was it bequeathed? And to what extent? This generation of the intelligentsia that displayed so neatly the classic features of the Russian intelligentsia and emerged as its first generation, was it not also the last?

Intellectuals in an Age of Modernity and Modernism

The study of Russian intellectuals as such from the early 1890's through 1917 meets with considerable difficulties because of intensity and pace of

138   MICHAEL CONFINO

social and intellectual processes, as well as the gaps still left in the research on several aspects of the period. Therefore, I will not venture beyond some cursory remarks.

The subject needs, first, a thorough semantic inquiry on the term "intelligentsia," for there are, quite clearly, important changes in its connotations from the 1870's to the 1890's and after. At the beginning of that period, the term seems clear, has positive undertones, and conveys a set of traits amounting to what may be called "the nihilist ethos," plus a subsequent layer of populist attitudes, which is similar to the features of the intelligentsia described at the beginning of this essay. Around the 1890's these connotations become ambiguous, and the term shifts more and more to the meaning of "intellectuals" in a broad sense. Two examples are in Chekhov's letters: "Our only topic is Zola and Dreyfus. The great majority of the intelligentzia [in France] are on the side of Zola and believe in the innocence of Dreyfus."[63] "Intelligentsia" here clearly stands for "intellectuals"; note also that for Chekhov this is not a unique Russian phenomenon. Even more stressed is the following use: "You ask my opinion of Zola and his trial. I first of all take the obvious into consideration: on the side of Zola is all the European intelligentzia."[64] Further, publicists currently use the term with an adjective, in which case the context is meaningless if "intelligentsia" is not understood as "intellectuals." Thus, for instance, Lenin used adjectives such as "advanced," "liberal," "democratic," "bourgeois," "petty-bourgeois," "radical," "conservative"; Orgeiani, the anarchist theoretician, used "the toiling intelligentsia" (*trudovaia intelligentsia*),[65] in contradistinction to well-to-do or "exploiting" *intelligenty*, that is, "intellectuals."

Moreover, "intelligentsia" is now often a word of abuse and denigration, and the group it designates does not fulfill a prestigious historic mission anymore. According to Chekhov:

The whole intelligentzia is to blame, all of them, sir. While they are still students they are a good honest sort, they are our hope, they are the future of Russia; but no sooner do they enter on an independent life and become grown up than our hope and the future of Russia turn into smoke, and in the filter there remains only doctors who own villas, hungry officials, and thieving engineers. Remember that Katkov, Podebonoszev, Vishnegradsky, are nurslings of the universities, that they are our professors, not upstarts, but professors, luminaries . . . I do not believe in our intelligentzia; it is hypocritical, false, hysterical, uneducated and lazy; nor do I believe in it even when it suffers and grumbles, since its oppressors come from its own midst.[66]

"Intelligentsia" was consistently used by Lenin to imply: impotent, inconsistent, compromising, selling itself, weak-willed, disgusting. The features of the intelligentsia are instability, flabbiness, wishy-washiness, opportunism, and anarchist phrase-mongering. For Lenin there was no doubt that the intelligentsia could barely lead itself, let alone the peasants, the workers, or, *horribile dictu*, the party.[67] The anarchists, displaying more civility and restraint than Lenin, consistently used "intelligentsia" as an equivalent of "intellectuals," and declared that it was "not a socio-eco-nomic group, neither a socio-ethical notion."[68] From the other end of the spectrum came the devastating criticism of the *Vekhi* group (Berdiaev, Frank, Struve, Bulgakov) against those who "gave themselves the name of 'the intelligentsia.' "[69] Although these critics still see themselves as "in-telligentsia," there is ample lexicological and ideological evidence that they mean "intellectuals."

Another sign of the increasing ambiguity is the heated debate, from the early 1900's, on the theme "What Is the Intelligentsia?" After thirty years of use, it suddenly became clear that the term "intelligentsia" needed definition. In these attempts, only the neopopulists and a few liberals still believed in the intelligentsia's existence and in its typical moral quali-ties and historic mission. But in their writings there was more nostalgia and romanticism than hope and sociological analysis; and they stressed the intel-ligentsia of the 1870's above the stratum of their own day. They were faithfully defending "the purity of its ideas" and its great strength, to which Lenin was replying that "the 'purity' of its ideas" was exactly why it was, and had always been, impotent.[70] He could have argued that, anyway, it ex-isted no more, but he did not, because he had in mind the intellectuals, whereas the neopopulists still meant the intelligentsia.

An attempt to explain these changes of meaning between the 1870's and the 1900's would involve a vast inquiry, obviously beyond the scope of this essay. Any such attempt should consider a series of complex back-ground developments: rapid industrialization with its manifold by-products; transformations in the patterns of political action, entailing, after 1905, wider possibilities for political and social organizing, publishing, and struc-turing autonomous activities in all intellectual fields; the renaissance usu-ally referred to as the Silver Age or the Second Golden Age, with its great creativity, richness, and vitality in all areas of cultural, intellectual, and spiritual life; and a conspicuous quantitative increase of the intellectual stratum, a growing diversification of occupations, and a greater speciali-zation in every field.

An important change of the 1860's and 1870's is the growing number and importance of the non-state-service intellectuals and the decreasing influence of the traditional bureaucratic intellectuals. To be sure, their proportion within the intellectual stratum was still relatively high. It seems clear that the following period witnessed a great increase of intellectuals of the "pure" cultural specialization—of freelance, unattached, independent intellectuals—and the formation of several strong centers conceiving of intellectual activity as free and autonomous and of spiritual activity as standing in no need of external justification. This new intellectual stratum included a large and dynamic group of artists, poets, writers, and painters; a well-organized and effective group of urban professionals—lawyers, en-gineers, physicians, university professors, scientists; a large group of rural professionals—agronomists, statisticians, physicians, teachers. Some of the latter, although working in local government institutions (*Zemstva*), considered themselves as serving the people, not the state, and used their institutional location not for furthering central state policy, but in order to limit its hold at the local level. The *Zemstvo* intellectuals were a most active and articulate group in the political and social sphere.

Against this background, what were the trends and changes in attitudes toward tradition, toward the intellectuals' traditions, and toward the powers? Several hypotheses seem possible.

Notwithstanding the relatively considerable evidence to the contrary, it is worth exploring whether intellectuals were not the main modernizing force in Russian society. One obvious exception that comes to mind is industrialization, which was carried on by government decision and policy. One might learn, however, that after the initial decision and first stage (which coincided with the weakening of populist influence on intellectuals in matters of economic development), the distribution of roles between the powers and the intellectuals was somewhat different from the customary assessment.

The intellectuals' role and influence were carried on through various centers, channels, institutions, and organizations, rather than through political parties or conventional political action. It might well appear that in parties and political groups (whether oppositional or traditionalistic) intellectuals represented negligible minorities, although the Liberal party (Kadets) and the Battle Organization of the S.R.'s may be exceptions.

In spite of the current belief that intellectuals played a leading role in revolutionary parties, those who did were a minority in the intellectual stratum as a whole, as well as in the membership of these parties. A new assessment of their qualitative role is also needed. It seems clear that not every professional revolutionary was necessarily an intellectual, and an elite of professional revolutionaries was not an elite of intellectuals, let alone an intellectual elite.

The role of the bureaucratic intellectuals in the center should be thoroughly studied. How did they influence the formation and crystallization of the cultural and social forms? What were their responses to conformity as compared to the different kinds of autonomous or critical attitudes developed in other segments of the intellectual stratum, including the *Zemstvo* intellectuals? Different kinds of attitudes among bureaucratic intellectuals in the center are worth noting because changes, innovative trends, criticism, and the breaking of traditions in areas with marginal political relevance were viewed less and less by the powers as fields of resistance and conflict.

The three main groups having the greatest influence in shaping the cultural order are: the scientific intellectuals, who displayed high specialization coupled with wide humanistic interests, and felt that "true scientists combine supreme intellectual endeavour with a profound dedication to humanity";[71] the philosophers and religious thinkers, who reappraised Russia's tradition, criticized the intellectuals' traditions, and gave new content to religious thought and experience; and the artists, writers, poets, and composers—decadent, independent, soul-searching, open-minded, apolitical although rebellious and considering it a disgrace to support the powers—who broke taboos in the arts, leading to their wider role in the cultural order.

Finally: what were the attitudes of the intellectuals toward the traditions of the intellectuals or, for that matter, of the intelligentsia? This must be studied on two levels, the ideological and the sociopsychological.

Authorities agree that with regard to philosophy and general theoretical premises, the orientations of this generation represent a break with the previous one; it rejected the so-called ideological heritage of the intelligentsia, or, to put it more accurately, this heritage ceased to be the main concern of many nonbureaucratic intellectuals. The rejected philosophies and theories were: materialism, positivism, ultilitarianism, antiaestheticism, realism. In this respect the more traditional and conservative groups around 1910 were the neopopulists and the Marxists; the most innovative were the various constellations of men in the arts and religious philosophers. However, this heritage was not totally rejected, even by its critics, and parts of it continued to influence the thought of those who rebelled against it, very much as populist political ideology influenced Lenin's Marxism, for instance.[72]

At the sociopsychological level the subject is much more intricate. In a sense it may be formulated in the following ways: what did remain from the nihilist ethos (with its subsequent populist layer of the 1870's)? Do the traditional features of the intelligentsia typify this generation too, or a major part of it? On most points the fragmentary evidence is contradictory or ambiguous. A few assumptions nevertheless seem plausible.

A large segment of the intellectual stratum did not identify itself either with the powers or with the state. This attitude was not a by-product of political opinions; it went deeper and beyond them. It may be seen among many creative intellectuals in the world of art, where dissent was basically apolitical; it is noticeable also in liberals and in the *Vekhi* group. (This critical attitude toward the state as such may lead to a reassessment of the scope of Marxist influence, and may uncover some latent anarchist tendencies.) There seems also to be no stress on guilt feeling, as well as a weaker propensity to turning political problems into moral ones. Other aspects need much more additional investigation in order to be assessed. Was there a peculiar immediacy in human relations? An uncompromising stand in matters of truth (*pravda* and *istina*) and of personal integrity? Neglect and disdain for one's personal interests? Deep concern? Moral passion? Conforming one's behavior and way of life to one's way of looking at the world and society?

Among the many variables that should be assessed, one seems fairly clear: Marxism had a disrupting effect on the traditions of the intelligentsia and contributed to the rejection or refraction of several. The focus of this kind of influence was its realism and relativism, as opposed to the romanticism of the populists. Marxism helped dismiss the guilt feeling and curtailed the propensity to turn political problems into moral ones. Instead, there were classes and class struggle, historical inevitability. The guilt was in others—in the exploiters, in the bourgeoisie, in the reactionaries and deviationists. Lenin's Marxism turned political problems into moral ones only for its adversaries.

Marxism helped weaken the sense of obligation to arrive at ultimate conclusions. Ultimate conclusions in life were petty bourgeois attitudes, the weak-willed impatience of people looking for individual salvation instead of fighting the right way for changing the whole fabric of society— utopian Dukhobory setting up equalitarian communities instead of preparing the overthrow of capitalism. Marxism helped to reduce the alienation of the intellectual from society by giving him a good conscience: henceforth he could live in the rotten bourgeois society, which was doomed anyway, and wait until revolution came.

Lenin's Marxism slackened also the sense of personal deep concern. Lenin's thought was first and foremost a political strategy, which required pragmatic and opportunistic attitudes. Fighting here and now for higher wages for the sake of wages was an aberration. Economism was a deviation. So was terrorism. And for the same reason. Terrorists do not understand that their ultimate conclusion in matters of revolutionary theory and practice is a fallacy. They do not understand the need to postpone. The only valid and moral ultimate conclusions are those emerging from the correct analysis of the situation, coming from the party.

"Correct analysis" meant no personal deep concern for general problems of public interest. The humiliated, the offended, the poor, the wretched, and the peasants were problems that could not be solved by philanthropy and good feelings. Were they a reservoir, a useful instrument, an ally, a force? That was what counted—force—not personal deep concern. In Lenin's words: "Agreement with a *force,* but the intelligentsia is not a force"[73]—the "intelligentsia," that is, the intellectuals.

What may have happened, then, to the intelligentsia during this phase, and to the intellectuals toward its end?

The term "intelligentsia" was probably loosely used from the late 1860's through the 1890's, that is, during a period when, as a result of the reforms of Alexander II and economic development, a new type of intellectual was emerging. Yet the group was not large; it had no clearly defined place in the social structure and estates system. There was a gradual formation of new intellectual roles and sporadic attempts at their legitimation, with some new patterns of participation in social and political movements. Thus, a vague term, loosely used and never defined, served with no difficulties in the political jargon of publicists and in the everyday slang of university students in the 1870's and 1880's, a time when these groups were imbued with populist beliefs. Thus the major connotations of the word came from two sources: the nihilist ethos and the populist creed. The intelligentsia itself was emerging within a relatively simple social structure, and, for that phase, the "two Russias" theory has a certain validity.[74] But not for long: twenty to thirty years later there were already many more than two.

Within three decades the social, economic, and institutional processes mentioned above were well under way. The intellectual stratum became more clearly structured; its roles and functions were differentiated; its place in society was unquestioned. At that time the word "intelligentsia" was becoming obsolete,[75] and the first result of that obsolescence was the emergence of the problem of definition, briefly stated as "What is the intelligentsia?" This marked the end of the intelligentsia, owing mainly to the numerical expansion of the intellectual stratum and its diversification and specialization, and the combined ideological blows of Marxism and the partial rejection of the intelligentsia's traditions by the Second Golden Age artists and religious thinkers.

Thus, in a sense, the intelligentsia of the 1860's to 1880's was not only the first generation, but also the last. Its heirs were intellectuals, or professional revolutionaries, not another generation of the intelligentsia. It nevertheless created a tradition and bequeathed a heritage, and further research would certainly permit us to assess and evaluate its scope and content during the Second Golden Age.

The dramatic epilogue to this phase argues the need for such research. For, as the intelligentsia of the 1860's to 1880's was a last generation, so were the intellectuals of the Golden Age. But interest in them should not be motivated by the well-known propensity to inquire mainly into the history of the victors. October 1917 was a victory neither for the intelligentsia, nor for intellectuals. The Bolshevik party was not "preeminently a party of intellectuals," as a recent scholar has it,[76] and the Bolshevik government was not "a government of intellectuals," as Volin and his fellow anarchists believed.[77] Rather, intellectuals, like the anarchists themselves, were among the most defeated victims. In this respect, too, there was a certain historical and logical continuity with the old nihilist-populist intelligentsia, and with the new modernist and individualist intellectuals of the Golden Age.

REFERENCES

1. Recent important contributions on this subject include: I. Berlin, "A Marvellous Decade, 1838-1848: The Birth of the Russian Intelligentsia," *Encounter,* 4 (June 1955); "The Russian Intelligentsia," *Dædalus* (Summer 1960), ed. R. Pipes (especially the following articles: M. Malia, "What Is the Intelligentsia?" L. Schapiro, "The Pre-Revolutionary Intelligentsia and the Legal Order"; B. Elkin, "The Russian

Intelligentsia on the Eve of the Revolution"; R. Pipes, "The Historical Evolution of the Russian Intelligentsia"; and L. Labedz, "The Structure of the Soviet Intelligentsia"); R. Pipes, "Russia's Exigent Intellectuals," *Encounter*, 22 (January 1964); A. Pollard, "The Russian Intelligentsia: The Mind of Russia," *California Slavic Studies*, 3 (1964); V. C. Nahirny, "The Russian Intelligentsia: From Men of Ideas to Men of Convictions," *Comparative Studies in Society and History*, 4 (July 1964); G. Fischer, *Russian Liberalism: From Gentry to Intelligentsia* (Cambridge, Mass.: Harvard University Press, 1958); L. H. Haimson, *The Russian Marxists and the Origins of Bolshevism* (Cambridge, Mass.: Harvard University Press, 1955), chap. 1; M. Raeff, *Origins of the Russian Intelligentsia: The Eighteenth-Century Nobility* (New York: Harcourt, Brace, 1966). The subject is touched upon also in numerous works dealing with various aspects of Russia's social and intellectual history; some of them are mentioned below.

2. This feature seems somewhat less typical when one reads descriptions such as the following: "Now this polarizing tendency was especially marked in Germany. In Germany there has always existed a tendency to go to extremes in pushing logical arguments to their ultimate conclusions—a tendency which has not existed in such a marked fashion in the European countries outside Germany." K. Mannheim, "Conservative Thought," in *Essays on Sociology and Social Psychology* (London: Oxford University Press, 1953), p. 79.

3. Important features are stressed in Professor Pipes's formulation: "But for all its diversity, the intelligentsia did share certain common beliefs. (1) Those who considered themselves *intelligenty* were committed to public affairs, and conceived the emancipation of the individual only in connection with the general emancipation of Russian society and democratisation of the Russian State. (2) They were historically-minded; *i.e.*, they regarded history as a meaningful and regular process, whose general course could be scientifically studied and even predicted. (3) They believed in the historic mission of the intelligentsia: they thought of themselves as the vanguard of the forces of freedom, as a group destined to point the way towards a general liberation of society." "Russia's Exigent Intellectuals," p. 80.

4. E. Shils, "Intellectuals," *International Encyclopeadia of the Social Sciences* (New York: Macmillan, 1968), VII, 399-415; S. N. Eisenstadt, "Intellectuals and Tradition," in this volume; E. Shils, "Intellectuals, Tradition, and the Traditions of Intellectuals: Some Preliminary Observations," in this volume. I wish to express my gratitude to Professor Shils and Professor Eisenstadt for their extensive comments and criticism on the preliminary draft of this paper; unfortunately, for lack of time and space, many a good remark of theirs is not reflected in the present version.

5. For an example of discussion on that point, see E. Morin, "Intellectuels: critique du mythe et mythe de la critique," *Arguments*, 4 (October 1960).

6. See A. Vucinich, *Science in Russian Culture: A History to 1860* (Stanford: Stanford University Press, 1963), Part I, a work which I found extremely valuable for this study; K. V. Ostrovitianov, ed., *Istoriia Akademii Nauk SSSR* (Moscow, 1958), I, 13-19.

7. The degree of success and failure is an issue not relevant to the point under discussion.

8. With one important exception: the preservation of serfdom.

9. See J. P. Nettl, "Ideas, Intellectuals, and Structures of Dissent," in Philip Rieff, ed., *On Intellectuals* (New York: Doubleday, 1969).

10. A. Besançon, *Le tsarévich immolé: La symbolique de la loi dans la culture russe* (Paris: Plon, 1967).

11. Alexander Herzen's expressions.

12. See Raeff, *Origins;* M. M. Shtrange, *Demokraticheskaia intelligentsia Rossii v XVIII veke* (Moscow, 1965).

13. See my "Le paysan russe jugé par la noblesse au XVIIIe siècle," *Revue des Etudes slaves,* 38 (1961).

14. Among the Russians elected to the St. Petersburg Academy during its first fifty years, none was of gentry origin; until the middle of the nineteenth century the nobility produced 25 per cent of its total membership. See Vucinich, *Science,* p. 80. On the nobility's lack of interest in university studies, see *ibid.,* pp. 49, 80, 127-128, 134.

15. See my "Histoire et Psychologie: A propos de la noblesse russe au XVIIIe siècle," *Annales E. S .C.,* no. 6 (November-December 1967).

16. M. Speransky, "Draft of Introduction to the State Laws" (1809), in J. Mavor, *An Economic History of Russia* (London and Toronto: J. M. Dent and Sons, 1914), I, 333.

17. A. Herzen, *O razvitii revoliutsionnykh idei v Rossii* (Moscow, 1958), p. 47.

18. See Vucinich, *Science,* pp. 30-31, 62-64; A. G. Mazour, *Modern Russian Historiography* (Princeton: Van Nostrand, 1958), pp. 9-49; H. Rogger, *National Consciousness in Eighteenth-Century Russia* (Cambridge, Mass.: Harvard University Press, 1960), pp. 186-252.

19. M. Raeff, *Imperial Russia, 1685-1825: The Coming of Age of Modern Russia* (New York: Knopf, 1971), p. 146; see also V. O. Kliuchevsky, "Vospominanie o N. I. Novikove i ego vremeni," *Sochineniia* (Moscow, 1959), VII, 223-252.

20. See A. McConnell, "Radishchev's Political Thought," *American Slavic Review,* 17 (1958), 439-453.

21. I should hasten to add that until the October Revolution, Radishchev's kind of suicide was rather rare among Russian intellectuals; see A. Gaiev, "Suicides d'écrivains soviétiques" and I. Krotov, "Trois suicides," *Le Contrat Social,* 12 (December 1968).

22. See Herzen's testimony on himself and Ogarev in *Byloe i dumy* (Moscow, 1962), I, 84-91.

23. I owe the idea of this subtitle to Sir Isaiah Berlin's brilliant essay "The Marvellous Decade."

24. A. Herzen, N. Ogarev, N. Stankevich, V. Belinsky, M. Bakunin, N. Turgenev, V. Passek, N. Ketcher, N. Sazonov, A. Savich, N. Satin, A. Lakhtin, T. Granovsky, and a few others.

25. Herzen, *Byloe i dumy,* I, 364 (Herzen's emphasis).

26. See Nahirny, "The Russian Intelligentsia." The one major exception is Belinsky, who stands out clearly with regard to attitudes and psychological make-up.

27. A. Herzen, "Bazarov. Letter II," in *My Past and Thoughts: The Memoirs of Alexander Herzen,* trans. Constance Garnett (London, 1927), VI, 206.

28. "*Slova poeta sut' uzhe ego dela*" (The poet's words are his deeds).

29. Herzen, "Bazarov," p. 208. The "seven years" were the period of political reaction in Russia, extending from the 1848 revolutions through the death of Nicholas I in 1855.

30. T. Granovsky to Alexandre and Natalie Herzen, Moscow, [June] 1849, *Byloe i dumy*, II, 621. (Belinsky died in 1848.)

31. Berlin, "The Marvellous Decade," p. 34.

32. See above, p. 118.

33. Berlin, "The Marvellous Decade," p. 34.

34. I shall not discuss here the history and etymological aspects of the term "nihilism"; although a reconsideration of several points may be useful, such a discussion would extend this paper beyond any reasonable length. As to the periodization, according to established custom in Russian historiography, the "sixties" represent the period from the mid-1850's to the mid-1860's.

35. Such is the current Soviet view; for two examples in Western works see E. Lampert, *Sons against Fathers* (Oxford: Clarendon Press, 1965), p. 85; Malia, "What Is the Intelligentsia?" p. 452.

36. For some scattered data, see V. R. Leikina-Svirskaia, "Formirovanie raznochinskoi intelligentsii v Rossii v 40-kh godakh XIX v.," *Istoriia SSSR*, no. 1 (1958), 83-104. In the 1850's and 1860's, compared to the enrollment of students from the lower and middle classes, the representation of the gentry in the universities was rising. In the academic year 1860-1861, at St. Petersburg University there were 1,228 students of gentry origin and 203 of more modest origin. V. V. Grigoriev, *Imperatorskij S. Peterburgskij universitet v techenie pervykh piatidesiati let ego sushchestvovaniia* (St. Petersburg, 1870), p. 306. Fragmentary data in a recent publication are contradictory; some of them tend to confirm the present assessment; others hint at the possibility that the *raznochintsy*'s breakthrough in the universities might have happened only in the late 1860's or early 1870's. See L. V. Kamosko, "Izmeneniia soslovnogo sostava uchashchikhsiia srednei i vyshei shkoly Rossii (30—80-e gody XIX v.)," *Voprosy istorii*, no. 10 (1970), 203-207; see also Pollard, "The Russian Intelligentsia," pp. 26-27.

37. N. K. Mikhailovsky, *Sochineniia* (St. Petersburg, 1896), II, column 623 (the essay appeared in 1874). Oddly enough, he also adds that the *raznochintsy* were, however, immediately followed by "the other social element which at first played only a subordinate role, but afterwards dominated the entire scene. I refer to the repentant noblemen . . . Pisarev was, at least in literature, the figure most representative of this sect" (*ibid.*, 647). On the whole question, see the excellent analysis of C. Becker, "*Raznochintsy*: The Development of the Word and of the Concept," *American Slavic and East European Review*, 18 (February 1959), 70-74, who aptly remarks that for Mikhailovsky, "in literature (and by implicit reference, in the radical movement) the *raznochinets* arrives late on the stage in the late 1850's and leaves it mysteriously in the late 1860's"; this author points out too that Mikhailovsky "regarded the word as something he was consciously putting into circulation" (*ibid.*, p. 71). However, the real mythmakers appear to have been Ivanov-Razumnik and Lenin. See also Pollard, "The Russian Intelligentsia," pp. 10, 26.

38. See for example: A. Coquart, *D. Pisarev et l'idéologie du nihilisme russe* (Paris: Institut d'Etudes slaves, 1946); Sh. M. Levin, *Obshchestvennoe dvizhenie v Rossii v 60—70-e gody XIX v.* (Moscow, 1958); L. A. Plotkin, *Pisarev i literaturno-*

obshchestvennoe dvizhenie 60—kh godov (Moscow and Leningrad, 1945); B. P. Koz'min, " 'Raskol v nigilistakh' (Epizod iz istorii russkoi obshchestvennoi mysli 60-kh godov)," in *Iz istorii revoliutsionnoi mysli v Rossii. Izbrannye trudy* (Moscow, 1961), pp. 20-67; F. C. Barghoorn, "D. I. Pisarev: A Representative of Russian Nihilism," *Review of Politics,* 10 (April 1948), 190-211, and "Nihilism, Utopia, and Realism in the Thought of Pisarev," *Harvard Slavic Studies,* 4 (1957), 225-235; J. A. Rogers, "Darwinism, Scientism, and Nihilism," *Russian Review,* 19 (1960), 10-23.

39. F. Venturi, *Roots of Revolution: A History of the Populist and Socialist Movements in Nineteenth-Century Russia* (New York: Knopf, 1960), p. 325.

40. S. V. Utechin, *Russian Political Thought* (New York and London: Praeger, 1963), pp. 112-114.

41. Herzen convincingly argued that nihilism "has brought forth no new principles" ("Bazarov," p. 209).

42. This kind of criticism implies too a tribute to the ideas of the "men of the forties," for it means that they had valuable thoughts, *but* refrained from acting in order to implement them. If not so, the criticism regarding the lack of action would have been pointless. I shall discuss below what the nihilist meant exactly by "action."

43. Pisarev's attitude on this issue may seem ambivalent, for, on the one hand, he advocated action, and, on the other hand, he opposed political organizing, stressing the importance of learning, consciousness, acquiring knowledge, and thinking. This apparent contradiction receives at least a partial explanation when examining the specific content that Pisarev and his fellow nihilists attributed to action, and which was different in several respects from the views of Chernyshevsky and Dobroliubov. For a good treatment of the differences between the two groups, see Koz'min, " 'Raskol v nigilistakh.' "

44. I follow here R. A. Nisbet's analysis and definition of "modernist revolt" in his introduction to *Tradition and Revolt: Historical and Sociological Essays* (New York: Random House, 1970), pp. 3-5.

45. The expression is used here as in Nettl's "Ideas, Intellectuals, and Structures of Dissent." The case under discussion shows clearly, I believe, the limitations of this model.

46. This part of the essay is based on extensive contemporary reports and testimonies: diaries, letters, memoirs, and so forth. For some especially useful examples see: E. N. Vodovozova, *Na zare zhizni: Memuarnye ocherki i portreti,* 2 vols. (Moscow, 1964); S. V. Kovalevskaia, *Vospominaniia detstva i avtobiograficheskie ocherki* (Moscow, 1945); L. F. Panteleev, *Vospominaniia* (Moscow, 1958); N. V. Shelgunov, L. P. Shelgunova, M. L. Mikhailov, *Vospominaniia,* 2 vols. (Moscow, 1967); N. Belogolovyi, *Vospominaniia i drugie stat'i* (St. Petersburg, 1901); P. D. Boborykin, *Vospominaniia,* 2 vols. (Moscow, 1965); A. V. Nikitenko, *Dnevnik* (Moscow, 1956), II-III; I. Khudiakov, *Opyt avtobiografii* (Geneva, 1882); E. Breshkovskaia, *Iz moikh vospominanij* (St. Petersburg, 1906); I. M. Krasnoperov, *Zapiski raznochintsa* (Moscow and Leningrad, 1929); P. Kropotkin, *Memoirs of a Revolutionist,* 2 vols. (London, 1899); Stepniak [S. Kravchinsky], *Underground Russia* (New York, 1883).

47. Kropotkin, *Memoirs,* II, 90.

48. Kovalevskaia, *Vospominaniia,* p. 68; see also Vodovozova, *Na zare,* II, 99, 221; and Shelgunov, *Vospominaniia,* I, 139-140.

49. Kropotkin, *Memoirs,* II, 89.

50. For a detailed analysis of these political groups see Venturi, *Roots of Revolution;* A. Yarmolinsky, *Road to Revolution: A Century of Russian Radicalism* (New York: Macmillan, 1962).

51. Stepniak, *Underground Russia,* p. 4.

52. See, for instance, D. Pisarev, *Sochineniia* (Moscow, 1955), II, 120-126.

53. See Vodovozova, *Na zare,* II, 9.

54. *Ibid.,* p. 486.

55. Among those who married at that time, especially the women, many developed a keen interest in child rearing. Subjects of discussion were, for instance, hygiene, physical culture, liberty in artistic education, and swaddling or not swaddling babies. Some of the important (and "modernistic") new trends and reforms in Russian pedagogical thought and practice were initiated by these circles or under their influence. See Vodovozova, *Na zare,* II, 197-198; Shelgunov, *Vospominaniia,* I, 137-138.

56. See Vodovozova, *Na zare,* II, 29; Kropotkin, *Memoirs,* II, 84.

57. See, for instance, letters to aunt (December 29, 1854) and to Blagobrazovs (April 20, 1855), in K. T. Soldatenkov, *Materialy dlia biografii N.A. Dobroliubova* (Moscow, 1890), I, 190, 210.

58. See Vodovozova, *Na zare,* II, 282.

59. Raeff, *Origins,* p. 173n.

60. This counterculture had some abstract theoretical components: positivism, scientism, antiaestheticism. But they were coincidental, adopted by this generation because of the accidental junction of two sets of facts: the education received in their formative years; the discovery of these theories as *dernier cri* around 1855-1860. Moreover, while the function of this set of theories was essential, their specific content was not. Actually, there were, within this generation, various subgroups professing slightly different social, political, and philosophical theories, while fulfilling— socially and culturally—the same role and function and keeping homogeneous the generational framework with its distinct role and place in society (transcending the political tendencies and almost unaffected by them). On a similar issue, R. Pipes argues convincingly that the rationalism of the critical intelligentsia "was a historical coincidence, . . . the essence of this group [being] the critical spirit of which 'rationalism' is merely one expression," and could be exercised from many different positions. "The Historical Evolution," p. 497.

61. S. N. Eisenstadt, "Intellectuals and Tradition."

62. Marxism presents some peculiarities which will be mentioned in the next section of this essay.

63. To F. D. Batiushkov, from Nice, January 23, 1898, in S. S. Koteliansky and Philip Tomlinson, trans. and eds., *The Life and Letters of Anton Tchekhov* (London, 1928), p. 253.

64. To his brother Mikhail, from Nice, February 22, 1898, *ibid.,* p. 256.

65. K. Orgeiani [G. Gogelia], *Ob intelligentsii* (London, 1912), pp. 4, 12.

66. To I. I. Orlov, from Yalta, February 22, 1899, *Life and Letters,* p. 265. Note also

that Chekhov considers Katkov, Pobedonostsev, and Vyshnegradsky as belonging to the intelligentsia.

67. Compare this position of Lenin's with the role which Plekhanov attributed to the intelligentsia in the "Programme of the Social Democratic Emancipation of Labour Group" (1884).

68. Orgeiani, *Ob intelligentsii*, p. 17.

69. N. Berdiaev, *Dostoievsky* (1934), pp. 163-164.

70. V. I. Lenin, "Ekonomicheskoe soderzhanie narodnichestva i kritika ego v knige g. Struve," *Sochineniia* (Moscow, 1941), I, 401.

71. I. Mechnikov's expression, in A. Vucinich, "Politics, Universities, and Science," in T. G. Stavrou, ed., *Russia Under the Last Tsar* (Minneapolis: University of Minnesota Press, 1969), p. 178.

72. See R. Pipes, "Russian Marxism and Its Populist Background: The Late Nineteenth Century," *Russian Review*, 19 (1960), 316-337.

73. V. I. Lenin, "Obshchij plan reshenij III s'ezda," *Sochineniia* (Moscow, 1947), VIII, 162 (Lenin's emphasis).

74. The "two Russias" theory essentially means: (1) the simultaneous existence of two cultures in Russia, the one Westernized (however superficially) within a small elite from among the nobility and the bureaucracy, the other popular, indigenous, traditional, well-rooted in the Russian past and ethos; (2) a very simple class structure—on the one hand the nobility and bureaucracy, on the other the peasantry, a conspicuous feature being the lack of a middle class.

According to this theory, the intelligentsia emerges within this twofold social-cultural context, and the role it would have to fulfill is almost inevitably determined *par la force des choses*. (1) Culturally, it would. try to bridge the gap between Western enlightenment, progress, and science, and the Russian popular values, native culture, and so forth. (2) Socially, it would fill the vacuum between the upper and lower classes of society, although it would not perform what is sometimes considered as the traditional and congenial role of a middle class. Just the opposite.

Some of the ultimate conclusions of this theory (such as "permanent state of isolation and alienation," "profound unhappiness") are speculations of the mind, much more than results of precise research.

75. See L. Labedz, "The Structure of the Soviet Intelligentsia," p. 505.

76. L. S. Feuer, *Marx and the Intellectuals: A Set of Post-Ideological Essays* (Garden City, N. Y.: Anchor Books, 1969), pp. 56-57, 67-68.

77. Voline [V. M. Eichenbaum], *La révolution inconnue: Russie 1917-1921* (Paris: P. Belfond, 1969), p. 205.

THOMAS F. O'DEA

The Role of the Intellectual in the Catholic Tradition

Catholicism and the Development of Modern Intellectual Life

THE COUNCIL of Trent (1545-1563) reformed the Catholic church and secured the foundations of its discipline and its spiritual life. Following Trent religious life, which had been in a deplorable state when the Reformation commenced, experienced a profound renewal among Catholics. If the statistics of canonization constitute a reliable index of Christian vitality, as many Catholic scholars would assert, then the post-tridentine spiritual revival was an authentic one, for there was at that time an abundance of canonizations. The saints were drawn from all classes of society and were of all ages. The less central position of the church in the post-medieval world turned its life inward and made it more exclusively a school of sanctity.[1]

This period was not without its seamier side, as may be seen in the continuing need for and effort to achieve reform in the early years of the seventeenth century. During the years from the Peace of Westphalia to the French Revolution reform was urgently needed, but attempts to achieve it usually failed.[2] Nevertheless, the first quarter of the seventeenth century produced some exemplary figures as well as an exacting ideal of the priesthood. Christian piety, however, reflecting the changed relation of the church to the world about it, tended to develop in isolation from daily life, a tendency that would increase over time.[3] Post-tridentine piety continued the emphasis of the *Devotio moderna*. This movement, which originated with Gerhard de Groote (1340-1384) and found its classical expression in the *Imitation of Christ* of Thomas à Kempis (1380-1471), stressed feeling, sincerity, and humility over intellectual qualities. This was in part a reaction against the intellectualism, often arid and sterile, of late scholasticism. Although the *Devotio moderna* was well received by no less a mind than Erasmus, it possessed potentially anti-intellectual characteristics.

Trent itself was an intellectual effort of considerable proportions. In responding to the challenge thrown down by the Reformation, the Catholic church emphasized more than ever the importance of intellectual explicit-

151

ness in matters of belief. The Council reviewed the greater part of Catholic doctrine and reaffirmed it, taking pains to give precise definition at those points that had been questioned by the reformers. The work took four and a half years and the product was more voluminous than that produced by all the preceding eighteen councils recognized by the Roman church as ecumenical. Moreover, at Trent Thomas Aquinas came into his own as the *doctor communis* among theologians.[4]

The post-tridentine period saw a great flowering of theology in many centers. The excessive verbalism of late scholasticism and the attacks of the nominalists upon its essentialism led to a reaction against the earlier speculative theology and a turn toward positive theology based upon the Bible and the fathers. Father Sarpi's history of the Council tells of the protest of the older style schoolmen against the onset of this trend, a protest that won little favor with the pope or the assembled fathers. Yet the high intellectual caliber of Trent is beyond question. Sacred studies thereafter became more differentiated, and separate disciplines evolved such as exegesis, patrology, history of dogma, and ecclesiastical history. A more practical moral theology developed, one that made use of intellectual distinctions to bring the moral law into contact with the realities of daily life. This casuistry was itself liable to abuse and open to attack. Pascal considered it one of the two chief dangers to the church, threatening it from within as freethinking threatened it from without.[5] The post-tridentine period saw profound theological controversies concerning the Catholic understanding of grace and free will, as may be seen in the conflicts concerning Molinism in the sixteenth century and Jansenism in the seventeenth. It also saw a flowering of the mystical life, and the writings of such figures as St. Teresa of Avila and St. John of the Cross constitute important intellectual as well as religious creations.

It is especially important to note, however, that these developments all took place in a situation in which the Catholic church had been put on the defensive. After Trent, the church's "first care henceforward was her own defense." It had been transformed into a "beseiged city" and although the vast intellectual improvement of the theological scene at Trent and afterwards made possible a "counter offensive of Catholic orthodoxy" the posture of defense remained fundamental.[6] As Lord Acton put it, Trent impressed upon the church "the stamp of an intolerant age."[7] However, Trent was "in some respects less rigid, defensive and anti-Protestant than the post-tridentine Catholicism it helped to mold."[8] Thus was initiated the first great countermovement of modern times—the Counter Reformation. The Counter Reformation added to the dimensions of the intellectual role in the Catholic milieu the characteristics of a counterposition—of a stance against—a marked defensiveness, an emphasis upon discipline and loyalty, and a counteroffensive polemicism.

While these developments were in the making, others of even greater eventual significance were taking place. Science was about to come into its own. Science had deep roots in the Christian culture of the Middle Ages. Whitehead has insisted that "faith in the possibility of science, generated antecedently to the development of modern scientific theory, is an unconscious derivative from medieval theology." He saw at the same time that science was also part of an antirationalist trend which itself was a "very necessary corrective to the unguarded rationalism of the Middle Ages," but one that ran "to extremes." The scientific activity of the Middle Ages and the Renaissance came to fruition in the scientific outburst of the seventeenth century, the century of genius.[9] Out of this development there emerged the idea of man starting all over again—of beginning anew. Bacon spoke of "minds washed clean of opinions" and Descartes attempted to "unload himself of all the teaching which had been transmitted from the ancient world."[10] This notion of newness was related to the somewhat inconsistent idea that time itself made a difference, that we could know more now, and that the present age surpassed classical antiquity in its accumulated knowledge. Giordano Bruno, before the beginning of the seventeenth century, had already stated that his generation were the ancients and that ancient Greece belonged to the infancy of mankind.

To this tendency to see the past as over there was an active and a passive expression. The latter may be seen in the *Essays* of Montaigne, whose combination of fideism, skepticism, neostoicism, and a profound mistrust of rationality appears to have been a reaction of fatigue to the intellectual controversies and religious wars of the time following the Reformation.[11] The active expression may be seen in Descartes who not only based philosophy upon methodological doubt but also was a significant contributor to that great transformation of thinking characteristic of the age—the mathematicization or geometricization of thought.[12]

Moreover, Descartes was surprisingly clear about the practical implications of science, stating that with it we would be able to "render ourselves the lords and possessors of nature."[13] Scientific technique would lead to a new kind of relationship between European man and his world, to an unprecedented ability to manipulate and control, while the mathematicization of thought would have two further consequences. It made the experience of quality come to appear illusory. It was a view of the world "framed by mathematicians for the use of mathematicians," a construct composed of abstractions and conducive to "eliciting from them clear-cut demonstrative trains of reasoning, entirely satisfactory so long as it is these abstractions which you want to talk about."[14] If you preferred to talk about something else, you were, so to speak, out of the game. Thus everything not subsumable under abstract mathematical formulation became unreal and an entire world of aesthetic response and human relationships were accounted outside genuine knowledge. This dubious experiential and epistemological character was extended to religion. The analytic geometry of Descartes and the infinitesimal calculus of Newton and Leibnitz made possible the New-tonian breakthrough. The Newtonian breakthrough changed Western man's relation to his world and altered radically his style of thought. In the next century the philosophes popularized this new way of thinking among a receptive bourgeoisie.

The consequences of these developments created a difficult set of cir-cumstances for traditional religion, although the early scientists themselves had little awareness that such would be the issue. Bacon himself remained a "discriminating, yet orthodox member of the Church of England,"[15] and Descartes was always a Catholic. Even in his own lifetime he complained that his *Discourse* was being misunderstood and cautioned against wide-spread use of his method.[16] There took place nevertheless a secularization of the Western outlook. This was the case in part because the new mathematized science was based upon an epistemological stance capable of acting as an acid solvent of tradition and of qualitative thinking generally. But there were other reasons as well. We have already alluded to the skeptical literary tradition of which Montaigne is an example. This tradi-tion popularized science and did so in a secular and irreligious context. Fontenelle, for example, presented science in the context of skepticism and cynicism. Thus was introduced a bias not found in the earlier scientists and one Descartes would have repudiated.[17]

That too is but part of the story. Not only was there a group of literary transmitters available who would secularize the implications of science, but there was as well a literate public predisposed to accept the product. In the new middle classes there existed a type of man ready to hail the new science in secular garb and to reject the excessively otherworldly religion preached by the church. Thomas Aquinas had discovered an autonomous realm of nature, but in subsequent centuries Catholic thought had done little to work out the fundamental implications of his discovery. The result was a failure to do justice to this world that made it almost inevitable that the rise of middle classes would entail considerable apostasy. The new breed of man, the eighteenth-century bourgeois, "lost the character of ordi-nary believers. These were people who argued and wanted to analyze before believing . . . The clergy were at a loss in the face of the pretensions of this new man," who was "out of place in the Christian universe." Indeed the bourgeois constructing his own world "was entering into competition with the God of the Christians." From that competition the bourgeois "went on to the conquest of power without the cooperation of the Church."[18] The popularization of the Newtonian breakthrough gave these middle classes a world they could understand and manipulate. The concept of mystery was exorcised and with it the common ground with traditional religion.

Yet even before these developments, the potential of science as a com-petitor and antagonist of religion became discernible. It is significant not only that the early scientists were men of religious convictions and religious interests, but also that they found the opportunity for the expression of the former and pursuit of the latter in science rather than in the traditional religious context. Fontenelle's biographies of scientists suggest that there were prominent among them men from middle-class background. Moreover, it appears repeatedly that they had been intended for the church and that their fathers had insisted on an education in theology. "But over and over again, the same pattern occurs in the biographies—the youth finds the prevailing educational methods irksome, finds that he is being given an education in mere words and not in real things."[19] It should also be noted that much of the novel speculation found in the early scientific milieu was of a sort to raise religious suspicions. Almost everywhere in the writings of sixteenth-century astronomers and in those of Galileo himself there is expressed the opinion that the vastly expanded universe scientists now perceived could not have been created solely for man. When such notions led to ideas like Bruno's plurality of worlds and his immanentist pantheism, they were suppressed by the Inquisition.

It is against this background that the trial of Galileo must be assessed. Copernicus had been a canon of the Catholic church and important churchmen were associated with the publication of his *De revolutionibus orbium coelestium* in 1543. Pope Clement had approved an outline of the work in 1531. Galileo too had been encouraged by men in high places in the church. But by the beginning of the seventeenth century things had changed. The church had assumed its post-tridentine counterposition and churchmen tended to see much of the novel speculation of scientific circles as dangerous to faith. The Jesuits were directed by their general to shun ideas that would weaken Aristotelianism with which so much theology had become entwined.[20] Moreover, there prevailed a kind of literalist attitude which saw the Bible as a source of all kinds of knowledge. When Galileo suggested that the Bible tells us how to go to heaven and not how the heavens go, his point was not grasped. In 1616 the Congregation of the Index declared the heliocentric theory heretical.[21]

Between 1625 and 1629 Galileo wrote his dialogues on *The Two Principal World Systems*. It was a general attack upon Aristotelian science and included an assertion of and support for the heliocentric hypothesis. After a trial in 1633, the Holy Office pronounced Galileo to be "vehemently suspected of heresy, namely, of having believed and held the doctrine—which is false and contrary to the sacred and divine scriptures—that the Sun is the center of the world and does not move from east to west and that the earth moves and is not the center of the world; and that an opinion may be held and defended as probable after it has been declared and defined to be contrary to the Holy Scriptures."[22] While there was more than a little ecclesiastical politicking in this condemnation and while the condemnation apparently had little effect on arresting the progress of astronomy, even among Catholic scientists, the fact is that the church was helping to set up the conflict between science and religion. As Lecomte du Nouy put it, when the church should have understood it failed to do so. "The Church became frightened; it doubted."[23] The Galileo case, with some justification, became for the advocates of an antireligious secularism and scientism the favorite club with which to thrash the church. A new conflict had emerged and the church developed what almost amounted to another counterposition —an attitude of caution and reserve toward scientific breakthroughs.

The most traumatic experience for the church arrived in 1789. In that year, beginning with a Mass of the Holy Ghost at which the assembled estates of France prayed that the Spirit might enlighten their deliberations, the French Revolution erupted and a year later the French church "appeared to lie in ruins."[24] The Revolution gave rise to a campaign of violent de-Christianization in which the church was despoiled and its ministers hunted, arrested, and even massacred. This great shock came upon a church completely unprepared. It lacked spiritual vitality; its clergy was influenced by current rationalist and secularist ideas. For many it could be said that becoming timid, their "faith was declining and disappearing; the Enlightenment, triumphing in their minds, was withering what were called 'ancient prejudices.' " The laity, like the clergy, imbibed the current rationalism, the science of the encyclopedists, Voltaire's "mockery of superstition," Rousseau's "sentimental deism."[25] Yet under the blows of persecution the church in France produced heroes and martyrs; "amid insult, suffering and death willingly endured . . . the Church bore her witness." Consequently the church recovered its prestige in the eyes of Frenchmen and experienced a great spiritual renascence.[26] Thus was enacted for the first time the archetypal drama of modern times—the revolution versus the church, a drama that would be repeated again and again in Europe and Latin America in the nineteenth century and throughout the world in the twentieth. To the church's posture of Counter Reformation, to its suspicion and defensiveness in the face of science, there was now added the stance of counterrevolution. A new counterposition came to characterize the relation of the church to developing modernity.

The nineteenth century found the church alienated from the spirit of the age. It seemed to some churchmen that the course of modern history was "nothing but a horrible perversion." Yet there were those Catholics who "felt the attraction toward political liberty, the independence of peoples, the nationality and unity of states, freedom of religious conscience and of the Church herself, the spread of culture, technical and industrial improvement; they experienced currents of approval and sympathy for the creations of modern philosophers, writers and poets, and took up the study and the independent scrutiny of history and even of the history of the Church . . . This effort toward accord and reconciliation, varying and often different in spirit in the several countries and variously tempered and fused, was called Liberal Catholicism."[27]

In fact, between the Congress of Vienna and the outbreak of World War I, there took place at least six significant attempts to rethink aspects of the church's relation to developing modernity.[28] Three of these, occurring in France, attempted to reconcile the church with the "principles of 1789" and to develop a liberal Catholicism in the political sphere. The first was led by Lamennais (1782-1854) and was condemned by Pope Gregory XVI in the encyclical *Mirari vos* in 1832. The second, led by Montalembert (1810-1870), was condemned by Pope Pius IX in 1864. A third attempt to reconcile the church with the working-class movement and to foster a Christian democratic movement was led by Marc Sagnier and was condemned by Pope Pius X in 1910. In Germany the nineteenth century saw two impressive attempts to bring Catholic life into contact with intellectual developments in history and science. The first was the Catholic Tübingen school which flourished from 1817 to 1840. Influenced by Schleiermacher (1768-1834) it sought to reconcile modern science and philosophy with Christianity. Its leader Johann Adam Mohler (1796-1838) and his colleagues took an approach to modern thought that was both sympathetic and critical. After 1840 the center shifted to Munich and there Ignaz Dollinger (1799-1890) set forth a program to update Catholic intellectual life. In 1863 he organized an impressive Congress of Catholic scholars at Munich and put forth a program to modernize Catholic thinking, bringing it into close relation with developments in philosophy and historical studies. The congress defended the independent rights of scholarship in history, philosophy, and science, and discussed the relation of these disciplines to theology. While the efforts of the Catholic Tübingen school were never condemned by church authorities, those of the Munich group were in effect. Pope Pius IX sent a brief to the archbishop of Munich stating that scholastic philosophy was required of theologians and that the decisions of the Roman congregations were binding on scientists and scholars.

Finally, at the turn of the century Catholic scholarship became aware of the methods and findings of modern biblical study and church history. There developed an impressive Catholic effort in these fields. Catholics, long self-segregated from modern trends, were unprepared to assimilate the impact of this experience. When extreme positions were taken, ecclesiastical authority, obviously gravely threatened, reacted violently. The result was the Modernist crisis and the condemnation of Modernism by Pope Pius X in 1907 in the encyclical *Pascendi Gregis* and the decree *Lamentabili*. The latter condemned the "fervor for novelties" characteristic of the times and some sixty-five propositions drawn mostly from the works of Alfred Loisy (1857-1940).[29]

Most characteristic of the stance of the church in the nineteenth century was the Syllabus of Errors and the First Vatican Council. The Syllabus and the encyclical *Quanta Cura* that accompanied it presented a general condemnation of modern ideas and social and political practices. It was a collection of statements of the pope, removed from the concrete context in which they had been uttered and presented as the church's position. Pius IX had come to the See of Rome as a liberal. He had attempted to compromise with the revolutionaries in Rome but failed because they would not compromise with him; consequently, he became conservative. Throughout his long pontificate he combatted liberalism, nationalism, socialism, and the efforts of liberal Catholics within the church. The First Vatican Council (1869-1870) proclaimed the infallibility of the pope in matters of faith and morals. It thereby asserted the independence of Catholic Christianity in the face of rising nationalisms that often sought for themselves some religious expression. It at the same time defined the church largely as a centralized clerical hierarchy.[30]

The church stood in relation to the modern world as half progenitor and half alien. Its fundamental position was based upon two dominating counter-positions—Counter Reformation and counterrevolution. Nowhere is its status of half progenitor and half alien so strikingly evident as in its relation to science. The church always maintained and constantly asserted its belief in human reason; it would not reject truths if it were convinced that they were indeed truths. But the church was obviously threatened by the development of modern science and it took its stance with respect to it with extreme caution. At first there had been many important scientists who were Catholics, but this condition changed in the eighteenth and nineteenth centuries. Thus we see the church during this period developing a high degree of alienation from the spirit of the age and an increasingly peripheral status in relation to the significant enterprises of Western man.

This condition was complex and profound and I cannot do justice to it here. Yet it must be noted, for it constitutes a strategic element in our topic. A new mode of human awareness and of relationship of man to his world was evolving and in many of its crucial *notae* and in its over-all character it differed most significantly from the world view and the mode of "being there" in which the Christian faith had long been embedded. The most important intellectual development of early modernity was the rise of science which impressed upon the thought patterns of later times the needs and ideals of the new scientists. The most significant societal development of the period was the commercial revolution which hastened the great transformation from status to contract, from traditional society to modern dynamic society.[31] Both contributed to what is sometimes called the disenchantment of the world or the demythologization of thought. Moreover, both emphasized doing as against contemplation and relationship. The modern stance stressed elements like doubt, distance from phenomena, manipulation rather than relationship, quantity as the "really real" or the index to it, abstraction as against immediate experience, a flat rationality as against a sense of mystery. In the face of the rise of such a modern outlook, the church tried to defend its older cultural contexts—to prevent the rending of the cultural garments in which faith had long been clad. It did this in order to defend faith itself. When romanticism arose with its own defense of faith, the church turned to defend its own conceptions of the proper character and role of reason and rejected what it considered a "neofideism" and therefore an obscurantism. It could accept neither extreme of the modern argument.

The older Catholic view of man's situation differed in strangely contrasting ways from that which developed in modern society. Modern thought was promethean and optimistic whereas the church accepted what it considered the ills and limitations inherent in the human condition and held to an otherworldly orientation that rendered its view of man in this life a pessimistic one. Yet it is equally true that modern thought developed a profound pessimism on a deeper level which eventually issued too often in despair and meaninglessness. Modern philosophy became in Nietzsche's words a school of suspicion. In an important sense it left man less at home in the world he now successfully manipulated and to which he was no longer related as prime form among its hierarchy of forms than was the case with otherworldly religion. The church on the other hand maintained an over-all optimistic estimation of man's deeper meaning, of his belonging-ness in the world, his rootedness in being. It saw him called to relationship with God and fellowship with the Saints, a view based on creationist premises that made the earth a home for man in one sense while in another he remained a stranger and a sojourner here below.

Against this background it becomes clear that the disarticulation between the Catholic church and modernity was not a superficial one, that the stance of Counter Reformation and counterrevolution and the attitude of distrust toward science derived from a profound condition of deviance and disparity. "What was lost in the modern age, of course, was not the capacity for truth or reality or faith nor the concomitant inevitable acceptance of the testimony of the senses and of reason, but the certainty that formerly went with it. In religion it was not belief in salvation or in a hereafter that was immediately lost, but the *certitudo salutis*—and this happened in all Protestant countries where the downfall of the Catholic Church had eliminated the last tradition-bound institution which, wherever its authority remained unchallenged, stood between the impact of modernity and the masses of believers."[32] The church saw the new view as a kind of "epistemological vertigo" which involved the loss of a place to stand and in consequence of which men were uprooted in a most radical sense.

In the nineteenth century Catholics concerned with the intellectual life to varying degrees divide roughly into two groups. The alienation of the church from the world and the tendency within the church to separate faith and devotion from the intellect combined to make the intellectual life a constrained and difficult pursuit and to place it now in actual, now in potential, conflict with authority. In this situation most Catholics responded in terms of the counterpositions, and the events of that century were such as to elicit such responses and reinforce them. They tried simultaneously to defend the faith and the cultural forms in which it had become embedded. A smaller group, as we have seen, aware that such defensiveness is at best a temporary recourse and that history, like Galileo's earth, does move, attempted to meet the intellectual challenge of the church's condition. This latter group was composed of men of the sort that we usually characterize as intellectuals—men who give centrality to intellectual understanding and judgment. They were also mostly intellectuals in the professional sense, academicians, theologians, philosophers, and scholars. The church itself and the larger defensive-minded group that dominated the clerical leadership made use of authority to enforce an increasingly protective cultural self-segregation. Nowhere is this more vividly to be seen than in the aftermath of the Modernist crisis, when a repressive authoritarian response stifled intellectual life in the church. With respect to biblical studies "stringent measures of defense were adopted by the Church authorities, and for some years anything that savored of 'novelty' in exegesis became suspect." Indeed at this time the ecclesiastical leadership in the United States "became so antimodernist that the infant intellectual life of the Church was retarded."[33]

The counterpositions and their attendant mind-sets evolved under circumstances of severe conflict and hence increased the significance of loyalty and authority and reinforced the residual position of the layman. Thus the clerical and authoritarian character of the church was exaggerated. Churchmen had come to handle crisis situations in terms of that attitude caricatured by Acton: "Authority must overcome history!"[34]

Despite the difficulties of this highly unpropitious situation of the intellectual in the church and the church in the world, the efforts to rethink the church's response to modernity continued, while the modern world beset with its own profound crisis began to question some of its own assumptions. As a consequence of a changed situation in the world and in the church, revisionist efforts found fruition in the Second Vatican Council (1962-1965). For Vatican II represented precisely that; it initiated an epoch of profound rethinking of the church's understanding of itself and its relation to the evolving "postmodern" world of the late twentieth and the twenty-first centuries. The Counter Reformation is over and is replaced by ecumenical fraternity and intellectual exchange; the counterrevolution gives way to more open and more sophisticated attitudes toward contemporary politics, even when anti-Christian elements are involved. Vatican II legitimated what we have called liberal Catholicism, if by this term we mean the effort to develop attitudes and policies that, while Christian in content and Catholic in emphasis, will no longer be encumbered by historically conditioned attitudes and interests not appropriate to reality. Most significant is the abandonment of the older defense-motivated constraints upon intellectual endeavor. Vatican II recognized the "rightful independence of science" and declared that independence to be not only a necessity for modern man but the will of God. The official council document which made this statement carried a notation referring to a two volume study on Galileo published in 1964 by the Vatican Press. That document also stressed the significance of the lay enterprise in the world and of the laity in the church.[35]

The Second Vatican Council which initiated this new situation in the church was itself the work of intellectuals. It was in a sense the victory of a small group, the conciliar *periti*, in cooperation with important Council fathers under conditions favorable to a liberal issue. This small minority were in a very real sense the spiritual descendants of those pioneers in France and Germany in the nineteenth and early twentieth centuries. In the Council these intellectuals found their opportunity. Discourse always favors the intellectuals and a council is a discursive body. Discourse before the world favors those intellectuals who have something to say that is relevant. The vast development of communications in our century ensured that the Council would meet within reach of the world's eyes and ears. The difficult post-World War II years in which Catholic intellectuals in Europe and America continued their attempt to confront modern issues ensured that there be men present with something significant to say. Moreover, the world that would follow this Council was a world much less hostile to the church than was the world of 1869-1870 in which Vatican I took place. This circumstance removed the pressures of external restraints and made loyalty and caution appear less significant. In short, bishops called to council are no longer bureaucratic administrators in chanceries; they are parliamentarians involved in discourse. Hence, once a council convened the progressive theologians found themselves possessing enormous leverage.[36] The favorable relationship of intellectuals to decision-makers was not maintained once the bishops returned to their sees and to accustomed settings and set procedures. Yet the precedent had been established. Vatican II initiated a development destined to bring about a major transformation in the church the shape of which cannot be discerned at present. The role of the Catholic intellectual today is also completely transformed. It is now full of creative possibilities but it also faces new and indeed formidable problems.

The post-Vatican II situation finds the church back in the world, and within the church, faith and devotion are once more developing a living contact with what happens in intellectual life. The church no longer looks on with prudent reserve at the efforts of modern man. The immediate consequence of this situation is conflict and confusion. Beneath the surface lies the deeper problem. Can the church develop a sympathetic and cooperative relationship with the significant endeavors of contemporary man— the man of the remainder of the twentieth and the twenty-first centuries— without losing its own proper Catholic essence and identity? Can it assimilate the authentic breakthroughs of contemporary consciousness and still remain a "school of sanctity"?

So far we have considered the character of intellectual life in the Catholic church in the modern period. It is abundantly clear that the lot of the intellectual became an increasingly unhappy one as time went on. It was burdened by interior anguish and institutional constraint. To see more clearly the ambiguities, ambivalences, strains, and tensions that have typically been incumbent on the role of the intellectual in the Catholic tradition it is necessary to look more closely at three aspects of the problem. First, we shall deal with the general character of the intellectual role in all cultures where it exists. Second, we shall consider the specific way that role came into existence and became institutionalized within the Catholic milieu. Third, we shall consider how secularization and especially the break-up of the older medieval clerical monopoly of learning affected the intellectual role in the church. We shall then be in a position to return to the contemporary situation and assess its problems and its possibilities.

The Intellectual Role and the "Socratic Tension"

When Immanuel Kant proclaimed "Dare to know!" (*Sapere aude*) and called men to an "exodus from self-incurred tutelage,"[37] he recognized that knowledge could of itself prove threatening to a deeper personal composure. When he wrote to Moses Mendelssohn that he had thought many things he did not have the courage to say but that he never said anything he did not think,[38] he recognized that thinking could threaten the stability of human institutions. We see here an indication of the inevitable ambiguities characteristic of intellectual life. Reason versus life, spontaneity versus reflection, confidence versus criticism—these are three conflicting pairs that may be said to describe the ambiguity of the place of reason in human existence. When there takes place an institutionalization of reason, that is to say a recognized and legitimated intellectual role is established as part of the activity structure of a society, those contrarieties become strains incumbent upon those who perform that role. They then constitute a basic tension that we shall designate as the "Socratic tension."

Aristotle declared that "all men naturally desire knowledge" and it is this condition that makes intellectual activity intrinsically rewarding and the intellectual himself highly esteemed by the other members of his society. But as T. S. Eliot observed, "people cannot stand too much reality." As one who attempts to recognize reality and do justice to it the intellectual can appear to be a source of danger to others and can experience within himself an insecurity that threatens the stability of his selfhood.[39] The intellectual role represents a societal acceptance of the Socratic dictum that "the unexamined life is not a fit life for man." Such examination may indeed threaten significant interests and at times societal survival itself. Socrates is not only the prototype of the intellectual but of the martyr as well, for his contemporaries saw his activity as a threat.

The examination of life, which involves the examination of the cultural and institutional context in which life is lived, may threaten other elements in society. Consequently there remains, despite institutional acceptance, an abiding ambiguity with respect to the intellectual role. Under stress of threat or conflict, that ambiguity can give rise to a virulent anti-intellectualism. The intellectual enhances society by increasing its knowledge; he embellishes it by adding to its cultural heritage. For these activities he is honored. He carries on traditions and for this he is esteemed. But breakthroughs to new knowledge can threaten old beliefs; new cultural creations may undermine old assumptions. And in transmitting traditions the intellectual may subject them to historical or philosophical criticism. And for these consequences of his activity the intellectual is suspect, disliked, and feared. The ambiguity is a real one although it is often expressed in confused forms. In Greece the sophists made genuine contributions to intellectual life and to the professionalization of education, but they also contributed to the erosion of values and the evolution of cynicism. Socrates was not a sophist but he was confused with them by conservatives like Aristophanes.

This central ambiguity and the Socratic tension to which it gives rise is the cause of conflict within the intellectual and tension and strain in his relation to society. Three antinomies are involved: (1) traditionalism versus rationality, (2) stability and continuity versus innovation and creativity, and (3) institutional legitimation versus critical evaluation. The consequences of these antinomies tend to erode established "credibility structures" or "plausibility structures" and to undermine established forms of consensus.[40] Furthermore, since rationality implies universalism and since intellectual activity is concerned with value as well as with being, the intellectual often finds himself in conflict with the various forms of in-group allegiance prevalent in his milieu. Since he shares the values and prejudices of that milieu to some extent, that conflict will produce an inner anguish.

For the religious intellectual examining religious matters this Socratic tension is intensified by the religious element itself. This may be strikingly seen in the Western religious traditions. For the Jew or Christian or Muslim the demands of the religious relationship—the I-Thou relationship to God— implies an attitude variously designated as obedience, humility, or submission, and this attitude may conflict with the disciplined objectivity and assumption of mental distance demanded by intellectual activity. Since religion is concerned with what matters ultimately, examination in the religious sphere may threaten not only the stability of society and its normative consensus but the very stability and integrity of the self. Moreover, when we deal with religion we deal with the "holy" (*qadosh, ayios, sacer, sanctus*) which the religious man experiences as both appealing and fascinating but evoking a peculiar dread and repulsion.[41] In that sacred realm intellectual confrontation and examination may be experienced as sacreligious or blasphemous, and the intellectuals appear like the seventy men of Bethshemesh who deserved to be slain by divine retribution "because they looked into the Ark of the Lord" (I Samuel 6:19). Catholics have at times tended to see intellectual examination as an intrusion in the realm of the holy and the intellectual as Saint Bernard saw Abelard, as a "scrutinizer of Majesty and fabricator of heresies."[42]

These problems become greater in the case of Catholicism because the Catholic understanding of the act of faith gives tremendous centrality to the element of intellectual assent to formulated doctrines. All Christians see faith as possessing both an intellectual and a voluntaristic element. Saint Augustine defined it as thinking with assent (*cum assentione cogitare*). For Luther the chief element was trust (*fiducia*). A generation after him Lutheran theologians distinguished three elements, knowledge (*notitia*), assent (*assensus*), and trust (*fiducia*), and made trust by far the most important. Catholics see faith as the act of both mind and will by which statements are taken to be true. The church is seen as having a "declaratory power" to "determine what pronouncements are to be received on the immediate authority of God"—a power "infallibly to propose the content of Christian revelation to the world."[43] The Council of Trent declared that fiducial faith did not suffice for salvation but that it was necessary to have a dogmatic faith as well, consisting of the acceptance of the truths of revelation on the authority of God revealing.[44] Vatican I based its teaching on Aquinas and understood faith to be "an intellectual assent under the impulse of the will."[45] It defined faith as "a supernatural virtue by which we, with the aid and inspiration of the grace of God, believe that the things revealed by him are true."[46] While this understanding of faith enhances the value of the intellect, at the same time by that very same token it makes the critical and creative functions of the intellect more of a risk, for such activities can threaten the basic act of faith on which the entire Catholic religion rests. Consequently the abiding Socratic tension is magnified.

The Emergence of the Intellectual Role in the Church

As early as the second century the church encountered Greek culture and from it "received that tendency to intellectualism which has clung to it ever since."[47] Christians came to see the Greek philosophical ideals of *paideia* and the good life in terms of biblical religion and biblical religion in terms of these ideals. Education and character formation became significant Christian activities, a fact important for the development of monasticism, the humanism of the Middle Ages and the Renaissance, and even for the eventual emergence of secular humanism.[48] Moreover, the church took over and made use of the Greek philosophical mode—its vocabulary and its technique—to state its beliefs in a manner that held in check affect-laden images and achieved objectivity and clarity. The achievement of the patristic period and the early councils was to transform the mode of statement of faith from the more existential and experiential mode of the Bible to the propositional mode of the councils—"from the *quoad nos* of the Scriptures to the *quoad se* of the councils."[49]

The church was influenced not only by Platonism and Stoicism, with which Christianity had profound elective affinities, but by Gnosticism as well. Here too significant affinities existed, but they concealed great dangers for the complete subversion of biblical faith.[50] Since the Gnostics were the first systematic theologians, the church had to emulate their methods in order to fight them. "The struggle against Gnosticism compelled the church to put its teaching, its worship, and its discipline into fixed forms and ordinances, and to exclude everyone who would yield them obedience."[51] The development of doctrinal definition was inevitable in the Christian situation in any case, but the Gnostic confrontation hastened it and started it off in an atmosphere of threat. This circumstance inevitably increased the closeness of relationship between intellectual activities, defense against heresy, authority, and discipline.

The conciliar and patristic achievement to be seen in the Christological statements of Nicea (325) and Chalcedon (451) represents an authentic triumph of *logos* over *mythos*. As a consequence rationality was esteemed in the Catholic tradition and intellectual activity given a high value, a condition that was never reversed, even when the concrete historical circumstances made them a serious threat. Antirational figures like Saint Peter Damian (1007-1072) were never able to prevail,[52] and, as we have seen, when modern scientism became a most serious threat the church took a stance of extreme reserve but did not allow itself to be propelled into obscurantism. The conciliar and patristic achievement, however, had other consequences whose significance was more complex and more ambiguous, as would eventually become clear. Catholic intellectual activity with respect to man's relation to transcendence—Catholicism's "Hellenic" explication of the meaning of its "Hebraic" religious experience—would heighten consciousness of the difference between faith and knowledge on the one hand and between faith and conventional belief on the other. It would make men aware of how vastly "other" was the subject of our religious experience and how frail was the human contact with it through faith. Following the Epistle to the Hebrews, Christians recognized faith as concerned with things unseen and things hoped for.[53] Saint Augustine had written that "faith is a virture whereby we believe what we do not see." Saint John of Damascus called faith an "assent without inquiry." Hugh of St. Victor speaks of faith as "that certainty of the mind about absent things which surpasses opinion but falls short of science." Saint Thomas speaks of "the firm adhesion of the intellect to the non-apparent truth of faith." He sees faith as an act proceeding from both the intellect and the will and therefore conditioned by the desire of the former for truth and the latter for the good. He pointed out that on the part of the believer faith is less certain than knowledge "because matters of faith are above the human intellect."[54]

The Catholic church as a religious institution has as its psychological base the act and habit of faith on the part of its members. Intellectual definition and clarification of the content of that faith reveals the tenuousness of that base. There is always a sufficiency of experiences in life to make men aware of that tenuousness, but with the acceptance of rationality and making it a central value, that awareness was increased. Because of this tenuousness, faith required that as a basis for a Christian civilization it should receive the secondary support of a civilizational environment— institutional forms, consensually validated beliefs and values, rational apologetics. As Voegelin states:

Uncertainty is the very essence of Christianity. The feeling of security in a "world full of gods" is lost with the gods themselves; when the world is de-divinized, communication with the world-transcendent God is reduced to the tenuous bond of faith, in the sense of Heb. 11:1, as the substance of things hoped for and proof of things unseen. Ontologically, the substance of things hoped for is nowhere to be found but in faith itself; and, epistemologically, there is no proof for things unseen but again this very faith. The bond is tenuous, indeed, and it may snap easily. The life of the soul in openness toward God, the waiting, the periods of aridity and dulness, guilt and despondency, contrition and repentance, forsakenness and hope against hope, the silent stirrings of love and grace, trembling on the verge of a certainty which if gained is loss—the very lightness of this fabric may prove too heavy a burden for men who lust for massively possessive experience.[55]

Intellectual clarification revealed this tenuousness more clearly. Moreover, intellectual activity brought the critical and self-transcendent dynamic of reason into direct contact with all attempts to state the substance of faith and thereby legitimated questioning and inquiry even in this most sacred realm. Such a legitimation made doubt more probable, though such doubt may be justified as leading to a purer faith.[56] Furthermore the development of doctrinal definition contributed to an eventual objectification of the content of faith in propositional form, thus producing a vast cognitive map of "things unseen and hoped for" and of the human condition in relation to them. Such rational objectifications inevitably run the danger of losing resonance with interior religiosity and becoming alienated.[57] The whole structure could become an enormous *impedimenta* for the Christian mind. Thus we see that unlike Jewish religious rationality, which focused upon proper behavior (*orthopraxis*), Christian religious rationality, adopting the Greek mode of thought, focused upon belief (*orthodoxa*). Consequently Jewish religious rationality was basically ethical and legal, while Christian religious rationality became basically ontological, thus further revealing and intensifying the abiding Socratic tension. The Catholic intellectual role continued to have a close interrelation with authority and discipline—one often characterized by tension.

In these first centuries the role of the intellectual in the Catholic milieu was established and given a central importance, but this was not done without opposition which witnessed the reality and presence of the Socratic antinomies. There were those who felt with Tertullian that Athens had nothing to do with Jerusalem.[58] Moreover, the church was always basically conservative, adhering to what it regarded as the Apostolic faith. Innovation was ever to be rejected and it was not admitted when it took place. The period from Athanasius' struggle against Arianism (ca. 339-369) to Chalcedon (451) was a great epoch in theology and the product of that epoch became the defined faith. It was the work of a small number and does not seem to have been highly regarded by the majority of bishops. According to Harnack, the creative theologians themselves, "in proportion to their piety, conceived their task to be compulsory, dangerous, and ensnaring them in guilt."[59] Yet the Catholic tradition legitimated definition as a justifiable activity and always continued to recognize it as such.

The legitimacy given the intellectual role testified to the continuation of the tradition of classical education within the Christian community. The church did little to change the rhetorical system of education prevalent at the time, and accepted much from the Platonists and the Stoics. Ancient empiricism, however, was rejected and the science, history, and criticism of antiquity was largely neglected.[60] This was not particularly Christian but was in line with the dominant spirit of the period. Christian education came to rest on two foundations, the older classical literature and the new specifically Christian literature. In the Byzantine East this education continued for centuries and there always remained a class of educated laymen who studied Homer and Plato as well as the fathers. The Cappadocian Fathers, the two Gregories, and Saint Basil (330-379) are the products of this education in the East as is Saint Augustine in the West. It would be difficult to exaggerate the significance of Saint Augustine in the intellectual history of Catholicism. Combining profound intelligence with profound religiosity, he was theologian, philosopher, historian, and psychologist. He was also a bishop, an ecclesiastical functionary, who defended the church and developed significant ideas in ecclesiology.[61] It may truly be said that the medieval theological enterprise rested upon the foundation of Augustine.

The history of the West differed in important ways from that of the East. In the West the church remained the sole carrier of high culture and no lay educated strata survived the Fall. The church assumed the enormous task of providing Western Europe a moral education and in converting the northern peoples to Christianity. It also brought many elements of the culture of Mediterranean antiquity to the Teutonic and Celtic peoples. Lay higher education did not survive, but the church preserved the liberal arts because they provided the basis for ecclesiastical studies, without which the church could not have survived.[62] Monasticism became the bearer of Christian education and its foundations the centers for the gradual conversion of the rural areas. The monastic schools developed plans of study like that of Cassiodorus (496-575) in which the Latin classics and the old tradition of learning found a haven.[63] These monasteries also became both the source of tremendous artistic creativity,[64] and of reform of the church. From the ninth century on they gave rise to a series of reforming movements.[65] The Cathedral schools began in the tenth century at Liege and Rheims and in the eleventh century expanded and took over the leadership of education, reflecting the rise of cities and the increasing importance of city life.

The issue of all this was the new institution of the university with its characteristic lectures and disputations and its new practice of conferring degrees.[66] In the university setting three significant developments took place. First was the rise of scholastic philosophy at the University of Paris and the theological enterprise based upon it. Second was the rediscovery and reappropriation of Roman law at the University of Bologna, which became as eminent in legal studies as Paris was in theology.[67] Third was the rise of science. This was a matter both of the accumulation of new facts and the theoretical critique of Aristotle, the latter eventually leading to the overthrow of Aristotelianism and a new conception of the kinds of questions proper to science.[68]

In these developments we see the church, in Paul Tillich's words, as the schoolmistress of Europe, sponsoring both the appropriation of antique culture and the achievement of authentic advances in the development of the European consciousness.[69] Here too we see the antinomies of the Socratic tension. We have already noted them in Saint Bernard's remarks about Abelard. We see them in the banning of the works of Aristotle by popes in 1215 and 1231, although these bans were not effective. We see them in a statement by Saint Bonaventure: "When I was a student, I heard it said that Aristotle posited the world as eternal, and when I heard the reasons and arguments quoted to that effect, my heart began to beat, and I asked myself: how is this possible?"[70] But perhaps the most dramatic expression of the Socratic tension in that period is to be seen in the Omnibus Condemnation of 1277. This was a radical censure by the Bishop of Paris and the Archbishop of Canterbury and later approved by Pope John XXI. One of its chief aims was to condemn the "doctrine of double truth" put forth by Siger of Brabant, Boetius of Sweden, and the Latin Averroists. It also aimed to condemn naturalism, which made reason superior to faith. In that condemnation the church affirmed its commitment to one truth and hence to the universality of reason, while affirming the superiority of faith. The event, however, testifies to the risks involved in intellectual activity and the presence of the Socratic antinomies. In fact after the Omnibus Condemnation the fruitful collaboration between philosophy and theology that had made an Aquinas possible came to an end and each discipline went its own separate way.[71]

There are several things to be said about these developments. As the church had dealt with the intricate theological problem of grace and nature by suggesting a complex interaction of the two, so it worked out its solution to the enduring problem of Christ and culture by fostering the growth of a Catholic culture bringing together Christian with classical and Northern European elements.[72] There can be no doubt of the cultural importance of medieval education "as an intellectual discipline that moulded the Western mind and this was clearly recognized in the Middle Ages when *Studium*, or Learning, was ranked alongside of *Imperium* and *Sacerdotum* —Empire and Priesthood—as one of the three great powers that ruled the Christian world." There arose an intellectual elite almost independent of wealth and birth because many were of humble origin. Those who could manage the twelve years needed for a doctorate in divinity at Paris or Oxford, or of Law at Bologna, were able to attain the highest offices in church and state.[73]

The church was the central institution in medieval culture. It was first of all a teaching institution, a *magisterium*, and that fact affected significantly its relationship to the intellectual role. It accepted that role and made it part of its own structure. This meant that it both nurtured it and at the same time exercised a degree of control—of constraint—over it. It imparted to it a degree of ideational and institutional responsibility; it subjected it in ultimate matters—matters of faith—and at times for prudential reasons—reasons of defense most often—to authority. However, the Catholic intellectual was and is a man of "two conversions," and his loyalties to each cannot but intensify the Socratic tension for him. He remains a critic, as we have seen in the role of the monasteries in agitating for reform and in the university scene in the Middle Ages. As a critic he is not so much the collaborator with authority—although at times he may be—as its opponent, or at least he finds himself suspect by it. As theologian to the church—adviser to duly constituted teaching authority— he is likely to find himself a collaborator at one time and a critic at another. The intellectual was important as a conserver and transmitter of tradition and in that function he was in harmony with the conserving function of the church; he was also important as an innovator and as such was seen as dangerous to the church or was believed to be so. The Omnibus Condemnation also condemned a number of Thomist propositions.[74]

The church was not only an authority structure but as a consequence a juridical structure as well, one "which created for itself a specific legal system."[75] The law became an important specialized intellectual role. Here too the intellectual found himself a collaborator with authority. The rise of the state in the Middle Ages gave him another option; he could and often did become the collaborator of emperors and kings who were struggling against the church for autonomy and indeed for state control over the church. In this role the intellectual as legist was a strategic element in one of the central societal conflicts of the medieval Catholic community.

Despite the centrality of the church, there arose as a consequence of the church's educational activity a lay culture in which Catholic and native northern elements mixed. Thus there began the lay education that transformed the barbarian feudal warrior into Chaucer's "verray parfit gentil knight." This new lay culture exercised "a civilizing and educative influence on the ruling classes who regarded learning as the business of the clerks." Although it embodied much that was not Christian, its Christian character in so many other respects indicated how "the native tradition of the semi-barbarian West had become modified and transformed in the course of centuries by the influence of Christian culture." The thirteenth century produced a number of eminent lay writers of whom Dante is the greatest.[76] This marks the beginning of a lay literary culture, whose significance would be vastly increased in the Renaissance.

The Middle Ages created an intellectual elite drawn from diverse strata of society, but it kept that elite within the church and employed many of its members as "attached intellectuals."[77] The tutelage state of the laity that began in the early church had been strengthened and confirmed by the exigencies and accidents of the medieval experience. With the further strengthening of the clerical character of the church in the Counter Reformation the lay intellectual role could not easily emerge to full legitimacy in the Catholic milieu.[78] Finally among restrictive elements in the situation of the Catholic intellectual we should note that the continual definition of dogma gradually closes off questions and realms with final answers. It therefore in a sense continually narrows down the area in which theology can really be done.

Secularization: Politics, Humanism, and Science

The late medieval and the early modern periods were extremely complex. What actually happened was that the sacral society of the Middle Ages had created the conditions that made possible and to some extent necessary a secular civilization. The significance of this situation will be grasped if we recall the uncertainty and tenuousness of faith and the consequent necessity of supporting it with a civilizational order of a Christian character. By the fourteenth century the Christian (or really semi-Christian) order that had evolved was changing into a secular one. Yet the older forms with respect both to institutions and ideas remained and were still the structural framework of the civilization. The church was still central in many ways but it was challenged by the state and by new ideas and was itself the arena for the fighting out of conflicts which had both religious and civilizational significance. Beneath the rivalry of church and state—

ostensibly a struggle over spheres of competence—and beneath the struggles within the church itself, there actually lurked different human ideals, different conceptions of society, and different ideas concerning the value of life in the world. The church stood for the maintenance of the older *respublica christiana*, while the state embodied the thrust of lay upper classes toward secularization. The more conservative in the church did not see how to bring about change, while those who saw the need for reform did not agree either substantively or tactically on what should be done. Cities were important from the high Middle Ages on and cities meant trade. Indeed the medieval city was founded for purposes of trade.[79] The new city middle classes represented a new life experience whose implications would challenge the established interpretations of the Christian faith.

Every society is an acted out answer to the implicit question: what ought man to be doing on this earth being the kind of being that he is? It is an answer acted out under the press of circumstances and conditioned by situational exigencies. It is an answer which elicits some sides of the human potential, neglects others, and indeed represses some others as well. The latent and the repressed always remain possible and therefore a possible threat to the established order. The church was older than the society of Western Europe; it was in a certain sense its progenitor. It brought to the rise of Western European civilization its own formulated beliefs, its own established organization, and its own patterned ritual forms. Thus the society of Western Europe was in a sense two societies in one; it was the sacral society brought from the earlier period and from Mediterranean antiquity and the Western European society arising in the specific historical circumstances of its own time and place. There were two authority structures in Western European society but their respective jurisdictions was a cause of confusion and conflict. New developments within the society, new activities such as commerce, new evaluations such as an increasing this-worldly interest,[80] and a new lay spirit[81] were at the same time developments within the church. Yet while the society was evolving, the church was relatively set and patterned in organization and belief. In its established form it did not elicit and esteem sides of man that were finding expression in the new developing medieval civilization, although it was the sponsor and inspiration of significant cultural values.

One evidence of all this can be seen in the failure of the conciliar movement to achieve reform. While Europe was still Christian, the city of man was slowly declaring its independence and asserting the dignity and worth of this-worldly activities against the marked other-worldly cast and emphasis of the church's preaching. However, on a deeper level the issues here were never clarified. Different visions and different versions of man's calling—different answers to the constitutive question "what ought man to be doing?"—and consequently different ideas concerning order and authority mingled with vested interests and ambitions to produce conflict. In this situation the church became increasingly clericalist, while a militant secularism evolved in the world. Curiously enough in both the church and the political society the democratic tendencies of the Middle Ages were largely smothered by absolutist ideas nourished on Roman imperial law, and an authoritarian centralism evolved. But underneath it all that which was neglected or repressed was asserting itself; those who did the work of the world were revolting against the technicians of the spirit. "The various priesthoods of second causes rose against the alienation of their domain into the hands of the priesthood of the First Cause. A superabundance of proofs could be adduced that this is the true, profound meaning of the lay movement—and of the modern world too . . . It would be embarrassing to have to choose among all the statements of leaders in the priesthoods of second causes—statesmen, philosophers, scholars, medical men, philanthropists."[82]

Important intellectual developments reflected and expressed this rebellion. Marsiglio of Padua (1275-1342), rector of the University of Paris, supporter of the emperor against the pope, wrote the *Defensor Pacis* which declared that the state was the basic human institution and community, that it derived its legitimacy from the people, while the church had no inherent jurisdiction either temporal or spiritual, and should be subordinate to the civil authority. William of Ockham (1300-1349), the "invincible doctor," member of the Franciscan Order at that time in conflict with the pope, supported the emperor in his antipapal struggle. Living in a period when old conceptions and old institutions had become ambiguous and when formulated ideas tended to become a verbalism removed from reality, he initiated an acid solvent intellectual critique known as nominalism which further dismantled what had once been common intellectual premises.[83] Francesco Petrarch (1304-1374), declaring himself to be a Christian as Cicero would have been had he known Christ, revived interest in classical literature but at the same time wrote his *De Contemptu Mundi* as a series of dialogues with Saint Augustine concerning this-worldly and other-worldly orientations.[84] Erasmus, associated with Brothers of the Common Life, Christian and humanist, reformer and loyal to the old church, friend of Thomas More and opponent of Luther on free will, advanced scriptural study and made fun of scholastic philosophy and many common pious practices of the time.[85] Of Galileo and science we have already spoken.

The neglected was asserting itself; the repressed was in rebellion in the souls of European men. In that process the normal "healthy disarticulation" characteristic of the relation prevailing between a religion of transcendence and the society in which it exists[86] was being gravely exacerbated by the conflict and confusion inherent in this evolution. The sociologist may distinguish four foci around which human activity becomes patterned and human consciousness becomes structured. The first is relational and elicits a many-sided diffuse response involving psychosexual elements and the acting out of archetypal relationships. The second is environmental, to which men respond both as constructive workers and as aesthetic creators. In archaic society the tool is always the implement of both the worker and the artist. The third concerns order and belongingness; it is the realm of authority, community, and power, the political realm in the broader sense. The fourth is religious. It involves man's response to the call of the Beyond. In primitive and archaic societies these foci and the responses they elicit tend to be fused together. In the constitutive symbolism of archaic cultures they are mixed together in compact symbolic expressions. In the history of the West they have become symbolically, conceptually, and institutionally separated.[87]

The victory of Yahwism in Elijah's confrontation of the priests of Baal (I Kings 18:18-46) symbolizes the suppression of the first with respect to manifest religious significance for the Judeo-Christian tradition. The separation of the third and fourth is symbolized with special poignancy in the prophet Jeremiah's opposition to military resistance and with special urgency in the social critique of the prophet Amos. The second—the environmental—long remained the humble domain of *homo faber* and did not really assume dynamic historical significance until the development of modern technology. It did however provide the basis in both ancient and early modern times for a commercial capitalism that played its part in the demythologization of thought and the disenchantment of the world.[88]

What had happened in medieval society was that the fourth of these foci was given central importance. Christian values were otherworldly; the church was the keeper of the public conscience and the tutor of souls and minds. The fact that the church came into the new Europe already formed and that it possessed not only a religious dignity but the remaining luster of classical culture made this outcome inevitable. But such an emphasis involved the neglect of aspirations and values concerned with the other foci; in the concrete circumstances of the time that meant the denigration and disvaluation of this-worldly pursuits. The religious ideal as it evolved could not provide a representative ideal for human potentiality because it rejected too much that was necessary for full human growth.[89] There was a dynamic or historical irony in this situation. The dominant role of the church made the rise of civilization possible, but precisely to the extent that the civilizational development sponsored and nourished by the church advanced, the possibility of the church playing this central role diminished. Moreover, the tenuousness of faith of which we have already spoken exacerbated the problem. The great overarching spiritual and cultural edifice of the church rested on this frail foundation. As a consequence, in the midst of confusion and conflict the position of the church would appear less than self-evidently justified and the appeal of this-worldly callings and ideas would be enhanced. Under the circumstances the church proved unable to grasp and handle the deeper latent structure of its problem. The church tended to stand pat while the forces working for secularization, some degree of which had become necessary, became at first anticlerical and finally anti-Christian.

The first severe break came with the Reformation. That movement represented an attempt to renew religious life by emancipating it from the now rigid and overinstitutionalized ecclesiastical context in which it had become embedded. Yet it was also an attempt to return to the conditions of the earlier now hardly appropriate sacral society.[90] With the Lutherans this led to surrendering the "world" to secular forces and segregating the church as an otherworldly community. The result was a vastly increased secularization. Among the Calvinists there was the effort to build a Christian community with the state and all spheres of life subordinate to the church. Despite the dynamism of the Calvinist movement, neither Geneva nor the English Commonwealth proved viable for the evolving modern world. Regardless of the aspirations of the reformers the unintentional consequences of the Reformation involved a great increase in secularization. The Catholic church was now being thrust to one side in the evolution of Europe; it was being put on the defensive; it would be more and more seen as standing for the past. From progenitor it was being made into an alien. Its position was being changed into a counterposition.

In this process laicization was a diffuse and subtle development. The church had brought from the ancient world and developed further in its own setting a concern with knowledge and thought. It had sponsored education and created an intellectual elite. Although the members of that elite were overwhelmingly clerics, they were susceptible to the laicization process. The clerical monopoly of intellectual life was transformed from within. It was destroyed in form after it had ceased to exist in spirit. The intellectual role was not simply institutionalized in the church but in the general society as well. It was a part of the earthly city now declaring its independence. "From a sociological point of view the decisive fact of modern times, in contrast with the situation during the Middle Ages, is that this monopoly of the ecclesiastical interpretation of the world which was held by the priestly caste is broken, and in the place of a closed and thoroughly organized stratum of intellectuals, a free intelligentsia has arisen."[91] There evolved a new relationship of the intellectuals to authority and to tradition.

The Catholic intellectual is now progressively out of the mainstream. In this transformed situation he faces new problems. His responses are constrained by the counterpositions. His general situation is greatly affected by the fact that intellectual life develops by leaps and bounds outside of and increasingly hostile to Catholic Christianity. For the role of the specifically Catholic intellectual, history was creating an enormous task— the task of working through this complicated and anguish-laden history in order to understand it and to undo its disfiguring effects upon the Catholic community. It would be some time before this task would be recognized and the first attempts to formulate its problems would appear to those in authority—now defensive in terms of the counterpositions and the reserved attitude toward science—to be threats to the church and the Catholic tradition itself. Moreover, under the circumstances they would possess aspects quite justifiably interpreted as such. The tendency to separate devotion from the intellect and to see them in some way disarticulated was increased and in turn itself increased the difficulties involved.

The Role of the Catholic Intellectual Today

The lay intelligentsia of the eighteenth century supported the middle classes in their struggle against the church, the monarchy, and tradition, but their own aspirations went far beyond those of their allies. They gradually came to see history as going somewhere and themselves as having a role in achieving man's emancipation and fulfillment. These ideas represented a radical secularization of the biblical conception of history, since man making use of science would be his own savior. These intellectuals believed that they had discovered in "reason," as they conceived of it, "a new and marvellous instrument" with which they felt men could proceed to an increasing control of the conditions of their lives, to the reform of society, and even to their own regeneration.[92] They challenged accepted beliefs, as may be seen in the popularization of the critical study of the Bible done by Richard Simon made by Pierre Bayle in his *Dictionary*, or in the merciless criticism to which the theology and ethics of the church were subjected in the eighteenth century. They tended to see man as throwing off the intellectual shackles with which tradition had fettered him and assuming for the first time a conscious responsibility for his destiny.

What was advocated was, in the words of Saint Simon (1760-1825), that men come to be able "to do consciously, by direct effort and with more fruitful results what they have hitherto been doing, as it were, unintentionally, slowly, indecisively, and with little success."[93] They sought also "to free the elite from the bondage of authority," although like Voltaire they usually considered "the rabble" as "apt for every yoke."[94] They preferred the active life to the contemplative, and industry and work were their most highly prized actions.[95] They believed that man could change his world and could eliminate what the church called the consequences of original sin and Kant called "radical evil." They found themselves in rebellion against biblical religion, what Voltaire called "this infamous superstition," and against tradition and authority. They advocated freedom of scientific inquiry and were in conflict with a church that too often represented "privileged and persecuting orthodoxy."[96] In England this rationalist spirit had been received with sympathy but in France, despite its penetration into the clergy, it was persecuted by church and state.

The ideas and aspirations of these men may best be seen in the *Encyclopedia* of Diderot and D'Alembert. Leading French scientists and men of letters supported this project, but it elicited the hatred of the ecclesiastical party for the way it handled religion. The work was "a *summa* of the new learning" and an encomium to science and industry, seen as the twin engines of progress. The section on technology, written by Diderot himself, and illustrated by an excellent set of plates, shows how these intellectuals had become aware of the coming of the age of the machine decades before the actual beginning of the industrial revolution.[97] The work asserts that the welfare of the common people should be the chief concern of government; it sees religious freedom and intellectual freedom as indispensable to progress. The *Encyclopedia* was suppressed by the authorities in 1759, three decades before the storming of the Bastille, yet despite its massive size it continued to circulate.[98] Ideals of progress, the unity of humanity, prosperity, peace, and some kind of popular sovereignty had come to replace older ideas of Europe as Christendom and society as a hierarchy of orders. These ideas were carried over into the nineteenth century. Said Renan, "By every way open to us we begin to proclaim the right of human reason to reform society by means of rational science."[99] Moreover, in the nineteenth century, ideas that had previously been the concern of salon discussion became the property of mass movements. Many of them found a new formulation in liberalism which confronted Catholicism as a rival "religious" belief.[100] They became associated with the rising nationalisms, which also constituted competing religion surrogates possessing great attraction for European men. However, these ideas found their quintessential nineteenth-century formulation in the works of Karl Marx. Marx saw work as man's central activity, accountable for his development and the basis for his eventual achievement of full maturity. Reinterpreting Hegel he saw the industrial working class as the instrument for achieving human emancipation, an end that "can be attained only by the forcible overthrow of all existing social conditions."[101] Marx replaced the deism of the Enlightenment with an unexamined atheism and the criticism of religion became central to the Marxist point of view. Like the Enlightenment, however, Marx's primary concerns were practical. "The philosophers have only *interpreted* the world in various ways; the point however is to *change* it."[102]

Marxism represented a combination of Prometheanism and a secularized and immanentized apocalypticism. The latter had a long genealogy going back to Jewish Messianism. Throughout Christian history one can distinguish two Christian traditions—the tradition of the church with its emphasis upon man's limitations and the tradition of chiliasm with its utopian regenerationist hopes.[103] Since the Joachimite movement of the Middle Ages, there had been intermittent reassertions of such apocalyptic expectations of a renewed earth and a regenerated mankind.[104] Voegelin suggests that one reason for the longlivedness of this tradition is to be found in the fact that such movements "overcame the uncertainty of faith by receding from transcendence and endowing man and his intramundane range of action with the meaning of eschatological fulfillment."[105] Behind the aspirations of the eighteenth century there lurked in secularized form important traces of these ideas. Marx systematized this heritage into a secular ideology and made militant atheism a part of it, as he had earlier made the "confession of Prometheus 'In a word, I hate all the gods'" his own in his doctoral dissertation.[106]

Not only was the church alienated from science and scholarship, but the new political movements were against her. To these aspirations of the nineteenth century the church did not simply offer those qualifications demanded by the Catholic faith or dictated by wisdom. She opposed them. They had arisen under circumstances which made anti-Christian orientations appear essential to them. They were preached in militant anti-Christian formulations. Thus was the revolution continued, while the church faced it in the posture of counterrevolution.

The church's idea—"the root idea of Pius IX"—was that "humanity had taken the wrong road," an idea that informed all modern papal social thinking until John XXIII.[107] The church was on the defensive and it was in close alliance with conservative political forces from whom it expected protection. It was distrustful of science, and the new scholarship of the nineteenth century was not understood in Rome. However, the French Revolution had truly demolished the old Europe and not all the efforts of conservative statesmen could alter this situation. For the church the suffering of the revolution had been like a refiner's fire. Beneath all the manifest destruction there had taken place a partial achievement of what the church needed most. The church was partially deinstitutionalized; it was pried loose from the older societal and political contexts that it long assumed to be necessary for its mission and even its survival. This new condition caused increased difficulty at first but slowly and gradually it enabled churchmen to distinguish authentic aspirations from vested interests. As in the period of the Counter Reformation, so now, as the stance of counterrevolution became strategically central for Catholic action, the church developed an intense inner life; it became again a "school of sanctity." This religious authenticity was however generally tragically separated from intellectual life as the church was removed from the significant developments of the age.

As we have already seen, this situation was not propitious for the development of intellectual life in the Catholic milieu. Yet, there did take place a series of attempts to initiate a revision of the church's stance. And finally, these efforts came to fruition in the Second Vatican Council, thereby initiating an altogether transformed situation within the church.

As we have seen throughout this study, the situation of intellectual life in the church always stands in close relation to the situation of the church in the world. In the half-century since the Modernist crisis of 1907, the position of the church improved and the prestige of the papacy rose. This changed situation was important for the liberal issue of Vatican II. The effort to rethink the church's stance began again and, although chided in *Humani Generis* (1950), continued. Moreover, Catholic biblical studies revived and in 1943 were given a new freedom of operation by the encyclical *Divino afflante Spiritu* of Pope Pius XII. The effort to rethink the relationship of Catholicism and modernity added two new functions to the role of the Catholic intellectual. We may designate them as the *resourcement* function and the "mediating" function. The first is based upon the insight that the required rethinking of the past must be done in close relation to the sources of the Christian faith and the Catholic tradition—the Bible, the fathers, and the documents of the liturgy.[108] The second is based upon the equally important insight that the past must be worked through intellectually. It must be brought to a different issue so that its authentic latent meaning and its genuine contributions can be assimilated.[109]

Moreover, the history of the modern period is not simply the record of intellectual expansion and material growth. Science and technology may or may not have fulfilled the dream of Descartes of making men the "lords and possessors of nature," but they have been gravely misused by unregenerate man in war and in mass murder. As a matter of fact, modern philosophy did not reflect that scientific confidence. The contrast between scientists and their optimism and the secular humanists and their pessimism has been a striking characteristic of the recent period.[110] Science has "been credited with a demonstrable, ever-quickening increase in human knowledge and power . . . Yet the same phenomenon is blamed with equal right for the hardly less demonstrable increase in human despair."[111] Against this specifically modern nihilism[112] the church maintained its own conviction of man's rootedness in being, his capacity for reason, and his call to a relationship with God. The defense of this more balanced traditional position against a scientistic overconfidence on the one hand and modern nihilism on the other was carried out in the constrained condition of the counterpositions which made it impossible for Catholic thinkers to do justice to their position. It follows that the function of the Catholic intellectual in the new situation involves both enabling the church to assimilate the authentic contribution of modernity and enabling a civilization in crisis to assimilate the genuine wisdom of the Catholic tradition.

One consequence of the defensive stance of modern Catholicism and its alienation from intellectual life was that it tended to become unaware of history in a deeper sense. It came to confuse the vertical dimension of its religious experience of transcendence with a spurious sense of being somehow not really embedded in history. The modern sense of history was thus long lost to Catholic thinking. But today, again, Catholic thinkers are making the sense of history and its implications their own. They are recognizing "the need for the finite, historical inquirer to conduct a critique of his own possibilities of meaning and those of other cultures and epochs."[113]

The relative deinstitutionalization of the church, the intensity of its religious life, and the improved status it had come to occupy in recent decades prepared for a second phase of relative deinstitutionalization. It began with the accession of Pope John XXIII; it involved nothing less than the dismantling of the counterpositions. That process started with the encyclical *Mater et Magistra* (1961). Modern papal social teaching, which came on the scene late in the day, was concerned with social justice in an industrial society, but its view was static and basically conservative. It tended to see the class structure of Europe as Leo XIII (1878-1903) saw it—as ordained by God. *Mater et Magistra* expanded Leo's idea of a human right to livelihood and extended its applications so far beyond what any pope had said before that it seemed to many to be socialistic and revolutionary.[114] The encyclical accepts the modern state as an agent of social change in the service of human betterment. Vatican II, having not yet embarked upon its own project that issued in *Gaudium et Spes*, ignored this letter and John issued another, the *Pacem et Terris* (1963). This letter covered much of the same ground, except that where the first had stressed social and economic matters, this one gave centrality to politics and international relations.

Pacem et Terris made three points strategic to undoing the counterpositions. It declared that it no longer makes sense to use war in the nuclear age to restore rights and to repair violations of justice.[115] It reasserted the rights of conscience and stressed the right of the individual to practice his religion privately and publicly.[116] It approved the collaboration of Catholics with unbelievers "in the pursuit of objectives that are of their nature good." It repeated and stressed the distinction between "error and the person that errs" and confirmed the inviolable rights of the latter despite error. Moreover, it declared that movements originally anti-Christian in ideology may prove to be "readily susceptible to change" and declared that it was permissible for Catholics to discuss questions with their members and even to some extent to collaborate with them.[117] Such statements go a long way toward abandoning the stance of counterrevolution. They create an open situation in the realm of political thought and action.

The great event of the second phase of the church's relative deinstitutionalization was, of course, Vatican II. There the crisis of the modern world was recognized, but it was characterized as a "crisis of growth" and as part of a broader and deeper revolution in which the "scientific spirit exerts a new kind of impact" to bring to men improved self-knowledge and great technological capacities. The Council recognized that the times raised the fundamental question of the meaning of life. Dynamic and continual change was seen to be a fact of the human condition in the present age and the passing away of established forms was seen as inevitable. *Gaudium et Spes*, the document that reflects most adequately the thrust of the Council, declared, "Persons and societies thirst for a full and free life worthy of man—one in which they can subject to their own welfare all that the modern world can offer them so abundantly."[118]

This new situation in the church means that while not losing sight of the special nature of its own pilgrimage and the unique character of its own proclamation the church has become involved in the common venture of modern man. It has joined that venture not to lead it but to serve men. The church is freeing itself from the procrustean bed of the counterpositions; it is discovering how to act rather than react. It recognizes freedom for scientific and scholarly inquiry and it seeks to help in utilizing technology to produce a more peaceful and more prosperous world. For the Catholic intellectual this means that he confronts the non-Catholic world of learning and science with a new openness of mind and freedom of action. He confronts the contemporary world with the conviction that the ideals of the *Encyclopedia* and those of Christianity need no longer stand in opposition, but rather exist in a state of creative tension. Cardinal Newman once said, "Great minds need elbow room, not indeed in the domain of faith, but of thought. And so indeed do lesser minds, and all minds."[119] The elbow room now exists. Indeed one can now say that theology is being done once again and not merely talked about as already done.[120]

The Catholic intellectual in his new freedom faces profound challenges from every side. Religious meaning and its statement, the relation of propositional to existential truth, the problems that are discussed under the rubrics of "demythologization" and of "dehellenization,"[121] history and the social sciences, biblical studies—all these and a host of immediately and remotely related questions are on the intellectual order of the day. Moreover, the role of the Catholic intellectual is undergoing a significant change on the organizational level. There is far less self-segregation; ecumenical dialogue is a reality and is being embodied in institutional forms. With respect to intellectual activities the distinction between clergy and laity is losing its former significance.

Yet as might be expected, the relative breakdown of precedent which these changes entail not only provides a vast expansion of opportunity and a new freedom, but by that very token introduces new problems inherent in a loss of established structures. Perplexity, confusion, and conflict are the consequence. This molting process will not be easy nor will it be accomplished soon. The fact is that the church is undergoing the greatest crisis of its ruling and teaching authority since the sixteenth century.[122] As the earlier defensive position involved a truncation or disfigurement of Catholic intellectual life, so now the new and unaccustomed liberty proves to be a heady wine. It elicits from no small number of Catholics a tendency toward an epistemological giddiness that finds expression in fads and novelties. The ultraconservatism of so much in the past is now counterbalanced by a kind of anarchy. Maritain has charged that the ultraconservatism of the past "has been spreading among us during the nineteenth century and the first decade of our own. Now, with a crash, the pendulum is swinging to the opposite extreme," to a "childish anarchy in the opposite direction."[123]

It has been said that if the church thoroughly assimilates the Johannine encyclicals, "she will, in effect, be abandoning her attitude of suspicion towards the claims of the liberal and socialist state and entering into a partnership with it in promoting a new phase in the life of society,"[124] lines presumably written with the West and the third world in mind but not unmindful of possible change within the Communist camp itself. We can say of the intellectual developments we have described that if the church succeeds in thoroughly assimilating them, she will place herself in a co-operative and creative relationship with all who share the contemporary experience. The church will bring her religious message, her tradition, and her wisdom into contact with all the authentic achievements of modernity. She will thereby be enabled to work together with the secular world for the solution of the tremendous problems of our age, problems upon whose solution the survival of humanity depends, while remaining herself a "sacrament or sign of intimate union with God and of the unity of all mankind."[125] In the realm of politics it has been said that the church has abandoned the "idea that she must resist those governing powers which she can no longer control."[126] In the realm of scholarship and science the church also is abandoning the idea of control and constraint; it is learning to live with the Socratic tension.

The position of the intellectual in the Catholic church has been completely altered. The present situation is an open-ended one; it is one of uncertain issue. Who can say where all this will end? Has the church started upon a course of deinstitutionalization that will lead to a new, more flexible, more adaptable, more creative, and more vital Catholicism? Is this deinstitutionalization the prelude to a new more appropriate institutionalization? Or has Catholicism entered upon a process of "self-liquidation"?[127] The present disarray in Catholic ranks shows signs pointing in both directions. In the midst of this risk and uncertainty, we see the tenuousness of faith exposed without the support of a traditional civilizational context. How will the Catholic intellectuals meet these new challenges? Will they prove themselves both creative and responsible? The answer to that question only they can give. Should they prove up to it they will be able in the words of Pope Paul VI to make their contribution to the creation of a "new humanism which will enable modern man to find himself anew by embracing the higher values of love and friendship, of prayer and contemplation."[128]

REFERENCES

1. Henri Daniel-Rops, *The Catholic Reformation* (Garden City, N.Y.: Image Books, Doubleday, 1964), II, 158, 163.

2. G. R. Cragg, *The Church and the Age of Reason, 1648-1789* (Baltimore: Penguin Books, 1966), p. 15.

3. Daniel-Rops, *The Catholic Reformation*, pp. 177, 163.

4. Philip Hughes, *The Church in Crisis: A History of the General Councils, 325-1870* (Garden City, N.Y.: Image Books, Doubleday, 1964), p. 352.

5. Cragg, *The Church and the Age of Reason*, p. 41.

6. Daniel-Rops, *The Catholic Reformation*, pp. 139-140; Bertrand Van Bilsen, *OFM, The Changing Church* (Pittsburgh: Duquesne University Press, 1966), p. 23.

7. Lord Acton, "The Vatican Council," in Lord Acton, *Essays on Freedom and Power* (New York: Meridian Books, 1955), p. 276.

8. George A. Lindbeck, *The Future of Roman Catholic Theology* (Philadelphia: Fortress Press, 1970), p. 4.

9. Alfred North Whitehead, *Science and the Modern World* (New York: New American Library, 1948), pp. 14, 10, 39.

10. Herbert Butterfield, *Origins of Modern Science, 1300-1800* (New York: Macmillan, 1951), p. 83.

11. Daniel-Rops, *The Catholic Reformation*, pp. 152ff.

12. Butterfield, *Origins of Modern Science*, p. 83.

13. Basil Willey, *The Seventeenth Century Background* (Garden City, N.Y.: Anchor Books, Doubleday, 1953), p. 96.

14. Whitehead, *Science and the Modern World*, p. 57.

15. F. L. Cross, ed., *The Oxford Dictionary of the Christian Church* (London, New York, Toronto: Oxford University Press, 1963), p. 118.

16. Butterfield, *Origins of Modern Science*, p. 83.

17. *Ibid.*, pp. 127-128.

18. Bernard Groethuysen, *The Bourgeois: Catholicism versus Capitalism in Nineteenth Century France* (New York, Chicago, San Francisco: Holt, Rinehart and Winston, 1968), pp. 5-6, 7, 139, 181, 233.

19. Butterfield, *Origins of Modern Science*, p. 124.

20. Giogia Di Santillana, *The Crime of Galileo* (Chicago: University of Chicago Press, 1955), p. 118.

21. Charles Journet, *The Church of the Word Incarnate* (New York: Sheed and Ward, 1955), I, 355.

22. Santillana, *The Crime of Galileo*, p. 310.

23. Lecomte du Nouy, *The Road to Reason*, trans. and ed. Mary Lecomte du Nouy (New York: Longmans, 1948), p. 208.

24. Henri Daniel-Rops, *The Church in an Age of Revolution* (Garden City, N.Y.: Image Books, Doubleday, 1967), I, 21.

25. E. E. Y. Hales, *The Catholic Church in the Modern World* (Garden City, N.Y.: Image Books, Doubleday, 1958), quoting volume 20 of Jean Leflon's *Histoire de l'Eglise* (Paris, 1951), p. 29; Alec R. Vidler, *The Church in an Age of Revolution* (Baltimore: Penguin Books, 1961), p. 13.

26. Daniel-Rops, *The Church in an Age of Revolution*, p. 54.

27. Benedetto Croce, *History of Europe in the Nineteenth Century*, trans. Henry Furst (New York: Harcourt, Brace, 1963), pp. 23-24.

28. The following summary is based upon chapter 3 of Thomas F. O'Dea, *The Catholic Crisis* (Boston: Beacon Press, 1968) and Alec R. Vidler, *The Modernist Movement in the Roman Church* (Cambridge, Eng.: Cambridge University Press, 1934).

29. See E. E. Y. Hales, *Pio Nono* (Garden City, N.Y.: Image Books, Doubleday, 1962) and Alec R. Vidler, *The Church in an Age of Revolution* (Baltimore: Penguin Books, 1961).

30. See Hales, *Pio Nono,* and Daniel-Rops, *The Church in an Age of Revolution.*

31. Karl Polanyi, *The Great Transformation: The Political and Economic Origins of Our Time* (Boston: Beacon Press, 1957).

32. Hannah Arendt, *The Human Condition* (Garden City, N.Y.: Anchor Books, Doubleday, 1959), p. 252.

33. R. A. Dyson and R. A. F. MacKenzie, S.J., "Higher Criticism," in *A Catholic Commentary on Holy Scripture,* ed. Bernard Orchard, Edmund F. Suttcliffe, S.J., Reginald C. Fuller, and Ralph Russell (London and New York: Thomas Nelson and Sons, 1953), p. 63; Robert D. Cross, *The Emergence of a Liberal Catholicism in America* (Cambridge, Mass.: Harvard University Press, 1958), p. 215.

34. Acton, "The Vatican Council," p. 298.

35. "Pastoral Constitution on the Church in the Modern World" (*Gaudium et Spes*), article 36, Walter M. Abbott, S.J., and Very Rev. Msgr. Joseph Gallagher, eds., *The Documents of Vatican II* (New York: Guild Press, Association Press, 1966); Msgr. Pio Paschini, *Vita e Opere di Gelileo Galilei,* 2 vols. (Rome: Vatican Press, 1964); *Gaudium et Spes,* chaps. III and IV; Abbott and Gallagher, *Documents of Vatican II,* pp. 231-248.

36. See O'Dea, *The Catholic Crisis,* pp. 121ff.

37. Ernst Cassirer, *The Philosophy of the Enlightenment,* trans. Fritz C. A. Koelln and James P. Pettigrove (Boston: Beacon Press, 1951), p. xi.

38. Quoted by Theodore M. Greene, in his introduction to Immanuel Kant, *Religion Within the Limits of Reason Alone,* trans. Theodore and Hoyt H. Hudson (New York: Harper Torchbooks, Harper and Row, 1960), p. xxxvii.

39. Aristotle made the statement quoted at the beginning of the *Metaphysics.* T. S. Eliot, *The Cocktail Party.* For a discussion of the Socratic tension and how it operated in preconciliar American Catholicism see Thomas F. O'Dea, *American Catholic Dilemma* (New York: Sheed and Ward, 1957).

40. The term "plausibility structure" is taken from Peter L. Berger and Thomas Luckmann, *The Social Construction of Reality* (Garden City, N.Y.: Anchor Books, Doubleday, 1967).

41. See Rudolf Otto, *The Idea of the Holy*, trans. J. W. Harvey, 2d ed. (London: Oxford University Press, 1950); Mircea Eliade, *The Sacred and the Profane*, trans. Willard R. Trask (New York: Harcourt, Brace, 1959); and Emile Durkheim, *The Elementary Forms of Religious Life*, trans. Joseph Ward Swain (Glencoe, Ill.: Free Press, 1954).

42. Quoted from H. O. Taylor, *The Medieval Mind*, 4th American ed. (New York: Macmillan, 1925), I, 416-417.

43. Journet, *Church of the Word Incarnate*, p. 161.

44. Ludwig Ott, *Fundamentals of Catholic Dogma* (St. Louis: Herder, 1954), p. 251.

45. John L. McKenzie, S.J., *The Roman Catholic Church* (New York: Holt, Rinehart and Winston, 1969), p. 189.

46. "Dogmatic Constitution Concerning the Catholic Faith," Vatican Council I, Session III, April 24, 1870, quoted from the thirteenth edition of Henri Denziger's *Enchirodion Symbolorum (The Sources of Catholic Dogma)* (St. Louis and London: Herder, 1955).

47. Adolf Harnack, *What Is Christianity?* trans. Thomas Bailey Saunders (New York: Harper Torchbooks, Harper and Row, 1957), p. 212.

48. Werner Jaeger, *Early Christianity and Greek Paideia* (London, Oxford, New York: Oxford University Press, 1961).

49. David Tracy, *The Achievement of Bernard Lonergan* (New York: Herder and Herder, 1970), p. 255.

50. See Hans Jonas, *The Gnostic Religion: The Message of the Alien God and the Beginnings of Christianity*, 2d ed. (Boston: Beacon Press, 1963).

51. Adolph Harnack, *History of Dogma*, trans. Neil Buchanan (New York: Dover Publications, 1961), I, 228; Harnack, *What Is Christianity?* p. 207.

52. Philip Hughes, *A History of the Church* (New York: Sheed and Ward, 1952), II, 268.

53. The King James Bible stated Hebrews 11:1 in this way: "Now faith is the substance of things hoped for, the evidence of things unseen." The Revised Standard Version says: "Now faith is the assurance of things hoped for, the conviction of things not seen." Compare Romans 8:24-25: "hope that is seen is not hope. For who hopes for what he sees? But if we hope for what we do not see we wait for it with patience."

54. Saint Thomas Aquinas, *The Summa Theologica*, II, II, Question IV, article 1, quoted from *The Basic Writings of Saint Thomas Aquinas*, ed. Anton C. Pegis (New York: Random House, 1945), II, 1096; Question IV, article 2, pp. 1097-1098; Question IV, article 8, p. 1107.

55. Eric Voegelin, *The New Science of Politics* (Chicago and London: University of Chicago Press, 1952), p. 122.

56. See the interesting treatment of the closeness of faith and doubt in Paul Tillich, *Dynamics of Faith* (New York: Harper Torchbooks, Harper and Row, 1957).

57. See Thomas F. O'Dea, *Sociology and the Study of Religion: Theory, Research, Interpretation* (New York: Basic Books, 1970), pp. 240ff.

58. Etienne Gilson, *Reason and Revelation* (New York: Scribner's, 1938).

59. Adolph Harnack, *History of Dogma,* trans. Neil Buchanan (New York: Dover Publications, 1961), III, 146.

60. Ernst Troeltsch, *The Social Teaching of the Christian Churches,* trans. Olive Wyon (London: Allen and Unwin; New York: Macmillan, 1931), I, 142-143.

61. See Whitney J. Oates, *Basic Writings of Saint Augustine,* 2 vols. (New York: Random House, 1948).

62. Christopher Dawson, *The Crisis of Western Education* (Garden City, N.Y.: Image Books, Doubleday, 1965), p. 13.

63. Christopher Dawson, *Religion and the Rise of Western Culture* (Garden City, N.Y.: Image Books, Doubleday, 1958), p. 45.

64. It is interesting to note that Saint Bernard not only opposed the rationalism of Abelard but the aesthetic splendor of Cluny as well, which he saw from a highly puritanical perspective. "There appears on all sides so rich and amazing a variety of forms that it is more delightful to read the marble than the manuscripts and to spend the whole day in admiring these things, piece by piece, rather than in meditating on the Divine Law." Quoted from Kenneth Clarke, *Civilisation: A Personal View* (London: British Broadcasting Company and John Murray, 1971), p. 40.

65. Frederich Heer, *The Medieval World* (New York: New American Library, Mentor, 1963), p. 63.

66. Etienne Gilson, *History of Christian Philosophy in the Middle Ages* (New York: Random House, 1955), pp. 246ff.

67. Taylor, *The Medieval Mind,* II, 260ff.

68. See especially A. C. Crombie, *Medieval and Early Modern Science* (Garden City, N.Y.: Anchor Books, Doubleday, 1959), II, chap. 1; and Butterfield, *Origins of Modern Science,* chap. 1.

69. There were significant outside influences upon these developments, especially from the Muslim world. Indeed J. Ribera Y Tarrago, a Spanish scholar, has maintained that much in the medieval university was influenced by the educational system of the Arabs. See Heer, *The Medieval World,* p. 235.

70. Gilson, *History of Christian Philosophy,* p. 402.

71. *Ibid.,* pp. 405ff. The Omnibus Condemnation did not simply condemn Averroist propositions. At least twenty of those condemned were Thomist. Some of the condemned statements were of unknown and possibly oral origin and have a shockingly modern ring about them. For example, *quod lex christiana impedit addiscere* (The Christian religion is a hindrance to education), *quod fabulae et falsa in lege christiana, sicut in aliis* (There are myths and falsehoods in Christianity as in all religions), and *quod sermones theologi fundati sunt in fabulis* (What the theologians talk about is based upon myths).

72. See H. Richard Niebuhr, *Christ and Culture* (New York: Harper Torchbooks, Harper and Row, 1956), esp. chap. 1, pp. 1-44.

73. Dawson, *The Crisis of Western Education,* pp. 19-20.

74. See note 64 above.

75. Troeltsch, *Social Teaching of the Christian Churches,* I, 96.

76. Dawson, *Crisis of Western Education,* pp. 22-23. Among these were Conon of Bethune, Thibaut of Champagne, John of Joinville, Geoffrey de Villhardouin, Wolfrom von Eschenbach, Snorri Sturlason, and Walter von der Wogelweide.

77. On attached and unattached intellectuals see Robert K. Merton, *Social Theory and Social Structure: Toward the Codification of Theory and Research* (Glencoe, Ill.: Free Press, 1949), pp. 161ff. It is interesting that university faculty are considered "unattached." See note 7 on page 385.

78. This situation is changing rapidly at the present time. See the final section of this essay.

79. Max Weber, *The City* (Glencoe, Ill.: Free Press, 1958); Lewis Mumford, *The City in History: Its Origins, Its Transformations* (New York: Harcourt, Brace, 1961); and Henri Pirenne, *Medieval Cities* (Garden City, N.Y.: Anchor Books, Doubleday, 1965).

80. See Amintore Fanfani, *Catholicism, Protestantism and Capitalism* (London: Sheed and Ward, 1935); and R. H. Tawney, *Religion and the Rise of Capitalism* (New York: Penguin Books, 1947).

81. See especially Pirenne, *Medieval Cities.*

82. Yves M. J. Congar, O.P., *Lay People in the Church,* trans. Donald Attwater (Westminster, Md.: Newman Press, 1957), pp. 33, 19.

83. Gilson, *History of Christian Philosophy,* pp. 524ff, 489ff.

84. E. H. Wilkins, *The Life of Petrarch* (Chicago: University of Chicago Press, 1961).

85. Johan Huizinga, *Erasmus and the Age of the Reformation* (New York: Harper Torchbooks, Harper and Row, 1957).

86. See the discussion of the "healthy unadjustment" characteristic of the relation between religions of transcendence and the "world," in O'Dea, *Sociology and the Study of Religion,* pp. 55ff.

87. See Bernard J. F. Lonergan, *Insight: A Study of Human Understanding* (London and New York: Longman's and Philosophical Library, 1957), chap. VI on the Biological, Aesthetic, Intellectual and Dramatic Patterns of Experience, pp. 181-190; Christopher Dawson, *Progress and Religion* (Garden City, N.Y.: Image Books, Doubleday, 1960), Part II, chaps. V and VI; Eric Voegelin, *Israel and Revelation* and *The World of the Polis,* vols. I and II of *Order and History* (Baton Rouge, La.: University of Louisiana Press, 1956 and 1957); Talcott Parsons, *Societies: Evolutionary and Comparative Perspectives* (Englewood Cliffs, N.J.: Prentice-Hall, 1966); and Robert N. Bellah, "Religious Evolution," *American Sociological Review* (June 1964).

88. See, for example, Tawney, *Religion and the Rise of Capitalism.*

89. "Great as the achievements of axial religion were, lasting as their influence remains, they rested in some degree on illusion. The type of personality they sought to impress on mankind as a whole is not, in fact, a universal one. In its over-

emphasis of the 'cerebral' and spiritual, the axial personality is a valuable corrective to the extraversion and shallowness of more common types: but it is not, in its isolated perfection, a sufficiently representative ideal of human potentiality, for it rejects too much that is needed for full human growth." Lewis Mumford, *The Transformations of Man* (New York: Harper and Row, 1956). Who can doubt the reality of the problem propounded here? Who also can doubt the deleterious effects of overinstitutionalization on the whole problem as it existed in European history. See O'Dea, *Sociology and the Study of Religion*, pp. 240-270.

90. Ernst Troeltsch, *Protestantism and Progress: A Historical Study of the Relation of Protestantism to the Modern World* (Boston: Beacon Press, 1958), pp. 85ff.

91. Karl Mannheim, *Ideology and Utopia* (New York: Harcourt, Brace, 1949), p. 10.

92. Cragg, *The Church and the Age of Reason*, pp. 235ff.

93. As quoted in Thomas Molnar, *The Decline of the Intellectual* (Cleveland and New York: Meridian, World Publishing Company, 1961), p. 48.

94. Cragg, *The Church and the Age of Reason*, p. 241.

95. See Arendt, *The Human Condition*, pp. 225ff.

96. Cragg, *The Church and the Age of Reason*, pp. 241, 240.

97. Dawson, *The Crisis of Western Education*, p. 48.

98. Cragg, *The Church and the Age of Reason*, p. 246.

99. Molnar, *Decline of the Intellectual*, p. 57.

100. Croce, *History of Europe in the Nineteenth Century*, pp. 20ff.

101. Karl Marx and Friedrich Engels, *The Communist Manifesto*, quoted from Emile Burns, ed., *Handbook of Marxism* (New York: International Publishers, 1935), p. 59.

102. Karl Marx, "Theses on Feuerbach," quoted from Burns, ed., *Handbook of Marxism*, p. 231.

103. Walter H. Capps, ed., *The Future of Hope* (Philadelphia: Fortress Press, 1970), pp. 32ff.

104. See Norman Cohn, *The Pursuit of the Millennium* (New York: Harper Torchbooks, Harper and Row, 1961).

105. Voegelin, *New Science of Politics*, p. 129.

106. Karl Marx and Friedrich Engels, *On Religion* (New York: Schocken Books, 1964), p. 15.

107. E. E. Y. Hales, *Pope John and His Revolution?* (Garden City, N.Y.: Image Books, Doubleday, 1965), p. 50.

108. Roger Aubert, "The Catholic Church," in Guy S. Metraux and François Crouzet, eds., *Religion and the Promise of the Twentieth Century* (New York: New American Library, 1965), pp. 66-67.

109. There are many important names associated with this effort—Lamennais, Lacordaire, Montalembert, Mohler, Dollinger, D'Hulst, Acton, Murri, Sturzo, Sagnier, Loisy, Tyrrel, Blondel, and so forth.

110. See, for example, C. P. Snow, *The Two Cultures and the Scientific Revolution* (New York: Cambridge University Press, 1962).

111. Arendt, *The Human Condition,* p. 237.

112. Paul Tillich, *The Courage To Be* (New Haven: Yale University Press, 1952), pp. 46ff, 139ff.

113. Davis Tracy, *The Achievement of Bernard Lonergan* (New York: Herder and Herder, 1970), p. 193.

114. Hales, *Pope John,* p. 56. Hales points out how John extended the idea "human right, of what is necessary to the development of human personality" that he got from Leo XIII's *Rerum Novarum* (1891) and extended it so far "that not only Leo, but Pius XI or Pius XII would have been astonished by the claims he was making." Hales, *Pope John,* p. 57.

115. John XXIII, *Pacem in Terris,* paragraph 127.

116. *Ibid.,* paragraph 14, National Catholic Welfare Conference edition quoted. See also the Vatican II documents which carry forward these policies. First of all is the *Gaudium et Spes* which gives a major restructuring of the position of the church in the modern world. Like the encyclicals of John it is optimistic and confident and expresses openness. The church becomes once again positively related to the venture of modern man. See also the Dogmatic Constitution on the Church which defines the church as a "pilgrim people," a definition more in accord with the changed conception of the church's relation to the world. Also there are the "Declaration on Religious Freedom," and the "Declaration on the Relationship of the Church to Non-Christian Religions," which set forth new positions. See Abbott and Gallagher, *Documents of Vatican II,* pp. 199ff, 14ff, 675ff, 660ff.

117. John XXIII, *Pacem in Terris,* paragraphs 157, 158, 60.

118. "Pastoral Constitution on the Church in the Modern World," articles 4, 5, 10, 6, 7, 9.

119. John Henry Cardinal Newman, *The Idea of a University* (Garden City, N.Y.: Image Books, Doubleday, 1962), p. 429.

120. See the excellent summary of Catholic theology in its contemporary situation by Daniel J. O'Hanlon, "Concluding Reflections," in Donald J. Wolf, S.J., and James V. Schall, S.J., eds., *Current Trends in Theology* (Garden City, N.Y.: Image Books, Doubleday, 1966), pp. 259-265.

121. On this topic see Leslie Dewart, *The Future of Belief: On Theism in a World Come of Age* (New York: Herder and Herder, 1966); also Leslie Dewart, "God and the Supernatural," Bernard J. F. Lonergan, "The Dehellenization of Dogma," and Justus George Lawler, "The Future of Belief Debate," in Martin E. Marty and Dean G. Peerman, *New Theology,* no. 5 (New York: Macmillan, 1968), pp. 142-190.

122. John L. McKenzie, S.J., "Authority Crisis in Roman Catholicism," in Clyde L. Manschreck, ed., *Erosion of Authority* (Nashville and New York: Abingdon Press, 1971), pp. 37-58.

123. Jacques Maritain, *The Peasant of the Garonne* (New York: Holt, Rinehart and Winston, 1968), p. 162.

124. Hales, *Pope John,* p. 61.

125. *De Ecclesia,* article 1. See Thomas F. O'Dea, "The Church as *Sacramentum Mundi,*" in *Concilium,* vol. 8, no. 6 (October 1970).

126. Hales, *Pope John,* p. 61.

127. For an interesting discussion of the self-defeating elements in many Christian attempts to come to terms with secularization and the profoundly upsetting character of secularization and pluralism for the churches on a deeper level, see Peter L. Berger, *The Sacred Canopy: Elements of a Sociological Theory of Religion* (Garden City, N.Y.: Doubleday, 1967), part II.

128. Pope Paul VI, *Populorum Progressio (On the Development of Peoples),* United States Catholic Conference edition (Washington, D.C., 1967), paragraph 20.

Notes on Contributors

ROBERT N. BELLAH, born in 1927, is Ford Professor of Sociology and Comparative Studies and chairman of the Center for Japanese and Korean Studies at the University of California, Berkeley. He is the author of *Tokugawa Religion* (New York, 1957), *Beyond Belief* (New York, 1970), and "Continuity and Change in Japanese Society," in Bernard Barber and Alex Inkeles, eds., *Stability and Social Change* (Boston, 1971).

MICHAEL CONFINO, born in 1926, is professor of Russian history and director of the Russian and East European Research Center at Tel Aviv University. He is the author of *Domaines et seigneurs en Russie au 18e s. Etude de structures agraires et de mentalités économiques* (Paris, 1963), *Systèmes agraires et progrès agricole aux 18e-19e s. en Russie. Etude de sociologie et d'économie rurales* (Paris, 1969), and numerous articles on the Russian nobility and peasantry, intellectual history, and Russian anarchism.

S. N. EISENSTADT, born in 1923, is professor of sociology at Hebrew University, Jerusalem. He is the author of *From Generation to Generation* (Glencoe, Ill., 1956), *The Political Systems of Empires* (New York, 1963), *Modernization, Protest and Change* (Englewood Cliffs, N.J., 1966), *Israeli Society* (London, 1968), *The Protestant Ethic and Modernization* (New York, 1968), *Political Sociology* (New York, 1971), *Social Differentiation and Stratification* (Glenview, Ill., 1971).

THOMAS F. O'DEA, born in 1915, is professor of sociology and religious studies at the University of California, Santa Barbara. He is the author of *The Mormons* (Chicago, 1957), *American Catholic Dilemma* (New York, 1958), *The Sociology of Religion* (Englewood Cliffs, N.J., 1966), *The Catholic Crisis* (Boston, 1968), *Alienation, Atheism and the Religious Crisis* (New York, 1969), *Sociology and the Study of Religion* (New York, 1970).

BENJAMIN I. SCHWARTZ, born in 1916, is professor of history and government at Harvard University. He is the author of *Chinese Communism and the Rise of Mao* (Cambridge, Mass., 1951), *In Search of Wealth and Power: Yen Fu and the West* (Cambridge, Mass., 1964), and *Communism and China: Ideology in Flux* (Cambridge, Mass., 1968).

EDWARD SHILS, born in 1911, is professor of sociology and social thought at the University of Chicago and a Fellow of Peterhouse, Cambridge University. He is the author of *The Present State of American Sociology* (Glencoe, Ill., 1948), *The Intellectual Between Tradition and Modernity* (The Hague, 1961), and *Selected Papers*, vol. I, *The Intellectuals and the Powers* (Chicago, 1972).

FREDERIC WAKEMAN, JR., born in 1937, is professor of Chinese history at the University of California, Berkeley. He is the author of *Strangers at the Gate: Social Disorder in South China* (Berkeley, 1966) and editor of *Nothing Concealed: Essays in Honor of Liu Yü-yün* (Taipei, 1970).

191

Intellectuals and Change

PART II

of

Intellectuals and Tradition

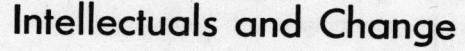

Intellectuals and Change

PART II

LESZEK KOŁAKOWSKI

Intellectuals Against Intellect

THE WHOLE of the spiritual and technological culture of our world is based on the belief in the *universality of Reason* in the *double meaning* of the word. The universality of Reason may mean, first, that the same rules of bivalent logic and the same rules of empirical verification are applicable to all questions that may occur to the human mind. Second, it may mean that the value of knowledge is determined *entirely* by the correct application of these rules, independent of its ethnic, social, religious, or psychological origin, and that all human beings are able, in principle, to think according to the same rules. This means that in all questions where the use of reason is possible, communication, discussion, and dialogue are also possible.

The belief in the universality of Reason in both senses came to articulation over centuries, slowly and not without difficulties. We find the full expression of this belief in the developed bourgeois culture of the seventeenth century. However, it must be noticed that the first form of the belief in the universality of Reason does not logically follow from the second; that is, one may, without contradiction, accept the second while rejecting the first. Criticism of the universality of Reason is sometimes directed toward the first and sometimes toward the second meaning, and the attacks are so differentiated in results and motivations that it is doubtful that we could give them a common historical meaning.

Criticism of the universality of Reason in the first sense, that is, criticism of the universal applicability of the rules of *positive* thinking, was associated with the defense of religious faith against rationalist and skeptical erosion. But its social sense is far from being always the same. Criticism of reason may be a defense of an establishment with ideological claims that must protect itself from rational skepticism. Criticism of reason may be a weapon of the oppressed and uneducated classes to whom the instruments of rational discussion are inaccessible; intellectual rigors, logic, and education itself, monopolized as they are by the privileged orders, often appear to these classes as a perfidious device of the devil. That is why they oppose their own spiritual poverty as a mark of superiority to the existing social order.

1

Every establishment protects itself against criticism, but not all need anti-intellectual ideologies for this purpose. Any criticism of the establishment is criticism of a certain consecrated tradition, but not all of them undermine the tradition of universalist rationalism. In the history of Christianity we find many examples of aggressive antirationalism that appears now as a tool of the conservative resistance of the ruling apparatus against the critique of intellectuals, now as a weapon of the unlettered exploited classes that assail the sanctified order together with its cultural and intellectual superstructure. Christianity has defined itself as opposed to secular and rationalist culture; it appeared as a movement of unenlightened people who have sanctified their own ignorance as the hallmark of a higher enlightenment whose origin is divine. At the same time, however, Christianity defined itself, in opposition to Jewish particularism, as a movement with universalist claims. This first ideological variant of Christianity, as articulated in Paul's letters, contained simultaneously vehement assaults against pagan intellectual culture and the belief in the basic unity of the human species—a position that was intended to serve and did effectively serve as an instrument of reconciliation with pagan culture. The history of Christianity considered from this standpoint is ambiguous: it marks a radical discontinuity with the foregoing culture while it maintains a belief in the unity of human nature sanctified in God, a belief that favors the acceptance of reason as a universal tool. That is why the assimilation of Greek culture started early and why the open hostility to reason, common to writers who represented "the plebeian side" of the Christian tradition, coexisted almost from the beginning with efforts of adaptation by those who looked to pagan culture as a natural preparation for the supernatural revolution, and who sought to adjust Christian ideas to the needs and level of the enlightened privileged classes.

This ambiguity—this belief in the basic discontinuity of human culture, interrupted in a miraculous way in the Resurrection of Christ, together with a belief in the basic goodness of human nature, involving a partial acceptance of pagan culture—is deeply rooted in Christianity. The whole of its history confirms this ambiguity. The moment a new urban culture arises, there is an unavoidable consequence: the emancipation of intellectuals. The Christian establishment begins by defending its anti-intellectual superiority over the new secular wisdom, but eventually it assimilates this wisdom, doing so with extraordinary ability, and making it an instrument of its own. In the eleventh-century controversy between dialecticians and antidialecticians we notice a situation that may never reappear with such sharpness of outline. Peter Damiani wrote in a small treatise, *De perfectione monachorum,* that monks who study secular science are like men who flee from an honest wife to a harlot. In the treatise *De sancta simplicitate scientiae inflanti anteponenda,* he observed that the devil was the first teacher of grammar since he taught our progenitors to inflect the word "God" in plural (*eritis sicut Dei*). His was an extremely well-aimed intuition. Four centuries later, from the end of the fifteenth to the end of the seventeenth centuries, grammarians were in the vanguard of the critical attack against tradition through their philological analysis of the Bible. The period from Antonio de Lebrixa and Erasmus to Spinoza and Richard Simon was one of the most important in the ideological corrosion of Christianity, whatever were the motivations of those who wrote in the way they did.

The open anti-intellectualism, protecting tradition against rational criticism, considerably weakened once Christianity succeeded in absorbing and assimilating in its own way the philosophical inheritance of antiquity, including the logical abilities that gave Christianity a weapon of its own. When the Thomist principle, holding that truth of faith is *supra non contra rationem*, prevailed within the Church, and the powers of logic were at the service of Orthodoxy as well as its critics, militant irrationalism was more often a weapon of the plebeian movements that fell on godless reason as an ally of social privilege. It was natural that in a situation where education was a privilege and rational philosophy and theology were used in ideological protection of that privilege, that reforming and revolutionary movements of the oppressed classes took the form of attacks against reason. Intellectuals who articulated this anti-intellectualism usually did not oppose Reason to Unreason, but contrasted the perverted human reason to the living faith of the regenerated. Savonarola was certain that any country gammer knew more than Plato and Aristotle since she knew what was most important and was inaccessible to pagan wisdom—she knew the Savior. Luther wrote that whoever tried to apply human logic to the Holy Trinity would unavoidably stop believing in it. Peter Gonesius, an ideologist of early Polish antitrinitarianism, stated that whoever deals with dialectics is the brother of the Turk.

The attacks of the Reformation on the value of Reason were in most cases limited; what mattered was not just any kind of intellectual activity but the scholastic techniques of validating faith with rational efforts, that is, the use of reason in religious questions. Criticism of the intellect that tries to inquire into divine secrets and that imagines it can really understand or justify the truth of faith was a consequence of a basic mistrust during the Reformation of human nature and human natural forces. This criticism was related to the idea of a democratic Church, a Church liberated from the distinction between an educated clergy and an ignorant crowd of believers who require a human mediator in their communication with God; in matters of faith all people are equally ignorant, or—what is the same—equally capable. To trust scholastic reason means to feed human pride; as such, this trust not only fails to support the believer in his faith, but actually perverts it. The simpletons' faith, that is indifferent to the subtle distinctions of theologians, and insensitive to the growing mass of arguments and counterarguments, resists temptation better than scholastic wisdom that holds up to ridicule the divine mysteries while trying to support them with its syllogisms.

To be sure, criticism of the universal applicability of reason is not a feature specific only to the Reformation. All variants of Christianity (except late deist doctrines that do not belong to any Orthodoxy) assumed that there were at least some elements of faith which could not be known except by revelation. Philosophers, however, differed widely about what in religion might be accessible to reason—from those who believed, as Anselm did, that almost everything in religion may have a rational validation, to those who rejected any rational justification in this domain. Christian mystic-pantheists, such as Meister Eckhart, or simple pantheists, such as Nicholas Cusanus, denied that there was any value in Aristotelian logic outside the finite world and argued that thinking about divine reality cannot be submitted to the principle of contradiction. Fourteenth-century nominalists rejected all attempts to turn faith into knowledge and so did their inheritors—the founders of the sixteenth-century Reformation. All later efforts to protect faith against rationalist criticism—from Pascal to Cardinal Newman—articulated different kinds of limitation in the universal applicability of scientific rules of thinking; philosophers who undertook these efforts tried to show that Reason was passing beyond its valid limits whenever it wanted to decide about questions properly reserved for the order of faith.

This kind of criticism of reason cannot properly be called anti-intellectualism. It is not criticism of the intellect but rather criticism of *scientism*, that is, criticism of the belief that all meaningful problems may be resolved with scientific methods, that their susceptibility to such solution properly defines the meaningfulness of problems, and that we must not profess any convictions which fail to keep this condition. In this century, criticism of the universality of Reason so conceived is a constant topic of philosophy and appears outside specifically religious thinking—in intuitionist philosophy, in *Lebensphilosophie* as a whole, and in existential meditation as well (especially in Karl Jaspers and Gabriel Marcel). The idea that analytical reason and the rigors produced by the sciences are inapplicable in the reflection about God, about human existence (in the peculiar existential meaning of the word existence), about Being as a whole transgressing the sum of particular beings, does not belong to the anti-intellectual but rather to the antiscientist tradition. Otherwise, everything in the history of culture that is not strictly in line with positivist scientism would be included under the rubric anti-intellectualism.

Criticism of the universal claims of analytical reason may be, and used to be, based upon rational arguments. A sharp distinction needs to be drawn between the criticism of the universal aspirations of analytical reason and the properly anti-intellectual criticism based on the idea that in questions where rational discussion and controversy are possible, final decisions depend on social, ethnic, religious, or psychological commitment, and that the object of conflicts is not truth in the current meaning but the function, value, or origin of ideas.

It is one thing to maintain that meditation on those aspects of existence which escape discursive thinking may be justified and fruitful; it is another to claim that in most important social, religious, or philosophical questions there are rights and wrongs founded not on arguments but on origin or function, and that a right of this kind may be imposed as a truth of a higher grade regardless of whether common ways of arguing are possible. In the first sense criticism of the universality of Reason is not necessarily dangerous to the culture, since it neither questions the possibility of dialogue nor denies the value of normal ways of arguing in domains accessible to scientific inquiry. Criticism of the universality of Reason in the second sense is dangerous. This second universalism assumes that all people participate in the same "rational nature," to speak in Aristotelian-scholastic language, or, to speak in a modernized way, that basic structures of thinking are qualities of the human species (without prejudging the origin of this identity), and that we are therefore allowed to believe in the continuity and universality of human spiritual culture that makes understanding possible and the ideas of criticism and tolerance rational. If the universalism of Reason in that version is undermined, fanaticism, intolerance, and refusal of discussion inevitably follow.

Certainly the distinction between these two kinds of attack against reason was not clearly articulated for a long time in the history of Christianity. At the time of the Reformation both kinds of criticism existed, interwoven in such a way that only analysis by a historian can separate them. Actually, the Reformers often criticized not only the attempts to apply logic and reason to questions reserved for faith, but the pagan culture as a whole. Precisely because it was pagan, they denied its intellectual and moral achievements; these derived from pagan, or "natural," sources and were not of divine inspiration. On this point the controversy between Erasmus and Luther is important. Dispute about the virtues of pagans—that is, about whether the moral values of the pre-Christian world were real values though they emanated from human natural forces (as Erasmus claimed)—was part of a larger dispute, which in philosophy was centered on the value of pagan philosophical thought and logic. Attitudes differed widely on this point. The extremists of the Reformation assumed that a pagan simply as pagan could not be right and that in stating this no further inquiry was needed, not unlike the statement that the demon is a liar by definition and therefore lies even when he tells the truth. Simplifying, we may say that the idea of the limited validity of reason, especially the rules that eliminated religious questions from the competence of analytical reason, were arising from the bourgeois culture within modern Christianity while

plebeian variants of Christianity were rather anti-intellectual in the proper
sense, that is, they rejected cultural continuity and all criteria—intellectual
or moral—that could claim universal validity and would be independent of
the opposition between paganism and Christianity.

The question of whether there are criteria for intellectual work that
are universally valid for all societies and all historical epochs is far from
being obsolete; on the contrary, we are witnessing its growing vitality in
this century. When Hugo Grotius, one of the outstanding minds of Christian bourgeois culture, wrote that there was a Christian theology, but no
Christian surgery, Christian geometry, or Christian political science, he was
articulating a problem that would revive in our own century in almost
exactly the same form. The oppositions "pagan-Christian," not unlike "Jew-
ish-Aryan," "bourgeois-proletarian," or "black-white," if they are taken to
cover the culture as a whole, and especially its intellectual values, serve to
raise questions about the cultural continuity of man and the unity of the
human species. The belief that these or similar oppositions are valid any-
where (needless to say, some are valid in certain domains of culture) is one
of the greatest dangers for humanity.

To be sure, the opposition between proletarian and bourgeois culture,
or rather between the culture of exploited classes and the exploiters, is not
absent in early variants of socialism. There is a striking similarity between
the mental structure found in the nineteenth-century anarchist movement,
in particular in Mikhail Bakunin and his followers, and that of various
plebeian Christian movements. Bakunin is not free from a certain inconsistency on this point. However, his idea of the "revolt of life against science," his attacks on universities as bulwarks of elitism, his faith in the
Lumpenproletariat as the leading force of revolution—all this forms a consistent whole. The Polish anarchist Jan Wacław Machajski (who wrote
principally in Russian) was even more radical in this respect than Bakunin.
He claimed that the Marxian idea of socialism was a product of particular
interests among the intelligentsia who aimed to take the place of the existing privileged classes and to preserve untouched the system of inequality
and exploitation. It was for this reason that the egalitarian society had to
begin by expropriating the capital of the intelligentsia, that capital being
knowledge. Knowledge, accessible only to the privileged minority, would
be a weapon in the struggle for privilege. One may find even stronger formulations of this idea in other, less known anarchist writers. Dislike for
intellectuals and for science is present also in other elements of the nineteenth-century workers movement, especially among the Proudhonists.

Georges Sorel, at the beginning of the twentieth century, formulated in
the clearest way the objections that the plebeian movement—the movement of the working class—needed to have to oppose the tradition of intellectualism and rationalism and intellectuals as such. They may be summarized briefly as follows:

First, intellectualism is unable to rise above the worship of utilitarian values; it shatters in a natural way traditional tribal solidarity, favoring the efficient and rational productive organization. Only within irrational tribal communities do the supreme human values flourish: devotion, heroism, contempt for immediate gain. Intellectualism views society through theories of social contract, variously formulated, and it is precisely for this reason that human dignity and spontaneous solidarity find no place among its views.

Second, reason is a natural ally of determinist doctrines. It aims to grasp the world as a system essentially determined in its evolution by natural laws, thereby weakening human belief in the strength of will and the possibility of true creativity.

Third, intellectualism and reason itself are natural allies of social reform against the idea of revolution. Partial changes and gradual reforms can be justified, foreseen, planned, and organized in a rational way, but the Apocalypse of the global revolution cannot look for support to rationalist doctrines and rational justification. It needs a myth, the only force capable of organizing the energy of the proletariat necessary for the struggle. One of the most important tasks of the proletariat is not to be blinded by the values of rationalist bourgeois culture—it must seek to escape the fate of Germans who sought learning from the conquered Romans and let themselves be dominated by their culture instead of overcoming it; it must escape the fate of the Reformation that in a similar way destroyed its own energy in assimilating the values of humanism.

Fourth, the values of intellectualism belong not only to the privileged classes but are themselves put at the service of the privileged, who assume that the highest human values are precisely those which can be shared only by a privileged elite. Hence, they sanctify inequality and oppression as necessary conditions for the flourishing of culture.

There are in Sorel's attacks some well-taken points that ought not to be disregarded. It is not only that the sets of values he opposed to each other have been contradictory throughout the history of culture. We cannot be certain whether they are not permanently contradictory, and whether a culture is possible that would be dominated entirely by this type of intellectualism Sorel fought against—a culture that would be scientistic and utilitarian in all respects. It is incontestable that intellectualism and the worship of reason are natural foes of the belief in the value of tradition; the link is obvious, it is confirmed historically, and is logically clear. But it is also incontestable that we can scarcely imagine how certain essential values, indispensable for society, can effectively survive without some form of cult to surround the tradition. It is obvious that, although the rationalist doctrine does not itself necessarily imply determinist belief, the psychological and historical link between the two is too strong to be considered unimportant. Rationalist ideologies are not simply affirmations of reason as a distinguishing mark of the human species; they have an inherent underlying belief in the unlimited capacity of reason to assimilate the world, a belief that in principle everything can be submitted to rational interpretation. Therefore, rationalist ideologies have a natural tendency to maintain that the world in all of its aspects is in principle predictable, and they are hostile to the idea of creativity (in the Bergsonian sense). Determinism is natural to rationalism. On the other hand, it may be a discouraging doctrine for those who wish to believe in the value of human initiative, irrespective of whether or not certain alleged historical laws guarantee its success. It is true that determinism was a part of Marxism in its evolutionist version, dominating in the period of the Second International, and that many Marxist theorists of that time (George Plekhanov, Karl Kautsky, Antonio Labriola) tried to show that historical determinism did not contradict the need for individual engagement; on the contrary, that it furnished the strongest reason for such engagement, giving the fighters a certitude that history was on their side (or, at least that they were on the side of history). In this respect, however, Antonio Gramsci's idea seems to be more accurate—that belief in the historical laws which guarantee victory to the struggling proletariat is rather the expression of the fact that the proletariat is still a class incapable of independent initiative and requires comfort in doctrines that promise victory than that it is an explicit appeal to struggle.

Whatever is correct in Sorel or in those anarchists with similar ideas can only be turned against the most expansionist version of intellectualism, against any ideology that assumes the reduction of all values to those accepted in the tradition of utilitarianism and the reduction of all admissible human convictions to those that fulfill conditions imposed by scientistic theories. But Sorel's appeals for a complete break with bourgeois culture— one of the reasons for the rather disgraceful success of his writings among Italian fascists—are by no means defensible by arguments which speak in favor of the value of tradition and of nonutilitarian virtues. That human reason must capitulate before certain questions that mankind cannot be rid of; that rational means do not allow for legitimizing the hopes that are needed for humanity; that universal determinism is an ideology as any other—these facts offer no justification for breaking the theme of cultural continuity. Sorel is only an example of the aberration to which intellectuals succumb when they succeed in persuading themselves that solidarity with the oppressed classes requires that they admire, not heal, what has been the great misfortune of these classes, their inability to participate in the development of spiritual culture.

It is incontestable that the position of intellectuals is a form of privilege, and that those who see their ideal in the absolute equality of mankind in every respect must demand the destruction of culture. If equality in every respect is the highest value, then the most important task of society is to press all people down to the level of its least enlightened parts. It resembles the ideal of certain eighteenth-century totalitarian utopias, the exact opposite of the doctrine Marx called scientific socialism. Marx sought to abolish privilege resulting from command over the means of production and to abolish also the privilege of education insofar as this was a consequence of the privilege of ownership; his purpose was to provide access to culture for everybody. That is why the cult of, and the striving for, knowledge were characteristic traits of the labor movement at the time that it was under the strong influence of Marxian theory. Movements which propagated equality in all respects as their principal ideal aimed at a very different end; their purpose was to liquidate rather than to spread culture and knowledge. Even if we believed in Trotsky's prophecy that in a socialist world everybody would be able to achieve the spiritual level of Aristotle, Goethe, and Marx, we would assume that to achieve this ideal the unenlightened strata of the population would have to rise first to the level of its present elites, and, then, that cultural differences would exist for a long time, the abolished inequalities in ownership notwithstanding. This obviously contradicts the ideals of anarchism and all those other socialist utopias that have had envy rather than a striving for justice as their underlying motivation and that put forward as their aim the pulling down of the whole of mankind to the level of its most ignorant strata, thereby glorifying illiteracy as a proper road to the liberation of humanity.

This kind of mentality appears to be spreading in our culture. It has always depended on the obviously reasonable observation that spiritual culture is linked to material privilege. Indeed, throughout human history inequality and exploitation have been the source of cultural progress or—what is much the same—the condition of culture was the free time that a minority enjoyed because it was denied to the majority.

Certain formulations of Marx suggest that he believed in the particular class character of the culture as a whole. It is certain, however, that Marxism, in its fundamental presuppositions, conceives of socialism as a continuation of the spiritual work of mankind, as the inheritor and not the destroyer of the existing bourgeois culture, in its intellectual, artistic, and technological dimensions. To the overwhelming majority of intellectuals in the last decades of the nineteenth century and the first two decades of this century access to Marxian socialism was access to universal culture. Socialism presented itself as a carrier of spiritual universalism, and so did Marxism, conceived as the ideological and theoretical articulation of socialism. To the intellectuals of the Second International (with a few exceptions), being a socialist or being committed to the cause of the working class did not mean being an advocate of an essentially different culture which broke the spiritual continuity of humanity and which had different rules of thinking and different moral values. On the contrary, it was a proletariat which—conforming to Marx's idea—had to be the spiritual inheritor of everything that the privileged classes had created, that they had kept as their privilege, and that they were no longer capable of preserving. There was no question of an essentially different "proletarian culture" opposed as a whole to the "bourgeois culture" and to bourgeois values.

In this respect the Russian Left of the Second International also shared this essential belief in the continuity of culture. It is confirmed by the clearly unsympathetic attitude of both Lenin and Trotsky toward the theory and practice of Soviet "Proletcult." That belief assumed that the proletariat in power, instead of assimilating and enriching the achievements of the existing culture, would create from nothing, by virtue of its peculiar mission, an essentially different culture of its own in which all previous institutional forms of social life as well as all earlier criteria of intellectual and artistic valuation would lose their validity. Proletcult was a barren formation; it remained as a historical curiosity without leaving any value that would be worthy of notice. However, its liquidation came less as the result of the triumph of the traditional socialist idea of cultural universalism and more as the result of the growing nationalist character of the new Soviet state. This state, rather than serving as the carrier of universalism, became a continuation of Great-Russian chauvinism. As such, Soviet culture admitted the principle of selective cultural continuity while virtually limiting that continuity to specific Russian features that began to be proclaimed as the supreme incorporation of the new socialist culture. Specifically socialist canons of art appeared to be, in the Stalinist period, dogmatization of the petit bourgeois tastes of the new privileged class, which cut itself off almost completely from the bourgeois tradition of the West.

This fact, so obvious today, was by no means so clear during the prewar years. That is why many Western intellectuals—especially during the years of the Great Depression and the fascist threat—still motivated by traditional ideas of universalism, supported Marxism and socialism, and saw the Soviet Union as its principal carrier. The need to believe in the existence of a movement representing this universalism was of such extraordinary strength that it blinded even the most outstanding minds to facts that —it seems now—ought to have been apparent to the most superficial observer. From the present perspective the reaction of many Western intellectuals to the Moscow trials, for example, seems unbelievable. These clumsy, fantastic spectacles, full of contradictions, where stupidity, cruelty, and lies seemed to cry for the vengeance of heaven, gained the support or sympathy of people like Romain Rolland, Henri Barbusse, Bertolt Brecht, and Leon Feuchtwanger. It is impossible today to read without horror the panegyric of Sidney and Beatrice Webb—brilliant and incorruptible beyond doubt— who, in the days of the most ferocious Stalinist terror, glorified the democratic Soviet regime and proclaimed its superiority over the British democracy. This blindness, unbelievable as it seems today, emanated from a desire to believe that there was still on earth a power representing or embodying traditional longing for cultural universalism whose agent would be the working class. These were unforgivable and fantastic mistakes, but anti-intellectualism was not necessarily involved in the attitude.

Of a quite different character were the conversions of intellectuals to Hitlerism or Stalinism, which were conscious conversions to barbarism, known and accepted as such. In fact, there were virtually no other kinds of conversions to Hitlerism, since it had no such phraseological veil inherited from universalist tradition as Stalinism used to exploit. Moreover, Stalinism also attracted some people as an embodiment of Marxist universalism, and tempted others as a march of the "splendid Asiatics" called to destroy decaying European civilization. There remains something enigmatic in the problem of conversions of the latter kind, not unlike the problem of active Hitlerites in intellectual circles. Our generation, which has seen the fall of men of such caliber as Knut Hamsun or Gerhart Hauptmann, which reads texts of Martin Heidegger putting his metaphysics at the service of fanatical criminals, during the life of which Nobel prize winner Philipp Lenard wrote his famous racist *German Physics*—this generation cannot be satisfied with the simple (and true) statement that every system and every movement finds intellectuals to serve it. It seems, as it were, that in many intellectuals there is something like "Naphta's component" (from *The Enchanted Mountain*): an independent intelligence impeded by its own independence and looking for an authority originating in other, nonintellectual sources. The fascination by barbarity, the cult of force, and the cult of authority are not new inventions among intellectuals. We observe similar cases in the history of early conversions to Christianity among Roman intellectuals; they acceded to the new faith aware of its primitivism and accepted it as such, feeling that they voluntarily submitted to a supreme authority, ashamed, so to speak, of their own human wisdom and ready to renounce it on behalf of "the madness of faith." The period of the Reformation and Counter Reformation furnish examples of similar attitudes. When studying the religious history of the seventeenth century, for instance, I was struck by the fact that an obscure French prophetess, a complete ignorant, Antoinette Bourignon, was suddenly acknowledged as an incorporation of the supreme divine wisdom. She was thought to be a spiritual authority, and acknowledged as such by men from the highest intellectual elite of Europe, including Johannes Komensky, Jan Swammerdam, and Pierre Poiret. The attitude of Florentine humanists toward Savonarola was similar. We may explain conversions of this type, in psychoanalytic terms, as a vengeance of id upon the excessively developed ego or, in social terms, as a result of the alienation that almost every intellectual experiences and that forces him to look for community other than the elitist République des Lettres, giving him the sense of confidence, spiritual security, and authority that is lacking in intellectual work. Whatever the explanation, one may be sure that any religious or social movement representing the most aggressive anti-intellectualism will find the enthusiastic support of a certain number of intellectuals brought up in Western bourgeois civilization who ostentatiously discard its values to humble themselves before the splendor of a sound barbarism.

Socialism of the Soviet brand is no longer a center of attraction for conversions of this type. It has been replaced by Maoism and the cult of backward countries, the latter, for some intellectuals, being saviors who are showing new ways to humanity. It seems almost incredible that the cult of primitivism combined with the belief in the revival of mankind through its least developed segments should commonly appear under the label of Marxism. I do not maintain that there is only a single "genuine" Marxism and that the others are "distorted" or "falsified"; on the contrary, I think that there are several incompatible versions or varieties of Marxism that can lay claim to continuing in certain respects the Marxian tradition. Nevertheless, there is no doubt that certain elements of the Marxian vision of the world were formulated so clearly and belong so obviously to the very core of the doctrine that it is impossible to discard them and to maintain the pretense of being Marxist. The idea of Marx that the industrial proletariat of highly developed countries should be the vehicles for socialist transformations is one such central theme. One may believe that social developments in this century do not permit this hope to be maintained; but if this is so, then one must admit that Marxism is a doctrine inapplicable to the modern world and that it has nothing to offer us. It is a pure verbal game to give the name of Marxism to a statement that mankind will be liberated from oppression, exploitation, and misery thanks to masses of illiterate peasants from the most backward parts of the world. Marxism without the industrial proletariat is like Christianity without God, and though even that phenomenon exists nowadays, there is no reason to consider it as anything but a play on words.

Let us leave aside the unimportant problem of denominational labels. I maintain that contemporary conversions of intellectuals to Maoist or similar faiths cannot be interpreted simply as an act of solidarity with the poor and the oppressed, and that it is not to be compared with the assent that intellectuals, once upon a time, gave to traditional Marxism. The latter was access to a movement that seemed to represent the continuity of culture, a respect for knowledge, and a regard for intellectual values. The contemporary enthusiasm of intellectuals for peasant and *Lumpenproletarian* movements or for movements inspired by the ideology of national minorities is an enthusiasm for that which in these movements is reactionary and hostile to culture—for their contempt of knowledge, for the cult of violence, for the spirit of vengeance, for racism. Racism is still racism even when it is the racism of a discriminated minority, as is the case of certain forms of the American black movement. It is one thing to take the side of discriminated elements of mankind in their efforts to overcome misery and humiliation; it is another thing to support every form of barbarism and violence provided that these are carried out by the discriminated strata, and to proclaim as "progressive" every movement that claims to be an "enemy of the bourgeoisie." (Did not the fascist movements also often draw their energy from the revolt of the discriminated *Lumpenproletariat* and use antibourgeois phraseology?) It is one thing to criticize Western democracies because of exploitation of poor countries or because of their inefficiency in coping with the misery of the third world; it is another thing to make of this criticism the pretext for admiring the most obscure dictatorships, provided only that they threaten the white world with destruction. It is one thing to fight for equal rights in education and another to kneel before black racists who stigmatize the existing intellectual tradition as "irrelevant white knowledge" (as stated in the proclamation of the Black Students Union), and to see a mark of particular supremacy in the cultural backwardness of the black population. Certainly, one cannot completely exclude the possibility that contemporary admirers of barbarism represent a real tendency in the historical process and that all the technological and spiritual achievements of modern times will be destroyed in an unprecedented cataclysm, compared to which the fall of the Roman Empire will seem a trivial stumble, and that the surviving part of mankind will, for centuries, be thrown into primitivism and misery. Such apocalyptic visions excite the childish imaginations of certain intellectuals, but they have little to do with the idea of helping oppressed and suffering humanity.

We have now, in the light of twentieth-century ethnological inquiry, good reason to presume that basic patterns of thinking are invariable throughout the history of the human species, and that they are independent of the vicissitudes of human civilizations. It is irrelevant in this context, important though it might be from a philosophical standpoint, how this universality may be explained: by genetic circumstances (it may be argued, for example, that basic rules of probabilistic thinking simply articulate the way the conditional reflexes are produced and extinguished); by the nature of language; by divine will; or by the structure of transcendental rationality. However, even if these basic patterns are common to people of all cultures and all ages, the same cannot be said about the *awareness* of this universality. From the fact that we share the same logic, it does not automatically follow that we know we do. On the contrary, the awareness of such a community is the product of a particular culture and perhaps only a particular perspective of that culture.

This awareness of universality being visible only from a particular perspective makes it difficult to separate the universal and the particular in our own consciousness, since to grasp our participation in universal patterns we are bound, perhaps, to belong to one particular civilization. Probably we would not be able to discover what is universally human in ourselves had we not lost, in general, belief in the superiority and exclusive value of our culture (though it is still ours). We imagine today that we are able to absorb specific values of all ages and all civilizations, that we can be at the same time Japanese of the twelfth century, Aztecs of the fifteenth century, ancient Greeks, Polynesians, and cave dwellers of Altamira. But this openness, this flexibility or ability to absorb, is a product of that unique civilization which produced a sort of indifference to its own specific values. Our universalism is another name for our indifference, for lack of belief in *any* specific cultural values. In cultures which did not articulate the universality of patterns of thinking (even if people actually were following them), the feeling of belonging to one's own culture could be much more total and all-embracing than it is for us. We usually make a distinction between the order of cognition and the order of values, between what is *true* (justified with the help of universal rules of deductive and probabilistic logic) and what is *valid* (what cannot be justified without appeal to tradition). However, this distinction cannot remove all doubts about what elements in our culture belong to what domain. This belief in the universality of certain cultural patterns (including patterns of thinking) runs against the need for "total commitment" or for "global belonging" to one particular culture or subculture or to a militant group (provided that the ideologies of a universally human cause are usually expressed also in groups with particular vested interests). Total commitment is difficult if we remain aware that we share with our enemies some basic values, even intellectual ones. The feeling of total commitment allows us to claim that what seems wrong from the standpoint of alleged universal criteria of thinking may be right or may turn out to be a higher truth from the perspective of supreme values. Strongly militant groups—be they religious or political, be they a threatened establishment or a revolutionary movement—often produce this tendency to deny any kind of universality. If all groups that need an ideology stressing such a denial find intellectuals responding to this demand, it may be partly explained by the peculiar social position of intellectuals themselves. In other words, it may be argued that intellectuals not only happen to express anti-intellectual tendencies arising in different milieus, but that their own situation produces this tendency as well. Precisely because social functions of intellectuals include the acceptance of universally valid patterns of thinking as obligatory norms, intellectuals are unable to constitute a group giving to its members that feeling of total commitment, or the sense of belonging that many religious and political groups are able to supply. Briefly, what is usually called the alienation of intellectuals, their often described feeling of being uprooted, of not belonging, may produce ideological needs which are expressed in joining and articulating anti-intellectual tendencies in existing movements.

This feeling of not belonging may be extremely strong and is produced not only by the peculiar situation of intellectuals, but also by all circumstances that make life in contemporary societies more and more dependent on rationally organized technological and administrative systems, which destroy all remnants of the tribal community and all village-like communication. The longing for global commitment and the desire to withdraw from a society where the communication is being carried out more and more through these intermediary systems are among the dominating motives of many philosophical, religious, political, and social phenomena in our culture. An individual may try to satisfy this need in different ways: in political participation, in mysticism, in drugs. (I do not suggest that all these kinds of commitments have the same social meaning or the same value, only that similar individual motivations may work in all of them.) Drugs may be a way of breaking the cultural continuity on an individual level, a desperate attempt to return to the lost union with the world, but the ideology of drugs may express some socially determined requirements for such a break. (One can hear American revolutionaries explaining that the American establishment is fighting against drugs for political reasons, because drugs enable people to get rid of the internalized values of the establishment, inoculated in education; the values and the ideas of the establishment are so deeply rooted and internalized that except for drugs there is apparently no other way of liberating oneself from them.)

Intellectuals are by no means called to govern the world. Their most important function is to maintain and to convey the accumulated stock of human spiritual culture as common stock; in other words, their work is meaningful only in terms of the assumption that despite all struggles and conflicts the human species participates in essentially the same intellectual structure, and that all the world's conflicts do not destroy the continuity and unity of human intellectual effort. The idea of the universality of Reason implies that the concept of *Truth* is different from the concept of *validity* as applied to values, institutions, mythologies, morals. It does not imply that the normative criteria of validity in other domains (in the realm of myth, among others) must not be employed, but it forbids *replacing* the criteria of truth by them. It forbids, briefly, replacing thinking by commitment. To violate this interdiction means what may properly be called the betrayal of intellectuals. The idea that mankind should "liberate" itself from its intellectual heritage and create a new "qualitatively different" science or logic is a support for obscurantist despotism.

MENAHEM MILSON

Medieval and Modern Intellectual Traditions in the Arab World

I

IN MEDIEVAL times the most important factor affecting the nature of intellectual traditions in the area now known as the Arab World was Islam. It should be noted therefore that the term "Arab World" used in the title of this essay reflects the modern situation which is discussed in part II.

The Supremacy of Religious Knowledge

Our discussion of intellectuals in Arab countries in the modern period must include some consideration of the intellectual elite in these countries in premodern times. The religious scholars, the 'ulama', comprised that elite. 'Ulama' is an Arabic word meaning "scholars" or, more precisely, "those possessed of knowledge" (in Arabic, 'ilm). The term 'ulama', however, came to signify quite early in the Muslim era "those possessed of *religious* knowledge," and it is in this sense that the term will be used throughout this paper.

Consideration of the 'ulama', their intellectual traditions and their social position, will afford us one necessary perspective for viewing the situation of the modern intelligentsia which has taken their place as the generally recognized intellectual elite in Arab countries. The inclusion of the 'ulama' in our purview is all the more important, since the 'ulama' retained their established position until the end of the nineteenth century.

The intellectual tradition of 'ulama' was multi-faceted, comprising methods of study and interpretation, rules of validation and refutation, criteria of excellence, and needless to say, a canon of sacred texts, which were believed to be the source of all religious knowledge. The 'ulama' maintained special educational institutions—madrasas—for the transmission and further development of their intellectual traditions. To be sure, nonreligious sciences were also known and pursued in the Muslim world. Muslim writers in the Middle Ages distinguished between religious and nonrelig-

17

ious sciences. Sometimes the dichotomy was presented as religious or traditional, in contradistinction from philosophical, rational, or foreign.[1]

Because of the general religious bent of Islamic civilization, religious knowledge was given preference over other types of knowledge. As a covenantal religion, Islam's most important manifestation is the Sacred Law (the *shari'a*), which in theory is all-embracing. Consequently, jurisprudence (*fiqh*) occupies a central position among the religious sciences.

Abu Hamid al-Ghazali, one of the most authoritative Muslim scholars, draws up the order of priority of the various sciences; his views are very instructive for the discussion at hand.[2] Having established a broad division between praiseworthy or commendable knowledge and blameworthy or reprehensible knowledge, he proceeds to distinguish—within the category of praiseworthy knowledge—between various types of knowledge according to their inherent value. Of the highest value is religious knowledge (and especially knowledge of the religious law), for it constitutes a personal obligation[3]: every Muslim is required to acquire that religious knowledge which is relevant to the occasion.[4]

Next in order of value comes knowledge which is considered a collective or communal obligation[5]—that is, there should be a sufficient number of persons with this type of knowledge to meet the needs of society. Included in this category are medicine and mathematics. It is noteworthy that Ghazali gives as the reason for the "communal obligation" to possess mathematical knowledge the fact that it is needed to implement the requirements of religious law in certain matters, such as division of estates and bequests and other business transactions.

Third in order of value is that knowledge which, though praiseworthy, is not included in the obligatory category, and is thus supererogatory. According to Ghazali that class includes "penetrating deeply into the subtle points of mathematics and the innermost truths of medicine and the like, *which can be dispensed with;* nevertheless, this [kind of knowledge] has the benefit of adding to the capacity in the required matter."[6]

The order of value seems clear: the nonreligious sciences are considered necessary only as *applied* sciences and derive their value from advancing the objectives of religious law. The value of pure or basic research is subsumed under applied science, which is itself subservient to religion. This order of priority, expressed by Ghazali as theological doctrine, had concrete social consequences; it was reflected in the predominance of the *'ulama'* as the uncontested intellectual elite in Islamic society. The centrality of religious knowledge (with jurisprudence as its axis) is demonstrated by the fact that many Muslim scholars who were creative in the nonreligious sciences also engaged in the religious sciences and often held prominent positions as *'ulama'*.

This is true mostly with respect to scholars in the "Arabian" sciences, because these sciences, though nonreligious, were nevertheless considered indigenous and were incorporated in the intellectual traditions of the *'ulama'*.[7] Still more remarkable is the fact that this was occasionally the case with scholars of the "rational-foreign" sciences.[8]

The inferior status of the nonreligious, "foreign" heritage—a phenomenon which was correlated with the supremacy of the *'ulama'* tradition—resulted in the decline of the "philosophical" or "rational" sciences.[9]

Scholars and Princes

A popularly held notion is that in Islam church and state are one. Insofar as this phrase means that the only truly Islamic political community is the *umma,* the community of believers, it is true. However, using the Western terms "church" and "state" one may be misled into thinking that the ruling institution and the religious institution are intermixed or are one and the same, and that is far from true.

Some historical studies point out that the *'ulama'* quite consciously and deliberately kept apart from the political institution.[10] This process of separation began quite early in Islamic history, probably immediately after the period of the Righteous Caliphs—the first four successors of the Prophet Muhammad (632-661). Following these caliphs, political power and the religious intellectual elite parted ways. At first this separation was not quite conscious and for a while some religious scholars did not give up hope of influencing the strictly political spheres of life. However, later on, in the Abbasid period, this separation became clear and the religious scholars recognized the situation and even preferred it. The religious scholars realized that by remaining detached from the actual exercise of political power, they retained prestige without becoming contaminated by the faults of the princes and therefore could better cultivate their intellectual traditions. A tacit concordat seems to have evolved between the *'ulama'* and the princes. Certain spheres of influence were left in the hands of the religious scholars, such as the regulation of all matters relating to personal status, moral behavior, and education. Other more strictly political matters were left to the princes: foreign policy, taxation, jurisdiction over criminal affairs. These matters were not considered under the jurisdiction of the *'ulama',* even though theoretically the *'ulama'* as representatives of the Holy Law, the *shari'a,* should have a say over every aspect of life.

This type of concordat made it possible for the rulers, on the one hand, and the *'ulama',* on the other, to cooperate for many centuries. A symbiotic relationship evolved between the two institutions, cooperating but distinct. The *'ulama'* legitimized the power of the Muslim rulers, who, for their part, recognized the supremacy of the Sacred Law.

In return, the *'ulama'* were allowed to exercise their influence in certain spheres and were also materially rewarded by having positions as judges in the courts and by receiving a share in various religious endowments. The *'ulama'* carefully tried to avoid direct involvement in politics and, as a result, a very strong tradition emerged in the Muslim world: the idea that worldly politics (in Arabic, *siyasa*) is essentially corrupt and contaminated by too many mundane considerations; hence scholars should be on guard against being tainted by excessive contact with the sultans. Related to this notion is another, the image of political power which evolved in Muslim tradition: namely, that such power rests basically on one sanction, military force. This notion is clear in the writings of al-Ghazali and of later writers[11] and may have persisted into the modern period. Still another concept which forms part of the tradition of the *'ulama'* is their self-image. The *'ulama'* are the guides of society. A saying which expresses this idea, and is ascribed to the Prophet Muhammad, is that "the *'ulama'* are the successors of the prophets." Another saying states, "Nothing is mightier than religious knowledge: kings have jurisdiction over people but the *'ulama'* have jurisdiction over kings." Notwithstanding the actual division of power between rulers and religious scholars, and the fact that the direct influence of the *'ulama'* was confined to well-defined spheres, the *'ulama'* viewed themselves as the guides of society, since their authority emanated from a higher source than that from which political power was derived, that is, the authority of the Holy Law.

The intellectual traditions of the *'ulama'* were enriched and expanded by additional cultural materials which, although of different origins and of another nature, were nevertheless adopted by the *'ulama'* and modified to accord with their traditions. This extension not only gave variety to their intellectual tradition, but also strengthened their social position, since it provided additional maneuverability and more opportunities for influence. The extension was in two directions. The *'ulama'* adopted and adapted within their own cultural framework another tradition—originally quite alien: namely, the literature about the education, etiquette, and ethics of the scribes at the Sassanid Court of Persia. In the early days of the Abbasids, during the reign of al-Mansur (745-775), the alien nature of that tradition was keenly felt, but within a few generations, religious scholars had absorbed and adapted many elements of this Sassanian court literature. This is clearly reflected in the writings of a religious scholar such as Ibn-Qutayba (d. 889), who manages to integrate this alien implant with Arab-Islamic tradition.[12]

This early association between religious scholarship and the education of the court scribe was of great importance, since thus, most of the persons trained in the tradition of the *'ulama'* were also conversant with the scribal arts and hence capable of filling positions in the bureaucratic hierarchy. We notice here a contradiction between the ideological position of the *'ulama'* on the one hand and the pressures of reality on the other. Although there was a very strong tradition that scholars should avoid excessive involvement in the ruling institution, throughout the Middle Ages one can find *'ulama'* occupying administrative positions in the service of Muslim rulers.[13] Later, in the Ottoman period, we find that many high positions in the administration (not exclusively in the juridical system) were still filled by persons trained in the *madrasas*.

In another direction, *'ulama'* tradition was extended to embrace the mystical tradition of the Sufis. Although these two strands in Islamic thought—the juristic and the mystical—represent two distinct types of religious approach, yet in reality they were not separate. This association, too, took place relatively early. The best-known representative of the integration of the two traditions is the aforementioned Ghazali (d. 1111), but this attitude of bridging the gap between the mystical and the juristic has its origins earlier in the history of Islamic thought. The great masters of Islamic mysticism—Junayd, Abu Talib al-Makki, Sulami,[14] to mention only a few—all insisted on the need to observe the Sacred Law and not to separate the mystical from the juridical. It is certainly no mere coincidence that the founders of the great Sufi orders (mystical brotherhoods) were also prominent teachers of jurisprudence. The founder of the Suhrawardi order, Abu al-Najib al-Suhrawardi (d. 1168), was a teacher of Shafi'i law. The founder of the Qadiri order, 'Abd al-Qadir al-Jilani (d. 1166), was an authority of the Hanbalite school of jurisprudence.

Withdrawal from worldly affairs is of course very important to the mystical outlook, and the association between the mystical tradition and that of the *'ulama'* may have reinforced a tendency already inherent in Islamic religious thought: namely, withdrawal from politics. On the other hand, Sufism exerted exceptional appeal upon the minds of the laity, and large numbers from all walks of life (including members of the ruling classes) joined the Sufi orders as "lay members." Consequently, Sufism reestablished some kind of community between rulers and ruled. Hence, the accommodation of Sufism by the *'ulama'* increased their influence over the masses.

In summary, the *'ulama'* had a very strong position as the representatives of the Sacred Law in a society dedicated to the realization of that law on earth. Their influence and status were greatly enhanced by the fact that their tradition included education for scribal offices (as previously stated, originating in foreign sources), so that they could supply administrative personnel. By incorporating the mystical approach into their religious outlook, they improved their capability to reach the uneducated laity and exerted strong moral influence upon them. Thus, even though they gave up the idea of directing the policies of the state, they were in a highly strategic position: placed, so to speak, between princes and masses, they served as intermediaries between the two groups. They were willing to legitimize the sultans and keep the masses docile, and did so, as long as the sultans allowed them to exercise that authority which they considered essential for maintaining the important elements of religious law and preserving the essentials of their way of life.

II

The following discussion deals with modern intellectual traditions in the Arab World, mainly as they are reflected in literature.

The Social Bases of Modern Arab Intellectual Tradition

Although modern Arab intellectuals are highly heterogeneous as a group in various aspects, such as religious origin, educational background, and political affiliation, they nevertheless seem to share some characteristic attitudes with regard to their society and to modern civilization. The present discussion is concerned with these common attitudes, which can be abstracted from their works. To be sure, the broader subject of Arab intellectuals in modern times also involves a study of (1) the various types of modern Arab intellectuals (namely, reformist *'ulama'*, Western educated Muslims, and Christian Arabs)[15] and (2) the specific circumstances in the various Arab countries which differ in regard to the pace of modernization. However, this certainly goes beyond the scope and purpose of the present essay, which is intended to deal with the major issues concerning Arab intellectuals in general.

The emergence of the modern Arab intellectual tradition came in response to the challenge posed by Western civilization to the Arabs (as well as to Muslim peoples in general). This challenge was a function of the military and political superiority displayed by European powers in relation to Muslim states and particularly to the Ottoman Empire. Napoleon's invasion of Egypt strikingly signaled that superiority, thus beginning a process of intervention and conquest called the Impact of the West.

In order to fully gauge the significance of that impact as perceived by Muslims, we must recapitulate the ideal collective self-image held by Muslims. This ideal self-image is based on the notion that God promised the Muslims victory and superior status in relation to other religious communities in this world. Islam was validated at the beginning of its history by means of the victory that Allah vouchsafed to the Prophet Muhammad's army at the Battle of Badr in 624, and that validation was repeatedly confirmed in a series of victories and conquests in the course of the first Islamic century. This story of success has become part of Islamic religious consciousness. The idea of Muslim superiority was particularly undermined in the second half of the nineteenth century, when the Ottoman Empire suffered various military setbacks at the hands of the Russians, and when Muslim countries in the Middle East fell under the domination of European Christian powers: Tunisia in 1881 under French rule and Egypt in 1882 under British rule. These events had an extremely unsettling effect upon the minds of Muslims; from the Muslim point of view, it seemed as though history had been deflected from its preordained course. In response, Arab-Muslim intellectuals asked certain questions and proposed some answers concerning the situation of their society in the modern world, thus laying the foundation of what we may call—to borrow a term from Edward Shils—the "original tradition" of modern Arab intellectuals. The realization of inferiority in power vis-à-vis Europe (or the West, or the Christian powers—as the other camp is variously defined) is the formative experience underlying the original tradition of modern Arab intellectuals.

The immediate aspect of the Western challenge was military and political; however, its cultural aspect soon became apparent as well, and has had more pervasive and lasting effects. Although Arab countries are no longer subjugated to European colonial powers, the sense of being in an inferior position persists. The continuation of that experience, which gave rise to the original tradition of modern Arab intellectuals at the end of the nineteenth century, may account for the fact that some of the central themes of that tradition persist in contemporary intellectual production.

To Muslim modernizers in the nineteenth century—of the ruling class and of the intellectual elite alike—it seemed that Europe possessed the secret of power. Hence, in order to regain lost power and glory, Muslim states had to emulate the European powers in military technology and methods of state administration. Muslim rulers, intent on effecting these modernization plans, set out to build Western-trained personnel, capable of carrying out such reforms. Thus, military and administrative reform prompted the emergence of a new educated elite.

Among those in the nineteenth century who called for modernization and contributed to the formation of the original tradition of modern Arab intellectuals, we find both members of the 'ulama' and members of the governing classes. An outstanding example of the first type is the Egyptian scholar and writer Rifa'a Rafi' al-Tahtawi (d. 1873).[16] Of the second type one should note the Tunisian statesman Khayr al-Din al-Tunisi (d. 1889).[17] Still faithful to the Islamic world-view, both Tahtawi and Khayr al-Din hoped that the 'ulama' would continue to play an important role as an intellectual elite, and they tried to convince them of the need for modernization.

In contradistinction from the attitudes which became predominant toward the end of the nineteenth century, the writings of Tahtawi and Khayr al-Din do not reflect that mixture of acute envy, hostility, and suspicion of the West which becomes a salient feature in the writings of modernizing intellectuals later in the nineteenth century. This is undoubtedly attributable to the fact that Tahtawi's and Khayr al-Din's attitudes toward European civilization were formed before the experience of European intervention and occupation in the 1870's and 1880's, which exacerbated suspicion of and hostility toward Europe.

Before we proceed to describe the characteristic features of the tradition

of modern Arab intellectuals, we must underline a fundamental fact,
namely, that the *ulama* as a group lost their position as an uncontested intellectual elite in the Arab world. When viewed in retrospect, the
ulama's loss of status appears to have been inevitable. However, throughout the nineteenth century this was not yet evident. The *ulama* were
involved in the "original tradition" of modern Arab intellectuals in two
ways: (1) some *ulama* (notably, Tahtawi and Muhammad 'Abduh)
played a leading role in laying the foundations of that tradition; (2) the
early modernizing intellectuals addressed themselves to two groups—rulers
and *ulama*. They attached particular importance to the attitudes of the
ulama in view of their position as spiritual leaders of society; they hoped
that the *ulama* would modernize themselves and thus lead their society to modernization. This hope, however, was not realized; the *ulama*,
as a group, were unable to modernize. There was a radical difference
between the moral and intellectual assumptions underlying modern civilization and the *ulama*'s belief system. But except for a few bold spirits, such
as Tahtawi and 'Abduh, the *ulama* responded to the challenge of modernity by withdrawing into a defensive conservatism. In the meantime, another
type of educated class evolved: the Westernized intelligentsia.[18]

The modern intelligentsia is different from the *ulama* also in its collective self-identity. In contrast with the *ulama*, who represent Islamic consciousness, the modern intelligentsia views itself as Arab. This is related, of
course, to the rise of Arab nationalism which came to replace the former
Islamic collective identity. The emergence and growth of Arab nationalism
and the various ways in which it replaced the earlier Islamic identity is
beyond the scope of this essay. However, it should be briefly noted that
this change from Islamic to Arab identity which took place among educated
Arabs in the Middle East was facilitated by the well-known close association between Arabism and Islam, an association harking back to the very
origins of the Islamic religion in Arabia.[19]

It should be noted that some intellectuals in the Arab countries have
propagated ideologies upholding nationalist identities other than Arab:
in Egypt, Egyptian nationalism and in Syria and Lebanon, Syrian nationalism. In both cases, an attempt was made to relate the particularist nationalist ideology to a national myth antedating the Islamic era. These ideologies
had little popular appeal and were swept aside by the tide of pan-Arab
nationalism. These particularist views, conflicting with the prevalent current
of opinion, have been submerged but not totally eliminated; they constitute
"small traditions" which may yet resurge. Small groups of intellectuals still
continue to favor "particularist" cultural identity, although this position is
not publicly acceptable.

The transition from Islamic to Arab identity was not immediate and
the early modernizing intellectuals such as Jamal al-Din al-Afghani and
'Abduh still speak in the name of an Islamic resurgence and Islamic unity,

but later on this changed. One of the factors inducing this change was the influence of the European notion of collective identity based on non-religious grounds. Secular nationalism was obviously "modern," and the modernizing intellectuals, by definition, preferred all that seemed modern. There were political developments, extraneous to the preferences of Arab intellectuals, which also prompted this change. The adoption by the Young Turks of a modern nonreligious concept of Ottomanism, in substitution for the traditional concept of the Ottoman Empire as an Islamic state, weakened the Islamic bond. This process culminated in the collapse of the Ottoman Empire and the establishment of a secular Turkish national state.

Related to the change from Islamic to Arab identity is the coalescence of Arab Muslims and Christians in the original intellectual tradition of modern Arabs. The tendency to coalesce was mutual, though more intense on the Christian side. Arabic-speaking Christians in the Middle East lived as members of minority communities which were tolerated, but could never aspire to a position of full citizenship in an Islamic state. Under the influence of modern ideas, educated young Christian Arabs aspired to break the confines of minority status and participate in the experience of society at large, in order to gain more economic and political opportunities. They saw the way to coalescence with their Muslim neighbors in their common denominator: the Arabic language and its literary heritage. Since modernity involved a decline in the influence of religion, it was now easier for educated Arabic-speaking Christians to relegate their confessional identity to a secondary place and emphasize those linguistic and literary elements which facilitated cooperation and unity with the Muslim majority. On the side of the majority group, modernizing Muslims, also influenced by modernity and European currents of thought, lost many of their more strictly theological beliefs, while retaining a strong attachment to Islam as a form of collective identity and a symbol of national pride.

They continued to cherish the historical glory of Islam: the military achievements of the Arab tribes, the accomplishments of the great Islamic empires, and the flourishing medieval civilization. Arab nationalism was able to encompass these traditionally Islamic elements, and thus to satisfy emotional needs of the Muslims while creating common ground between Muslims and their Christian neighbors. It supplied a nationalist formula apparently modern rather than medieval.

For modernizing Muslim intellectuals, this change was relatively easy because the heroes of Arab nationalism are also Islamic heroes: the Prophet Muhammad, the Caliph 'Umar, the great general Salah al-Din (of Kurdish ethnic origin). Christian intellectuals must also cherish the glory of Islam and admire its great past if they want to be truly identified with Arab nationalism. On this point we should quote Michel Aflaq, the chief ideologue of the Ba'th party. Aflaq, himself a Christian, says, "The Ba'th party is a national movement which addresses itself to all Arabs irrespective of religion, and it respects freedom of religious belief. However, it sees in Islam a national aspect which has had a very significant role in shaping Arab history and Arab nationalism, and it believes that this aspect has a very strong connection with the spiritual heritage of the Arabs and the components of their genius."[20] He states that "Islam is an Arab movement which meant the revival and fulfilment of Arabism."[21] According to Aflaq, "The life of the Prophet Muhammad represents the Arab spirit in its true sense."[22]

Muslim intellectuals, while striving to modernize, nevertheless have a sense of allegiance to their Islamic heritage, and they feel keenly the need to maintain it in order to retain their identity and self-esteem. In contrast, Christian intellectuals incline to advance much further in the direction of modernization without excessive regard for a heritage to which they feel no inner allegiance, as it is not truly their own. The following lines by Hisham Sharabi succinctly describe the situation of Christian Arab intellectuals in this respect:

> It was impossible for the Christian Arab not to wish for a way to Westernize society. Theoretically there could be no limit to what the Arabs might borrow from the West. To the Christians, the Islamic reformists' limitations on borrowing could not be valid. Nevertheless, Christian intellectuals had to be especially aware of these limitations and reservations, and they always tried to see the West with Muslim eyes in order to determine these limits. These conditions determined the scope of the Christian intellectual contribution.[23]

Christian Arabs realize that they must pay homage to the Islamic heritage if they wish to remain within the fold of Arab nationalism. They are thus under certain constraints which they can hardly overcome.

Heritage Versus Modernization

Having opted for modernization, which in fact means borrowing from the West, Arab intellectuals had to face serious ideological and psychological conflicts. In order to withstand the West, the Arabs must learn from the West. To be on the receiving end in the process of borrowing is to be somehow inferior. Thus modernization—desired by the Arabs to help them in restoring their lost power and national pride—also had the effect of undermining self-esteem. Further exacerbating the ambivalence toward Western culture was the lurking fear that cultural borrowing might result in the loss of national identity. Modern intellectuals had to look back to the glorious past for pride and reassurance. True, history was the story of not only achievement but also decline. The causes of decline, however, were identified and isolated. The responsibility for the decline was attributed to a non-Arab group, the Turks, who, even when they had been converted to Islam, were not truly imbued with its spirit. In addition, religious accretions of foreign origin (Jewish, Christian, or Persian) were also deemed to be a detrimental factor, since they were held to have distorted pristine (Arab)

Islam. Specifically, these foreign accretions are described as the source of fatalism, which in turn led to lethargy and stagnation. This particular approach to the interpretation of Islamic history has become characteristic of the modern intellectual tradition.

Contemporary Arab writers bestow great praise upon their medieval ancestors, who cultivated the heritage of Greek philosophy and science and, in transmitting it to Europe, enabled that continent to achieve the Renaissance. This notion, already found in the works of early modernizing writers such as 'Abduh and Afghani, has percolated to school textbooks and to journalistic writing and is, in a way, accepted as "common knowledge" among Arabs today. Interestingly enough, although the glorification of medieval Arab science has assumed such ideological importance, there seems to have been no great interest in the actual study of this subject in modern Arab universities. The notion that European science is derived from medieval Arab science is intended to legitimize and facilitate cultural borrowing, for it implies that (1) Arabs borrow from Europe what they had previously given to it (hence, no inferiority is involved), and (2) the borrowed science cannot be alien in principle (hence, there can be no danger of losing cultural identity). We may wonder whether modern Arab scientists actually accept this notion or whether they feel that, ideology aside, the modern science in which they are engaged is Western-based and has very little to do with the medieval science of their ancestors.

Emphasis on the importance of science was a central theme in the original tradition of the modernizing Arab intellectuals, for science seemed to be the key to the acquisition of military and political power. The modernizing intellectuals stressed that Islam is the religion of reason and science. To uphold this view, modernizing intellectuals and reformers such as Afghani and 'Abduh quoted various sayings of the Prophet in praise of science and knowledge: "Seek knowledge ('ilm) even if it be in China," or "The search for knowledge is a personal obligation incumbent upon every Muslim." Such sayings occur originally in contexts which make it clear that the knowledge intended is religious. The modernizing intellectuals use these sayings with the intention of making science more readily acceptable to their Muslim society and demonstrating that Islam favors science. This practice seems to serve the double purpose of the modernist: (1) legitimization of reform, and (2) apologia for Islam.

Using these traditional sayings in praise of knowledge or science (as 'ilm may be variably translated), the modernists glossed over the essential difference between modern science and traditional knowledge. This ambiguity serves ideological purposes, but does not help bring about the change in values necessary for a scientific approach. When we read of the need to acquire science in the writings of many modern Arab intellectuals, we cannot help feeling that they think of science as they would of some commodity, rather than as the internalization of new attitudes and values.

Partly as a result of this attitude toward science, as an instrument that can be acquired and then put to use in order to regain strength and greatness, the modern Arab intellectuals, who have adopted some of the traditions of Europe, were not so successful in adopting others (those concerning method and discipline in particular).[24] In addition to the factor of attitude toward science, there is a social factor that may also account for this failure to adopt certain primary components of Western intellectual tradition. The outside intellectual control on scholarly production in Arabic is minimal: European scholars cannot read works written in that language in their field of specialization. Whereas the Arab readers, who are the primary consumers of this intellectual production, cannot usually compare what is written in Arabic with parallel products in European languages.

We have already mentioned the particular approach to Islamic history characteristic of modern Arab intellectual tradition. We should refer here to one specific theory, forwarded by some Arab writers, which illustrates the ideological orientation of this type of historical thought. According to this theory, European civilization borrowed from the Arabs not only in the Middle Ages, but even earlier, in ancient times, and Arab civilization actually precedes that of Greek and Hebrew antiquity. This argument is based upon another, that the Aramaeans and Phoenicians were in fact Arabs, and so, since the Greek script is derived from the Phoenician script, it follows that Greek civilization is derived from and based upon Arab civilization.[25]

In innumerable writings, modern Arab intellectuals stress the need to preserve and revive their heritage. This frequently means the literary heritage, but in other instances we cannot be sure whether the heritage to which the writer refers is the literary or the scientific one. We should also note that the writers who call for preservation of the heritage hardly ever specify which elements within this heritage are viable in a modern situation. Though they constantly refer to the spirit of Arabism inherent in the heritage, they do not explain the nature of that spirit. The heritage is described in general terms as a source of national pride and self-esteem. It must be cherished because, so the argument goes, no nation separated from its historical origins and its national heritage can survive. The following quotation from Professor Nasir al-Din al-Asad may well represent this extremely popular theme: "The heritage of every nation is [the embodiment of] its spirit, its characteristic qualities and its history; and any nation abandoning its heritage kills its own spirit . . . It is not true that the adoption of modern civilization requires the destruction of the heritage . . . on the contrary, in truth, the nation's progress comes into being from its inner self and emerges from its heritage."[26]

Few Arab writers declare outright that modern civilization is totally different from their traditional indigenous culture and that one should be completely oriented toward modernity without nostalgia for a past which is no longer relevant. This was the attitude of Salama Musa (d. 1958), the Egyptian Coptic writer and social critic. The same view is held by Ghali Shukri, a contemporary literary critic, also of Coptic origin. The Lebanese poet and literary critic Adonis also calls for critical examination of the heritage, and proposes that if the latter constitutes an impediment to modernization it should be relinquished. Adonis states that "the infantile attachment of modern Arab intellectuals to the belief that the heritage is infallible may be the cause for the failure of modernizing efforts in the past fifty years."[27]

It is probably no mere coincidence that both the Egyptian writers who so boldly advocate the need to modernize without being held back by attachment to the heritage and the Lebanese writer who speaks in a similar tone are not members of the Sunni ("orthodox") Muslim majority group, but belong to religious minorities: the Egyptians are Copts and Adonis comes from a Shi'ite family. Therefore they do not share the general loyalty to the great tradition of Islam. Their views encounter fierce opposition on the part of nationalist intellectuals who represent the predominant ideology. Those who have not shown allegiance to the heritage are accused by nationalist writers of mental enslavement to Western culture.[28]

The inner conflict between the attraction exerted by Western culture and loyalty to the traditional heritage is clearly expressed by a modern Arab intellectual as follows:

The task of the revolutionary intellectual with respect to universal currents of thought is difficult and complicated, because he should harmonize between national faith and his humanistic inclination. He is, on the one hand, compelled to be conservative with regard to his ethical and historical values and, on the other, he must satisfy his desire to develop his backward society.[29]

Thus the dichotomy of heritage versus modernization presents a bipolar syndrome of agonizing ambivalences and conflicts.

The cultural attraction of the West seems to nourish an idea current in the writing of modernizing Arab intellectuals: namely, that Western powers wanted not merely to conquer the Eastern lands physically, but also culturally, and even religiously. Even if such an accusation could be leveled at French colonialism, it hardly applies to the British variety. In any case, this kind of motive does not seem central in the considerations of modern colonizing powers in the Middle East. This accusation could reflect the consciousness of modernizing Arab intellectuals that they have in fact been conquered culturally. The Arab intellectuals, strongly attracted to Western culture, now project this situation, thus attributing what is in fact the result of a cultural process to the evil intentions of the colonizing powers.

A concept taken from European history, namely the idea of *renaissance* (in Arabic, *nahda*), offered reassurance and hope to the Arab intellectuals. Having studied European history, they became fascinated by the experience of the Renaissance: revival of the scientific tradition of antiquity brought Europe out of the Dark Ages and made possible its great achievements of culture and power. Arab modernists hoped that their countries could effect a similar *renaissance* and regain power and grandeur. This theme is very powerful in the early formative period of the original intellectual tradition, in the late nineteenth and early twentieth centuries.

In more recent writings the term *nahda* is not in great favor. Since Arab intellectuals used the word with such high hopes at the turn of the century, and no great renascence followed to bring the desired effects, the use of the word now would be a reminder of failure. Some modern intellectuals in recent years speak of the *renaissance* as beginning not, as was previously thought, at the end of the nineteenth century, but actually later under the revolutionary regimes, the earlier stages being only preparatory.

Western culture has proved highly attractive for many modern Arab intellectuals, and their acquaintance with it led to deep dissatisfaction with and sometimes even repulsion for their own indigenous civilization. This is reflected particularly in novels, some of them autobiographical or partly autobiographical. An example is the autobiographical work of the Egyptian writer, Tawfiq al-Hakim, *Zahrat al-'Umr*. The book consists of letters written to a French friend, in which he constantly speaks with admiration about European culture and expresses his dissatisfaction with the Egyptian environment and the culture of Egypt. The following passage from one of the letters reflects the author's cultural preference: "I am afraid that my love for European music results from the fact that it is primarily an intellectual structure, whereas our oriental music which is based on sensual pleasure and physical impression does not interest me at all."[30]

The modernizing intellectuals who have become acquainted with Europe are faced with another problem: they realize that European culture, which is supposed to be a model for emulation, itself suffers from various faults and that they should determine which elements are good and which are bad. However, it is difficult for them to discern and select. An Arab professor, discussing the crisis of Arab intellectuals, refers to "the lack of self-confidence [on the part of the Arab intellectual] in his capacity to distinguish between that which is beneficial and good and that which is damaging and destructive among world currents of thought."[31]

In another autobiographical novel, *'Usfur min al-Sharq* (A Bird from the East) by Tawfiq al-Hakim, the young protagonist, an Egyptian student in Paris, has conversations with a Russian expatriate. The time is shortly after World War I, and the young Egyptian hears sharp criticism of European civilization. His Russian friend tells him that the pure source of spiritual culture is the East and that to the East the young Egyptian should return. The Egyptian, however, knows well that this image of the East is false. He thinks, "There is no longer a pure source there . . . The beautiful and noble clothes of the East are today a strange mixture of European attire which causes laughter, like the appearance of monkeys who snatch the clothes of tourists of all sorts, put them on and climb a tree, imitating the gestures of the owners." He concludes his thought, "The East no longer exists today. It is a jungle on whose trees there are monkeys putting on Western clothes—without method, order, understanding, or perception."[32]

Imported modern technology cannot alleviate the feeling of the Arab intellectual that "he lives under the shadow of a backward civilization."[33] The progress achieved in the industrial and technological spheres only widens the gap between the external material conditions in which he finds himself and the inner aspect of mental attitudes which has not adequately changed.[34]

A very interesting feature of the original tradition of Arab intellectuals is that while attracted to Western civilization and desiring to emulate it, they still pejoratively characterize European civilization as materialistic, and praise Arab civilization as spiritual. They ascribe the colonialist tendencies of European culture to materialistic ambitions, which are of course blameworthy. We should note, however, that there are also intellectuals in Arab countries who try to stress the common elements in the intellectual traditions of Europe and of Islam and see in these elements a basis for a new humanistic Arab culture that would eliminate the tension between indigenous and foreign cultures. This is especially the attitude of the Egyptian writer and thinker, Taha Husayn.[35] But this seems to have remained a minority attitude, because of the nationalistic tendencies so important in the intellectual tradition of modern Arabs.

The Crisis of the Educated

For some fifteen years now, Arab intellectuals have been writing and speaking about "the crisis of the educated" (azmat al-muthaqqafin).[36] The sense of crisis is not limited to Arab intellectuals living under conservative or "reactionary" regimes, but is also acutely felt in the progressive or revolutionary Arab states. In fact, the phrase azmat al-muthaqqafin has been made current by, and in reference to, Egyptian intellectuals. On the face of it, there is a consensus between the Egyptian intelligentsia and the political leaders in regard to the great national goals. However, although the progressive regimes subscribe to the ideas of nationalism and social reform propagated originally by the intellectuals, there is, nevertheless, an intense tension between the two groups. One may wonder what is the source of the malaise of the Egyptian intelligentsia. In view of the ostensible consensus in ideology between rulers and intellectuals in Egypt, one tends to conclude that the crisis may have its roots in the very nature of the modern Arab intellectual elite.

The major factor responsible for the deep malaise of Arab intellectuals seems to be their alienation. Alienation is, of course, a phenomenon characteristic of intellectuals everywhere. But the alienation of Arab intellectuals goes beyond that of the learned man who feels separated from the uncultivated masses. The modernizing Arab intellectual, having adopted Western education and Western values, cuts himself off from his family background and the experiences of his own childhood. The resultant alienation is very acute. Occasionally the Western-educated young man discovers that the cultural gap makes it difficult for him to communicate with his wife or fiancée. Egyptian literary works amply illustrate this experience.[37]

To be sure, the experience of alienation extends beyond the family circle; the modern Arab intellectual is estranged from the masses. His estrangement is often aggravated by disdain toward their backwardness and imperviousness to change. The result is a conflict between the ideological outlook of the modernizing intellectual and his immediate feelings toward the people. A short novel by the Egyptian writer Yahya Haqqi tells the story of a young Egyptian doctor returning home upon completion of his studies in England. The young hero loves his country, but he feels that, "The more his love for Egypt grew, the more he became exasperated with the Egyptians."[38] This kind of paradox is not unique to Arab intellectuals; it is familiar in other modernizing societies and revolutionary movements.

Yahya Haqqi's story illuminates yet another important issue, namely, the question of the terms upon which the modernizing intellectual is reaccepted in his society. In the story, the young doctor is infuriated by the superstitious beliefs of the people. His offensive outburst against customary beliefs is met with violent opposition. He still hopes to prove the superiority of his modern scientific techniques over the customary (superstitious) way by effecting a dramatic success in the treatment of his first patient. Unfortunately, the first attempt ends in failure. The young doctor is about to lose his self-confidence, having previously lost the confidence of the people. He then realizes that "there is no science without faith." He makes his peace, at least outwardly, with the customary beliefs. In this way he regains the confidence of the people; he now resumes the treatment of his first patient, this time with success. The happy end of the story is that the doctor continues to practice medicine in his native neighborhood, "relying on Allah as well as on his science and his hands, so Allah blessed his science and his hands."[39]

The story may be taken as an object lesson for modernizers: new techniques can be successfully introduced, if they are not presented as opposed to traditional beliefs. Conversely, it also reveals that although the Western-educated professional may be accepted by the people on a practical basis, yet his world-view remains alien and incomprehensible.

True, the modern intellectuals speak and write Arabic, that is to say, they formulate their ideological positions in a language which is read by the people. The question is how much of this intellectual production is really understood by people who are but slightly Westernized, if at all.

Understanding is difficult to measure quantitatively. But we may suppose that the masses who read papers and listen to the radio understand best and adopt most readily those elements which appear familiar to them linguistically as well as conceptually. In other words, the audiences actually do not transform their ideas to the modern, partially Westernized outlook of the Arab intellectuals; rather, they pick from this intellectual production published in Arabic those sections which include, or seem to resemble, traditional phrases and formulations. Those phrases are the ones which appeal most to the emotions and consciousness of the masses.

Consequently, although there is linguistic contact between the Westernized intelligentsia and the people, that contact is very tenuous. The more sensitive intellectuals are certainly aware of this gap. Ghali Shukri, for example, complains that modern Arab writers, who are themselves educated in the West or have adopted modern culture, write for people who still live in a culture which is four centuries behind. This may be something of an exaggeration; nevertheless, it may point to a very real situation.

The alienation of the intellectuals is accentuated by yet another factor: their political peripherality. They accuse the politicians of having removed the intellectuals from the realm of planning as well as that of implementation.[40] The political ineffectuality of the intellectuals in Egypt—as well as in other Arab countries—is due in part to the relatively minor international significance of the Arab academic and scientific community.

The fact that Arab governments, when they need scientific aid, can, and indeed have to, rely on foreign sources means that they depend only slightly on the indigenous academic community for these concrete purposes. This certainly deprives the intellectuals of an important leverage for political influence. The preoccupation of the Arab intellectual with ideological questions at the expense of technology and science seems to have undermined the position of the Arab academic and intellectual community as a whole.

In the thirties and forties the intellectuals led the struggle for independence by means of the written and spoken word. They were in the forefront of the movements which called for complete independence and social reform; many of them were active in political parties and parliament. But once the revolutionary regimes were established by military men, these intellectuals seemed left out. Paradoxically enough, the intense involvement of the modern Arab intellectuals with political ideology may have contributed to their political peripherality, once the ideology which they had created triumphed.

Under colonialist or imperialist rule the intellectuals acted as social critics. But now that they live in national "revolutionary" and independent Arab states, they find it somewhat difficult to act vigorously as social critics, for that would mean, in many cases, to criticize a government which shares, at least formally, the same ideology that they do. And that criticism would appear to be an act of disloyalty or even treason, especially since the Arab world still views itself as in the midst of a struggle against external enemies. So that Arab intellectual is handicapped as a critic within his own society.

It should be noted, however, that some Egyptian writers expressed their misgiving about various aspects of life under the revolutionary regime through fiction.[41] They have occasionally also resorted to allegory in order to express their criticism of the social and political conditions in Egypt. Since the death of Nasser, Egyptian intellectuals have begun to feel somewhat freer to criticize the conditions in their country.

Unlike traditional 'ulama' in medieval Islam, the modern Arab intellectuals are not indispensable as legitimizers of political power. The military officers can address the masses directly, using the same ideological formulations which were originally produced by the intellectuals. The officers may be able to use them even more effectively than the intellectuals themselves, since they have greater cultural affinity with the masses.

To be sure, there are intellectuals in Egypt who continue to carry out the task of explaining to the public the policies of the government in reference to the accepted ideological formulas and to reinterpret ideology in the light of political contingencies. However, the range of this process is limited by the positions of the regime and by attitudes which have come to be accepted as unquestionable national dogma. It seems that the ideological views of the intellectuals are accepted within certain limits: the masses respond to them inasmuch as they understand them, and the rulers use them to the extent that these views suit them politically. In other words: Arab society has accepted the solutions of the intellectuals on its own terms.

To qualify our observation on the decline in the significance of modern Arab intellectuals as legitimizers of political power, we should call attention to the fact that modern Arab governments, unlike traditional Muslim rulers, need also some measure of external legitimization. By virtue of their Western education and the resulting affinity with foreign attitudes, modern Arab intellectuals have assumed the role of obtaining external legitimization for their governments.

Being relegated to a state of political peripherality would not have been a distressing experience to traditional 'ulama', since such a situation does not clash with their world-view. In contrast, the modern intellectuals, having adopted the Western notion of nation-state, wish to influence the direction of the nation through their association in the ruling institutions. However, they now find themselves relegated to a marginal role in politics, far removed from their hoped-for role as the "vanguard of leadership."

REFERENCES

1. See L. Gardet and M. M. Anawati, *Introduction à la théologie musulmane* (Paris: J. Vrin, 1948), pp. 101-124.

2. See Ghazali, *Ihya 'ulum al-Din,* I (Cairo: 'Isa al-Babi al-Halabi, 1957), pp. 14-18.

3. Arabic: *fard 'ayn.*

4. Ghazali says, "The meaning of the word knowledge (*'ilm*) in the saying of the Prophet Muhammad, 'Every Muslim is under obligation to seek knowledge,' is knowledge of the practice which is patently obligatory for Muslims." Ghazali, *Ihya 'ulum al-Din,* I, 16.

5. Arabic: *fard kifaya.*

6. Ghazali, *Ihya 'ulum al-Din,* I, 17.

7. The prevalence of this phenomenon in Islamic civilzation makes it useless to list examples. However, two outstanding cases will be mentioned here by way of illustration. Ibn Hazm (d. 1064), the famous Andalusian poet and writer, best known for his book on love, also wrote on jurisprudence. Ibn Khaldun (d. 1406), the historian and philosopher of history, served most of his life in religious offices: as *qadi* (judge), teacher of jurisprudence, and head of a Sufi convent.

8. Ibn Rushd (Averroës, d. 1198), "the Commentator of Aristotle," held for a number of years the religious office of *qadi.*

9. See G. E. von Grunebaum, "Muslim World View and Muslim Science," in *Islam,* 2d ed. (London: Routledge, 1961), pp. 111-126. Especially pertinent to our point are his following observations:
    "No matter how important the contribution Muslim scholars were able to make to the natural sciences, and no matter how great the interest with which, at certain periods, the leading classes and the government itself followed and supported their researches, those sciences (and their technological application) had no root in the fundamental needs and aspirations of their civilization . . . This is why the pursuit of the natural sciences as that of philosophy tended to become located in relatively small and esoteric circles and why but few of their representatives would escape an occasional uneasiness with regard to the moral implications of their endeavors—a mood which not infrequently did result in some kind of an apology for their work. It is not so much the constant struggle which their representatives found themselves involved in against the apprehensive skepticism of the orthodox which in the end smothered the progress of their work; rather, it was the fact, which became more and more obvious, that their researches had nothing to give to their community, which this community could accept as an essential enrichment of their lives." (p. 114)

10. See H. A. R. Gibb, "An Interpretation of Islamic History," in his *Studies on the Civilization of Islam* (Boston: Beacon Press, 1962), pp. 10-14; and cf. Gibb, "Government and Islam under the Early Abbasids: The Political Collapse of Islam," *L'Elaboration de l'Islam,* Colloque de Strasbourg, June 1959 (Paris: Presses universitaires de France, 1961), pp. 115-127.

11. See H. A. R. Gibb, "Constitutional Organization," in M. Khadduri and H. J. Liebesny, eds., *Law in the Middle East* (Washington: Middle East Institute, 1955), pp. 19, 23.

12. The blending of Arab-Islamic tradition and that of the Persian court scribes is demonstrated in his book, *'Uyun al-Akhbar.*

13. In illustration of this point two examples are noteworthy. Ibn Hubayra (d. 1165), a scholar of the Hanbalite school who wrote books in the religious sciences, distinguished himself as a powerful vizier in Baghdad. Al-Qadi al-Fadil (d. 1200), educated as a religious scholar, served as the vizier of Salah al-Din.

14. Junayd (d. 910), Abu Talib al-Makki (d. 996), Abu 'Abd al-Rahman al-Sulami (d. 1021).

15. See a discussion along these lines: H. Sharabi, *Arab Intellectuals and the West* (Baltimore: John Hopkins Press, 1970).

16. See Albert Hourani, *Arabic Thought in the Liberal Age, 1798-1939* (London: Oxford University Press, 1962), pp. 68-82.

17. See L. Carl Brown, *The Surest Path: The Political Treatise of a Nineteenth-Century Muslim Statesman* (Cambridge, Mass.: Harvard University Press, 1967); see also Hourani, *Arabic Thought,* pp. 83-94.

18. A special term signifies the new intelligentsia, *muthaqqafun.* The word *muthaqqaf,* which is in itself a neologism, means "an educated person" but it is used to signify exclusively "a person with modern education."

19. W. C. Smith, *Islam in Modern History* (Princeton: Princeton University Press, 1957), p. 94.

20. Michel 'Aflaq, *Fi Sabil al-Ba'th,* 3d printing (Beirut, 1963), p. 89.

21. *Ibid.,* p. 54.

22. *Ibid.,* p. 53.

23. H. Sharabi, *Arab Intellectuals and the West,* p. 60.

24. See von Grunebaum's pertinent observation: "It should be added here that the results of Western research are more easily transferable than its methods, and that the Western research mentality, as one of the most singular characteristics of our culture, can only very gradually be instilled into the thoughts and the feelings of the impatient young nationalists of the Near East." *Modern Islam,* p. 266.

25. See 'Abbas Mahmud al-'Aqqad, *Al-thaqafa al-'arabiyya asbaq min thaqafat al-yunan wa-l-'ibriyyin* (Arab culture is earlier than that of the Greek and the Hebrews) (n.p., n.d.), p. 29 et passim.

26. Nasir al-Din al-Asad, "Al-turath wa-l-mujtama' al-jadid" (Heritage and modern society), *Al-Adab,* 13 (Beirut, March 1965), 26.

27. Adonis, "Al-ra'is jamal 'abd al-nasir wa-l-thaqafa," *Al-Adab,* 16 (Beirut, June 1968), 5.

28. 'A'isha 'Abd al-Rahman (Bint al-Shati), *Qiyam Jadida li-l-Adab al-'Arabi* (Cario, 1970), p. 174.

29. Abu al-Qasim Sa'dallah, "Azmat al-muthaqqaf al-thawri fi al-watan al-'arabi" (The crisis of the revolutionary intellectual in the Arab homeland), *Al-Adab,* 14 (Beirut, April 1966), 4.

30. Tawfiq al-Hakim, *Zahrat al-'Umr,* 2d printing (Cairo, 1944), p. 166.

31. Abu al-Qasim Sa'dallah, "Azmat al-muthaqqaf al-thawri fi al-watan al-'arabi," p. 4.

32. Tawfiq al-Hakim, *'Usfur min al-Sharq* (Cairo, 1938), pp. 229-231.

33. Ghali Shukri, *Shi'runa al-hadith ila ayna* (Cairo, 1968), p. 18.

34. See *ibid.,* p. 19.

35. On Taha Husayn, see Hourani, *Arabic Thought*, pp. 324-340.

36. On the meaning of the term *muthaqqaf*, see note 18 above.

37. For example, *Adib* by Taha Husayn, *'Usfur min al-Sharq* and *Zahrat al-'Umr* by Tawfiq al-Hakim, and *Qindil Umm Hashim* by Yahya Haqqi.

38. Yahya Haqqi, *Qindil Umm Hashim* (Cairo, n.d.) (*Iqra'* Series, no. 18), p. 34.

39. *Ibid.*, p. 57.

40. See Adonis, "Al-ra'is jamal 'abd al-nasir wa-l-thaqafa," p. 4.

41. Especially noteworthy in this respect is the novel *Miramar* (published in 1967) by Najib Mahfuz. The villain in this story is a high-ranking official in an Egyptian nationalized company who is also an important member of the Arab Socialist Union, Egypt's only political party.

NIKKI R. KEDDIE

Intellectuals in the Modern Middle East:
A Brief Historical Consideration

INTELLECTUAL LIFE in the Middle East, influenced by Islam, has a long and varied history. There has been a rich intellectual life in the Muslim world, especially in its first few centuries and again in the last two.

Traditional Islamic Intellectuals

The first centuries of Islam saw the development of an increasingly complex and differentiated class of intellectuals. Much of the earliest intellectual effort was devoted to the Qur'an and the Prophet Muhammad. A definitive Qur'anic text had to be established; it needed to be interpreted for believers; Muhammad's life, sayings, and practices needed to be recounted. The early rise of sectarian movements guaranteed that intellectual effort would be made in establishing their defenses. The Shi'a, or partisans of Muhammad's cousin and son-in-law 'Ali and his descendants, devoted their efforts to proving the intellectual as well as religious superiority of their particular claims; the Kharijites or "seceders," who rejected both the Shi'ites and the Umayyad caliphs, did the same.

The Islamic world, influenced by Hellenistic thought coming in from the conquered Near East, necessarily became more sophisticated in its intellectual endeavor. Hellenistic influence first appeared in theology, where Hellenistic logic was used to defend the rationality of Islam against the rationalist claims of Christianity and of other religions. The Mu'tazilites, the first theologians of Islam, argued for the unity and justice of God. In doing so, they set up a theory of natural law and of rational good and evil which competed with Christian theology on its own ground. The Mu'tazilites believed in a created rather than eternal Qur'an; in this they were going against the dominant Muslim opinion. Popular orthodoxy soon reasserted itself despite the protection given Mu'tazilite doctrine by the early 'Abbasid caliphs. After this, Greek logic was used by theologians in a more conservative way. They argued for the omnipotence and inscrutability of God, whose ways are not subject to earthly concepts of justice, and who creates good and evil by His own will, rather than following rationally knowable good and evil.

Just as theology became more conservative after its early intellectual flowering, so also did law, the central science of Islam. In the first Islamic period, law adopted, though sometimes in altered form, a good deal from prior local law and custom, and also from the necessities of the day. As time went on, however, a need was felt to Islamicize legal practices. Nearly all of them came to be traced back to Muhammad himself. This was done through the medium of *hadiths* or Traditions—sayings attributed to Muhammad via a chain of authorities whose names were cited to validate a Tradition. Intellectual effort by jurists came to be limited to analogy from the Qur'an or Traditions. Once all the usual cases had been decided by the Qur'an, Tradition, analogy, or consensus of the jurists, the legal codes were virtually frozen in the four orthodox schools of law. Nevertheless, more probably remained open to the judgment of jurisconsults as expressed in *fatwas* (judgments) than recent Oriental scholars have admitted. In any case, the intellectual activities of the leading jurists continued to provide leadership to the community, and legal scholars played the central role in the traditional Islamic educational system. Law continued to expand and to adapt itself to new conditions; this was accomplished through the medium of opinions or *fatwas* granted by judicial leaders in answer to new or difficult questions, and through administrative rulings outside the *shari'a* (Islamic law).

The first centuries of Islam witnessed significant economic and social expansion characterized by the growth of cities, the development of trade, the increased importance of the commercial bourgeoisie, and the extension of agriculture. There was a corresponding intellectual ferment, in part at least the consequence of these new economic and social needs. Science and mathematics developed beyond the level they had achieved with the Greeks and the Romans; these served the needs and the curiosity of the expanding society; the same was true in the fields of medicine and philosophy. In all these areas a debt was owed to the Greeks, and to a lesser extent to the Persians and the Indians. In all fields there were also new achievements.

The early 'Abbasid period (beginning A.D. 749) saw a series of officially sponsored translations from the Greek and the Persian which greatly expanded the intellectual horizons of the educated classes. The cultivated man came to be educated in the *Adab* "culture"; he had access to refined poetry, prose literature (often dealing with morality), and the rudiments of science. Intellectual experimentation and free thought were possible. The widespread sectarian movements gave ideological content to revolts among the discontented masses. Greek philosophy became known to some of the intellectual elite.

The Muslim philosophers, the most sophisticated intellectuals of their time, took over the neo-Platonic and neo-Aristotelian theories of Hellenistic times and adapted them to the Islamic environment, and, in addition, made original contributions of their own to philosophy. In the relatively free tenth century A.D., there were a variety of philosophies based on different Greek schools, extending to a radical rejection of religion in a few known cases. The Shi'ites in this period also made use of Greek philosophy in their religious theories, and the influence of Greek thought permeated beyond strictly philosophical circles.

In the eleventh century economic and social changes occurred that ended the first expansive state of Islamic society and culture. The invasion of Turkish nomads into the eastern part of the Middle East and of Arab Bedouins into North Africa brought major changes in economic life. There was a trend toward greater nomadism and a decline in agricultural production and trade. Deforestation and salinization of irrigated soil preceded this agricultural decline and made agricultural recovery to former levels exceedingly difficult. The Mongol invasions of the thirteenth century only accelerated trends that had been operating since the eleventh century. A form of military feudalism based largely on nomadic tribes took over where formerly there had been relatively centralized states. Many of the urban centers declined. These economic, social, and political changes were accompanied by major cultural changes. As the age of feudalism had been the age of religion in the European West, and the age of commerce the age of free thought, so it was in the Muslim East, except that there the time periods were reversed, with tribal feudalism coming second. In the eleventh century religious orthodoxy began to take over the entire educational system. Even civil servants who had formerly received a partly secular education came increasingly to be educated in religious schools. Religious orthodoxy displaced free thought, and philosophy became more suspect than it had ever been. Even the less radical philosophers were suspect; they were subject to abuse and penalities at the hands of the orthodox. The philosophers developed a sort of protective coloration. They expanded on their earlier argument that philosophical thought was designed only for a restricted elite, and that a literalist and unquestioning orthodoxy was best for the masses. Philosophy was declared to be consistent with the Qur'an when the Qur'an was interpreted according to reason, but such rationalist allegorical interpretations were to be available only to the philosophers. Not even theologians were to indulge in such interpretation; for them to do so would confuse the masses and make them question the faith that had kept them orderly and obedient in this world through fear of punishment in the next.

This theory entered Western Europe along with Averröes' philosophy and came to be known as the theory of the "double truth." In fact, as others have pointed out, there was only one truth, the rational truth known to the philosophers. The masses were given a distorted version of reality, together with a mythology about physical heaven and hell and God's human attributes, making religion comprehensible to them in terms accessible to them and thereby leading them to behave in accord with the religious law.

Orthodox theologians considered that theology was only for the educated and should be kept from the masses as it would only confuse them. The famous theologian al-Ghazali (d. 1111) wrote a treatise on the need of keeping theology from the masses. The Islamic mystics, or Sufis, similarly restricted their higher truths to the initiated, as did many of the Shi'is. It was the philosophers, however, who worked the theory out most elaborately. Their ideas deserve attention because in some degree they persist into the modern Muslim world. Following certain hints in the Greek philosophers, the Muslim philosophers, faced with a religious orthodoxy of a kind the Greeks had never known, created a series of defenses that found their most classic expression in certain of the writings of Avicenna and Averröes. Insisting that their Greek-based philosophy was enjoined on them by the Qur'an, they offered a few appropriately interpreted verses to support their view. They also adopted the idea that humanity was divided into a small elite capable of understanding philosophy and a large mass who could not be exposed to it, lest it upset their literalist faith. They insisted that philosophy was intended only for a restricted intellectual elite, and that the rest of mankind might properly be moved with parables and rhetoric that served a useful social purpose.

The notion that society is divided into a mass and an elite permeates the Islamic world of the later Middle Ages, and leaves a great residue among modern Islamic intellectuals and politicians. In class terms no less than in intellectual terms, medieval Muslim authors saw their society as divided into two great classes, the large mass and the small elite. The words used for the mass and elite classes—'amma and khassa—are the same as those used by the philosophers and others to describe the intellectual elite and the common mass.[1]

In late medieval times, apart from the small class of innovating intellectuals—the philosophers and the few innovating theologians such as al-Ghazali and Ibn Taimiyya—the religious scholars and jurists, or ulama, and the chief governmental scribes and advisers were the closest thing to an intellectual class. The later ulama operated within an Islamic tradition that held innovation (bid'a) to be a sin. They made strenuous efforts to show that they were not being original. Their position was precisely opposite to the one taken by most intellectuals in modern times. This emphasis on preserving the past was not peculiar to the Middle East, though the weight of the Qur'an, of religious Traditions supposedly emanating from the mouth of Muhammad, and of religiously based law—the all-encompassing shari'a —may have made Islam especially resistant to innovation. The belief that the Qur'an was the literal word of God, and hence infallible, and the quasi-infallibility of at least the "strong" (that is, well-attested) Traditions from the mouth of Muhammad gave intellectual endeavor within the Muslim world a very special cast. Almost to the present, innovation has had to be represented as interpretation of the Qur'an and Traditions. Inevitably, new ideas came out in highly traditional forms.

A partial exception to the relative rigidity and traditionalism of late Islam is found in Twelver Shi'ism—the state religion of Iran after 1501. Not only did Twelver Shi'ism incorporate a rationalist Mu'tazilite theology, but Iran maintained a live Avicennan philosophical tradition uninterrupted into the nineteenth century, with a number of original philosophical minds developing this tradition within the Shi'i framework. In the western Islamic world, by contrast, the philosophical tradition was persecuted out of existence, though it seems to have existed underground for some time after Averröes, to reappear, as Muhsin Mahdi has shown, in the social thought of the last great original thinker of the traditional Muslim West, the fourteenth-century Ibn Khaldun.[2] In Iran, even religious thought was touched by rationalist philosophy, and religious innovation was justified by the theory that in the absence of the "Hidden Imam," the twelfth in the line of 'Ali, the leading religious thinkers, or *mujtahids*, could exercise individual endeavor, or *ijtihad*, to solve questions of law or religion. Their solutions were merely probable, so that the same question might be solved differently by a different *mujtahid*.

The practical difference in rates of innovation between Iran and the lands to the west were in fact not as great as this theoretical difference might imply. Iran, more nomadic and less economically developed than the Ottoman Empire, did not have any great social impetus for intellectual innovation. Even the Ottoman Empire at its height did not witness intellectual adventuresomeness comparable to what had been present in the first centuries of Islam. Most of the empire's economic, social, and scientific needs were answered within a framework of adapted Islamic traditions, though there were some fundamental innovations in the realm of law and government.

The First Modern Intellectuals

The Ottoman Empire, following on its first great military defeats by the West, recorded in the Treaty of Karlowitz of 1699, experienced in the early eighteenth century a brief period of incipient Westernization. A few Western books were translated into, and printed in, Ottoman Turkish and some Ottomans became conscious of the need to adopt Western military methods. The chief intellectual of the period, and the one responsible for most of the printed translations, was a converted European Unitarian, Ibrahim Müteferrika.[3] After his death and the resumption of conflicts with Europe, a reaction against the nascent Westernization set in. The reaction

44   NIKKI R. KEDDIE

pointed up what was to be a recurrent problem in the intellectual life
of the Middle East—the psychological difficulty of responding positively to
a West seen to be an attacker and the abode of infidels.

The real break with the past did not occur until the beginning of
the nineteenth century; it was Napoleon's invasion of Egypt in 1798
that started the process. The first major innovations occurred on the governmental level; they had to do largely with military reform. It was soon
discovered that military change necessitated at least partial educational
change, and this was responsible for opening the intellectual dikes.

Nineteenth-century Muslims, in reconsidering traditional modes of
thought, had the choice of setting up parallel systems with scant reference
to traditional ways, or trying to reinterpret the old, employing modern
ideas that necessitated new interpretations of traditional writings. Both
methods were in fact employed. The first innovators—rulers and governmental men—were largely concerned with self-strengthening. Their reforms
were practical; they had scant concern for Islamic justifications. Muhammad
'Ali, the ruler of early nineteenth-century Egypt, established numerous new
schools and a translation bureau without ever trying to justify them as
Islamic. Rifa'ah at-Tahtawi, the Egyptian Muslim *shaikh* who accompanied
the students Muhammad 'Ali sent to Paris to oversee their religious behavior,
was a pioneer in advocating Western ideas and practices. He did not
devote much time to reconciling what he advocated with the Qur'an.
Tahtawi was fortunate enough to write at a time when Western imperialism
was not yet making serious incursions into his native Egypt. He did not
face the dilemma that wracked so many later Muslim intellectuals—how
to advocate modernization without encouraging servility to the West and
discouraging confidence in one's own cultural resources. Tahtawi became an
ardent advocate of Westernization; he had none of the apologetic tone so
common with so many of his successors.

Sultan Selim III, who came to the Ottoman throne in 1789, introduced
a "New order" (*Nizam-i jedid*) in the army and elsewhere, but conceived
of his acts as any traditional Ottoman reforming sultan might have done.
He showed little concern with justifying his reforms by Qur'anic precedents. The reforming Sultan Mahmud II, whose modernization program
included the destruction of the traditional janissary corps in 1826, asked
his *ulama* to secure justifications from the Qur'an and Traditions for his
military policies, but this was a minor concern for him. After his death
the centralizing and modernizing ministers Reşid, Ali, and Fuad Paşas
took the lead in introducing Western reforms in the bureaucracy, in the
judiciary, and in the schools. These ministers generally tried to introduce
reforms without reference to the Qur'an and Traditions; ironically, it was
against these ministers that Ottoman reformists spoke up in defense of
certain elements of tradition.

The first generation of Ottoman intellectuals appeared in the 1860's.

Among the so-called new or Young Ottomans, the most prominent was the writer, Namik Kemal. Writing for and editing newspapers, first in Istanbul, then from their Paris exile, these men set forth a program of reform that placed constitutionalism at its center. Reforming ministers had no great interest in such a program. Opposed to a regime that had already made significant moves to Westernize and centralize the government, the Young Ottomans were very different from the reformers in most Middle Eastern countries, who were still arguing against traditional and reactionary regimes. The Young Ottomans had their own idealized modern version of Islam and of traditional Ottoman society. Namik Kemal argued that the separation of powers had existed in the old Ottoman state; the *ulama* had been the judiciary; the janissaries (in the eighteenth and nineteenth centuries, a large urban militia) had existed as a countervailing force. The regime of Ali and Fuad was criticized for its blind imitation of the West and for its overcentralization of power. The proposed remedy was primarily a constitution and a parliament. Under Kemal and others the opposition press became a force for the first time. Kemal is generally given credit for popularizing such terms as *watan* (fatherland), *hurriet* (liberty), and *millet* (nation)—Arabic words nationalized in Turkish, but taking on new meanings in the Arab world after the Turkish innovations.

If modern Egypt's intellectual life may be said to have started with Tahtawi, who welcomed nearly every Western innovation, it continued in a new way with the young oppositionists of the 1870's. The principal figure was Sayyid Jamal ad-Din al-Afghani. His peripatetic life led him to influence many countries in the Muslim world, but his most important work was done in Egypt, where he lived from 1870 till the time he was exiled in 1879.[4] In Egypt, as in the Ottoman capital, the first innovators borrowed from the West without trying to justify their borrowings intellectually. As in Turkey, it was a group of opponents of the government—in this case the government of the spendthrift Khedive Isma'il—that constituted the first body of independent intellectuals that that society had seen. Though there is no evidence of direct influence either way, Afghani, like Namik Kemal, saw much of the ideal society as having existed in the Islamic past. He called on Muslims to cast off their apathy and to build societies as strong as those that had existed in early Islam. Working to find Islamic precedents for the reforms he advocated, Afghani's real concern was to find arguments that would mobilize the masses so that they would defend their country's independence against the now encroaching West. Where, as in Egypt, the West appeared both as an enemy to be feared and as a model to be emulated, a strong ambivalence toward the West developed. There was a keen desire not to admit open borrowing.

In this situation, Jamal ad-Din was an ideal leader for young and aware Egyptians and also for Syrians in Egypt. His circle included young men who were to figure among Egypt's most prominent intellectuals and most important politicians. Jamal ad-Din was born and raised in Iran in a Shi'ite family, but from the time of his expulsion from Afghanistan by its new ruler in 1868 until his death in 1897, he claimed to be from Afghanistan, except when he lived in Iran in the late 1880's and early 1890's. He probably put forth this claim to make himself appear as a born Sunni and thus to be acceptable in the Sunni lands to which he traveled. From the time he first appeared on the historical scene, on his only trip to Afghanistan in the 1860's, he figured as one who hated the British. He resented their encroachment on Eastern and Muslim lands—most particularly India— where he had lived as an adolescent at the time of the Indian mutiny. In Afghanistan he showed the same desire to strengthen Muslim lands against foreign aggression. After his expulsion from Afghanistan, Afghani went briefly to Egypt and then to Istanbul. Here, in a speech on crafts delivered in the manner of the medieval Muslim philosophers, whom he had learned of in Shi'i circles and who had come to have great influence on him, he referred to prophecy as a craft on almost the same level as philosophy. He drew comparisons between philosophers and prophets, and the talk aroused considerable anger among the religious conservatives. It was at their prodding that the government deported Afghani in 1871.

He went to Egypt, where a leading government official arranged a stipend for him. In his eight years there Afghani offended the religious conservatives, but he was more circumspect than he had been in Istanbul and managed to get into less trouble. Among his young disciples were many who were to become important intellectuals—including, especially, his closest disciple, Muhammad 'Abduh, later the grand mufti of Egypt and a major religious reformer; also, journalists like James Sanua and Adib Ishaq and political men like Abdullah Nadim and Sa'd Zaghlul (prominent in later years as a nationalist leader). Just as the circle of Young Ottomans who lived precariously in exile made up the nucleus of the first independent group of Turkish intellectuals, so Afghani's Egyptian circle can be regarded as the first independent intellectual group in that country.

Afghani taught his disciples to use rational arguments to confront the outmoded policies and religious forces of the opposition. Much of his teaching consisted of oral commentaries on Muslim philosophers, virtually untaught in Egypt and in other western Sunni lands. Just as the philosophers had used reason in their approach to the traditional religious texts, Afghani taught his pupils to do the same, though his purpose was to give a more modern meaning to those texts. Afghani also adopted from the philosophers their division of humanity into an elite, capable of taking in the whole rationalist truth, and a mass, who had to be dealt with in quite different terms, in a style more rhetorical. Afghani may be regarded as the first man in the Islamic world to recognize the importance of the mass media—newspapers, public speeches, and leaflets were all crucial for him. He pushed his followers in Egypt to publish newspapers; these became a kind of opposition press, limited only by the dangers incurred in criticizing the government of Isma'il and the encroachments of foreigners. Afghani was one of the first to detect in the ready-made structure of Freemasonry in Egypt the possibility of creating a political secret society. He converted one of the masonic lodges to which he belonged into a secret political group with ties to the heir apparent to the khedivate, Taufiq. When Taufiq assumed power after the British and French had brought about the deposition of his father Isma'il in 1879, Afghani expected greater influence for himself and for his followers. He was sorely disappointed. Continuing to make fiery speeches against the foreigners, he was deported by Taufiq, whose power depended on foreign support. Afghani's followers, however, went on to become important men in Colonel Ahmad 'Arabi's revolutionary government in 1882; men like 'Abduh and Sa'd Zaghlul had important later careers.

Afghani's group, like the Young Ottomans, illustrates the close ties between intellectual life and politics in the modern Middle East. Nearly all the men who can be pointed to as intellectuals also have a political role. While this may be thought to reflect the myopia of the scholar who refuses to dignify as intellectuals those among the *ulama* who were doing the same old thing in the same old way, the prejudice has some basis in fact. Only the man who is capable of looking at the traditions of his society with a critical, though not necessarily jaundiced, eye can be properly called an intellectual. Because the *ulama* were not all blindly bound to a traditional mode of thought, more study needs to be made of their leading men and writers. In Egypt and Iran, and probably in the rest of the Middle East as well (which has not been studied with this question in mind), many of the leading *ulama* sent their sons to foreign universities and gave them the modern training that served as their entrée into lucrative and powerful positions.

Recent studies on the *ulama* and Sufi orders support the above observation, and also show the traditional and continued use of education in religious sciences for entrée into the *ulama* class by sons of the peasants and other relatively poor groups. Entry into the *ulama* has been shown to be the chief traditional vehicle of social mobility, but now that the more powerful and lucrative posts lie outside the *ulama* class, the religious higher schools tend to be patronized by the poorer classes, while the *ulama* may regard continuation of *ulama* status for the family as something for the third son to take up, but not the first or second.[5] Original writing by the traditionalist *ulama* is rare, although not so rare as Western concentration on the modernizers would make it seem.

A modernist member of the *ulama* class who had great intellectual influence was Afghani's chief disciple, Muhammad 'Abduh. Giving up on political activity after he left Afghani in 1885, 'Abduh became the founder of the school of Islamic modernism. Returning to a quasi-Mu'tazilite interpretation of Islam, he tried to prove that modern science and other modern principles were encompassed in the Qur'an. In his practical activity, he sought to modernize Egyptian law and education. His own chief disciple, Rashid Rida, persisted in believing that all the principles necessary for modern life were to be found in a return to the truly understood principles of the Qur'an and of the earliest Muslims. As time went on he became increasingly conservative, expressing admiration for the puritanical Wahhabis of Saudi Arabia. His influence dwindled even before his death in 1935. The highly political and revolutionary principles of Afghani were used by his most immediate descendants in directions that became increasingly reformist and in time conservative. A theory of religiously-based change which seemed revolutionary in the 1870's appeared outdated or even reactionary in the 1930's.

This is not to say that all such thought became conservative. In the hands of the Islamic reformist Qasim Amin, Islamic modernism was used to justify the emancipation of women, a growing cause among many progressive thinkers of the twentieth century. There were others of 'Abduh's school who similarly used Islamic reformism to justify modernizing change.

The Ideas and Expression of Modern Intellectuals

Modernization in its earlier phases encouraged the development of a relatively independent intellectual class, though that class was often stifled by censorship like that of the more traditional despots, as, for instance, under Sultan Abdülhamid II. In the early phases of modernization, Western thought inevitably came to influence educated Middle Easterners; modernization created new groups amenable to Western ideas. New military and technical schools, translation bureaus, and Western-model schools on all levels, in addition to education abroad, helped to create a growing class of modern or semimodern intellectuals. No longer were the *ulama* class and the government the only channels of entry for talented and educated men, though expanded government operations meant that many intellectuals were in fact in the government. There were also jobs for the educated in law, medicine, and, increasingly, in business enterprises and in other new professions. The writer, found primarily in newspapers in the late nineteenth and early twentieth centuries, could increasingly move to the novel, the short story, the modern poem, play, or essay. Much of this writing was directly political, but in times of repression writers could use fiction to express critical attitudes in the way that had been done in Russia in the nineteenth century.

In the late nineteenth and early twentieth century there was a belief in modern constitutions and parliament as the key to achieving the status of the West. Particularly after the Russo-Japanese war, when the only constitutional state in Asia defeated the one European great power that had no constitution, there was a growth of interest in parliaments and constitutions. The revival of the Ottoman constitution in 1908, the Persian constitutional revolution of 1905-1911, and the Arab parliamentary regimes of the period between the world wars all attest to this faith. In the period since World War II there has been increasing disillusionment with parliamentary regimes. These are seen as representative of a limited ruling class of landlords and the rich. Nationalism and socialism have appeared as the new panaceas. Nationalism was a much later development in the Middle East than is generally realized; pan-Arab nationalism is an even more recent development. Its post-World War II triumph could not have been predicted with confidence before 1939.

Middle Eastern intellectuals, seeing the weakness and inefficiency of their own traditional regimes, turned to nationalism after the deposition of Sultan Abdülhamid II in 1909. Arab intellectuals developed into separatists only after the succeeding Young Turk government discriminated in favor of the Turks and against the Arabs. The exact nature of Arab separatism varied over time and place. The Arab nationalists who opposed the Ottoman Empire generally wanted a single large Arab Asian state; Egypt was rarely considered a candidate for membership in this state until World War II. Local Lebanese, Syrian, and Egyptian nationalist movements flourished in the interwar years; so, also, did nationalist theories put forth by intellectuals. Only since the creation of the state of Israel has pan-Arabism become the dominant trend among both intellectuals and the masses.

After the death of constitutionalism as a panacea, increasing emphasis was put on nationalism by both intellectuals and governments. In Turkey, the key figure was Mustafa Kemal Atatürk, who created a new nation out of Anatolian Turkey, and whose military success was followed by major reforms. His success attracted intellectuals as much as others; intellectuals were harnessed into supporting Anatolian-Turkish nationalism, which had scarcely existed before Atatürk took power. The dominant form of Turkish nationalism before this had been pan-Turanianism, which aimed at annexing Russia's Turkish territories. Atatürk even found intellectuals to back his laudable campaign for Anatolian nationalism with a less intellectually honest, but perhaps necessary, campaign to prove that earlier peoples in Anatolia, notably the Hittites, had in fact been Turks. The original language of mankind was said to be a form of Turkish (which could make the Turks relatives of any desired people). Turkish intellectuals since World War II have not been pressured into supporting theories of this sort.

Egyptian nationalism became a major intellectual trend early in the twentieth century, with the romantic Mustafa Kamil and the liberal constitutionalist Ahmad Lutfi as-Sayyid. After World War I the nationalist movement was led by the chief of the leading nationalist Wafd party, Sa'd Zaghlul. Egyptian nationalism was at first quite separate from Arab nationalism, and until approximately World War II the word "Arab" had the meaning of "Bedouin" in Egypt. Mustafa Kamil's nationalism was pro-Ottoman, but after the breakup of the Ottoman Empire nationalism tended to be limited to Egypt and to be anti-British in its emphasis. In the interwar period Egyptian liberals developed the Pharaonic view of Egyptian civilization, emphasizing the continuity of Egypt from Pharaonic times to the present. The great intellectual Taha Husain, in *The Future of Culture in Egypt*, argued that Egypt was a Western, Mediterranean civilization, with no ties to the East.

This liberal view of nationalism was part of a secularism characteristic of many Egyptian intellectuals, particularly in the 1920's. This secularism sometimes went beyond the bounds tolerated by a still powerful religious establishment and public opinion. Taha Husain's early book on pre-Islamic poetry, which claimed that much of it had been forged by later Islamic authors for their own ends, created such a furor that it had to be withdrawn and revised. A book by 'Ali 'Abd al-Raziq, suggesting that Islam was not concerned with politics and that Muhammad had not headed a state, caused a similar outcry. Despite such setbacks, reformist and secularist writing continued, though many more gestures were made in the direction of Muslim orthodoxy.

Broadly speaking, these nationalist intellectuals represented a new bourgeoisie. They were largely a landed, professional, and commercial rather than industrial bourgeoisie, who owed much of their position to new types of trade with the West. The Egyptian bourgeoisie in the early twentieth century was optimistic about the possibilities of liberal nationalism, and this optimism was reflected in the chief contributions of its liberal intellectuals. As constitutionalism was shown to be a farce in practice, and as the demands of the lower classes came increasingly to the fore, the higher bourgeoisie and certain of the liberal intellectuals became increasingly conservative, irrationalist, and pessimistic. Taha Husain changed from optimistic radicalism to emotional conservatism. With certain of the other intellectuals the change was even more marked.[6] At the same time the lower classes and the petty bourgeoisie were beginning to find their organized intellectual expression in the Muslim Brotherhood, which expressed both their frustrations and their utopian aspirations in those religious terms that were most familiar to them.

Arab nationalism began, as Sylvia Haim has demonstrated, only in the early twentieth century.[7] It received its major impetus from the Turkish nationalism of the Young Turk government and from World War I, which influenced the Arab revolt and the Arab separation from the Ottoman Empire. Arab nationalism's chief ideologist was Sati' al-Husri, whose many books were dedicated to promoting nationalism and pan-Arabism. Other nationalists wrote suggesting that all ancient Near Eastern empires were Arab achievements. Intellectuals became increasingly caught up in the pan-Arab cause, and in place of the many nationalisms, local as well as pan-

Arab, we find a single pan-Arab nationalism taking over both the masses and the intellectuals in the post-World War II period. The virtual unanimity of Arabs, intellectuals and masses, on the Arab-Israeli question helped forge a consensus and a dislike of heresy among Arabs that was in certain ways reminiscent of the orthodoxy of the premodern period. Arab intellectuals, having for a brief period differed, were partially returned to the mold of unanimity. This unanimity, however, ought not to be exaggerated; even on the Arab-Israeli question, a variety of practical and impractical approaches exist about what ought to be done, and these may even outweigh the unanimous feeling that something must be done.

In the "progressive" countries—Iraq and Syria—as well as in those that have had more recent revolutions, Arab socialism is the dominant ideology of intellectuals. The same is true of Egypt, where the form of socialism is somewhat different. In Iraq and Syria, where communism was known earlier, the Ba'th party, which originated during World War II, has been the chief representative of socialist thought; it has helped provide an ideology for Egypt as well, though this is not always admitted. The Ba'th's original ideology, expressed by its first leader Michel Aflaq, combined a moderate socialism with a strong nationalism. This blend suggested a downgrading of the idea of class struggle and an emphasis on national unity and integration. With the rise to power of more leftist factions of the Ba'th, Marxism and the class struggle have taken a more prominent place in Ba'thist thought. Certain thinkers have tried to integrate not only Arabism but also Islam with socialism. As Islam had once been portrayed as being constitutional, democratic, and scientific, so now it is claimed to be socialist.

Socialism made its first appearance in Egypt after World War I with intellectuals like the Coptic Christian Salama Musa and organizations like the small and divided Communist party. Only since World War II, however, has socialism come to the fore as a major force. The discrediting of the constitutional regime and of the monarchy, particularly during the first Palestine war, led to a revolutionary situation that came to a head in 1952. Since 1961 socialism has been the order of the day, though it is generally proclaimed to be of a special kind—Arab socialism—which retains a utopian, nationalist, and even Islamic tinge. Arab socialism is held to avoid class struggle and the sacrifice of the current generation to future ones, though in practice these things turn out to be less easy to achieve than is suggested by theory.

The continued emphasis on Islam in the Arab countries, considerably more vocal than anything characteristic of Turkey or Iran, is not only to be explained by the fact that the Arabs were the first Muslims and therefore feel an identification with Islam in an almost nationalist way; the Turks felt almost as much identification with Islam. This defensiveness about Islam and use of Islam in modernization is also caused by the fact that the

Arabs, unlike the Turks and Iranians, were colonized by Europeans, and had to emphasize their ideological distinction from European Christianity and secularism as part of their anti-imperialistic ideology.

In Turkey, the intellectuals' position has been different because of Turkey's noncolonial background and also because the Turks were about a generation ahead of the Arabs in modernization and development. The variety of intellectual trends common to the Turks before 1922 is roughly comparable to what the Arabs experienced in their own liberal interwar period. Just as the Arab intellectuals at that time wondered whether to support pan-Arabism or separatism, with Egypt as an entity returning to the Pharoahs, and Lebanon as a unit going back to the Phoenicians, so Turkish intellectuals before 1920 argued whether Ottomanism, pan-Islamism, or pan-Turkism ought to be the dominant trend for them. Just as the Arab new regimes claiming a mass appeal have clamped down on intellectuals, limiting the variety of permissible solutions, so Turkish intellectuals under Kemal Atatürk were drawn to the Anatolian-Turkish nationalism discussed earlier, which had the pragmatic value of limiting the strivings of Turks to territory they controlled or regained after World War I. The major difference between the Anatolian nationalism that became official Turkish policy and the Arab nationalism of the post-World War II period is that the former was based on a realism that did not require the Turks to annex new territory, which the pan-Turanianism of certain Turkish intellectuals would have done, and which the ideology of pan-Arabism requires. The defeat of Israel imposes obligations that are beyond the capability of Arab governments; these obligations only lead to increased frustration.

Kemal Atatürk encouraged ideas with less intellectual plausibility than pan-Arabism, but these were positions that permitted pragmatic accomplishments; pan-Arabism and belief in the ultimate defeat and dismemberment of the Jewish state have as yet led to no comparable pragmatic accomplishments. Turkey, having never been a colony or a mandated territory, finds few psychological obstacles to taking over Western thought systems in their entirety; Arabs, having suffered from colonialism in various forms, and seeing Israel as the final chapter of Western colonialism in their territory, find it more difficult to take over unchanged thought systems from the colonial West. The Arabs identify more strongly with Islam than do the Turks, but it must be realized that this was not always the case, and that a non-Muslim Turk is seen by many Turks as an impossibility, whereas non-Muslim Arabs abound.[8] The archaicizing nature of much Arab thought probably has more to do with the Arabs' hostile attitude toward the West than with stronger traditional identification with Islam. Both the Arab countries and Turkey have vacillated between intellectual conformity and greater intellectual freedom.

Important in the development of Arab thought has been the special role of the Arab Christians. Sent to foreign or local missionary schools before their Muslim compatriots, they were the first to develop a Westernized viewpoint. They tended also to be secularist and to be scientifically oriented in their publications. They did not have to confront the humiliation of their people in quite the same way as did the Muslims. They pioneered in setting up newspapers and other modern institutions in Arab countries. Despite these early secularizing tendencies, Christian writers and politicians recently have identified themselves with the Islamic past and have shown a reverence for Muhammad. Even Arab Christians, then, recognize a tie between Islam and Arab nationalism, and few have tried to divorce the two. Lebanon, however, remains different from the other Arab countries with their large Muslim majorities.

Arab intellectuals today are frustrated not only by the problems faced by their countries, but by their marginal importance in the Arab world. Most recent regimes are either traditional monarchies or military revolutionary states; neither has turned much to intellectuals for help; neither has feared intellectuals sufficiently to devote great attention to them. The military regimes have usually worked out their ideologies with little help from the intellectuals, who have joined the movements rather than initiated the ideologies. The modern intellectuals are unlike the traditional *ulama* who had a clear role in society, recognized by government and masses alike. The frustrations and the alienation of the intellectuals ought not, however, to be overemphasized. They hold major positions on newspapers, and have influence as writers and professors. The secular authorities rarely heed them, but this is hardly a situation unique to the Arab world.

The intellectuals of the late nineteenth and early twentieth centuries were in a position to claim credit for an influence on society, for helping to transform the social order. In the traditional class structure the *ulama* operated as a buffer between the masses and the secular rulers and as the maintainers of the status quo. Attacks on the status quo and the old class system came largely from the new intellectuals, who tended to express the interests of the new middle classes and professional groups. New theories were brought to the Middle East by intellectuals in the first instance and were later taken up by other groups in society. Constitutionalism, democracy, higher status for women, nationalism, socialism—these were all causes first advocated by intellectuals and then supported by broader strata of the society. Even the military rulers of the Arab countries were influenced by the new climate of opinion that owes so much to the pioneering of intellectuals. Nationalism has been the most important meeting ground for intellectuals and new rulers; nationalism is a twentieth-century phenomenon in the Middle East, which spread with great rapidity after being initially espoused by a small group of intellectuals. Socialism, as an idea, spread even more rapidly; its first advocates were small numbers of intellectuals, of whom Salama Musa of Egypt ought to be singled out.

The intellectuals were pioneers in communicating new political theories and in making them palatable by insisting that they were Islamic (or Arab, Turkish, or Persian) in origin. The new middle class tended to take up the theories of nationalism, while the petty bourgeoisie of the bazaars and the lower classes looked more for a new interpretation of Islam such as the one offered by the Muslim Brotherhood. Such individuals and groups saw all the difficulties of modern times as stemming from a turning away from traditional Islam. Traditional Islam still motivates the lower classes, though sometimes in unlikely combinations with socialism and nationalism. The demand for intellectual conformity in most of the Arab world and in Iran now affects all classes, though it is felt to be particularly galling by the intellectual class.

Iran, like Turkey, has alternated between periods of intellectual conformity and periods of freedom. The rhythm, however, has not been the same. In the late nineteenth and early twentieth centuries a strong censorship existed in both Iran and Turkey. Iran was in a relatively backward social and intellectual state; the intellectuals who were the analogues of the Young Ottomans, who first published newspapers abroad and smuggled them into the country, appeared later, in the 1870's to 1890's. Iran achieved its first constitution in 1906-1907 through a revolution that made a free press possible. A great variety of antiautocratic, constitutional, and modernizing newspapers developed, along with others that took quite opposite views. After a period of intellectual freedom in the first years after World War I, Reza Shah, who copied Kemal Atatürk in many ways, began to suppress independent liberal thought and encouraged a form of official nationalism that had its roots in the Achemenid and Sassanian past. This type of nationalism, based on pre-Islamic emphases but without the conservative official bias, had been favored by advanced Iranian intellectuals since the late nineteenth century, when Mirza Aqa Khan Kirmani published his anti-Arab, anti-Islamic, and radical Iranian nationalist works. He, however, had looked back to Mazdak, the fifth century A.D. religious rebel and communist, for inspiration, and not to the rulers of early Iran. Similarly, the radical nationalist Democratic party of the early constitutional period that continued through World War I had taken the legendary blacksmith and warrior Kaveh as its hero. Kaveh had saved Iran in the distant past. Reza Shah and his son, the present Shah, prefer to look to the ancient monarchy. The nationalist intellectual Ahmad Kasravi, who tried to free Persian of Arabic words and to reject Shi'ism as a harmful alien importation, was assassinated in 1946 by a member of the Fida'iyyan-i Islam, a fundamentalist organization with appeal similar to the Muslim Brotherhood. As in much of the Middle East, religious orthodoxy has become a class phenomenon, adhered to by many of the lower classes and by the petty bourgeoisie, but not by the intellectuals or upper bourgeoisie.

In Iran the brief periods of intellectual freedom and free political life that followed the two great wars of the twentieth century each time have culminated in an absolutist monarchy that imposed strict censorship and worked to keep intellectual expression under firm control. In Iran, as in the Arab countries and Turkey, censorship has led intellectuals to seek the ambiguous spheres of fiction and poetry rather than to risk open political dissent. The literature of modern Iran, like that of the Arabs and that of modern Turkey (excellent, but still undiscovered in the West), deserves greater study by those who wish to learn what intellectuals are in fact thinking. In Iran today there is far more oppositional thought among intellectuals than appears on the surface, or impresses itself on the outsider bedazzled by the sometimes real and sometimes public relations achievements of the Shah.

Everywhere in the Middle East, as in much of the rest of the world, nationalist loyalties have largely taken the place of religious loyalties among the educated classes. The appeal of secular nationalism as opposed to nationalistically tinged religion has been much more limited among the masses. The continued strength of religious fundamentalism among the people is shown by the popularity of the fundamentalist Muslim Brotherhood in Egypt until its suppression, or the expression of religious loyalties among Turkish peasants in their electoral behavior when Kemal Atatürk's Republican Peoples' party ceased to have a political monopoly. Arab nationalists have associated their nationalism with an appeal to Islam, which in its beginnings was a religion of the Arabs. The Turkish and Persian nationalists have generally made no such connection, and, especially since World War II, have been faced by opposition movements among the *ulama* and/or the common people.

Intellectuals in the modern Middle East have introduced a wide variety of new ideas to their countries—liberalism, parliamentarianism, nationalism, and socialism in all their permutations. Since the late nineteenth century, as circles of mutually reinforcing individuals, they have often formed "schools" favoring particular trends. The modern intellectuals have broken decisively with the Islamic past, most particularly in Turkey and Iran, where religion is generally considered, in the tradition of the philosophers, to be good for keeping the masses orderly, but not suitable in its rules and dogmas for the well educated. Only in a few periods have intellectuals been free to express all their thoughts openly in print.

The fluctuation between periods of censorship and periods of freedom has moved more frequently toward intellectual controls than to intellectual freedom. One can only hope that the current situation in Iran and most of the Arab countries will give way to one where intellectuals will feel greater possibilities of openly discussing important affairs. Privileged Westerners should realize, however, that intellectual freedom often seems a distant luxury to rulers who seek to modernize and improve living standards rapidly. The intellectual must often suffer when these goals preclude intellectual freedom, and it is all too easy to condemn all interference with intellectual freedom without recognizing the forces that make such interference attractive to new regimes.

The bravado of much of the nationalist appeal often masks a profound frustration and uncertainty about the national virtues that are so loudly proclaimed. In the Arab countries in particular, the twentieth century has been a time of serious defeats, for which a certain consolation is sought in ideology. Arab intellectuals, and often their Persian and Turkish counterparts, have taken refuge in the glorification of the distant past, which serves as a balm for the pains of the present. The Golden Age of Muhammad and the first four caliphs is constantly celebrated by Arab intellectuals, as are the achievements of the early 'Abbasid caliphate and the final outcome of the Crusades. Later years are seen as a deviation from the Arab essence—they may be discarded. Recently, socialism has been added to the nationalist ideology, but not always with great clarity of purpose.

Intellectuals in the Arab countries have a more difficult task than their peers elsewhere, and we should not be surprised that many of them choose exile, silence, or cunning as ways to overcome their predicament. Hope for a changed climate among Arab intellectuals depends largely on whether their countries achieve either solutions or new attitudes to their major domestic and foreign policy problems. So long as Arabs, with partial justification, consider themselves to be ill-used by the West and Israel, so long will the restrictions on intellectual freedom and the frustrations of daily life lead certain intellectuals and publicists to romanticize about the past and the present. Others will choose to express their realistic views in literature and art, where freedom is the greatest.

There has been, since the six-day war, the development of more radical thought concerning what is wrong with the Arab world. The rise of socialist ideologies and the opposition to neo-imperialism has cut into the intellectual gap between the elite and the masses, which was already undermined by mass nationalism. If the Arab masses, the leading intellectuals, and the governments can unite around practical socialist programs, there will be hope for a more rapid economic, social, and cultural development in the future.[9]

REFERENCES

1. For further details see Nikki R. Keddie, "Symbol and Sincerity in Islam," *Studia Islamica*, 19 (1963), 27-63.

2. Muhsin Mahdi, *Ibn Khaldûn's Philosophy of History* (London: Allen and Unwin, 1957).

3. Niyazi Berkes, *The Development of Secularism in Turkey* (Montreal: McGill University Press, 1964), pp. 36-46.

4. On Afghani see Nikki R. Keddie, *Sayyid Jamāl ad-Dīn "al-Afghānī": A Political Biography* (Berkeley: University of California Press, 1972) and *An Islamic Response to Imperialism: Political and Religious Writings of Sayyid Jamāl ad-Dīn "al-Afghānī"* (Berkeley: University of California Press, 1968).

5. Nikki R. Keddie, ed., *Scholars, Saints, and Sufis: Muslim Religious Institutions in the Middle East since 1500* (Berkeley: University of California Press, 1972), particularly my preface and the papers by L. C. Brown, Kenneth Brown, and Afaf Lutfi al-Sayyid Marsot.

6. See Nadav Safran, *Egypt in Search of Political Community* (Cambridge, Mass.: Harvard University Press, 1961).

7. Sylvia G. Haim, ed., *Arab Nationalism: An Anthology* (Berkeley: University of California Press, 1962), introduction.

8. See Bernard Lewis, *The Emergence of Modern Turkey* (London: Oxford University Press, 1961), chap. 1.

9. For fundamental studies of Arab intellectuals see Albert Hourani, *Arabic Thought in the Liberal Age, 1798-1939* (London: Oxford University Press, 1962) and G. E. von Grunebaum, *Modern Islam: The Search for Cultural Identity* (Berkeley: University of California Press, 1962).

JUAN J. LINZ

Intellectual Roles in Sixteenth- and Seventeenth-Century Spain

AFTER UNIFICATION under the Catholic Kings in 1474, the conquest of Granada in 1492, and the incorporation of Navarre in 1512, Spain became one of the first large European monarchical states.[1] This political modernity, however, was not accompanied by other processes of modernization, most specifically a flourishing national capitalism. Spain could have been one of the first national monarchies had it not become enmeshed soon after unification in a two-fronted imperial adventure. The grandson and heir of the Catholic Kings, who became Charles I of Spain in 1516, was, when elected emperor in 1519, confronted by both the Lutheran challenge and the Turkish threat in Vienna and the Mediterranean.[2] In those same years navigators and conquistadores were creating a transoceanic empire that would soon extend to the Philippines and incorporate most of America. The meaning and purpose of empire in Europe and overseas, and specific policy questions such as the treatment of the Indians, would engage intellectuals in fierce disputes and important political roles. Politically Spain experienced basic changes in the two centuries of Habsburg rule: it moved from a rising power with a new sense of mission, optimism, and dignity, to a period of frustrating and costly struggles inherited from that moment of zenith, ending in defeat, crisis, and decline.

Religion occupies a central role at the time of the Reformation and Counter Reformation in Spain; it is impossible to find more than isolated cases of secularized intellectuals such as those in eighteenth-century France.[3] The medieval coexistence and conflicts among Christians, Muslims, and Jews created unique problems, problems that have led Américo Castro to interpret Spanish culture and society almost exclusively from that perspective.[4] Centuries of a crusading tradition left a mark; the forced conversion of large populations and their resistance to assimilation created unique problems to which the Inquisition was one response; concern for *limpieza de sangre* (clean blood, that is, no descent from Jews or Moors) and conflict between old and new Christians had profound implications for society and culture. This unique religious constellation led to a pre-Reformation religious reform that had close ties with Erasmianism and helps explain

the failure of the Protestant Reformation in Spain and the role of its intellectuals in the Catholic Reformation (or Counter Reformation).[5] In fact,
it is impossible to separate religious and intellectual roles, not only because
clerics, monks, and even inquisitors played important roles in cultural and
intellectual life, but also because lay intellectuals were deeply involved in
religious questions and political-legal or economic problems are debated
in religious-moral terms. Without the religious context—the confrontation
with the Muslim and particularly the Jewish heritage, the missionary task
in the New World, and the defense of Catholicism against the Protestant
heresy—Spanish culture would make little sense. In this essay, therefore,
I will be dealing with religious intellectuals, post-Reformation Catholic
intellectuals living in a religious society rather than a secularized world.

Culturally Spain was often the crossroads of the main currents of the
time: the Renaissance and humanism blend and conflict with a variety of
medieval heritages; Erasmianism and scholasticism, innovation and continuity, face each other and often fuse.[6] Cultural life is at the center of the
transition from the Renaissance to the post-Renaissance, or baroque, era.
The Counter Reformation had a strong Spanish component, at least in
the sixteenth century. The Jesuit order, its agent, was founded by a Span-
iard, although it was not always in favor in Spain. The Jesuits and their
system of education contributed a new type of religious-intellectual role,
quite different from that of medieval monks. Spanish mystics and saints
play an important role until Frenchmen assume intellectual and organizational innovative roles in the seventeenth century.

Within this unique historical, political, religious, and cultural context,
Spain offered men of ideas—the creators or manipulators—a large number
of roles, some old with a new content, others emerging at the time.

Intellectuals as Guardians and Innovators, Not Deviants

A theme will soon emerge as central for the two centuries under consideration, one quite different from any during the last two and a half
centuries: intellectuals identified with an order, religious or political. This
identification as guardians of a tradition did not imply subservience, lack of
innovation, or even criticism of that tradition, particularly in the first half
of the sixteenth century. Men responding to a new situation (the Reformation, the conflict between emperor and Pope, the discovery and colonization
of America) gave creative formulations in literature and the arts to its
ideals, criticizing imperfections in the social order, while defending it
against its enemies. Obviously the emphasis on one or another role varies
in different men and over the two centuries, but the majority of the men
we will be discussing do not present the disjunction between society and
culture to which we are so accustomed in our time. Some might argue that
this situation was ultimately in conflict with the most genuine role of the

intellectual, with real breakthrough and innovation, and in the last analysis was the result of constraint, of a closed society, of conscious or unconscious self-censorship of which we have only an insufficient record.[7] This might be true in some areas of intellectual endeavor (scriptural criticism, certain expressions of religious sentiment, for example) and in certain periods (such as the last years of the Erasmians).[8] With the exception of Bartolomé de Las Casas, who became a bishop, was listened to in the highest circles, and was not persecuted or silenced in his lifetime, few leading minds questioned the legitimacy of authority to the point that we could call them radical intellectuals. A few, who were not central figures, went as far as real heresy to die at the hands of the Inquisition, and many more encountered suspicion or persecution (accused by fellow intellectuals, not always lesser minds). A few preferred to live abroad, like Luis Vives, or exile, like Juan de Valdes, but one cannot speak of an intellectual emigration (and certainly powers hostile to Spain would have welcomed real dissidents). How is it possible to account for this combination of "basic" conformity and "real" creativity—a creativity based on issues concerned with central values? The answers are not easy and are certainly subject to controversy.

I would stress that a culture whose boundaries are fundamentally religious (even when politically supported) leaves a wide area for cultural creativity, perhaps because a book religion and a tradition based on it cannot be expanded or stretched too far by the intellectuals to limit creativity outside of its particular content. Despite similarities between the Spain of those centuries—in fact of Catholic and much of Protestant Europe—and contemporary totalitarian societies (a point stressed by Barrington Moore in his analysis of Calvinist Geneva),[9] the fact that those societies were based on religious rather than political-secular values makes such comparisons risky when attempting to study the life of intellectuals in them. The duality,[10] paradoxically, often protects those who question other authorities on the basis of arguments derived from the religious sphere. Las Casas' criticism of colonization, of the authority of kings to engage in the conquest of America, was possible because he appeared moved by evangelical zeal. As long as a man identifies with the religious community he can go far in his criticism of the powerful and of society, or of intellectual tradition and its authorities.

Innovation within an order is perceived as less disruptive and irresponsible than a situation where there is no established public allegiance to some basic consensus. Those concerned with the role of intellectuals in "closed" societies today should consider the possibility of conclusions other than the inevitable destructive conflict between power and intellectuals. Why not consensus on a fairly well-delineated range of beliefs, values, and ideologies, and creativity within the area defined by those boundaries? One basic difference from contemporary closed societies is that the Spaniards of the sixteenth and seventeenth centuries had few if any models of a freer society.

Another explanation for this widespread cultural consensus—one that does not speak in terms of repression or fear—might be that Spaniards did not turn their attention to certain problems or push their questions beyond a certain point as the result of latent self-censorship. Such an interpretation is offered by many who admire the works of Spanish intellectuals, without either ignoring or stressing their limitations or the gaps in their contribution to Western civilization. There are variations in this approach, ranging from a comparison of the sum total of the intellectual effort in those two centuries (a balance in which the plus in art and literature would be contrasted with a minus in philosophy and science) to a comparison of the work of men pursuing similar intellectual problems or forms of aesthetic creation, accounting for the differences in the boundaries set to the travels of their mind by their different basic commitments and the pressures of the societies supporting them. It would be a tempting but hazardous task, for example, to compare Shakespeare with the almost contemporary Spanish theater in those terms. The comparison between Spanish, Italian, and English science would appear as a more fruitful example, but would have to await much more scholarly work on the history of Spanish science. Certainly such research would be central to a test of Robert K. Merton's theory of Puritanism and science as well as the theories of his critics. The risks of such an approach become evident when we realize that scholars have discovered important Spanish contributions which had previously been attributed to other countries, or had been independently arrived at almost simultaneously in Spain, or had been diffused from Spain. The case of the contributions of Spanish moralist-economists to the understanding of the European and particularly Spanish inflation caused by the American treasury is a good example. Those who refer only to Bodin, Botero, Serra, Davanzati, Sully, Montchrestien, and Montaigne ignore, as Pierre Vilar has stressed,[11] the contribution of the Spaniards Martín de Azpilcueta, Tomás del Mercado, Luis Ortiz, Martín González de Cellorigo, Pedro Fernández de Navarrete, and Diego de Saavedra Fajardo. The same seems to be true in some other scientific fields. A social history of science should distinguish the issue of intellectual discovery from that of institutionalization of scientific endeavors, diffusion, continuity in efforts, and practical application and use of technology before accounting for the gap between Spain and other countries at the onset of the industrial and scientific age. The issue might then shift into an analysis of the direction of the total effort of the society, given its ideological and political commitments and its use of economic resources, and the values of the society in determining them, rather than the role of the individual intellectual. It would turn the question away from queries about the impact of society on intellectuals, scholars, and scientists, themselves, into queries on the response of political, social, and economic institutions to their work. Modern scholarly histories of Spanish universities and science from a comparative perspective would be important in this context.

Chronological comparative tables of developments in different realms, such as those of Pierre Chaunu,[12] clearly show that the Spanish contribution was outstanding in the late sixteenth and the seventeenth centuries in literature and the arts and some forms of religious thought and expression, but not fully comparable in philosophy and probably less so in science and music. Even when gaps in scholarship may account for some of the differences in visibility, there can be little doubt that few of the great philosophers, scientists, and musicians who shaped European civilization from then on were Spaniards. Even if it were only a question of the diffusion and reception of the work in some of those fields by Spaniards making simultaneous and independent discoveries, the question would remain: what barriers—cultural and sociological—would account for the lack of diffusion, visibility, institutionalization? On the other hand, there is little record of persecution or censorship of efforts in those fields in Spain in indices of the Inquisition, records of trials by the Suprema, or even the limited information on university life.[13] In fact, there is some evidence (for example, on the toleration of Copernican teaching) of less inquisitorial concern with new scientific ideas than in Italy. The course of intellectual life was apparently shaped more by positive than negative sanctions, by incentives rather than by proscription or even prescription. Selective, permissive tolerance, with largely invisible but effective boundaries, channeled the efforts of intellectuals—or, as the defenders of Spanish culture would argue, there was deliberate and free choice of certain alternatives even when others were possible.

Spain in the post-Renaissance and Counter Reformation period offers an example of intellectual life characterized by integration into the society—shaping society and being shaped by it—rather than in conflict with it. Some periods of the Middle Ages, the era of Louis XIV, Germany in certain decades of the nineteenth century, and prolonged periods in non-Western civilizations were perhaps similar in combining creativity and the absence of crisis—a period when intellectuals were often influential, highly respected (ignoring their economic complaints), integrated without necessarily being subservient to the powers of the society, even critical of specific aspects of the social order without questioning its basic assumptions. How this became possible is an interesting question, one that should include, however, the question of the cost of such a pattern to the society and long-term intellectual development. Such a perspective certainly would make sense in studying German idealism and culture at the turn of the nineteenth century, or academic and scientific life in imperial Germany until close to World War I. Claudio Sánchez-Albornoz has noted: "We had no religious wars in the sixteenth century but we had them in the twentieth."[14]

An important aspect of the heritage of those two centuries is the conflict in Spain over the interpretation of its cultural achievements in view
of the fact that the successful nations of Europe followed a different path
and that regardless of the value of their heritage, Spaniards could not
continue their unique culture in a creative way into the eighteenth century
(except, perhaps, in the arts, with Goya). Glorious achievement and
decadence are inextricably linked and are a source of permanent ambivalence for nineteenth-century intellectuals. The polemic of the two Spains[15]
—defined more or less narrowly and projected into the past—is the key to
post-Enlightenment Spanish culture and, together with economic and social
problems, to the deep divisions underlying instability and civil wars. We
may surmise that this problem of relating a glorious past to later main-
streams of a Western civilization imposed on all by its political, military,
technological, and economic success also plagues other intellectuals in
non-Western societies, particularly Islam.

The basic Catholic consensus in the Spanish culture, particularly of
the seventeenth but even of the sixteenth century, turns out as central to
Spanish intellectual and political debate in the twentieth century, when secularization of the culture has moved very far. We cannot resist quoting a
historic speech of Prime Minister Manuel Azaña in defending article 26
of the Constitution of the Republic outlawing the Jesuits and forbidding the
religious orders to engage in education. Even this great secularizer feels
pride in the Spanish Catholic culture, to the point of suggesting that perhaps Catholicism owes more to Spain than Spain to Catholicism, and he
argues that the nation was Catholic because its culture was Catholic
while "Spain has stopped being Catholic," whatever the number of believers, because then (1931) its creative culture was not Catholic. Few
texts reveal better the complex identification between religion, culture,
and nationality that those creative centuries have left as a heritage for
intellectuals and politician-intellectuals.

I cannot admit, honorable gentlemen, this to be called a religious problem.
The authentic religious problem cannot go beyond the ·limits of the personal
conscience, because it is in the personal conscience that the question on the
mystery of our destiny is formulated and answered. This is a political problem,
of the constitution of the State, and it is just now when this problem loses even
a resemblance to religion, to religiosity. Unlike the old state that took upon itself the tutelage of consciences and provided a means to push the souls, even
against their will, on the way to their salvation, our State excludes all otherworldly concern and any care about faithfulness, and withdraws from the church
that famous secular arm that rendered it so many and large services. The question
is nothing but to organize the Spanish state on the basis of the premises that I
have just established. *In order to affirm that Spain is no longer Catholic we have
the same reasons, I mean reasons of the same nature, as to affirm that Spain was
Catholic in the sixteenth and seventeenth centuries.* It would be a useless argument to examine now what Spain owes to Catholicism, which is the favorite
subject of the apologetic historians; I rather think that it is Catholicism which

is in debt to Spain, because a religion doesn't live in the written texts of the concilia or in the folios of its theologians, but in the spirit and the actions of the people who embrace it, and the Spanish genius spread all over the moral expanses of Catholicism, as its political genius spread all over the world in the enterprises we all know. Spain, in the apogee of her genius, when Spain was a creative and inventive people, she created a Catholicism to her own image and resemblance, in which shine above all the traits of Spain's character, certainly very different from the Catholicism of other large Catholic powers; so different, for example, from French Catholicism. Then there was a Spanish Catholicism for the same psychological reasons that created a Spanish novel, a Spanish painting, a Spanish theater, and a Spanish morality in which the penetration of the religious faith is so visible. And this is so true that there is still by chance the Society of Jesus, a Spanish creation, the work of a great example of our race, and that proves to what extent the genius of the Spanish people has affected the direction of the historic and political government of the Church of Rome. But now, honorable gentlemen, the situation is just the opposite.

Therefore I have the same reasons to say that Spain is no longer Catholic as to say the opposite of the old Spain. Spain was Catholic in the sixteenth century in spite of the fact that there were many very important dissidents, some of whom are the glory of Castilian literature, and Spain has stopped being Catholic despite the fact that there are millions of believing Catholics in Spain. And could the Spanish state, could any state in the world in its organization and thought be dissociated, divorced, turning its back, hostile to the general sense of civilization, of the present situation of its people? No, honorable gentlemen.[16]

A Profile of Intellectual Production

A quantitative or qualitative analysis of the total intellectual contribution in the sixteenth and seventeenth centuries is outside the scope of this essay, but a few facts can provide a profile of intellectual life. To form a collective portrait of intellectuals I have compiled a biographical file on 321 authors writing between 1500 and 1700. To add to the data on this "elite" we have the index of the *Bibliotheca Hispana Nova* of Nicolás Antonio, the seventeenth-century Spanish bibliographer-scholar, which classifies authors and works published between 1500 and 1584. The statistics composing this profile of intellectual life are presented in table 1.

Our quantitative analysis revealed, to an extent we did not expect, a shift at the turn of the century from the scholarly—be it scientific, humanistic, or theological-philosophical—to the expressive literary artistic culture. Many factors must account for such a dramatic change, among them the decline of the universities and the drop in enrollment (as stressed by Richard Kagan[17]) in the less professional and practical disciplines. Our data confirm Kagan's in that the shift was not only away from an incipient scientific culture—mathematics, natural history, and medicine—but also simultaneously away from theology, scholastic philosophy, and even the classical humanities. Our rough quantification even shows the shift from a legal-philosophical-theological analysis of power to a more secular treatment of

Table 1.   Classification of "elite" authors of the sixteenth and seventeenth centuries by main area of endeavor; classification of "mass" authors and/or works listed under comparable subject headings in Nicolás Antonio's *Bibliotheca Hispana Nova* (in percentages).

Field	Elite authors						Nicolás Antonio's mass authors, 1500–1584	
	Sixteenth century		Seventeenth century		Both centuries			
Theology	4.9		0.9		3.4		30.6	
Philosophy	1.5	6.4	—	0.9	0.9	4.3	2.5	33.1
Classical humanities	10.2		2.6		7.5		7.5	
Legal thought	9.3		—		5.9		8.7	
Political thought	13.7		15.5		14.2			
Economics	2.9	16.6	2.5	18.0	2.5	16.7	1.7	1.7
Natural science	2.4		—		1.6		1.2	
Medicine, science	7.3		0.8		5.0		4.5	
Mathematics	3.4	13.1	—	0.9	2.2	8.9	3.3	9.0
Morals	1.5		0.9		1.2		7.5	
Mystic	2.9		2.5		2.8		—	
Ascetic	4.4		0.9		3.1		—	
Religious, devotional	3.4	12.2	0.9	5.2	2.5	9.6	—	7.5
History	13.6		5.2		15.9		15.4	
History of Indies	7.8		0.9		0.5		—	
History of saints and religious orders	—	21.4	—	6.1	—	16.4	7.8	23.2
Poetry	18.0		25.9		21.0		6.5	
Theater	7.3		28.5		15.0		1.1	
Religious theater	0.5		0.9		0.6		1.2	
Novel	3.9		10.3		6.2		—	
Rogues novels	1.0		8.6		3.7		—	
Social description	2.4		4.3		3.1		—	
Literary theory	1.5	34.6	1.7	80.2	1.6	51.2	—	8.8
Total number of authors	205		116		321		10,807	

SOURCE: See Note on Quantitative Data at end of essay.

those subjects by the lay baroque writers, as pointed out by José Antonio Maravall.[18] The basic religious and philosophical ideas were not too different from those formulated by theologians and philosophers in the sixteenth century, but the form of expression changed. The strange symbiosis between writers and their public, particularly in the theater, shows how the hard-won consensus, the consumption society created by inflation, the treason or defeat of the bourgeoisie, and the mixture of court, aristocratic, and bureaucratic culture with the populism of the old Christians gave priority to living ideas rather than searching for them.

The contrast between the aesthetic creativity of the seventeenth century and the relative barrenness from then until the late nineteenth century leads conservative, nativist critics to perceive cultural decadence as the result of an effort to link with traditions of intellectual effort that had become neglected and that therefore appear foreign. However, our data suggest that the break had taken place much earlier and that the explosion of aesthetic creativity in the seventeenth century hid the decadence already affecting other forms of intellectual life. The apparent lack of correspondence between cultural glory and political power and wealth that we felt existed in the Spain of the seventeenth century is, in view of these data, partly spurious.

The Societal Context

It is not easy to describe briefly the social structure of Spain in the sixteenth and seventeenth centuries. Social and economic historians have accumulated much information,[19] and literary historians and essayists have offered their quite contradictory interpretations. Obviously, the social structures of the different kingdoms and even of different parts of the Crown of Castile were quite heterogeneous. In addition, a great number of economic, social, and even cultural changes took place between the reign of the Catholic Kings and the death of the last Habsburg. We can only list some basic characteristics and then explore how they affected the recruitment of the intellectual elite broadly understood and particular sectors of it.

The first question that arises is the degree to which society was feudal or bourgeois. Using those terms in a somewhat strict sense—that is, rejecting the Marxist expansion of the concept feudal and linking the term bourgeois to certain forms of economic organization, at least of incipient capitalism—I would argue that the dominant structures of Spain were neither feudal nor bourgeois; both are, however, important components of the social structure.

The Reconquista of a large part of the area north of Toledo was accompanied by settlement by free peasants. The large-scale participation of the population in the struggle against the infidel gave to many, in some provinces the overwhelming majority of the population, the status of nobility: *hijodalgos*. This status did not imply wealth or a seigneurial relation over anyone. Most cities were under royal rather than noble or ecclesiastical lords. The Southern Reconquista, carried out by the military orders and by a nobility that was granted authority over an Islamic population, created a quite different social structure.[20] The cities of Castile, on the basis of wool production, the textile industry, and trade with northern Europe, were at some point becoming bourgeois centers, but a number of economic and political changes soon weakened that development.[21] The important role of the church, particularly the religious orders, and of the *letrados*[22]—lawyers trained at the universities—created strata close to the center of power that only in part overlapped with the nobility, or at least

with the titled nobility. The special role of the formerly Muslim population
in many of the manual and artisan activities, and in some sections in agriculture, introduced a cultural-ethnic stratification that might in part, particularly after the notion of purity of blood becomes institutionalized,
be considered a caste structure. A large Jewish minority[23] in business, the
administration of kings and lords, and certain professions such as medicine
constituted a pariah people, in Max Weber's terms, powerful in many
respects, but increasingly perceived as alien and hated by the little people.
The end of the Reconquista in 1492, after over a century of conflicts,
antisemitic riots, and perhaps a populist element in the royal policy, left
the Jewish population with a choice between conversion and expulsion.
The fact that a large number, particularly the more secularized privileged
segment, opted for a more or less sincere conversion created a new group:
the *conversos* or *cristianos nuevos*. This group was increasingly the object
of discrimination and suspicion. In Spain we are confronted with a plural
society, subject to a giant political-religious-cultural effort of integration or,
perhaps better, homogenization.

It is within this context that we must analyze the men whom we might
call intellectuals. The fact that most of them entered their roles through
the university and/or the church, which only to a point required noble status, allowed for some social mobility,[24] even though the mass of peasants
were far from having equality of opportunity to become literate. Legally
the church and the convents were open to men of all classes and the
universities had colleges for those of limited means,[25] but throughout this
period they discriminated increasingly in favor of those of privileged
background, even violating their statutes, although the servants of wealthy
students often had an opportunity to obtain an education. Most of those in
intellectual activities probably came from the lesser nobility, the *hidalgos,*
a numerous class in Spain, or, to a lesser extent, from an incipient office and
merchant bourgeoisie.

One disability must have weighed seriously for the new Christians in
precluding entry into many professional and intellectual pursuits: that of
the requirement of *limpieza de sangre* in cathedral chapters, for officers of
the Inquisition, for many benefices, in the most distinguished colleges at the
universities, and, after some resistance, in the religious orders, even among
the Jesuits who opposed it strongly and did not accept it outside of Spain.[26]
(The successor of Saint Ignatius came from a *converso* family.) Even so, a
number of outstanding figures in letters and scholarship had known Jewish
ancestors, something that their personal enemies did not fail to note, and
others probably "passed" by obtaining false genealogical backgrounds.[27]

Américo Castro suggested that the intellectual elite in the sixteenth
century had ties with a *converso* milieu. Our data (see table 2), obviously
incomplete since they cannot take into account those "passing" successfully
and the many for which biographical data are scant, do not show such a

Table 2.   New Christian background or suspicion of it in elite intellectuals
(in percentages).

Background	Sixteenth century	Seventeenth century	Both centuries
Converso or crypto-Jew	—	1.7	0.6
Of *converso* family	4.4	2.6	3.7
Accused of *converso* background with high probability of being so	1.5	—	0.9
Accused of *converso* background, probably unjustly	1.5	3.5	2.2
Modern scholars have reasonable suspicions of *converso* background	3.4	—	2.2
Modern scholars provide circumstantial evidence on *converso* background	1.0	1.7	1.2
Total number	205	116	321

SOURCE: See Note on Quantitative Data at end of essay.

high proportion as his, though they show a larger number in the sixteenth (9 per cent) than in the seventeenth century (4 per cent). However, the "probably unjustly accused" more than doubled from one century to the next, perhaps reflecting the heightened concern with *limpieza de sangre*. These figures are the more surprising considering the fact that an estimated 250,000 *conversos* lived untouched by the Inquisition after the expulsion among the 7.4 million inhabitants calculated for 1541 (that is, 3.3 per cent of the population)[28] and the fact that the Jewish population was of an urban character and disproportionately engaged in intellectual callings.

The caste element that the distinction between *cristianos viejos* and *nuevos* introduced must have had important psychic consequences, regardless of the Jewish cultural heritage that they may have received and reworked within a Christian framework (for instance, in an Erasmian Christianity or a mystical "Protestantism") or in literary forms that expressed alienation.[29] Paradoxically, the distinction between old and new Christians created a sense of equality among old Christians, even commoners, reflected in literature and often noted by foreign observers. In fact, the emphasis on the *limpieza de sangre* had at its roots the hostility of upward mobile strata toward an aristocracy that often had intermarried with wealthy Jews, toward all economically or professionally privileged strata, and therefore encountered the resistance of parts of the elite.

The aristocracy of birth, from the poorest *hidalgo* to the *grandees* of Spain, retained its status privileges, enhanced its wealth and power (particularly in the period of decadence), maintained a style of life, even without means, by indebtedness, and reinforced its self-esteem through a complex process of rejection of incipient bourgeois values and ways of life. Economic decline, inflation, depopulation of the countryside, and consumption rather than saving made Spain less bourgeois than other European societies of the time. The situation profoundly affected its culture, its literature, and its market for the theater and the arts.[30]

The importance of a nonaristocratic clergy and of the professions, particularly lawyers and nonaristocratic servants of the state, does not allow us to consider Spain a feudal society even when feudal values and structures were evident. In a sense we are dealing with intellectuals in neither fully traditional nor modern society—an agrarian society, which is neither feudal nor bourgeois nor peasant-egalitarian, but one in which religion, religious-racial prejudice, monarchical authority, and even education introduce elements of egalitarianism and achievement. The economic dependence of the intellectual, scholar, and writer on officeholding in the bureaucracy or the church did not affect his self-esteem nor that granted to him by his contemporaries of all classes. In addition, the imperial assertion of Spain's power had very early established the dignity of intellectual work in the vernacular rather than Latin, doing away with any distinction between scholars and writers.[31]

In a period in which noble family background was widespread in all elites—often falsely claimed, if for no other reasons than to escape taxes—in which the population of entire regions claimed noble status, we cannot be sure that biographers always recorded it. Our data therefore must underestimate the noble background, but they are nevertheless indicative. The titled nobility, from princes and dukes to *señores,* was not heavily represented among intellectuals (between 4 and 5 per cent), even when those of noble background or *hidalgos* constituted at least 19 per cent more. Proportions of intellectuals from the titled nobility, the *hidalgos,* and those of noble background without specification, as well as those donning the crosses of one of the military orders (requiring proof of nobility), increased markedly among those born after 1575. (Those with some information on noble background were 21 per cent before that date and 27 per cent afterwards.) The number of *caballeros* of the military orders increases from 5 per cent to 19 per cent. Considering an average of one noble for every ten inhabitants in the population,[32] this proportion, while high, does not seem so remarkable. Intellectual positions were far from dependent upon noble birth.

Birthplace and Travel

The birthplace of intellectuals, particularly the elite among them (see tables 3 and 4),[33] tells us much about the milieus favorable to cultural creativity. It is certainly not the marginal and poor Spain of the northern seaboard—where the use of vernaculars like Galician and Basque must have been an obstacle—nor large parts of the poorer interior, from which academics and men of letters came. Most of them came from urban centers, particularly the rich emporium of the Atlantic trade: Seville, the other large Andalusian cities, the old imperial city of Toledo (in the sixteenth century), some of the bourgeois cities of Old Castile, and, increasingly, Madrid, capital of the empire. One-third of the intellectual elite was born in the seven largest cities of Castile. Maps of economic activity[34] and intellectual activity show striking resemblances.

The participants in the Council of Trent (1545-1563)[35] allow us to compare a top religious-scholarly elite with sixteenth-century elite intellectuals in general. The Basque areas, Navarre, and Old Castile are represented disproportionately, while the south, so rich in literary intellectual life, is underrepresented. The areas that today constitute the core area of Spanish Catholicism are overrepresented. Perhaps the more recent conquest, a different style of life, and a less intellectualized religiosity account for the north-south differences.

An outstanding characteristic of these intellectuals is geographic mobility (see table 5), a reflection of the imperial character of Spain. In the sixteenth century, up to 64 per cent had traveled outside of Castile or Aragon, a figure reduced in the seventeenth century to 35.5 per cent. One of every ten had even crossed the Atlantic. Italy, partly dominated by Spain, seat of the Pope, center of humanistic learning, location of Bologna and Naples, two of the universities open to Spaniards after 1558, and on the route to the Habsburg north, was visited by more than one-third in the sixteenth century and over one in four in the seventeenth century. Flanders, the fatal inheritance of the Habsburgs, was seen by almost one in ten as a result of its frequent wars. In the sixteenth century, France and specifically the Sorbonne attract many visitors, as does England after the British marriage of Philip II. One of the most surprising facts is the considerable intellectual exchange between Castile-Aragon and Portugal in the sixteenth century and the cessation of those contacts in the seventeenth century, despite the union of the crowns until 1640, perhaps an indication of increasing cultural nationalism in the neighboring country soon to become independent. The retrenchment of Spain, the increased cultural isolationism, is reflected in the decreasing contacts of intellectuals within foreign countries, with the exception of those such as Naples, Sicily, and Flanders, and to a lesser degree the Habsburg domains, tied to the empire.

Among motives for foreign travel or sojourn (see table 6), study and teaching were important in the sixteenth century but nearly disappeared in the seventeenth, reflecting the change from the internationalism of Renaissance Europe to the growing national and religious boundaries of later days. Charles V, in his constant travels, was often accompanied by men of letters, but the later Habsburgs stayed in Spain; correspondingly travels as diplomats became more important for a minority of intellectuals. The great debates of the Counter Reformation offered another opportunity for international contacts. Only one reason for travel did not decline: war. More Spaniards go abroad to fight in the seventeenth century than in the

Table 3. Birthplace of elite and mass intellectuals, region's per cent of total population, ratio between figures, birthplace of Spanish participants in Council of Trent (in percentages).

Region	Elite			Mass[a] (1500–1584) (B)	Per cent of total population (C)	Ratios		Participants in Council of Trent
	Sixteenth century	Seventeenth century	Both centuries (A)			Elite (A/C)	Mass (B/C)	
Madrid, city	4.4	25.0	12.0	5.9	1.8	6.68	3.28	2.3
Castilla la Nueva, including Madrid province	15.0	14.0	15.0	16.0	14.2	1.05	1.26	8.6
Sevilla	9.3	7.8	8.7	7.6	6.4	1.36	1.34	2.3
Cadiz, Huelva	—	—	—	1.0ᵉ	—	—	—	—
Cordoba	4.4	2.6	3.7	3.0	2.6	1.42	1.11	2.3
Jaen	0.5	1.7	0.9	2.2	3.1	1.29	1.71	3.1
Granada	2.9	1.7	2.5	3.0	2.7	1.26	1.30	1.6
Malaga, Almeria	0.5	1.7	0.9	1.6	—	—	—	—
Andalucia	17.6	15.5	16.7	18.4	14.8	1.11	1.21	7.0
Castilla la Vieja (Santander, Burgos, Logroño, Soria)	2.0	5.2	3.1	5.6	7.5	.41	.75	18.7
(Avila, Valladolid, Segovia, Palencia)	8.8	6.0	7.8	9.0	10.6	.73	.85	14.0
Salamanca	2.9	0.8	2.2	2.6	3.6	.61	.72	5.5
Leon, Zamora	4.3	1.7	3.4	2.3	5.2	.66	.44	7.0
Extremadura	4.4	0.8	3.1	4.2	6.3	.49	.67	3.1
Asturias	1.0	1.7	1.3	0.3	1.9	.68	.16	—
Galicia	0.5	0.9	0.6	1.2	7.0	.09	.17	0.8
Basque country	1.0	0.9	0.9	2.0	2.2	.41	.91	3.9
Navarra	1.9	0.9	1.5	2.2	1.6	.94	1.37	4.7
Murcia	1.5	1.7	1.5	0.7	1.6	.94	.44	—
Albacete	—	0.9	0.3	0.5	—ᵇ	—	—	—
Aragon	4.4	2.6	3.7	11.4	4.5	.83	2.54	9.4
Cataluña	2.4	3.4	2.8	6.6	5.0	.56	1.32	3.1
Baleares	—	—	—	1.3	1.5	—	.88	2.3
Valencia	6.3	4.3	5.6	7.7	5.0	1.12	1.54	7.0
Crown of Aragon	13.1	10.3	12.1	27.0	16.0	.76	1.69	21.8
Spanish America	2.4	2.6	2.5	3.4ᶜ	—	—	—	—
Portugal	2.9	2.6	2.8	—ᵈ	—	—	—	—
Other foreign countries	0.5	—	0.3	—	—	—	—	—
Without information	16.1	10.1	14.0	—	—	—	—	—
Total number	205	116	321	2,586	8,120,337	—	—	128

SOURCE: The data on population are from Antonio Domínguez Ortiz, *La sociedad española en el siglo XVII* (Madrid: Instituto Balmes de Sociología, CSIC, 1963), pp. 101–157. The censuses and estimates for the different kingdoms and provinces are of uneven quality and are from somewhat different dates; the best ones are for the kingdom of Castile from the census ordered by Philip II at the end of his reign. The figures are for the date closest to 1600. The sixteenth century is generally a period of population increase, while the seventeenth century represents a drop. There are obviously important regional differences in the demographic trends from region to region and city to city which we could not take into account—for example, the rapid rise of Madrid at the end of the sixteenth century and the decline of Toledo around 1600 and of Seville at mid-seventeenth century (see graph III, p. 155). The data for eighteen regions or provinces within Castile around 1591 have been taken from

Felipe Ruiz Martín, "La población española al comienzo de los tiempos modernos," in *El tránsito de la edad media al renacimiento en la historia de España, Cuadernos de Historia*, I (Madrid: Instituto Jerónimo Zurita, CSIC, 1967), pp. 189–202, second of the appended tables. The lack of correspondence between the present provincial division and the historical provinces has forced us to combine data for those born in different provinces to calculate the ratios and a margin of error exists in the case of those born in the rural areas or small towns due to boundary changes between regions. Another source of error is the nonallocation of those of the elite whose birthplace we ignore, for we include them in calculating the percentages.

The data on the participants in the Council of Trent (1545–1563) refer to 128 of 163 participants, for whom we have birthplace and certitude of their participation. Spaniards constituted the largest group, after the Italians, and played a prominent role (of fourteen theologians sent by the pope, eleven were Spaniards). Data from C. Gutiérrez, S.J., *Españoles en Trento* (Valladolid: Instituto Jerónimo Zurita, CSIC, 1951), pp. lxix-lxx, 1050–1053.

[a] Nicolás Antonio, *Bibliotheca Hispana Nova*; see table 1 and Note on Quantitative Data at end of essay.
[b] The province of Albacete was not a separate unit; it was divided among different regions.
[c] Based on all those listed in the Peninsula and overseas: 2,679.
[d] Nicolás Antonio lists Portugal and its authors born overseas, which represent 26.7 per cent of his total listing of 3,604 authors by birthplace.

Table 4.   Type and size of birthplace of elite intellectuals.

Region	Sixteenth century (per cent)	Seventeenth century (per cent)	Population		Per cent of total population	
			1530	1594	1530	1594
Madrid	4.4	25.0	4,060	37,500[e]	0.05	0.40[e]
Castilian cities:						
over 20,000 in 1530[a]	22.4	17.2	192,290	253,455	2.60	3.00
	26.8	42.2				
10,000 to 19,999 in 1530[b]	4.9	2.6	101,360	138,630	1.30	1.60
3,000 to 9,999 in 1530[c]	4.9	1.7	87,700	128,830	1.20	1.50
	36.7	46.5			5.15	6.50
not included above, now provincial capitals	9.8	11.2				
Cities of the crown of Aragon and Navarre[d] now provincial capitals	4.9	2.6				
All present Spain: small towns and important villages	17.1	15.8				
small villages	11.2	7.8				
America, Portugal, foreign countries	5.8	5.2				
No information	14.5	11.2				
Total number	205	116	7,414,000	8,485,000		

SOURCE: Ramón Carande, *Carlos V y sus banqueros: La vida económica en Castilla (1516–1556)* (Madrid: Sociedad de Estudios y Publicaciones, 1955), I, 60; see also Note on Quantitative Data at end of essay.
[a] Includes Seville, Toledo, Valladolid, Jaen, Cordoba, Medina del Campo. Only Medina del Campo drops below 20,000 at the end of the century. This group does not include the cities of the kingdom of Granada; Granada city had a population of between 18,000 and 50,000 in the seventeenth century. The population for Seville used here is 19,000, but turn-of-the-century estimates go as high as 150,000, including transients, to drop again in the mid-seventeenth century to 65,000.
[b] Includes Segovia, Salamanca, Baeza, and Ubeda (which at the end of the century have over 20,000), and Murcia, Alcazar de San Juan, and Medina de Rioseco.
[c] Includes Burgos, Avila, Alcala, Toro, Palencia, Talavera, and Ciudad Rodrigo (all over 10,000 at the end of the century), and Zamora, Guadalajara, Soria, Santiago, Orenso, Vigo, Tuy, and La Coruña.
[d] Includes Barcelona, with about 50,000, Zaragoza, with between 25,000 and 30,000, and Valencia, with approximately 50,000, in the seventeenth century.
[e] Maximum estimate for Madrid in the seventeenth century is 165,000 or 1.8 per cent of the total population.

Table 5. Travels of elite intellectuals (in percentages).

Place visited	Sixteenth century	Seventeenth century	Both centuries
America	13.2	7.8	11.2
Naples and Sicily	7.8	8.6	8.1
Rome	12.7	5.2	10.0
Rest of Italy	16.1	4.3	11.8
Italy unspecified	6.3	7.8	6.9
Total Italy	42.9	25.9	36.8
Flanders	9.8	9.5	9.7
Germany, Austria	8.8	5.2	7.5
France	13.7	7.6	11.5
England	5.4	0.9	3.7
Muslim countries	7.3	4.3	6.2
Portugal	10.2	3.5	7.8
Other countries	1.0	—	0.6
Those having visited places outside the Peninsula	63.7	35.5	47.1
Total number	'205	116	321

SOURCE: See Note on Quantitative Data at end of essay.

sixteenth. Some 11 per cent of the intellectual elite had seen action some-where outside the peninsula, a factor not to be neglected when we try to understand the heightened national and imperial consciousness in their work.

Universities and Intellectuals

One might consider intellectuals as those men trained at the thirty-three universities of the realm—eighteen of them founded in Castile alone between 1475 and 1620—or at foreign universities before the prohibition by Philip II in 1559.[36]

The outstanding work of Richard Kagan[37] on Spanish universities based on matriculation records allows us to describe the university attendance in the period. Kagan estimated 20,000 students annually in the late sixteenth century, which would be 3.7 per cent of the fifteen- to twenty-four-year-old males, and 6.3 per cent of those seventeen years old, a figure that would have to be raised slightly if taking into account students being educated by the Jesuits in arts and grammar at the university level. This proportion would be higher than that for England and probably the highest in Europe at that time. In fact, such proportions were not exceeded in modern nations until the late nineteenth century and in many countries until a few decades ago. Kagan estimates, in view of the large proportion of students of noble (particularly *hidalgo*) origin and the proportion of that class in the population, that perhaps one-quarter or one-third of Castile's

Table 6.   Motives for foreign travel of elite intellectuals (in percentages).

Motive	Sixteenth century	Seventeenth century	Both centuries
Study	15.0	1.8	7.1
Teaching	7.8	—	5.0
Council of Trent	6.3	—	4.0
Business of religious orders	6.3	0.9	4.4
Diplomacy	3.9	5.2	4.4
Travel with			
kings	6.4	—	4.0
nobles	3.4	6.0	4.4
ecclesiastics	2.4	0.9	1.8
family	1.9	1.7	1.9
Ecclesiastical position	2.9	0.9	2.2
War			
Italy	5.4	6.9	5.9
Flanders	2.9	5.2	3.6
Armada Invincible and			
British pirates	1.0	0.9	1.0
France	2.4	0.9	1.8
Turks and Africa	5.4	4.3	5.0
America	2.5	2.6	2.5
Germany	1.5	2.6	1.9
Portugal	2.4	—	1.6
Total in any war[a]	13.2	8.6	11.2
Exile	2.9	1.7	2.5
Adventure	0.5	1.7	0.9
Total number	205	116	321

SOURCE: See Note on Quantitative Data at end of essay.
[a] The same individual, obviously, can have participated in different campaigns.

young noblemen may have received some form of university or university-level education. Most of the students were of urban background, from the north and center of the peninsula, areas with the highest *hidalgo* concentration. With the exception of Alcalá, Salamanca, and Valladolid, Castile's universities drew the vast majority of their students from the diocese or province in which they were located. The three mentioned were in many ways the "imperial" universities of the Habsburgs; their graduates enjoyed a majority of places and in many offices a virtual monopoly.

Within the three imperial universities the graduates of the six Colegios Mayores started to dominate the chairs and crown and clerical offices. Between 1566 and 1700 over half of the members of the Councils of Castile and the Indies, and nearly 40 per cent of the Castilian bishops during the seventeenth century, were graduates of the Colegios. Since these students were a privileged minority, others must have been discouraged from studying. Two additional factors accounting for the sharp drop in university enrollment are the increase in the sale of offices by the crown under the

late Philips and the revival of aristocratic ideals with the great wars of the
1630's and 1640's and the policies of Olivares. In addition the religious
orders, particularly the Jesuits, offered in the seventeenth century an alternative to university education.[38] It is probable that these circumstances,
together with population losses, economic decline, mounting taxation, fiscal
chaos, atrophy of urban economic activities that reduced professional opportunities for lawyers, and the displacement of private teaching by the
orders, account for the fall in the number of students. By 1660, Alcalá,
Salamanca, and Valladolid attracted fewer than half the number of students
they had had a century before, a downward trend that continued into the
eighteenth century. Kagan's time series for Castile's universities by faculty
therefore offer another clue to the fluctuations of cultural life and the onset
of Spanish decadence. It would seem that, with some delay, the curves of
academic life and cultural creativity, considered in terms of the number of
outstanding figures born at different times, reflect the economic and subsequent political crises of Spain.

Obviously many of those who obtained their *bachiller, licenciado,* or
even doctorate entered pursuits that did not involve the use of knowledge
and ideas. Some became conquistadores or adventurers, but most were probably professionals: lawyers, doctors, civil servants, and ecclesiastics. The
functions of the universities were listed in a royal privilege of 1659: "they
have been since their foundation, seminaries of eminent men of letters, the
source of the highest dignitaries of the Church, and for the administration
of justice in our royal name and with your representation on our tribunals
and councils."[39] Therefore, not all those with academic degrees can be considered intellectuals, even in a broad sense of the term.[40] The rosters of
faculty, graduates, and students of the leading universities should allow us
to answer two complementary questions: how many of the men that shaped
Spanish culture and society were connected with universities and how many
of those who sat in their classrooms contributed more or less creatively to
shape that culture? Our data allow some tentative answers to the first of
these questions (see tables 7 and 8).

Six out of ten of the elite intellectuals of these two centuries attended
at least sometime, often without obtaining a degree, some university. However, that proportion changes markedly from 48 per cent in the sixteenth
century to 28.5 per cent in the seventeenth. This shift reflects the change
from a humanistic renaissance and scholarly academic-scientific culture
to a more literary and expressive one, from the Renaissance (or late
medieval) to the baroque. It also corresponds well with the conclusions of
Kagan on the decline in enrollment over the period. The universities attended and the courses of study followed also tell us much about the intellectual milieu. Among those born before 1576, 11 per cent attended foreign
schools, compared to 3 per cent afterwards. Undoubtedly, the prohibition of
Philip II in 1559, together with other factors, had some impact. Within

Table 7. Universities attended by elite intellectuals (in percentages).

University	Born before 1525	Born 1525–1575	Sixteenth century[a]	Seventeenth century	Both centuries
Salamanca	37.0	19.8	26.8	12.1	21.5
Alcalá	19.0	16.2	15.1	12.1	14.0
Valladolid	2.4	2.3	2.4	3.1	2.8
"Imperial Universities"	58.4	38.3	44.4	27.6	28.3
Sevilla	3.7	4.6	3.4	3.5	3.4
Granada	2.4	5.8	3.4	1.7	2.8
Osuna and Baeza	—	3.5	1.1	1.7	1.6
Other Castilian universities	1.2	3.5	2.4	0.9	1.9
Catalan and Aragonese universities	3.7	9.3	5.8	1.7	4.4
Valencia	1.2	3.5	2.4	0.9	1.9
Foreign universities	19.9	5.8	11.2	2.6	8.1
No record of university education	29.8	36.0	37.0	53.5	43.0
Total number	81	86	205	116	321

SOURCE: See Note on Quantitative Data at end of essay.
[a] Includes those sixteenth-century intellectuals for whom there is no record of birth date.

Spain, 38 per cent attended one of the three universities Kagan has called imperial—Salamanca, Alcalá, and Valladolid—often more than one of them. In the sixteenth century Salamanca was attended by 27 per cent, a figure reduced to 12 per cent in the seventeenth, while Alcalá, closer to the court, retained much of its attraction (15 per cent and 12 per cent, respectively). The figures for the elite clearly reflect the drop in enrollment after the peak in the 1580's and the decline of the universities as centers of learning—and even, as we will see in the case of Francisco de Quevedo, reaction against

Table 8. University studies of elite intellectuals (in percentages).

Field	Born before 1525	Born 1525–1575	Sixteenth century	Seventeenth century	Both centuries
Humanities	30.1	18.6	21.8	17.3	19.3
Theology	15.8	17.4	17.1	9.5	14.3
Civil law	12.1	10.5	17.1	18.1	20.2
Canon law	7.3	3.5	7.3	8.6	7.7
Medicine	8.6	10.5	9.8	3.4	7.5
University studies with no information on discipline	6.2	15.2	9.3	6.1	8.5
Total number	81	86	205	116	321

SOURCE: See Note on Quantitative Data at end of essay.

the university-educated and exaltation of the men of action and the aristocracy against the *noblesse de robe*. These trends occur even when the proportion born in university towns remains stable at around one-fourth. There are indications that some must have preferred a Jesuit college education to the disorderly universities (the proportion triples from one to the other century, but is still low). The Andalusian universities did not train a large proportion of the intellectuals but those proportions remained almost unchanged, in contrast to those of the kingdom of Aragon, which without exception came to play a much smaller role.

Kagan also documents how the enrollments in different faculties show a steady shift, beginning in the middle years of the sixteenth century, away from the study of arts and theology to the study of law, particularly canon law, gateway to both clerical and secular careers. In Alcalá the number of law students equaled that of theology by 1550, and by the opening of the seventeenth century, jurists outnumbered theologians almost two to one, a ratio that doubled before the century was out. At Salamanca and Valladolid the theology faculty fared even worse. As Kagan says: "In this light the old, popular assertion that a one-sided, conservative preoccupation with theology thwarted educational and scientific progress in Spain and her universities is not borne out . . . the almost exclusive pursuit of law and office-holding careers would be a more credible answer." Our data on the intellectual elite are fully congruent with his findings.

The Occupations of Intellectuals

The occupations of intellectuals (see table 9) provide us with many insights into their way of life, their social contacts, and their experiences. Obviously many made their living with activities very directly related to their written work, but others had to engage in a great variety of activities to assure it.

The most intellectual of all occupations, university teaching, was practiced by one out of every four intellectuals in the sixteenth century, the age of splendor of the universities, but it becomes almost insignificant in the seventeenth century. Certainly there were still professors at the universities of the realm, but few of the cultural elite, as we have defined them, were occupying the chairs. Private teaching had already been an important activity in the 1500's, but it became more important in the next century relative to university teaching, a fact probably not unrelated to the shift of the cultural center to Madrid, a city without a university. The masters holding chairs, particularly at Salamanca and Alcalá, were often not only creative intellectuals but were also called on to act in other roles: to be advisers to the crown and its councils, the church, and the Inquisition; to settle controversial issues—moral and legal questions such as the conquest of America and the treatment of the Indians—and to answer questions of heresy

Table 9.   Main occupations of elite intellectuals (in percentages).

Occupation	Sixteenth century	Seventeenth century	Both centuries
University teaching	25.9	1.7	17.1
Private teaching, including			
religious colleges	8.3	4.3	6.8
Total academic	34.2	6.0	23.9
Chronicler	6.8	6.0	6.5
Archaeologist, artist	1.5	0.9	1.2
Actor	2.9	0.9	2.2
Income from writing	1.5	—	0.9
Continuous support by maecenas	1.0	1.7	1.2
Censor	.5	3.5	1.6
Total "intellectual"	14.2	13.0	13.6
Ecclesiastical office	19.5	17.2	18.2
Religious order	19.0	9.5	15.6
Preacher	4.9	2.6	4.0
Inquisitorial office	3.9	6.9	5.0
At service of church without			
being cleric	1.5	1.7	1.5
Total religious	48.8	37.9	44.7
Rentier	2.4	6.0	3.7
Medicine	8.3	1.7	5.9
Law	2.0	4.3	2.8
Notary	2.4	0.9	1.9
Total free professions	12.7	6.9	10.6
Court positions	16.1	12.9	14.9
At the service of the nobility	8.8	14.7	12.0
Total court service	24.9	27.6	26.9
Government office:			
Executive	6.8	12.1	8.6
Finance	5.4	6.0	5.6
Judiciary	4.9	3.5	4.4
Diplomacy	1.5	3.5	3.1
Other public employment	2.4	4.3	3.1
Total public office	21.0	29.4	23.9
Military:			
Officer	7.8	10.3	8.6
Service as officer	3.4	3.4	3.4
Soldier	5.4	2.6	4.4
Total military	16.6	16.3	16.4
Business, commerce	1.5	—	0.9
Printer	0.5	0.9	0.6
Artisan	1.5	—	0.9
Total "bourgeois"	3.5	0.9	2.4
No information on occupation	7.3	19.0	11.6
Total number	205	116	321
Average number of positions for those with information	2.1	1.7	1.9

SOURCE: See Note on Quantitative Data at end of essay. The biographies are far from adequate on the activities of intellectuals. Multiple activities were frequent and we have considered all of them, rather than attempt to identify one main occupation and secondary ones, or take into account the time spent in each.

and occasionally technical problems. There was movement from the universities into important offices; for example, a humanist professor at Alcalá —Juan de Vergara—became secretary to the archbishop of Toledo and canon of the cathedral. This practice became so frequent in the seventeenth century that faculty turnover contributed to the crisis of the university. Sometimes professors were influential writers and poets as well as academic experts, as in the case of Fray Luis de León. Professors often became bishops and church dignitaries. Theologians were often heads of powerful religious orders or held office in them; some of them participated as experts in the Council of Trent. In contrast to modern times, the university influenced public affairs not only through its members, but also as an institution expressing its opinion corporatively, though the practice was probably less common in Spain than at the Sorbonne or Louvain. Although the Inquisition may have shifted the function of thought control from the universities to censorship and the expurgation of books by that organization, it also, however, turned to well-known men, highly respected (then, and some even today) for their learning and creative contributions.

In addition to teaching, a variety of activities associated with cultural life, from royal or city historian to theater censor or actor, provided a living to another 14 per cent. Few are reported as living from the product of their published works, nor did private fortune support many of them. Support was less from individual patrons or even positions in the entourage of the nobility, than in court or public offices and, probably most often, through ecclesiastical benefices demanding little attention and often held in absentia. The church, particularly in the sixteenth century, was the support of close to half of the intellectual elite, mainly through the religious orders. After they lose importance for cultural life in the seventeenth century, church offices still provide support to close to two in ten.

Positions in that unique bureaucracy, the Inquisition, became increasingly important, assuring its members at least a tax exemption. The free professions, particularly medicine, were relatively important, but could not compare in either period with public office as a source of income. The administration of the state, the Indies, and the municipalities, and the diplomatic service, provided many intellectuals not only with social status and an income, but also with interesting experiences to use in their work, particularly that of the seventeenth-century political and economic thinkers. From governors of provinces, members of the highest councils of the realm, to modest tax collector positions—such as the one Cervantes held—the public sector provided the economic base for creative work and leisure. Obviously we cannot determine how many of the 21 per cent in the sixteenth and 29 per cent in the seventeenth century holding such positions won them by learning, professional capacity, and dedicated effort and how many held such positions more on account of their noble status or local family prestige. However, the two columns of a bureaucratic empire—state and church—as opposed to a market for intellectual products such as the university, were the supporters of the creators of ideas. Obviously this dual support did not encourage overly critical ideas about those institutions, criticism such as could be encouraged by autonomous corporate institutions such as universities, or a market for books supporting their authors. The surprising fact is the freedom of mind of many of these men in view of their social position. The military involvements of Spain in that period account for the large number who either as officers or soldiers spent years of their life in the army or navy of the king. Bourgeois occupations such as merchant, banker, or artisan were full-time occupations and did not allow the leisure to think and write that benefices of the church and offices in the bureaucracy provided. Few of the elite made a living in the incipient bourgeois society, and the number decreases from one century to the next.

The Religious as Intellectuals

Priests and members of religious orders, some without university education, were often intellectually active outside religious roles. Many of them taught, others wrote, preached, and advised the powerful as confessors, often without limiting themselves to religious activities. Much of profane literature was written by clerics, though one must distinguish carefully between those who obtained only minor orders to be eligible for ecclesiastical benefits as a source of income and those who were priests. The boundaries between laymen and clerics in those centuries were much less precise.

Antonio Domínguez Ortiz[41] has described the extremely complex structure of ecclesiastical society, the secular and regular clergy, the offices, the financial bases, the relation to different aspects of the social structure and public life. For the end of the sixteenth century he reports a figure of 29,745 secular and 32,698 regular clergy in Castile. An estimate that seems plausible for the late seventeenth century is 150,000 clerical persons, including nuns, which would be about 2 per cent of the population and 5 per cent of the active population.[42] In 1630 in Castile and Leon there were 343 high church offices, 928 canons, and 585 *raciones* in the cathedrals; adding those of the kingdom of Aragon, a reasonable estimate for Spain is 2,500. A variety of other "benefices" could raise the figure to some 3,650.[43] There is no doubt that many intellectuals held such positions, but from the figures it is also clear that only a small proportion of those holding them must have been creative intellectuals. We have no figures for the number of convents in the seventeenth century, but in the eighteenth century 2,104 male convents are reported to have existed. Some of them in the sixteenth century had been centers of learning, like San Esteban of Salamanca, and many served local schools. Quite a few men of all walks of

life, among them some famous writers (such as Lope de Vega), in their
advanced age became priests or entered cloisters.

In many ways clerics, particularly those of the secular clergy, were less
differentiated and isolated from the lay world and its worldliness than they
are today: their dealings with women and children, their attachment to the
household of powerful aristocrats, their political offices as viceroys and
governors, and their positions in the court assured them a much closer
contact with the whole society, a contact that allowed them to share and
understand the problems of laymen, from love and politics to the emerging
capitalist market and monetary system. Those men approached their tasks
from a religious perspective, and at the same time they brought to the
religious sphere the problems of the world and their direct knowledge of
them. It is not an accident that some of the most interesting contributions
to economic analysis at the time were the work of clerics, moralists who
as preachers and confessors could observe directly in a place such as
Seville the consequences of the arrival of specie from the Indies.[44] The
authors of religious-educational plays—the *autos sacramentales*—and of plays
with deep religious-philosophical meaning were also authors of profane
comedies and dramas.[45] There were undoubtedly, after the Reformation, pressures to limit certain intellectual activities of religious significance to those
specifically trained (particularly after the translation of the Scriptures into
the vernacular was forbidden and their commentary increasingly suspect),
but even so the literature written by laymen has a deep religious component.
The fear of the *iluminados* and lay mysticism, of the excesses of conven-
ticula outside the control of the church, of an intimate religiosity neglecting
or rejecting the sacramental and public manifestations, of the impact of
Erasmian devotion weakening the role of religious functionaries and threatening the monopoly of religious virtuosi controlled by church institutions[46]—
all put a limit to lay devotional literature and scriptural scholarship, but
not to the more aesthetic manifestations, poetry and theater. For a better
understanding of the religious life it would be interesting to know how
many religious officeholders were also intellectuals in one sense or another;
for a sociological study of intellectuals it would be interesting to know how
many were linked with the church.

Our data allow some tentative answers to the second of these questions
(see table 10). While in the Middle Ages to be an intellectual was almost
identical with clerical status, the Renaissance brought with it the secular
intellectual in the royal and noble courts and in the universities, who, with
the invention of printing, increasingly wrote for the market or an audience.
Four out of ten among the intellectual elite were clerics, almost equally
divided among the secular and the regular clergy. Obviously many of those
men had received orders late, sometimes as widowers. There are significant
differences between the sixteenth and seventeenth centuries in the number
of members of the regular clergy (23 per cent as opposed to 13 per cent)

Table 10. Membership in religious orders of elite and mass intellectuals (in percentages).

Religious order	Elite			Mass (1500–1584)[a]	
	Sixteenth century	Seventeenth century	Both centuries	Per cent of authors	Per cent of members of order
Benedictine	—	—	—	2.7	4.8
Cister	—	—	—	2.8	4.2
Dominican	5.4	0.9	3.6	11.2	16.5
Franciscan	5.9	1.7	4.3	16.1	23.8
Carmel	1.5	—	0.9	4.8	7.2
Capuchine	—	—	—	0.6	0.9
St. Augustin	2.4	—	1.5	6.1	9.0
St. Hieronymus	1.0	0.9	0.9	0.9	1.3
Jesuit	5.4	4.3	5.0	14.9	21.9
Merced	—	0.9	0.3	5.4	7.9
Other orders	1.5	4.3	2.5	2.7	3.9
Total members of religious orders	45.4	32.8	40.7	67.9	100.0
Secular clergy	22.0	18.1	20.5	11.6	—
Minor orders	1.0	1.7	1.2	—	—
No record of clerical status	54.0	64.5	59.0	20.5	—
Total number	205	116	321	3,604	2,449

SOURCE: See Note on Quantitative Data at end of essay.
[a] Nicolás Antonio, *Bibliotheca Hispana Nova*; see table 1 and Note on Quantitative Data at end of essay.

and even a slight drop in the secular clergy (from 23 per cent to 20 per cent). Undoubtedly the decline in the humanistic and academic fields and the decrease in the number of university trained intellectuals had something to do with this change. Significantly, Spain, without an internal war of religion, political secularization, or even a lessening religious emphasis in its culture (except in the type of religiously oriented culture), undergoes a process of secularization of its intellectual elite. However, among the "mass intellectuals"—those classified by Nicolás Antonio—the proportion of members of religious orders is appreciably larger than among the elite (68 per cent as opposed to 41 per cent). Among the regulars we see the decay of the mendicant orders, particularly the Dominicans, but also the Carmelites who had brought mysticism to its height. The Jesuits contribute in the seventeenth century one-third of the regulars with distinguished contributions (one of every twenty intellectuals). Their share among the elite was disproportionately large. A finding of interest for a sociological study of culture is the considerable parallelism between the number of authors from different orders among the "mass" (including "second raters") and their contribution to the small minority of outstanding writers, our "elite."

The Religious Role of Intellectuals

Within the church the following intellectual roles existed: professors of theology, scholastic philosophy, moral theology, scripture, and canon law, mainly at Salamanca and Alcalá. Many of those teaching were also members of religious orders. It should be remembered that only in the nineteenth century were ecclesiastical studies separate from the university. In addition, there were the centers of education and learning of the religious orders, of increasing importance in the seventeenth century. The famous preachers, especially at the court, who often also wrote, were another type using and diffusing ideas.

A special category of "religious intellectual" not found in later centuries are the ascetics and mystics, whose writings are an important part of literature and who had a wide impact in shaping the ideas and values of the time as they were reflected in more profane literary expressions such as poetry and the theater. Their role was particularly frought with ambiguities and dangers as religious virtuosi without institutional charisma either of office or education, rebelling as divinely inspired reformers against the *Veralltäglichung* of the religious orders. Despite the deep suspicions of authorities and "qualified" religious experts and moments of persecution,[47] these men and women and their writings were soon recognized and their early sanctification legitimized their endeavors. The fact that such a style of religious creativity has little importance after 1700 indicates the deep discontinuity in Spanish culture and the uniqueness of the preceding period. The continuity that many scholars have noted between the medieval or pre-Reformation and the Catholic Reformation or baroque (or Counter Reformation) mystics, despite the apparent discontinuities in the cultural policies of the Inquisition at the time of the ascent to the throne of Philip II,[48] is one of the strong arguments for the basic unity of Spanish cultural life in those centuries. Obviously the question can be asked: Is it legitimate to stretch the term intellectual as far as to include mystics like Saint Theresa or Saint John of the Cross? Certainly for men like Quevedo—whose role probably would fit any narrower definition—such an approach (separating different types of creativity) would make no sense. To understand the impact of ideas on society, its central institutions and its elites, that approach would not suffice either.

The church, however, not only molded culture and society through its teachers, scholars, preachers, and mystics, creating and diffusing ideas, it also proscribed, deleted, and punished "heretical ideas" (see table 11). In the broad sense of the term "intellectual," part of the role of the inquisitors was intellectual: to judge the compatibility of new ideas with a dogmatic religious-philosophical heritage, subjecting to their control the works of the elite, including those of men close to power and even high church digni-

Table 11. The Inquisition and elite intellectuals (in percentages).

Inclusion in the Spanish *Indices Librorum Prohibitorum*	Seventeenth century	Eighteenth century	Both centuries
Opera omnia or several works forbidden	3.9	—	2.5
One work forbidden	4.4	1.8	3.4
Chapters, parts, or paragraphs expurgated	5.8	5.2	5.6
Some lines or quotations expurgated	3.9	1.8	3.1
Special cases	1.0	—	0.6
Total authors included	19.0	8.6	15.2

Actions other than inclusion in the indices	Seventeenth century	Eighteenth century	Both centuries
Interrogated but not prosecuted	1.0	—	0.6
Denounced but absolved	1.5	—	0.9
Prosecuted or jailed but finally absolved	3.9	0.9	2.8
Minor sentence	—	1.7	0.6
Major sentence (over 5 years) or burned in effigy	1.0	1.7	1.2
Exiled out of fear of the Inquisition	1.5	0.9	1.2
Total authors affected	8.9	5.2	7.3
Collaborators with the Inquisition[a]	1.9	0.9	1.6
Total number	205	116	321

SOURCE: The information on the inclusion in the indices has been obtained by checking the names of the elite authors against the indices of the Inquisitors: Fernando de Valdés (1559), Gaspar de Quiroga (1583), Bernardo de Sandoval y Rojas (1612), Antonio de Sotomayor (1667), and Agustín Rubín de Cevallos (1790). The indices of Antonio Zapata (1632), Diego Sarmiento de Valladares and Vidal Marín (1707), and Francisco Pérez de Prado (1747) could not be consulted. The index of 1790 reproduces the index of 1747 with additions up to 1789. The omission of the indices of 1632, 1707, and 1747 should not affect our findings too much, since later indices carried over the works included earlier, even when some works might have been dropped in the meantime. Some of the sixteenth-century authors were included only in the seventeenth and a few in the eighteenth centuries. Therefore the figures do not refer to authors affected in their lifetime, nor do they take into account that some works were included in only one index or only temporarily until they could be studied more thoroughly. The data on personal persecution and collaboration with the Inquisition have been gathered from the biographical sources listed in the Note on Quantitative Data at the end of the essay. The information on this aspect might not be complete.

a The majority of these also had difficulties with the Inquisition on account of their own works.

taries.[49] The pattern of censorship that generally did not condemn all the works of an author, nor whole books, but that "expurgated" them, deleting paragraphs or sometimes even isolated sentences, required an intellectual effort. So, for example, in Cervantes' *Quijote* only one sentence was found objectionable.[50] The indices of forbidden books, the deletions in different editions, and the records of the trials of the Inquisition are basic sources for the study of intellectuals and their relation to society. The impact of the Inquisition as an institution, the social control climate supporting and reinforced by it—through the appeal to denunciation of the *edictos de la fe*, what Unamuno has called the "immanent inquisition," the conscious or unconscious self-censorship on intellectuals and scientists—will continue to be debated.

The summary conclusion of Otis Green offers a balanced judgment:

It would be possible to draw, for Spain, an imposing picture of official leniency, and to balance this with a sobering account of the "immanent inquisition" which not only might, but sometimes suddenly did, introduce into a writer's life a period of terror (usually relieved by absolution). Yet this much can be asserted with assurance: the Spain of the sixteenth century was not created by the Inquisition; it developed, used, and abused the Inquisition as a means of strengthening, and later defending, its cherished way of life.[51]

However, our data on the changing emphasis within the religious culture from the first half of the sixteenth century to the second half and, even more, during the seventeenth century, suggest that social controls might have contributed to a shift from an intellectual-scholastic or intimate-mystical focus to a more literary-aesthetic-public style, very congruent with the age of the baroque.

The record of the overt activity of the inquisitors is complex: works included in the Roman Index of Paul IV were not included in the Spanish; some works were allowed in Latin but not in vulgar languages (because certain ideas were dangerous for the masses but not for the elite); there was tolerance of political thought (like that of Juan de Mariana and Francisco Suárez) considered sufficiently dangerous in other European countries to be burned; they were not overly concerned with some types of criticism of rulers; and they were far from puritan (as the treatment of *La Celestina* shows) despite the appeals of some intellectuals against light and useless literature. Of over a hundred picaresque novels, a risqué genre, only two were permanently forbidden and four expurgated.[52] Obviously political considerations, personal animosities, guilt by association, the personalities of the grand inquisitors, and the *converso* family background of the author enter into the particular cases; but, not without some ambivalences and shifts in emphasis, there is an undeniable consistency and logic in this thought control institution. Certainly the boundaries between the censorship and the creative activities of intellectuals in those centuries were far from neat, the same men sometimes playing the two roles. Unfortunately, we have no clear record of their motivations and feelings in doing so. However, we should remember that censorship, evaluation of thought from some fixed standards, need not always be the task of hacks, second-rate minds, as it became in the eighteenth-century Inquisition and is probably generally true in our time. A high degree of consensus on an orthodoxy, relatively clear standards to define it, an idea of order that excludes an absolutization of the idea of intellectual freedom, these are probably the conditions for a censorial function by creative intellectuals. From that perspective the inquisitor role can be an almost legitimate intellectual role and our implicit assumption of the equation of censorship with anti-intellectualism turns out to reflect a unique historical situation.[53]

Political Roles of Intellectuals

For the contemporary reader the political roles of intellectuals are probably more interesting than the religious roles, even though such an analytical distinction would make little sense to most men of the sixteenth and seventeenth centuries, and even less to Spaniards of those centuries. Even when Charles V and his advisers were involved in a bitter feud and war with Pope Clement VII, the issue was perceived and argued in religious terms: the proper role of a Pope and the need to call a church council to face the Lutheran heresy and to unite the Christians against the Turkish menace. The occupation and plundering of Rome by mutinous imperial troops is interpreted both by a humanist imperial secretary, Alfonso de Valdés,[54] and a popular poet as the just punishment by God of the Pope and the Roman Church for their deeds. The distinction of the charisma of the office from the person of the incumbent, which allows so much criticism (direct or indirect in literary forms) of rulers, including the Pope, allows for a defense of that act by the Erasmists. High officials and theologians who were consulted about the unprinted but widely circulating *Diálogo de las cosas ocurridas en Roma* (1527), objected mostly to particular sentences, not to the spirit. However, what is important about this work is its religious-political character as an important document by an intellectual in the service of the emperor. Political theory in those centuries is also moral-religious theory. The separation of political from religious and moral thought and the secularization of politics that was initiated with the Renaissance in many European countries did not go far in Spain.

Within this general framework intellectuals responded to a variety of problems, often in bitter conflict with each other. They played a number of roles. The uncommitted humanist[55] was politically concerned and sometimes influential, but unwilling to attach himself to any ruler in a permanent way or to intervene directly in the great debates. Erasmus, avoiding partisanship in disputes and policy decisions, despite his connection with emperor, Popes, rulers, and other more committed humanists and theologians, is the model for that role. Among Spaniards, Luis Vives, who lived principally abroad in Bruges, fits this role.

The committed humanist was active as a political adviser, writer of official statements, and propagandist of the position of his ruler. He maintained contact with his more apolitical peers, encouraged learning and scholarship, fought more or less overtly the more traditionalist or scholastic clerics and monks, and hoped for an irenic solution to the religious conflict. A few Spaniards looked with understanding on the Reformation but ultimately supported the Catholic position of the emperor and turned against the reformers. The more Erasmian or more Italian background of their humanism shades into their positions, as the contrast between an Alfonso de Valdés and a Ginés de Sepúlveda[56] would show. It is these men who formulate the new and at the same time old imperial ideas of Charles V, against the appeals of many members of the Castilian Cortes to center his attention on the national kingdom. They combined ideas of a Christian peace under the leadership of the emperor to face the Turkish threat with calling a council to reform the church and if necessary stand up to the Pope, who was overly interested in his Italian power politics. International politics among emerging modern states, particularly in relation to France, is justified by them in ideological terms that combine a variety of historical and intellectual heritages.

Max Weber has summarized the sociology of the humanists and the monumental work of Bataillon, *Erasme et l'Espagne,* in an excellent documentation of his conclusions for the Spanish case.

The sociology of the Humanists, particularly the transformation of a feudal and clerical education into a courtly culture based on the largesse of patrons, is not without inherent interest . . . The ambivalent attitude of the Humanists toward the Reformation was primarily caused by ideological factors. Insofar as Humanists placed themselves in the service of building the churches of either the Reformation or the Counter-Reformation, they played an extremely important, though not decisive, role in organizing church schools and in developing doctrine. But insofar as they became the carriers of particular religiosity (actually a whole series of particular types of faith), they remained without permanent influence. In keeping with their entire pattern of life, these Humanist groups of the classically educated were altogether antipathetic to the masses and to the religious demagogy of priests and preachers; on the whole they remained Erastian or irenic in temper, for which reason alone they were condemned to suffer progressive loss of influence.[57]

More specific is the role of those asked to debate basic policy alternatives in theological-moral-philosophical terms and to contribute more or less directly in transforming their positions into policies and legislation. The legitimation of Castilian rights over the New World and the legislation about the rights of the conquistadores and the Indians in the new domains of the crown is a classic example of such a role. A man like the Dominican professor Francisco de Vitoria of the University of Salamanca, considered one of the founding fathers of international law, represents this type well.[58]

The two preceding roles are, to use Theodor Geiger's expression,[59] legitimizers and rationalizers (a better English translation would be institutionalizers) of power, but are far from mindless servants without independent judgment and influence, and are genuinely concerned about the uses and abuses of power. They are not, however, moral prophets standing up in protest against power, any power, in the name of higher principles or ideals. Obviously this type is not frequent, and has little place in Spanish intellectual life once basic choices have been made in the reign of Charles V and Philip II has fully committed himself to a Spanish policy and worldview within the framework of the Counter Reformation. The "prophetic Christian," like Father Las Casas,[60] not without an element of megalomania, lack of realism, even intolerance or rigidity, incarnates this position. It is not an accident that this author of memoranda, distorted history, self-apologias, should have been less scholarly and academically learned than his antagonists: Ginés de Sepúlveda or the moralists and legal advisers shaping the compromise legislation of the Indies. Weber's notion of the prophet[61] would lead us to expect him to be less the pure intellectual.

The prophetic-moral critic, legitimized by a religious mission, is quite different from another type of critical intellectual, found in the seventeenth century and closer to some of our contemporary writers. These men do not question the ultimate values of society, nor even the specific policies, but rather satirize in literary forms, particularly dreams or pamphlets, rulers and their abuses: the *validos*—the universal ministers, favorites of the king—who usurp (due to the weakness or laziness of the monarchs) their power. Some of the works of Quevedo,[62] which cost him considerable persecution, fall into this category. This political role of intellectuals is again closer to that of modern lay intellectuals than to that of the religiously inspired moralists who contributed potentially radical political theories.

Another manifestation of intellectual concern with politics, or more specifically policy, is the type called at the time *arbitristas*,[63] those who offered panaceas to problems, particularly the financial problems of an indebted monarchy. There were some frauds among them, but they provided the beginnings of economic science and practical suggestions for the reform of government. The works of Martín González de Cellorigo[64] and Pedro Fernández de Navarrete[65] are good examples. Again this type of thinking is most frequent between 1600 and 1626 and reflects an increasing awareness of crisis, even decadence. After 1640, with the Catalan and Portuguese rebellions, the character of this literature changes from a search for remedies to a mood of defiance or *laudatio temporis acti*.[66]

Just as in the religious intellectual effort we found aesthetic creators diffusing the basic values of society for the masses in their poetry and in the theater, we find playwrights exulting a distinct concept of monarchical authority, glorifying the giant efforts of the nation in its wars. Many of the plays of Lope de Vega and Calderón perform this function. The defense and restitution through poetic justice of a political-moral order—in contrast to the work of Shakespeare which was more concerned with human passions—limits the tragic elements in politics.[67]

Finally, we may note how the embattled position of Spain stimulates a continuous tradition of defense of its culture and values: first with the assertion of the Castilian language against Latin, and later the defense against foreign criticism that was partly based on the dissidents or prophetic critics who were received with enthusiasm abroad. This line of nationalist intellectual response to the external world[68] becomes increasingly important as a feeling of decline, defeat, and exhaustion from trying to meet the great commitments of a superpower with limited resources set in. In the eighteenth century this defensive role was central and was a continuous strain in Spanish culture, increasingly combined with an awareness of the need to assimilate important elements from other cultures to overcome decay and backwardness.

Debates on the Conquest of the Indies and the Status of the Indians

Few issues exemplify better the role of intellectuals in politics than the disputes about the rights of the Spanish crown to conquer America and the status of the Indians. Those disputes have been symbolized in the works of Las Casas, Ginés de Sepúlveda, and Francisco de Vitoria, but as Lewis Hanke has shown,[69] many theologians, legal scholars, and historians both in Spain and overseas participated, and their positions were echoed in the actions of administrators, bishops and clergymen, and even common Spaniards. It is impossible to summarize even the main outlines of the arguments used by all the parties to the dispute or the impact of their positions on declarations of principle, legislation, policies, and ultimately social reality. It is impossible to do so not only because of the complexity of the issues, but also because of the bitterness of the disputes between contemporary scholars, who generally took sides for or against one of the protagonists, and the difficulty of learning and evaluating the realities of Spanish rule. Ultimately modern scholars attempting to analyze the role of those learned and passionate men of the past face the question: How different would Spanish rule have been without the agitated polemics and inquests in the universities and royal councils; how much did different posit. .is influence the legislation; and, finally, how far did that legislation get implemented overseas? On all those questions we find a variety of often contradictory responses by respectable scholars.

However, a few facts stand out and deserve to be noted in a study of the role of intellectuals in the Spanish empire. First, the rulers allowed and even encouraged discussion of their rights, duties, policies, and laws, in a search for legitimacy, information, and policies. As Weber stressed, like all others who enjoy advantages over their fellows, men in power want to see their position as "legitimate" and their advantages as "deserved," and to interpret the subordination of the many as the "just fate" of those upon whom it falls. It was up to the intellectuals of the time to find, largely through scholastic debate and the collective decision of learned men, convincing arguments within the theological and humanistic cultural traditions of the time, and it was up to the legal experts to translate those claims into normative declarations. Normally the legitimizing effort is directed more toward the subjects than toward satisfying the conscience of rulers, but the difficulty in making those claims understandable to the natives, and the fact that the conquistadores to a large extent did not feel a need for legitimacy when their rewards were so immediate and tangible, gives those disputes their unique quality. The considerable freedom granted to those debating the issues suggests that this legitimizing function of intellectuals cannot be performed—even for the ruler himself—without it.

Second, the controversy exemplifies the difficulties in linking disputes by intellectuals about ultimate values, principles, and laws with social realities—and the subsequent distortion of reality. The nature of the Indians, their psychology, and their customs are described (even by those who were in close contact with them) in terms of the positions taken, and we find little reference to the varieties of Indian civilization, customs, peoples, or situations in the conquest. Examples were chosen and generalized to fit intellectual arguments. In contrast, an administrator like Antonio de Mendoza, the first viceroy of New Spain, recommended in a memorial to his successor:

Treat the Indians like any other people, and do not make special rules and regulations for them. There are few persons in these parts who are not motivated, in their opinion of the Indians, by some interest, whether temporal or spiritual, or by some passion or ambition, good or bad.[70]

Whatever conclusion we reach about the impact of the ideas of theologians and moralists on the laws, basic policy declarations, and specific experiments to implement certain ideas, the striking gap between them and the reality of the colonization is undeniable. The feedback of resistance to the implementation of values enjoying authoritative sanction in the further elaboration of laws and policies and even more their implementation should warn us against overestimating the role of intellectuals in shaping social reality. The difficulty of answering the question how things would have been without their presence, their justification, their criticism, their solutions, is a persistent problem in the study of the role of men of ideas in any society.

Third, the range, variety, and complexity of positions of men sharing largely a common culture, often using the same authorities and concepts in their arguments, often linked with the same or similar institutions, illustrates how difficult it is to derive ideas from a sociocultural context, how many of the same cultural materials can be used for opposite purposes, and how even a limited freedom of intellectuals rather than strict hierarchical subordination makes consensus among them difficult. The main antagonists never convinced each other. The fourteen judges called to Valladolid in 1550-1551 never reached a clear decision; they scattered after the final meeting, exhausted and confused, and for years afterward the Council of the Indies struggled to get them to give their opinions in writing. As late as 1557, Melchor Cano, one of the most influential among them, was still being asked to submit his answer. Indirectly, however, the dispute had a great impact.[71] Sepúlveda's books and apologies[72] on his doctrine of the Indians as slaves by nature and his justification of Spanish rule were never allowed to be published and did not appear until the end of the eighteenth century; the work that was the immediate cause of the Valladolid dispute did not reach print until 1892 and his earlier works were suppressed. On the other hand, Las Casas was able to publish in 1552 a galaxy of provocative treatises including the *Very Brief Account of the Destruction of the Indies*,

a strong indictment of Spanish rule, that circulated freely until it was withdrawn first in Peru and when his papers were collected in 1571 and kept
closely watched by the chief historian of the Indies. The *Destrucción* was
forbidden by the Inquisition in 1659 as offensive to the Spanish nation.[73]
The general ordinance of 1573 by Philip II incorporated some of the ideas
emerging from the dispute. The word "conquest" was to be substituted
by "pacification" and no license was given to enslave the captives if war
was necessary. The idea that the Indians were slaves by nature, childlike
creatures, was rejected; they were to be accepted as men capable of becoming Christians and incorporated into Spanish civilization with legal
rights. In some respects those developments exemplify something we find
often in the role of intellectuals: their tendency to take extreme positions
when asked for advice by rulers, the difficulty of formulating a consensus
among intellectuals after their arguments are aired, the lack of resolution
of the issues, the silencing or ignoring of some opinions, the partial incorporation, without explicit reference to them, of some of the ideas debated
into policies, an ebbing of interest, and, finally, the renewed interest centuries later from the perspective of other times, leading to a reliving of old
battles among another generation of intellectuals.

Fourth, the debates and arguments provide evidence of a proposition
that Marx formulated for revolutions and that might be extended to politi-
cal-intellectual conflicts. New issues and new situations are discussed in a
language using concepts and categories of the past, even when their
meaning is likely to be different. The title of a work by Lewis Hanke,
Aristotle and the American Indians,[74] reveals how new answers were
sought not on the basis of new concepts, which emerge only slowly, but by
debating the meaning of natural slavery and by arguing that new facts do
not fit the old concept. This might be characteristic only of a traditional
society, but we suspect that it is a more general pattern, particularly when
dealing with questions of legitimacy, morality, and law.

Fifth, there is also a shift, that would be interesting to document
chronologically, from debates about questions of principle to more descriptive and factual efforts—writings that today would be considered
anthropological, even efforts to reconstruct with a political purpose the pre-
conquest history. Francisco de Toledo, a wise lawgiver, energetic administrator, and the greatest ruler Spain ever sent to Peru (1569-1582), conscious
of the "books of the fanatic and virulent bishop of Chiapa [Las Casas]
[that] served as the spearhead of the attack on Spanish rule in America,"
attempted to counteract that influence. He inspired the composition of a
treatise against the bishop's ideas, arranged for the "true history" of Peru's
past by Pedro Sarmiento de Gamboa, and embarked upon an investigation
of the justice of Inca rule by collecting the so-called *Informaciones*. These
were a formal inquiry into the ancient history of the Incas, their conquests,
the institution of the Curacas, and religious beliefs and customs, particu-

larly sacrifices. Information was taken down, by the means of interpreters, from two hundred Indians at eleven different points during an inspection of the realm between November 1570 and March 1572. Those inquiries have been published and their nature and value are debated by scholars, since their conclusion was foregone: "Your majesty is the legitimate ruler of this kingdom and the Incas are tyrannical usurpers"—an interesting example of the use of "facts" collected to answer the questions of intellectuals. That did not end the arguments, even in Peru. The effort to obtain a correct history led to the Indian history of Sarmiento de Gamboa, which was read to the principal and most able descendants of the Incas and to the surviving colleagues of Pizarro who, under oath, were called to tell the truth and make the necessary corrections. After their approval it was sent to the king of Spain, but was not published until 1906.[75]

One of the most fascinating roles in these debates of theologians and lawyers, religious men and humanists, against the background of king, royal officials, and conqueror colons, is the one assumed by Bartolemé de Las Casas, that of the prophet in the sociological sense of the term. The contradictory portraits of the man by his followers and his critics—for example, Ramón Menéndez Pidal in a recent biography—can be harmonized if we look at his role and personality in this light. Las Casas, through his many published and unpublished writings, through his constant pleading before the authorities and at councils of experts including some of the most learned men of his time, through his polemics with scholars like Sepúlveda, through the influence of his thought on many writers of his time, through his echo abroad and to our day, can certainly be considered an intellectual. However, neither his training (he probably did not have a bachelor's degree) nor his late scholarly reading made him an equal to those learned advisers. Prophecy in the context of sixteenth-century and overseas colonial society could not be addressed to the masses; it had to be directed to the elite and it had to take intellectual forms. Menéndez Pidal[76] makes the mistake of analyzing the scholarly efforts, the arguments, the historical writings of Las Casas by applying to them the standards that might be valid to judge the works of a legist or a historian. The impact and the audience that this bitter, even intolerant, critic could find can be understood only in terms of his prophetic role. The critique of his role as a bishop, of his lack of interest in missionizing day-by-day to the Indians, in learning their languages, and in living among them, makes sense only if we cast him in the role of the exemplary prophet rather than that of the ethical prophet—again to use Weberian terminology.

We shall understand "prophet" to mean a purely individual bearer of charisma, who by virtue of his mission proclaims a religious doctrine or divine commandment . . . the personal call is the decisive element distinguishing the prophet from the priest . . . It is characteristic of the prophets that they do not receive their mission from any human agency, but seize it, as it were . . . the afore-

mentioned assumption of power, came about as a consequence of divine revelation for religious purposes . . . The philosophical ethicist and the social
reformer are not prophets in our sense of the word, no matter how closely they
seem to resemble prophets . . . [they] lack that vital emotional *preaching* which
is distinctive of prophecy, regardless of whether it is disseminated in the spoken
word, the pamphlet, or any type of literary composition . . . The enterprise of
the prophet is closer to that of the popular leader (*demagogos*) or political
publicist than to that of the teacher.[77]

There are obviously many aspects of Weber's description that are missing in the role created for himself by Las Casas, but there is an affinity
between him and the "titans of the holy curse" when he threatens the royal
advisers and the king with doubts about their salvation, when in his *Con-
fesonario* as a bishop he denies the sacraments to those unwilling to res-
titute and give up their exploitation, when in 1542 he prophesies God's
punishment and destruction of Spain, when he writes "and for those sins,
from what I read in the Holy Scripture, God shall punish with terrible
punishments and perhaps totally destroy all of Spain." His demagogic ser-
mons from the beginning of his career, his demonstrative acts as a bishop,
particularly his excommunications, his passionate accounts of Spanish cruelty,
his one-sided view of the qualities of the Indians, his denial of the right of
conquest even with royal authority, his confidence in God's protection, all
fit into this prophetic role. His testament summarizes well this self-image
that carried such conviction that while he was often hated and seen as a
fool he was not dismissed by the powerful, nor silenced by the Inquisition.
He was listened to and given opportunities to carry through his more or
less utopian (in the circumstances of the New World) experiments; he
was sometimes ignored, but not perceived as mentally abnormal or a
"Quijote," as Bataillon noted, criticizing the hostile view of Menéndez Pidal.[76]

Las Casas' position is found in letters, in memorials to the Council of
the Indies, and in his *History of the Indies*. Menéndez Pidal, commenting on
these texts, without any sympathy, notes the imitation of the style of Isaiah,
and points out that some of his ecclesiastical admirers of the time likened
him to the prophet Elias. He concludes by stressing Las Casas' megalomania
and split personality and by complaining bitterly that he does not prophesy
like Isaiah a "restoration in justice." Like the prophets of Israel described
by Weber, Las Casas included himself among the sinful. For many younger
monks he was "the candle that set everything on fire," as one of his contemporaries wrote warning the authorities.[79]

Undoubtedly this prophetic intellectual, who did not even attempt to
create a community of followers outside the institutions of the church, or a
political movement, or dissidence, generally using the language of the
scholastic and the legist and trying to work through the institutions, is the
best evidence of the limits that an existing social order based on tradition
and self-interest and with the support of other intellectuals can place on
its most passionate critics. Scholars still debate how much his strident voice

contributed to shaping policies and laws and arousing the public conscience, as compared to those arguing and working for reform from more moderate premises.

Decadence and Providentialism

The seventeenth century sees a change in the role of intellectuals in their relation to politics and society. The great debates about the ultimate goals of the polity, the imperial role in Europe and America, and the legitimacy of power had been resolved. We no longer find humanists reinterpreting Roman and medieval ideas as advisers of the emperor, nor theologians, moralists, and lawyers arguing about the mission of Spain when confronted with the prophetic critique of a Las Casas. Other roles and human types appear, as the country faces new and different problems. There is no question about goals, but great concern about means; administration, finances, monetary policy, and economics become the concern of intellectuals. Occasionally some of the most intelligent spontaneously offer their advice, suggesting an end to the imperial drive that overtaxes the resources of the country and consolidation of the empire, but for pragmatic reasons rather than doubts of its legitimacy. Two of the most interesting political thinkers and critics of the seventeenth century had considerable diplomatic experience: Quevedo in Italy and Saavedra Fajardo as negotiator of the Peace of Westphalia.

In contrast to Charles V, who traveled constantly over his European domains, the later Habsburgs stayed in Spain and increasingly in Madrid, partly due to financial difficulties that limited the travels of the court. This inward shift is reflected in the data presented above on the travel of the intellectual elite in the sixteenth and seventeenth centuries. The foreign world with which Spain is at war most of the time is perceived as hostile and the success of writings critical of Spanish society, its colonization, its Inquisition, its persecution of the Jews, leads to a new type of literature: the defense of Spain. This self-affirmation is not the pride of a new power, of a new language equal to the classical languages, of its contribution to humanistic learning, but the defense of a mission questioned by others, of a culture considered stagnating or intolerant, of a Catholicism asserting itself against the consolidated Protestant Reformation. The extreme form of this defensive reaction is a feeling of being God's chosen nation, the elected people, a messianism that overcomes all the doubts that the economic decadence, corruption of government, and military defeats might create. The baroque rhetoric of priests, monks, and preachers substitutes for the rigorous theological debates of previous generations and the intimate creativity of the mystics. The period of political decadence initiated around 1600, fully evident with the rebellions of Catalonia and Portugal in 1640 and the Peace of Westphalia in 1659, slowly turns also into one of cultural decadence. The years from after the death of Calderón in 1681 until 1730 when the eighteenth-century renewal began (though some of the political and economic changes of the new Bourbon dynasty had been instituted earlier) are a low point in Spanish culture.

Quevedo is a fascinating type of intellectual: poet, novelist, political philosopher, satirist, apologist of the monarchy and Catholicism, influential diplomat and politician, persecuted and imprisoned for his criticism of the king's favorite, defender of Spanish culture and foreign policy, but also conscious of the twilight of Spanish power. Witty, sarcastic, moralist and opportunist, "in his personal life a deviant who did not wish to be a deviant," with some exaggeration it has been said that all by himself he played the role which is played by the press of the political opposition. His satire was literary as well as social and political; it varied with the ups and downs of the author's needs and aspirations. At the same time, in his serious political treatise, *Política de Dios y Govierno de Christo*,[80] he sought to apply the principles of ethics to politics, attacking the idea of a reason of state as a satanic invention of which Pilate is a prime example. He is not the academic or clerical expert—in theological or legal matters—at the service of the state, but the layman, diplomat, politician, moral critic of the foibles of the society, hard, brisk, and often brutal in his style.

Juan Marichal[81] has noted how Quevedo, despite the fact that he was the son of the queen's secretary and had aspirations to a bureaucratic career, identifies with the more dynamic segment of the aristocracy—the Duke of Osuna—and in his writings turns against the *noblesse de robe*, against the university educated, the "negotiators," with their *civilidades* (courteous formulas), in favor of the men of action. As Quevedo wrote: "Monarchies maintain themselves with the customs on which they were built. They always have been acquired by captains, always corrupted by *bachilleres* . . . armies, not universities gain them and defend them . . . The battles give kingdoms, the letters, degrees and caps." And in another place: "Rome [in its rise] did not use doctors, nor books, but soldiers and lances. Everything was impetus, nothing studied. After Cicero and . . . Caesar introduced words and discourses [decadence began]."[82] It is probably no accident that he should have been an advocate of the apostle Santiago—Saint Jacques, so closely associated with the Reconquista, patron saint of Spain against those favoring the mystical doctoress Saint Theresa. The military defeat of Spain arouses the hostility of an intellectual against a government run largely by graduates, using summas rather than aphorisms, theologians rather than men of experience and cunning.

Quevedo's darts are often directed against the powerful, their vices and abuses of power, but without questioning the legitimacy of the monarchy, the monarch, or the ultimate values of the society. Far from him is the prophetic wrath of Las Casas that indicts a whole society. In contrast to the Erasmians who were questioned or persecuted by the Inquisition for the religious implications of their scholarly activities, he was the victim of political persecution, being exiled and made a prisoner of the state. The duality of king and *valido*, universal prime minister and king's favorite, in an age of crisis, allows a successful writer with some independent means to play the role of an independent intellectual who calls attention to the woes of the state without however questioning the legitimate authority of the king—something that would have been more difficult when the kings also governed. Divided authority, semi- or illegitimate authority, even in a highly consensual society, allows the emergence of the critical intellectual. Persecution in this case does not threaten the honor of the person, as the suspicion of heresy did, but after the fall of the *valido* becomes a source of pride. Ultimately the bitter experiences of politics, intellectual feuds, influence and defeat, and ups and downs of fortune lead to the philosophical attitude toward life that we find in many of Quevedo's works.

The first page of the *Panegírico a la Majestad del Rey nuestro Señor Don Felipe IV en la caída del Conde Dugue* (1643) praises the monarch after the years in which his light reached us weakly until the day he "subjected to him alone all the citizens" saying:

It cannot be noted against you that you have elected ministers who have been an obstacle to you. Your majesty should consider that Christ not only selected twelve disciples, of which Peter denied him, Thomas doubted him, Judas sold him; but he himself told them: "I elected you, and not you me" . . . Who shall wonder that in the one [selection] your Majesty made in the desire of the whole common good there should be among the selected some neglectful, etc. so that it is convenient that you deserve to be such a great king, that you should be it alone.[83]

The praise followed by hopes for the future does not prevent him from expressing his despair in a private letter to a friend (1645):

The worst news keeps coming in from everywhere, and the worst of all is that everyone expected that kind of news. I cannot be sure, dear Don Francisco, whether things are breaking up or have finally broken up. God knows! There are many things that, though they seem to exist and to have been, are now mere nothing, a word or an image.[84]

Only six years before a priest, mathematician, and jurist, Francisco Mateu, wrote in an *Antipronóstico a las victorias que se pronostica el reino de Francia:*

As long as Spain administers justice with equity, favors the ecclesiastical estate maintaining its immunities, obedient to the Roman Pontifex, furthering the Holy Tribunal of the Inquisition, diffusing the faith . . . and would keep it with the customary purity . . . I say and reaffirm myself that it shall triumph not only of France but of as many enemies shall oppose it.[85]

Mateu is not alone; others like Pellicer, Jauregui, Céspedes y Meneses, Quiñones de Benavente, in their works and pamphlets, reassure the nation.[86]

The reactions of despair and its opposite, foolhardy providentialism of a chosen people, were the literary expressions of the crisis. Another response was the pragmatic one of administrative and economic reformers, who with rare exceptions did not question the goals of the nation but attempted to propose more rational means to achieve them. New kinds of intellectuals were at the point of appearing, but they were without a well-defined role, without an organized and theoretically elaborate body of knowledge on which to base their advice despite important theoretical insights, without a defined social position; these new intellectuals and economists were the fiscal and administrative reformers. Writers were concerned with problems: the depopulation of the country from 8.4 million in 1591-1594 to 7.5 million in 1713 (as a result of wars, migration to America, expulsion of the *moriscos* —converted Moors—pests, and the large number of celibate priests and monks), the unfavorable balance of trade and decay of industry, the copper money inflation, the drop in productive population particularly in the countryside, the dominance of consumption values in the ruling classes, administrative corruption and inefficiency, and economic inequality of classes and regions. Some of these writings make real contributions to understanding the economic and social mechanisms that produced the seventeenth-century European, and particularly Spanish, inflation and economic decadence. A changing society in crisis, which does not encourage criticism of its ultimate values, which feels no guilt for its actions, seems to be particularly favorable to the emergence of empirical social science analysis and reformism. (There might be here an analogy with post-Napoleonic bourgeois France, post-Bismarckian Germany, post-depression United States.)

This concern with more pragmatic problems, even when often the solutions proposed are unrealistic, coincides with a certain weariness with the load of empire. So, for example, Bartolomé Leonardo de Argensola (d. 1631), canon of Zaragoza, who negotiated to bring Galileo to Spain, writes in an officially sponsored history, *Conquista de las Islas Malucas* (1609), on the Philippines:

> People said that the Monarchy, spread far and wide and separated by so many seas and climates, can scarcely be held together, nor is human providence able to bind into a unit . . . provinces which Nature set so wide apart . . . ; that these reasons are not sophistic, but born of experience . . . ; and that the most suitable action would be for the king to increase his strength in Europe.[87]

But the response of Philip to these people, the ministers of finance, was that all efforts should continue, as Otis H. Green summarizes the account of Argensola:

> The history proclaims the king's zeal to maintain inviolate the faithfulness of his subjects in the Indies . . . (and the) determination to introduce into all corners of the earth "our vigilance," ever at the service of this mythical empire, so that in the end it might triumph. The natives of the Spice Islands are exposed to the heresies of the Dutch and the abominations of Islam; the "cause of the Faith" does not permit the abandonment of that Asiatic outpost. Even though in

the enterprise of preaching the Gospel there are intermixed at times "the avarice and the excesses of our captains and soldiers," such excesses do not render the cause less just; nor can the Spanish nation listen to "reasons of state."[88]

On their public record, Spanish intellectuals did not question the attitude reflected in this text. When three and a half centuries later another empire found itself confronted with overexertion and the option to abandon an outpost in the struggle for an ideology, politicians responded like Philip II but intellectuals took a completely different stance. A counterideology of a religious character (if we accept the notion of Counter Reformation) probably gave the historical process a meaning acceptable to many intellectuals that a secular counterideology might not be able to provide.

A Note on Quantitative Data

To provide a collective portrait of intellectuals I have compiled a biographical file on 321 authors writing between 1500 and 1700, which will be expanded and improved in future research. In the absence of a standard national biography, such as the one used by Theodor Geiger in his research on Danish intellectuals, I have based my selection of names on several criteria. First, I considered those receiving more than passing mention in three leading histories of literature: Angel Valbuena Prat, *Historia de la literatura española*, 4 vols. (Barcelona: Gustavo Gili, 1968); Juan Hurtado and Angel González Palencia, *Historia de la literatura española*, 2 vols. (Madrid: SAETA, 1940); and Guillermo Díaz-Plaja, ed., *Historia general de las literaturas hispánicas*, 6 vols. (Barcelona: Barana, 1953). As histories of literature their references to philosophy, theology, political thought, science, and so forth are limited. To compensate I included the authors mentioned in the works of José María Maravall, *Carlos V y el pensamiento político del renacimiento* (Madrid: Instituto de Estudios Políticos, 1960) and *La philosophie politique espagnole au XVIIe siècle dans ses rapports avec l'esprit de la Contre-Réforme* (Paris: Librairie Philosophique J. Vrin, 1955); in the monograph by Luciano Pereña Vicente, *La universidad de Salamanca forja del pensamiento político español en el siglo XVI*, in *Acta Salamanticensia, Historia de la Universidad*, vol. I, 2 (1954), which includes most of the theologians, philosophers, and jurists; in Alain Guy, *Les philosophes espagnoles d'hier et l'aujourd'hui* (Toulouse: Privat, 1956); in Gregorio Marañón, "La literatura científica en los siglos XVI y XVII," in Díaz-Plaja, ed., *Historia general de las literaturas hispánicas*, III, 933-966, with special reference to the medical literature; and in Julio Rey Pastor, *Los matemáticos españoles del siglo XVI* (n.p.: Biblioteca Scientia, n.d., about 1914), for the history of mathematics. In future work I intend to take into account some of the recent research in the history of Spanish science, unfortunately inaccessible now. The Catalan language literature, of limited importance in this period, was likely to be underrepresented with histories of literature centered on writings in Castilian and I therefore included those authors receiving more than passing mention in: Jorge Rubió Balaguer, "Literatura Catalana," in Díaz-Plaja, ed., *Historia general de las literaturas hispánicas*, III, 729-930; Joan Ruiz i Calonja, *Historia de la literatura catalana* (Barcelona: Teide, 1954); and the intro-duction by Martín de Riquer, *Resumen de literatura catalana* (Barcelona: Seix Barral, 1947). The biographies of the authors so listed were taken principally from Félix Torres Amat, *Memorias para ayudar a formar un diccionario crítico de escritores catalanes y dar alguna idea de la antigua y moderna literatura de Cataluña* (Barcelona: Verdaguer, 1826). The biog-raphies of Valencian authors were completed with the classic work of Vicente Ximeno, *Escritores del Reyno de Valencia* (Valencia: Estevan Dolz, 1749). If anything, my data give a somewhat disproportionate weight to the authors in Catalan. The biographical data for all the authors so listed were completed from a great variety of sources, particularly the *Diccionario de Literatura Española*, edited under the direction of Germán Bleiberg and Julián Marías for the Revista de Occidente, Madrid, 1949, and the *En-ciclopedia Universal Ilustrada Europeo-Americana*, edited by Espasa Calpe (the Spanish National Encyclopedia), Barcelona, 1905. The work of Nicolás Antonio, *Bibliotheca Hispana Nova sive Hispanorum Scriptorum qui ab anno MD. addMDCLXXXIV floruere notitia*, reprinted in two volumes in Madrid by Joachimi de Ibarra in 1788, was an indispensable source. In addition, I consulted a spate of bio-bibliographic lexica on the illustrious sons of various provinces, most published around the turn of the century. On the Jesuit authors, Petri Ribadeneirae, S.J., *Bibliotheca Scriptorum Societas Iesu* (Antverpiae, 1643) was useful.

Certainly a further search through monographic sources would supply missing information, and it is reasonable to assume that on many character-istics the figure would be higher, but I do not feel that the general trends would be modified. The percentages should be read with this relative lack of information, particularly on lesser figures, in mind.

I divided the elite intellectuals into those born in or before 1575, whose productive years would fall mainly into the sixteenth century, and those born after that date, whose writings would fall into the reigns of the last three Habsburgs (1598-1700). The authors whose birthdates were unknown were classified into one or the other century on the basis of the date of their first published work. It might have been interesting to use 1556—the date of the abdication of Charles V and ascent to the throne of Philip II—as another dividing line, but this would have further complicated the tables. My analysis of data on the first generation suggests that what I say about the sixteenth century is particularly true for the first half.

The excellent indices of the monumental work of the seventeenth-century scholar Nicolás Antonio, giving place of birth, membership in religious orders, and sex for 3,604 authors—925 native of Portugal and its possessions

SIXTEENTH- AND SEVENTEENTH-CENTURY SPAIN

and 93 of the Castilian Americas, leaving 2,586 born in the area of present day Spain plus some parts of today's France—have contributed data on persons outside my small elite. I call those persons, for brevity's sake, "mass" intellectuals. In addition, his index of twenty-three main subjects of works, a list of some 10,807 entries, has allowed me to characterize in general terms the intellectual production of the men writing between 1500 and 1584 whose work was considered worthy of notice by one of their most learned and informed contemporaries. The data of Nicolás Antonio permit some interesting comparisons between "elite" and "mass" intellectuals (without taking those terms too seriously).

I want to thank my wife Rocío Terán de Linz for her collaboration and Pedro González Blasco for research assistance.

REFERENCES

1. Basic sources on the political, social, and economic history of the period are: Juan Reglá, *Historia social y económica de España, Imperio, Aristocracia, Absolutismo,* Vol. III of the *Historia social y económica de España y América,* ed. Jaime Vicens Vives (Barcelona: Teide, 1957); J. H. Elliot, *Imperial Spain, 1469-1716* (New York: St. Martin's Press, 1964); John Lynch, *Spain under the Habsburgs,* 2 vols. (Oxford: Basil Blackwell, 1965-1969). For a critical review of the rich literature on the economic and social structure, specifically that with a quantitative emphasis, see Juan J. Linz, "Five Centuries of Spanish History: Quantification and Comparison," in Val Lorwin and Jacob M. Price, eds., *The Dimensions of the Past: Materials, Problems and Opportunities for Quantitative Work in History* (New Haven: Yale University Press, 1971). For the sixteenth century see also Ramón Carande, *Carlos V y sus banqueros: La vida económica en Castilla (1516-1556),* vol. I of a three volume work, 2d rev. ed. (Madrid: Sociedad de Estudios y Publicaciones, 1955).

2. On the political, economic, social, and cultural structures of southern Europe at the time see the beautiful book by Fernand Braudel, *La Méditerranée et le monde méditerranéen à l'epoque de Philippe II,* 2 vols., rev. ed. of work first published in 1949 (Paris: Armand Colin, 1966).

3. There is no work on religious ideas, movements, and practices in Spain comparable to the great work of Henri Bremond, *Histoire littéraire du sentiment religieux en France depuis la fin des guerres de religion jusqu' à nos jours,* 9 vols. (Paris: Armand Colin, 1967) (first ed., 1923). However, Luis Sala Salust, "La espiritualidad española en la primera mitad del siglo XVI," *Cuadernos de Historia, Anexos de la revista Hispania,* 1 (Madrid, 1967), 169-187, provides a brief overview of the variety of spiritual currents in Spanish Christianity in the first half of the sixteenth century, with a good critical bibliography.

4. Américo Castro, *The Structure of Spanish History* (Princeton: Princeton University Press, 1954) and *De la edad conflictiva: El drama de la honra en España y en su literatura* (Madrid: Taurus, 1961). See also his *Aspectos del vivir hispánico: Espiritualismo, mesianismo, actitud personal en los siglos XIV al XVI* (Santiago: Cruz del Sur, 1949); *Cervantes y los casticismos españoles* (Madrid: Alfaguara, 1966); and *Hacia Cervantes,* 3d rev. ed. (Madrid: Taurus, 1967). Castro's work

has aroused bitter polemics, particularly Claudio Sánchez Albornoz, *España. Un enigma histórico*, 2 vols. (Buenos Aires: Ed. Sudamericana, 1956) and "Las cañas se han tornado lanzas," *Cuadernos de Historia de España*, 27 (1958), 43-66.

The outstanding modern scholarly work on the Jews in society is Julio Caro Baroja, *Los judíos en la España moderna y contemporánea*, 3 vols. (Madrid: Arion, 1961). On the "purity of blood" statutes and the bitter controversies surrounding their introduction, see Albert A. Sicroff, *Les controverses des statuts de "pureté de sang" en Espagne du XVe au XVIIe siècle* (Paris: Didier, 1960).

5. Unfortunately we cannot go into the question to what extent Spanish cultural development was a continuation of the pre-Protestant reform of the church initiated by Cardinal Jiménez de Cisneros or a reaction to the Reformation, an antimovement, a counterreformation. Much of the argument hinges on the reading of the work of Marcel Bataillon on the Erasmianists and the degree to which the period 1530-1540 and the change of generations coinciding with it is considered a breaking point. A comparison between the Spanish and the Italian counterreformation in this respect, and between Spanish and French Catholicism in the late sixteenth and seventeenth centuries, would also be rewarding. For an introduction to the problem, the lectures of H. Outram Evennet, *The Spirit of the Counter-Reformation* (Cambridge, Eng.: The University Press, 1968), with a postscript by John Bossy on the concept of counterreformation, are an interesting point of departure.

For a review of the problems and positions on the place of Spanish history in the context of European historical periodizations, see Quintín Aldea, "Límites y valoración del tránsito de la Edad Media a la Moderna," *Cuadernos de Historia, Anexos de la revista Hispania*, 1 (Madrid, 1967), 1-36, with special reference to the ideas of Ortega y Gasset, Américo Castro, and Sánchez Albornoz.

6. The monumental work by Otis H. Green, *Spain and the Western Tradition: The Castilian Mind in Literature from El Cid to Calderón*, 4 vols. (Madison: University of Wisconsin Press, 1965) rejects the narrow perspective of the literary historian and includes philosophical and political thought, even scientific developments, in an effort to understand Spanish culture in its uniqueness as well as in the context of the great streams of European civilization. See the review by Manuel Durán, "Otis H. Green and Spanish Culture: 'Spain and the Western Tradition,'" *Hispania*, 50 (December 1967), 1012-1018.

7. The "censura inmanente" of which Unamuno wrote in *En torno al casticismo* (Madrid, 1916), p. 185. For a discussion of some of these problems see Henry Kamen, *The Spanish Inquisition* (London: Weidenfeld and Nicolson, 1965). For a moderately conservative Spanish view see Miguel de la Pinta Llorente, *La Inquisición española y los problemas de la cultura y de la intolerancia* (Madrid: Cultura Hispánica, 1953). See also Green, *Spain and the Western Tradition*, IV, 163-164, and Castro, *The Structure of Spanish History*, pp. 636-637, on the Mariana comment on the trial of Fray Luis de León.

8. Marcel Bataillon, *Erasme et l'Espagne. Recherches sur l'histoire spirituelle du XVIe siècle* (Paris: E. Droz, 1937). There is an expanded Spanish translation published by the Fondo de Cultura Económica in Mexico.

9. Barrington Moore, "Totalitarian Elements in Pre-Industrial Societies," *Political Power and Social Theory* (New York: Harper Torchbooks, 1958), pp. 30-88.

10. This aspect has been central to Weber's analysis of Western civilization in his *Economy and Society*, ed. Guenther Roth and Claus Wittich (New York: Bedminster Press, 1968). While there are strong tendencies toward what Weber calls Caesaro-

papism in Spain, there are in this period a number of situations in which segments of the church, like some religious orders, or the Inquisition, acted very independently and even against the wishes of the sovereign.

11. "Los primitivos españoles del pensamiento económico: 'Cuantitativismo' y 'Bullonismo,'" in *Crecimiento y desarrollo. Economía e Historia: Reflexiones sobre el caso español* (Barcelona: Ariel, 1964).

12. Pierre Chaunu, *La civilisation de l'Europe classique* (Paris: Arthaud, 1966), pp. 530-567.

13. See Kamen, *The Spanish Inquisition;* Pinta Llorente, *La Inquisición española;* Bataillon, *Erasme et l'Espagne.* For example, the teaching of Copernicus at Salamanca in 1561, Green, *Spain and the Western Tradition*, III, 234, and Irving A. Leonard, *Books of the Brave: Being an Account of Books and Men in the Spanish Conquest and Settlement of the Sixteenth Century New World* (Cambridge, Mass.: Harvard University Press, 1949), esp. chap. 7, "Light Literature and the Law."

14. Sánchez Albornoz, *España. Un enigma histórico*, II, 562.

15. Ramón Menéndez Pidal, *The Spaniards in Their History* (New York: W. W. Norton, 1950), pp. 102-143; Franz Niedermayer, "Zwei Spanien? Ein Beitrag zum Gespräch über spanische Geschichtsauffassung," *Saeculum,* 3 (1952), 444-476.

16. "Política religiosa: El artículo 26 de la Constitución," speech in the legislature on October 13, 1931, in Manuel Azaña, *Obras Completas,* ed. Juan Marichal (Mexico: Oasis, 1966), II, 51-52. Emphasis added.

17. Richard Kagan, "Universities in Castile, 1500-1700," *Past and Present,* 49 (November 1970) and his unpublished Ph.D. dissertation, "Education and the State in Habsburg Spain," Cambridge University, 1968.

18. José Antonio Maravall, *La philosophie politique espagnole au XVIIe siècle dans ses rapports avec l'esprit de la Contre-Réforme,* trans. Louis Cazes and Pierre Mesnard (Paris: Librairie Philosophique J. Vrin, 1955). See pp. 30-31 on the change in social background and intellectual style of the political writers in the sixteenth and seventeenth centuries.

19. The most important scholarly study of Spanish society in the seventeenth century is Antonio Domínguez Ortiz, *La sociedad española en el siglo XVII*, vol. I (Madrid: Instituto Balmes de Sociología, CSIC, 1963). For the sixteenth century, Carande, *Carlos V y sus banqueros* is an excellent study of the social structure.

20. Edward E. Malefakis, *Agrarian Reform and Peasant Revolution in Spain: Origins of the Civil War* (New Haven: Yale University Press, 1970), pp. 50-61.

21. See the works of Ramón Carande, Earl Hamilton, Pierre Vilar, among others. The essay by Pierre Vilar, "El tiempo del Quijote," in *Crecimiento y Desarrollo,* originally published as "Le temps du Quichote," *Europe* (January 1956), pp. 3-16, summarizes well those developments and their intellectual reflection.

22. See José Antonio Maravall, "Los 'Hombres de Saber' o letrados y la formación de su conciencia estamental," *Estudios de historia del pensamiento español* (Madrid: Cultura Hispánica, 1967), pp. 347-380, for the early development of their status consciousness; Bartolomé Bennassar, *Valladolid au siècle d'or. Une ville de Castille et sa campagne au XVIe siècle* (Paris: Mouton, 1967), pp. 357-373, esp. 365-372; and José Antonio Escudero, *Los secretarios de Estado y del despacho, 1474-1724,* 4 vols. (Madrid: Instituto de Estudios Administrativos, 1969).

23. See Caro Baroja, *Los judíos en la España moderna*, I, 182-189, for the various estimates of the Jewish population at the end of the fifteenth century and the number of expelled and converted. His estimate is 160,000 expelled, 240,000 new converts, of which 50,000 were tried by the Inquisition in the first half-century of its activities.

24. See the map on page 80 of Antonio Domínguez Ortiz, *La sociedad española en el siglo XVIII* (Madrid: Instituto Balmes de Sociología, CSIC, 1955), with the proportion of nobles in relation to the total population in 1797.

25. See, for example, some of the Constitutions of the Colleges of the University of Alcalá, quoted by José de Rújula y de Ochotorena, Marqués de Ciadoncha, *Indice de los colegiales del Mayor de San Ildefonso y Menores de Alcalá* (Madrid: Instituto Jerónimo Zurita, CSIC, 1946), pp. viii-ix, xvi.

26. Sicroff, *Les controverses des statuts de "pureté de sang,"* pp. 270-290.

27. See Castro, works cited in note 4; Caro Baroja, *Los judíos en la España moderna;* Bataillon, *Erasme et l'Espagne.*

28. For estimates of the Jewish population and the *conversos* remaining after the expulsion see Caro Baroja, *Los judíos en la Espagña moderna*, pp. 182-189, and his concluding estimate, p. 189. The ratio to population is based on the figure given for Spain by Carande, *Carlos V y sus banqueros*, I, 67.

29. On the affinities between a new Christian background and illuminism and Erasmianism, see Bataillon, *Erasme et l'Espagne.*

30. Vilar, "El tiempo del Quijote," pp. 444-448; Bennassar, *Valladolid au siècle d'or*, chaps. V to VIII.

31. See Green, *Spain and the Western Tradition*, II, 11-16, on Nebrija, father of Spanish philology and author of the *Gramática de la lengua castellana* (1492), the first grammar of the romance language written with all the rigor of the new philology.

32. This estimate is based on Domínguez Ortiz, *La sociedad española en el siglo XVII*, p. 169. This work constitutes the best study of the role of the nobility in Spanish society of the seventeenth century.

33. We have used the information on the place of birth rather than where a person spent his formative years, or the main place of residence, because that information was available more frequently than any other. However, the data on places lived show for both centuries, but particularly the seventeenth, the attraction of the capital, with 31.2 per cent and 53.5 per cent, respectively, having spent time in Madrid. The number having lived in Seville is also slightly higher than for those born there. Unfortunately, the information on the place of death is so incomplete that we could not, as we intended, use this information to study more precisely the internal migrations or the "brain drain" from the periphery to the center. In addition, a number of writers must have retired in their old age to their ancestral homes or quieter places than the court, a fact that would limit the validity of the indicator.

34. See José Gentil da Silva, *En Espagne, Développement économique, subsistance, déclin*, avec représentation graphique des information par Jacques Bertin (Paris: Mouton, 1965), maps in appendix and tables pp. 82ff.

35. The data are from C. Gutiérrez, S. J., *Españoles en Trento* (Valladolid: Instituto Jerónimo Zurita, CSIC, 1951); see map on p. lxviii.

36. On November 22, 1559, Philip II issued an order to all Spaniards studying or teaching abroad to return within four months, the only exceptions being those at particular colleges in Bologna, Rome, Naples, and Coimbra. In the future, no Spaniards were to be allowed abroad to study except at those colleges.

37. Kagan, "Universities in Castille." The figures quoted here are revised estimates that Professor Kagan was kind enough to communicate to me.

38. See Alberto Jiménez, *Ocaso y restauración. Ensayo sobre la universidad española moderna* (Mexico: El Colegio de México, 1948), pp. 26-28, on the reaction of the universities to the creation of the Colegio Imperial in Madrid in the first years of the seventeenth century. See also José Simón Díaz, *Historia del Colegio Imperial de Madrid* (Madrid, 1952).

39. A *Real Cédula* of April 8, 1659, quoted by José de Rújula y de Ochotorena, *Indice de los colegiales*, p. vii. In 1766 the Marquis of Alventos, in his history of the college of San Bartolomé in Salamanca, summarized the achievements of the students of the six Colegios Mayores (four in Salamanca, one in Valladolid, and another in Alcalá). Summarizing the count in thirty-four groups given by José de Rújula y de Ochotorena, *ibid.*, p. xii, we can classify the 6,093 colegiales into the following groups:

Saints, venerables, and persons of special virtue	156	2.6 per cent
Ecclesiastical dignitaries	2,173	35.7
High executive government officials	1,398	22.6
High judicial officials	1,553	25.6
Titles and nobles	612	10.0
Writers and teachers of princes	228	3.8
	6,093	100.3 per cent

Some of those in the "nonintellectual" categories, such as those in the clerical group, the forty-five participants in general church councils, could be considered intellectuals. Even so, the proportion is low. Nicolás Antonio lists only 118 writers who were graduates of the Colegios, confirming that those elite colleges served more to train civil and church officials than intellectuals.

40. The indexes of students and professors in those centuries published for a number of universities and colleges would allow an analysis of this type. These listings have been used to determine if leading writers attended the universities, if they received degrees, and the type of courses in which they matriculated. An indication of the prestige attached to university education is that sometimes it can be proved that claims were not quite true; so, for example, Lope de Vega attended Alcalá, but apparently did not receive a degree. Américo Castro and Hugo A. Rennert, *Vida de Lope de Vega (1562-1635)* (Salamanca: Anaya, 1968), pp. 24-26.

41. For a sociological-historical study of the church see Antonio Domínguez Ortiz, *La sociedad española en el siglo XVII*, vol. II, *El estamento eclesiástico* (Madrid: Instituto Balmes de Sociología, CSIC, 1970).

42. *Ibid.*, pp. 7-8.

43. *Ibid.*, p. 39.

44. This point is emphasized by Pierre Vilar in his essay, "Los primitivos españoles del pensamiento económico," pp. 183-184.

45. See, for example, Angel Valbuena Prat, *El teatro español en su Siglo de Oro* (Barcelona: Planeta, 1969).

46. Max Weber has emphasized this problem in *Economy and Society*, pp. 1168-1173.

47. See Green, *Spain and the Western Tradition*, III, 165-167 on the orthodox mystics and pp. 161-165 on the heterodox mystics.

48. On that discontinuity see Bataillon, *Erasme et l'Espagne*, particularly chap. IX on the persecution of the Erasmianists. A change reflected in the correspondence of Luis Vives and Rodrigo Manrique, the son of the Inquisitor, was part of a general European change in the religious political climate. Vives writes to his friend Erasmus in 1534: "We pass through difficult times in which one cannot speak nor be silent without danger. In Spain Vergara and his brother Tovar have been arrested, not to mention other very learned men. In England, the bishops of Rochester and London, and Thomas More. I pray heaven to give you an easy old age." Rodrigo Manrique writes from Paris to Luis Vives on the occasion of Vergara's imprisonment: "You are right, our country is a land of pride and envy; you may add: of barbarism. For now it is clear that down there one cannot possess any culture without being suspect of heresy, error, and Judaism. Thus silence has been imposed on the learned. As for those who take refuge in erudition, they have been filled, as you say, with great terror . . . At Alcalá they are trying to uproot the study of Greek completely."
   For an interesting example of a critical reaction to the change and a plea for a more tolerant policy see José Antonio Maravall, "La oposición político-religiosa del siglo XVI. El erasmismo tardío de Felipe de la Torre," *Homenaje a Xavier Zubiri* (Madrid: Editorial Moneda y Crédito, 1970), II, 297-320.

49. An archbishop of Toledo, Carranza, was subjected to persecution, as were Priuli, Flaminio, Pole, and Morone in Italy.

50. See Bataillon, *Erasme et l'Espagne*, p. 826. The expurgated text was in the Second Part, chap. 36: "The works of charity that are made lukewarmly and slackly have no merit and are not worth anything" (Index of 1632). See Américo Castro, "Cervantes y la Inquisicion," *Modern Philology*, 27 (1930), 427-433.

51. Green, *Spain and the Western Tradition*, III, 333.

52. Gerhard Moldenhauer, "Spanische Zensur und Schelmenroman," *Estudios eruditos in memoriam de Adolfo Bonilla y San Martin*, 1 (Madrid, 1927), 223-239, quoted by Green, *Spain and the Western Tradition*, III, 460.

53. On the role of inquisitor see Julio Caro Baroja, "El señor inquisidor," in *El señor inquisidor y otras vidas por oficio* (Madrid: Alianza Editorial, 1968), pp. 15-63, who stresses the consequences of the legal, rather than theological, training preferred for the "career" and of the dependence of the judges in the more important "intellectual" cases on the opinions of experts.

54. Bataillon, *Erasme et l'Espagne*, pp. 395-466. See also José Antonio Maravall, *Carlos V y el pensamiento político del renacimiento* (Madrid: Instituto de Estudios Políticos, 1960), pp. 206-224.

55. The position of Erasmus when faced with the conflicting demands of Catholics, Protestants, and even Charles V is paradigmatic. See Bataillon, *Erasme et l'Espagne*.

56. See Angel Losada, *Juan Ginés de Sepúlveda a través de su Epistolario y nuevos documentos* (Madrid: Instituto Francisco de Vitoria, CSIC, 1959).

57. Weber, *Economy and Society*, II, 513-514.

58. See Pierre Mesnard, *L'essor de la philosophie politique au XVIe siècle* (Paris:

Librairie Philosophique J. Vrin, 1969), with chapters on Francisco de Vitoria, Juan de Mariana, and Francisco Suárez.

59. Theodor Geiger, *Aufgaben und Stellung de Intelligenz in der Gesellschaft* (Stuttgart: Ferdinand Enke, 1949), chap. II.

60. The literature is so extensive that a special bibliography has been published: Lewis Hanke and Manuel Giménez Fernández, *Bartolomé de las Casas, 1474-1566. Bibliografía crítica y cuerpo de materiales para el estudio de su vida, escritos, actuación y polémicas que suscitaron durante cuatro siglos* (Santiago, 1954). Lewis Hanke, *The Spanish Struggle for Justice in the Conquest of America* (Philadelphia: University of Pennsylvania Press, 1959) provides an excellent account of the historical context and the controversies of the time. His *Aristotle and the American Indians: A Study in Race Prejudice in the Modern World* (Chicago: Henry Regnery, 1959) focuses more specifically on the intellectual battles and debates. Marcel Bataillon has collected his papers in *Etudes sur Bartolomé de las Casas* (Paris: Centre de Recherches de L'Institut d'Etudes Hispaniques, 1965), which includes a chapter on "Charles-Quint, Las Casas et Vitoria," a subject also treated by Ramón Menéndez Pidal, "Vitoria y Las Casas," in *El P. Las Casas y Vitoria con otros temas de los siglos XVI y XVII* (Madrid: Espasa-Calpe, Col. Austral, 1958), pp. 9-48. See also Menéndez Pidal, *El Padre Las Casas, su doble personalidad* (Madrid: Espasa-Calpe, 1963).

61. Weber, *Economy and Society,* II, 439-451.

62. Francisco de Quevedo y Villegas, *Obras completas,* vol. I, *Obras en prosa* (Madrid: Aguilar, 1966), with an introduction and notes by Felicidad Buendía. For a biography see Luis Astrana Marín, *La vida turbulenta de Quevedo* (Madrid: Editorial "Gran Capitán," 1945).

63. On the Spanish contributions to economic theory, see Vilar, "Los primitivos españoles del pensamiento económico," pp. 175-207.

64. *Memorial de la política necesaria y útil restauración de la República de España* (Valladolid, 1600).

65. *Conservación de Monarquías y discursos políticos sobre la gran consulta que el Consejo hizo al señor rey Don Felipe Tercero* (1626).

66. See Vilar, "El tiempo del Quijote," p. 443.

67. Green, *Spain and the Western Tradition,* IV, 250.

68. See *ibid.,* pp. 6-9, on Saavedra Fajardo.

69. Hanke, *The Spanish Struggle for Justice,* leads to some of the relevant literature.

70. *Ibid.,* pp. 12-13.

71. Hanke, *Aristotle and the American Indians.*

72. *Ibid.,* chaps. 5 and 6.

73. Menéndez Pidal, *El Padre Las Casas,* pp. 358-380.

74. See note 60.

75. Hanke, *The Spanish Struggle for Justice,* pp. 162-172.

76. Menéndez Pidal, *El Padre Las Casas,* chap. VIII, esp. pp. 324-335 on his prophetism.

108 JUAN J. LINZ

77. Weber, *Economy and Society,* II, 439-451.

78. Bataillon, *Etudes sur Bartolomé de las Casas,* pp. xvi-xvii. See also Lewis Hanke, "More Heat and Some Light on the Spanish Struggle for Justice in the Conquest of America," *Hispanic American Historical Review,* 8 (1964), 313.

79. Menéndez Pidal, *El Padre Las Casas,* p. 347.

80. Francisco de Quevedo Villegas, *Política de Dios y Govierno de Christo,* ed. James O. Crosby (Madrid: Castalia, jointly with the University of Illinois Press, 1966); an excellent critical edition of the text.

81. Juan Marichal, "Quevedo: El escritor como 'espejo' de su tiempo," *La voluntad de estilo* (Barcelona: Seix y Barral, 1957), pp. 149-162.

82. Quoted *ibid.,* p. 158.

83. Quevedo, *Obras completas,* p. 947.

84. Quoted by Green, *Spain and the Western Tradition,* IV, 6.

85. Quoted by Palacio Atard, *Derrota, agotamiento, decadencia en la España del siglo XVII* (Madrid: Rialp, 1956), p. 156.

86. Palacio Atard refers to these authors and quotes them. Vilar, "El tiempo del Quijote," p. 443, refers to this generational shift in the response to the state of the nation. Another important source on the ideas of the period is José María Jover, *1635: Historia de una polémica y semblanza de una generación* (Madrid, 1949).

87. Green, *Spain and the Western Tradition,* III, 49-51.

88. *Ibid.,* p. 50.

FRANÇOIS BOURRICAUD

The Adventures of Ariel

ARIEL IS not only the biblical name for certain human-headed lions, or the sylphlike character of *The Tempest* created by Shakespeare as the wise Prospero's companion. It is also the title of an excellent book, published in 1901 by the Uruguayan José Enrique Rodó, which gives a highly idealized description of the intellectual and his mission in Latin American societies. I shall place the following observations under the invocation of Ariel in order to emphasize the continuity of this mission, or of a pretension to such; yet I am well aware that the symbol so expressed has undergone quite evident transformations.

We must first ask whether it makes sense to consider the role of the Latin American intellectual *in general.* I shall not hide my skepticism as to the stereotypes concerning "Latin America." In fact, the geographical area thus designated manifests an extraordinary heterogeneity when social and economic factors are taken into account. The differences between such obviously underdeveloped countries as Bolivia or Paraguay, and Argentina, southern Brazil, or even Chile are striking, whether one considers individual productivity, rate of urbanization, or education. In addition, there is little exchange within the countries of that particular zone, and I refer not only to the flow of goods, services, or capital, but also to the exchange of ideas and intellectual contacts.

During the nineteenth century, intellectual life in the new Latin American republics was characterized by two features: compartmentalization of small national (one is tempted to say provincial) intellectual markets and dependence on the international centers of diffusion, situated in Europe and the United States. Today, intellectual life in Latin America tends to be organized around Latin American themes; dependence on themes imported from the center seems, at least at first sight, to have diminished. Just how seriously should one consider these apparently important transformations?

I am not unaware of the arbitrary nature of dividing history into periods. Yet I feel that it is far more justifiable to attribute the awakening of consciousness to the 1920's than to the time of Independence, which constituted a false start for almost all of the new states, followed by a long period of disillusionment, characterized by the setting aside of the very ideals in whose name the *Libertadores* had fought and by a pronounced degradation of the most elementary conditions of civility.[1] The period that followed saw an increased exposure of ever-greater sectors of the society to the impact of modern ideas and modern techniques of production. There was a growth in foreign investment, an activation of foreign exchanges, and finally the substitution of American imperialism for British imperialism. The crisis expressed itself culturally in the rise of indigenous art, the formulation of the Indian-American theme, and the affirmation of populism. These are characteristic expressions of a search for identity, a trait common to societies struggling with major transformations.

So, for example, positivism, of the French or Spencerian version, had repercussions first in Mexico, and, with some delays, almost everywhere on the Latin American continent. What is significant is that there was no exchange or interaction between the European positivists and their Latin American disciples; the ideas circulated only one way. The Latin American contribution to the decisive points of the positivist conception of intellectual life (the relation between science and its technical, moral, or political applications; the autonomy of knowledge with regard to religion, culture, and values) added no original element later adopted by either France or England. During the entire nineteenth century, and probably until World War I, Latin American culture remained provincial, in that the learned culture had been drawn either from the hispanic background or from French and Anglo-Saxon sources, while the popular culture survived on a latent basis, forced into a sort of limbo by the censorship of a Westernized elite.

With the advent of the Mexican revolution, this period, which some, such as José Carlos Mariategui or Victor Raúl Haya de la Torre, called "neocolonial," gave way to an intellectual, political, and university movement which spread from Córdoba during the 1920's. This was the trying experience of discovering a Latin American identity. Although observations that attempt to treat the entire American subcontinent as a meaningful unit are questionable, a more or less analogous combination of circumstances did take place throughout Latin American history, occurring in the various areas with no more than thirty years difference in time. Thus between 1850 and 1880, most countries put into effect policies of modernization founded on the free entry of foreign capital. In like manner, between 1930 and 1960, these development policies *hacia afuera* were abandoned in favor of industrialization based on the substitution of imports, protectionism, and the creation of a more or less extensive State sector.

The 1920's mark a delimitation in intellectual and ideological activity; it seems reasonable to speak of a "Latin American conjuncture" from 1920 on, in which the problems of dependence and identity were dominant. In the main, these two concerns were expressed through the *indigenismo* movement, which was of interest first to those countries in which a strong native minority subsisted, then through the intellectual movements, which after Córdoba affected all the universities of the continent in varying degrees.

Interest in "indigenous" life is now fully accepted, but the history of this interest illustrates the difficulties with which several generations of intellectuals had to struggle in their effort to grasp the originality of the Latin American situation. From 1860 on, in Mexico and Peru, the question of what should be done about the Indians preoccupied not only philanthropists and other "do-gooders," but also those concerned with the material development of their country. One may even ask whether, from the very beginning, sensitivity to the indigenous was not—in addition to radical criticism of a society guilty of tolerating such injustices—a sort of reactionary love of the past,[2] a more or less avowed longing for the colonial period, when the Indians were "protected" by the church and the Spanish monarchy from the abuses of land grabbers, who, after independence, were given by liberal legislation the means to enrich themselves at the expense of the indigenous communities and the church. However that may be, the radical indigenous cause underwent serious transformations; having at first demanded a policy of promotion (education) and protection (concerning land), the movement eventually turned the Indian into the symbol of national identity (and in the final analysis, continental identity).

The *indigenista* claims were not set forth by the natives themselves, who during this entire period could neither express themselves nor be heard, except through outbursts of "decentralized violence,"[3] but by the enlightened elements of a mainly provincial middle class. In Peru during the 1920's, for example, a tight network of channels connecting Lima and the capitals of the provinces (especially Le Cuzco) was established through the *Asociacion Pro Indigena* and the subscribers to several magazines such as *Amauta* and *La Sierra*. This system brought the intellectuals of the capital—those who had a concern for the indigenous problem and who had access to the power groups in Lima—into touch with others of similar sympathies in the provinces. Having access to the ministries, they could at one and the same time assume the role of protector of a community suffering the abuses of some *gamonal* and press for progressive legislation. Communications existed, but there was always the threat of misunderstanding and distrust between those who had already "arrived," and were near the seats of power, and those who, bitter or resigned, remained isolated in the provinces.

The *indigenista* protest offered the intellectuals a rallying point. It gave them a mission, and, indeed, painters, folklorists, and *indigenista* "instructors" contributed much toward giving the natives, particularly the brighter among them, a vital sense of their own dignity.[4] For this reason, it is impossible to dismiss the indigenous movement as simply folkloric, as was the case with certain similar movements in Europe at the end of the nineteenth century. This is not to say, however, that the *indigena* culture did not have serious shortcomings. Two were particularly obvious.[5] First, it lacked sufficient conceptual and analytical tools, not only in the technical or scientific realms, but also in the areas of cosmology and philosophy. No fully developed intellectual tradition comparable to Confucianism or Buddhism existed any longer in Latin America—assuming that any such tradition had existed, even before the conquest. Second, the indigenous culture, even if still remarkably alive within the confines of village life, did not provide a convincing model of political and social organization for countries asserting their participation in the race for modernization. For this reason, more lucid persons involved in discussions of "Inca socialism" in Peru generally concluded that pre-Colombian "socialism" had little to do with that modern socialism defined by Lenin as "democracy plus electricity."

The combination of a certain number of indigenous and local elements —what Robert Redfield would call "folk culture"[6]—with modern elements, ideas emanating from Paris, London, or New York, inevitably rendered the *indigenista* ideology highly unstable. The Latin American intellectuals of the 1920's vigorously affirmed the need for an original synthesis. This synthesis, however, already precarious, was threatened even more by certain characteristics of the hispanic tradition, which, in spite of the *indigenista* group's railings against Spanish colonial rule, continued to serve as the medium making possible a familiarity with European and North American ideas.

It is difficult to appreciate the contribution of the Spanish cultural tradition to the intellectual life of Latin America. Distrust of Spain, denunciation of the colonial administration's crimes, and condemnation of clerical obscurantism are themes that recur frequently in *indigenista,* Mexican or Peruvian, literature. Except during the Second Spanish Republic, *los hispanizantes,* those who claimed as a point of reference the traditional hispanic culture, generally identified themselves as conservatives. However, the vehicle of traditional Spanish culture was more important than the symbolism of ideological affiliations. During the whole of the nineteenth century and the first half of the twentieth century, Spain had no great philosophical systems, no original social or political doctrines, and no important technological or scientific innovations to export. This did not mean that intellectual life in Spain was dead. Its development, however, proceeded along the lines of the polemic and the essay (perhaps even in the academic storing of knowledge), but not by research procedures and theoretical analysis.

Frenchmen writing about politics, in particular the French of the eighteenth century, are considered to be very prone to generalization; Tocqueville pointed out the consequences of this tendency toward abstraction and deduction on the part of the French intellectual. The Spanish of the nineteenth and twentieth centuries cultivated the essay; Unamuno and Ortega excelled in the use of this form. What the essay has in common with the French "politics of literature" is a basic lack of concern for facts and experience. The difference, however, is that while the French claim to deduce and prove, the Spanish writers willingly assume the role of visionary or magician, multiplying mirror tricks and spotlight effects endlessly, resorting to all the artifices of a baroque affectedness.

One should add to the preceding observations the fundamentally *innerweltlich* orientation of the Latin American intellectual. He is generally uninterested in pure learning or theoretical knowledge. This is demonstrable in many ways. Thus, for example, a comparison of the Latin American crisis of the 1920's, which centered on the search for identity, and the ways in which Europe came to modernity in the sixteenth, seventeenth, and eighteenth centuries will show the difference. All the questions so passionately examined by Erasmus as well as Voltaire—the relations between positive thought, tradition, and faith; the capacity of Reason to organize human society according to its own criteria; the limits imposed on Reason by tradition and the past—were barely considered by Latin American intellectuals, and if considered, only in the most conventional manner. Their interest focused almost exclusively on problems such as dependence and national identity, leading them to question the social mission of the intellectual, rather than the critical function of intelligence.

It is interesting to compare this pragmatic orientation with the constant weakness of the mystical element in Latin American Catholicism. The secular or regular church has remained strictly ritualistic until recent times. Today, however, it seems that the church is abandoning its traditionalism to launch itself into revolutionary activism. The transition to modernity, for clergy as well as laymen, seems to have been accomplished less through the development of critical thought than through an intense feeling of the urgency of an inevitable *compromiso* (commitment).

The possibilities of realizing this *compromiso* depend on the relation between the Latin American intellectual and the various institutions in which he participates. It is for this reason that an analysis of the Latin American student movement is so essential. Generally speaking, the intellectual associates with (1) learned societies or academies; (2) institutions of teaching and research (universities, for example); (3) public and private organizations in which he has a professional role; (4) political organizations, political parties, political movements. The effectiveness of the intellectual's participation in such groups depends on the nature of his attachment to them, and the help such organizations give him in realizing his objectives. For example, the role of the intellectual will differ greatly according to whether he can maintain active communication and systematic discussions with his colleagues or whether he is condemned to solitude by the narrowness, hostility, or inconsistency of his social environment. As a last resort, the intellectual may feel impelled to search outside of—perhaps even in opposition to—his own social group for people with whom he may converse, persons who were not formed in the same disciplines as he was, but whose energies he will seek to capture to accomplish his mission. He will turn to the youth, workers, peasants.

I

The most positive feature of empirical sociology is its ability to rid us of preconceived ideas. There are two particularly strongly-held stereotypes of the Latin American intellectual. On the one hand, he is represented as a guerrilla-obsessed, revolution-loving romantic; on the other, he is described as a lover of the past, forever hostile to technical progress and the modern organization of industrial societies. As with all stereotypes, these do hold an element of truth. Indeed, if one questions Latin American students, particularly those in sociology, one finds that they locate themselves on a scale of radicalism as "very much to the left." However, if one takes the trouble, as Glaucio Soares did, for instance, to separate the social science students from others—medical students, law students, students of agronomy—one finds that these last groups situate themselves at lower levels of radicalism. If one seeks to further the analysis by studying the motivations of social science students, one discovers that although 30 per cent of the students of the University of Colombia's sociology department chose this discipline out of a desire to change society, 50 per cent of the students chose sociology in preparation for a professional career—which may be unrealistic, but it does not imply an exclusively or even primarily ideological motivation, at least at first sight.

In that respect, Gloria Cucullu's research on the values held by intellectuals is quite revealing. Her study, conducted in Argentina, consists of two samples, the first randomly selected among people in the literary field, the second composed of those individuals selected by the first sample as the most distinguished literary personalities.[7] Three open-ended questions were asked of this intellectual elite. The first concerned the connotations associated with the following terms: industrialization, mechanization, and technology. The second solicited the respondent's opinion on the increasing interest among students in technical and scientific careers. The third evoked the effects of accelerated industrialization on the future of the writer and his public. The answers of both sample populations to each of the above questions were favorable to the stereotypes of industrial society. In the first sample, favorable associations outweighed unfavorable ones by 47 per cent, in the second by 55 per cent; negative associations occurred among 24 per cent in the first sample and 20 per cent in the second. For example, 29 per cent and 34 per cent (first and second samples, respectively) considered industrialization as "progress"; only 10 per cent and 3 per cent spoke of "standardization," "massification," or "mechanization." Gloria Cucullu left an option open to those who would rather hold a middle-of-the-road position, such as the following: industrialization is like Aesop's tongue, the very best or worst of things. Only 16 per cent of the respondents chose this cautious answer. The sum of favorable responses to the second question was even greater than for the first. Sixty-one and 62 per cent of those questioned approved the technological and scientific orientation of studies. The development of scientific and technical studies is of course a prerequisite to a more general development. Yet the difference between the two samples is particularly marked in reference to this point; 37 per cent of the literary personalities held this opinion, as against only 25 per cent of the first sample. On the last question, concerning the future of literature in an industrial society, the great majority of literary notables were optimistic (58 per cent). This optimism was somewhat less evident in the first sample (44 per cent), yet pessimistic reactions were only 15 per cent and 12 per cent respectively.

One must not attempt to draw more conclusions from these data than warranted. The answers given do not guarantee that the subjects' conceptions of industrial society are realistic. In addition, the second question is quite surprising: It would seem, at first sight, that it is not the growth of technological and scientific establishments which is problematic in Argentina, but rather the rapid increase in the number of literary persons. The worth of Gloria Cucullu's study lies in its suggestion that we not content ourselves with the stereotypes of the Latin American intellectual's persistent past-loving and humanist orientations.

The work of Frank Bonilla reveals the special difficulties of the intellectual's situation, especially a remarkable article in which he demonstrated that intellectuals could not be clearly distinguished from professionals (or more generally, from the urban upper-middle class), whether one considered social origin, career profile, possibilities of promotion and mobility, or opinions and attitudes.[8] Bonilla encountered a major methodological problem in the rigorous identification of intellectuals. Does this qualification apply indiscriminately to all persons having either undertaken or completed certain studies? Or should it be reserved for those who so identify themselves? Finally, assuming that it is possible to delimit a group whose existence is affirmed by both its members and outside observers—by combining purely objective facts, such as level of studies and length of training, and subjective data, such as attitudes and opinions—the coherence of this group and the power it can dispose of in relation to other groups must yet be determined.

Using data from Argentina, Chile, Mexico, and Brazil, Bonilla shows the extent to which the intellectual (self-identified or objectively recognized) resembles the other professional group closest to him on the scale of social stratification. Bonilla took care to assess his comparisons at all levels of the social scale. He thus extends the range of his observations (which include the relatively low categories of intermediate technicians) and also avoids conferring elite status on all intellectuals merely on principle. His conclusions are thereby far more pertinent, as they apply to all categories of intellectuals, regardless of hierarchical position, and because of the rigorous correspondence established between the intellectuals and their professional homologues: same origin (rising urban middle class), little difference in years of schooling and revenue, same class identification. The score does not differ greatly for a doctor or a laboratory researcher, a student leader or an intermediate executive in a firm. In any case, the difference in score is less between intellectual and professional of the same level than between intellectual and intellectual, professional and professional of different levels. What is even more remarkable is that both intellectual and professional express the same attitude toward commonly-held values (the degree of legitimate competition in a good society, the degree of confidence in industrial society, the degree of adherence to one's nationality).

I shall not undertake a thorough examination of the relationship between intellectuals and professionals, even though this relationship constitutes one of the most important elements in studying not only industrialized countries, but also developing countries. The professionalization process combines in a very complex way a certain number of partial trends: a high level of qualifications (consequently a considerable initial investment), continual adaptation, retraining of the professional in an increasingly demanding organizational framework, frequent loyalty conflicts between the organization's hierarchy and the authorities in the profession. The result of this process is a certain reconciliation of intellectuals and professionals, and at the same time a specialization of each group according to different functions, even if this means that the relations and contacts are tighter and more continuous. It is thus not very surprising that Bonilla should find marked similarities among researchers, industrial executives, and university professors, since all in all these categories belong to the same body, or to the same population, if only because of common education and the increasing importance given to intellectual training for professionals.

What is more surprising, however, is the conformity Bonilla notices among intellectuals. "The intellectuals I have studied reveal, behind a façade of radicalism and nonparticipation, a profound adherence to middle-class values, and seem to have been conditioned by bourgeois sentimentality as to appropriate behavior and the worth of a good reputation." Bonilla thus not only shows the relationships between professionals and intellectuals, but also maintains that both are "petit bourgeois."

I would agree, but with certain reservations. The so-called "bourgeois" values do not constitute a coherent and complete ethical system, such as that of the Puritans, or even that of the French petit bourgeois at the end of the nineteenth century. Bonilla gives three indicators of conservatism which describe the "attitudes of several Latin American professionals." The first concerns adherence to Catholicism, which is very strong, since 70 per cent of the medical students, 75 per cent of the students in economics, and 42 per cent of those in the sciences[9] claim to be practicing Catholics. The second indicator concerns the subject's optimism and satisfaction, both of which are also high (and without the variations found in relation to religious practice, conspicuous among students in the sciences). The third indicator measures the degree of satisfaction attained through the subjects' participation in their everyday activities. The smallest percentages of satisfaction are revealed by the medical students; this would seem to be in accord with the marked reticence of this group concerning the conditions of competition.

Can conservatism be presumed on the basis of the practice of Catholicism, the subject's optimism as to his private life and future, and his satisfaction with his chosen career and profession? Bonilla does not speak of "conservatism," but rather of adherence to "petit bourgeois" values. These values do not apply merely to professional life; they also refer to the subject's attitude toward his home life, his obligations toward his wife and children, his concept of what is desirable in this area. Obviously, similar expectations bring the intellectual and professional closer together.

Is conservatism, or even cultural authoritarianism (in other words, a more or less implicit adherence to common values, in the most rigid and constrained way), associated with political conservatism? Cultural conservatism, or even authoritarianism, is quite evident in Bonilla's data, especially in certain political answers. Of the Mexican intellectuals questioned, 64 per cent stated that the popular majority cannot influence the course of the country's affairs. (Only 15 per cent of the members of parliament replied similarly.) The interpretation of this answer is ambiguous, however, so long as one cannot determine whether the respondent considers such a situation "normal" or "scandalous." When asked which obstacles seem to prevent national unity, between 82 and 88 per cent of the subjects cited the "absence of civic culture among the masses." This absence, considered a "cause of underdevelopment," is mentioned by all categories questioned and is placed before "the pressure of foreign governments," which comes immediately after "the operations of international monopolies," and "the egoism of national land-owners and businessmen." According to available data, the extent of national identification or nationalism is remarkably strong; if one adds this element to the above observations, the over-all picture becomes quite clear: distrust of those who govern, contemptuous condescension toward the "uncultured masses," a distinct though somewhat weaker tendency to project the blame for underdevelopment on foreign capitalism and local interest.

But these "petit bourgeois" are also political radicals; they favor vast property transfers, extension of state control over the economy, nationalization, and state planning; they express their distrust of imperialism and the ruling classes. It seems, then, that there is in fact consensus regarding the different points enumerated above, and moreover, that it exists more intensely among intellectuals *stricto sensu*, particularly among students, than among professionals. The coherence of this consensus, however, is another matter, and we shall later explain why, lacking strictly logical coherence, it tends to be formulated in paroxysmic terms, at the end of a radicalizing process.

Suffice it to say for the moment that though these petit bourgeois intellectuals give all the appearances of being political radicals, they are cultural conservatives (anti-imperialists and at the same time authoritarian and elitist). Two facts explain this disjunction. First, it must be remembered that radical criticism in the realm of ethics, religion, and morals was probably not as pervasive in Latin American societies as it was in France and the United States. I find the absence of such a radical tradition indicated in the missionary style of political preaching in Latin America, the insistence on the *compromiso,* the suffocating moralism of the most radical movements—as in the Cuban example—and the failure, at least until now, of hippie-type movements. The astonishingly large proportion of students, professionals, or intellectual radicals who declare themselves practicing Catholics and, in general, the adherence to middle-class values by people *de avazanda* themselves underscore the persistence of conventional morality.

Second, it must be understood that there is no true conservative tradition in South America. Of course, vested interests ardently defend themselves, but they have never succeeded, or even tried to succeed, in legitimizing their action or presence. It is true that toward the end of the nineteenth century, civilian governments (called *civilistas* in Peru until President Leguia's second term) established almost everywhere a sort of democratic legitimacy, which although limited and very constrained, assured the reign of vested interests, and also the presence of well-bred people in parliament, the ministries, and even the presidency. But that which Jorge Basadre calls the *Republica aristocratia* belongs to the past. Except for that period, Latin American conservatism has assumed essentially two political forms, one which we shall call, as does the Venezuelan Valenilla Lanz, "democratic Caesarism"; the other I propose to call "cynical economicizing" (not intended pejoratively). According to democratic Caesarism, one's only resort in societies constantly threatened by dissolution is to call on a strong leader. Caesar, whether he be called Porfirio Diaz or Juan Vicente Gomez, plays the part of a democrat, and in general does not respect the traditions entrusted him. In addition, to the extent that the conservative leaders are generally cultivated and cosmopolitan, they can hardly be pleased by the governments which shut down newspapers and behave badly toward foreigners, who usually end up in exile. Unlike liberal politicians whose weakness engenders disorder, Caesar asserts his ability to assure, first, personal security, then the safety of goods, then common prosperity. He encourages the initiatives of both foreigners and national capitalists.

The cynical type also emphasizes the need to produce wealth, but he distrusts Caesar as he would any formidable demagogue. His aim is the preservation of the economic sphere from the improvisations of politicians, the whims of the "man on horseback," and the pressures of the "blind masses." The clever maneuvers of the cynic are rarely very effective today. As to the "man on horseback," he no longer wishes to serve as the "oligarchy's watchdog," an expression well known among the Peruvian military.[10]

We are thus confronted with two facts: the weakness of conservatism as a political ideology and the strength of conservative attitudes and culture. We must therefore resolve the paradox arising from a juxtaposition of an authoritarian cultural background with a political orientation that is far more radical than conservative, and at the limit is frankly activist.

First, let us recall that only a minority of Latin American intellectuals (or intellectuals of other nationalities) are political activists. This point is particularly well established with regard to students. Only a minority of them participate in political organizations, be it as sympathizers, members, or leaders. Similar results show up when the observer examines student participation in the administration of jointly governed universities. Everyone knows that the level of electoral participation is quite low, varying between 20 per cent and 30 per cent of those registered.[11] Although, to my knowledge, there is little data available on the political commitment of professionals, I would tend to believe that the two propositions confirmed in the case of students—low partisan participation and low corporate participation—would be equally true. In considering whether these two types of participation are linked, we find that students who are politically motivated and active are also those who participate as candidates or delegates in the Department or University Councils. Finally, it would be interesting to determine if (as I believe, even in the absence of evidence) the most politically engaged professionals are to be found among those who qualify themselves as intellectuals.

To understand the nature of activism, it is essential to differentiate between activism and extremism. All those who are "engaged" are not necessarily rabid; all politically active Latin American intellectuals are not communists, Trotskyites, Castroists, or Maoists. The term "extremist" includes a series of attitudes of which at least two must be specified here. On the one hand there is an extremism of nihilistic inspiration, which wantonly exaggerates the severity of its choices; on the other hand, there is an extremism which feels compelled willy nilly to "go to the limit" without experiencing the exquisite sensation which envelops the nihilist facing the desired end—annihilation of the other and of self. A "reformer" may be induced to advocate extremely drastic policies he had not initially planned to support, or that he would even have disapproved of or condemned. The radical intellectual can be led into a situation in which he loses control of an action undertaken without having properly estimated his own capacities and with little knowledge of the world in which he attempts to function. Thus, if certain "committed" become "rabid," it could be more the result of repeated failures than a deliberate choice. In the end, we can say that one suffers extremism as a fatality, rather than choosing it as a destiny.

This kind of proposition is obviously very difficult to prove. We could attempt to do so only if a great deal of autobiographical material were available. Personal information on guerrilla fighters would be most valuable for this task. But when we look at the material actually available—the research on students—we realize the scarcity and poverty of our information. Yet, these studies do reveal the Latin American intellectual's extreme ambivalence in relation to his society.

Students who are politically engaged are almost all progressive; what is striking is the diversity, the rivalry among the parties or factions which they support. Many could not possibly be labeled extremist. In the Peruvian university elections, until the military coup d'etat of 1968, the *aprista* federation of students sometimes won, and even when beaten by a coalition formed of all its opponents, it constituted an important minority, along with the communist groups of various doctrines, the Christian-Democrats, and the "independents." The Christian-Democratic groups are well entrenched in the Chilean and Venezuelan universities. However, it is important to realize that this partisan pluralism coexists with an ideological consensus, which is readily conducive to situations of unanimity (for instance, against the "imperialist threat"), particularly if the explosive potential is exploited by clever manipulators.

We have already noted that Latin American professionals agree on the causes of the underdevelopment of their country. A study comparing answers given by a sample of Chilean students[12] belonging to two different groups, Christian-Democrats and the Popular Front (FRAP), discloses a similarly remarkable convergence on interpretations of the Chilean situation, its causes and its remedies. Referring to a list of the most important issues relevant to Chile today, 20 per cent of the Christian-Democratic students and 20 per cent of the FRAP students cite "inequality of opportunity"; 23 per cent of FRAP students and 37 per cent of the Christian-Democratic students point out the "monopoly of the upper classes." The most significant difference is revealed in two responses: (1) "imperialism's" baneful role is mentioned by only 2 per cent of the Christian-Democrats, whereas 29 per cent of the *frapistas* assert this; (2) the "necessity of a social revolution" is acknowledged by 11 per cent of the *frapistas* and by only 4 per cent of the Christian-Democrats. Let us add, though, that on the question concerning the veto which could nullify a party's victory at the polls (Must the party which has won the elections, regardless of which party it is, be allowed to assume power?), both *frapistas* and Christian-Democrats agree to accept the majority's decision. Furthermore, the Christian-Democrats are more numerous in recognizing this rule of the democratic game: 73 per cent as against 63 per cent of the *frapistas*.

It is unwise to generalize from this Chilean data without due precaution. For instance, respect of the majority is much less prevalent in a country like Peru, where the military has more than once annulled electoral results it disliked, with little resistance or opposition from civilians in general, or from the intellectuals among them. However, from the data collected by Myron Glazer, it is possible to distinguish among Latin American intellectuals the grounds for consensus as well as the outlines of several important cleavages. They more or less agree on the necessity of development, "structural" reforms, the egoism of the privileged, the masses' passivity and lack of culture, and the perversity of foreign interests. Cleavage revolves around two issues: the resources and the identity of the group—party or institution—on which devolves the historical responsibility of accomplishing change.

For example, among the Chilean students studied by Glazer, *frapistas* and Christian-Democrats seem divided on the desirable extent of reforms: Should they be "moderate," "considerable," or "structural"? The *frapistas* are more structuralist than the Christian-Democrats. In all probability, the problem of the extent of reform is linked to that of its implementation. Those who believe in "revolution in liberty," to use Eduard Frei's expression, do indeed intend to "change the structures," but they believe that this change should come about according to a rate and procedure fixed by law, that is to say, under circumstances whose legitimacy cannot be challenged by those who stand to lose because of the change. On the second divisive issue—which party leader, which group appears best qualified to advance "structural reforms" or to "make the revolution"—this question, which implies partisan sympathies and loyalties, evidently varies in form according to the time and place. But one may wonder—though this hypothesis is by no means proved—if this search for those most capable of "making the revolution" does not become progressively more radical as the deceptions and errors accumulate and intensify.

The Latin American intellectual's "extremism" should be examined from this angle. If we are to assess the problem correctly, we must take into account the existence of two kinds of consensus: one cultural—in the sense of fundamental common values—characterized by a high degree of conservatism if not authoritarianism; the other political, concerning those problems which Latin American societies in their present state of development must deal with, and find solutions for, if they are to be brought out of their present crisis. Conservatism or cultural authoritarianism, radicalism or political progressivism—these theoretically define independent attitudes; yet, they seem to be associated, with at least moderate intensity, by most subjects, though often in an unstable and ambiguous way.

II

I suggest that we call "activism" that very unstable combination which is first perceived as a most ambitious project, "integral" as the Latin Americans say, and yet at the same time incapable of assuring its full realization. In the following pages, I shall attempt to connect the successive forms of activism to the evolution of the relation between professional and intellectual, and consider the extent to which the intellectual has entered the administrative and political systems.

The most obvious and naïve form of intellectual activism is what one could call the Latin American variety of "pulpit idealism,"[13] or, to use a more current expression, "arielism." The following remarks are borrowed from Rodó,[14] though I do not propose to describe fully the Uruguayan *Pensador*. I consider him a model, a type. The idea of his work that one may infer from the following may seem to some more of a caricature than a portrait. We know that Rodó contrasts the utilitarianism he attributes to the North Americans—whose technical mastery he admires, but whose "spirit of possession and acquisition" he condemns—with devotion to the values of Beauty and Truth. The manner in which he opposes "Society" and "City" is as follows: "The society organized once and for all, which limits its project of civilization to elements of material prosperity, and its idea of justice to equitable redistribution between partners, will not manage to make the cities it inhabits anything other than beehives or anthills. But the *City* is great in the sense that its days are more than the invariable repetition of a same echo . . . that in it something exists which rises up over the crowd, when among the lights burning in its night, there is also the lamp which comforts the solitude of him who watches, kept alert by his thoughts, and in whose spirit begins the formation of the IDEA which shall burst forth under tomorrow's sun, transformed into a cry which summons and a force which guides souls."

Rodó's vocabulary—the light, the lamp, the sun, tomorrow, the cry, the force, the anxiety—is obsolescent. But regardless of how ridiculous the *Pensador* may seem in our day and age, even to many Latin American intellectuals, his message deserves attention, not only because of his influence on generations formed at the time of the Córdoba Manifesto, and during the crisis that followed, but also because of the permanence of certain arielist themes which even today have not lost all their vigor. Is the opposition between city and society a replica of the *Gemeinschaft-Gesellschaft* opposition? In any case, this opposition includes a condemnation of industrial society, especially the Anglo-Saxon variety, echoes of which one could easily find today among revolutionaries as well as among "humanists" of Christian inspiration. We must however add that Ariel's idealism, the indifference or contempt for technical matters and industry, has been vigorously attacked by professors and other writers, who also bear the title "intellectual."

Rodó sees the *Pensador*'s role as a mission of censorship and denunciation; he is awarded the vocation of being the archetype. The function of censor proceeds in the name of values that have been slighted; it is less a social criticism than a moral protest. The *Pensador* thus comes to conceive of his action on society not as a series of piecemeal interventions, but as an "integral" reform, a total change, which has all the traits of a philosophical conversion. The methods of this action are essentially pedagogic, if we assume this term to mean that the master presents himself as the model and that his sole presence on the ramparts is like a flame whose light will suffice to keep alert the spirit of the citizens.

The insistence on the Socratic relationship between "master and disciple" is clearly linked to the aristocratic aura of *arielismo:* "As the multitude passes by, I observe that though it does not look up at the sky, the sky watches it. Something from on high descends upon the masses, indifferent and obscure as the furrowed earth. The fluttering of the stars resembles somehow the motion of the sower's hand." According to the arielist conception, political action consists essentially of preaching. And it so happens that the supreme preacher is the university professor. This coincidence, this convergence of two otherwise independent elements in the same role deserves attention. Rodó's *Pensador* borrows much from the Germanic *Denker:* the same concern with vast panoramas, what today we would call "totalizations," the same combination of idealism and aristocratic tendencies, more or less reconciled within the educational mission. In Germany, however, where the thinker is also a professor, the pulpit is more than just a tribune. The professor is specialized in a given field, and the thinkers' aristocratic tendency to separate themselves from that which is common is reinforced by the esoteric style of the "Seminar," in which the disciples gather around the master, who reserves for them alone the rare elixir of his science. No such thing existed in the Latin American universities at the end of the last century, since intellectual specialization was minimal. The professors' essential activity was to give a veneer of general culture to future professionals in law and medicine. The "Thinker" was a sort of specialist in generalities, who, in an effort to consolidate his prestige, willingly resorted to all the seductive potential of "inspired" style.

Anxiety and curiosity found their expression in the rhetorical and brilliant evocation of ideas rather than in empirical research or through methodical discourse with experts of a life specialty. It is possible, however, that in the Latin American societies of the late 1900's, the university, because it still had an almost religious prestige—well indicated by the Spanish word *claustro*—was the only refuge where a certain kind of abstraction (the "generalities" of the French) could be discussed. The fusion within the *Pensador*'s role of a "generalizing" orientation (the *Pensador* is able to recognize Good, Beauty, and Ugliness, condemn or exalt civilizations) and of an aristocratic orientation (the *Pensador* is the only one capable of fulfilling this sovereign office and is responsible for his message only before History) would thus be explained.

The dark legend woven around the pre-Córdoba universities does not allow us to discern the ideological ferment which probably made many of them far more animated than is generally admitted today. The students there were not the only source of anxiety; the tremor perceptible at the beginning of the twentieth century was not the only omen heralding the confrontations and troubles that were to come. Almost everywhere around 1910, professors—some of whom were truly remarkable[15]—came into the universities with "new ideas." Most were influenced by arielist thought, some by pragmatism of the Anglo-Saxon variety.

Let us not disparage too quickly the Latin American version of pulpit idealism. Rather, let us attempt to understand how the concept of the *Pensador* as *vates* led to a new definition of the relation between the intellectual and politics. I shall not attempt to describe the movement which, while originating in Córdoba, had its most remarkable consequences outside the Argentine, and attained cultural significance for the whole of Latin America. The arielist hue is apparent in the Córdoban Students' Manifesto: "Youth lives in constant search of heroism. It is disinterested, it is pure. It has not yet had the time to become corrupt. It never errs in the choice of its own masters." Youth is now identified with those values whose defense Rodó had entrusted to the *Pensador*. Youth is elevated to the dignity of Ariel; it becomes a collective *Pensador*.

We should dwell a moment upon this metamorphosis, for which a precedent can be found in the romantic exaltation of the student during the nineteenth century. The lectures given by Jules Michelet at the Collége de France[16] between December 1847 and April 1848 evoked some of the essential themes of the Argentine Students' Manifesto of 1918: There was an important difference; Michelet was not a youth, but a visionary addressing young people. He said, "You are, as it were, at the center of the times . . . You relate more easily to the various classes, through sympathy, or at least benevolence. You are at the center of everything, at the hub of things. You have, in more than one way, the custody of unity, and with this custody, the duty to fortify, extend, and establish this unity which has as yet but little progressed."[17] According to Michelet, the student was a link between the past and the present, a mediator between the different social classes. In the role Michelet assigned youth, as in the role the Córdoban youth assigned itself, the common element was a value-carrying role as harbinger of modernity as well as the mediator between the future and the past, between the still "barbaric" masses (to use Michelet's term) and the socially and culturally well-endowed elites. The romantic idealization of the European student of 1848 and the Latin American student of the 1920's has a great many causes, only some of which are identical.

In both cases, the phenomenon occurs at a time when the social actors, if not the most active and the most immediately affected by the process, are at least those most able to reflect upon it, give a meaning to it, and in general foresee some of its consequences; in short, those individuals most preoccupied with the aftermath of industrialization and urbanization, with the resulting changes in work and life styles, are recruited from school youth, because on the one hand, their "capacities"[18] supposedly enable them to assume the greatest responsibilities, and on the other, as a result of their youth, they are not guilty of the errors and egoisms of the past, are unsoiled by compromises with those in power, and are open to all alliances with the "vital forces" pushed aside for so long by the oligarchies.

The ethereal branch of Ariel is embodied in the student. This embodiment of spirit in a social movement, although inconclusive, can perhaps best be studied in Peru between 1919 and 1931, because during the 1920's university life and the beginnings of mass-party organization met and intersected, though the modern forms of mass politics did not break through. I shall mention only three of the most characteristic aspects of the Peruvian process, which I analyze further in a study of the formative years of Apra[19]; relevance goes far beyond the Peruvian case. The first problem encountered by the movement during its formation concerned its capacity to reform the university and to become the driving force of the reformed university. This attempt failed quite rapidly, not only because of resistance on the part of the old university oligarchies and the distrust of the political authorities, but also because of difficulties inherent in the "reformist" project. The reformers tried to make of the university a center of ferment and discussion, a center of popular education open to all without restrictions or qualifications, a research center of the highest quality—in short, a combination of Spanish Ateneo, Socratic-Platonic academy, German seminar, and, of course, a revolutionary thought and action group. The movement, totally incapable of reforming the university from within, tried from without to create a counteruniversity, called a "popular university," which lasted only a few years.

The movement continued to claim "revolutionary capacity," but this had to be proved. This is the most serious problem that Haya de la Torre and then Mariategui had to deal with. Both of them, although by different methods, sought to establish a working solidarity between intellectuals and workers. Since the school youth organized itself as the "vanguard of the masses," it could not just speak for the masses, it also had to communicate with them, or at least have some contact with them. This was particularly difficult in countries such as Peru, composed of a great majority of Indian peasants and a very small urban proletariat. The *indigenista* movement then seems to have been an attempt by intellectuals to assert their own identity through rediscovery of the historical continuity and geographical extension of the popular tradition. The famous *pueblo continente* or Indo-America myth is an illustration of this pathetic effort to find oneself by meeting others. If one wishes to follow the Peruvian movement's course to the end, one must find out how, after the university reform adventure, the attempt to establish an alliance with the manual worker and the Indians eventually resulted in the constitution of a populist party that, despite many setbacks, still exists today.

Regardless of the ambiguity that might result from applying the same term to the Mexican regime, the Peruvian *aprista* party, as well as the Perónist movements, I believe it is possible to speak of "populist" movements, if the term is taken to mean the combination of a certain number of original orientations: (1) a dose of "anti-imperialism," especially in relation to the United States; (2) a concept of autonomous development, *hacia adentro;* (3) a demand for the "integral" participation of those social forces which the traditional oligarchic governments had held back; (4) a preference for coalitions or "fronts" rather than for "class" action in the Marxist-Leninist sense. These items form but an outline, and the "extended participation" as understood by Haya in 1930 differs from the conception held by Perón in 1943; the *hacia adentro* development generally indicates a policy of import substitution, but the expression may also be applied to more or less successful, and more or less methodical, attempts at autarchic planning. Whatever the diversity of the positions covered by each item mentioned, whatever the problems involved in harmonizing these different orientations at the operational level of concrete policies, they are organized around the rejection of "oligarchic power" and "dependence on imperialism"; they affirm and claim an autonomous capacity of development.

The intellectuals' situation during the period of predominantly populist orientations was not always easy. One need only mention the brutal interventions of Perónist authorities in the press and in university life. The intellectual atmosphere was extremely strained in Peru between 1945 and 1948, when an uninterrupted succession of skirmishes and confrontations occurred, during which time the *apristas* intellectuals were constantly opposed to all other sectors of the intellectual community who were leagued against Haya de la Torre's party. If one attempts to sift from the mass of arguments and accusations the reasons for the hostility between the populist intellectuals and all other groups of the intelligentsia, one retains several indefinitely repeated themes which criticize populism both as a method of action and as a style of thought.

The first criticism I shall consider later. The second refers to a certain rhetorical redundancy, a certain idealistic verbosity, which seems even more vulnerable given the intellectual intentions and claims of the populist movement. When Colonel Perón disguised himself as the *Pensador,* his chances of being taken seriously were slim. But Haya de la Torre—great orator and well-known essayist—was not much more convincing when, imagining himself following in Einstein's footsteps, he commented on *el espacio-tiempo historico.* Haya and the intellectuals of his generation were extremely critical of Rodó, arguing against his unrealistic intellectualism. Yet they were also fond of generalities; they were thoroughly satisfied with an "integral" vision, and despite their declarations on the need for the elaboration of scientific politics, their frames of reference remained essentially literary.

Meanwhile, Ariel pursued his metamorphoses. He had yet to add to all his ambitions that of vying with Prometheus. Even if until about 1950 the *tecnificación* theme of government by experts and scientific policies was composed mainly of rhetorical developments—with the notable exception of the Mexican *cientificos*—it soon became far more important, particularly given the initial disdain of pulpit idealism for technical matters. The North American—who, according to Rodó, was technical civilization's most finished product—lived for the immediate reality, for the present, and subordinated all his activity to the egoism of personal and collective welfare. However, this condemnation was in truth already weakened, with the realization that technology—in the area of production as well as that of organization and control of social relations—was a condition of progress. Would it not suffice to subordinate technology to an ideal, for it to acquire a value (derived evidently, but still valid)? This issue had been raised by the Mexican positivists of the 1880's, when they asked whether it was not best for them, given their ideal, to support an authoritarian government—that of don Porfirio—which, they argued, was the only one capable of undertaking the accelerated modernization of their country.

They were mockingly called *cientificos* and the name stuck. It illustrates well the conviction that the alliance of power and science is the basis for political legitimacy—a theme recurring frequently among Latin American intellectuals and one substantially distinct from the concept which founds democratic legitimacy on civility. In order to fully comprehend the *cientificos* position, one must first determine with which science they were in fact affiliated. During the 1880's, economics and sociology were not, as they are today, applied sciences. The *cientificos* were schooled either in law or technical engineering, and in both cases steeped in a philosophy more or less derived from the French positivist conceptions of societal development. It is difficult to assess the role assumed by the *cientificos* in the development of Mexico because it evolved mainly during the government of don Porfirio and because the *cientificos* claims as against their real achievements, and the "dark legend" spread by their opponents, render a balanced appraisal of their role impossible. We can say that they were advisers, *asesores,* who tried more or less efficiently to promote a certain number of progressive reforms in the areas of education, judicial and administrative organization, and public works.

However, it must be pointed out that most were not true civil servants, but "part-time advisers," who, while keeping their private concerns in their *bufetes,* dedicated a part of their time to advising the administration. They were involved in the technical preparation of laws and in the elaboration of major developmental projects, as well as the structural organization of roads, railroads, agricultural production, and mining. They probably acted as intermediaries and "promoters" in these different roles. In the first place, they helped spread a certain number of new ideas and techniques on organization and production that they had learned abroad. Second, they helped establish the dialogue between the federal government and foreign interests, probably the most criticized aspect of their activity. Their influence on don Porfirio and the increasingly small circle of his intimate associates should, however, not be exaggerated: the "Porfiriato" was never, even in its best moments, the *cientificos* government. In addition, it is doubtful whether they formed a homogeneous group, trying to impose themselves on other groups who shared in the management of affairs.

The *tecnificación* process, which was inevitably stopped during the period of violence and instability that marked the first twenty years of the revolutionary era in Mexico, progressed more vigorously than ever after 1945 through almost the whole of Latin America. With respect to Mexico, Raymond Vernon[20] suggests an image of the post-revolution *tecnico* that provides an important comparison with the *cientifico.* The *tecnicos* are mainly economists working for the federal government. Their situation differs from that of the *cientificos* in that they are obliged to live and work in the context of a bureaucratic organization. They are not independent professionals lending their services to the administration in an accessory and irregular fashion. Whatever their exact judicial status, it is related to that of civil servants. In addition, because of the peculiarities of the Mexican regime, they are the agents of an executive who is not only powerful but also stable, whose operation is continuous, and who is consequently able to decide and control the execution of that which has been decided. Thus, Vernon states, the *tecnicos* are not, and cannot claim to be, policymakers, even if they are closely associated with the decisions made by politicians. While they may claim that their strength lies in their ability to prescribe a political line, in fact it lies in their ability to elaborate the technical alternatives which are submitted for decision to the political leaders.

They possess a certain fiscal or budgetary know-how which allows them to participate in the definition of major national alternatives on the level of governmental programs; they also have a more or less well-defined conception of the government's task, of the goals it proposes, and of their urgency and priority. Strictly speaking, as technicians they are more or less specialized and more or less competent. But the very nature of their work leads them out of the narrow field of their own technical capacity and into the consideration of the major options of national politics. They are even more so inclined if apart from their particular competence they are influenced by a certain number of generalities or ideological trends. Vernon gives a rich and detailed description of their ideology: "They are far from agreeing on all economic problems. They are separated by several doctrinal differences. A small minority is committed to the Marxist dogma . . . the others favor a mixed economy, but one in which the public sector would increase. And even among this last group, large differences subsist as to policies of intervention. And yet, they do have a common ideology."[21]

This ideology is evidently related to the populist trend. Industrialization, agrarian reform, lessening of dependence on imperialism—this is a language which can be understood by an *aprista* of the 1930's, a Mexican *cientifico* of the 1950's, or any of General Velasco's *asesores* in 1971. But as these themes move progressively away from their populist origin, they undergo a sort of split into two parts, through a technocratic transposition. On the one hand, they become commonplace, and, indeed, in the early 1970's, the major populist themes are indiscriminately accepted by almost all sections of opinion. The experts become aware of the fact that there is not just one possible industrialization policy, but several, and that the lessening of dependence on the foreigner may be realized in quite different ways.

This consensus is given a certain efficiency, a certain regulatory capacity, precisely because the government for which the *tecnicos* work is relatively aware of its goals and methods. They have a double advantage in that their responsibilities are carried out in an administrative framework and under the control of political leaders. First, since the administrative machinery is discriminating and efficient, their action has predictable and attributable consequences. A certain apprenticeship thus becomes possible, which allows the accumulation, at the organizational level, of knowledge, experience, and a tradition; this assures the formation of a highly qualified team of leaders and civil servants. Second, the role of the intellectual undergoes decisive revision; the efficiency of intervention in the political order no longer seems exclusively dependent on ideological preaching or partisan commitment, but rather on the ability to cooperate in the prosaic setting of an organization where the intellectual contributes less by his inspiration and charisma than by his competence, information, and judgment. But this hypothesis is advanced with considerable hesitation. Even if this transformation in the intellectual's role is confirmed, it is to be expected—though the signs are still rare and ambiguous—that it will in all probability be the beginning of a new crisis, one more mishap in the story of Ariel.

For the *tecnificación* process is not, as suggested by the Mexican example analyzed by Vernon, limited to the advent of a responsible and qualified economic administration. In fact, the Mexican example notwithstanding, this process can lead to far greater difficulties with regard to control over a society whose development the intellectual is conceived to promote. It may be relevant to mention briefly another group of *tecnicos,* who might be called the "developmental technicians." I have had ample opportunity to observe them in Peru during the last ten years. In the intellectual area, their rise is explained by the rise of the social sciences; in the administrative domain, by the multiplication and growth of organizations charged with the realization of a certain number of developmental programs: an agrarian reform institute, *cooperación popular,* regional management, planning, and so forth.

The training received by members of these organizations is a function of the prodigious expansion of university enrollment, particularly in social science departments, from the end of the 1950's on. Theoretical and methodological tools imported from the United States and Europe were superimposed on "progressive" ideological orientations. Although this combination was quite unstable, it had the great merit of giving applied sociology and anthropology certain techniques of observation and intervention, along with vague principles justifying their use. It seems that the developmental technicians in Peru have generally been able to find their niche within the political system, which in the end was almost as dependent on them as they were on it.

Recent Peruvian administrations, lacking tradition, and having expanded greatly since the beginning of Belaunde's presidency, recruited a highly heterogeneous group. Among them were a certain number of Belaunde's followers; personal loyalty to the president and membership in his party, or in a given faction of his party, or in one of the splinter groups more or less connected with his party, constituted the principal if not unique title of recommendation. In these developmental agencies, there were also technicians from the various ministries: Health, Agriculture, Education, Public Works. The students fresh from the university—in particular from the anthropology and sociology departments—were conspicuous in these organizations. Though they were restricted to contractual status, without guaranteed employment, they generally received higher wages than the permanent employees of the classic administrations and were often given extensive responsibilities dealing with coordination and administration, either in Lima or in the field. It is not surprising that such tasks, assumed by the "generalists," often youthful, who had full liberty in the way they executed their responsibilities, yielded all sorts of resentment from the "classic" bureaucrats.

The heterogeneity of recruitment and training which seems characteristic of the group of "developers" explains in part, but only in part, its fragility and its vulnerability to ideological "commitment." It is not very difficult to explain why the theme of *compromiso,* whose major interpreter is Orlando Fals Borda,[22] has once again become fashionable. After a long period of acceptance on the part of the social science specialists, the objectivity and neutrality extolled by empirical methodology—the precept of "axiological neutrality"—becomes almost unbearable in countries where the intellectual's mission appears less one of understanding the world than of changing it. The consequences of the exaltation of the *compromiso* for the definition of the intellectual's role must yet be examined.

It is no longer a matter of writing, or speaking from the heights of a pulpit, or even of participating in the organization—by education or indoctrination—of the popular masses. There is only one duty left: to make the revolution! I am well aware that in Spanish the word *revolución* is extremely ambiguous, since it equally designates the most commonplace military coup d'etat and the most decisive social transformation. It seems to me, though, that three attitudes which prevail through the recent analyses of Fals Borda can be discerned within the new *compromiso*, and that these are held by the most radical, the most revolutionary of Peruvian intellectuals.

First, I would underline their pessimism, or even nihilism. In truth, one is hardly surprised, this attitude colors so naturally the way in which the intellectuals judge their own societies—often called neocolonial—and imperialism, which they blame for the state of underdevelopment. The intensity of the pessimism seems to vary a good deal. Though it was checked by an almost fanatical confidence in the final success of the "cause," it was very pronounced, for example, in the 1930's among Peruvian intellectuals committed to the *aprista* party, which was persecuted at the time; it was probably less intense during the postwar years. Even if the democratic interlude in Peru lasted only from 1945 to 1948, even if the *aprista* party was again obliged to descend into the catacombs of clandestinity, hope still existed for the possibility of development, or at least of change. And this hope was strengthened greatly at the beginning of the 1960's by the Alliance for Progress. Although American imperialism was still perceived and denounced as inherently perverse, the Alliance, through various programs, provided assistance in the areas of education, health, housing, and regional planning, which benefited directly (through jobs), and indirectly (through foreign posts, periods of instruction, retraining) the early developmental technicians. The outlook was not completely bleak: One felt something could be done.

This relative euphoria died down noticeably from about 1965 on, for multiple and even contradictory reasons, both local and international. The failure of the Alliance for Progress was not the only factor involved; the failure of Castroism also added to the depressive effect. Increasingly pronounced and widespread skepticism toward the possibilities of industrialization and the modernizing capacities of the "national bourgeoisie" was one of the manifestations of this pessimism. In the populist ideologies, condemnation of capitalism and imperialism accompanied exaltation of the "national bourgeoisie," which would be given the means of expansion and consolidation by the popular state, what Haya de la Torre[23] calls the anti-imperialist state. Now, though, this confidence in the "national bourgeoisie" is gradually disappearing,[24] while at the same time confidence in reformism and the worth of formal democracy declines. The Latin American economists, on their side, grow increasingly more skeptical of the merits of the substitution-of-imports policy. The sociologists and political scientists insist on the *total* dependence of the local elites on the major national interests. During the 1950's, it was fashionable to expect a great deal of the "national bourgeoisie." The fashion today is to deny that it ever existed. Most of the committed intellectuals consider the ruling classes of their own countries to be only the puppets of major foreign interests. Meanwhile, the revolutionary potential of the masses seems increasingly doubtful, particularly since the decline of Castroist influence. The only organized movements seem willing to participate in the game of reformist demands or action, and the belligerency of unorganized marginal groups is quite restricted.

Disappointed by the national bourgeoisie, but also by the masses, certain revolutionary intellectuals may come to believe that the system excludes any serious possibility for change, and that it is necessary to "break the system" in order to make change possible. This conviction takes several different forms, but all have a common latent dimension, which I shall call "volitionalism." The goal of breaking the system can be expressed in the humanist rhetoric of the Christian-Democrats as "structural conditions" or "revolution in liberty." It can also be attained by what Fals Borda calls *subversion*—that is, by overthrowing the established order, through violent action, even if sporadic, and protest by the masses, even if these are incompletely mobilized. However, if breaking the system becomes the primary goal, all methods are good, guerrilla tactics as well as the "call upon the soldier."

I call "voluntaristic" the attitude underlying these different positions as they are held by the intellectuals. I consider this term to mean, as does Karl Deutsch,[25] the claim of an individual or a group to impose its own preferences, without taking into account—unless in a purely tactical way— the preferences of other groups, or the "resistance of the environment." Volitional politics combine, in varying proportions, elitism (or counter-elitism) and progressivism. If their will is that of the State, a considerable— and eventually excessive—portion of the collective resources may be put at the disposal of the bureaucratic apparatus so that the "plan" may be accomplished. The will of a "counterelite" tends first to organize into sects or small groups, hoping later to eliminate all opposition and eventually become the only party. In both cases, the collective resources are ultimately concentrated relentlessly, and controlled by a minority, self-defined as avant-garde or a "universal class," which legitimizes its action by invoking the interest of the "people" or of the "working class."

The voluntaristic inflexibility expresses both the urgency of the *compromiso* and the impossibility of its realization through other than exceptional and drastic measures. It is unstable and fragile because of its paroxysmic character. It can take either the constraining form of hierarchical control, or the exalting form of appeal to spontaneity. The spell cast by Castro on many intellectuals is due to the combination, in both his regime and personality, of these two aspects. He is at once the orator whose breath pulverizes "imperialism" and the organizer "planning" the development of his country. The charm, though obviously weaker, exerted by the present military junta on certain Peruvian intellectuals,[26] results from the convergence of a task—a duty—and an instrument of power, which providentially occurs in order that what has long been but a dream may be realized.

An impression of increasing anomie among the intellectual group emerges from this description, progressing as the urgent need for the *compromiso* is perceived as more intense and as the choice of strategies becomes more confused. Two evidences of this anomie may be cited; first, the growing fascination with violence, exemplified by intellectuals and students not only at the university, but also in clandestine action, guerrilla warfare, and urban terrorism—the various modes of action which receive if not the blessing, at least increasingly evident toleration from the Catholic Church. There is also an extreme instability in alliances among those intellectuals involved in political life. I refer particularly to certain Peruvian intellectuals whose intricate maneuvers between an allegiance to the revolutionary movements and their actual allegiance to the military regime are so baffling. They justify their support of the junta by saying that a great number of the military became aware of the army's special responsibilities in respect to developmental policies. The concept of development set forth by the military was indeed close to that of the intellectuals because the former borrowed it from the latter, or rather because both evolved it from common sources. And yet the style, the manifestly authoritarian concept of power which the Army Command shows no signs of abandoning, does not appear to have repulsed those intellectuals who feel most attracted to the junta. They simply proclaim even more vigorously their unwavering commitment to the principles of the left.

This analysis is incomplete for obvious reasons. We are, in truth, unable to distinguish those among the developers who would qualify as the most radical, or to identify the characteristics of this group and give its numerical importance. In fact, we know neither how many are the revolutionaries—the active few—nor exactly who they are. If we take the group as a whole, however, we can determine the shift of the developers toward radical themes, which we have tried to describe and attempted to relate to the developers' experiences in the organizations where they work. In this way, our hypothesis about the importance of the formation of the intellectuals' ideology, their roles, and, particularly, the professional roles they perform in their society might be verified.

Does my description exaggerate the importance of the *compromiso* in Latin American intellectual life? I have shown Ariel in his pulpit, trying to organize the masses, fascinated by revolutionary violence, making his way through the labyrinth of modern bureaucracies, simultaneously client and adviser to the Prince. But I did not give him the opportunity to speak of his artistic or literary dreams. I have shown him more as lusting for power than tortured by conscience. Is he beginning to deliver himself from his didactic and moralistic bonds, as Octavio Paz suggests, to enjoy his own solitude, to perceive it not as the result of his powerlessness, but as the symbol of his destiny? I feel that this conversion may be accomplished only if certain conditions, some concerning Ariel, others concerning his society, are realized. First, the intellectual's way of relating to politics exclusively through the compulsive *compromiso* must be exorcised. Second, the values of popular culture can no longer be ignored and disdained, or experienced with remorse and obsession, as they were for a long time by the *indigenista* intellectuals. Can they not be grasped in all their richness, thereby liberating those who delve into them, bringing them fullness and development?

In setting forth this problem, I return to the issue raised in the first few pages of this essay: the cultural dualism that has characterized the Latin American intellectual's situation since Independence. The first manifestation of this dualism was the opposition between popular culture and learned culture in the nineteenth century. Even if, from World War I on, popular culture was acclaimed and glorified by the *indigenista* movement, even if the elimination of internal and external dependence was extolled by the various populisms as the paramount task, the gap subsisting between the project and its realization is still so great that the *compromiso* takes on an increasingly intense volitionalist hue. The distance between the intellectual and his society used to carry with it the shameful acceptance of those differences separating the small enlightened minority from the rest of the population. Today, this distance tends rather to lead the intellectual to proclaim the project of "suppression of dualism," yet it continues to be experienced as the impossibility of accomplishing such.

Perhaps Ariel has yet to explore the possibility of aesthetic conversion? But can he, who is so infatuated with power, become an artist; in other words, can he become reconciled with the world and with himself, trying less to transform the world than to transfigure it through the mediation of images with which he can identify? In the aesthetic realm, will we not once again come across the problems of Latin American dualism, if until now, as I suspect, aesthetic creativity has been confined entirely within the popular culture, which Ariel continues to exalt, but to which he is probably more and more a stranger?

REFERENCES

1. This interpretation has little relevance to Chile, Argentina, or Uruguay. However, it is applicable to Mexico, the Andean countries, and, with many reservations, to Brazil, of which case no mention will be made in this essay.

2. For example, in Victor Andres Belaunde's answer (*La Realidad Nacional* [Paris: Editorial "Le Livre libre," 1931]) to Mariategui's thesis in *Siete ensayos sobre la realidad peruana* (Lima: Amauta, 1928).

3. To use Albert O. Hirschman's expression in *Journeys Toward Progress* (New York: The Twentieth Century Fund, 1963).

4. See Ciró Alegría, *El mundo es ancho y ajeno* (Mexico: Giana, 1953), chap. 20.

5. I feel that these observations apply equally to the Mexican case.

6. For example, in *Peasant Society and Culture* (Chicago: University of Chicago Press, 1956).

7. "El estereotipo del intelectual latino-american: su relación con los cambios económicos y sociales," in Juan F. Marsal, *El intelectual lat* (Buenos Aires: Solar, 1968), pp. 73-101.

8. Frank Bonilla, "Intelectuales y liderazgo," *Aportes,* 5 (July 1967), 123-147.

9. This concerns Argentine students in the first and last years of the disciplines considered.

10. See my book *Pouvoir et société dans le Pérou contemporain* (Paris: A. Colin, 1967), part II, chap. 2.

11. Aldo Solari, *Estudiantes y politica en América Latina* (Caracas: Monte Avila, 1968), pp. 18-24.

12. M. Glazer, "Estudiantes y politica," *Aportes,* 5 (July 1967), 42-80.

13. The term "idealism" should not be understood here in the technical sense of the word, which reduces the being to a mere phenomenon and emphasizes the activity of the mind in the knowing process. I consider this term to designate the attitude, very like that developed during the same era by a French philosopher, forgotten today, Alfred Fouillée, under the name *Idées-Forces,* which credits "ideas" with the ability to assure *an sich für sich* their own realization. This attitude is compatible with historicism, since the realization of ideas is not immediate, and history acquires its meaning from such.

14. Kalman Silvert devoted chap. 7 of his *Sociedad problema* (Buenos Aires: Paidos, 1962) to Rodó. The texts cited are from this chapter.

15. For Peru, one would have to mention Villaran and Deustua, who engaged in a most interesting argument on the social functions of education.

16. Jules Michelet, "L'Etudiant," *Le Seuil* (Paris, 1970).

17. *Ibid.,* pp. 57-58.

18. This is the expression used in France at the end of the July Monarchy to designate the members of liberal professions whose training should have qualified them to dispose of the franchise but whose insufficient income prevented their political participation.

19. In a forthcoming work on the formative years of the Apra party.

20. Raymond Vernon, *The Dilemma of Mexico's Development* (Cambridge, Mass.: Harvard University Press, 1963), esp. chap. 5.

21. *Ibid.*, p. 137.

22. See *La subversión en Colombia* (Bogotá: Universidad Nacional, 1967) by Fals Borda, and the discussions which took place around this work, in particular the debate between Fals Borda and Solari (in *Aportes*).

23. Haya de la Torre, *El anti-imperialismo y el Apra* (Santiago: Ediciones Ercilla, 1936).

24. See Fernando Henrique Cardoso and Enzo Faletto, *Dependencia y desarrolla en América Latina* (Santiago: Ilpes, 1967).

25. Karl W. Deutsch, *The Nerves of Government* (New York and London: The Free Press, 1963), esp. pp. 105-111.

26. See my article in *Aportes* (April 1970), "Militares porque y para que?" and in *Mundo Nuevo* (December 1970), "Los militares peruanos mano a la obra."

SEYMOUR MARTIN LIPSET AND RICHARD B. DOBSON

The Intellectual as Critic and Rebel: With Special Reference to the United States and the Soviet Union

MODERN SOCIETIES—both Communist and non-Communist—face a growing dilemma posed by the fact that key institutions and their elites are increasingly dependent upon intellectuals, particularly those in universities, research institutes, and the cultural apparatus generally. Yet, the leaders in these same social units are among the major critics of the way in which the society operates, sometimes calling into question the legitimacy of the social order and its political structure. A ruling elite, even one that is conservative and anti-intellectual, cannot respond to such challenges by crushing the intellectuals, unless it is willing to incur the punitive costs which such suppression entails. As the Polish "revisionist" philosopher Leszek Koła-kowski wrote while still a member of the Communist party, "the spiritual domination of any ruling class over the people . . . depends on its bonds with the intelligentsia . . . ; for the less one is capable of ruling by intellectual means, the more one must resort to the instruments of force."[1] Decades earlier, the liberal economist and sociologist Joseph Schumpeter argued that under capitalism the dominant economic class must protect the intellectuals, "however strongly disapproving" they are of them, because they cannot repress intellectual criticism without initiating a process of repression which will undermine their own freedom.[2]

The word "intellectual" is fraught with ambiguities. The meanings attached to it are diverse. In the loosest sense in which the word is used in common parlance today, intellectuals may be said to be all of those who are considered proficient in and are actively engaged in the creation, distribution, and application of culture. This conception, however, is too diffuse for analytic purposes; it is desirable to distinguish between several types. We prefer to emphasize the much smaller category of "creative intellectuals," whose principal focus is on innovation, the elaboration of knowledge, art, and symbolic formulations generally. Included in this group are scholars, scientists, philosophers, artists, authors, some editors, and some journalists, as distinguished from the more marginally intellectual groups

137

who distribute culture, such as most teachers, clerics, journalists, and performers in the arts, as well as those who apply knowledge in the course of their work, such as practicing physicians, lawyers, and engineers. The creative intellectuals are the most dynamic group within the broad intellectual stratum: because they are innovative, they are at the forefront in the development of culture, and the other marginal groups are dependent upon them for the ideational resources they use in their work.

A qualitatively more exclusive group is the "critical intelligentsia" whose members are recruited from the ranks of creative intellectuals. The critical intelligentsia is composed of those who not only have the ability to manipulate symbols with expertise, but who have also gained a reputation for commitment to general values and who have a broad evaluative outlook derived from such commitment. The characteristic orientation of these "generalizing intellectuals" is a critically evaluative one, a tendency to appraise in terms of general conceptions of the desirable, ideal conceptions which are thought to be universally applicable. Such generalizing intellectuals have been described by Lewis Coser as follows:

Intellectuals exhibit in their activities a pronounced concern with the core values of society. They are the men who seek to provide moral standards and to maintain meaningful general symbols . . . Intellectuals are men who never seem satisfied with things as they are, with appeals to custom and usage. They question the truth of the moment in terms of higher and wider truth; they counter appeals to factuality by invoking the "impractical ought." They consider themselves special custodians of abstract ideas like reason and justice and truth, jealous guardians of moral standards that are too often ignored in the market place and the houses of power.[3]

It appears that since his appearance as a recognizable social type, the creative intellectual has frequently assumed the role of generalizing intellectual, often acting as a severe critic of the society in which he lives and engaging in political activism in order to transform it. What explains this phenomenon? In this essay, by examining the Soviet and American cases, we seek to demonstrate how certain features inherent in the role and social organization of intellectual life give rise to critical activity, promote the formation of a critical intelligentsia, and help produce what Lionel Trilling has perceptively called the "adversary culture" of the intellectuals.[4] Moreover, the rising prestige of the institutions of knowledge production and creative intellectuals, along with the interdependence between these social units and other key institutional structures, leads to the rapid diffusion of critical ideas and values, thereby amplifying the impact of such activity.

The United States

The opposition or adversary role of American intellectuals is, of course, not new. Many[5] have called attention to this phenomenon, seeing it as a continuing one in American history. Richard Hofstadter described their stance of alienation as "historical and traditional," and pointed out that "even the genteel, established intellectuals of the mid-nineteenth century were in effect patrician rebels against the increasing industrialization and the philistinism of the country. So that it has been the tradition of American intellectuals of all kinds and stamps to find themselves at odds with American society: this, I think, to a degree that is unusual elsewhere." A century ago, Whitelaw Reid, the editor of the *New York Tribune*, pointed to the role of the American "Scholar in Politics" as a foe of the "established," and a leader of the "radicals."[6]

Policy-makers have expressed concern over this phenomenon since the beginning of the Republic in spite of the fact that the first generation of American political leaders have justly been described as intellectuals. Thus, in 1798, President John Adams argued against admitting foreign scientists or philosophers, saying: "I really begin to think, or rather to suspect, that learned academies, not under the immediate inspection and control of government, have disorganized the world, and are incompatible with social order." And in a less directly political context, Thomas Jefferson wrote even earlier, in 1787: "State a moral case to a ploughman and a professor. The former will decide it as well, and often better than the latter, because he has not been led astray by artificial rules."[7] In a preinaugural memorandum to President Nixon advising him what to expect, Daniel Patrick Moynihan suggested the tension began somewhat later, stating that since "about 1840, the cultural elite have pretty generally rejected the values and activities of the larger society. It has been said of America that the culture [the intellectual elite] will not approve that which the polity strives to provide."[8] An earlier Republican president, Herbert Hoover, writing of the situation in the late 1920's, discussed "the growing left-wing movement embracing many of the 'intelligentsia.' "[9]

Lest it be thought that the intellectuals' opposition to the "polity" has been limited in modern times to periods when Republicans have been in office, or when there were very exceptional circumstances, as, for example, under Lyndon Johnson, it should be noted that in October 1961 James Reston felt moved to write a column discussing the discontent of the intellectuals with John F. Kennedy.[10] He noted that after nine months the new regime was being described as "the third Eisenhower administration." Reston reported that the intellectuals were "disenchanted by the absence of new policies, the preoccupation with political results, the compromises over education and the techniques of appointing conservatives to put over liberal policies and liberals to carry out conservative policies." Reston reminded his readers that an earlier liberal Democratic president who had sought to appeal to the intellectuals, Woodrow Wilson, had had comparable difficulties with them. Wilson had pointed to an inherent "perennial misunderstanding" between "the men who act . . . [and] the men who write."

Long before he took office as Richard Nixon's foreign policy adviser, Henry Kissinger reiterated Woodrow Wilson's complaint and analysis: "[For] intellectuals outside the administrative machines . . . protest has too often become an end in itself. Whether they have withdrawn by choice or because of the nature of their society, many intellectuals have confused the issues by simplifying them too greatly."[11] More recently, America's leading novelist, Saul Bellow, has acknowledged the validity of the complaint of the political leaders. "American intellectuals don't enter government service very willingly, and they look upon government as a cold-blooded monster. They're separatist and radical by education, and they feel they're serving higher ideals—to resist, to stand aside. States are distrusted, establishments attacked."[12]

Although scattered groups of right-wing intellectuals have emerged at times, the record seems to validate Richard Hofstadter's generalization that for almost all of this century the political weight of American intellectuals has been on the progressive, liberal, and leftist side.[13] Quantitative data derived from attitude surveys, the earliest dating back to before World War I, plus assorted other reports of the political orientations of the American professoriate, strongly indicate that American intellectuals have consistently leaned to the left.[14] This bias, to a considerable extent, reflects the absence or weakness of a legitimate national conservative tradition in America. National identity and national ideology are linked to a value system, stemming from an elaboration of those principles enunciated in the Declaration of Independence, that emphasizes egalitarianism and populism. Thus, when American intellectuals point up the gap between the real and the ideal, whether represented by what was (in a bygone Jeffersonian laissez-faire utopia of equal yeoman farmers) or what should be (a classless participatory future), they challenge the system for not fulfilling the ideals implicit in the American Creed.[15]

It may be argued, of course, that the "leftist" orientation of American intellectuals is in fact largely liberal rather than radical. If so, then it is in harmony with the preponderant national tradition. While there can be little doubt that a majority of those involved in intellectually-linked occupations have been liberals or progressives rather than supporters of the extreme left, it is also true that no other stratum in America has even approached intellectuals in their support of leftist, third party, socialist, and Communist activities, broadly defined. The record suggests also that the more involved individuals have been in genuinely creative intellectual activities, the more they have tended to support the left. One would hardly anticipate that in a country where leftist movements have never secured more than a fraction of the national vote that many intellectuals would stand on the political extreme. Yet, their obvious preference for opposing the existing authorities, whether economic or political, is clearly reflected in all the information that exists on the comparative strength of radicals among different strata of the society.

Academics were involved in antiwar agitation during the Spanish-American War, and they agitated for Filipino independence during the Filipino insurrection. While the war was still on, Oliver Wendell Holmes, Jr., commented to a friend: "I confess to pleasure in hearing some rattling jingo talk after the self-righteous and preaching discourse which has prevailed to some extent at Harvard College & elsewhere."[16] An article in the *Atlantic Monthly* in 1902 reported that college professors had acquired a reputation for taking obstructionist political positions. "Within a twelvemonth college teachers have been openly denounced as 'traitors' for advocating self-government for Filipinos. In many a pulpit and newspaper office, last September, it was declared that the utterances of college professors were largely responsible for the assassination of President McKinley."[17] Whitelaw Reid, who in 1873 had praised the antiestablishment role of American scholars, complained in a speech at Stanford in 1901 that it is a misfortune for the country that its college "instructors are out of sympathy with its history, with its development, and with the men who made the one and are guiding the other."[18] In the next decade, observers, both foreign and domestic, commented on the strength of socialism among the faculty of leading American universities.[19] The most influential young socialist intellectual of pre-World War I days, Randolph Bourne, while still an undergraduate at Columbia in 1912, explained the spread of socialism in the colleges as reflecting the fact that for a typical undergraduate, "his education, if it has been in one of the advanced universities, will only have tended to confirm his radicalism."[20] John Reed, active in the Harvard Socialist Club, reported that it was supported by many professors.[21] Although we have no quantitative measures to validate these impressions, a highly sophisticated survey of the religious opinion of American academics in 1913-1914, a period in which most adult Americans belonged to churches, indicated that the large majority did not believe in God or immortality. And reinforcing the generalizations that faculty radicalism was strongest in the leading schools, this survey found that the more distinguished faculty were much more irreligious than their less eminent colleagues.[22]

Large numbers of socialist and progressive intellectuals were swept away by the Wilsonian crusade to make the world safe for democracy. Yet by "1918-20 the doubts of many intellectuals about both the war and Wilsonian idealism turned to violent and bitter revulsion."[23] Considerable enthusiasm was expressed in many intellectual circles for the Bolsheviks and the Russian Revolution. The growing discontent on the campuses led many in business and politics, including the then vice-president-elect, Calvin Coolidge, to denounce the radicalism of college faculties.[24] Granville Hicks, perhaps the foremost Communist literary intellectual of the 1930's, saw the twenties as preparing the way for the Communist gains in the next decade.

There was in that decade [the twenties] a loose kind of united front against the *status quo*. The intellectuals were almost unanimous in their distaste for a business civilization and in their willingness to accept as allies all enemies of the existing order. Russia, with all its faults, was regarded as being on "our" side because it represented something new in the world and because it was hated and feared by the proponents and beneficiaries of the *status quo*.[25]

Although much of the renewed "alienation" of intellectuals in the period took on a nonpolitical, strongly antimaterialistic, and antibourgeois orientation, the protests against the conviction of Sacco and Vanzetti for murder which grew gradually through the decade and reached a crescendo in 1927, the year of their execution, eventually mobilized and radicalized a substantial number of intellectuals both on and off the campuses.[26] As David Felix put it: "The Sacco-Vanzetti case belonged to the intellectuals."[27] The large-scale protest movement only magnified the conflict between the intellectuals and the powers.

Thus when writers and professors began to voice . . . doubts, it seemed to many conservatives only another proof of dangerous radicalism among the intellectuals. And the writers and the professors, bringing out fact after fact which showed the prejudice and perjury involved in the conviction, came increasingly to feel that the leaders of business and government were not interested in evidence but only in teaching the radicals the brutal lesson that there was no room for dissent in America.[28]

The explicit involvement of large numbers of prominent intellectuals in various forms of left-wing politics, particularly in Communist and Communist-front groups, during the 1930's resulted in extravagant evaluations of the strength of Communism among intellectuals.[29] In 1932 a significant number of the more prominent intellectuals of the country endorsed the Communist presidential ticket.[30] However one estimates the actual proportion of intellectuals who went so far as to back the party, no one seriously doubts that the party's most obvious success during the 1930's was among the intellectuals and their "apprentices," the college students. As Daniel Bell has written:

Except for its success in attracting an important section of the intellectual fringe and the student youth, the Communist party never achieved a wide mass following in America during the depression years . . . It did have for many years a disproportionate influence in the cultural field. At one time, from 1936 to 1939, through the fellow travelers in the publishing houses, radio, Hollywood, the magazines, and other mass media, it exercized influence on public opinion far beyond the mere number of party members.[31]

The one serious attempt at a quantitative evaluation of the backgrounds of members of the Communist party agrees with these impressions. Ernst and Loth report that "the proportion of Party members who have been to college is very high. Even more striking is the great number of college degrees among them . . . In fact, the Communist party in America seems to be such a highly educated, non-manual laboring group that at times there would seem to be more rejoicing in its headquarters over the recruiting of one common laborer than over ten Ph.D.'s."[32] Given the paucity of data, it is difficult to form any conclusive statistical judgment about the distribution of opinion among intellectuals in this period. It is possible, of course, that although the Communist party and other radical groups drew the bulk of their support from intellectuals, as well as from their fellow-travelers among the well-educated, that most intellectuals were in fact unaffected, as the limited membership of such groups suggests. Certain data imply the contrary. A repeat in 1933 of the 1913 survey of academics on religion, to which samples of writers and business and professional people listed in Who's Who were added, indicated that irreligion had grown among the professors during the twenty-year interval. The more distinguished academics were again shown to have a greater propensity to be irreligious than their less eminent peers. Writers were also heavily atheistic (62 per cent), while substantial majorities among the business and professional communities—of those sampled—were shown to be believers. Although attitudes to religion are not flawless indicators of political preferences, many studies indicate high correlations between being irreligious and having left views, at least in the United States. A Chicago survey in 1937 found academics to be much more liberal or radical on various socio-economic issues than those in other occupational groups, even manual workers. A study of party registrations in suburban San Francisco found one quarter of the writers registered as members of minority political parties, mainly Communist or Socialist.[33] The one national survey of college student opinion in the 1930's, conducted by the Roper Poll, saw 24 per cent express sympathy for "socialism," 6 per cent for "communism," 45 per cent for "liberalism," 15 per cent for "conservatism," and 2 per cent for "fascism."[34]

A contemporary (1938) effort to account for the leftist views of the more intellectually oriented undergraduates of the 1930's by two psychologists, Gardner Murphy and Rensis Likert, suggested that to be "bookish" meant to be exposed to radical thought.

To be bookish in this era has meant to steep oneself in the disillusioned gropings of postwar thinkers, most of whom, from philosophers to lyricists, are clearly "radical" . . . The literary groups to which these men belong, the day-by-day conversations in which they train one another to think and to feel, are full of the modern doubt and disquietude, and even more frequently, of the modern challenge and rebellion. To be bookish today is to be radical.[35]

The support given by intellectuals to organized leftist groups, particularly the Communists, was highly unstable. The various dramatic shifts in the party line along with events in the Soviet Union—from the famines imposed by enforced collectivization to the purges of the Soviet leadership and the Moscow trials of 1936 and 1938—leading finally to the Hitler-Stalin pact of 1939, which enabled the Germans to go to war, served to alienate almost all the intellectuals from the party. (Ironically, just before the Hitler-Stalin pact was signed, over four hundred intellectuals signed a manifesto published in the *Nation* on August 19, 1939, testifying to their faith in the *bona fides* of the Soviet Union.) Except during the period of the Hitler-Stalin pact (1939-1941), the Communist party from 1936 on had strongly urged all leftists to adopt a "defensist" posture, to support the United States and the other Western democracies. The Communists, joined by many socialists and liberals, argued that fascist totalitarianism was so dangerous that intellectuals and other critics of Western democratic systems had an obligation to restrain themselves and to defend their very imperfect societies against an attack from a much worse system. The Popular Front tactic, uniting all antifascist forces, pushed intellectuals to become supporters of the domestic status quo.

The end of the antifascist war was followed, ironically, by a renewed concern for Western democracy, again under totalitarian attack. This time the threat was thought to come from an aggressive expansionist Stalinist totalitarianism. Open anti-Semitism in Russia, the Czech coup, the Berlin blockade of 1948—these and other developments served to undermine any lingering faith in a Communist utopia. Many intellectuals, including most avowed socialists among them, were led to continue or to revive the policy previously urged on them by the Communists—to defend the existing society against an external threat. Philip Rahv, who had been an editor of *Partisan Review*, the principal radical literary-political magazine of the 1930's (pro-Communist in the beginning, later sympathetic to Trotskyism), pointed to these shifts in orientation in 1952.

Among the factors entering into the change, the principal one, to my mind, is the exposure of the Soviet myth and the consequent resolve (shared by nearly all but the few remaining fellow travelers) to be done with utopian illusions and heady expectations. In their chastened mood American democracy looks like the real thing to the intellectuals . . . Whether capitalist or not, it has so far sustained that freedom of expression and experiment without which the survival of the intelligence is inconceivable in a modern society . . . In the palmy days when it was possible to take democracy for granted—that is, before the rise to global power of Hitlerism and then of Stalinism—the intellectuals were hardly aware of the very tangible benefits they derived from it. Now, however, only the most doctrinaire types would be disposed to trade in those benefits for some imaginary perfection of good in the remote future.[36]

Throughout the West, not only in the United States where Senator Joseph McCarthy pressed his advantage against the intellectuals, the same pattern of response developed. As Lipset noted at the end of the 1950's:

The political issue of the 1950's has become freedom versus Communism, and in that struggle many socialist and liberal intellectuals find themselves identifying with established institutions. This identification comes hard to intellectuals who feel called upon to reject conventional stupidities, and results in a feeling of malaise which takes the form of complaining that everyone, including the intellectuals, is too conformist . . . Their solution to this dilemma is to continue to feel allied with the left, but to vote Democratic; to think of themselves as liberals—and often even as socialists—but to withdraw from active involvement or interest in politics and to concentrate on their work, whether it be writing poetry or scholarly articles.

. . . In spite of the powerful conservatizing forces, the inherent tendency to oppose the *status quo* will still remain . . . Any *status quo* embodies rigidities and dogmatisms which it is the inalienable right of intellectuals to attack, whether from the standpoint of moving back to traditional values or forward toward the achievement of the equalitarian dream.[37]

This period came to an end with the breakdown of one of the principal ideological justifications for the cold war—the threat of a monolithic Communist movement. Destalinization in the Soviet Union set a dynamic process in motion within the Communist world which made internal conflict within various countries and among the bloc nations very visible. Protest was more common; the Sino-Soviet split gave the final lie to the idea of Communist unity. As monolithic totalitarianism broke down, the image of Stalinist society—expansionist and oppressive—was weakened. Many of the pressures that had prevented intellectuals in the West from attacking their own societies ceased to exist. As ideological anti-Communism lost its strength, many older once-leftist intellectuals turned back in some measure to their earlier beliefs. More significant, perhaps, was the emergence among younger intellectuals and students of widespread social criticism. This began in the civil rights area, expanded substantially because of the Vietnam war, and ultimately came to touch a host of issues that affected almost all major American institutions. The new generations who knew neither Hitler nor Stalin, and had no first-hand experience of the 1948 Czech coup or the Hungarian revolution, found no reason to hold back in their criticisms.

The movement of the late 1960's differed substantially from that of the 1930's. Its most striking feature, perhaps, was an absence—there was no single radical group or combination of groups at the center; there was no equivalent to the Communist party of the 1930's. Many hundreds of thousands of persons—possibly millions—identified with the various militant radical protests. A sense of alienation was widely diffused; there seemed to be a rejection of authority; many spoke of the need for a new noncapitalist social order. Yet, with the exception of the short-lived conglomerative antiwar organizations, no group recruited more than a few thousand members. No new radical political party of any substance emerged. At the heart of the movement perhaps were the many hundreds of New Left or "underground" papers, of which the most influential was the "aboveground" *New York Review of Books.*

In spite of its loose level of organization, the different elements of the movement succeeded in challenging the system in a variety of ways and on a number of issues. Universities became staging areas; liberal and left faculty, followed by student activists, looked for a mass response. There were over 600,000 professors and 8,000,000 students in the colleges and universities of the country; ideas originating in these places circulated quickly. New forms of student activism and confrontation became common. As John Kenneth Galbraith noted:

It was the universities—not the trade unions, nor the free-lance intellectuals, nor the press, nor the businessmen . . .—which led the opposition to the Vietnam war, which forced the retirement of President Johnson, which are forcing the pace of our present withdrawal from Vietnam, which are leading the battle against the great corporations on the issue of pollution, and which at the last Congressional elections retired a score or more of the more egregious time-servers, military sycophants and hawks.[38]

The evidence that the critical, often radical, role of the universities has stemmed from its most creative segment—those most successfully involved in research and publication and located at the most distinguished universities—has been reported in a variety of independent surveys of faculty opinion. All these confirm the early findings in the Leuba studies of religious belief. Those scholars who are at the most eminent schools (as judged by rankings of faculty, by the test scores of their students, and by funds available for research and library facilities), who have published the most (studies indicate a relationship between quantity and quality; those who publish more, on the average, also publish more highly regarded work), who have secured research funds, are generally in their political views much to the left of their less productive and less successful colleagues. Although younger faculty are generally to the left of those who are older, the age gap is lowest in the most prestigious universities. Conversely, those faculty who are most involved in and concerned with teaching, which might be thought to be a less intellectual (creative) role, are among the most conservative members. A national survey conducted by the National Opinion Research Center in 1966 found the most successful academics already opposed to the Vietnam war. A more comprehensive study conducted for the Carnegie Commission on Higher Education in 1969 reiterated this finding. Surveys of persons who signed advertisements protesting the Vietnam war suggested that a disproportionate number were located at the better schools.[39]

In spite of Galbraith's emphasis on the influence of the universities, attention needs also to be paid to the literary intellectuals. They, too, have played a critical role in fostering the antiestablishment mood. Lionel Trilling, writing in 1965, emphasized their "adversary" role:

Any historian of the literature of the modern age will take virtually for granted the adversary intention, the actual subversive intention, that characterizes modern writing—he will perceive its clear purpose of detaching the reader from the habits of thought and feeling that the larger culture imposes, of giving him a ground and a vantage point from which to judge and condemn, and perhaps revise, the culture that has produced him.[40]

While no opinion data exist for this group as a whole at all comparable to the surveys of faculty, their "house organ" in the 1960's, the *New York Review of Books*, has been as systematically radical and supportive of movement causes both at home and abroad as any other journal in the country. A 1970 survey of 147 "leading intellectuals" indicated that they were far more likely to mention the *New York Review of Books* as influential than any other single magazine. Half the respondents mentioned the biweekly as the one they and their friends discussed most frequently; its closest rival received only 20 per cent of the choices. Not surprisingly, given its role as an organ of literary as well as political criticism, the New *York Review* was considerably more influential among English professors and "nonacademics" than among social scientists or other academics.[41]

Quantitative data support the general impression that the intellectual elites are considerably to the left of all other strata in the American population. Various national surveys of the general public taken in 1969-1970 indicate that when asked to identify themselves by degrees of "liberalism," "conservatism," or "middle-of-the-road" status, only 20 to 30 per cent describe themselves as liberal or very liberal, between 40 and 50 per cent see themselves as conservatives. Among those in intellectually-linked occupations who were polled, the proportion who see themselves as liberal or left is 75 per cent for the leading scholars in the humanities or social sciences in elite schools (but 45 per cent for the professoriate as a whole), 86 per cent among a select group of 110 major intellectuals both within and outside of the university, 78 per cent among a sample of influential "culture critics" employed by major media outlets (as contrasted to 57 per cent of the group nationally), and 63 per cent among the editors of important publications and broadcast stations (as compared to 40 per cent generally). Although close to half the adult population choose to describe themselves as "conservatives," less than 15 per cent in any of the groups of leading intellectuals, professors, critics, or editors do so.[42] Over four fifths (80 per cent) of the high achieving scholars supported the terms for ending the Vietnam war proposed by Hanoi and the FLN.

The "critical" role of the American intellectuals is obviously significant. Unlike other groups who have challenged the system at various times, their antagonism does not appear to be reduced by success and the rewards it brings. If "adversary" tendencies flow in part from the fact that intellectuality tends to emphasize creativity, originality, and rejection of the traditional and the accepted, it follows that the cast of mind necessary for intellectual creativity will remain associated with support for social change and a rejection of the status quo. Such is what men as diverse as Thorstein Veblen, F. A. Hayek, and C. P. Snow have long argued.

The Soviet Union

The 1960's have, of course, also witnessed the widespread diffusion of opposition tendencies among Soviet intellectuals. Given the absence of quantitative materials on the attitudes and behavior of Soviet intellectuals, and the limited knowledge among the public concerning the adversary culture in the USSR, we devote more attention to describing its actual content there than we did for the more familiar American story. The very notion that intellectuals are inherently at odds with the political system has apparently become so common within the country that it was the subject of open discussion at the Twenty-Fourth Congress of the Soviet Communist party in April 1971. Aleksandr Chakovsky asserted the obligation of intellectuals to support the system and urged them not be be influenced by the idea fashionable in the West that "every sincere artist must be inevitably in opposition to the state in which he lives." "We can understand the opposition of an honest artist to a bourgeois society and state based on violence, oppression and lies, but we cannot tolerate the attempts of anti-Communists to spread this fraudulent view equally to the opposing system, on the basis of which social justice exists."[43]

Russian intellectual dissidence, too, has a long history. The very word "intelligentsia," which first gained currency in the 1860's and 1870's in Russia, denoted those who represented "consciousness" or "enlightenment." As such, the conception was linked with criticism and dissent.[44] In its early meaning, the word came to be closely associated with the names of Chernyshevsky, Dobroliubov, Tkachev, and the "nihilists" and Populists—all of whom were opposed to the existing order. Yet, by the end of the nineteenth century, as the educated group grew in size and its work became more differentiated, a new definition based on objective criteria—skilled non-manual work or possession of higher education—came to vie with and even supplant the conception of the intelligentsia as, in effect, "the conscience of the nation," bound together by common ideals and sentiments.[45]

The victory of the Bolshevik revolution and subsequent rise of Stalinism had a profound impact on creative intellectuals. Ideological uniformity was established over intellectual life, if necessary through the liquidation of those of heretical views. In the years following the revolution, though, many intellectuals joined forces with the Communists, seeking thereby to implement their values and create a new social order and culture. For many, there was the strong conviction that an unprecedented era had dawned. In her memoirs, Nadezhda Mandelstam (wife of the outstanding poet Osip Mandelstam, who died in a Stalinist labor camp) castigates these intellectuals for their "capitulation":

The intellectuals, meanwhile, set about a leisurely "revaluation of all values." This was the period of mass surrender when they all took the path marked out by the pre-revolutionary extremists and their post-revolutionary successors of the Averbakh type—though, needless to say, they tried to avoid the fanaticism and crudity of the vanguard. The capitulationists were led by men of about thirty who had been through the war, and the younger people followed them . . . The basic premise behind the surrender was that the "old" had given way to the "new," and anybody clinging to the former would go to the wall. This view was rooted in the whole theory of progress and the determinism of the new religion. The proponents of surrender attacked all the old concepts just because they were old and had outlived their usefulness. For most of the neophytes, all values, truths and laws had been done away with—except for those which were needed at the moment and could conveniently be given a "class" label.[46]

By supporting the Communists in this great "social experiment," these intellectuals at the same time undermined the basis for the existence of an independent critical intelligentsia. In Nadezhda Mandelstam's estimation, "it was the twenties in which all the foundations were laid for our future: the casuistical dialectic, the dismissal of older values, the longing for unanimity and self-abasement. It is true that those who shouted loudest were then the first to lose their lives—but not before they had prepared the ground for the future."[47]

But the tradition of the Russian intelligentsia as an independent social force has lived on, as has the haunting memory of the "surrender" of the intellectuals. The latter theme is embodied in the novel *Doctor Zhivago*, which caused such an uproar in the late fifties, leading to Pasternak's expulsion from the Writers' Union in 1958. As the editors of *Novy Mir* wrote, explaining their reasons for refusing to allow publication of the novel two years earlier,

You are no stranger to symbolism, and the death, or rather passing of Doctor Zhivago in the late 1920's is for you, we feel, a symbol of the death of the Russian intelligentsia, destroyed by the revolution. Yes, it must be admitted that for the Doctor Zhivago you depicted in the novel the climate of the revolution is deadly. And our disagreement with you is not over this but, as we have already mentioned, over something quite different.

To you, Doctor Zhivago is the peak of the spirit of the Russian intelligentsia.

To us, he is its swamp.

To you, the members of the Russian intelligentsia who took a different path from the one Doctor Zhivago took and who chose the course of serving the people betrayed their true calling, committed suicide and created nothing of value.

To us, they found their true calling on precisely that path and continued to serve the people and to do for the people precisely the things that had been done for them—in laying the groundwork for the revolution—by the best segment of the Russian intelligentsia, which was then, and is today, infinitely remote from that conscious break with the people and ideological renegacy of which your Doctor Zhivago is the bearer.[48]

Against this background, the "rebirth" of the critical intelligentsia which has gradually taken place during the past two decades should be viewed.

As Andrei Amalrik observes in his essay *Will the Soviet Union Survive Until 1984?* several stages in this process may be discerned. A cultural opposition began to manifest itself slowly in the years following the death of Stalin. Writers and artists who had obediently followed party directives or who had withdrawn from public life began to express themselves more freely and to create works that did not conform to the party's prescriptions. Novels such as Ehrenburg's *The Thaw* (1954) and Dudintsev's *Not By Bread Alone* (1956) helped set a new, more critical and searching tone for published works and elicited heated debate. Independent artists like Anatoly Zverev and Oskar Rabin began to exhibit abstract art; young poets attracted large crowds at public readings. Singers like Okudzhava, Galich, and Vysotsky expressed in their songs the skepticism and suffering of those who had endured the Stalinist labor camps. During these years, unpublished works such as Pasternak's *Doctor Zhivago* and the typewritten literary magazine *Syntax*, edited by Alexander Ginzburg, began to circulate in manuscript form. Despite the government's attempt to suppress such challenges to the party's dictatorial role in cultural affairs, the opposition assumed a broader and more critical form in the years that followed.[49] As Andrei Amalrik notes, the increasingly widespread circulation of "underground" manuscripts with a more pronounced social and political content marked a qualitatively different stage in the growth of the oppositionist movement in the late fifties and early sixties.[50] The word *samizdat* (self-publication) came to describe this development.

While the trial of Siniavsky and Daniel in 1966 made clear the government's intention of eliminating the dissident writers, it also galvanized the intellectual community, producing an unprecedented number of protest demonstrations and petitions.[51] In the course of this continuing struggle between the dissident intellectuals and the government, numerous critics have been arrested and sentenced; countless others have been subjected to informal administrative measures (for example, firing from work, expulsion from the Writers' Union, denial of permission to travel abroad, loss of scholarship funds). Among those who have suffered most conspicuously are Viacheslav Chornovil, sentenced in 1967 for compiling an account of political trials in the Ukraine; Yuri Galanskov, condemned in 1968 for editing the anthology *Phoenix;* Alexander Ginzburg, prosecuted for gathering and editing documents on the trial of Siniavsky and Daniel; and Anatoly Marchenko, prosecuted for writing memoirs of life in prison camps in the post-Stalin period.[52]

The struggle has given rise to what has come to be called the Democratic movement. As Amalrik points out, though the movement lacks a formal organization and embraces very different ideological orientations, it is united by a common devotion to the establishment of the rule of law and basic civil rights. Within this rather diffuse movement, Amalrik identifies three distinct, though frequently intermingling, ideological currents—genuine Marxist-Leninist, Christian, and liberal.[53] Identified as representatives of the genuine Marxist-Leninist approach are Alexei Kosterin, Peter Grigorenko, and Ivan Yakhimovich, all of whom avowedly seek to return to the true principles of the party's revolutionary doctrine.[54] Supporters of Christian ideology, such as I. Ogurtsov, leader of the All-Russian Christian Union, maintain that society must return to Christian moral principles, which are sometimes interpreted in a Slovophile spirit, to stress the noble spiritual qualities of the Russian people.[55] Proponents of liberal ideology include Pavel Litvinov, grandson of Maxim Litvinov, and Andrei Sakharov, the noted physicist, who are said to seek the establishment of a democratic republic, while accepting public ownership of the means of production.[56] While these may be the dominant currents, there are also numerous groups seeking more particularistic objectives—Ukrainians wishing to strengthen their cultural heritage, Jews wanting to emigrate to Israel, Crimean Tatars seeking to return to their homeland, and so on. Realizing the importance of the rule of law for them to be able to achieve their ends, these groups, too, enter into the broad Democratic movement.

The principal *samizdat* organ for the Democratic movement as a whole appears to be the *Khronika tekhushchikh sobytii* (The chronicle of current events).[57] The fact that the *Chronicle* has appeared on a bimonthly basis since 1968 testifies to the considerable continuity in the movement in spite of government repression. The establishment of the Committee for Human Rights by Andrei Sakharov, Andrei Tverdokhlebov, and Valery Chalidze, three physicists, in November 1970 may provide a nucleus for the coordination of the diffuse movement's activities. The Committee is devoted to strengthening the rule of law and ensuring civil rights, in accordance with the Universal Declaration on Human Rights adopted by the United Nations, by cooperating with the government in the establishment of legal guarantees and by engaging in criticism of the legal system. Hoping to create an organization which would retain its autonomy and would be able to speak for general principles rather than the interests of specific groups, the founders exclude from membership "members of political parties or other organizations laying claim to participation in the government, or of organizations whose principles permit participation in orthodox or oppositional political activities."[58] The main consequence of this clause, obviously, is the exclusion of members of the CPSU. Soon after its founding, the poet and singer Alexander Galich and the novelist Alexander Solzhenitsyn were elected as "corresponding members," while the physicist Boris Tsukerman and the historian Alexander Yesenin-Volpin were elected as "experts."[59]

In effect, the guiding role of the Communist party of the Soviet Union is being challenged by a new intelligentsia—not the stratum of white-collar workers hailed by Stalin in the thirties as the creation and servant of the party—but by a conscious, amorphously organized group of intellectuals who dare to speak their minds and engage in independent activity in support of their ideals. The sources of contemporary protest are clearly reflected in Andrei Amalrik's analysis of the occupational distribution of those who signed letters of protest against the trial of Galanskov, Ginzburg, Dobrovolsky, and Lashkova in early 1968. Though the documents may not be entirely representative, their findings highlight a general phenomenon: those in the academic professions in particular—teachers and researchers— and those in intellectually-oriented occupations in general constitute the major source of support for the Democratic movement. Of the 738 persons signing these documents, the occupations of 700 are known. The percentage breakdown by occupational field is as follows: academics, 45 per cent; persons engaged in the arts, 22 per cent; engineers and technical specialists, 13 per cent; publishing house employees, teachers, doctors, and lawyers, 9 per cent; workers, 6 per cent; and students, 5 per cent.[60]

Accompanying the growth of dissent has been the resurgence of the idea of the intelligentsia as an autonomous critical force, serving as the "conscience of the nation." Such conceptions depart from the standard Soviet formulation, which defines the intelligentsia in terms of education and type of work (that is, qualified mental labor).[61] The sociologist, S. A. Kugel', for example, expresses doubts about the standard Soviet definition of the intelligentsia: "Is possession of a diploma of higher education sufficient for automatic inclusion in the composition of the intelligentsia? . . . It is well known, for example, that far from all specialists with higher and secondary education possess the capacity for independent thought and sufficiently creative social activity, corresponding to their cultural upbringing."[62] Others define the intelligentsia in terms of "intellectuality"—a high development of the intellect, wide mental horizons, and an elevated level of culture. For Iu. A. Kurnosov, the intelligentsia is above all "those people of high culture and morals" who actively participate in social life.[63]

In an insightful essay devoted principally to the American intelligentsia, the Soviet sociologist Igor Kon grapples with the problem of defining the intelligentsia. He argues that the growth of the educated group, the expansion of its functions and its accompanying internal differentiation, but also the interdependence between intellectual workers and their employers, all bring into question the conception of the intelligentsia as a lofty elite somehow standing above the basic social classes.

Intellectual activity lost its former aura of exclusiveness: it was transformed from a calling into a mere occupation. Separate groups within the intelligentsia began to live in accordance with their own particular interests, which are sometimes very far from and even opposed to the interests of the remaining society . . . The model of the intellectual-ideologue, the social critic, can no longer claim universality.

However, the need for such people exists, and is quite vital. Not fortuitously, in most recent American works, the intellectual is defined specifically as a thinker and critic of society (as distinguished from the technical specialist or the expert).[64]

Kon's conclusion—that there is a vital need for a critical intelligentsia—is particularly interesting because of the many similarities between his description of the problems of American intellectuals and those of Soviet intellectuals (for example, the restraints upon intellectuals in bureaucracies, the dogmatism and philistinism of political authorities, political repression during the McCarthy period resembling in milder form that of the Stalin period, the effect of censorship in politicizing and radicalizing writers, and so on). The article, appearing in the liberal journal *Novy Mir*, while ostensibly about the United States, was doubtlessly interpreted by some readers as an appeal for the self-assertion of a critical intelligentsia within the Soviet Union.

Clearly, the view of the intelligentsia as an autonomous critical force is one shared by members of the Soviet intelligentsia among themselves, even if it is not explicitly represented in the pages of the controlled press. *Message from Moscow*, a revealing anonymous account of Soviet society purportedly written by a foreign student who has been studying in Russia, claims that critically-minded, educated Russians speak of themselves as "the one per cent," thereby expressing their sense of eliteness, alienation, and isolation within Soviet society. The author writes: "Russian intellectuals themselves speak of the 'Soviet intelligentsia' as distinct from intelligentsia in the traditional sense: they mean engineers, even doctors and lawyers, who have acquired the technical skills of their professions but not the instincts of cultural and political enlightenment—people with a literate veneer over their essentially peasant cast of mind."[65] The intelligentsia, "the one per cent," though filled with pessimism regarding their ability to affect political decisions or realize structural change in society, think of themselves as the principal force of enlightenment.

Similarly, prominent members of the scientific community refer to the crucial role of a critical intelligentsia as a humanizing force in Soviet society. The renowned physicist Andrei Sakharov takes this position in his manifesto *Progress, Coexistence, and Intellectual Freedom*, which circulated originally in manuscript form in the USSR and was published in 1968 in the West. Sakharov addresses himself to what he sees to be the burning issues of the day—the threat of universal nuclear war, famine, militaristic police states, "bureaucratized dogmatism," and stupifaction induced by "mass culture." In view of these dangers, he asserts, "Only universal cooperation under conditions of intellectual freedom and the lofty moral ideals of socialism and labor, accompanied by the elimination of dogmatism and pressures of the concealed interests of ruling classes, will preserve civilization."[66] These beliefs, he tells us, "were formed in the milieu of the scientific and scientific-technological intelligentsia, which manifests much anxiety over the principles and specific aspects of foreign and domestic policy and over the future of mankind."[67]

Sakharov clearly regards the intelligentsia as a social group crosscutting occupational and class divisions in society that ought rightfully to play an active role in influencing policy. In his judgment, "the most progressive, internationalist, and dedicated element of the intelligentsia is, in essence, part of the working class, and the most advanced, educated, internationalist, and broadminded part of the working class is part of the intelligentsia." For this reason, it is senseless for the party to demand that the intelligentsia subordinate itself to the will and interests of the working class. "What these demands really mean," Sakharov asserts, "is subordination to the will of the party or, even more specifically, to the party's central apparatus and its officials." In the absence of a critical, committed intelligentsia, he asks, who will guarantee that the party officials are responsible to the working class and serve the genuine interests of progress rather than their own narrow interests?[68]

Although Sakharov stresses here the coincidence of interests of the intelligentsia and the working class, other scientists seemingly take a more elitist view of the intelligentsia and its social role. One such exponent is Zhores A. Medvedev, a prominent biologist who in recent years has become an outspoken critic of Communist policy, particularly with respect to scientific and cultural affairs. In his recent essay "Fruitful Meetings Between Scientists of the World," Medvedev says:

> There is only one social group of people in the world which, not only on account of its position in society but simply on account of the humane qualities inevitably inherent in it, on account of its selection of people for these qualities and on account of the character of its daily activity, is connected in a worldwide mutually dependent, mutually advantageous, mutually respecting system in friendship independent of national frontiers, constantly sharing among itself all possible help and *interested to the utmost in the progress of mankind, of which it is the standard-bearer and motive force.* This group consists of the scholars, the scientists, the *intelligentsia, in the sense of the scientific, technical and culturally creative intelligentsia,* and not simply that class of people who have had a secondary or higher education.[69]

Medvedev emphasizes the international cooperation carried out by specialists from many nations and notes that "inter-state and international relations among scientists and those who are culturally active are the wisest and most trustworthy." Referring to the intelligentsia's progressive role, he points out that "if we take the American corporate scientific body as a whole, it constitutes the principal opponent to the war in Vietnam, while the universities and colleges are centres of the movement of the intelligentsia for peace." The cause of progress and peace can be best served by strengthening such international cooperation among members of the intelligentsia, thereby fostering "a truly intellectual and moral society" in which "any aspect of public activity is considered on the principle of the maximum benefit for the whole of humanity and the whole world."[70]

It is impossible to estimate with any precision the number of intellectuals who are dissidents and who engage in cultural or political activity with the intention of changing their society. Documents which have reached the West may indicate simply the tip of the iceberg of widespread opposition. According to three leading figures in the democratic movement (A. D. Sakharov, V. F. Turchin, R. A. Medvedev), "the overwhelming majority of the intelligentsia and youth understands the need for democratization" and, though also acknowledging the need for the gradual implementation of reforms, "cannot understand or condone actions which are clearly anti-democratic in character," such as the imprisonment of critics and the persecution of independent minded writers.[71] Somewhat more conservatively, Jonathan Harris estimates that throughout the Soviet Union, "there are probably hundreds, if not thousands, of groups [of intellectuals aspiring to "independent thinking"] who gather to discuss the nature of their own social and political system."[72] In view of the available evidence, it would appear that the conception of the critical intelligentsia as "the one per cent" of the Soviet population is not far from the mark. Yet, the evidence clearly suggests that a considerably higher proportion of those persons engaging in intellectual work, especially the more creative members of the scientific and scholarly community, are dissidents who identify themselves with the critical intelligentsia. Statistically, the incidence of conscious radical dissent in the Soviet Union may not be very different from that in the United States. It should be borne in mind that only one per cent or less of the American adult population have identified themselves as "radical" in public opinion polls in recent years, but that the proportion of intellectuals and students who have done so is invariably much higher. In the United States, where open dissent is more readily accepted, critical radical intellectuals are much more conspicuous.

To understand why a growing intellectual opposition emerged in the late 1950's, and why it grew to significant proportions in the 1960's, it is necessary to reflect on the consequences of destalinization. As has already been noted, in undermining the image of a single monolithic Communist power, destalinization weakened the ideological constraints on intellectual opposition in the United States and other Western countries. This development had even greater importance in the Communist world itself.

Just as the Russian intelligentsia emerged in the nineteenth century as a distinct social group during a period of uncertainty, sweeping reform, and enlivened public debate, so in a similar way, destalinization—the most momentous reform in the history of the Soviet Communist party and, indeed, of the World Communist movement—has been a crucial catalytic process for the reemergence of a critical intelligentsia in the Soviet Union today. The process began with Stalin's death; the demise of the infallible leader who had ruled his country with an iron hand for decades provoked widespread uncertainty about future policies. At that time, as the poet Yevgeny Yevtushenko recalls, "the whole of Russia was one immense sea of doubt stretching all the thousands of miles between the Baltic and the Pacific . . . Something, I knew, was breaking down . . . The Babylon that was falling to pieces on Russian soil was the guilded papier-maché city of lies built upon gullibility and the habit of blind obedience. It was as if a blind people were recovering its sight."[73]

As initial uncertainty gave way to an official policy of destalinization— most notably, of course, with Khrushchev's speech to the Twentieth Party Congress in 1956—new problems arose. By condemning Stalin and thereby broaching the issue of the legitimacy of Stalin's deeds, Khrushchev raised doubts about the complicity of Stalin's heirs and brought to light the equivocal position of the leaders with respect to the establishment of the rule of law. If Stalin was condemned, ought his living accomplices to be deemed blameless and go unpunished? More than that, how could recurrences of the abuse of power be prevented except through the institutionalization of legal norms protecting individual rights and constitutional constraints on party leaders? At the same time, Khrushchev's affirmation of collective leadership effectively shattered the monolithic façade that Stalin had imposed on political life. Collective leadership, even when consensual, could not be as unitary as a one-man dictatorship; cleavages were inevitable. Such leadership necessitated a constant search for new support. Alignments more frequently shifted. To maintain a ruling coalition, there was a need for the kind of bargaining that increased the possibilities of an incipient pluralism within the political structure.

The winds of reform were felt particularly strongly by certain social groups—the entrenched Stalinist bureaucrats who feared any manifestations of "liberalization," which appeared to endanger their power and privileges; the inmates of labor camps, the most obvious victims of political repression; and the creative intellectuals who had been decimated by Stalin's purges and subjected to the most stringent political and ideological constraints. For a variety of reasons, intellectuals achieved greater prominence during this period and came to play a more independent role in political affairs. This resulted in part from the fact that certain intellectuals— writers, artists, and historians—whose occupational task is the interpretation of experience, showed themselves especially sensitive to the normative ambiguity that accompanied the reforms. Others looked to them for a clarification of the meaning of the times; willingly or unwillingly, writers, artists, and others professionally concerned with the interpretation of experience found themselves in a position of social leadership.[74] Also, the conditions of collective leadership and the leaders' perpetual need of support enhanced the position of those intellectuals who provided vital services to the regime. To the extent that some gained greater autonomy in exchange for services they rendered, the give-and-take between the political authorities and the intellectuals contributed to the emergence of a critical intelligentsia. Their relative autonomy, in turn, facilitated the free expression of ideas. It may be argued, furthermore, that intellectuals are particularly sensitive to the need for the rule of law and for social predictability combined with personal freedom. Not only is the rule of law necessary for their work, but they require it to protect their relatively privileged position from arbitrary acts by those who have political power.[75] Thus, in many cases, the intellectuals have tried to strengthen the rule of law and to curtail the scope of the party leaders' prerogatives.

In the Soviet Union, as in the United States, the resurgence of dissent derives in some measure from the critical activity of the younger generation. For thousands of young Soviet citizens who had learned quite literally to worship Stalin, destalinization was a shattering experience, discrediting the Communist regime and calling into question the actions of their elders. Not having known the Stalinist terror at first hand, they were also less likely to be submissive.

As Nadezhda Mandelstam observes:

Among the new intelligentsia now growing up in front of our eyes, nobody blithely repeats old sayings like "You can't swim against the tide" or "You can't make an omelet without breaking eggs." In other words, the values we thought had been abolished forever are being restored, and they must be taken account of, even by people who could quite well do without them. This has come as a surprise both to those who never gave up these values and to those who tried to bury them once and for all. Somehow or other they lived on underground, taking refuge in all those hushed homes with their dimmed lights. Now they are on the move and gathering force. The initiative in their destruction belonged to the intelligentsia of the twenties, which, as a result, ceased to be itself and turned into something different. At the present day we are witnessing the reverse process . . . the main thing is this: these young intellectuals have appeared and the process is now irreversible—it cannot be stopped even by the physical destruction which the representatives of the past would love to visit on them. Nowadays the persecution of one intellectual only creates dozens more. We saw this during the Brodski affair.[76]

Not surprisingly, the young intellectuals pose problems for the party and Komsomol organizations which are supposed to guide their behavior and attend to their proper indoctrination. For instance, in an article entitled "Party Concern for the Upbringing of the Scientific-Technical Intelligentsia," which appeared in the journal *Kommunist*, the author comments: "Party and Y.C.L. organizations should devote more profound study to the needs and attitudes of young scientists and should struggle more persistently against personality traits that are unsuitable for young builders of communism, such as aloofness, skepticism and apoliticalness, which are sometimes encountered in scientific collectives. One cannot fail to be disturbed that certain young scientists picture democracy, individual freedom and humanism as some sort of abstract, nonclass categories."[77]

Like the Russian intelligentsia of the past century, the contemporary critical Soviet intelligentsia has emerged in the wake of a major reform, when the basic problems of social life have been brought into the foreground. The intellectuals, confronting these problems, have articulated those values they believe necessary to guide men's actions and shape the social order. Because the Stalinist tyranny stands for the more critical intellectuals as the virtual antithesis of everything they believe in, they define their position with reference to the Stalinist past and struggle against every manifestation of neo-Stalinism. As the outspoken critic Andrei Sakharov affirms: "Our country has started on the path of cleansing away the foulness of Stalinism. 'We are squeezing the slave out of ourselves drop by drop' (an expression of Anton Chekhov). We are learning to express our opinions, without taking the lead from the bosses and without fearing for our lives."[78]

Internationally, the impact of destalinization has been far-reaching and profound. The most immediate effects were felt within the Soviet bloc, where unity gave way to "polycentricism" and schism. Throughout the Communist world, the initiation of destalinization elicited a vocal response from the intellectuals, who emerged as prominent critics of the existing order. Reviewing the events in Eastern Europe, one commentator writes:

[In Hungary and Poland following destalinization] the writers, supported by the professors, economists, artists, the majority of journalists, and the teachers, took the lead in the mass movements for democratization . . .

In Czechoslovakia, as in other dictatorships of the left or right, the struggle for democratization began with the fight of the writers, the artists, the students against censorship, for free expression. In 1967, the "liberals" won a majority in the Writers' Union . . . In January 1968, the writers, journalists, economists, historians, artists, joined with a growing part of the intelligentsia to force through a transformation of the regime into a pluralistic socialism.[79]

At the same time that destalinization was underway in the Soviet Union, and dissent was becoming more manifest in the Communist countries to the west, the leaders of Communist China thought it expedient to loosen the ideological fetters on their own intellectuals. The official slogan of the campaign in 1956-1957—"Let the hundred flowers bloom, let the hundred schools contend"—was meant to suggest that intellectuals were to be allowed an undefined degree of freedom of expression. The outcome of the Hundred Flowers episode was revealing, though hardly what the leaders had anticipated. As Benjamin Schwartz has written:

Not only were the literary and cultural policies of the regime attacked; not only did professionals challenge the authority of the Party within their areas of competence; but there were even those who raised the dread question of power itself. The very grounds on which the Communist Party claimed political infallibility were challenged. In raising the question of political power, the "civism" of the Chinese intelligentsia went beyond anything that has occurred in the Soviet Union [in the fifties] since the inauguration of the "Khrushchev era."[80]

In the face of overt dissent on the part of the critical intelligentsia, the Chinese leaders decided to tighten the reins again. Their experience with their own intellectuals probably strengthened their conviction that Stalin deserved great credit for what he had done. This was one more factor helping to create a schism between the Soviet Union and the People's Republic of China.

The United States and the Soviet Union: Academic Intellectuals

The sixties, quite obviously, were a time of intellectual ferment both in the West and in the East. The United States and the Soviet Union, which had long appeared to differ from the countries of the third world by their political quietism and the absence of major ideological debate, emerged again as arenas of dissident activity. In both countries, intellectuals—or at least the critical intelligentsia—appear to be ideologically inspired, actively committed to the implementation of certain values and the achievement of structural change. The differences between the intellectuals of the two countries in their traditions, social conditions, and objectives are fairly obvious. The Americans seek the end of American participation in the war in Vietnam, the expansion of egalitarian opportunity, and the reform of the political system, to make it more responsive to citizen participation; in the Soviet Union the main thrust of the intelligentsia is toward institutionalizing basic rights and establishing the rule of law.

What attributes of the social structure contribute to the formation of such a critical intelligentsia? How is one to explain why autonomous social movements derive such support from those engaged in the "cultural apparatus"? The relationship between the two is by no means self-evident. As organized culture creation has increased in size and in social impact, cultural work has become more differentiated. The intellectual stratum itself has become more heterogeneous, and the individual practitioners have become less autonomous. These conditions would seem to militate against the creation of a critical autonomous intelligentsia, proposing and seeking to implement values of universal scope. Yet, any such inference would be superficial and misleading. There are other important features which, individually or in combination with other variables, contribute to the creation of a critical intelligentsia. To account for the emergence of such an intelligentsia, we must first isolate factors that induce intellectuals to adopt a broader stance—that is, a larger world-view and a commitment to general values. We must then show how they are able to gain sufficient autonomy to maintain their commitments.

It appears that various elements in the institutionalized reward structure for scientific and scholarly pursuits contribute to the fostering of a critical intellectual class. Intellectual life tends to be highly competitive;

there is, in both Communist and non-Communist countries, a marked emphasis on the few in every category or field who win recognition for significant achievement. It has been argued that the vast increase in numbers of those involved in intellectual activity, both inside and outside the university, has heightened the possibilities of frustration and consequent political alienation.[81] The academic community itself is stratified; highest status and eminence go to a few in major universities or academy institutes or to those who win special recognition for specific scholarly achievements. The majority of scholars probably feel a sense of relative deprivation or even failure in relation to these more distinguished academics. Even those who have secured good posts or attained eminence in the past often find themselves pressed by younger men who are better suited to doing the original work that is required in new circumstances. Because of competitive demands, the increase in the status of the academic profession as a whole, and the greater recognition accorded the successful, the sense of frustration by others is probably increased. Hence, the growth in numbers may give rise to a more influential, though more alienated, intellectual stratum.

To understand the political and social activity of intellectuals, those factors inherent in scientific and scholarly activity and intellectual creativity in general are certainly more important than those which affect the distribution of reward or status. Among these are the variety of normative patterns associated with science and scholarship or related to intellectual life more generally. As Robert Merton has noted in analyzing the role of the scientists, the normative pattern of "organized skepticism" demands a "suspension of judgment until 'the facts are at hand' and the detached scrutiny of beliefs in terms of empirical and logical criteria."[82] Merton stresses also the importance of "universalism"—"the canon that truth claims, whatever their source, are to be subjected to *preestablished impersonal criteria*: consonant with observation and with previously confirmed knowledge."[83] Adherence to such norms of scholarly work may engender a critical attitude toward judgments and beliefs outside of the particular field of inquiry—a doubting of the conventional verities and reigning myths.

Maintenance of the norms of scientific and scholarly inquiry requires a certain autonomy from outside interference. As the authors of a significant study conducted under the auspices of the Czechoslovakian Academy of Sciences stated: "Science calls for quite a different type of management, working regime, different standards and rules in society's everyday life, than those suited to industry, because it involves a much higher degree of inner subjectivity and responsibility, a greater measure of initiative and self-realization. There has to be much greater 'reliance on man,' on his creative abilities and powers. In contrast to the hierarchy of the industrial system, science reaches a state in its development where it demands a fuller implementation of democratic principles."[84] Though perhaps of limited scope, such autonomy constitutes a necessary condition for the emergence of informal structures, such as those of a critical intelligentsia.

The most creative intellectuals in various disciplines often feel impelled to keep abreast of current developments outside their individual fields. In doing so, they establish informal contacts with their peers in other disciplines and develop a more comprehensive view of their work and its significance. In the Soviet context, for instance, Academician Pyotr Kapitsa asserts that neither the scientific councils nor any other existing formal organization can replace the *kruzhok*, the informal social circle, as the appropriate setting for the free and spontaneous exchange of ideas.[85] To the extent that scientists and scholars feel themselves to be alienated—separated from the means of effectively realizing themselves through their activity—they may be inclined to develop a critical orientation to their activity and to generalize ideological propositions. Bureaucratic social arrangements may have dialectical potentialities—at once limiting the scholars' creativity while fostering in them a critical mentality.

The very expansion of knowledge creation has resulted in an increasing concentration of intellectuals within certain social and geographical settings. Such concentration facilitates the dissemination of unorthodox ideas and may serve to foster a sense of corporate identity, solidarity, and eliteness. Students of the American scene have pointed to such concentration as one of the conditions contributing to the spread of radicalism within the academic world.[86] In the Soviet Union, scientists and scholars are even more concentrated, the trend toward greater concentration being particularly evident in the establishment of "science towns" and scientific "satellite-towns" such as Dubna, Pushchino, Obninsk, Cernogolovka, Rukovo, and others on the outskirts of Moscow.[87] The largest of these science towns is the *Akademgorodok* at Novosibirsk—an urban area with a population of over 40,000, where more than twenty specialized institutes are located.

While such settlements may serve to isolate scientists and scholars from the rest of the population, they also seem to afford a fertile setting for the gestation of critical thought, and they clearly pose new obstacles to the party's persistent efforts to maintain ideological controls. For instance, as the First Secretary of the Sovetskii Borough Party Committee stated in August 1970: "Ideological work in Academy City has its special features, conditioned above all by the youth of the collective (the average age of scientific personnel here is 32), territorial isolation and the absence of direct, everyday ties with production. All this creates a particular social climate that leads a certain portion of the young scientists to hold an exaggerated conception of their role in society. In their opinion, the scientific and technological revolution is the work of a rather small 'intellectual elite' alone. This mistaken self-appraisal is explained in large measure by the fact that the life path of some young scientists has been: school, university, then work in an academic institute. And, since their social and life experience has been quite limited, sometimes distortions arise in their outlook."[88] In 1969 more than 3,000 foreign intellectuals visited the center. "Along with scientific literature," we are told, " 'information' designed to serve the purposes of psychological warfare sometimes reaches the intelligentsia."[89]

Attempts by political authorities to impose their will on scholars creates a conflict situation conducive to the generalization of specific values. In the United States, many academics are cushioned from direct manipulation by political authorities by the institutionalization of academic freedom; but in allocating research funds, for instance, political authorities obviously have an impact on the choice of problems by scientists and scholars.

The relation of scholars to the political authorities in the United States differs significantly from that of the Soviet Union. There, the Communist party, deriving its legitimacy from Marxist-Leninist ideology, seeks to incorporate scientific achievements and scholarly explanations within its world-view, while at the same time attempting to exert a guiding influence over the whole of social life, including academic work. In the eyes of the party, the scientist or scholar, like every Soviet citizen, is in the first instance a builder of Communism, an unflagging fighter for the Communist cause, rather than a disinterested seeker of truth. Science, scholarship, and education are regarded as political pursuits, contributing either to the advancement of socialism or the defense of the imperialist-capitalist system.

Time and again, the party has attempted to thwart the spread of new ideas and theories—Freudianism, mathematical modeling in economics, cybernetics, sociology, genetics.[90] Yet, the party's intrusion into science and scholarship clashes with the very norms that define the nature of the scholars' work and provide standards for the evaluation of their performance. Scientists and other scholars are loath to permit the party's persistent surveillance of their intellectual work and personal lives. They resent limitations on their right to engage freely in inquiry along lines suggested by their discipline or beyond it.

It would appear that certain academics are becoming increasingly aware of their common position vis-à-vis the party authorities and are developing a sense of solidarity that cuts across lines established by individual disciplines and specialties. Recognizing the importance of such values as freedom of discussion and inquiry, "universalism," and cognitive rationality for their common endeavor, they are gaining a keener understanding of the political implications of such values. In being arbitrarily constrained by political authorities and finding themselves in a situation of conflict, they tend to generalize the values inherent in their academic work and to establish ties with other intellectuals, including writers, who are similarly constrained.

The party representatives appointed to supervise intellectuals can become symbols of the cleavage between the party and themselves. Andrei Sakharov, for example, attacking party tutelage of science, singles out a prominent party appointment—the director of the Science Department of the Party's Central Committee, Sergei Trapeznikov, whose views "are basically Stalinist (from our point of view, they reflect the interests of the bureaucratic elite)" and "differ fundamentally from the dreams and aspirations of the majority and most active section of the intelligentsia, which, in our opinion, reflect the true interests of all our people and progressive mankind. The leadership of our country should understand that as long as such a man . . . exercises influence, it is impossible to hope for a strengthening of the party's position among scientific and artistic intellectuals. An indication of this was given at the last elections in the Academy of Sciences when S. P. Trapeznikov was rejected by a substantial majority of votes, but this hint was not 'understood' by the leadership."[91] Thus, ironically, the very attempt of the Communist party to control science and to prevent the formation of an intelligentsia—an autonomous group which articulates fundamental values—contributes to the emergence of such a group.

In the United States, during the McCarthy period (1950-1954) when various efforts were made to intimidate left-oriented intellectuals both on and off university campuses, political intrusion may have produced comparable results. A survey of the effect of McCarthyism on the beliefs and behavior of American social scientists concluded that they were relatively unintimidated; their heads were "bloody but unbowed." Paul Lazarsfeld and Wagner Thielens, Jr., suggest that it was more dangerous for the career of an academic to be a public supporter of McCarthy on a college campus than to be a bitter opponent.[92] Robert Nisbet has credited the McCarthy period with helping to legitimate and thereby stimulate campus political activism. The activism of the 1960's drew support from the politicized university faculties which had resisted McCarthyite pressure during the 1950's.

No single figure, no single issue . . . had ever seized the minds of faculty members as did the person of Senator Joseph McCarthy and the cause he represented in the 1950's . . . For McCarthy's enemy, his declared enemy, was not labor, not labor unions, not the people—in the Populist sense—but almost strictly and exclusively the intellectuals in this country, academic intellectuals especially.

Given his assaults in so many intellectual areas, his challenging of the loyalty of intellectuals, his threats to "get" Harvard and other universities, it would be extraordinary if the mind of the American faculty had not become visibly radicalized in the 1950's.[93]

The impulse to react critically to the larger society must not, however, be seen primarily as a function of deprivation or punitive experiences, though these may contribute to the *activization* of an opposition movement at a given time and place. Both logic and evidence suggest that the principal component of intellectual endeavor—its concern for creativity, for originality, and for rejecting the traditional and the established— presses those most favorably endowed to challenge what is received and accepted in the larger society. As noted earlier, all systematic quantitative efforts in the United States to relate intellectual achievement (as reflected in recognition by one's peers, record of relative accomplishment in publications, and position at the more prestigious universities as judged by rankings of faculty generally or by the test scores of students) agree that those who rank high on these indicators of academic status are among the most left-inclined professors. Those faculty who are primarily oriented to and concerned with teaching are more conservative than those more involved in the research culture.

Although no comparable published surveys exist for the Soviet Union or for any other Communist country, a variety of reports by foreign scholars who have spent time in Russia, impressionistic though they be, together with accounts of findings in still unpublished studies by Soviet scholars, indicate that a similar pattern exists there as well. It seems certain that scholars who are members of the Soviet Academy of Sciences, whose institutes correspond to the more prestigious research-oriented graduate schools in the United States, are much more likely to exhibit antiestablishment thought and behavior than those who teach in the relatively low status, non-research-oriented Soviet universities and the specialized technical institutions of higher education. The Soviet authorities have had more difficulty with their best scholars and scientists, and with intellectuals generally, than with those who *distribute* intellectual products as teachers. Soviet science institutes and "science cities" tend to be centers of opposition; they are among the principal supporters of free intellectual life and the "underground press."

These reports do not, of course, demonstrate that activities associated with intellectual creativity press men to take a more critical political position. They are also congruent with the assumption that the kind of mind or background which impels men to question the society of which they are a part also makes for success in intellectual activities. An argument of this kind was made by Thorstein Veblen over a half century ago in his attempt to account for the "intellectual pre-eminence of Jews."

The first requisite for constructive work in modern science, and indeed for any work of inquiry that shall bring enduring results, is a skeptical frame of mind. The enterprising skeptic alone can be counted on to further the increase of knowledge in any substantial fashion. This will be found true both in the modern sciences and in the field of scholarship at large . . . For [the intellectually gifted Jews] as for other men in the like case, the skepticism that goes to make him an effectual factor in the increase and diffusion of knowledge among men involved a loss of that peace of mind that is the birthright of the safe and sane quietist. He becomes a disturber of the intellectual peace.[94]

A comparable thesis was put forth fifteen years ago by Lazarsfeld and Thielens in their effort to explain why those faculty who were at high quality American schools had the most liberal and left views. Pointing out that such institutions "attract more distinguished social scientists," they said:

The original and creative minority among them will often have analytical minds which do not automatically accept current beliefs, minds willing to entertain unorthodox ideas as to how a modern society can best function. Next to the creative leader comes the competent teacher and productive research scholar. Even if he might be by nature more amenable to the general currents of public opinion, he is more directly in communication with the leaders of his profession, and his thinking is shaped by the process of mutual interaction among primary groups [of other high quality scholars] . . . Thus he too will add to a permissive [liberal] climate when appointed to a distinguished institution.[95]

Radical and liberal social scientists in the West naturally find it ego-enhancing to discover and explain links between their leftist political views and intellectual creativity. Hence, the way in which the conservative economist F. A. Hayek accounts for the same phenomenon is of considerable interest. Writing in 1949 before most of the studies cited above were made, and without apparent awareness of the early ones completed by Leuba, Hayek stated: "on the whole the more active, intelligent, and original men among [American] intellectuals . . . most frequently incline toward socialism, while its opponents are often of an inferior caliber . . . Nobody, for instance, who is familiar with large numbers of university faculties . . . can remain oblivious to the fact that the most brilliant and successful teachers are today more likely than not to be socialists, while those who hold more conservative political views are as frequently mediocrities. This is of course by itself an important factor leading the younger generation into the socialist camp."[96]

In seeking to explain this phenomenon Hayek understandably rejected the hypothesis that more intelligent people tend to become socialists. Rather, he suggested that the more intelligent among those who were inclined to support the status quo sought out nonintellectual pursuits, while the "disaffected and dissatisfied" rejected occupations linked to the business system and were more inclined to find a career in intellectual activities. Hayek wrote: "It is therefore probably the fact, not that the more intelligent people are generally socialists, but that a much higher proportion of socialists among the best minds devote themselves to those intellectual pursuits which in modern society give them a decisive influence on public opinion."[97] Hayek, like Veblen, found a relationship between the factors that lead Jews to intellectuality and to leftist political views.[98]

Such hypotheses, advanced to account for the association between intellectual achievement and propensity to "disturb the peace" of society, may be regarded as mutually reinforcing, rather than as contradictory explanations. They suggest that the attributes of mind which lead men to reject the established order are closely linked with those that foster scholarly or artistic creativity. Certain evidence from surveys of student attitudes and occupational preferences reinforces these generalizations. A number of American studies indicate that as the opinions or partisan identification of undergraduates move to the left, the more likely are they to exhibit qualities defined by researchers as "intellectuality" and to indicate a desire for an academic career. Those inclined to become intellectuals exhibit cultural tastes with regard to athletics, books, media habits, and politics distinctly different from other youth long before they have finished college.[99] It is highly doubtful that the relationship is solely a function of selection. As Lazarsfeld and Thielens have argued, absorption in the high level intellectual culture in the United States has, particularly for young people, inevitably meant association with the adversary culture orientation. Not only do the brighter among the more leftist-oriented tend to opt for intellectually related vocations, but the intellectually motivated who are initially nonleftist discover a link between their activities and a critical stance.

There are, of course, other sources of variation among scholarly intellectuals which affect their political orientations. Discipline or subject matter are particularly important. In the United States, a variety of surveys of academic opinion indicate that the social sciences and humanities are toward the left end of the spectrum, the natural sciences near the middle, and the more applied professions (education, business, engineering, and agriculture) farthest to the right. In general, these findings lend support to the hypothesis that those fields which are more "intellectual" rather than practical—that is, the liberal arts, as contrasted with the professional or applied disciplines—tend to foster a leftist or liberal political orientation. Within the natural science fields, the pure or theoretical approaches tend to be associated with a more liberal outlook, while among the social sciences and the humanities, the more politically relevant disciplines—political science and, above all, sociology—appear to be the most liberal according to a number of independent surveys of academics in different fields.[100]

As for differences among Soviet scholars, reports by foreign scholars and students, together with documents published in the West, lead one to believe that political dissidence and critical activity are more pronounced among students and faculty in the natural sciences than in the social sciences and the humanities.[101] Significantly, it is not scholars in the humanities and social sciences, but Andrei Sakharov, Andrei Tverdokhlebov, and Valery Chalidze, three prominent physicists, who founded the Committee for Human Rights, an organization devoted to the strengthening of legal norms and basic civil rights. The principal reason that natural scientists are relatively more critical and more politically active appears to be that the more politically relevant fields, such as the social sciences and the humanities, are particularly hampered by ideological controls. Philosophy, by and large, means Dialectical Materialism, which is endowed with the sanctity of revealed truth; social science tends to be "applied" and is generally subordinated to ideological tenets; fields in the humanities are tailored to serve the needs of "political upbringing." At a recent conference (December 21, 1971) of the heads of Social Science Departments of Higher Educational Institutions, M. A. Suslov, the Secretary of the Central Committee of the CPSU, reiterated the party's position on these matters. After pointing to the task of the social sciences to produce knowledge dealing with "the problem of management in the broadest sense, from the management of the individual enterprise to management on the enormous scale of the entire country," and contributing "to the more effective utilization of the latest machinery and of labor," Suslov described their ideological role:

The most important conditions for the fruitful development and effective utilization of the social sciences in communist construction are the allegiance of these sciences to Marxist-Leninist methodology, a creative approach to the elaboration of urgent problems, and interaction with other spheres of scientific knowledge.

The growing role of the social sciences makes higher demands on the level of the teaching of these sciences in the higher schools and calls for intensifying the Marxist-Leninist tempering of all Soviet students.

If Marxist-Leninist revolutionary theory is to be presented to students in all its vital force, teachers in the social sciences must be in the forefront of the ideological struggle and must be able to use the latest achievements of Marxist-Leninist thought. The central part of this task is the creative understanding and propaganda of the decisions of the 24th Party Congress.[102]

Being subject to such forms of ideological control, liberal arts fields that might otherwise be controversial and intellectually engaging are neither. Because of limitations on original and innovative work, the more creative or intelligent are often drawn to the sciences. In many cases, the student's or young scholar's search for promising areas of inquiry is simultaneously a flight from politics.[103]

While the natural sciences produce more critics than the social sciences—a situation that also existed in Czarist Russia through much of the nineteenth century—this may now be in the process of changing. Sociology, banned in all Communist countries during the Stalinist period as a "bourgeois" discipline, has become an important field of inquiry both in Eastern Europe and the Soviet Union. Having previously been regarded as somewhat heretical, it has become attractive to the more critically minded among students and younger researchers. In Eastern Europe, there is a general consensus that sociology students have been in the forefront of student protest. In Poland and Czechoslovakia, senior sociologists stood out among "revisionist" and "non-Marxist" elements. In the Soviet Union, where the party regards sociology as an instrument for rationalizing its rule, the theoretical conceptions and empirical findings nonetheless tend to undermine ideological dogma and officially sponsored images of society. Zev Katz observes that the party leaders "—and, indeed, the sociologists themselves—find themselves in a painful dilemma. For if sociology is to be a truly effective instrument for improving the Soviet system, it must be allowed to be somewhat independent and critical, to point out where the failings of the system lie . . . The party is as yet reluctant to do this, and it therefore continues to try to keep sociology within safe bounds."[104]

Writers and Artists as Critical Intellectuals

In concentrating on scientists and scholars, that is, on knowledge producers, there is no implication that writers and artists do not play a significant social role or form a vital constituent part of the critical intelligentsia. Of course, they differ from the former group both in their social organization and type of work. Writers and artists are much more likely to be freelance or unattached intellectuals who are not employed within an organization. Also, their creative work is typically more evaluative and expressive than scholarship or science, bound by norms of "objectivity," cognitive consistency, and empirical verification. But among these groups, too, the nature of their work and of their social relationships tend to foster a critical, skeptical outlook which has important political implications. Jean-Paul Sartre has argued that the creative writer is inherently engaged in an activity that undermines the stability of society by making it "self-conscious."

If society sees itself and, in particular, sees itself as *seen,* there is, by virtue of this very fact, a contesting of the established values of the regime. The writer presents it with its image; he calls upon it to assume it or to change itself. At any rate, it changes; it practices dishonesty; thus, the writer gives society a *guilty conscience;* he is thereby in a state of perpetual antagonism toward the conservative forces which are maintaining the balance he tends to upset . . .
Only the governing classes can allow themselves the luxury of remunerating so unproductive and dangerous activity . . . They want to retrieve themselves, and they charge the artist with presenting them with their image without realizing that he will then make them assume it . . . But, functionally, he moves in opposition to the interests of those who keep him alive. Such is the original conflict which defines his condition.[105]

One of the fundamental dilemmas for intellectuals generally has been to obtain the resources necessary to pursue creative activity without "selling out," without tailoring one's creative and intellectual work to the demands of director, patron, or consumer. In modern times in the West, the emphasis on originality and innovation and on following the logic of development in various creative fields—be it painting, music, literature, or drama—has been responsible for a recurrent conflict between intellectuals and their patrons, who pay for their works or exert control through the state, churches, businesses, or other institutions. Intellectuals have often felt themselves to be dependent on philistines, while wanting to do whatever they liked according to the logic of their field.[106]

Much of the discussion concerning the political propensities of unattached intellectuals has focused on the tensions created for the artist by his relation with those who determine his rewards. It has been asserted "that free-lance intellectuals are more receptive to political extremism than are other types of intellectuals . . . [since] the free-lance intellectual . . . has been dependent on an anonymous and unpredictable market . . . Rewards are much less certain to be forthcoming for the free-lance intellectual, the form of reward less predictable, and the permanence of the recognition more tenuous . . . [They] tend to be more dependent on their audience over which they have relatively little control, and to feel greater social distance from it."[107]

Out of this tension between the intellectual and the patron have come various political tendencies, both reactionary and radical. Since the beginning of the nineteenth century, the right-wing critique has depicted mass society or democracy as coercive and corrupting for intellectual activity. Such societies are said to pander to the masses who destroy genuine creativity. Tocqueville feared that a democratic society would produce mediocre intellectual elites precisely because these elites would be greatly influenced by the demands of the masses. Charles Eliot Norton was typical of many nineteenth-century American humanists who deplored "the loss of cultural standards in an era of democracy."[108] In their quest to realize their values, many American intellectuals expressed their rejection of the vulgar commercial civilization around them by glorifying the supposed virtues of the more cosmopolitan European cultures, and by attacking the "bourgeoisie." The dominant ideological trends among the most creative writers were "adversary," either disdainfully reactionary, or more commonly an elitist intellectual opposition to capitalist industrial society. Referring to the intellectual climate at the turn of the century, Joseph Gusfield observes that Henry Adams was a perfect representative of this view. "In his anti-democratic and anti-business attitudes he mirrored a persistent theme in American intellectual life."[109] Adams also illustrated a dominant theme among elitist intellectuals, that their main antagonism was directed against the bourgeoisie. Writing in the nineties, Adams voiced sentiments that were to lead some writers to back fascism or communism in the 1920's and 1930's:

For my part, hating vindictively as I do our whole fabric and conception of society, against which my little-self squeaked protest from its birth, and will yet protest till its death, I shall be glad to see the whole thing utterly destroyed and wiped away. With communism I could exist tolerably well, for communism is favorable to social consideration apart from wealth; but in a society of brokers and Jews, a world made up of maniacs mad for gold, I have no place.[110]

Antibourgeois, elitist, or overtly antidemocratic sentiments led a small minority of leading American humanists and other intellectuals to find reason to praise Italian fascism. Some who wrote in extremely positive terms were avowedly on the left, and sometimes also pro-Soviet. The *New Republic*, for example, during the last years of the twenties urged a "sympathetic hearing" for the Italian system which promoted "national cohesion and national welfare." The "liberal" weekly even justified fascist violence as necessary to end internal strife and disunity and compared it to the use of force and bloodshed to save the Union during the American Civil War. Its editors at the time included Herbert Croly (who wrote the pro-fascist editorials), Bruce Bliven, Alvin Johnson, Robert Littell, Robert Morss Lovett, George Soule, and Stark Young. Among the prominent Americans who wrote favorably of fascism were writers such as Wallace Stevens and Henry Miller, a variety of humanistic scholars, including Irving Babbitt, Charles Beard, Shephard Clough, Carlton J. H. Hays, Horace Kallen, William Lyon Phelps, George Santayana, and Herbert Schneider, and former "muckrackers" S. S. McClure, Ida Tarbell, and Lincoln Steffens.[111]

Although, as noted earlier, the thirties pressed almost all politically involved American intellectuals to identify with the left, the rightist formulations of the antibourgeois critique had considerable strength among major literary figures in Europe. In Germany, one thinks of Stefan George, Ernst Junger, Friedrich Junger, Gottfried Benn, and Moeller van den Bruck as central figures, almost all of whom came close to identification with the Nazis. In France there were a variety of Catholic reactionaries such as Paul Claudel, Georges Bernanos, Gabriel Marcel, plus the philo-fascist right, Celine, Henri de Montherlant, and Drieu la Rochelle. In the English language world, there were W. B. Yeats, D. H. Lawrence, Wyndham Lewis, the American expatriates T. S. Eliot and Ezra Pound, all of whom held antidemocratic elitist points of view. Almost all of these figures, however, loathed the materialistic world of commerce and industry.

What has been termed the "aesthetic movement" in literature exhibited their thinking well. John Harrison observes:

> The aesthetic movement, ostensibly the least political of all literary "movements," nevertheless had a profound effect on the political beliefs of many writers and artists . . . Poets in the early nineteenth century tended to retire to a private world where they cultivated the belief in their superiority to practical life . . . Contempt for the taste and judgment of the public can easily become contempt for the public itself, particularly when that public is becoming more numerous and self-assertive.

. . . The critics of democracy believed that the privileged aristocracies of old, despite their inequities, did preserve a taste for higher human quality and forms of refinement by their traditions. Ortega y Gasset's *Revolt of the Masses* epitomizes the fear and hatred aroused by the developing mass society. This attitude was widespread among the literary intelligentsia who gave it its most articulate expression.[112]

On the other side, the leftist literary view predominant in the United States for much of the century suggests that conditions of the market place and the power of the privileged class and the state prevent the intellectual from being free; his creativity is thwarted. Writing about the constraints on intellectual creativity, both conservative and leftist intellectuals often cite the same examples, but locate the source of the problem differently. Both, for instance, attack movies, television, or the other mass media for catering to essentially low tastes and suppressing true creativity. Yet, while the conservatives blame the phenomenon on the vulgar values of the mass audience, the leftists attribute it to the bad taste and profit-making motives of the businessmen who own and control these forms of mass communication.

Some have recently argued that the power relationships have been reversed to a marked degree in the United States—that the artist is no longer dependent on a patron, that it is the other way around. James Ackerman says that wealthy consumers now agree to buy art that is judged as the most creative by the leading experimental artists. As a result, there is no longer an avant-garde in the old sense, since the most advanced and esoteric work is quickly bought at high prices by art patrons.[113] Daniel Bell, currently engaged in an in-depth study of the relationship between culture and social structure in the United States, also stresses the power of the creators: "The middle-class audience, or even the buyer alone, no longer controls art. In painting, in film (perhaps less so in advanced music), the artist, and usually the *avant-garde* artist, now dominates the cultural scene. It is he who swiftly shapes the audience and the market, rather than being shaped by them."[114]

The increased power, status, and income of the cultural elite has not appreciably tempered their opposition to the larger society. They still see themselves at war with a "repressive" society. The "adversary culture" is more widespread today than at any time in the past; it finds support among the educated wealthy, where it has taken the form of "radical-chic," an involvement usually on the fund-raising level, with participation in well-publicized social events for causes identified with the most exploited elements in society.[115] As Lionel Trilling notes, "the adversary culture of art and thought . . . has detached a considerable force from the main body of the enemy and has captivated its allegiance."[116]

The situation of writers and artists in the Soviet Union differs in many ways from that of their counterparts in the West. To begin with, they are corporately organized and are "officially" dedicated to art as a specific ideological form. To be recognized as a writer and to be published in the Soviet Union, for example, requires that one be a member of the Union of Soviet Writers. Under Stalin, the Writers' Union served as one of many organizational "transmission belts" for communicating decisions from above and mobilizing, in Zhdanov's memorable phrase, these "engineers of the soul."[117] Membership in the Union carried with it—as it does today—certain obligations. One of the articles of the Union's statute specifies "socialist realism" as the basic, obligatory approach of Soviet writers. As the party ideologues reiterate on numerous occasions, only when the writer is guided by party spirit (*partiinost'*) can he understand his place in the historical process and his role and responsibility in the struggles of his time. According to the political authorities, party control is not restricting; rather, it is the very condition of true creative freedom.[118] Literature is necessarily ideological and propagandistic; it must conform to a host of conditions in respect to plot structure and character portrayal, never straying from the party line of the moment. As Andrei Sinyavsky stresses in his essay "On Socialist Realism," Soviet literature and the whole official culture is teleological through and through: its purpose, its very raison d'être, is to speed the coming of Communism.[119]

Needless to say, many talented writers chafe under such limitations. The plethora of underground writings published in the West and the trials of dissident authors tell their own story. Indeed, the tension between writers and patrons common in the West is aggravated in the Soviet Union by the stringent censorship and by the long tradition that imposes a civic obligation on those who choose to write. Yevgeny Yevtushenko asserts: "Perhaps more than the poets of any other nation Russia's poets have been remarkable for their high civic spirit . . . It is no accident that Russia's tyrants regarded Russian poets as their most dangerous enemies . . . To a Russian the word 'poet' has overtones of the word 'fighter.' Russia's poets were always fighters for the future of their country and for justice."[120] The tradition of realistic, *engagé* literature and of the writer as a social critic lives on, shaping the writers' conception of their vocation and thereby contributing to the formation of a critical intelligentsia.

A milestone in the struggle for freedom of artistic expression was the letter submitted by Alexander Solzhenitsyn to the Fourth Congress of Soviet Writers in May 1967, which called for the abolition of censorship.[121] No action was taken on Solzhenitsyn's proposal. Not allowed to publish any of his works in the USSR since the mid-sixties, Solzhenitsyn was expelled from the Writers' Union in November 1969. Yet, the very limitations that censorship and political controls impose upon writers create a degree of solidarity and ideological consciousness among those who feel the restrictions. Not fortuitously, Andrei Sakharov applies an observation from Lewis Coser's *Men of Ideas* to the situation of the Soviet writer: "Many an author who was initially apolitical was drawn to the political left in the United States because the left was in the forefront of the battle against censorship. The close alliance of avant garde art with avant garde political and social radicalism can be accounted for, at least in part, by the fact that they came to be merged in the mind of many as a single battle for freedom against all repression."[122] Just as Coser believes that censorship contributed to the alienation of intellectuals in France and the United States, so Sakharov suggests that such is occurring in the USSR today. If this is so, then the very stringency of censorship and party control is partly responsible for the fostering of a politically conscious and critical intelligentsia.[123]

Several facts testify to the strong links between the critical intellectuals in the arts and those in the academic world. Several of the most widely publicized protests by academics centered around the trials of writers. As we have noted, the trial of Sinyavsky and Daniel in 1966 marked a watershed in the development of the oppositionist movement. Because of the attention which their works may receive, writers in particular may become symbols of the struggle for creative freedom and civil rights in the Soviet Union. Such is the case most notably with Solzhenitsyn, whose "portrait hangs in prominent places in [intellectuals'] living rooms: it is a kind of membership of the 'opposition.' "[124]

Academic intellectuals also make up an important part of the public supporting experimental, original, and critical writing and art. Academicians such as Pyotr Kapitsa, Lev Landau, Igor Tamm, and Nikolai Semyonov publicly supported and defended abstract art, though it was denounced by Khrushchev himself.[125] Noting that young or prominent members of the scientific elite are among the most ardent patrons of abstract art, some have attributed this fact to the congruence between theoretical research and a more "intellectual," less representational form of art.[126] Likewise, scientists and other intellectuals tend to be conspicuous among those favoring more innovative forms of literature. The poet Andrei Voznesensky commented while traveling in France in 1962:

In today's world, in which Sputniks and other extremely complex machines are constructed, there are a vast number of people interested in such things. The people who especially like modern poetry are the young physicists, the young scientists, men who, while they appear very uncomplicated and ordinary, do complex things and are complex people. Thus they don't want overly simple poetry, just as they are not interested in primitive tools.[127]

In short, the Soviet "adversary culture" gains strength from and unites intellectuals in the academic world and those in the arts.

The Power and Influence of Intellectuals

A number of the variables mentioned here as determinants of an intelligentsia have been specified by others as explanatory variables for the creation of class consciousness vis-à-vis the political authorities. It is obvious that certain segments of the intellectual stratum may have an international character and are bound to an international community that extends beyond the borders of any single nation. Although there are parallels between an intelligentsia deriving its principal support from the intellectually involved stratum and the fully conscious working class described by Marx, the differences are significant. Whereas the proletariat engages in material production, the intellectual is employed in the production of nonmaterial objects, in the creation and elaboration of ideas and symbolic forms. The industrial working class has been thought to have revolutionary potential because it is a large class whose members are exploited, share a common low status, and are deprived of effective political power. In contrast, though growing at a rapid rate, the intellectual stratum is much smaller and is relatively "well-to-do," if not privileged, with respect to income and prestige.

Yet, to the extent that intellectuals constitute a critical intelligentsia, they have great potential for inducing social, political, and cultural change. This point was emphatically argued by C. Wright Mills, among others. In "The Decline of the Left," written in 1959, Mills said:

No other group of men is as free [as are intellectuals to make political decisions about their work]; no other group, just now, is as strategically placed for possible innovation as those whose work joins them to the cultural apparatus; to the means of information and knowledge; to the means by which realities are defined, by which programs and politics are elaborated and presented to publics . . .

Intellectuals have created standards and pointed out goals. Then, always, they have looked around for other groups, other circles, other strata to realize them. It is time, now, for us in America to try to realize them ourselves—in our lives, in our own direct action, in the immediate context of our own work.

. . . As intellectuals, we should conduct a continuing, uncompromising criticism of this established culture from the standpoint of—what so-called practical men of affairs call—utopian ideals . . . If we, as intellectuals, do not define and redefine reality, who will?[128]

In his article "The New Left" published the following year, Mills expressed even more forthrightly his conviction that intellectuals should be regarded as the revolutionary class, in effect, by the nascent left movement. Distinguishing himself from contemporary Marxists who regard the working class as the historic agency of radical change, Mills minced no words in pointing to "the really impressive historical evidence that now stands against this expectation" and characterized the belief as a "labor metaphysic," "a legacy from Victorian Marxism that is now quite unrealistic." He proposed that those on the left direct their attention to "the cultural apparatus, the intellectuals—as a possible, immediate, radical agency of change."[129]

To appreciate the intellectuals' potential for social change, it is necessary to consider their functions and their relationships to other social elites and to the body politic generally. A key function of intellectuals is to provide symbolic formulations for the cultural construction of reality. Hence, they have potential for the "restructuring" of man's conception of himself and his society. Beyond that, they may be able to apply sanctions to motivate others to act toward their favored ends. The sanctions which they possess are principally three: power derived from the threat of withholding needed services, influence derived from its possession of high prestige, and value commitments generated through the elaboration of ideology.

With respect to the first sanction, power, it is clear that intellectuals supply services vitally needed by various social collectivities and their elites. At the same time, they are dependent on others for resources, particularly financial support in the form of remuneration or grants. By virtue of this interdependence, they are, at least potentially, not without power. The extent to which they come to exercise power depends on the degree to which their services are needed, the degree to which they constitute a unified monopolistic supplier (that is, control the market), and the degree to which they themselves are dependent upon other services or resources which others supply. Although the state, in the United States and the Soviet Union, is dependent on intellectuals for skills and expertise in many areas, including military research and development, they are, for the most part, many separate suppliers rather than a single monopolistic force. For that reason, their power vis-à-vis the state has been obscured by the more manifest power of the political authorities over them. The relationship, however, is not a constant and may not always be so asymmetrical. Intellectuals, particularly when organized, may be able to exercise considerable leverage vis-à-vis other elite groups, including political leaders.

Contributing to the increased political importance of intellectuals has been the growing significance of science and other branches of knowledge, evidenced by the rapid expansion of those occupational groups that are engaged in knowledge production. These changes, as well as growing numbers in the "service" sector, have led some to posit the beginning of a new social era. Daniel Bell speaks of a "post-industrial" society in which theoretical knowledge becomes the principal source of social and economic change, the "matrix of innovation," and in which the scientific-technological intelligentsia gains great prominence, prestige, and power.[130] In a similar vein, Zbigniew Brzezinski writes of the onset of a "technetronic" age, in which technology and especially electronics increasingly become the principal determinants of social change, altering social structure, values, mores, and the global outlook of society.[131]

The impact of the "scientific-technological revolution" has been gaining greater attention recently by scholars in Communist countries, including the Soviet Union. The most comprehensive and significant of these studies, perhaps, is that conducted by Radovan Richta and his associates in the mid-sixties under the auspices of the Czechoslovakian Academy of Sciences. According to the authors, the work, entitled *Civilization at the Crossroads: Social and Human Implications of the Scientific and Technological Revolution,* was "conceived in an atmosphere of critical, radical searching and intensive discussion on the way forward for a society that has reached industrial maturity while passing through a phase of far-reaching socialist transformation."[132] The central thesis of the study is that "science is emerging as the leading variable in the national economy and [is] the *vital dimension* in the growth of civilization. There are signs of a *new* ("post-industrial") *type of growth,* with a new dynamic stemming from continual structural changes in the productive forces, with the amount of means of production and manpower becoming less important than their changing quality and degree of utilization. Herein lie the intensive elements of growth, the acceleration intimately linked with the onset of the scientific and technological revolution."[133] Amplifying this point, the authors write:

Today it is a commonplace to see the upsurge of science as the feature of our age. Fifty years ago there was nothing in the world to compare with the research centers of today, the network of laboratories, the new towns catering for scientists and universities. Science has penetrated the foundations of contemporary society, infused the dynamics of historical movement so thoroughly that the whole pattern of change appears as a "research revolution" and the coming age as one of "scientific civilization" . . . We discover that the crux lies in the *new status of science.* This type of human activity, which has hitherto served primarily as a factor of *social consciousness,* is now fully and self-evidently proving its worth as a *productive force.*
. . . *all* productive forces are being converted in one way or another into applications of science, which is emerging as the most revolutionary and widespread—and ultimately in effect universal—productive force in society. Therein lies the basis for the new status assumed by science in current civilization processes . . . Science does not operate solely as a factor in the production of things and as an instrument for satisfying wants; it serves equally as a source generating new types of human endeavour, as an initiator and producer of new wants. That is to say, it is a productive force that can create new demands, conflicts and outlooks.
Science owes its new status primarily to its exceptional power of *generalization.* In contrast to other products, a scientific finding is not consumed by use, on the contrary it is improved on—and then "it costs nothing." Moreover, science possesses a peculiar *growth* potential. Every finding is both a result, and then a starting point for further research; the more we know, the more we can find out. This intrinsically exponential quality distinguishes science sharply from all traditional activities of the industrial type.[134]

Coinciding with the scientific-technological revolution are major changes in the occupational structure. Demonstrating the "disparity between the scientific and technological revolution and industrialization," the authors point out, is "the turn to a relative *decline* in the amount of labour absorbed by *industry* and associated activities" and the prospect that the tertiary sector will encompass 40 to 60 per cent of the national labor force in industrial countries in the coming decades, as is already the case in the United States. Particularly noteworthy is the trend of rapid expansion of the labor force engaged in science, research, and development: until recently a fraction of one per cent, these experts now constitute about two per cent in the technologically advanced countries; by the end of the century they may account for 10 per cent, and in the first half of the next century 20 per cent or more.[135]

"The fantastic forecast of a drastic, tenfold expansion in scientific activity made by Prof. Bernal in 1939—received with incredulity at the time— was soon outdone by reality," comment Richta and his associates. "In most industrial countries the work force in science, research and development is doubled within eight to twelve years, and in the USSR in seven years."[136] In the United States, the number of engineers rose from 217,000 in 1930 to nearly a million in 1964, whereas during the same period, the number of scientists increased from 46,000 to 475,000. Otherwise stated, whereas between 1930 and 1965 the general work force increased by about 50 per cent, the number of engineers increased by 370 per cent and that of scientists by 930 per cent.[137] In the Soviet Union the growth of the numbers of scientists and scholars (nauchnye rabotniki) has also been very rapid.[138] Numbering 96,000 in 1939, they increased to 162,500 in 1950, 354,200 in 1960, and 927,400 in 1970.[139] In the past decade, the growth rate has accelerated.[140]

Not only have the knowledge-producing occupations been increasing in number at a phenomenal rate, but such intellectuals have become more conscious of their social role and more widely valued by the general population. A signal event in the United States was the Soviet Union's successful launching of Sputnik in 1957. As Richard Hofstadter observed: "The Sputnik was more than a shock to American national vanity: it brought an immense amount of attention to bear on the consequences of anti-intellectualism in the school system and in American life at large . . . In 1952 [during the height of McCarthyism] only intellectuals seemed much disturbed by the specter of anti-intellectualism; by 1958 the idea that this might be an important and even a dangerous failing was persuasive to most thinking people."[141] In the Soviet Union, too, the success of Sputnik and subsequent achievements have heightened men's awareness of the importance—and "power"—of scientists.

In appraising the social significance of the expanding intellectual stratum, it is important to realize that though the scientist's or scholar's specialized knowledge may be comprehensible only to a relatively few, his personal prestige is widely appreciated. That prestige may provide the basis for the exercise of influence, in the sense specified by Talcott Parsons, or social leadership more generally. According to Parsons, when given information suggesting a course of action but not offering a clear inducement is transmitted by an actor, the receiver differentially appraises the information in terms of the actor's prestige. Prestige, as a code, changes not the content of information but the evaluation of it. If such information is transmitted by someone of higher status, action in accordance with it is more compelling than if it is transmitted by someone of lower status; that is, the message is more "persuasive."[142] Thus, people tend to "look up" to those whom they respect and to defer to their judgments on important matters. In this way, the prestige of knowledge producers contributes to the political and social importance of intellectuals and the critical intelligentsia, both in capitalist and Communist countries.

Significantly, Richta and his associates argue that under socialism it is even *more essential* for intellectuals to be accorded high prestige and allowed freedom of inquiry, since socialism seeks to limit material differences among occupational groups.[143] Yet, as we have noted, such conditions help promote a critical intelligentsia as an independent political force. The authors themselves seem to be aware of, but by no means disturbed by, that possibility. Before the Russian invasion in 1968, they applauded the idea that the expert might become a social critic under these conditions of intellectual freedom.

The expert is of service to socialist society when he points emphatically to the opportunities for advance and to the barriers, when he is fully informed about science, technology and cultural developments in other countries, when he breaks new ground with full confidence that what furthers socialism will find the recognition due to it. The expert who carries out instructions to the letter has no opinions of his own, avoids taking risks, or is timid, absorbed in his own worries and incapable of criticising superiors and subordinates when things need to be pushed ahead, is of no value to socialism. Today all types of society are facing a test of their ability to create the climate needed for free development and universal application of science.[144]

Not without reason, the authors say that the Communist party "will be equal to the task [of political leadership during the scientific-technological revolution] only if it oversteps the narrow bounds of rule by power and the corresponding means of administration," completely reshapes its internal structure, and evolves a "whole range of new, unorthodox approaches and forms." In their view, power pressures and administrative management "served their purpose," but "are incapable of arousing economic activity, stimulating rapid technological advance, and still less of generating scientific discoveries—in fact, they offer the best way of killing such prospects."[145]

The greater impact of intellectuals and the university community on the body politic of many nations is not a function simply of increased numbers, of the vital services provided, or even of increased general social prestige. Serving both to certify other elites as technically competent through their control of formal education, and helping to produce the ideational and cultural resources that various collectivities need, the culture-producing centers and intellectuals have been gaining in their ability to exercise great influence over the other elites, whether in government, the churches, business establishments, or the mass media. They are able more readily to disseminate their values and ideas and assure their acceptance by others in elite positions. Since in the United States the most prestigious within the intellectual world tend to be disproportionately to the left, they are able to influence the beliefs of other less intellectually involved people, both within and outside the university. The most visible and distinguished scholars and scientists constitute important reference individuals for those who respect intellectual accomplishment.[146] This process is more evident in the United States than in the Soviet Union, though even there the political elite is hard pressed to maintain its political hegemony and "charisma" in relation to the expanding, vital, and prestigious stratum of intellectuals.

In the West, the influence of the universities and the intellectual community generally appears with respect to the churches as another chapter in the historic process of secularization. Both the Protestant and Catholic churches are currently under severe internal tensions as they seek to adjust their identity, theology, and ritual to contemporary conditions. Although the complex changes occurring in the churches have a variety of causes, one of the major sources of change stems from the fact that increasingly the leaders of the churches—those concerned, above all, with questions of theology and dogma—conceive of themselves as "intellectuals" and include the secular intellectuals in their reference group.[147] Increasingly, the leaders of the churches appear to seek the approbation of the intellectual community located principally around the universities. While the university is a secular and critical institution which is modern in the sense of constantly being in the forefront of the elaboration of new ideas, churches by their nature emphasize continuity, tradition, and the legitimacy of revelation. Numerous dilemmas confront those churches seeking to maintain belief in revelation and tradition, while also aligning themselves with the critical, innovative approach of the universities. In general, the modernization of many religious denominations reflects the extent to which theology has become a subbranch of the broader intellectual life. Surely the changes in the church have important consequences for the value system of the larger society. Organized religion, rather than being simply a conservative institution, increasingly emerges as an institution pressing for broad social reform, often of a radical nature.

A somewhat analogous problem arises in the Soviet Union where the Communist party seeks to maintain the purity of its Marxist-Leninist ideology, by which the party's "historic" role is justified. In contrast to religious dogma, Marxist-Leninist ideology is purported to be "scientific"—that is, based on empirically verified generalizations rather than revealed truth. According to the official party view, dialectical materialism is sensitive to and dependent on all the accumulated wisdom of science. It is supposed to provide the individual branches of science with a codified world-view and an integrated philosophy. But certain problems are inherent in this identification of ideology with science. As Alexander Vucinich, an American scholar, points out:

It fails to perform the most important task of a philosophy preoccupied with the epistemological problems of science. "It is no accident," states Thomas S. Kuhn, "that the emergence of Newtonian physics in the seventeenth century and of relativity and quantum mechanics in the twentieth should have been both preceded and accompanied by fundamental philosophical analyses of the contemporary research tradition." In relation to science, dialectical materialism is essentially a conservative philosophy—a philosophy too much committed to the proposition of harmonious relations between established ideology and established science to search for and propose new avenues in the development of scientific theory. The primary task of dialectical materialism is to consolidate sacred and secular—ideological and scientific—thought, and to spell out, defend, and extol the superiority of science as a mode of inquiry and a world view. It overlooks the fact that science does not thrive on the dedication of uncritical worshippers but on the work of critical protagonists.[148]

This commitment of the party to the maintenance of ideology in all spheres of life lies at the heart of the troubled relationship between the party and the academics. A true dilemma confronts the party: on the one hand, in order to advance science it seeks to encourage initiative, criticism, and the free expression of original ideas; on the other hand, it attempts to obstruct the expression of ideas or theories which might challenge established ideology.[149] The creation of new knowledge and the construction of improved conceptual schemes carries the threat of "revisionism," whether through incremental emendations or the complete refutation of Marxist propositions. The official contention that Marxist ideology is "scientific" allows critics to challenge both the theory and the political policies on the grounds of science. For example, attacking the idea that it is an "ideological deviation" to express unorthodox ideas, Medvedev declares: "Scientifically speaking, it is senseless and absurd. If ideology is a science, if communism is a science, if Marxism-Leninism is a science, then any criticism of any proposition in these sciences is also a science and not a 'deviation.' In any science, if it is not a collection of empty dogmas, certain propositions are continually going out of date and need to be replaced, new ideas, new propositions are always appearing in connection with new circumstances, new conditions, new relationships."[150] In the long run, it appears likely that the continued cultivation of science in the Soviet Union and other Communist countries will lead to a gradual erosion of ideology, at least in its cruder dogmatic forms.

A second sphere of activity in which the elite shows strong signs of being affected by ties to the intellectual and university world is in the mass media. To an increasing degree in the United States and in other Western countries, the men and women who write for the major papers and journals and who are in charge of broadcasting have the same values and political orientations as the critical intellectuals. As noted earlier, a survey by the Harris Poll of mass media editors reports that 40 per cent describe themselves as "liberals," and only 13 per cent as "conservatives," a pattern which puts them far to the left of the public, but to the right of leading intellectuals. Harris reports, however, that 63 per cent of those in charge of major organs located in the major cities are liberal. It may be argued that those who have risen to prominent positions in the mass media wish to be accepted as intellectuals and, like many contemporary theologians, regard the critical intelligentsia as a key reference group. The change in the outlook of journalists, for instance, has recently been described by A. James Reichley:

> Since World War II the old reporters of the *Front Page* school, whose attitudes were at least as much anti-intellectual as anti-government, have gradually disappeared. The new journalists have tended to be better educated and more professional—and strongly influenced by prevailing currents of opinion in the academic community. The part played by the Ivy League in the intellectual establishment has no doubt been exaggerated, but it is worthy of note that almost one third of the nation's most influential journalists . . . turn out to be graduates of Ivy League schools. Even the top national journalists who are not college graduates . . . operate in a milieu in which liberal intellectual attitudes are pervasive. The suggestion of one critic that many national journalists now function as a kind of "lesser clergy" for the academic elite is not far from correct.[151]

Such men identify prestige with being at the summit of an intellectual institution, not with being successful in business. Since many who work in the mass media identify with the summits of the intellectual world, the "working press" is often composed of individuals sympathetic to social change. Consequently, though the most influential American mass media— the Columbia Broadcasting System, National Broadcasting Company, *Washington Post, New York Times,* and the like—are big business establishments, they increasingly present a sympathetic view of those who seek to change society from the left.

In the Soviet Union, the intellectual community does not exercise a comparable influence on the mass media managers and producers; the party continues to exercise control through agencies such as *Glavlit,* the system of *nomenklatura,* and the like. It would seem, in contrast to the American case, that not finding sympathetic supporters for their views, the Soviet intellectuals try to a considerable extent to circumvent the controlled media altogether. Unpublished Soviet sociological studies indicate that scientists in major research centers rely on foreign radio for reliable news and ignore the Soviet mass media.

A third elite group on which the intellectual community in the West exerts growing influence is the government bureaucracy. Commenting on the way in which the antibusiness values of the intellectuals were undermining the legitimacy of capitalism, Joseph Schumpeter stressed the "direct relationship between the intellectual group and the bureaucracy . . . Except for inhibitions due to professional training and experience, they are therefore open to conversion by the modern intellectual with whom, through a similar education, they have much in common, while the tinge of gentility that in many cases used to raise a barrier [particularly in Europe] has been fading away from the modern civil servant during the last decades. Moreover, in time of rapid expansion of the sphere of public administration, much of the additional personnel required has to be taken directly from the university."[152] The government bureaucracy has become increasingly dependent on the expertise cultivated by the university, so that it is now staffed, particularly at its upper levels, by men with close ties to the university world. Since many of them seek the approbation of that community, they, too, appear responsive to the changing orientations and generally leftist dispositions of prominent figures in the academic world.

In the Soviet Union, intellectuals do not exercise a degree of influence on the political elite which is comparable to that of intellectuals in most Western countries. Party control of institutions of higher education, the Academy of Sciences, and the various professional unions, as well as of the mass media, greatly limits the ability of intellectuals to influence diverse social groups. At the same time, stress upon the preservation of ideological purity and political reliability in the promotion of individuals in the party and state bureaucracies obstructs the spread of values and ideas articulated by critical intellectuals. Yet, it is certain that the governing authorities are relying to an increasing degree upon the specialized competence of highly educated personnel and that the latter are forming a growing proportion of the party membership. The incidence of party membership correlates positively with level of education: the more one's education, the more likely one is to be a member of the CPSU, and the higher one's position within it will probably be.[153] Whereas in 1956 "specialists" (those with higher or specialized secondary education) made up 26 per cent of the party membership, by 1965 they had increased to more than 34 per cent. Graduates of institutions of higher education have come to be particularly highly represented in the party. In 1965, 39 per cent of the 4.6 million graduates were in the party, as compared with 35 per cent of the 2.3 million graduates in 1956.[154] More than 90 per cent of the full members of the Central Committee elected at the Twenty-Third Party Congress in 1966 had a complete higher education.[155] It remains to be seen whether this increasing reliance upon the expertise deriving from education and research in universities and institutes will lead to intellectuals' exerting greater influence on the political leadership. At a number of points we have commented on the dilemma posed for the leadership as it tries to foster intellectual creativity and "development" in the broadest sense, while simultaneously seeking to maintain ideological orthodoxy and discipline. In view of the evidence reviewed, there is every reason to expect that the tension and conflict between creative intellectuals and the party authorities in the Soviet Union will continue.

In the United States, the leadership group most resistant to this trend is business management. One would expect business executives to provide support for conservative values since they manage the dominant economic institutions of the society. Yet, even business and management are beginning to face problems deriving from the functions and prestige of the university. Particularly in capitalist society, as Schumpeter noted, and as was later reiterated by the radical sociologist J. P. Nettl, the business establishment finds it necessary to protect the right of intellectuals to undermine the system. They argued:

> In capitalist society . . . any attack on the intellectuals must run up against the private fortresses of bourgeois business which, or some of which, will shelter the quarry. Moreover such an attack must proceed according to bourgeois principles of legislative and administrative practice which no doubt may be stretched and bent but will checkmate prosecution beyond a certain point. Lawless violence the bourgeois stratum may accept or even applaud when thoroughly roused or frightened, but only temporarily . . . because the freedom it disapproves cannot be crushed without also crushing the freedom it approves . . .
>
> From this follows both the unwillingness and the inability of the capitalist order to control its intellectual sector effectively . . . the intellectual group cannot help nibbling . . . and criticism of persons and of current events will, in a situation in which nothing is sacrosanct, fatally issue in criticism of classes and institutions . . .
>
> In defending the intellectuals as a group—not of course every individual— the bourgeoisie defends itself and its scheme of life. Only a government of a non-bourgeois nature and non-bourgeois creed—under modern circumstances only a socialist or fascist one—is strong enough to discipline them.[156]

One cannot preclude the possibility of a fascist reaction to severe challenges from the intelligentsia, but in the United States at least, as David Riesman has suggested, it appears that the top business executives show increasing respect and concern for "intellectual values" as articulated by those in universities.[157] Being respectful of intellectuals and sharing at least certain of their values, the business elite is significantly affected by criticism emanating from the academy and the intellectual world. Preliminary results from the Columbia University study of the American elite, directed by Charles Kadushin and Alan Barton, strongly reinforce these assumptions.

In the Soviet Union, the influence of the academic world and the critical intelligentsia appears weaker in respect to the state economic managers. For one thing, the process of self-selection noted by Frederich Hayek in the United States is probably even more pronounced in the USSR. The more "intellectual" and critical men and women prefer to engage in research far removed from the exigencies of management. Also, political reliability continues to be a major criterion for promotion in the bureaucracy; consequently, those at the top show a strong commitment to the established ideology and its principal tenets. Although some are critical of certain aspects of the economic system, their criticism is often of a narrow and technical nature. However, such a "technocratic" critique has some points of congruence with the ideological propositions of various members of the scientific community.[158]

Conclusion

Intellectuals and their apprentices, university students, have never been as numerous as they are today. Given the increased requirement of post-industrial society for university-trained people and continuing high levels of innovative research, the university is needed more than ever before. While the society is becoming more dependent on intellectuals, it is also more influenced by them.

It may be argued that the growth of critical intelligentsia disposed to support the "adversary culture" and reject the worth of dominant political and economic institutions is undermining the capacity of governing systems in modern societies to maintain social equilibrium. Leadership itself, the primary function of authority, is under question by intellectuals every-where. Castro, Mao, Tito, Franco, the Greek colonels, the leaders of West-ern Europe, no less than those who head the governments of the United States and the Soviet Union, find themselves at odds with their intellec-tuals.

The critical intellectual denies the possibility of participating in govern-ment without betraying the ideals of the society. Faced with attacks on their legitimacy from intellectuals and students, many in the governing elites exhibit a failure of nerve. They find it difficult to ignore or suppress groups whose values of scientific and intellectual progress they are com-mitted to. The basic tensions, the contradictions within the system, come increasingly from within the elite itself—from its own intellectual leaders supported by large segments of its student children. If in Hegelian terms the contradiction of capitalism was its dependence on an ever growing working class brought together in large factories, the contradiction of post-industrial society, whether Communist or non-Communist, may be its dependence on trained intelligence, on research and innovation, which re-quires it to bring together large numbers of intellectuals and students on great campuses and in a few intellectual communities located at the centers of communication and influence.

We would like to acknowledge a grant from the Ford Foundation for the study of intellectual life being conducted under the auspices of the Center for International Affairs of Harvard University. We have also drawn on data collected for the Carnegie Commission on Higher Education in its survey of the opinions and behavior of American academics, now being analyzed by Everett Ladd and Lipset with the support of the Commission.

REFERENCES

1. Leszek Kołakowski, "Intellectuals and the Communist Movement," in his *Marxism and Beyond* (London: Pall Mall Press, 1968), p. 179.

2. Joseph Schumpeter, *Capitalism, Socialism and Democracy* (New York: Harper Torchbooks, 1962), p. 150.

3. Lewis A. Coser, *Men of Ideas* (New York: Free Press, 1970), p. viii. For a discussion of various definitions see Ronald Berman, *America in the Sixties: An Intellectual History* (New York: Free Press, 1968), pp. 10-16.

4. Lionel Trilling, *Beyond Culture* (New York: Viking Press, 1965), pp. xii-xiii.

5. Henry May, *The Discontent of the Intellectuals: A Problem of the Twenties* (Chicago: Rand McNally, 1963); Richard Hofstadter, *Anti-Intellectualism in American Life* (New York: Knopf, 1963); F. A. Hayek, "The Intellectuals and Socialism," *University of Chicago Law Review*, 16 (Spring 1949), 417-433; Daniel Aaron, *Writers on the Left* (New York: Harcourt, Brace, and World, 1961); Reinhold Niebuhr, "Liberals and the Marxist Heresy," in George B. de Huszar, ed., *The Intellectuals* (New York: Free Press, 1960), pp. 302-307; Ludwig von Mises, "The Resentment and the Anti-Capitalistic Bias of American Intellectuals," *ibid.*, pp. 365-370.

6. Richard Hofstadter, "Discussion," in A. Alvarez, *Under Pressure* (Baltimore: Penguin Books, 1965), pp. 111-112; Whitelaw Reid, "The Scholar in Politics," *Scribner's Monthly*, 6 (1873), 613-614.

7. Charles Francis Adams, ed., *The Works of John Adams*, VIII (Boston: Little, Brown, 1853), 596. Thomas Jefferson, *Writings*, ed. A. E. Bergh, VI (Washington, 1907), 257-258, as cited in Hofstadter, *Anti-Intellectualism in American Life*, p. 155. For a discussion of the role of intellectuals in helping to form the American national identity after the Revolution, and the early use of "anti-intellectualism" by the politicians of both parties, see S. M. Lipset, "The Role of the Intellectuals," in *The First New Nation: The United States in Comparative and Historical Perspective* (Garden City, N.Y.: Doubleday-Anchor, 1967), pp. 75-85. For an analysis of the "desertion of the intellectuals" in Jacksonian America, of the emergence of "a pervading sense at once of alienation and of longing, which, one way or another, controls their work, directly if they are political writers, obliquely and at many removes if they are poets," see Arthur M. Schlesinger, Jr., *The Age of Jackson* (Boston: Little, Brown, 1946), pp. 369-390.

8. "Text of a Pre-Inauguration Memo from Moynihan on Problems Nixon Would Face," *New York Times*, March 11, 1970, p. 30.

9. *Memoirs of Herbert Hoover, 1920-1933* (New York: Macmillan, 1952), p. 202.

10. James Reston, "Washington on Kennedy's Discontented Intellectuals," *New York Times*, October 8, 1961, p. 10E. For a discussion of the bitterness of many intellectuals against Kennedy before the 1960 election as representing the same thing as Nixon, see Berman, *America in the Sixties*, pp. 4-5. Describing the nonemotional quality of John Kennedy before he took office, James MacGregor Burns stated prophetically: "If he should die tomorrow in a plane crash, he would become at once a liberal martyr, for the liberal publicists of the land would rush to construct a hero." James MacGregor Burns, "Candidate on the Eve: Liberalism Without Tears," *New Republic*, 143 (October 31, 1960), 16.

11. Henry A. Kissinger, "The Policymaker and the Intellectual," *The Reporter,* 20 (March 5, 1959), 34. On the intellectual as "counterexpert," see Peter Berger and Thomas Luckman, *The Social Construction of Reality* (Garden City, N.Y.: Doubleday, 1966), p. 116.

12. Israel Shenker, "U.S. Cast Saddens Novelist," *New York Times,* December 1, 1969, p. 43.

13. Hofstadter, *Anti-Intellectualism in American Life,* p. 39.

14. For a report of various studies bearing on this point see S. M. Lipset, *Political Man* (Garden City: Doubleday, 1960), pp. 310-343. A more recent comprehensive survey of analyses of the political attitudes and behavior of American academe closely linked to the concerns of this article is Lipset, "Academia and Politics in America," in T. J. Nossiter, ed., *Imagination and Precision in the Social Sciences* (London: Faber, 1972), pp. 211-289.

15. Lipset has elaborated on these themes in the American value system with reference to the work of analysts such as Tocqueville, Martineau, Bryce, Hartz, Riesman, and others in his *The First New Nation: The United States in Historical and Comparative Perspective,* and *Revolution and Counterrevolution* (Garden City: Doubleday-Anchor, 1970).

16. Frank Freidel, "Dissent in the Spanish-American War and the Phillipine Insurrection," in Samuel Eliot Morison and others, *Dissent in Three American Wars* (Cambridge, Mass.: Harvard University Press, 1970), p. 77.

17. B. P., "College Professors and the Public," *Atlantic Monthly,* 89 (March 1902), 286.

18. Whitelaw Reid, *American and English Studies,* I (New York: Scribner's, 1913), 241-242.

19. For references, see S. M. Lipset, *Rebellion in the University* (Boston: Little, Brown, 1972), pp. 148-151.

20. Randolph Bourne, *Youth and Life* (Boston: Houghton, Mifflin, 1913), p. 295.

21. John Reed, "The Harvard Renaissance," *The Harvard Progressive* (March 1939), p. 22. This essay was written in 1912.

22. James H. Leuba, *The Belief in God and Immortality* (Chicago: Open Court Publishing Co., 1921), pp. 219-287.

23. May, *The Discontent of the Intellectuals,* p. 19.

24. For references, see Lipset, *Rebellion in the University,* p. 162.

25. Granville Hicks, *Where We Came Out* (New York: Viking, 1954), p. 165. For a more recent analysis by a Marxist on the revived radicalism of the intellectuals of the 1920's, see Martin J. Sklar, "On the Proletarian Revolution and the End of Political-Economic Society," *Radical America,* 3 (May-June 1969), 23-36.

26. See David Felix, *Protest: Sacco-Vanzetti and the Intellectuals* (Bloomington: Indiana University Press, 1965).

27. *Ibid.,* p. 16.

28. Ernest Earnest, *Academic Procession* (Indianapolis: Bobbs-Merrill, 1953), p. 279.

29. See especially Eugene Lyons, *The Red Decade: The Stalinist Penetration of America* (Indianapolis: Bobbs-Merrill, 1941), p. 129.

30. Aaron, *Writers on the Left,* pp. 196-198.

31. Daniel Bell, "The Background and Development of Marxian Socialism in the United States," in Donald D. Egbert and Stow Persons, *Socialism and American Life,* I (Princeton: Princeton University Press, 1952), 353-354; see also Irving Howe and Lewis Coser, "The Intellectuals Turn Left," *The American Communist Party: A Critical History* (Boston: Beacon Press, 1957), pp. 273-318.

32. Morris L. Ernst and David Loth, *Report on the American Communist* (New York: Holt, 1952), pp. 3-4.

33. For these studies see Lipset, *Political Man,* pp. 314-318.

34. For a report on this study and other surveys conducted during the 1930's, see Lipset, *Rebellion in the University,* p. 184 and pp. 178-182.

35. Gardner Murphy and Rensis Likert, *Public Opinion and the Individual* (New York: Harper, 1938), pp. 107-108.

36. Philip Rahv, "American Intellectuals in the Postwar Situation," reprinted in his *Literature and the Sixth Sense* (Boston: Houghton, Mifflin, 1969), pp. 176-177.

37. *Political Man,* pp. 341-343.

38. John Kenneth Galbraith, "An Adult's Guide to New York, Washington and Other Exotic Places," *New York,* 4 (November 15, 1971), 52.

39. These studies are reported and cited in Lipset, "Academia and Politics in America," pp. 211-289.

40. Trilling, *Beyond Culture,* pp. xii-xiii. For documentation from novels, see John Chamberlain, "The Businessman in Fiction," *Fortune,* 38 (November 1948), 134-148.

41. Charles Kadushin, Julie Hover, and Monique Tichy, "How and Where to Find Intellectual Elite in the United States," *Public Opinion Quarterly,* 35 (Spring 1971), 1-18.

42. The academic data are from the massive (60,000 sample) survey of American professors conducted by the Carnegie Commission on Higher Education which is being analyzed by Everett Ladd and Lipset. References to various findings from that study are reported in Lipset, "Academia and Politics in America." The data on the major intellectuals are from the Kadushin study cited in the previous note. The information on the culture critics and editors is from a study conducted by the Harris Poll in 1969, as reported in a newspaper release issued by the United Church of Christ, March 16, 1970. The leading scholars from the Carnegie study are those who have published ten or more books or articles in the past two years and are located at "elite schools" as defined by their standards for admitting students and amount of research funds and revenue.

43. Bernard Gwertzman, "Brezhnev Is Given Ovation as Congress Votes Report," *New York Times,* April 6, 1971, p. 3.

44. On the early meaning of the word "intelligentsia" see Alan P. Pollard, "The Russian Intelligentsia: The Mind of Russia," *California Slavic Studies,* 3 (1964), 1-32. For further references see Michael Confino, "On Intellectuals and Intellec-

tual Traditions in Eighteenth- and Nineteenth-Century Russia," *Dædalus* (Spring 1972), pp. 117-149.

45. Confino, "On Intellectuals and Intellectual Traditions," pp. 138 ff. Cf. George Fisher, "The Intelligentsia and Russia," in Cyril E. Black, ed., *The Transformation of Russian Society: Aspects of Social Change Since 1861* (Cambridge, Mass.: Harvard University Press, 1967), p. 262.

46. Nadezhda Mandelstam, *Hope Against Hope: A Memoir,* trans. Max Hayward (New York: Atheneum, 1970), p. 165.

47. *Ibid.,* p. 168.

48. " 'Doctor Zhivago': Letter to Boris Pasternak from the Editors of *Novyi Mir,*" in Richard Pipes, ed., *The Russian Intelligentsia* (New York: Columbia University Press, 1961), p. 224.

49. On the literary ferment of the fifties, see Harold Swayze, *Political Control of Literature in the USSR, 1946-1959* (Cambridge, Mass.: Harvard University Press, 1962) and Robert Conquest, *The Pasternak Affair* (New York: Lippincott, 1962). On the literary situation in the early sixties, see Priscilla Johnson, *Khrushchev and the Arts: The Politics of Soviet Culture, 1962-1964,* with documents selected and edited by Priscilla Johnson and Leopold Labedz (Cambridge, Mass.: MIT Press, 1965); and Patricia Blake and Max Hayward, eds., *Dissonant Voices in Soviet Literature* (New York: Harper and Row, 1964) and *Halfway to the Moon: New Writing from Russia* (New York: Anchor Books, 1965).

50. Andrei Amalrik, *Will the Soviet Union Survive Until 1984?* with an introduction by Leopold Labedz, letters, commentaries, and notes (New York: Perennial Library, 1971), pp. 8-9. The *samizdat* materials (typewritten manuscripts or photo-copied material that are circulated through informal social networks) are diverse, ranging from verses by obscure poets and the unpublished works by Alexander Solzhenitsyn, to detailed accounts of recent political developments and of the trials of dissidents. See the following anthologies: Abram Brumberg, ed., *In Quest of Justice: Protest and Dissent in the Soviet Union* (New York: Praeger, 1970); *Samizdat I: La voix de l'opposition communiste en U.R.S.S.* (Paris: Combats, 1969); and Michel Slavinsky, ed., *La Presse clandestine en U.R.S.S., 1960-1970* (Paris: Nouvelles Editions Latines, 1970). The best available guide to published and unpublished *samizdat* materials in English and Russian appears to be *The Radio Liberty Register of Samizdat,* Reference Handbook No. 76, compiled by Albert Boiter and Peter Dornan, Research Department, Radio Liberty, February 1971.

51. Sinyavsky and Daniel were arrested in September 1965, and tried in February 1966, at which time they were sentenced to seven and five years respectively, in strict regime labor camps, for having published their books abroad. Documents on the trial are found in *On Trial: The Soviet State versus "Abram Tertz" and "Nikolai Arzhak,"* translated and edited with an introduction by Max Hayward, revised, enlarged edition (New York: Harper and Row, 1967). Works by Abram Tertz (Andrei Sinyavsky) include *Fantastic Stories* (New York: Pantheon Books, 1963), *The Trial Begins and On Socialistic Realism* (New York: Vintage Books, 1965), and *The Makepeace Experiment* (New York: Vintage Books, 1965). The story "This Is Moscow Speaking" by Nikolai Arzhak (Yuli Daniel) is found in Blake and Hayward, eds., *Dissonant Voices in Soviet Literature.*

52. Amalrik, *Will the Soviet Union Survive Until 1984?* p. 9. See Viacheslav Chornovil,

The Chornovil Papers (New York: McGraw-Hill, 1968); and Anatoly Marchenko, *My Testimony* (New York: Delta, 1971). Amalrik, too, was arrested, tried, and sentenced in 1970 for publishing "anti-Soviet" works—notably, his essay, cited above. His previous conviction and exile under the earlier "anti-parasite" laws are described in Andrei Amalrik, *Involuntary Journey to Siberia* (New York: Harcourt, Brace and Jovanovich, 1971). The trials themselves gave little evidence of the magnitude of the struggle being waged. On the widespread use of "administrative sanctions," see the recent account by An Observer, *Message From Moscow*, with a new Epilogue "Russian Intellectuals in the Leninist Year" (New York: Vintage Books, 1971), esp. pp. 44-90, 289ff; and the account of psychiatric detention for political reasons by Zhores A. and Roy A. Medvedev, *A Question of Madness* (New York: Knopf, 1971).

53. Amalrik, *Will the Soviet Union Survive Until 1984?* pp. 10–13. Amalrik dates the Democratic movement from 1968, the time of the extensive public protests over the violations of legality in the trial of Galanskov, Ginzburg, and others. Some of the documents from this period are found in Brumberg, ed., *In Quest of Justice*, pp. 93-182.

54. For some materials by and about Kosterin, Grigorenko, and Yakhimovich, see Brumberg, ed., *In Quest of Justice*.

55. Relevant documents are found in Michael Bourdeaux, *Patriarch and Prophets* (New York: Praeger, 1970).

56. See Pavel Litvinov, *The Demonstration in Pushkin Square* (Boston: Gambit, 1969) and Karel van het Reve, *Dear Comrade: Pavel Litvinov and the Voices of Soviet Citizens in Dissent* (New York: Pitman, 1969). See also Andrei D. Sakharov, *Progress, Coexistence and Intellectual Freedom*, with an introduction and notes by Harrison E. Salisbury (New York: W. W. Norton, 1968) and "Appeal of Soviet Scientists to the Party-Government Leaders of the USSR," an Open Letter from A. D. Sakharov, V. F. Turchin, R. A. Medvedev (dated March 19, 1970), *Survey*, 76 (Summer 1970), 160-170.

57. An English translation of *The Chronicle of Current Events* is published regularly by Amnesty International in London. A number of other serial *samizdat* "publications" have also appeared. Among these are *Iskhod* (Exodus), which is devoted to the struggle of Jews for their rights; *Politicheskoi devnik* (Political diary), which evidently circulates among those in political positions, perhaps within the party *apparat*; *Veche* (named after the ancient Russian popular assembly), which has a strongly Slavophilistic orientation; and *Obshchestvennye problemy* (Social problems), edited by Valery Chalidze, a founding member of the Committee for Human Rights, whose viewpoint and concerns it largely mirrors.

58. "The Committee for Human Rights in the USSR," *Chronicle of Current Events*, 17 (London, April 1971), 45-46.

59. *Ibid.*, p. 47, and Bernard Gwertzman, "Three in Russia Move to Defend Rights," *New York Times*, November 16, 1970, pp. 1, 8.

60. Amalrik, *Will the Soviet Union Survive Until 1984?* pp. 14-15.

61. Among Soviet sociologists, the most widely accepted and authoritative view appears to be that formulated by M. N. Rutkevich: "By intelligentsia (in the narrow, direct sense) in a socialist society we understand the social group, [or] segment (*sloi*), consisting of individuals who are professionally employed in the performance

190 S. M. LIPSET AND R. B. DOBSON

of highly-qualified mental labor which requires specialized secondary or higher education." M. N. Rutkevich, "Intelligentsiia kak sotsial'naia gruppa i ee sblizhenie s rabochim klassom" (The intelligentsia as a social group and its rapprochement with the working class), in Ts. A. Stepanian and V. S. Semenov, eds., *Sotsial'nye klassy, sloi, i gruppy v SSSR* (Social classes, segments, and groups in the USSR) (Moscow: Nauka, 1968), pp. 136-137. Most Soviet sociologists characterize the intelligentsia as a "segment" (*sloi*), rather than a social class (*klass*), and regard the main components of Soviet society as two classes of manual workers— the working class and the collective farm peasantry—and a nonmanual "segment." Occasionally, some sociologists still include all nonmanual workers in the intelligentsia (that is, both specialists and less qualified white-collar workers), while others define it more narrowly than Rutkevich. As noted, however, the dominant tendency is to follow Rutkevich in distinguishing between the intelligentsia composed of specialists and the less qualified white-collar workers (*sluzhashchi*). According to the criteria of Rutkevich's definition, some fifteen million persons would be included in the Soviet "intelligentsia." For an overview and critique of various social scientists' conceptions of the intelligentsia, see Stepanian and Semenov, eds., *Sotsial'nye klassy, sloi, i gruppy v SSSR*, esp. pp. 136-143, and P. P. Amelin, *Intelligentsiia i sotsializm* (The intelligentsia and socialism) (Leningrad: Leningrad University Press, 1970), esp. pp. 40-44. A detailed discussion of these problems is found in Zev Katz, *The Soviet Sociologists' Debate on Social Structure in the U.S.S.R.* (Cambridge, Mass.: Center for International Studies, Massachusetts Institute of Technology, December 1971). Complementing this study is his forthcoming *Part II: Soviet Dissenters' Views on Social Structure in the U.S.S.R.* We are particularly indebted to Dr. Katz for sharing with us his insights on the Soviet Union and bringing to our attention relevant material.

62. S. A. Kugel', "Izmenenie sotsial'noi struktury sotsialisticheskogo obshchestva pod vozdeistviem nauchno-tekhnicheskoi revoliutsii" (Change in the social structure of socialist society through the influence of the scientific-technological revolution), *Voprosy filosofii*, no. 3 (1969), 16.

63. Amelin, *Intelligentsiia i sotsializm*, pp. 41-44.

64. Igor Kon, "Razmyshleniia ob amerikanskoi intelligentsii" (Reflections on the American intelligentsia), *Novy Mir*, no. 1 (1968), 179.

65. An Observer, *Message From Moscow*, p. 199.

66. Sakharov, *Progress, Coexistence, and Intellectual Freedom*, pp. 27-28.

67. *Ibid.*, p. 25.

68. *Ibid.*, p. 30.

69. Zhores A. Medvedev, "Fruitful Meetings Between Scientists of the World," in *The Medvedev Papers*, trans. Vera Rich, with a foreword by John Ziman, F.R.S. (London: Macmillan St. Martins Press, 1971), pp. 170-171. Emphasis added.

70. *Ibid.*, p. 171.

71. "Appeal of Soviet Scientists to the Party-Government Leaders of the USSR," an Open Letter from Sakharov, Turchin, Medvedev, p. 165.

72. Jonathan Harris, "The Dilemma of Dissidence," *Survey*, 16 (Winter 1971), 107.

73. Yevgeny Yevtushenko, *A Precocious Autobiography*, trans. Andrew R. MacAndrew

(New York: E. P. Dutton, 1964), pp. 91-92. Indeed, no one in Russia was unaffected by the death of the dictator. For instance, as a retired school-teacher told Maurice Hindus in 1958: "In the time of Stalin, teaching history was a simple matter: all I had to do was to stick to Anna Pankratova's texts like a fly to paper and no one could make trouble for me. But soon after Stalin's death, academicians, historians, and ideologists began to denounce Pankratova's fables and to wrangle over how best to present our history to the younger generation. It was a trying time for history teachers." Because of the perplexities of the historians over a new history textbook, Hindus reports, there were no school examinations in the subject in the spring of 1953. Maurice Hindus, *House Without a Roof: Russia After Forty-Three Years of Revolution* (Garden City, N.Y.: Doubleday, 1961), pp. 325-326.

74. Furthermore, the task of rendering experience meaningful may easily merge with that of creating ideology, since such interpretations embody values, ideals which can be generalized. It is in terms of the generalization of values inherent in a creative work that one can understand the impact, for instance, of the short novel by Alexander Solzhenitsyn, *One Day in the Life of Ivan Denisovich*. The publication of his novel in the fall of 1962, during one of those ephemeral bloomings of "liberalization," was a literary event of the first magnitude. Solzhenitsyn's portrayal of the quiet dignity of a simple worker in one of the labor camps, based upon his personal experience, perhaps came closer to the life experiences of millions of Soviet citizens than any work which they had read. The condemnation of Stalinism contained in the work is implicit, but strong. In 1963, although he had reportedly given his personal approval for publication of the novel, Khrushchev stated with consternation that literary magazines had received about 10,000 novels, short stories, and memoirs on the theme of labor camps. Soon it was said, "Tell me your attitude about Ivan Denisovich, and I will tell you who you are." The last two points are reported in Mihajlo Mihajlov, *Moscow Summer*, introduction, notes, and biographical information by Andrew Field (New York: Farrar, Straus and Giroux, 1965), pp. 66, 128. Cf. Mandelstam, *Hope Against Hope*, pp. 287-289, and see "How People Read *One Day*" (A Survey of Letters, by Alexander Solzhenitsyn), in Leopold Labedz, ed., *Solzhenitsyn: A Documentary Record* (New York: Harper and Row), pp. 21-37.

75. Cf. Amalrik, *Will the Soviet Union Survive Until 1984?* p. 17. Amalrik asserts that as a consequence of their need and respect for law, professionals in general constitute "the basic stratum of any society on which a democratic regime bases itself."

76. Mandelstam, *Hope Against Hope*, pp. 331-333.

77. N. Sviridov, "Party Concern for the Upbringing of the Scientific-Technical Intelligentsia," *Kommunist*, 18 (December 1968), as translated in *The Current Digest of the Soviet Press*, 21 (January 22, 1969), 5.

78. Sakharov, *Progress, Coexistence, and Intellectual Freedom*, pp. 54-55.

79. François Fejto, "Les intellectuels et la politique: pays de l'est: revendication du droit à la critique," *Le monde diplomatique*, 19 (October 1970), 11-12. For detailed analyses of the Czech events see Dušan Hamšik, *Writers Against Rulers* (New York: Vintage Books, 1971) and Vladimir V. Kusin, *The Intellectual Origins of the Prague Spring: The Development of Reformist Ideas in Czechoslovakia, 1956-1967* (London: Cambridge University Press, 1971). For a discussion of the relationship of Communism to intellectuals in many countries, including the West,

In research, the obscure writer or thinker is preferred as a subject to the well-known one.

"In everything the light-weight peripheral project is preferred; it is less likely to attract attention, and hence there is a greater chance of honesty." An Observer, *Message From Moscow*, pp. 223-224.

104. Zev Katz, "Sociology in the Soviet Union," *Problems of Communism*, 20 (May-June 1971), 38-40. Katz notes, too, that "in contrast to the situation in the literary field, not a single piece of sociological writing suppressed in the USSR has been published abroad; there is not a single Soviet sociologist who is an expatriate in the West; nor do the signatures of Soviet sociologists usually appear on protest documents. This would seem to indicate that even the most critical members of the Soviet sociological community accept the basic principles of socialism as their point of departure, although many of them, one suspects, would like to see—and promote —an evolution of the system in the direction of the humanist ideals of Marxism and the Bolshevik Revolution. When they are critical, their criticism and their constructive proposals for change appear to be motivated by such a desire rather than by any thought of overthrowing the system altogether. Indeed, such an attitude may be an indispensible precondition for a major contribution by sociology to a positive transformation of Soviet society." (p. 28) It is possible that since many Soviet sociologists produce findings which often sharply challenge the official ideology in the course of their normal scientific work (for example, that school grades, dropping out, and university attendance correlate highly with parental socioeconomic status, that high school youth disdain manual and rural employment, and the like), they may feel it necessary to pretend to a greater formal ideological loyalty than do those whose work, as such, does not touch the party line. For a discussion of the factors which make sociology the most "adversary" discipline in western academe, see Lipset and Ladd, "The Politics of American Sociologists."

105. Jean-Paul Sartre, *What Is Literature?* (New York: Philosophical Library, 1949), pp. 81-82. Emphases in original.

106. Hannah Arendt, *Between Past and Future* (New York: Viking Press, 1961), pp. 201-204; see also pp. 197-226. For a general analysis, see Ferdinand Kolegar, "Literary Intellectuals and the Politics of Perfection," *Indian Sociological Bulletin*, 3 (October 1965), 79-90.

107. William Kornhauser, *The Politics of Mass Society* (Glencoe: Free Press, 1959), pp. 186-187.

108. William B. Hixson, Jr., *Moorfield Storey and the Abolitionist Tradition* (New York: Oxford University Press, 1972), p. 36. See also Kermit Vanderbilt, *Charles Eliot Norton: Apostle of Culture in a Democracy* (Cambridge, Mass.: Harvard University Press, 1959), pp. 194-220.

109. Joseph Gusfield, "Intellectual Character and the American Universities," *The Journal of General Education*, 14 (January 1963), 234.

110. Quoted in Wilson Record, "The American Intellectual as Black Sheep and Red Rover," *Bulletin of the American Association of University Professors*, 40 (Winter 1954-1955), 538-539. In commenting on the French scene in 1896, Adams wrote: "No common interest can ever reunite rich and poor, clerical and atheist, bourgeois and artist." W. C. Ford, ed., *Letters of Henry Adams* (Boston: Houghton, Mifflin, 1938), p. 114.

111. John P. Diggins, *Mussolini and Fascism: The View from America* (Princeton: Princeton University Press, 1972), pp. 209-260; see also Thomas Molnar, "The Intellectual as a Reactionary," in his *The Decline of the Intellectual* (Cleveland: Meridian Books, 1961), pp. 157-198.

112. J. R. Harrison, *The Reactionaries* (London: Gollancz, 1966), pp. 25-26.

113. James Ackerman, "The Demise of the *Avant Garde:* Notes on the Sociology of Recent American Art," *Comparative Studies in Society and History,* 11 (October 1969), 371-384.

114. Daniel Bell, "The Cultural Contradictions of Capitalism," *The Public Interest,* no. 21 (Fall 1970), 21.

115. Tom Wolfe, *Radical Chic & Mau-mauing the flak catchers* (New York: Farrar, Straus and Giroux, 1970).

116. Trilling, *Beyond Culture,* p. xv. For a description and analysis of the diverse forms of tension between the literary world and the "modern economic personality" from the early nineteenth century to the present see César Graña, "Social Optimism and Literary Depression," in his *Fact and Symbol* (New York: Oxford University Press, 1971), pp. 3-64.

117. On the political functions of the Writers' Union under Stalin, see Jack F. Matlock, Jr., "The 'Governing Organs' of the Union of Soviet Writers," *American Slavic and East European Review,* 15 (1956), 382-399.

118. For example, A. Rumiantsev, "The Party Spirit of the Creative Labor of the Soviet Intelligentsia," *Pravda,* September 9, 1965, translated in *The Current Digest of the Soviet Press,* 17, no. 36 (September 29, 1965), 3-6.

119. Abram Tertz (Andrei Sinyavsky), *The Trial Begins and On Socialist Realism,* pp. 150ff.

120. Yevtushenko, *A Precocious Autobiography,* pp. 88-89.

121. Document 49, in Brumberg, ed., *In Quest of Justice,* pp. 245-247. As Solzhenitsyn's letter states, in part, "Under the obfuscating label of *Glavlit,* this censorship—which is not provided for in the Constitution and is therefore illegal, and which is nowhere publicly labeled as such—imposes a yoke on our literature and gives people unversed in literature arbitrary control over writers . . . Literature cannot develop between the categories of 'permitted' and 'not permitted,' 'about this you may write' and 'about this you may not.' Literature that is not the breath of contemporary society, that dares not transmit the pains and fears of that society, that does not warn in time against threatening moral and social dangers—such literature does not deserve the name of literature; it is only a façade."

122. Sakharov, *Progress, Coexistence, and Intellectual Freedom,* p. 62. Sakharov derived the quotation from Kon, "Razmyshleniia ob amerikanskoi intelligentsii," 190-191.

123. Coser, *Men of Ideas,* pp. 95-97.

124. An Observer, *Message From Moscow,* p. 307.

125. Parry, *The New Class Divided,* pp. 263-264.

126. *Ibid.,* pp. 264-265.

127. Cited *ibid.*, p. 265.

128. C. Wright Mills, *Power, Politics, and People: The Collected Essays of C. Wright Mills,* edited with an introduction by Irving Louis Horowitz (New York: Oxford University Press, 1970), pp. 231-233.

129. *Ibid.,* p. 256.

130. Daniel Bell's views have been widely published. See, for instance, his recent articles, "Technocracy and Politics," *Survey,* 17 (Winter 1971), 1-24, and "The Post-Industrial Society: The Evolution of an Idea," *Survey,* 18 (Spring 1971), 102-168. For an alternative view, see Alain Touraine, *The Post Industrial Society* (New York: Random House, 1971).

131. Zbigniew Brzezinski, *Between Two Ages: America's Role in the Technetronic Era* (New York: Viking Press, 1971).

132. Richta and others, *Civilization at the Crossroads,* p. 21.

133. *Ibid.,* p. 39.

134. *Ibid.,* pp. 212, 213, 217. Emphasis in text.

135. *Ibid.,* pp. 120-124.

136. *Ibid.,* p. 217.

137. Daniel Bell, "The Measurement of Knowledge and Technology," in Eleanor Bernert Sheldon and Wilbert E. Moore, eds., *Indicators of Social Change: Concepts and Measurements* (New York: Russell Sage Foundation, 1968), pp. 201-202.

138. The Soviet category "scientific worker" *(nauchnyi rabotnik)* includes a wide variety of specialized workers. According to current usage by the Central Statistical Administration, the definition encompasses Academicians, full members and corresponding members of all academies, all persons with a higher degree of candidate or doctor of sciences or with the academic title of professor, associate professor *(dosent)*, assistant professor, senior research worker *(nauchnyi sotrudnik)*, junior research worker, irrespective of the place or nature of their work, and also persons conducting research work in research establishments or carrying out research and teaching in institutions of higher education, regardless of whether they have higher degrees or academic titles, as well as specialists without a higher degree who carry out research at enterprises and project organizations. E. Zaleski and others, *Science Policy in the USSR* (Paris: Organization for Economic Co-operation and Development, 1969), p. 543. On earlier definitions, see Alexander G. Korol, *Soviet Research and Development: Its Organization, Personnel, and Funds* (Cambridge, Mass.: MIT Press, 1965), pp. 76-78.

139. T. H. Rigby, *Communist Party Membership in the U.S.S.R., 1917-1967* (Princeton: Princeton University Press, 1968), p. 442; Central Statistical Administration, *Narodnoe Khoziaistvo SSSR v 1969 g.* (Moscow: Statistika, 1970), p. 694; Central Statistical Administration, *SSSR v tsifrakh v 1970 gody: kratkii statisticheskii sbornik* (Moscow: Statistika, 1971), p. 191.

140. Thus, from the end of 1960 through 1966—that is, in the course of six years— the number of scientific workers doubled, whereas during the fifties, such doubling took ten years. On the average, according to S. A. Kugel', the number of scientific workers has been growing by more than 12 per cent annually, faster than any other social-occupational group. In comparison, the number of workers and em-

ployees as a whole has been increasing by just 4.3 per cent a year, and industrial workers by 3.5 per cent. In some fields the growth rate has been even more intensive. During the early sixties, for instance, in the fastest growing fields—economics, technical science, and physics and mathematics—the number of scientists doubled in approximately four years. Kugel', "Izmenenie sotsial'noi struktury," 18.

141. Richard Hofstadter, *Anti-Intellectualism in American Life*, pp. 4-5.

142. Talcott Parsons, "On the Concept of Influence," in his *Sociological Theory and Modern Society* (New York: Free Press, 1967), pp. 355-382.

143. "Many specialists will lack the incentives existing under capitalism—social distinctions cannot be unduly sharpened. The greater then the need for socialist countries to contrive and safeguard a suitable regime for creative work, leaving people as free as possible to do their special jobs; the more important it is to raise the prestige of work in science and technology and, most important, to give the socialist expert a wide field for freely creative self-assertion." Richta and others, *Civilization at the Crossroads*, p. 232.

144. *Ibid.*, p. 233.

145. *Ibid.*, pp. 253-254.

146. See Lazarsfeld and Thielens, *The Academic Mind*, p. 250, for a discussion of this process within academe as it affects younger faculty and graduate students.

147. This reference group phenomenon is reflected symbolically in the proximity of major seminaries in the United States to university centers. For instance, the Union Theological Seminary and the Jewish Theological Seminary are across the street from Columbia; the Pacific School of Religion is up the hill from the University of California; and the Episcopal Theological Seminary is next door to Harvard. Various Catholic seminaries, such as Woodstock, have moved to secular academic communities. Not fortuitously, seminaries such as these are among the most innovative.

148. Vucinich, "Science," in Kassof, ed., *Prospects for Soviet Society*, pp. 345-346.

149. The party's dilemma was revealed, for instance, in an interview with V. P. Silin, Doctor of Physics and Mathematics and Secretary of the Party Committee of the Academy of Science's P. N. Lebedev Physics Institute in Moscow, which appeared in *Pravda* (December 2, 1970). In response to one question, Dr. Silin asserted that "conditions ensuring the broadest possible scope for initiative" are essential for the full development of the potentialities of young scientists. He made this point emphatically: "The scientist who asks, 'What should I do?' is a poor scientist. Maybe you're young, but you should have your own ideas. Our task—that of the Party organization and the entire collective—is to create an atmosphere in which you can boldly put forth your ideas and get an interested response, in which you can receive an opportunity to examine, investigate and experiment. This is the only way real scientists grow." V. P. Silin, "The Potential Is Practically Unlimited," interview by V. Kozhemyako, *The Current Digest of the Soviet Press*, 22, no. 47 (December 22, 1970), 8.

150. Medvedev, *The Medvedev Papers*, p. 280. At the same time, the ideology can be used to challenge the legitimacy of official policies. Medvedev also states: "If a

government which at a particular moment in time adopts a particular point of view uses illegal measures in its polemics against those who hold different views; encroaches upon the secrecy of correspondence, arbitrarily extends the legal functions of the censorship, dismisses people from work, prosecutes them, breaking the standards of legal procedures, commits slander, restricts civil rights, and so on, then this means of ideological warfare is an ideological deviation from the ideology of communism as a whole. The Marxist communist ideology is something international and universal, it extends in time into the past and future, it develops and becomes more complex with the inevitable increase of exchange of information. The chief aim of communism, as a political system, in the works [sic] of Karl Marx, consists of 'destroying all attitudes under which a man can be humiliated, oppressed or outcast.'" (p. 282)

151. A. James Reichley, "Our Critical Shortage of Leadership," *Fortune*, 84 (September 1971), 93. See also Daniel Patrick Moynihan, "The Presidency and the Press," *Commentary*, 51 (March 1971), 41-52; Edith Efron, *The News Twisters* (New York: Nash, 1971).

152. Schumpeter, *Capitalism, Socialism and Democracy*, p. 155.

153. For 1959, it is estimated that the percentage of party members in the Soviet Union according to level of education was as follows: primary or less, 0.3; incomplete secondary, 9.5; secondary and incomplete higher, 14.0; higher, 27.0. Rigby, *Communist Party Membership*, p. 407.

154. Boris Meisser, "The Power Elite and the Intelligentsia in Soviet Society," in Kurt London, ed., *The Soviet Union: A Half-Century of Communism* (Baltimore: Johns Hopkins Press, 1968), pp. 169-170.

155. Most of them (60 per cent) had specialized in the natural sciences, mathematics, or in applied technical fields. S. Voronitsyn, "The Present Composition of the Party Central Committee: A Brief Sociological Analysis," *Bulletin of the Munich Institute for the Study of the USSR*, 16 (June 1969), 24-25.

156. Schumpeter, *Capitalism, Socialism and Democracy*, pp. 150-151. Nettl comments on this statement that "this explains the social effectiveness of intellectuals in bourgeois society (as well as their effectiveness in transforming it radically)." J. P. Nettl, "Ideas, Intellectuals, and Structures of Dissent," in Rieff, ed., *On Intellectuals*, p. 57.

157. See David Riesman, "The Spread of 'Collegiate' Values," in de Huszar, ed., *The Intellectuals*, pp. 506-507.

158. On the social characteristics, values, and political role of the managers, see Jeremy Azrael, *Managerial Power and Soviet Politics* (Cambridge, Mass.: Harvard University Press, 1966).

COMMENTS ON AMERICAN AND SOVIET INTELLECTUALS

The Editors believed that there would be some interest in having others comment on the argument developed by Seymour Martin Lipset and Richard B. Dobson. Professor Jill Conway of the University of Toronto and Professor Martin Malia of the University of California, Berkeley, have acceded to our request to provide such comment.

JILL CONWAY

Intellectuals in America: Varieties of Accommodation and Conflict

SEYMOUR LIPSET's and Richard Dobson's discussion of the intellectual as critic and rebel in the United States is an interesting attempt to illuminate and interpret radical social criticism in that post-industrial society which many sociologists until very recently characterized as having moved beyond ideology. They assert that American academic institutions are centers of cultural activity critical of and divorced from the essential values and attitudes of American popular culture, inhabited by scholars and students alienated from the structures of power in America. This picture of the American intellectual and his relationship to his society is not easily recognized by scholars working from a historical rather than a sociological perspective. The notion that American scholars as a group hold ideas more to the left than their fellow Americans serves not to clarify but to confuse the picture. Both conservative and progressive views have been associated with a wide range of intellectual positions which cannot be fitted into the conventional categories used in the analysis of European thought.

The late Richard Hofstadter pointed out in the introduction to his *Social Darwinism in American Thought* that "the roles of liberal and conservative have so often been intermingled and in some ways reversed that clear traditions have never taken form."[1] Hofstadter's generalization came from his detailed study of American intellectual life in the post-Civil War period. In the Gilded Age the robber barons, who were interested in preserving property and controlling egalitarianism, were not conservative in intellectual matters. Quite to the contrary, they were outstanding economic innovators who with unparalleled skill and inventiveness built up the corporate structure of American business and industry with little if any reference to the past. On the other hand, those who revered the ideas and beliefs of agrarian America might properly be called conservative, for they were, often as not, unquestioning adherents of the Jeffersonian tradition in American thought, as convinced as the sage of Monticello that the principles upon which the republic was founded have a universal applicability. It was this group, true believers in the Jeffersonian teaching, that favored government intervention in economic life, an attitude that Europeans would characterize as left and progressive. Thus for the intellectual historian, the views of those academics whom surveys reveal as being on the political left must be examined much more closely before they are accepted as genuine critics of the American way of life.

The distinctive American experience and the resulting ambiguity of the words "liberal," "conservative," "progressive," and "reactionary" must always be borne in mind in any analysis of American intellectual life. The American intellectual is not a single social type. He may emerge as the expert or technocrat whose mind is at the service of the existing economic and political structures. This is often the case today. He may be the romantic democrat whose opposition to power and authority comes from an idealized vision of Jeffersonian America. He may be something else again. He may reject America and its values entirely and follow the long line of American expatriates to Europe. Henry James was an expatriate for profound aesthetic reasons, as was Ezra Pound. T. S. Eliot left for philosophical as well as aesthetic reasons, later reinforced by religious convictions. Henry Adams is a striking example of an exile who stayed at home. At the same time there are the artists such as Herman Melville and Walt Whitman who believed that the American experience possessed a classic universality. They remained to celebrate a democratic society. They and their successors glorified the common man, be he worker, ethnic, black, or booster from Main Street.

These were and are the artists. Those who live and work with ideas, on the other hand, the academics, the intellectuals, whether expert or romantic democrat, have experienced no rebellion against American political and social institutions but have accepted their promise as the only blueprint for an ideal world order. What changed the quality of intellectual life in American centers of learning in the 1930's and the 1960's has been the emergence of competing models of the ideal world order. However, with rare and not very influential exceptions, it is questionable whether these alternatives have done much to undermine the inner conviction of the most radical contributor to the *New York Review of Books* that he or she inhabits the center of the world. The acrimony of American intellectual life comes not from a genuine adversary culture questioning the legitimacy of both cultural and political institutions. Instead the battle rages because one style or another of approach to the promise of American society is in vogue at the seats of political power or may have greater appeal for popular culture. Those deprived of influence for the time being advance their opposing views. But they are adversaries about means and ends in realizing the American dream, not about its ultimate desirability. Certainly in their quest for the rewards of intellectual réclame, their preoccupation (overt or covert) with "making it," they are not exempt from the national obsession with success.

This raises the basic question. Can an activist society whose intellectual tradition is pragmatic produce a genuine adversary culture? In fact, can it even conceive of one? It was certainly the intent of the founders of graduate education in the United States and of the benefactors who endowed the first secular institutions of higher learning in the late nineteenth century to achieve within a bustling commercial culture a true academic enclave where reflection and social criticism would be possible and where scholars could be exempt from the national drive for pecuniary success. However, there were forces at work in the professionalization of higher education which frustrated this intent. Nothing could illustrate their influence more clearly than the history of sociology during its development as a field of academic specialization. The sociological mind in America, which Lipset and Dobson regard as the most radical in the intellectual spectrum, has an instructive history which is exactly contemporaneous with the rise of graduate education and the professionalization of academic life.

The point in American history when the concept of society replaced that of politics and the state in the elucidation of historical change came in the late nineteenth century with the generation of William Graham Sumner and Lester Ward. Their task, as they saw it, was to fit the eighteenth-century idea of progress arising from political institutions into the framework of evolutionary social science. Both succeeded admirably in ways which exemplify the basic configuration of intellectual types in the native American tradition. Sumner's reworking of the evolutionary scheme produced a justification of the unrestrained competition of American economic life in the second half of the nineteenth century. Ward, in justifying the interventionist state, asserted that intellect and social policy should control the dynamic of progress. Both were synthetic thinkers who left no academic successors, though Sumner taught within the established setting of Yale.

The institutional setting which was central for the development of the second generation of sociologists was the newly founded University of Chicago, where the availability of endowment, the opportunity to build a scholarly department, and the social service orientation of William Rainey Harper's university all fostered rapid growth. At Chicago the social factor seemed preeminent to a group of midwesterners for whom the growth of the industrial city appeared to be transforming the rural America of their youth and carrying it upon a path of development not provided for in American political or social thought. They believed it was the city rather than industrial capitalism which was undermining the basis of community and creating social conflict. Moreover, as citizens of a progressive republic they were not free to speculate about problems arising from the decline of religion, the anomie which comes from the absence or disintegration of norms. For them the problem of norms had to be dealt with under the study of the immigrant and his difficulties of assimilation and under the guise of speculation about "social control" in democratic societies. In focusing attention on the immigrant, none of the Chicago urban sociologists doubted that his assimilation was desirable to a way of life whose legitimacy and humane qualities they left unquestioned. Edward A. Ross, Robert Park, and William I. Thomas believed that the conflicts of assimilation came from the backward racial stock, religion, or culture of the immigrants. It did not occur to them that these conflicts might arise from the exploitive and alienating economic and political systems of the United States. It followed that their students engaged in the study of "human ecology" were obliged to undertake descriptive surveys because the major sources of social conflict could not be examined and the psychological dimensions of the disintegration of norms were blurred by the search for "democratic social control."

One might expect that a generation of describers and cataloguers would logically be followed by a new group of synthesizers in rebellion against the methods and interests of their predecessors. However, this did not happen during the era of Ernest W. Burgess and William F. Ogburn at Chicago and George Lundberg at the University of Washington. The work of these three men made Chicago and Washington the two centers of major development in sociology during the 1920's and 1930's. However, the aim and intention among members of this generation was to establish sociology as a science with the same precision in observation and measurement as a natural science. This ambition reflects a hierarchy of intellectual values which is characteristically American. It is at once a response to the pragmatic movement in philosophy and to the high value placed on science in intellectual endeavor. The result was a concentration on quantification and on the development of survey techniques which has been one of the characteristics of American sociology. Together with the passion for quantification came the development of academic specialization. This was the major institutional factor operating against any further concern with synthesis. Quantification and specialization meant that research projects in the 1920's and 1930's treated materials which were quantifiable and subjects which did not cross the boundaries of the conventional subspecialties which together made up the discipline of sociology. Industrial sociologists did not do research on social pathology, though they well might have in these years. Similarly, research on deviance separated the problem of prostitution from the study of the family and of property systems. As Robert

Lynd pointed out in *Knowledge for What?*[2] the net result of this fragmentation was the prevention of radical root and branch assessments of American society. Major efforts at synthesis could not be undertaken by a generation pursuing precision in ever more restricted areas of academic competence.

There were other factors militating against synthesis and radical criticism during these decades. Of these the most important were the extent to which the profession became involved in government work during the First World War and later during the great depression. Ogburn's work for the national War Labor Board during the First World War was to be followed by his presidency from 1930 to 1933 of Herbert Hoover's Research Committee on Social Trends, a natural position for one of the leaders in a profession responding to the enhanced prestige of government service. During the Roosevelt era of the 1930's sociologists were to be deeply attracted by the lure of planning the democratically controlled society and ready to put their skills at the service of established authority. Burgess' faith in the ability of sociology to bring about utopia was expressed in his presidential address to the American Sociological Society in 1934. He declared that the mores of the American people could be manipulated in a planned progression of change which would permit the United States to become the model democracy of a new world order. Lundberg's awareness of the extent to which government involvement blunted scientific detachment made his one of the few voices of the era raised against the tendency to merge research projects with political goals. Given the enthusiasms of the New Deal and the Second World War it is understandable, if unfortunate, that his warnings were not well received by his contemporaries.

The climate of opinion which developed in the late 1930's and the 1940's did nothing to reverse the trend which linked research in sociology with established authority. Instead the rise of fascism and the outbreak of the Second World War created a situation in which the capacity for social research could have great patriotic significance. Coincidentally, Paul Lazarsfeld brought to the United States the new research techniques necessary for surveying opinion and testing attitudes, techniques which were necessary for mobilizing a national population. Lazarsfeld's interests in market research which he had developed in Europe were to find their full institutional expression at Columbia University and its related research institute. Here was developed the first large scale research center utilizing the new techniques. This kind of institution, created, staffed, and maintained for conducting surveys, was to be the prototype of sociological development in the postwar period, of value alike to business and government and far more dependent on their support than earlier research had been. From such centers teams go out to quantify the alienation of the appropriate sample of the work force on the requisite five point scale. The capacity to do so however produces only meliorist criticism of industrial organization because of the very nature of the research operation.

Even so, the ability to scrutinize a national population and to describe not only the "human ecology" of a city or the deference system of a small town but states of mind as well did lead sociologists in the late forties and fifties to the spiritual malaise of the consumer society. It is debatable, however, whether the discovery of the anomie of the middle class has provoked a fundamental reassessment of American values among those who led the way in mapping the contours of the malaise. At the conclusion of *The Lonely Crowd* David Riesman professes a modified version of the American faith. "The idea," he says, "that men are created free and equal is both true and misleading: men are created different; they lose their social freedom and their individual autonomy in seeking to become like each other."[3] This statement implies a lost state of autonomy, like the independence of the Jeffersonian yeoman, to which all should desire to return.

In the fifties and sixties this sense of lost American innocence was to be still further intensified by renewed contact with European thought and the discovery of elites. The recognition of the existence of elites and the new concern with the nature of leadership came in a decade when the disasters of American foreign policy emphasized in the most unambiguous terms the dimensions of American economic imperialism. At the same time the cultural revolution in China proved infinitely attractive to American youth dissatisfied both with mass culture and the learning of cultural institutions where specialization and professionalism had constrained intellectual spontaneity and deadened both curiosity and ideological fervor. These external forces have contributed to the radicalization of a new generation in American sociology, so that in place of the once bland assumption of freedom from values, academic debate centers upon the political orientation of all research. Beneath the passionate search to unmask structures of power, lines of command, enclaves of privilege, and sexist domination—all seen as domestic dimensions of American imperialism—there lies an implicit assumption of subversion. Only treachery can explain why a once innocent republic should acquire such a massive drive for power and dominion. The theme of subversion is a recurrent one in the writing of American history, worked and reworked in moralistic terms in the nineteenth century, secularized in economic terms by the generation of Beard and Parrington, refined and restated by the new analysts of the cold war. Just as the conspiracies of the rich are necessary to explain America's decline from grace because the initial promise of the Revolution and the break from Europe cannot be questioned, so it is necessary for American intellectuals to establish the path to recovery, some liberation from the dream turned nightmare. The transformations of consciousness which will give us back the spontaneity of that once happy agrarian utopia will, we are told, come from technology, from the media, from the youthful counterculture, from "people's universities" and "free schools." The list is long. To it we must now add the "adversary culture" of the universities, which have suddenly become capable of generating fundamental criticisms of American society, criticisms directed at what Lipset and Dobson call structural change, though in fact the only changes they mention are expansion of economic opportunity and modifications of the political system. One final point must be made about Lipset's and Dobson's analysis of American intellectual life. They follow Schumpeter in assuming that a capitalist society is both unable and unwilling to control its intellectuals because of the reliance of bourgeois business upon free enterprise in goods and ideas.[4] What Schumpeter did not envision, steeped as he was in the values of European intellectual life, was the complexity and ambiguity of the intellectual's role in America. The truly alienated respond to the force of democratic sentiment by taking their explosive criticisms into exile. Those who remain are sufficiently steeped in the capitalist ethos to be controlled by the market for their ideas, strong enough believers in the American way to make them, as Santayana said, "clergymen without a church" who may dispute about dogma but who never question the revelation.[5]

REFERENCES

1. Richard Hofstadter, *Social Darwinism in American Life* (Philadelphia: University of Pennsylvania Press, 1944), p. 8. The introduction contains a brief essay on the role of the intellectual in America which is among the most enlightening on this complex subject.

2. Robert S. Lynd, *Knowledge For What?* (Princeton: Princeton University Press, 1939).

3. David Riesman and others, *The Lonely Crowd: A Study of the Changing American Character* (Garden City, N.Y.: Doubleday, 1953), p. 349.

4. See Lipset's and Dobson's note 156.

5. George Santayana, *Character and Opinion in the United States* (New York: W. W. Norton, 1934), p. 43.

MARTIN E. MALIA

The Intellectuals: Adversaries or Clerisy?

SEYMOUR LIPSET and Richard Dobson, in analyzing the role of "critical intellectuals" in the United States and the Soviet Union, give a pessimistic version of the "convergence theory" of Western and Russian developments. Their thesis is that in an advanced technological, or "post-industrial," order the key institutions of society are increasingly dependent for their functioning on professionally trained intellectuals; yet these intellectuals, because of the critical faculties required by their work, also become the bearers of a strident "adversary culture" which questions the very legitimacy of the order they serve. Indeed, since "the critical intellectual denies the possibility of participating in government without betraying the ideals of the society," his attitude becomes the chief "contradiction" of the post-industrial order: modern society clearly cannot live without its intellectuals, but it may not be able to live with them, either.

There is certainly much evidence for the period since the end of the cold war—evidence which Professor Lipset and Mr. Dobson marshal most persuasively—to support such a thesis; and the 1960's in particular may well go down as a major cultural divide in modern history. Still, we should not forget that the "end of ideology" was once prematurely proclaimed, in the 1950's; and it may be equally premature now to proclaim the definitive return of ideology. Just as destalinization and the fading of the cold war permitted a revival of ideological criticism, so too new international events may provoke another ideological recession; and, indeed, since Nixon and Mao have appeared in the media smiling benignly at each other, the critical intelligentsia in all countries is already somewhat less sure of itself. In any event, it is worth attempting to point out certain historical and social factors which could limit or diminish the recent impact of critical intellectuals in both East and West.

Professor Lipset and Mr. Dobson find the propensity of intellectuals to assume an adversary stance to lie in a variety of causes: the irritations of censorship and repression, the pressures of historical circumstances, the value system of the national tradition. But they find the basic cause in the nature of intellectual activity itself, in "its concern for creativity, for originality, and for rejecting the traditional and the established": skepticism and criticism of all received values, of all accepted norms, are intrinsic to intellectual creativity per se; and this characteristic is amplified many times over when intellectuals are mobilized massively in the "technostructure" and "culture apparatus" of advanced societies.

What is questionable in this view is the primacy as a causal factor accorded to the nature of intellectual activity per se; for, though all intellectuals live by exercising critical discernment, a *systematically* critical intelligentsia, directing its fire primarily at society, is a relatively rare—and recent—phenomenon, a special case in the long history of professional intellectuals. For such an intelligentsia to emerge a special concatenation of other factors—social, political, and historical—is required, so as to focus the critical temper of intellectuals with ideological obsessiveness on a limited range of sociopolitical issues. Indeed, Professor Lipset and Mr. Dobson recognize this multicausal pattern in their perceptive discussion of the fluctuating fortunes of the critical intelligentsia between the 1930's and the 1960's and of their dependence on the egalitarian and populistic value system of the United States, which obviously originated in a social and religious heritage quite independent of the intellectual class itself. Still, such factors deserve to be explored further, and in terms of other national examples, in an effort to assess more precisely the conditions under which the critical habits inherent in intellectual activity go the lengths of a full-blown "adversary" culture.

It should be noted, by way of introduction, that the existence of such a culture implies a number of attitudes, over and above a critical consciousness, on the part of intellectuals. It implies, first, self-consciousness as a group, defined by a sense of collective mission to society. By the same token, it implies a sense of opposition between the intellectuals and society, a sense of "we" and "they," of the enlightened and the benighted, the refined and the philistine, the progressive and the retrograde. It thus implies, also, a sense of historical movement, of progress founded on constant struggle between "right" and "left," an agonistic dynamic in which the intellectuals are the vanguard. It implies, finally, the belief in the following amalgam of values: that the life of the intellect yields not only scientific truth, but moral truth; that the moral truth is also inevitably social in nature; that there exists, therefore, a scientific or rational politics the aim of which is social justice, or equality; and that the men of intellect, by definition, are the chief bearers of this truth-which-is-justice. Intellectuals of this particular sort are best designated by the Russian term "intelligentsia," which, from the time of its emergence in the 1860's, has meant, basically, "critically thinking personalities" (in Pisarev's phrase) or "nihilists" (in Turgenev's term), in the sense of those who systematically question all traditional values in the name of reason, progress, and social justice.

Why such a term and group first emerged in backward Russia will be touched on later. For the moment suffice it to note that a similar group self-consciousness was much slower to emerge in the more advanced West. Elements of the above mentioned syndrome of attitudes were clearly present among the French Encyclopedists, in Marx, and on the nineteenth-century European left generally; but the feeling that these attitudes belong, or ought to belong, to *all* intellectuals is a relatively recent phenomenon. To stick to terminology as a convenient measure of collective self-consciousness, we first hear of *la classe intellectuelle* in France at the time of the Dreyfus affair. In the English-speaking world the term "the intellectuals" (invariably in quotation marks) appears only in 1914, with Bertrand Russell in Britain or with Walter Lippmann (then on the left) in America. It seems, moreover, to have been imported from France, in particular from the circle of Romain Rolland and other "intellectuals" opposed to the war. It was only after the war and the Russian Revolution that the term lost its quotation marks and became a part of the standard vocabulary everywhere, replacing the older and less potent designation of "men of letters." At the same time the terms "right" and "left," hitherto used only on the Continent, entered the Anglo-Saxon political vocabulary, giving a heightened sense of historical movement and indicating to the newly self-conscious intellectuals which side they should be on.

Thus it was the trauma of world war together with the Russian Revolution, and the concomitant spread of Marxism-Leninism (an ideology of the Russian intelligentsia, after all), that for the first time generalized belief in the responsibilities of militant, missionary, or moral intellectuals. For modern war seemed to menace the very existence of civilization at the same time that revolutionary Communism offered the mirage of a new type of civilization. And ever since 1914 we have lived with the same cycle of political and social issues—the fear of *Gotterdämmerung* and the hope of the ultimate utopia—with the result that the new type of political-moral intellectual has been with us just as constantly, from the *New Masses*, to the *Partisan Review*, to the *New York Review of Books*, at times driven to retrench, as at the height of Stalinism, but always ready to return in force whenever the issues of war and revolution came again to the fore.

But in other political and cultural circumstances the intellectuals can behave very differently. Let us begin with a situation that presents the clearest antithesis to the modern one: the period—say until the seventeenth century—when Western society was dominated by a religious culture articulated through established churches. In this situation the intellectuals, who were often also clerics, could be critical of received truths only within narrow limits and in selective fashion, arguing for one variant of religious tradition against another, as for example in disputes between Puritans and Anglicans or between Jansenists and Jesuits. Or when the intellectuals were rationalists, as in the case of Baconians or Cartesians, they always took care to reconcile, in some manner, the dictates of reason with the heritage of faith. Thus systematic, across-the-board criticism was simply out of the question for intellectuals of whatever stripe. This was so not only because society would not tolerate total or "heretical" dissent, but also because the intellectuals themselves had accepted and internalized the notion that the basic principles by which man lives must be beyond human questioning.

The existence of critical intellectuals, then, presupposes a predominantly secular, pluralistic, and liberal culture, which makes a positive value of free expression and of intellectual competition in the "market place of ideas." And this in turn presupposes not only institutional arrangements guaranteeing civil liberties, but also the triumph of modern science, which conferred on human reason—the prime faculty of all intellectuals—an authority and apparent infallibility it had never before possessed. Still, these developments, for the first time approximated in the eighteenth century, constitute the necessary, but not the sufficient, conditions for the emergence of a critical intelligentsia. It is political and social conditions, as well as the national tradition, which play the decisive role in orienting the energies of the intellectuals. For example, in the eighteenth century a liberal culture and the new science were certainly more advanced in England than in France, yet it was France which produced those first critical intellectuals known as the philosophes.

In England the new rationalism of science led to the empiricism of Locke and the skepticism of Hume, which emphasized the limits of human understanding almost as much as its achievements, combatting all "enthusiasm" and warning against the vagaries of mere "opinion"; while what reforming zeal existed in society was left to the religious sects and dissenters of an "unenlightened" sort. This was so, in large part, because after the Glorious Revolution of 1688 the majority of intellectuals were satisfied with the existing oligarchic, liberal order and wished to protect it from the assault of religious zealots left over from the turmoil of the Great Rebellion. In France, on the other hand, the existence of absolute monarchy, a monolithic established church, and a legal class hierarchy furnished social issues to the intellectuals that made it possible for the Encyclopedists to transform Locke's prudent empiricism into an instrument of radical criticism, the weapon of a militant *parti de la saine philosophie* in its struggle with the "superstition" and "irrationality" of the establishment. And this tendency was reinforced by the absence in France of a tradition of religious dissent to serve as an alternative outlet for reforming energies. Then, after 1789, the Revolution served to fix the French national myth predominantly on the left, while the British, reacting to the rationalistic follies transpiring in France (for example, Burke) fixed their national myth ever more firmly in the mold of the moderate, "organic" overturn of 1688 and of the prudent empiricism that stemmed from it.

Thus the same intellectual method, founded on critical adherence to the "facts" as established by modern science, led to very different intellectual traditions in the two countries, because of differing social, political, and national circumstances. And once these two traditions had become fixed, they largely defined the field of maneuver, and the range and tone of criticism, for all future generations of intellectuals. As a result, modern Britain, though it has had its Bertrand Russell, its Oxford Pledge, and the *New Statesman and Nation,* has never had an adversary intelligentsia on the scale of modern France, with large masses of intellectuals actually in "The Party" and others, such as Sartre and Merleau-Ponty, hovering anxiously on its fringes. This difference cannot be explained by the dynamic of intellectual creativity per se; it can only be accounted for by the total context in which the intellectuals exercise their creativity, and the targets for criticism offered by that context.

An even more telling example of this fact is furnished by modern Germany. Surely, no group of intellectuals in modern history has been more creative than that of Germany between the late eighteenth and the early twentieth centuries. Indeed, most of the great intellectual "isms" of the modern world, from Kant, Hegel, and Marx, to Nietzsche, Freud, and Weber are of German origin; and it is no exaggeration to claim that, in the domain of general social philosophy, mankind continues to live off the accumulated intellectual capital of pre-Hitler Germany (by comparison nineteenth-century British utilitarianism and French positivism have been paltry influences). Yet this great German tradition has leaned much more to the right than to the left; and it has displayed consistent ambiguity toward the role and power of reason in human affairs. There is, to be sure, the towering exception of Marx; but Marx (and the other "left Hegelians") can be accounted for, in part, by the one period of acute conflict, in the 1830's and 1840's, between the German establishment and the intellectuals. Otherwise, the German intelligentsia has supported, and indeed justified, the established and the traditional with all the power of its creativity.

Why this should be so is a very complicated matter, but a few crucial factors may be singled out. First, the religious heritage of Lutheranism, which abandoned control of the church to the territorial prince, has meant that in much of German thought freedom came to be associated with voluntary submission to authority—as in Hegel's (and Marx's) equation of liberty with the conscious and rational acceptance of historical necessity. Second, when German national culture began to stake out its identity in the period of the *Sturm und Drang* it was obliged to do so by combatting the universalistic pretentions of dominant French rationalism, thereby producing an unusually precocious and fecund critique of all reason in the name of romantic, intuitionist, and subjectivist modes of thought. Third, throughout the nineteenth century German society was in large part modernized, whether with respect to industrialization or to education, by state action from above rather than by citizen initiative from below, thereby creating a bizarrely mixed order that was at the same time progressive and undemocratic, dynamic and unegalitarian, ultramodern and yet tenaciously old regime. Indeed, it was autocratic Imperial Germany which pioneered in linking the universities with the research laboratory, industry, and the state bureaucracy, thus adumbrating the present-day "technostructure."

In this confused situation the intelligentsia of Imperial Germany divided. Some, such as the future members of the Frankfurt School, chose critical opposition and entered the Marxist subculture, which entailed automatic exclusion from the universities and from a national forum. But the majority, including the most creative minds of the period, found that the system embodied enough of the values of "culture" to opt for integration and careers as "mandarins." As a result, the creativity of German intellectuals was turned less toward criticism of established institutions and values in Germany than toward the criticism of "Western" (Anglo-French) rationalism, of liberalism, positivism, and individualistic capitalism. Indeed, this criticism of critical intellect became the stock-in-trade of the German intellectuals after 1870—when they had become the admiration and envy of the world. Thus most of the "mandarins" were frankly conservative, extolling and rationalizing the "organic" German synthesis of the modern with the traditional, as did Tönnies and Sombart, the *Kathedersozialisten* and Thomas Mann, Meinecke and Heidegger; while such vulgar Nietzschean publicists as Scheler, Spengler, and Moeller van den Bruck stridently complained that the existing order was not conservative enough.

If the differences of national traditions and social and political patterns between England, France, and Germany have been great, the differences between the United States and Russia are even greater. And even though these differences are in a sense "fairly obvious," it is worth belaboring the obvious a bit here, for the present role and impact of the intellectuals of the two countries is largely governed by these institutional and historical dissimilarities.

Professor Lipset and Mr. Dobson have appropriately emphasized the lack of a legitimate conservative tradition and the predominance of an egalitarian ethos in the United States. It might be added that these characteristics of the national value system are due, among other things, to the Puritan settlement of the more important colonies and the persistence, in secularized form, of a liberal, evangelical spirit; to the quasi-revolutionary origins of the Republic; to the enduring lack of a rigidly stratified social structure; to the unparalleled opportunities for individual advancement and social mobility offered by an entire continent to be developed; to a sense of moral mission as a "new" society opposed to the "corruption" of old Europe, and so forth. Another unique feature of American society which deserves to be emphasized is the exceptional importance of the judiciary as the guardian of the higher national values, construed as much in ethical as in legal terms, a situation which exists in no other country, not even in the motherland of civil liberties and judge-made law, England. All of these circumstances together have given exceptional institutional leverage to left liberal intellectuals of the adversary culture, whether in promoting civil rights, influencing national policy on Vietnam, publishing the Pentagon papers, or fighting the regents of the University of California on behalf of Angela Davis. Visiting European leftists, such as Jean-François Revel and Edgar Morin, are constantly amazed by, and envious of, the variety and potency of the means of action to effect change open to American intellectuals. And these circumstances, in conjunction with real issues whose time had come, such as civil rights and the Vietnam war, account for much of the impact of the critical intellectuals in the 1960's.

Yet these same circumstances, especially once the burning issues have passed (as they inevitably do), can also serve to blunt the impact of the critical intellectuals. For the very flexibility of American institutions and the means of action they provide constantly lead dissenters, despite some talk about the hopelessness of the "system," back into the institutions of that same system: the courts, elections, the reform or "capture" of the Democratic party. Ideological issues, moreover, become particularized: elaborate dissertations by Noam Chomsky in the *New York Review of Books* about "imperialism" for most readers boil down to "the war" and to voting for McCarthy or McGovern; the issue of "capitalism" tends to dissolve into concern for ecology and the environment, or Ralph Nader's "consumerism"; allegations of structural "racism" come in fact to focus on concrete electoral and economic grievances of blacks or chicanos (for Max Rafferty, after all, can be defeated by Wilson Riles as California State Superintendent of Education).

Indeed, one of the standard complaints of the New Left is the "system's" ability to "co-opt" radical personnel and issues, to fuse them into a "wishy-washy" reformism. And this allegation is largely true. To be sure, with each crisis, from the New Deal to the 1960's, the system gives way somewhat and moves a bit to the left, a few authentic "reds" creep into the left wing of the Democratic fold and a number of Henry Wallace types come prominently to the fore, while the right develops a panicky suspicion of sell-out and treason. Still, in each of these crises the adversary culture gives way much more than does the system, and most of its spokesmen wind up, *à la Partisan Review*, basically supporting the new national "consensus," while somewhat later the right, *à la* Nixon, takes up many of the economic and foreign policies of a John Kenneth Galbraith. This view, to be sure, represents the optimistic, centrist opinion that America has usually had of itself. Nonetheless, it possesses a very real basis in historical fact; and institutionalized capacity to readjust the national consensus, surely, provides the chief opportunity, and the principal limitation, for American intellectuals.

It should be needless to emphasize that no such flexibility and capacity for accommodation have characterized the Russian order, whether under the old regime or the new. And this circumstance has served to endow the Russian intellectual with a national heritage that combines the most exalted kind of critical ideals with a virtually complete lack of institutional means for implementing them—a situation, obviously, which is the exact antithesis of the American one.

Under the old regime the rigidity and the very real irreformability of the autocracy led to the emergence of a diamond-pure adversary intelligentsia of the sort that has already been defined. It was, moreover, the most extreme wing of this intelligentsia, the Bolsheviks, which gave to the new Soviet society its national myth and its norms of legitimacy. Thus the combined heritage of the old regime intelligentsia and of the October Revolution have given Soviet society the most left set of ideals of any modern nation—not only "rational" economic planning and material abundance, but the stateless and classless society—ideals so far left that no society could realize them. This circumstance, in conjunction with the Russian heritage of backwardness and Stalin's regimented modernization from above, have led to a uniquely wide gap between the ideal and the real in Soviet life.

In such a situation, the mass production of professionally trained intellectuals necessary for modernization would seem to favor the emergence of a thriving adversary culture. In reality, however, other circumstances have kept such a development to a minimum. And it should be emphasized that the number of active dissenters in the Soviet Union is extremely small. Although we obviously do not have the kind of survey data on Soviet intellectuals that we have for American intellectuals, it is clear from numerous reports of foreigners who have visited or resided in Russia that the dissident activities symbolized by such figures as Sakharov, Amalrik, Solzhenitsyn, or the brothers Medvedev are restricted to very limited circles in Moscow, Leningrad, Kiev, Novosibirsk, and a few other centers, and that these activities are quite unknown to the overwhelming majority of the population.

This impotence is due, in the first instance, to the complete lack of institutional leverage afforded to critical intellectuals by the Soviet political structure—the obvious absence not only of an independent judiciary and political parties, but even of elementary freedom of expression. *Samizdat*, however remarkable in the post-Stalinist context, is still a primitive, and very limited, means of disseminating information, and one that probably reaches more people in the West than in Russia. As I. F. Stone aptly said in a recent number of the *New York Review of Books*, the problem of free expression as it is now posed in the Soviet Union takes us back more than two hundred years to the English revolution of 1688. Under such circumstances the only leverage that Soviet critical intellectuals possess is the combined appeal to the literal meaning of the Soviet Constitution (the tactic of Sakharov's "Committee for Human Rights") and to international public opinion so as to exert pressure on the Soviet government. This tactic has produced results on occasion, as in obtaining the release of Jaurès Medvedev, and, especially, in producing the pardon of the Leningrad Jews tried in early 1971—at the same moment Franco pardoned the accused in the Burgos trial. Still, this technique of moral pressure is as primitive as is *samizdat;* and for its few known successes there is a far larger, and unknown, number of failures.

Moreover, the limited scope both of *samizdat* and of the technique of moral pressure depend entirely on the persistence of division of opinion within the Soviet hierarchy as to how far to tolerate such dissident activity. Moderates apparently feel the dissidents are not dangerous enough to make it worth the scandal of repressing them. But old Stalinist and neo-Stalinist elements clearly disagree, and these groups have been gaining strength since Khrushchev's fall, in 1964, in the administrative bureaucracy, the military, and even in the technostructure; for the Soviet establishment possesses unusually effective means for the co-optation of like-minded successors. How long these divisions of tactical opinion will leave to Soviet critical intellectuals their present narrow margin of maneuver is impossible to tell. What is certain, however, is that in a "crunch" all the leverage is on the side of the establishment and that, outside of a handful of *exaltés*, no one would attempt a "talent strike" against the system.

The Czechoslovak case in 1968 is here the touchstone, for despite the *national* union of the intelligentsia for reform, and their commitment to the premises of Radovan Richta, quoted by Professor Lipset and Mr. Dobson, the entire movement collapsed once autocratic pressure was applied—and society continued to function, inefficiently of course, but not much more inefficiently than Communist societies normally function. And both the Soviet government and the Soviet critical intellectuals are quite aware of this precedent. In short, the opinion of Joseph Schumpeter, quoted by Professor Lipset and Mr. Dobson, that, in effect, intellectual repression and advance technology cannot mix, does not hold under certain political structures; and what Leszek Kołakowski deplored as the "resort to the instruments of force" can, if necessary, close the gap between the two—at a low level of efficiency to be sure, but then the aim of such regimes is not economic efficiency as such, but that minimum of crucial productivity necessary to support international political power.

Another set of inhibiting factors for Soviet critical intellectuals lies not in the system but in themselves. Soviet intellectuals as a group are characterized, first, by a very low level of critical sophistication. The flat quality of Soviet intellectual life in most areas outside the natural sciences, the dead weight of official ideology, and the relative lack of contact with the West for some fifty years have conspired to deprive Soviet intellectuals of adequate concepts and models in terms of which to criticize their society. Their protest, therefore, is almost always a moral one, expressed moreover in literary terms. The key critics are poets and novelists, such as Pasternak and Solzhenitsyn, and not social scientists as in the West. The criticism of Soviet intellectuals thus almost never assumes the form of an *analysis* of the system, directed to the great and obvious questions: what went wrong with the Revolution, and why Stalinism? Roy Medvedev's *Let History Judge* is a reasonably well-documented study of Stalinist practices, but it is a complete failure as an effort to explain why such "aberrations" occurred. The only real attempt at an analysis of Soviet reality is Amalrik's *Will the Soviet Union Survive Until 1984?* but this is only the timid beginning of an enormous task.

A second constraint on the Soviet critical intelligentsia lies in its unique relation to Marxism-Leninism. Elsewhere Marxism-Leninism, in one or another version, and usually in a loose construction, provides the chief critical theory of adversary intellectuals, since it offers a "scientific" explanation of the principal moral scandals to the left—inequality and exploitation—which it accounts for by "capitalism" at home and "imperialism" abroad. Yet this theory is unavailable as a critical weapon to the Soviet left, in part because it has been preempted by the state, and in part because its categories are completely unadapted to the analysis of Soviet society. To be sure, as Amalrik informs us, the Soviet opposition, in addition to Liberals and Christians, is composed of "Marxist-Leninists," such as Grigorenko. But this group, which wishes to return to a mythical "democratic Leninism," as a practical matter has the same constitutionalist program as the Liberals; thus they use Leninism as a moral mystique, not as a mode of analyzing Soviet society. And the unavailability of Marxism-Leninism as a critical doctrine, in combination with the failure to produce a new mode of social analysis, leaves the Soviet intelligentsia without any sweeping, universalistic ideology, and hence with a diminished critical bite.

The same inhibiting confusion applies to the Soviet intellectuals' relationship to socialism. In the West and in the third world the ultimate ideal of the left, and the final goal of history, is held to be "socialism," in the loose sense of a world beyond private property and the profit motive, a world of justice and equality through nationalization. But this ideal cannot serve as a critical foil to reality for Soviet intellectuals, since "socialism," at least in the sense of nationalization, already exists in Russia and they all accept it as a *fait accompli*. The problem, then, is only how to make it work "correctly," to purge it of abuses. But this is viewed as a limited, practical problem, not as a question of "revolution" or of transition to a new historical stage. Thus, once again, ideology is evacuated and critical punch is lost.

Still other ideological avenues and critical utopias are closed to Soviet intellectuals. Among the principal utopias of the old regime intelligentsia was "the people," either the peasants, the workers, or both. But belief in the radical, redemptive power of the people is no longer possible in Russia, in part because the people have already had their metahistorical day, in 1917, and the results were disappointing, but even more because of the Stalinist formula of exploiting popular frustration, xenophobia, and obscurantism against the intelligentsia during the purges of the 1930's and the "anti-cosmopolitan" (that is, anti-Semitic) campaign after World War II. As a result of these experiences, the Soviet intelligentsia is, by and large, afraid of the masses as an unenlightened force and as an ally of the repressive state. And this is true despite a certain Slavophile populism in Solzhenitsyn's art and despite Sakharov's rhetorical assertion that the intelligentsia "properly understood" is a part of the people. As a practical matter, Soviet intellectuals know that they are alone in their struggle with the state, and virtually without allies or even understanding among the masses.

For similar reasons Soviet intellectuals harbor no romantic illusions about the might and purity of third world revolution, Ho Chi Minh, Cuba, and above all about China. Indeed, Sakharov finds China even more frightening than his own government, the ultimate expression of all the evils that Stalin visited upon Russia.

The critical horizon, then, of Soviet intellectuals is an extremely narrow one in every respect. Both the institutional and the cultural context in which they operate make their criticism far less sweeping and global than that of their more fortunate Western confreres. At the same time, these circumstances leave no room for the nihilistic vitriol which characterizes a part of the Western counterculture. Instead, the Soviet critical intelligentsia concentrates pragmatically on the "small deeds" of old-fashioned civil liberties and liberal constitutionalism. In theory, this is a crippling "contradiction" for the Soviet order. It could become such in reality, however, only if the people became responsive to the intellectuals' criticisms, and for the moment there is no sign that this is occurring.

Thus, for very different reasons, there is probably at least as much stability in the Soviet as in the American order, despite the rapid growth of the technostructure in both countries; and the critical potential of the intellectuals in the two societies will no doubt continue to be filtered fairly routinely through the peculiar national traditions and institutional patterns of each nation for a long time to come.

Notes on Contributors

FRANÇOIS BOURRICAUD, born in 1922, is professor of sociology at the University of Paris and will be visiting professor of sociology at Harvard University in the fall of 1972. His publications include *Equisse d'une théorie de l'autorité* (Paris, 1961), *Changements à Puno: étude de sociologie andine* (Paris, 1962), *El sindicalismo en Latinoamérica* (Barcelona, 1965), *Power and Society in Contemporary Peru*, trans. Paul Stevenson (New York, 1970, first published 1967), and *Universités à la dérive* (Paris, 1971).

JILL CONWAY, born in 1934, is professor of history at the University of Toronto. She is the author of numerous articles on American social and intellectual history and biographical essays for *Notable American Women, 1607-1950* (Cambridge, Mass., 1971). Mrs. Conway is at present writing on "The Place of Women in American Culture."

RICHARD B. DOBSON, born in 1944, is a graduate student in sociology and graduate associate at the Center for International Affairs at Harvard University.

NIKKI R. KEDDIE is professor of history at the University of California, Los Angeles. She is the author of *Religion and Rebellion in Iran: The Tobacco Protest of 1891-92* (London, 1966), *An Islamic Response to Imperialism: Political and Religious Writings of Sayyid Jamal ad-Din "al-Afghani"* (Berkeley and Los Angeles, 1968), and *Sayyid Jamal ad-Din "al-Afghani": A Political Biography* (Berkeley and Los Angeles, 1972).

LESZEK KOŁTAKOWSKI, born in 1927, is a fellow of All Souls College, Oxford. His publications include *The Alienation of Reason: A History of Positivist Thought*, trans. Norbert Guterman (Garden City, N.Y., 1968), *Marxism and Beyond: On Historical Understanding and Individual Responsibility*, trans. Jane Zielonko Peel (London, 1969), *Chrétiens sans église: la conscience religeuse et le lien confessionnel au XVIIe siècle*, trans. Anna Posner (Paris, 1969), and many works available only in Polish. Mr. Kołakowski was professor of the history of philosophy at Warsaw University until March 1968, when he was expelled for political reasons. He has been visiting professor at McGill University, 1968-1969, and the University of California, Berkeley, 1969-1970.

JUAN J. LINZ, born in 1926, is professor of sociology and political science at Yale University. He is the author of *Los empresarios ante el poder publico* (Madrid, 1966, with Amando de Miguel), "The Party System of Spain, Past and Future," in S. M. Lipset and S. Rokkan, eds. *Party Systems and Voter Alignments* (New York, 1967), "From Falange to Movimento Organizacion: The Spanish Single Party and the Franco Regime," in S. Huntington and C. Moore, eds., *Authoritarian Politics in Modern Society* (New York, 1970), *An Authoritarian Regime, Spain, Mass Politics*, ed. E. Allardt and S. Rokkan (New York, 1970), and many articles based on a study of Spanish business elites.

SEYMOUR MARTIN LIPSET, born in 1922, is professor of government and sociology at Harvard University. He is the author of *Political Man* (New York, 1960), *The First New Nation* (New York, 1963), *Revolution and Counterrevolution*

(New York, 1968), *The Politics of Unreason* (New York, 1970, with Earl Raab), and *Rebellion in the University* (Boston, 1972). Mr. Lipset is the recipient of the Gunnar Myrdal Award (1970). He is currently on a Guggenheim fellowship for the study of intellectuals, of which this article is a preliminary part.

MARTIN E. MALIA, born in 1924, is professor of history at the University of California, Berkeley. He is the author of *Alexander Herzen and the Birth of Russian Socialism, 1812-1855* (Cambridge, Mass., 1961).

MENAHEM MILSON, born in 1933, is senior lecturer in Arabic literature at the Hebrew University of Jerusalem. He is the author of *A Sufi Rule for Novices* (Cambridge, Mass., forthcoming), *Bibliography of Modern Arabic Literature* (Jerusalem, forthcoming, with S. Moreh), and various articles on modern Arabic literature.